D1033382

Cracking the Boards: USMLE Step 1

Cracking the Boards: USMLE Step 1

caballoo @ pois.com
Ryan Ley

Edited by

Michael Stein
Stanford University School of Medicine, Class of 1998

Gloria Hwang
Stanford University School of Medicine

Paul Zei
Stanford University School of Medicine, Class of 1998

Radhika Breaden
Resident in Internal Medicine, Stanford Medical Center

With

Paul Wheeler   Sheri Fink
Randall Rupper   Srinivas Akkaraju
Marc Lee   Kristin Weidenbach
Pooya Fazeli   Matthew Hanasono

Illustrated by Paul Wheeler, Brian Dunham, Scott Harris
and Iam Williams

Random House, New York
www.randomhouse.com/princetonreview

Princeton Review Publishing, L.L.C.
2315 Broadway, 3rd Floor
New York, NY 10024
E-mail: comments@review.com

Copyright © 2000 by Princeton Review Publishing, L.L.C.

All rights reserved under the International and Pan-American Copyright Conventions. Published in the United States by Random House, Inc., New York, and simultaneously in Canada by Random House of Canada Limited, Toronto.

ISBN 0-375-76163-2

Editor: Jeannette Mallozzi
Production Editor: Maria Dente
Production Coordinator: Stephanie Martin
Designer: Thane Kerner, Silverchair Science + Communications

Manufactured in the United States of America on partially recycled paper.

9 8 7 6 5 4 3 2

Third Edition

Acknowledgments

This book would not have been possible without the encouragement of many people. We thank our editor, Evan R. Schnittman, for his enthusiastic support throughout the entire process, as well as Rachel Warren and the rest of the staff at The Princeton Review. Many, many thanks also go to Jenn Nagaj, Jennifer Whitlow, and the staff at Silverchair Science + Communications for their beautiful work.

I would like to thank my parents and mega-cool sister for their love and support all these years; the SMS peanut gallery (JJ, Jen, Keith C., Keith H., and Ron) for making medical school so much fun; my roommate, Jeff, who always found new ways to surprise me; Radhika for recruiting me and making this book possible; Dr. Carolyn Walsh, who taught me the art of medicine; the Spiegls for their friendship and exquisite blueberry pancakes; the Stanford OSA for their warm smiles and limitless patience; all of my professors who challenged and inspired me; and, of course, Andrea, for bringing so much happiness into my life.

M.S.

Thanks to my fantastic parents, to Radhika for getting this whole adventure started, to George Martin for keeping the band together, and, last but not least, to "Smooth" Johnson, master of the carve.

P.Z.

I would like to thank my husband, Matthew Breaden, and my family, Neelam Sekhri, Amita O'Rourke, Dr. K.K. Sekhri, and Carol Sekhri, for all their support and encouragement. Many thanks to Shalini Dodds for her assistance in the book production as well.

R.S.B.

Contents

Introduction

Now that you've embarked on what is probably one of the most harried times in your life, studying for the USMLE Step 1, what can we tell you to make things a little less stressful? Well, not much that you don't already know. We just hope that this book will help make the whole process manageable and maybe even a little fun. We know that there are many review books out there already, so you might be wondering why we wrote yet another one. (We've asked ourselves that question many times during the writing process.) In our preparation for the United States Medical Licensing Examination (USMLE), we never found a review book that had everything we wanted, and all of us ended up buying way too many books and schlepping them around for months. We wanted to write a book that might approach the "perfect" Boards review book.

What makes a review book good? A comprehensive review book should cover all the topics you're required to know for the test but be concise enough so that you could actually read the whole thing. This book is a primary source of information, your home base. Obviously, we can't cover everything you've learned (and might have forgotten) in your preclinical courses, so use your course notes, syllabi, and textbooks for reference. The entire outline provided by the USMLE for Step 1 is covered in this book.

Unlike most of the other review books, our book primarily uses an organ system approach to presenting and synthesizing the material. We have chapters on general principles (e.g., biochemistry, pharmacology, microbiology), but pathology, physiology, histology, anatomy, microbiology, and pharmacology are discussed in the context of each organ system. The USMLE has over the past few years moved toward using clinical syndromes and case presentations to test your knowledge of the material. This is probably a good thing because that's how you will take care of your patients in the real world.

Where possible, we've also tried to present the material in an intuitive fashion because we feel that such an approach makes the material much easier to remember than list after list of facts to memorize. We've used a semicasual tone, so that things don't get too dry, although with some subjects that simply can't be avoided (e.g., biochemistry). We've also used bullets to describe signs and symptoms, diagnosis, and treatment of disease entities, and key points are highlighted or emphasized in the margins.

Just a few words of advice. Realize that your medical school's curriculum may have seemed exhaustive, but chances are that the USMLE will pose some questions that your courses didn't cover. This may become apparent as you're studying and doing practice questions. There are many strategies for studying: reading alone, using texts, using old notes and syllabi, doing lots of practice questions, and many more. Try several to see what works for you. Finally, remember that you've already learned almost all of this material before, and it's just a matter of re-acquainting yourself with it.

Description of the USMLE Step 1

The USMLE Step 1 is the first part of a three-step process to gain medical licensure in the United States. Starting in mid-May 1999, it has been offered as a one-day computerized exam administered by Sylvan Technology Centers®. Unlike in the past, when a written exam was offered only twice a year, the current USMLE Step 1 can be taken throughout the year, with the exception of major holidays.

The subjects tested on the USMLE Step 1 include anatomy (gross anatomy, embryology, neuroanatomy, and histology), biochemistry, behavioral sciences (including biostatistics and epidemiology), microbiology, immunology, pathology, pharmacology, and physiology. Over the years, the exam has become more interdisciplinary in nature, with many questions being posed in the format of a case presentation that spans different fields of knowledge. In addition, integrative topics such as nutrition, genetics, and aging will be covered.

To register for the exam, students can obtain registration materials from their medical schools or through the appropriate registration entity below:

> Students and graduates of United States and Canadian medical schools accredited by the Liaison Committee on Medical Education (LCME) or the American Osteopathic Association (AOA):

> NBME
> Department of Licensing Examination Services
> 3750 Market Street
> Philadelphia, PA 19104-3190
> Telephone: 215 590-9700
> Internet: www.nbme.org

> Students and graduates of foreign medical schools:
> ECFMG
> 3624 Market Street
> Philadelphia, PA 19104-2685
> Telephone: 215 386-5900
> Internet: www.ecfmg.org

Additional information on the examination can be obtained from the registration packet or the web site www.usmle.org. Test site information can be obtained from the web site www.sylvanprometric.com.

The USMLE is administered in blocks of 30 to 60 minutes over the course of an eight-hour day. Short breaks are given between blocks, and a break is provided for lunch.

Scores are made available to the registration entity (NBME or ECFMG) within two weeks of the date of the exam, at which time they are sent to the examinee. The score report contains both your overall score on Step 1 and a profile of your performance in each subject area.

The front page of your score report reveals that critical four-letter word (pass or fail), your score on a scale with a mean of 200 points, and your score on an alternate scale with a mean of 82. On the back of the score report, a topic-specific profile shows your performance in various areas. The profiles are meant for your information only and are not provided to residency programs or other institutions. The score required to pass the USMLE Step 1 is currently set at 179.

Test Format

USMLE Step 1 will be administered in seven timed blocks of about 50 questions per block. All questions will be multiple-choice, with a "one best answer" format. Generally, a brief case description is followed by a variable number of options. At times, the question is accompanied by a photograph or diagram. Most students agree that the majority of questions can be answered solely on the basis of the information provided in the question.

Breaks will be provided between examination blocks, and a lunch break is given. Because the entire examination day must take no longer than eight hours, longer breaks taken earlier in the day may result in no breaks between sections later in the day. If a section is completed early, then the extra time can be put toward breaks.

Just a Few More Pearls

Different students have different goals, so the amount of time students spend studying for the examination differs greatly. Informal surveys of medical students nationwide show study times ranging from two weeks to a year! Obviously, the right amount of time to study depends on your experience, your strengths, and your goals (not to mention the amount of time available). Here are a couple more recommendations that we have for Step 1 examinees:

- Use the USMLE practice computerized exams provided on our website and the exam offered through the USMLE web site. The same exam is also offered under simulated testing conditions for a fee through Sylvan Prometric.

  The sample items are similar to those that appear on the Step 1 and may even have been pulled from previous administrations of the test. Some students take the sample examination before they begin studying to reveal their areas of weakness, whereas others prefer to use it toward the end to simulate the examination and practice their pacing. Either way, you'll get a feel for the content, style, and pace of the test.

- Get comfortable with the computerized table of lab values; if you have the time, you might even want to memorize a few key values. The computerized format requires you to scroll through the table to find the value you want. If you don't know where to look, precious seconds may be lost during your search.

- Try to get a copy of the retired NBME questions. In addition to the sample items included with registration, there are two NBME publications that contain several hundred Step 1 questions that are out of print. Known as the *Retired NBME Questions* and *Self-Test Part I Questions*, these books have a total of 1,500 practice Step 1 questions that are excellent study tools (although the format of the questions is outdated). Many medical schools keep an old copy of these questions for students to use during Step 1 study, and "big sibs" often pass old copies from one class to the next. Locating one of these question sets is definitely worth the effort!

Good luck!

Strategic Guide for the USMLE Step 1

Basic Information

The USMLE is a three-step series of standardized tests that must be successfully completed in order to apply for medical licensure. The USMLE is administered by the National Board of Medical Examiners (NBME) and the Educational Commission for Foreign Medical Graduates (ECFMG). In the United States, a license to practice medicine is governed by individual medical licensing authorities ("state medical boards") who require successful completion of the USMLE as part of the licensing process.

The USMLE Step 1 is designed to test the basic biomedical sciences. In 1999, the USMLE was administered via computer at Sylvan Learning Centers worldwide. The new computer-based testing (CBT) will be comprised of seven 1-hour sections, each containing 50 items. Each section will test all subject areas and although each examinee will have a different exam, all exam administrations will be "content-equivalent." The total testing appointment is 8 hours long, during which the examinee must complete a 15-minute orientation and the 7 hours of testing, which leaves 45 minutes for breaks and lunch. The exam will be administered throughout the year, and students may take the CBT up to three times in a 12-month period.

The NBME has announced that initially, the computer-based exam will be linear (not adaptive) and that its goal is to introduce computer adaptive sequential testing (CAST) in 2000. In adaptive sequential testing, the examinee's performance on a given section influences the difficulty level of subsequent sections, and it is possible to go back to items or skip around within a section. Our research indicates that the exam will be adaptive with regards to subject matter; for example, if an examinee performs well in pharmacology, but poorly in physiology, the examinee will be administered harder pharmacology questions and easier physiology questions on subsequent sections. The NBME has stated that it does not plan to announce when the exam will switch to section-adaptive testing, but that the "students will know when they take the exam." Topic representation is randomly dispersed

This guide was prepared by John J. Mariani, M.D., Director of Research and Development, Medical Licensing Program; and David Kelley, Product Manager, Medical Licensing Program.

throughout the test. All CBT sections contain test items that cover anatomy, behavioral science, biochemistry, microbiology, pathology, pharmacology, and physiology. Interdisciplinary topics, such as nutrition, genetics, and aging are covered as well.

Scoring

The USMLE scoring process is complex; a raw score is converted into two equivalent scores, one on a three-digit score scale and one on a two-digit scale. Currently, the three-digit score of 179 is the minimum passing score for USMLE Step 1, which corresponds to the 7th percentile among U.S. and Canadian medical students, as published in *General Instructions, Content Descriptions and Sample Items*, the booklet you receive after you have registered to take Step 1. A complete distribution of scores on the three-digit scale from over 30,000 U.S. and Canadian medical school students is available in that booklet.

The NBME has stated that it will be scoring the USMLE Step 1 CBT on a "new" scaled score, so direct comparisons between the old paper and pencil administered exams and the CBT will not be possible. As of January 1999, it has not announced what this new 3-digit scaled score will be. It is assumed that the 2-digit scaled score will remain the same since this score is written into the individual state medical licensing laws for minimum competency criteria.

The ECFMG does not furnish score distribution information from the data on graduates of overseas medical schools. A two-digit score of 75 always corresponds to the minimum passing score on the two-digit scale. A two-digit score of 82 is always equivalent to the three-digit score of 200. Those are the only intersections of the two scaled scores that are published by either organization.

According to the NBME, any examinee must answer between 55–65% of the total items on the Step 1 correctly attain a passing score. That is the most specific information either organization provides on the subject of raw-to-scale conversion.

Why the USMLE is Different From Other Standardized Tests

The NBME has gone out of its way to prepare an exam that assesses only your readiness for the next step in your medical education or career, not how well you take a test. For some of you, this may be a relief. Many, many other standardized tests are intentionally written to trip you up, despite your command of the competencies their writers profess to examine. The NBME specifically steers its item writers away from defects in test writing, so students cannot employ strategies to get around the content-based objectives of the test. In this way, the USMLE tests are technique-proof, as compared to other standardized tests.

The Princeton Review Approach to the USMLE

As discussed, tricks or gimmicks won't help you much on the USMLE Step 1. It is a very well designed, content-based exam that requires comprehensive and detailed knowledge of basic medical science. So, we do not rely on standardized test-busting techniques or teach you how to trip up the test.

Content, Content, Content

Instead, The Princeton Review focuses on the highest-yield topics and teaches you to apply your knowledge to complex, interdisciplinary questions whose like you've never encountered before on standardized tests. Because we know this is a content-based exam, we carefully track the most recent changes in topic representation and item types on the USMLE. We revise our materials continuously to include the most recent basic science developments and changes in the USMLE.

We also need to train you to deal with some traditional issues caused by all standardized tests, including the USMLE, such as test-taking anxiety, careful selection of answer choices, and sudden memory loss.

Step 1 is an "indoor Olympic reading event." You've got to train to build your endurance and speed. Apart from drawing blanks, the single greatest impediment to not doing your best is *bad pacing*. Knowing the item formats well and practicing a few time-saving approaches will make the most of your hard review work and smarts.

Purpose of Techniques

So, our goals in this guide are to show you how to make the most of your time, acquaint you with the item formats and test language, and teach you when to cut your losses and move on. All Step 1 examinees can use specific, but limited techniques to maximize their performances. These techniques are not gimmicks that will magically give you a higher score; Step 1 is not vulnerable to typical strategies for cracking standardized tests.

You must practice the approaches we teach in this guide. At first, they may seem awkward, but with time and practice, these techniques will enable you to:

- Increase your reading pace

- Focus only on relevant details

- Eliminate more options when you are unsure of the correct answer

Because the timing on this exam is so critical, we recommend that you first try the techniques on practice exams or during timed sections prior to the administration of the actual exam. We want you to practice them so that they become second nature. **Unless these pacing techniques become second nature to you, they not only won't work, but may also actually slow you down.** We don't want you to concentrate on anything but how to choose the correct answer when you actually sit for the exam.

Training for the USMLE

The USMLE Step 1 is the Mount Everest of standardized tests. The process of preparing for this exam is not unlike an athlete preparing for an Olympic event. All Step 1 examinees need a strategy for studying, practicing, and sitting for this exam. Preparation for this exam can be broken down into three main areas: selecting review materials, studying, and practicing with USMLE-type questions.

Review Materials

Selecting review materials is critical. You must use your studying time and effort efficiently, neither spending time on material unlikely to be on the exam, nor skipping lightly over high-yield topics. Of course, we cannot predict what will be on the exam; we can only report what has been tested on previous exams and in what level of detail. Not all of the content of the book is directly tested, some of it is background information necessary to review complex concepts that are likely to appear on Step 1.

Studying

Studying for the Step 1 is a demanding challenge. The amount of information to be mastered is tremendous. Each student has a unique set of strengths and weaknesses that is determined by his or her individual background. While the material will be covered in a detailed and thorough fashion, ultimately, your own personal preparation will be the critical factor in how you score.

Practicing

It takes practice to get used to the way in which the questions are asked—which can stump even the best test-taker, the most diligent student, or the experienced physician—and how quickly you need to answer them. We wrote this guide to increase your confidence and advantage in this third aspect of boards preparation.

Anatomy of USMLE items

First, let's quickly run through a little USMLE vocabulary. This will help clarify questions later.

1. **Items** or **Item Stems**—all of the **information** following a number in the testing booklet. The items may present patient lab information, or

Strategic Guide for the
USMLE Step 1

lab information needed to compute a result. The items may have associated gross or microscopic findings, and radiographic images such as computed tomography (CT) scans or magnetic resonance imaging (MRI) findings. They may have complete or partial patient histories.

2. **Lead-in**—the **specific sentence or question** that asks you to find some connection between the stem and ONE of the options provided.

3. **Options**—lettered words or phrases provided as possible **answer choices**. They follow the lead-in or follow a small set of items. For each numbered item, only one option will be considered the correct answer. There is no partial credit on this test.

4. **Answer**—the single option for each item that will be scored as **correct**.

5. **Distractors**—all of the options that will be scored as **incorrect**. They are always wrong, but each is written so that if one or two pieces of information provided in the stem were just a bit different, each distracter could be correct. They're written not so much to confuse you (though they might), as they are to make sure you perceive the appreciable distinctions between each of them and the correct answer.

6. **Picture**—a gross or microscopic finding, chart, graph, radiograph, or any type of **visual element**.

Techniques

Fast Forward

You are looking at a new item. What's your first impression? Is it long or short? If the stem is longer than four lines, then read the very last sentence, phrase, or question before you start reading at the beginning. You need to first determine what this item is asking about. In NBME terms, the lead-in most often establishes the objective of the question. Knowing that right off the bat, you can screen the information presented in the stem or cluster header that isn't relevant to the lead-ins. Remember reading comprehension from the SAT and MCAT? The good news is that, on the Step 1, you will rarely have more than two questions based on the same "passage," which we call a cluster header. If you read the whole stem or cluster header before figuring out what hoop the NBME is holding in front of you, then you are wasting very valuable time and your score will suffer.

Computer-based Testing (CBT)

The USMLE Step 1 is now administered via computer. What does this mean to students who have been bubbling in answers on paper and pencil multiple-choice tests their whole lives, or to students who are more comfortable with essay or oral exams?

It actually isn't that big of a change. Initially, the CBT will look very much like the old paper and pencil USMLE Step 1, except that the testing interface is a computer screen. The item formats are the same as the old paper and pencil exams, so the only differences will be the mechanics of answering the questions on the computer and the new, single-day format of the exam.

One advantage of not having to "bubble in" an answer sheet is that you don't have to worry about skipping around and accidentally marking the wrong question or skipping an item. Frame-shift errors (accidentally skipping or inserting an answer on the answer sheet and therefore making each subsequent answer choice out of synch) will be impossible. You will have the ability to mark items for later review.

To Skip or Not To Skip

For paper and pencil exams, it has always been our advice to answer the questions in order so as to minimize the chance of making any sloppy answer sheet errors. With CBT, those errors are no longer a concern, so now we offer students a choice of techniques, **scanning and skipping** or **one-by-one**. We recommend that students try both techniques on the practice exams provided with their registration packets and decide what works best for them.

Scanning and Skipping

For some students, particularly students who have difficulty finishing all the items within a section, the option to skip around and decide which items they want to answer first will improve their efficiency. The items will be randomly distributed throughout the section with regard to topic representation and difficulty level. To maximize performance, some students may prefer to answer the questions they are more comfortable with first, and save the more difficult items for the end. The technique is to **scan** an item and decide if it should be answered now, or **skipped** and answered later. The logic behind this strategy is that if you waste time on difficult items early in the section (items that you are more likely to answer incorrectly), you may not have time to answer easier items that appear towards the end of the section. The idea is to maximize your time management, spending time on items that you are likely to get credit for. If you run out of time and the items that were unanswered were items that you were likely to get wrong anyway, you have used your time efficiently. The downside to this strategy is that it is necessary to invest time in **scanning** the item to decide whether it should be answered now or saved for later. If too much time is spent on **scanning**, the end result will be time wasted, not saved. And when a question is answered, **leave it alone**, it is a well-studied phenomenon that going back and changing answers is a bad strategy. Students are much more likely to change a correct answer to an incorrect one than an incorrect answer to a correct one.

One-by-one

Other students will feel more comfortable attacking the items **one-by-one**, answering each question in the order it appears in a section. This technique will benefit those students who are confident that they are going to finish all the items in the section in the allotted time. The advantages to going **one-by-one** are: (1) no time is spent deciding whether an item should be skipped or not; (2) it is easier to calculate how many more items remain in the section for pacing purposes; (3) the overall flow of the exam is smoother without any time or energy spent skipping around.

Process of Elimination (POE)

Your skills as a diagnostician depend on your ability to rapidly reduce the number of disease entities, causative agents, or injured systems, etc. en route to prescribing efficacious treatment. This principle of reasoning also applies to the task before you when sitting for the USMLE. A general concept in all standardized test taking is that distractors (or wrong answers) are easier to find than correct answers if you aren't already sure of the answer. With this in mind, you should immediately begin to strike down that which you know to be false.

Examine every option. You want to poke holes in them, one at a time. If any part of the item stem falls apart while you're considering a single option (lab values given in the stem don't match a lettered option, for example), move on—quickly. For example, if an item asks you to treat a patient with COPD, you should immediately eliminate an option that calls for 100% oxygen by face mask. Be suspicious of any answer options that use extreme terms like "always" or "never."

Process of elimination is one of the most powerful tools that you will employ on this exam. This strategy should be applied to every test item that you are not 100% sure about. Each time you can eliminate an answer option, the probability of getting the correct answer choice increases. For instance, if you flat-out guess on one answer out of five options, there is a 20% chance that you guessed correctly. If you can eliminate one option, the probability increases to 25%. If you eliminate two options, the probability is 33%. If you can eliminate three options, the probability is now 50%. You may wonder, "Who cares? I'm still guessing wrong a lot." This is true, but on a 350-question test, you will not know the answer to every question cold, so by using POE to increase your guessing percentage, you can significantly increase your score over the course of the entire exam.

POE is not a "trick;" when you are able to discount answer choices you are using your hard-earned knowledge to do so. POE is a systematic approach that should be used throughout the exam. You should never just be guessing randomly (unless you are literally out of time) or choosing the "letter of the day" when you don't know the answer. Using POE, you should always be able to eliminate at least one answer choice per question.

Guessing

The only time it is acceptable to randomly guess the answer to a question is when you are almost out of time (have only a few minutes left) and have not finished the section. THERE IS NO GUESSING PENALTY ON THE USMLE. It is always beneficial to fill in all of the answers. The most effective way to do this is to select a single letter such as "C," and mark the remaining questions with it. Obviously, the more answer choices there are available, the less likely you are to hit the bull's eye. Again, this type of guessing is only useful when there isn't enough time available for you to employ POE.

Pacing

This is a critical part of any standardized test performance. The USMLE Step 1 CBT sections require you to answer 50 items in 1 hour; that's an average of one minute and twelve seconds per question. In those 72 seconds, you must read the item and select an answer. Every time you spend more than a 72 seconds on a question, that time must be made up somewhere else in the section.

No Crusades

Don't spend too much time on any one item. Some Step 1 examinees reach a test item and say, "I knew this just yesterday, now I can't remember a thing about it, and I am going to sit here and answer this if it is the last thing I ever do!" Launching a crusade against any one test item is a big mistake. There are 350 questions on Step 1 and you are not going to be sure about the answer to every single one. There will be questions that you simply don't know the answer to, so accept that, and when you are about to start banging your head against the desk, use POE and move on. Wasting time on items you do not know the answer to will not allow you enough time to answer the questions that you do know the answers to. Learn to cut your losses when you are up against the wall, be rational, use POE, and MOVE ON!

Pictures

Some items are presented with additional information in the form of graphs, diagrams, slide and micrograph findings, photographs, or imaging studies. You must be very open-minded when approaching these items—do not get trapped, spending huge amounts of time (which on this test can be only 2 minutes) deciphering cryptic data representations at the expense of missing equally weighted, easier, nongraphical items. Bear in mind that the visual information is *not always necessary* to help you choose the correct answer. For some items, you absolutely *must* read the image properly in order to choose the answer. The key here is to have a system: at first, ignore the picture and try to answer the question without using the visual material. Then, after reading the item and the options, refer to the picture if necessary. **DON'T** look at the picture first and say, "I have no idea what this is and I will not be able to answer this question."

1. **Slides, Micrographs, Photographs, and Imaging Studies**—these images take the form of an imaging study like a CT scan or MRI, or a microscopic preparation like an electron or light micrograph. Sometimes these items can be answered without looking at the picture, as we have said. However, the picture can be useful in confirming an answer choice or in using POE. The best approach here is to read the item first, determine your answer choice, and then look for it, just as we indicated before. But, you may need to look for the best option if the answer doesn't immediately come to mind. Only once you have determined your favorite should you look at the picture to confirm your selection. If you have to look at the picture before determining an answer and still nothing jumps out at you, then you need to use POE with the picture in mind.

2. **Graphs and Diagrams**—these tend to be more central to the item than the above. However, they invariably contain some superfluous information that can take too much time to decipher or eliminate. Therefore, when you come across one of these, go straight to the item to first determine EXACTLY what you need to find in the graph. You will definitely waste time if you look at the diagram or graph prior to reading the item and lead-in. Remember, just because information is provided to you does not mean that it is relevant to answering the question. Think of it as being analogous to clinical medicine; not every piece of history, physical exam, or lab data is relevant.

Lab Values

A table of standard laboratory values is available on the USMLE CBT as a "pop-up" screen. You should have received your *Step 1 General Computer-based Content and Sample Test Questions* booklet if you've registered for the test already. The lab values you are expected to use on the actual test are provided in the "Sample Items" section of that booklet. Study them carefully. These are extremely helpful and should be consulted as you work through any practice items. Do NOT assume that the normal lab values you used in lab research will be the same on Step 1. Different hospital labs, different medical journals, and possibly even different faculty use different techniques and different units to present data. In order to avoid misinterpreting labs on the actual test, you've got to be clear on what the Step 1 regards as normal. So, if an item presents you with a lot of lab information, you should immediately check the normal values.

Adaptive Tests and Difficulty

Computer-adaptive sequential testing sounds a lot like section-adaptive testing. During *any* section-adaptive test, the computer selects items of varying levels of difficulty for each new section. Think of the distribution of item difficulty and score scale as a bell curve. Difficulty may be mixed or may ascend with the item numbers in each section, but each section should show some variety of difficulty levels.

Getting to Know You

When you sit down for the first section in a section-adaptive test such as we envision CAST, the computer does not know anything about you. So, it gives you a selection of items that represent the full range, or curve, of difficulty levels available in the entire pool. After the first section, it evaluates where on that curve your performance began to falter and where it was consistently correct. For the next section, it leaves out levels of difficulty that are clearly too high or low for you and decreases the variance in difficulty, focusing in on the median difficulty of your prior correct answers. Section after section, the computer tests the limits of your performance, until it is confident that it has accurately measured the best you can do in the time it has given you.

Cross-training

Bear in mind that most standardized tests measure performance across a number of subjects, whether it's math versus vocabulary, or biochemistry versus behavioral science. So, from one section to the next, the median difficulty of one subject may be greater than that of another subject.

Adapting to CAST

A good score on the USMLE paper and pencil test was the result of thorough preparation and an ability to perform multiple deductive steps under pressure. This is also true of good CBT and CAST scores, but CAST will require, at a minimum, a "defensive" test-taking strategy—not giving up any ground once you've claimed it. With each new section, the computer eliminates whole levels of difficulty (and score possibilities) because it believes you couldn't handle them in the last section. Just like people taking the GMAT CAT or GRE CAT, by the end of a section-adaptive test, you are basically haggling with the computer over one or two points. It is too late to make up for incorrect answers made during the first or second section at that point.

Cracking the CAST

After CBT for any step has been given for more than 6 months, all bets are off. The NBME has itself said that no advance notice will be given when CBT switches to CAST. So, if you are sitting for any step after it has been given as a CBT for more than 6 months, you should hedge your bets and use this approach. *Give the first section all you have*. If you need a couple of hours and/or a couple of cups of coffee to really wake up, then don't wake up an hour before you're scheduled to start CAST and not drink any coffee. The major difference between CAST and CBT is that with CAST, your performance on the first section proportionally has a much greater affect on your score. If you have a bad first section on CAST, it is much harder (and may be impossible) to recover compared to CBT or the old paper and pencil tests.

Item Format

Single Best Multiple Choice

All of the 350 items on the USMLE Step 1 CBT are multiple-choice items. This item type has changed recently. Currently, the answer options may range from A through J; in the past they only ranged from A through E. Most items using this format are still a standard five-option multiple-choice question, but a minority of them have more than five options. However, even if an item has more than five options, the principle is the same. Pick a single option as your answer choice.

Here are examples of standard single best-type items with five answer choices:

1. A 73-year-old African American man with long-standing hypertension and atherosclerotic vascular disease was recently prescribed captopril. He now presents with worsening renal function and even higher blood pressure. Physical examination reveals a bruit at the right costovertebral angle. Which of the following is most likely to be found in this patient?
    (A) Decreased plasma renin
    (B) Hyperkalemia
    (C) Hyperpigmentation
    (D) Increased urine sodium
    (E) Metabolic alkalosis

(E) is correct. This is secondary hyperaldosteronism due to renal artery stenosis. Hypoperfusion of the juxtaglomerular apparatus causes increased renin, which then results in increased aldosterone, resulting in (A) hyperreninemia, (B) hypokalemia (D) increased sodium retention, and metabolic alkalosis (aldosterone stimulates renal proton secretion) (C) is associated with hypoaldosteronism (adrenal cortex failure) (Addison's disease).

2. A 20-year-old Anglo-American man presents to the emergency department (ED) status-post blunt trauma after being struck by a car. The patient is evaluated and treated at a local hospital with a simple fracture of the right distal femur. After several weeks of ambulation on crutches, the patient returns to ED complaining of generalized extensor weakness of his right arm, particularly his right hand. The most likely etiology of his muscle weakness is
    (A) previously undiagnosed right mid-humeral fracture
    (B) previously undiagnosed surgical fracture of the right humerus
    (C) radial nerve compression at the level of the axilla on the right
    (D) radial nerve compression at the wrist on the right
    (E) right-sided compartment syndrome

(C) is correct. This is "wrist drop," palsy of the extensor muscles of the posterior compartment of the forearm secondary to radial nerve compression in the axilla by the crutches. (A) could cause the symptoms described, but is not likely considering that the patient has been ambulating with crutches for several weeks. (B) would compromise the axillary nerve, which supplies the deltoid and teres minor muscles. (D) the generalized extensor weakness on the right means that the radial nerve damage must be proximal to the wrist. (E) would have been a surgical emergency at the initial presentation that, if untreated, would have led to muscle and nerve necrosis soon after presentation.

3. A 27-year-old African American woman with a well-documented history of sickle cell anemia presents for a routine "check-up." The patient is without complaints. Physical exam is unremarkable. Complete blood cell count is pending. Which of the following should be considered in this patient?
    (A) Autologous bone marrow transplant
    (B) Hemoglobin electrophoresis
    (C) Karyotype analysis
    (D) Pneumococcal vaccine
    (E) Recombinant hepatitis C vaccine

(D) is correct. Patients with sickle cell anemia are susceptible to encapsulated organisms; *S. pneumonia* is a Gram-positive cocci with a capsule. The pneumococcal vaccine contains the antigenic components of multiple variants (23 types) of the pneumococcal capsule. (A) This would not be effective in a sickle cell anemia patient since the point mutation in the DNA is present in the marrow stem cells. (B) Hemoglobin electrophoresis is unnecessary in this patient, since she already carries the diagnosis of sickle cell anemia. (C) A karyotype would not reveal any abnormalities with regard to SS anemia. (E) There is no vaccine available for hepatitis C.

4.   A 32-year-old man presents with a 6-day history of fever, headache, malaise, and nonproductive cough. Physical exam is remarkable for an elevated temperature of 38.7C (101.7F) and isolated crackles heard over the left lower lung field. A roentgenograph of the chest demonstrates interstitial infiltration and subsegmental atelectasis of the left lower lobe. Which of the following drugs would most likely be an effective treatment for this patient?

(A)   Amphotericin
(B)   Ampicillin
(C)   Erythromycin
(D)   Nafcillin
(E)   Penicillin

(C) is correct. This is *Mycoplasma pneumoniae* causing the syndrome of atypical pneumonia (walking pneumonia). *M. pneumoniae* lacks a cell wall, so a bacterial protein synthesis inhibitor is the treatment of choice. Erythromycin binds to the 50s component of the bacterial ribosome and inhibits the translocation of tRNA. (A) Amphotericin is an antifungal drug. (B) Ampicillin (D) Nafcillin, and (E) Penicillin are all bacterial cell wall synthesis inhibitors.

5.   A 7-year-old boy presents with fever, diffuse rash, cervical lymphadenopathy, conjunctivitis, desquamation of the palms and feet, and dry, cracked lips. Workup reveals leukocytosis and an elevated erythrocyte sedimentation rate. He is treated with aspirin and high-dose gamma globulin. Without treatment, the most likely complication of this disease is

(A)   bloody diarrhea
(B)   coronary artery vasculitis
(C)   encephalopathy
(D)   lower lobe pneumonia
(E)   lymphoma

(B) is correct. This is the mucocutaneous lymph node syndrome (Kawasaki syndrome), an acute, febrile, multisystem disease of children. Autoimmune vasculitis of the coronary arteries and coronary artery aneurysm is associated with more serious cases. Treatment with aspirin and gamma globulin is standard. (C) is not associated with Kawasaki syndrome. This is neither an infection (A and D) nor a premalignant condition (E).

6. A 43-year-old woman with hemianopsia on physical exam is evaluated. A computed tomography scan reveals a 0.5 cm mass in the sella turcica and surgical management is indicated. During the surgical procedure to remove the mass, the pituitary stalk is partially severed. During the immediate post-operative period, which of the following would be most likely be present?

   (A) Elevated levels of estradiol
   (B) Elevated levels of luteinizing hormone
   (C) Elevated levels of prolactin
   (D) Elevated levels of thyroid hormone
   (E) Elevated levels of vasopressin

(C) is correct. Prolactin is the only pituitary hormone whose control by the hypothalamus is primarily negative. Dopamine secretion by the hypothalamus travels via the hypothalamic-adenohypophyseal portal venous system and inhibits the release of prolactin by the anterior pituitary. (A), (B), (D), (E) are wrong, because damaging the pituitary stalk would decrease production of all other pituitary hormone products.

The USMLE won't provide you with explanations like we have, but these are examples of the way this item type is likely to be used; a clinical scenario testing a basic science concept.

This next item is an example of a complicated clinical scenario. It contains more information than you need and requires discriminating judgment as to what information is relevant. When approaching a long item like this, you should initially ask yourself, "What is the actual question?"

7. A 35-year-old African American woman presents with complaints of long-standing generalized weakness and fatigue. The patient had recently been treated for a urinary tract infection with trimethoprim/sulfamethoxazole. Laboratory workup reveals a microcytic anemia. Bilirubin studies are normal. Menstrual history is unremarkable. Hemoglobin electrophoresis reveals significantly increased levels of hemoglobin A_2. Which of the following is the most likely cause of her anemia?

   (A) β-thalassemia major
   (B) β-thalassemia minor
   (C) Glucose-6-phosphate dehydrogenase deficiency
   (D) Iron deficiency
   (E) Pyridoxine deficiency

(B) is correct. Increased amounts of hemoglobin A_2 is diagnostic of β-thalassemia minor (β-thalassemia trait). (A) β-thalassemia major (Coolie's anemia) appear after the first 4–6 months of life, and even with modern therapies, those afflicted rarely survive into adulthood. (C) Anemia secondary to G6Pdase deficiency exacerbated by sulfa therapy would present with hemolysis (elevated unconjugated bilirubin), but not abnormal hemoglobin A_2. (D) Iron deficiency does cause a microcytic anemia, but would not cause elevated levels of hemoglobin A_2. (E) Pyridoxine (vitamin B_6) is required for transaminase reactions and is unrelated to microcytic anemia.

To figure that out, you want to go straight to the lead-in found at the very end of the item stem, and read it first. In this case, you immediately know that the patient has anemia and you will be looking for clinical clues in the rest of the stem to tell you the etiology. Scan the item stem looking for these clues. In this example, the recent antibiotic treatment is a distracting piece of clinical information. Know what you are looking for before the item stem leads you astray; not all of the information in the item stem is directly relevant to answering the item correctly. Sometimes, information is there only to make you waste time reading and trying to figure out where it fits in. Not every lab data, piece of history, or physical exam finding will be directly relevant to the item.

Think about this: once you're practicing, your patients won't know what they're supposed to tell you, so in a history, you'll be confronted with many pieces of information, medical or otherwise, that are irrelevant to diagnosing and treating the problem at hand. For the test, going straight to the lead-in will provide cues to help you find the discrete information needed to provide a diagnosis, or determine the best means of prevention, or indicate what you expect to see in the patient's labs.

Here is an example of the extended single best item type, where the option range is greater than the standard A–E:

8.   A 25-year-old Anglo-American man is referred to a psychiatrist. The patient has been unable to hold down a steady job, often missing days, and having many arguments with his superiors. The patient reports having a history of intense, unstable relationships, usually broken off by him. The patient states that he feels uncomfortable in social situations. The patient denies any hallucinations or other psychotic symptoms. Sleep habits and appetite are normal. This patient's most likely diagnosis is

(A)   agoraphobia

(B)   antisocial personality disorder

(C)   bipolar disorder

(D)   borderline personality disorder

(E)   cyclothymia

(F)   major depression

(G)   schizoid personality disorder

(H)   schizophrenia

(D) is correct. The key words here are "intense, unstable relationships," which, especially in the context of the USMLE, implies borderline personality disorder. (A) This disorder is characterized by the fear of being alone in public places, especially in situations from which a rapid exit would be difficult. (B) The patient would need to display signs of "lacking a conscience," committing acts against others without remorse. (C) Bipolar disorder is characterized by alternating cycles of mania and depression. This patient has no history to support this diagnosis. (E) This is a less severe form of bipolar disorder. The symptoms can often be almost as severe as in bipolar disorder, but may not be of sufficient duration to meet criteria for that of bipolar disorder. (F) The patient lacks any vegetative signs or symptoms. (G) This is characterized by a lifelong pattern of social withdrawal. Others often see them as being eccentric, isolated, or lonely. (H) Markedly peculiar behavior, abnormal affect, unusual speech, bizarre ideas, and strange perceptual experiences characterize schizophrenia.

This is a more difficult type of item if you do not know the answer straight away. After reading the item stem, try to answer the question without looking at the answer options. Once you have an answer option in mind, scan the options for your answer. If you are unsure or draw a blank, use POE. It is harder to narrow down the choices when there are more answer options, but POE always improves your chances of arriving at the correct answer when you are less than 100% sure.

The very worst thing you can do is to read the lettered options prior to reading the items. This will confuse your thinking and possibly induce a panic attack. You should also read only one numbered item at a time.

Calculations

Some items will require you to make simple calculations. In general, Step 1 is not a math test. However, there are some basic skills that you will need to master prior to the exam. Calculators are not allowed into the test center, so all calculations must be worked out by hand. A "white board" is provided for this purpose.

For example:

9. A screening test for a newly discovered infectious agent is performed on the sera of 100 volunteers. It is known that 10 of these volunteers are infected with the agent in question. The screening test results indicate that 10 of the volunteers tested positive for the infectious agent in question. A confirmatory test is performed on the sera of the patients who had a positive screening test for the infectious agent. The confirmatory test, which has a specificity of 99.9%, is positive in 90% of the tested sera. What is the sensitivity of the screening test?

    (A) 0.1%
    (B) 1%
    (C) 10%
    (D) 90%
    (E) 100%

(D) is correct. Sensitivity = true (+)/true (+) + false (–). The true (+) = 10 x 90% confirmatory test = 9. It was known that 10 of the original 100 were infected, so the screening test missed one of these cases, making the false negative # = 1. The equation is 9 / 9 + 1 = .9 = 90%. Specificity = True (–)/true (–) + false (+). Sensitivity is the ability to detect disease (low false (–)), specificity is the ability to exclude disease (low false (+)). Typically, good screening tests have a high sensitivity (low false (–)), and confirmatory tests have a high specificity (low false (+)).

In this case, you needed to know some basic formulas and how to plug in numbers. You will need to be familiar with scientific notation and understand how the pH scale works. The math in general is relatively easy; what is being tested is the application of the appropriate formula. Still, be careful. Wouldn't you hate to get a question wrong even when you know the concept and formula cold, but your math is wrong?

Interpreting Laboratory Values

Some items will offer the answer options as a group of lab values from which you must select the most appropriate option based on the clinical description in the item stem.

For example:

10. A 23-year-old woman presents to the emergency department with complaints of gradually worsening polyuria, polydipsia, and generalized weakness over the past week. She has a history of insulin-dependent diabetes and reports poor compliance with her prescribed insulin regimen. Physical exam reveals tachypnea, hyperpnea, and a "sweet" breath odor. Which of the following blood gas values would most likely represent this patient's arterial blood gas?

	pH	Pa_{O_2}	P_{CO_2}	H_{CO_3}
(A)	7.12	102	19	7
(B)	7.22	91	60	26
(C)	7.29	85	80	40
(D)	7.37	98	41	25
(E)	7.60	55	18	22

(A) is correct. This patient has diabetic ketoacidosis, which is characterized by a metabolic acidosis (low bicarb) secondary to ketone body formation, and hypocapnia (compensatory respiratory alkalosis). Complete respiratory compensation for a metabolic acidosis does not occur. (B) This is an acute respiratory acidosis. (C) This is a chronic respiratory acidosis with a compensatory metabolic alkalosis (elevated bicarb). (D) is a normal blood gas. (E) This is a respiratory alkalosis (hyperventilation) in response to hypoxia.

Experimental Items

Items can also ultimately end up unscored, even if the NBME intended to include them in its final score tabulations. If it tested well in another administration (probably as an experimental item), but you, and everyone else who took the test at the same time you did, all chose the same incorrect option, then it's pretty obvious that that particular item was poorly written. The NBME usually throws that item out and recalibrates everyone's final scores before they go out to you to make sure that the bad item doesn't count against you.

The most important thing to remember about experimental items is that you can't tell which they are when you are taking the exam. ASSUME THAT EVERY TEST ITEM COUNTS!

Remember...

- DON'T LEAVE ANY QUESTIONS BLANK! There is no penalty for guessing; you receive credit if you answer the question correctly, and there is no deduction from your raw score for wrong answers.

- NO CRUSADES! Hard questions count just as much as easy questions. If you don't know the answer, use POE and move on. Don't throw good time after bad. Cut your losses!

- TIMING IS EVERYTHING! Keep track of your pacing at regular intervals. The fear of not finishing in time will motivate you to keep up.

We absolutely do not want you to go back and re-evaluate—or worse, *change*—your choices. First guesses are more likely to be correct. If you go back and change your answers, you are likely to change correct answers to wrong ones. Never go back and change an answer choice. (The only rare exception to this rule is if an item stem provides you with the answer to a previous question.)

Keeping Faith

Preparing for the Step 1 is a very difficult exercise in self-discipline. Again, preparing for this exam is analogous to an athlete preparing for the Olympics. You must condition yourself for the big event. The amount of studying required is tremendous. The pressure of the USMLE Step 1 can feel crushing. Anxiety over the eventual outcome and its implications can be disabling.

To be an efficient and productive student, you must deal with these issues as they arise. Use your instructor and classmates as a resource. Keep a regular schedule and study habits. This is not an exam that you can cram for, so don't stay up all night only to sleep through class the next day. Pace yourself; slow and steady wins the race. Focus on what's in front of you, and don't worry about tomorrow, next week, or two years from now. If you stick to a schedule and work at it regularly, you will be able to move mountains (of books).

Anxiety is a normal state of mind for this process. If you aren't anxious, something is wrong. Use the anxiety to motivate your studies, not interfere with them. The key to success at this exam is an honest effort on a daily basis. The material needs to be chipped away at a little at a time, and if this is done regularly for a solid block of time prior to the exam, it can be manageable. Procrastination is a recipe for disaster.

Sleep regular hours. In the weeks prior to the exam, you should be getting up the same time you will need to be up for the exam. If you are in a pattern of staying up late and sleeping late, it will be hard to change right before the exam. Rest is just as important as studying

Be good to yourself. When you are not studying, DO SOMETHING FUN. It is important to maintain your mental health, so mix in some recreational activities with your studying. The key here is balance.

Test Day

Most of the rules you must adhere to when you arrive at the center will have been provided to you already in the *Step 1 Computer-based Content and Sample Test Questions* booklet, published by the NBME. On test day remember—bring the registration card given to you by your school or the ECFMG and photo identification. Do NOT expect to keep any calculators, beepers, cell phones, or books, or watches (the computer will provide a clock timer).

1. Arrive at the test center at least 30 minutes early.

2. Follow all instructions carefully.

3. Pay attention during the mandatory 15-minute computer orientation.

4. Look at the timer regularly. Adjust for pace. You should AVERAGE 72 seconds per item. All items are scored with equal weight. They don't care if you spent 7–8 minutes on a difficult item. It counts the same as an item that took you only 20 seconds to answer.

5. You are not penalized for wrong answers, so DON'T LEAVE ANY QUESTIONS BLANK. You may not be sure about every question, so when in doubt use POE and move on. If you find that you're almost out of time (only a couple of minutes left), choose one letter and fill in all of the remaining items with that letter.

6. BE COOL! Remember, this is a very difficult test for everybody. It is supposed to be difficult and you are supposed to feel rushed. Don't let the test intimidate you.

Good Luck!

CHAPTER 1

Biochemistry: Molecular Biology to Metabolism

DNA

DNA and RNA Structure

Let's start with a quick review of the fundamentals of life—that is, how information coded in DNA is transcribed to RNA, then translated into functional proteins. This process, known as the central dogma of molecular biology (Fig. 1-1), is used by organisms as simple as bacteria and as complex as human beings. (Viruses, which require hosts to replicate, do not necessarily follow this path.)

Genetic information is primarily stored as DNA and expressed as RNA. Picture DNA as a twisted zipper and RNA as a half-zipper. The teeth of the zipper are composed of bases that come from the families of **purines** and **pyrimidines** (Fig. 1-2).

An easy way to remember which DNA bases are pyrimidines is that their names, and the word "pyrimidine," contain the letter "y": cytosine and thymine. Purines do not contain the letter "y": they are adenine and guanine. An exception to this rule is the RNA base uracil (a pyrimidine), which takes the place of thymine.

Nucleosides are the result of linking a base with a pentose (five-carbon ring) sugar (Fig. 1-3). RNA uses ribose, which has an —OH at the $2'$ position; DNA uses deoxyribose, which has only an —H at the $2'$ position.

A **nucleotide** is simply a nucleoside plus one to three phosphates that have been added to the $5'$ position of the sugar (Fig. 1-4). You may want to quickly review the nomenclature for bases, nucleosides, and nucleotides (Table 1.1).

A DNA strand is built of multiple nucleotides linked by $3',5'$-phosphodiester bonds. The chain has a $5'$ end and a $3'$ end, with the deoxyribose-phosphate groups forming the backbone (Fig. 1-5).

Two DNA strands are paired to form a double helix. The strands are antiparallel (i.e., the $5'$ end of one strand aligns with the $3'$ end of the other), the deoxyribose-phosphate backbone is on the outside, and the bases, which are hydrophobic, are stacked within (Fig. 1-6). The two strands are held together noncovalently by hydrogen bonds between the bases. Adenine is always paired with thymine (or uracil in RNA) by two bonds, and cytosine is always coupled with guanine by three bonds. Because the base pairing is so predictable, one strand is said to be the **complement** of the other.

Adenine-thymine bond = 2 H bonds
Guanine-cytosine bond = 3 H bonds

Table 1-1. Nomenclature

Ribonucleic Acid (RNA)

Base	Nucleoside (base + ribose)	Nucleotide (base + ribose + phosphate)
Adenine	Adenosine	Adenylate (AMP)
Guanine	Guanosine	Guanylate (GMP)
Cytosine	Cytidine	Cytidylate (CMP)
Uracil	Uridine	Uridylate (UMP)

Deoxyribonucleic (DNA)

Base	Nucleoside (base + ribose)	Nucleotide (base + ribose + phosphate)
Adenine	Deoxyadenosine	Deoxyadenylate (dAMP)
Guanine	Deoxyguanosine	Deoxyguanylate (dGMP)
Cytosine	Deoxycytidine	Deoxycytidylate (dCMP)
Thymine	Deoxythymidine	Deoxythymidylate (dTMP)

Chromosomal DNA is organized primarily as a right-handed helix called the B form, with 10 bases per 360-degree turn (try curling your right hand inward—this follows the curve of the helix upward). Other forms of DNA have been discovered, however, including the A form (a right-handed helix dehydrated) and the Z form, which is a left-handed helix.

The two DNA strands separate if the pH is decreased or if the temperature is increased (**denaturation**). Strands that contain more C-G (cytosine-guanine) pairs denature at higher temperatures because more hydrogen bonds must be broken.

Prokaryotes (e.g., bacteria) contain DNA that is organized as a single circular chromosome. They also contain one or more tiny circular chromosomes called **plasmids** that may bear genes that confer antibiotic resistance and/or facilitate the transfer of genes between bacteria.

Human cells are eukaryotic (i.e., they have a nucleus). Human DNA is packaged into 46 separate chromatin fibers. Because the long strands of DNA must be packed efficiently in the nucleus, scaffolding proteins are used to aid in DNA packaging. First, each DNA double helix is wrapped around multiple proteins called **histones** in a "string-of-beads" formation (Fig. 1-7). Each "bead," called a **nucleosome**, contains two each of histones H2A, H2B, H3, and H4. Histone H1 binds the DNA between the nucleosomes and helps in packing the nucleosome-bound DNA into even more compact structures. DNA between histones is called **linker DNA**.

Heterochromatin is the condensed form of DNA and is transcriptionally inactive. **Euchromatin** is less condensed and is transcriptionally active. Histones are composed mostly of lysine and arginine, which give the proteins a positive charge. The histones form ionic bonds with negatively charged DNA (the ribose-phosphate backbone). During cell division, heterochromatin condenses even more to form chromosomes that can actually be seen under the light microscope. The ends of the chromosomes are called **telomeres**.

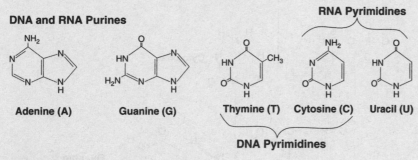

Fig. 1-1. Central dogma of molecular biology.

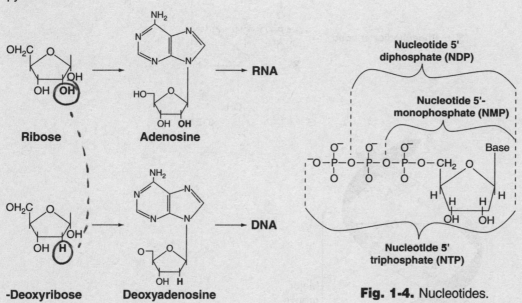

Fig. 1-2. DNA and RNA purines and pyrimidines.

Fig. 1-3. Nucleosides in DNA and RNA.

Fig. 1-4. Nucleotides.

RNA is a single strand of nucleotides linked by phosphodiester bonds. Remember that the nucleotides have a ribose (five-carbon) ring and use uracil instead of thymine. RNA comes in three major forms: messenger (mRNA), transfer (tRNA), and ribosomal (rRNA).

rRNA makes up 80% of all cellular RNA. It is associated with other proteins in the cytoplasm to form ribosomes, which are the site of protein synthesis.

After **mRNA** is transcribed (discussed later), it gets a **5′ cap** (7-methyl-guanosine attached by the third phosphate) and a **poly-A tail** (approximately 200 bases long) at the 3′ end, and its **introns** (noncoding regions) are spliced out.

tRNA base-pairs with itself to form a cloverleaf formation, then folds into an L shape. An amino acid is covalently attached to the 3′ end, and an anticodon region is exposed (Fig. 1-8). There is at least one tRNA for each amino acid. tRNA is used to facilitate the synthesis of proteins.

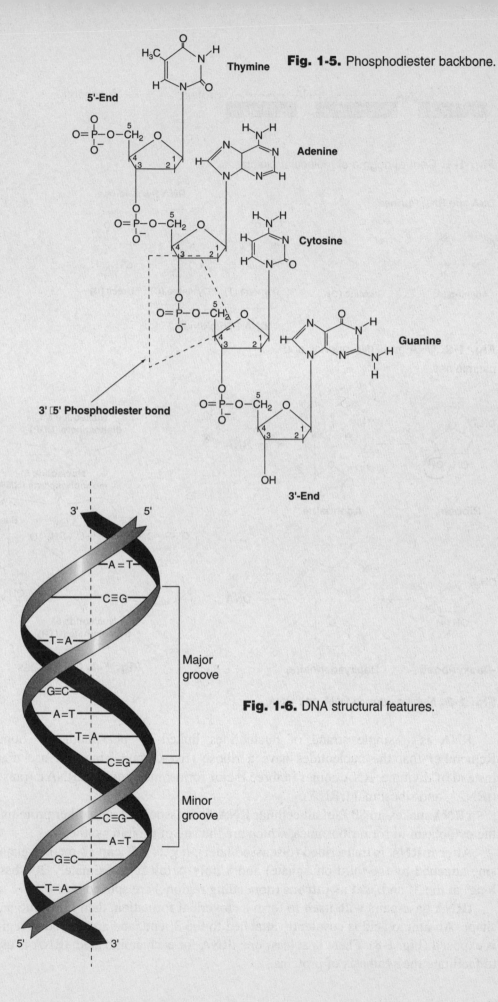

Fig. 1-5. Phosphodiester backbone.

Thymine

5'-End

Adenine

Cytosine

3' → 5' Phosphodiester bond

Guanine

3'-End

Fig. 1-6. DNA structural features.

Major groove

Minor groove

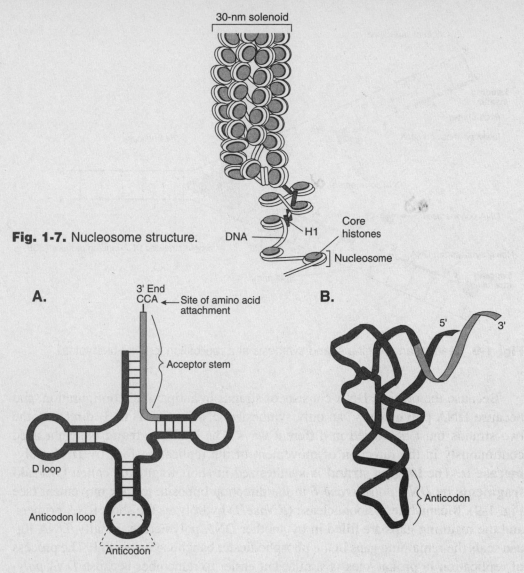

Fig. 1-7. Nucleosome structure.

DNA — H1
Core histones
Nucleosome
30-nm solenoid

A.

3' End
CCA ← Site of amino acid attachment

Acceptor stem

D loop

Anticodon loop

Anticodon

B.

5'   3'

Anticodon

Fig. 1-8. Transfer RNA structure. **A.** Schematic of tRNA base-pairing. **B.** tRNA folding.

DNA Replication

The genome must be duplicated faithfully in the S phase of the cell cycle, before cell division. Each strand of DNA in the helix serves as a template for the synthesis of a new strand. Replication is **semiconservative**, with each resulting double helix consisting of one parent strand and one newly synthesized, complementary daughter strand. Replication starts at an **origin of replication** and proceeds in both directions in a process called **bidirectional synthesis**. The circular prokaryotic chromosome contains only a single origin of replication, but eukaryotic chromosomes contain multiple origins of replication so that the large genome can be replicated quickly.

In eukaryotic replication, a *helicase* uses adenosine triphosphate (ATP) to unwind the double helix, and **single-stranded binding protein** (SSB) keeps the strands apart (Fig. 1-9). Because DNA polymerases can only extend pre-existing chains, another enzyme must be used to initiate chain synthesis. The primase subunit of *DNA polymerase* α makes short RNA primers, then the appropriate DNA polymerase extends the primer by adding DNA nucleotides to the 3′ end of the growing chain.

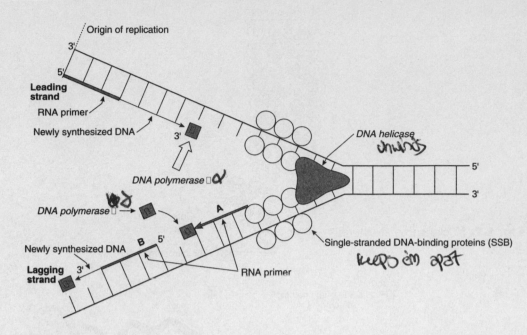

Fig. 1-9. Leading and lagging strand synthesis at a replication fork in eukaryotes.

Because the original DNA consists of strands in antiparallel configuration, and because DNA polymerases can only synthesize DNA in the 5′ to 3′ direction, the two strands must be copied in different ways. The **leading strand** is synthesized continuously in the direction of movement of the replication fork by **DNA polymerase** α. The **lagging strand** is synthesized in short fragments called **Okazaki fragments** by *DNA polymerase* δ in the direction opposite to fork movement (see Fig. 1-9). Meanwhile, a ribonuclease (***RNaseH***) hydrolyzes the short RNA primers, and the resulting gaps are filled in by another DNA polymerase. Finally, **DNA ligase** seals the remaining gaps in the phosphodiester backbone using ATP. The process of replication in prokaryotes is similar but easier to remember because *DNA polymerase III* synthesizes both leading and lagging strands. *DNA polymerase I* uses its RNaseH activity to remove the RNA primers and replaces them with deoxyribonucleotides, and *DNA ligase* uses nicotinamide-adenine dinucleotide (NAD) to seal the nicks.

DNA Repair

Although the replication process is very accurate, multiple repair systems exist in all cells to maintain the integrity of the genome. For instance, as DNA is replicated, DNA polymerase can make occasional mistakes by inserting an incorrect base into the growing strand. But these errors are typically detected by DNA polymerases that act as "proofreaders." *DNA polymerase* δ has 3′ → 5′ exonuclease activity that can remove the mispaired nucleotide and fill in the correct one.

Mechanisms exist not only to fix errors that are introduced during replication but also to remove lesions in DNA that are introduced by normal metabolism (e.g., superoxides), chemicals, ultraviolet (UV) light, ionizing radiation, X-rays and spontaneous loss or alteration of bases. Phenotypically detectable mutations in a gene can occur because of defects in either the protein coding or regulatory regions. Repair of DNA is largely possible because a lesion in one strand can be corrected

Fig. 1-10. Nucleotide excision repair of pyrimidine dimers in *Escherichia coli*. (Reprinted with permission from *Lippincott's Illustrated Reviews*: *Biochemistry*, 2nd ed., Champe, P.C. and Harvey, R.A. Philadelphia, Lippincott–Raven 1994. p. 374.)

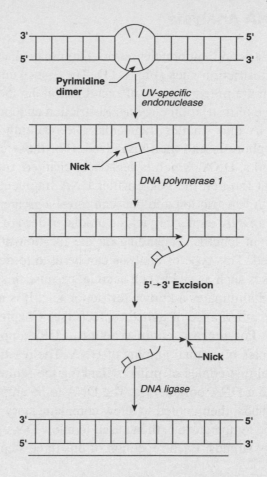

by using the undamaged complementary strand as a guide. Many repair systems operate by removing the damaged strand and then filling in the gap with a DNA polymerase. Others repair the damaged nucleotides directly. Many types of cancer are caused by defects in DNA repair mechanisms.

Nucleotide excision corrects bulky lesions, such as **pyrimidine dimers**, that occur as a result of exposure to UV light. UV light causes the covalent bonding of adjacent pyrimidines (usually thymine) on a strand. These dimers block replication and transcription until they are removed. In *Escherichia coli*, where this system has been studied best, a UV-specific endonuclease cleaves the damaged strand on the 5′ and 3′ sides of the dimer. A helicase then unwinds this damaged segment, DNA polymerase I fills in the gap, and DNA ligase seals the nick (Fig. 1-10). A similar pathway using *DNA polymerase β* (a repair-specific polymerase) exists in humans.

In the autosomal recessive skin disease **xeroderma pigmentosa**, an enzymatic defect in DNA nucleotide excision repair causes extreme photosensitivity to UV light, which leads to uncorrected mutations and skin cancers.

Another important system directly repairs lesions caused by **alkylating agents**, which attach extra methyl or ethyl groups to nucleotide bases. These lesions can be mutagenic and carcinogenic if left unrepaired, especially when they produce O^6-alkylguanine. On subsequent DNA replication, alkylated guanine pairs with thymine instead of pairing with cytosine, which introduces mutations. The enzyme that repairs these defects is O^6-*methyl guanine–DNA alkyl transferase*, which removes the alkyl group from guanine and transfers it to a cysteine.

DNA Analysis

Restriction endonucleases act like molecular scissors to cut double-stranded DNA at restriction sites (Fig. 1-11). These sites consist of short sequences of base pairs that are mirror images of each other along the chain and are usually unique to each type of restriction enzyme. Restriction endonucleases can be used to cut a stretch of DNA into smaller fragments. The resulting fragments are separated by gel electrophoresis and then visualized. (For those curious about how gel electrophoresis works, DNA, which is negatively charged, runs toward the anode when a current is sent through the gel. Smaller DNA fragments weave through the pores of the gel with less friction and thus can travel a greater distance toward the anode.) Analysis of a DNA sequence yields a unique pattern of bands that represent fragments of different lengths, depending on the location of the restriction sites and the enzyme used. This type of analysis can be used to detect genetic mutations that cause diseases such as sickle cell anemia, because this mutation occurs in the β-globin gene and eliminates a known restriction site. It is also used in linkage studies, to predict the inheritance of genetic defects (see Chapter 3).

Polymerase chain reaction (PCR) amplification is a way to make multiple copies of a small amount of DNA. The reaction mixture contains a DNA template, multiple copies of primers flanking the sequence to be amplified, free nucleotides, and a DNA polymerase. The DNA to be amplified is heat-denatured to yield single strands, then cooled to allow complementary primers to stick to the template DNA. The temperature is then raised to allow DNA polymerase to synthesize complementary strands. Each repetition of this three-step process doubles the amount of DNA,

DNA restriction analysis

A. 5' ----G|AATTC----3'   5' ----G 3'   5' AATTC----3'

3' ----CTTAA|G----5'   EcoRI digest   3' ----CTTAA 5'   3' G----5'

                                                  Sticky ends

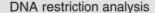

B.   2 kb   5 kb   1 kb

            EcoRI   HindIII

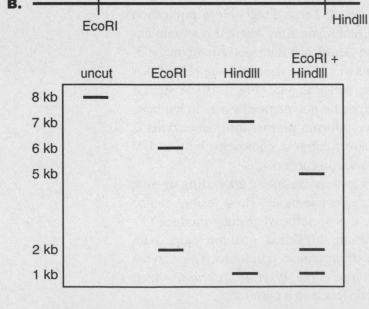

Fig. 1-11. DNA restriction analysis. **A.** Example of a restriction digest to yield two "sticky" ends, which can be used to anneal DNA fragments of different origins with each other. **B.** Restriction analysis of a DNA fragment yields a pattern of smaller fragments on gel electrophoresis.

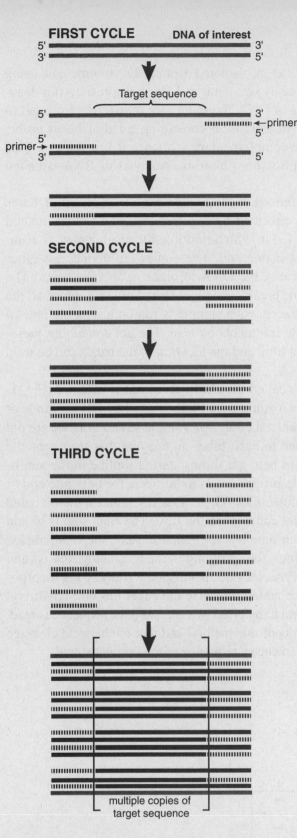

FIRST CYCLE   DNA of interest

Target sequence

primer

SECOND CYCLE

THIRD CYCLE

multiple copies of
target sequence

Fig. 1-12. One cycle of the process used in polymerase chain reaction. (Adapted from *Lippincott's Illustrated Reviews: Biochemistry,* 2nd ed., Champe, P.C. and Harvey, R.A. Philadelphia: Lippincott–Raven, 1994.)

so multiple cycles give exponential amplification of the original sequence (Fig. 1-12). This rapid and sensitive method of DNA duplication has many applications, including the detection of bacteria, viruses (e.g., early-stage human immunodeficiency virus), and mutated genes. It is also used in DNA sequencing.

Hybridization is the method used to locate a particular gene or nucleotide sequence on a strand of DNA. In this technique, a labeled, single-stranded DNA or RNA marker, called a **probe,** can be used to detect the presence of a complementary sequence in a sample. Hybridization is used in many RNA and DNA studies.

For example, an organism's DNA can be isolated from cells, fragmented using restriction enzymes, and then resolved by size using gel electrophoresis. After denaturing the DNA with heat, the bands of DNA fragments are transferred from gel to filter paper. This filter is incubated in a solution containing a radiolabeled probe, which hybridizes (or pairs) with the complementary sequence if it is present. This particular type of analysis is called Southern blotting. Analysis of RNA is called Northern blotting.

A stretch of DNA can be **sequenced** to determine the exact series of bases within it. DNA sequencing can be performed by two techniques. An older method is called **chemical cleavage** (Fig. 1-13) in which multiple identical copies of a single strand of DNA are radiolabeled at one end. The copies are divided into four tubes, and chemicals are added to cause the DNA to break at specific bases. The reaction is run so that, on average, one break occurs per strand of DNA. Once all the different-sized DNA pieces are produced, each sample is run on a separate lane of gel, and electrophoresis separates the fragments by size. The gel containing radiolabeled DNA can be used to expose a film, and the location of the bands can be used to determine the sequence of the DNA.

Another sequencing technique is called the **chain-terminator method** (Fig. 1-14). Instead of cutting up DNA, this method uses PCR to amplify DNA strands of different lengths. Again, multiple identical copies of a single strand of DNA are put in four tubes. The following is added to each tube: an enzyme that lengthens the DNA (DNA polymerase), a primer to help get things started (unlike in the amplification procedure described above, a primer needs to be made for only one end of the sequence of interest), normal nucleotides (G, A, T, and C), and a radiolabeled nucleotide so that each DNA segment can expose the film. The final step is to add a different dideoxynucleotide to each tube. As the reaction runs, the radiolabeled nucleotide will be incorporated into the growing strand, making the strand detectable on film. Once the dideoxynucleoside triphosphate (ddNTP) is incorporated, however, no other bases can be added (because the sugar has no 3' hydroxyl group). Each sample is run on a gel and transferred to a film, and the sequence is read. The only difference between the results of this method and that of chemical cleavage is that this technique gives the complementary sequence of the original strand.

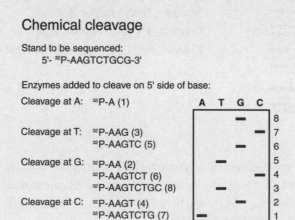

Chemical cleavage

Stand to be sequenced:
   5'- ^{32}P-AAGTCTGCG-3'

Enzymes added to cleave on 5' side of base:

Cleavage at A: ^{32}P-A (1)

Cleavage at T: ^{32}P-AAG (3)
                 ^{32}P-AAGTC (5)

Cleavage at G: ^{32}P-AA (2)
                 ^{32}P-AAGTCT (6)
                 ^{32}P-AAGTCTGC (8)

Cleavage at C: ^{32}P-AAGT (4)
                 ^{32}P-AAGTCTG (7)

Fig. 1-13. Chemical cleavage. The radiolabeled strands are broken by chemicals and separated by gel electrophoresis.

Chain-terminator method

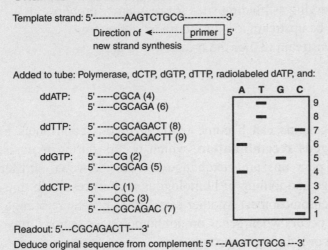

Template strand: 5'-----------AAGTCTGCG-------------3'

Direction of ◄-------- | primer | 5'
new strand synthesis

Added to tube: Polymerase, dCTP, dGTP, dTTP, radiolabeled dATP, and:

ddATP: 5' -----CGCA (4)
        5' -----CGCAGA (6)

ddTTP: 5' -----CGCAGACT (8)
        5' -----CGCAGACTT (9)

ddGTP: 5' -----CG (2)
        5' -----CGCAG (5)

ddCTP: 5' -----C (1)
        5' -----CGC (3)
        5' -----CGCAGAC (7)

Readout: 5'---CGCAGACTT----3'

Deduce original sequence from complement: 5' ---AAGTCTGCG ---3'

Fig. 1-14. DNA sequencing by the chain-terminator method. Dideoxynucleotides are added to PCR reactions to cause termination at a specific base.

Gene Structure

Genes are sequences of DNA that encode proteins and the regulatory sequences that control transcription of the proteins' mRNA. In eukaryotes, each protein is encoded by a gene that is self-regulating; the resulting RNA transcript is monocistronic, meaning that it specifies a single protein. In contrast, prokaryotic genes are frequently arranged as operons, which code for a cluster of metabolically related proteins under a single regulatory control system.

A typical protein-coding eukaryotic gene contains the following elements (Fig. 1-15):

- **Promoter**: the region where the transcriptional machinery (RNA polymerase and transcription factors) binds to start transcription. The TATA box is a highly conserved sequence found in most promoters.

- **RNA initiation site** (called +1): the nucleotide at which RNA synthesis begins.

- **Transcription unit**: the DNA that encodes the primary RNA transcript. The primary transcript includes the protein-coding sequence (exons); the intervening sequences (introns), which are removed in the mature mRNA; and the 5′ and 3′ untranslated regions.

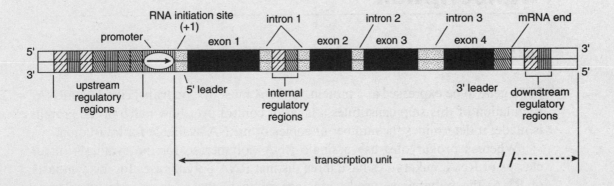

Fig. 1-15. Structure of a typical eukaryotic protein-coding gene.

- **Enhancers and silencers**: sequences on either strand that help regulate transcription by serving as binding sites for regulatory proteins. These sequences may be upstream (5′) of the transcription unit, within introns, or downstream (3′) of the transcription unit.

Genetic Exchange

In eukaryotes, genes in the genome can become rearranged; this contributes to genetic diversity. In **homologous recombination**, which occurs during meiosis, homologous chromosomes pair up, and exchange occurs between similar sequences. Enzymatic breakage and joining of homologous regions results in double-strand exchange between chromosomes. Another category of genetic rearrangement is **transposition**, which occurs when genes on nonhomologous regions move to a new position on the same or a different chromosome.

Bacteria can acquire new genetic information in several ways:

- **Transformation** is the uptake of DNA by a cell from its surrounding medium. The DNA may come from nearby dead organisms, or it can be placed into the medium in a laboratory.

- In **transduction**, DNA is inserted into the bacteria by **bacteriophages** (viruses that infect bacteria).

- **Conjugation** is the transfer of DNA by direct contact between bacterial cells. Such exchange is mediated by **plasmids**. Plasmids are small circles of DNA that possess their own origin of replication and can therefore replicate autonomously. Some plasmids, including those that contain genes that encode for resistance to antibiotics, also code for the formation of sex pili and other factors required for conjugation. The spread of antibiotic resistance is due in large part to the exchange of drug resistance plasmids between bacteria.

Other than plasmids, there are other categories of transposable elements. The simplest type is the **insertion sequence**, which has special sequences at its ends and can insert itself into any stretch of DNA using an enzyme called *transposase* (the gene that codes for *transposase* is included in the insertion sequence).

Transcription

DNA → RNA

For a gene to be expressed as a protein, its DNA must first be **transcribed** to mRNA. Regulation of this step constitutes a layer of control over how much of the protein is made; it determines the number of copies of mRNA available for translation.

Whereas prokaryotes use a single RNA polymerase for the synthesis of all classes of RNA, eukaryotes have three distinct RNA polymerases for the synthesis of RNA; the polymerase used varies according to the class of gene being transcribed. *RNA polymerase I* (*RNAP I*) produces large rRNA (for ribosomes). **RNAP**

II transcribes the genes that code for proteins, and it synthesizes small nuclear RNA (snRNA). *RNAP III* synthesizes tRNA, some snRNA, and small rRNA. The focus here is on eukaryotic mRNA made by *RNAP II*.

In the transcription of protein-coding genes, *RNAP II* and the basal transcription factors bind at the promoter to form the transcription initiation complex. Most promoters require these basal transcription factors for *RNAP II* to start transcription. Other transcription factors, described below, are needed for mRNA production above a baseline level. The RNA chain is synthesized just like DNA — except uracil substitutes for thymine—in the 5′ to 3′ direction. Only one of the DNA strands, called the **antisense strand**, is used as a template for mRNA synthesis. The RNA produced has a sequence complementary to the antisense strand and has the same nucleotide sequence as the DNA strand that was not used to make RNA, called the **sense strand** (except the substitution of U for T). Gene sequences are typically shown only as a sense strand, with the 5′ end to the left.

Transcription produces a primary transcript, which undergoes immediate modifications, including the following (Fig. 1-16):

- Addition of a **7-methyl-guanylate cap** at the 5′ end, soon after transcription begins

- Cleavage at a **poly-A site** at the 3′ end by an endonuclease, followed by the addition of a **poly-A tail** by the enzyme *poly-A polymerase*

- **Removal of introns and joining of exons** by the **spliceosome**, which is composed of proteins and snRNA

The modified transcript, called mature mRNA, is transported through the nuclear pores to the cytoplasm for translation (in eukaryotes). Mature mRNA contains three major regions:

- The **protein coding region**, located between the start and stop codons

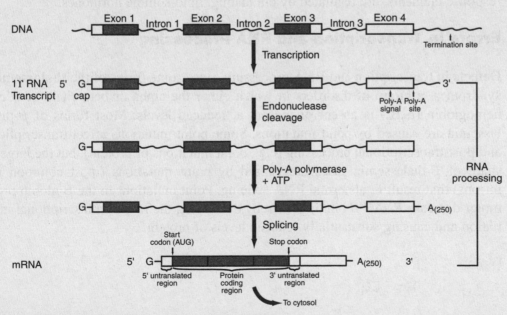

Fig. 1-16. Eukaryotic transcription of DNA to RNA.

- The **5′ untranslated region**, which precedes the start codon

- The **3′ untranslated region** that follows the protein coding region

The mRNAs for various proteins have varying life spans, measured as half-lives, before they are degraded by cellular ribonucleases (RNA cutters). Mammalian mRNAs have an average half-life of about 10 hours, although there is a substantial range.

Regulation

The regulation of gene expression is the basis for cellular differentiation. A particular cell type acquires its structure and function because of the genes it chooses to express. In particular, each cell uses regulatory sequences in the DNA to express the correct genes at the appropriate levels and at the right times. Most DNA in a eukaryotic cell is not expressed. Gene expression can be regulated at many points, from the beginning of transcription to after the formation of active protein. Typically, the principal regulatory step is at transcription initiation.

Transcription factors are proteins that are important in regulating the initiation of transcription. In contrast to the transcription factors described earlier, there are some factors that only act as promoters. These highly specific transcription factors bind to **enhancers** and **silencers** and are able to increase or decrease transcription of the associated gene. For example, factors bound at an enhancer can contact and stimulate the transcriptional machinery at distant promoters by making a loop of the intervening DNA. Promoter-selective transcription factors contain one of three motifs in their DNA-binding domains: a **leucine zipper**, a **zinc finger**, or a **helix-loop-helix**. These elements of the protein fit into the major grooves on the DNA helix. The regulatory proteins themselves can also be regulated, e.g., by phosphorylation.

Another type of regulatory sequence is the **response element**, which responds to signaling molecules, such as cyclic adenosine monophosphate (cAMP) and hormone receptors. The regulatory factors that bind to response elements can also be regulated. **Steroid hormone receptors**, for example, which bind to hormone response elements, are regulated by circulating, lipid-soluble hormones.

Errors in Transcription and RNA Processing

Defects in transcription and RNA processing cause some forms of the **thalassemia** syndromes, a group of disorders in which either the alpha or beta chain of adult hemoglobin ($\alpha_2\beta_2$) is absent or present at reduced levels. Most forms of β-thalassemia are caused by point mutations. Some point mutations affect transcription and post-transcriptional processing (e.g., point mutations of protein), but the largest share of β-thalassemia cases are caused by point mutations (most common in introns) that result in abnormal RNA splicing. Point mutations in the β-globin promoter decrease *RNAP II* binding, thereby decreasing the rate of transcriptional initiation and causing substantially reduced levels of protein.

thalassemia.
abnormal splicing

Translation

Genetic Code and Translational Machinery

The genetic code is the nearly universal dictionary that explains the relationship between triplet nucleic acid sequences, or **codons**, and the amino acids they specify. The code is nonoverlapping, so it is read starting from a specific start codon and stays in a specific frame. It is also **degenerate** because more than one codon can specify the same amino acid. There are 64 possible three-letter combinations: 61 specify amino acids, and three are stop codons that signal translational termination.

The adapters that translate the genetic code are **tRNA** molecules. These translators speak the language of both nucleotides and amino acids, converting genetic information from mRNA into proteins. There is at least one type of tRNA for each of the amino acids. tRNAs are a single strand of RNA (containing many unusual bases) with regions of intramolecular pairing that give them their characteristic two-dimensional cloverleaf structure (see Fig. 1-8A). The three-dimensional structure is L shaped, with the amino acid attached to one end and its corresponding anticodon loop at the other. The three-base anticodon loop pairs with the complementary codon sequence in the mRNA (Fig. 1-17). Specific aminoacyl-tRNA synthases charge the tRNA using ATP and catalyze the proper pairing of an amino acid with its tRNA.

Ribosomes, made up of rRNA and several proteins, are the site of protein synthesis in the cell. Eukaryotic ribosomes are composed of a 60S large subunit and a 40S small subunit (Fig. 1-18A). Ribosomes contain functional sites for mRNA binding and peptide bond formation. There is also an **A site**, where the *a*minoacyl-tRNA

tRNA · lots of unusual bases

Fig. 1-17. Schematic structure of tRNA-mRNA interaction.

Fig. 1-18A. A eukaryotic ribosome.

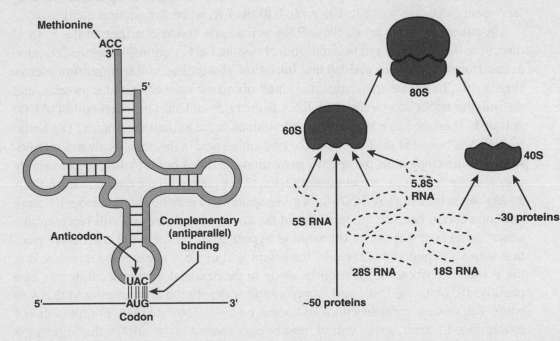

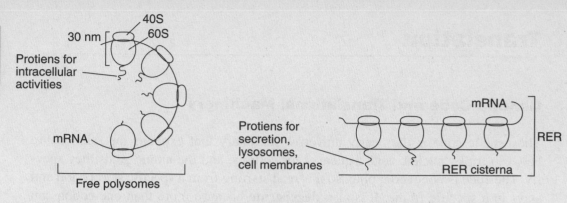

Fig. 1-18B. Polysomes. (*Cell and Tissue Ultrastructure: A Functional Perspective* Cross, P.C. and Mercer, K.L. New York, W.H. Freeman & Co., 1993. p 14.)

comes in to bind to the mRNA codon, and a **P site**, for binding of the *p*eptidyl tRNA. **Polysomes**, or polyribosomes, are formed when multiple ribosomes are simultaneously in different stages of translating the same strand of mRNA (Fig. 1-18B). They appear as clusters of ribosomes in electron microscopy.

Protein Synthesis

In prokaryotes, because there is no nucleus to serve as a barrier, translation begins as soon as the mRNA comes off the RNA polymerase. In eukaryotes, the mature mRNA travels from the nucleus into the cytosol, where ribosomes attach and mediate the process of translation. Proteins destined for the **endoplasmic reticulum** (ER), **Golgi bodies**, **lysosomes**, **plasma membrane**, or for secretion are synthesized on membrane-bound ribosomes that attach to the ER (known as rough ER) after synthesis begins in the cytosol. All other proteins are synthesized on free ribosomes in the cytosol. Many proteins contain signals, typically amino acid sequences, that direct them to particular cellular locations. Proteins to be translated on rough ER, for example, contain a stretch of hydrophobic amino acids at their *N*-terminal. Once this signal sequence is made, a **signal recognition particle** (a cellular "seeing-eye dog") directs the protein to the ER, where translation continues.

In eukaryotic translation, the mRNA is read one codon at a time in the 5′ to 3′ direction; the protein is synthesized from N-terminal to C-terminal using the 20 amino acids. Translation can be divided into **initiation**, **elongation**, and **termination phases** (Fig. 1-19). To initiate translation, the small ribosomal subunit, initiator proteins, and the initiator tRNA scan along the mRNA from the 5′ end until the **start codon (AUG)** is found. Then the large ribosomal subunit binds to the initiation complex. The initiator tRNA is bound at the P site, and the first amino acid in the chain is always **methionine**. During elongation, the appropriate aminoacyl tRNA binds to the complementary codon at the A site (i.e., the anticodon in the tRNA pairs with the codon in the mRNA by hydrogen bonding). A tRNA for a given amino acid may be able to recognize more than one codon because the last base in the codon may differ and still represent the same amino acid (known as **the wobble hypothesis**). The peptidyl transferase reaction forms a peptide bond between the amino acid in the A site and the amino acid at the P site. The ribosome then moves along to the next codon, translocating this new peptidyl tRNA to the P site and emptying the A site for the next aminoacyl tRNA to enter. The process continues until all codons on the mRNA are read. For translational termination to occur, a **stop codon** must be encountered in the mRNA that signals the end of the protein. A release factor then activates release of the protein.

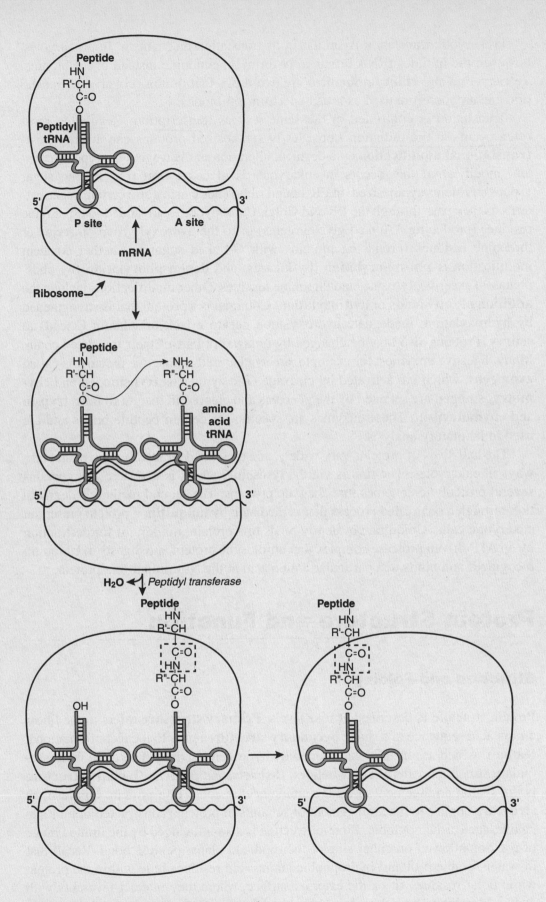

Fig. 1-19. Translation of mRNA to protein.

Prokaryotic translation is similar in its translation mechanism. In prokaryotes, however, the initiator tRNA brings in N-formyl-methionine instead of methionine. **Tetracycline** and **chloramphenicol** are two drugs that inhibit prokaryotic translation and are therefore used as broad-spectrum antibiotics.

Translation is controlled in the same way as transcription: Regulation most often occurs at the initiation step. Newly synthesized proteins can acquire **post-translational modifications** via covalent alteration or cleavage. One type of covalent modification that occurs in eukaryotes is **glycosylation** (i.e., adding sugar groups). Proteins synthesized on ER-bound ribosomes can acquire certain sugar patterns as they pass through the ER and Golgi. Carbohydrates are added to asparagine residues (producing *N*-linked glycoproteins) or to the hydroxyl group on serine or threonine residues (producing proteins with *O*-linked sugars). Another covalent modification is **phosphorylation** (by kinases) and **dephosphorylation** (by phosphatases) at serine, tyrosine, and threonine residues. Other modifications include the **addition of fatty acids** or **hydroxylation**. **Collagen** is a protein that is strengthened by hydroxylation; inadequate hydroxylation due to a lack of vitamin C leads to **scurvy**. Proteins also may be changed by removal of part of their translated chain. Many digestive enzymes, for example, are synthesized as inactive precursors called **zymogens**, which are activated by cleavage. The zymogens **trypsinogen** and **chymotrypsinogen** are secreted by the pancreas and cleaved in the gut to form **trypsin** and **chymotrypsin**. These enzymes are specific for certain peptide bonds and are used in laboratory analysis.

The half-lives of proteins vary widely, and they are degraded by two main pathways in eukaryotes. The first is via the **lysosome**, which is a vesicle that contains several proteolytic enzymes that chew up proteins. The second method is degradation through a controlled process that is mediated by **ubiquitin**, a protein present in eukaryotic cells. Ubiquitin covalently binds to a protein, marking it for destruction by an ATP-driven protease complex that unfolds the protein and digests it. Ubiquitin recognizes and binds to a particular amino acid at the N-terminal of a protein.

Protein Structure and Function

Structure and Folding

Protein structure is described at four levels. **Primary structure** refers to the linear amino acid sequence in a chain. **Secondary structure** refers to local conformational features, which are usually determined by hydrogen bonding. The three main secondary structural patterns are **α-helices**, **β-sheets**, and **β-turns**. **Tertiary structure** is the spatial arrangement of all the amino acid residues in a protein. **Quaternary structure** applies to the arrangement of subunits of proteins constructed of multiple chains, such as hemoglobin. Protein structure is also influenced by the limited range of rotation allowed on either side of the rigid and planar peptide bond. Recall that in water-soluble proteins, hydrophobic amino acid residues hide within the protein while polar residues sit on the external surface, where they interact favorably with water. Membrane-bound proteins, on the other hand, tend to have hydrophobic amino acids exposed in their transmembrane regions.

The three-dimensional structure of a protein is specified by its sequence. Proteins fold spontaneously with the help of two types of proteins:

- **Chaperone proteins** are molecular timers that bind to growing proteins and block incorrect interactions before synthesis is complete.

- Enzymes that catalyze intermolecular bonds. For example, disulfide isomerase catalyzes the formation of the proper disulfide bonds from the many possible arrangements that are available.

Protein Interactions

Proteins are unique in their ability to specifically recognize and interact with a wide array of other molecules. This ability arises from variations in the amino acids that compose the protein. Amino acid side chains contribute to unique structures and form complementary surfaces for binding specific molecules. Multi-subunit proteins, such as **hemoglobin**, depend on surface complementarity because the subunits come together spontaneously (self-assemble) based on their intrinsic fit. Complex macromolecular structures, such as **collagen**, also depend on self-assembly. Collagen, the most abundant protein in the body, is a staggered array of **tropocollagen** units. (Tropocollagen is made of three long polypeptide chains that form a triple helix.) Collagen molecules also spontaneously come together to form collagen fibrils.

Mutations in Proteins

DNA mutations can cause protein defects, with a range of possible outcomes that includes the addition, substitution, or deletion of amino acids. Such alterations can have structural and functional effects; again, consider the **hemoglobinopathies**. The most prevalent of the group is **sickle cell anemia**, which results when valine, a hydrophobic amino acid, is substituted for glutamic acid in the sixth position of the hemoglobin beta chain. This mutated hemoglobin polymerizes in low-oxygen conditions, resulting in deformed, sickle-shaped red blood cells (RBCs). Another abnormality is **cystic fibrosis**, in which mutations occur in a gene that codes for an integral membrane protein that functions as an anion (chloride) transporter. The most common defect in cystic fibrosis is a deletion of three nucleotides that code for the amino acid phenylalanine. This disease causes dysfunction of exocrine glands and secretion of thick mucus in affected organs, such as the respiratory tract, where it leads to obstruction and infection. In the autosomal dominant disease **familial hypercholesterolemia**, mutations occur in the receptor for low-density lipoproteins (LDLs). LDLs are a major form of transport for cholesterol in the blood, and the receptor is required for cells to internalize the LDL-cholesterol complex. In some cases, receptors are produced but fail to bind the plasma LDLs. Patients with this disease have high plasma cholesterol levels, which contribute to heart disease and heart attacks at a young age.

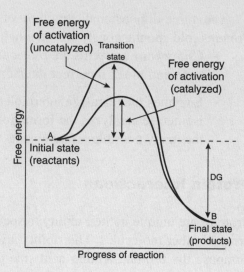

Fig. 1-20. Free-energy diagram for a reaction, showing the reduction in activation energy when enzyme is present.

Enzymes, Kinetics, and Regulation

Many proteins serve as enzymes, which are highly specific catalysts used in almost all reactions in the body. Some enzymes require a nonprotein cofactor, such as a coenzyme (organic molecule) or a metal ion. The **activation energy** of a reaction equals the energy difference between the transition state and the reactants (Fig. 1-20). Enzymes increase rates (i.e., they cause the reaction to occur more quickly) by decreasing the activation energy. Enzymes contain active sites for substrate binding. Recall that the Michaelis-Menten model can be used to analyze the kinetics of most nonallosteric enzymes. The **Michaelis constant (K_m)**, which is unique to a particular enzyme, is the substrate concentration at one-half maximal velocity (V_{max}) of the reaction. A high K_m indicates low affinity of an enzyme for its substrate, and a low K_m means high substrate affinity. Enzymes that follow Michaelis-Menten kinetics exhibit two types of reversible inhibition: competitive and noncompetitive. **Competitive inhibitors** compete with the substrate for binding at the active site and can be overcome with high substrate concentrations. **Noncompetitive inhibitors** bind to the enzyme but not at the active site; therefore, adding more substrate does not make the reaction happen any faster.

The catalytic activity of enzymes can be regulated in four main ways:

- **Reversible covalent modification**, such as phosphorylation, serves as a switch to turn an enzyme on or off.

- Allosteric enzymes can be regulated by **positive** and **negative effectors**, which bind reversibly at sites other than the active site.

- **Proteolytic activation** involves peptide bond cleavage, which transforms an inactive enzyme precursor into its active form; this occurs with digestive enzymes.

- **Control proteins** can regulate through activation and inhibition of the initial catalytic enzyme.

General Energy Metabolism

In contrast to kinetics, thermodynamic calculations are used to describe whether a reaction is energetically favorable. The overall change in free energy of a reaction, ΔG, is the main thermodynamic ruler. It depends only on the initial and final energy states; it is independent of the reaction mechanism and rate. Thermodynamic calculations might report that a reaction is energetically favorable but say nothing of how much time it takes for the reaction to occur. Note that enzymes increase the rate at which a thermodynamically favorable reaction achieves equilibrium. Enzymes do not change the equilibrium or ΔG, however. Recall that ΔG depends on the change in two variables during a reaction, enthalpy (ΔH) and entropy (ΔS): $\Delta G = \Delta H - T\Delta S$, where temperature ($T$) is in kelvin. If $\Delta G < 0$, the reaction is exergonic and proceeds spontaneously. If $\Delta G > 0$, the reaction is endergonic and is not spontaneous. At equilibrium $\Delta G = 0$.

To determine whether a compound is energy-rich or energy-poor, its **group transfer potential** is measured. Group transfer potential is the absolute amount of free energy released on hydrolysis. Energy-rich compounds have high energy bonds and high group transfer potentials. The more positive the group transfer potential, the more likely the molecule is to transfer the group to some acceptor. ATP is the main energy currency of the cell and contains two high-energy phosphoanhydride bonds. The standard free energy of hydrolysis ($\Delta G°$) of ATP to adenosine diphosphate (ADP) is about -7.3 kcal/mol. The energy released from ATP hydrolysis is used in reactions that require an input of free energy.

Metabolic pathways can usually be characterized as catabolic or anabolic. Catabolic pathways degrade complex molecules to simple ones and harvest energy (as ATP) and metabolic intermediates. In contrast, **anabolic pathways** require energy (by ATP hydrolysis) and synthesize complex molecules from simpler precursors. An important thing to remember about metabolism is that synthetic and degradative pathways are not simply the reverse of each other.

In catabolic pathways, fuel molecules such as glucose and fatty acids are **oxidized**, whereas in anabolic pathways, the starting molecules are reduced. In oxidative catabolic pathways, NAD^+ and FADH are the electron acceptors that are reduced, forming NADH and $FADH_2$. NADH and $FADH_2$ are electron carriers that ultimately donate these electrons to the electron transport chain for oxidative phosphorylation and ATP production. The reduced form of nicotinamide-adenine dinucleotide phosphate (NADPH) is the usual electron donor in pathways of reductive biosynthesis; it carries two high-potential electrons.

Metabolic pathways are regulated on two levels: (1) short-term signals arise intracellularly and act in local, immediate situations; and (2) global extracellular signals, such as hormones and the nervous system, coordinate the pathways occurring in different organs. These signals, in turn, influence the intracellular regulatory mechanisms. Both types of signals regulate metabolic pathways in three general ways: (1) They control enzymatic activity in ways previously described, (2) they induce or repress enzyme synthesis, and (3) they control substrate availability.

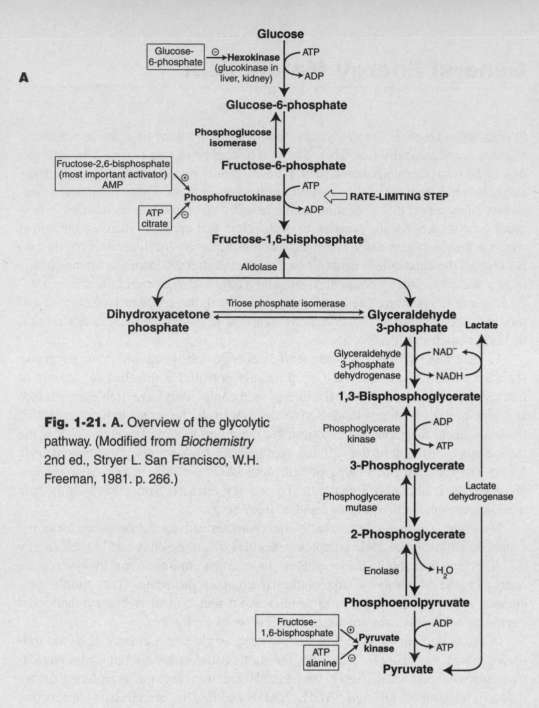

Fig. 1-21. A. Overview of the glycolytic pathway. (Modified from *Biochemistry* 2nd ed., Stryer L. San Francisco, W.H. Freeman, 1981. p. 266.)

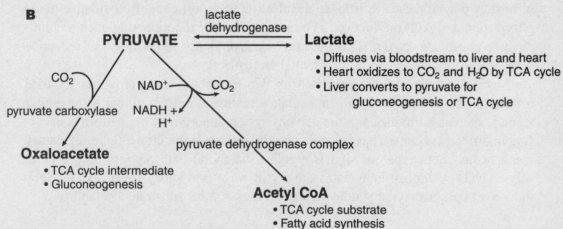

Fig. 1-21 B. Different fates of pyruvate in humans.

Energy Production

Glycolysis

Glycolysis is the central pathway for carbohydrate metabolism. This pathway breaks down glucose and creates energy in the form of ATP as well as intermediates for other pathways (Fig. 1-21). Many other sugars can also be funneled into this degradative pathway.

Some key points to know about glycolysis include:

- Glycolysis occurs in all tissues in the cytosol of cells.

- In **aerobic glycolysis**, pyruvate is produced and oxygen is required for reoxidation of the NADH produced from oxidation of glyceraldehyde 3-phosphate.

- In **anaerobic glycolysis**, lactate (the reduced form of pyruvate) is produced by skeletal muscle in the absence of adequate oxygen to reoxidize NADH. It is also produced in cells that have few or no mitochondria, such as red blood cells and white blood cells.

- The most important regulatory enzyme in glycolysis is *phosphofructokinase*, which catalyzes the rate-limiting step.

- Pyruvate may be metabolized to **oxaloacetate** or **acetyl coenzyme A** (acetyl CoA).

- Overall reaction for glycolysis (P_i = inorganic phosphate):

    Aerobic: $Glucose + 2\ P_i + 2\ ADP + 2\ NAD^+$

    $\rightarrow Pyruvate + 2\ ATP + 2\ NADH + 2\ H^+ + 2\ H_2O$

    Anaerobic: $Glucose + 2\ P_i + 2\ ADP \rightarrow 2\ lactate + 2\ ATP + 2\ H_2O$

Glycogenolysis

Glycogenolysis in the breakdown of **glycogen**, which is the branched, storage form of glucose, for energy use (Fig. 1-22).

- The most important stores of glycogen are in **liver** and **muscle**, where increased breakdown occurs during exercise and between meals. Glycogenolysis, like glycolysis, occurs in the cytosol. *Glycogen phosphorylase* and a debranching enzyme degrade glycogen to *glucose-1-phosphate*, which is converted to **glucose-6-phosphate** by *phosphoglucomutase*. The liver contains *glucose-6-phosphatase*, an enzyme that removes the phosphate group and allows free glucose to exit the liver, thereby raising blood glucose levels. Muscle tissue lacks this enzyme, so all the glucose-6-phosphate that is produced is used locally in the muscle tissue.

- The main regulatory enzyme in glycogenolysis is *glycogen phosphorylase*.

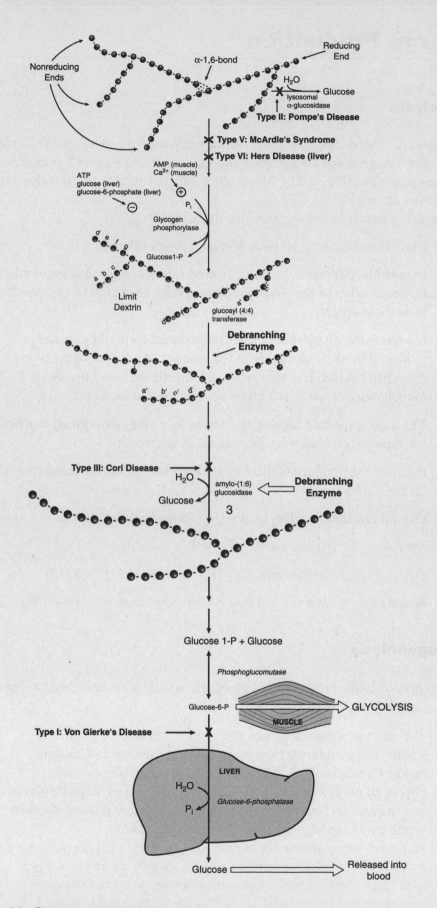

Fig. 1-22. Glycogen degradation.

Table 1-2. Glycogen storage diseases

Disease	Enzyme deficient	Metabolic effects	Results in	Notes
Type I: Von Gierke	Glucose-6-phosphatase	Increased amount of glycogen (normal structure) stored in **liver, kidneys**	Liver enlargement Severe hypoglycemia Failure to thrive	Most important example of hepatic glycogenoses Autosomal recessive
Type II: Pompe	Lysosomal α-glucosidase (acid maltase)	Excessive deposition of glycogen (normal structure) in **liver, heart, muscle**	Massive cardiomegaly Pronounced hypotonia Cardiorespiratory failure often results in death by age 2	Autosomal recessive
Type III: Cori	Amylo- (1:6) glucosidase (debranching enzyme)	Increased glycogen (short outer branches) in muscle and liver	Like type I but milder	Autosomal recessive
Type IV: Anderson	Glucosyl (4:6) transferase (branching enzyme)	Normal amounts of glycogen (long outer branches) in **liver, spleen**	Hepatosplenomegaly Progressive hepatic cirrhosis; liver failure Early death	Autosomal recessive
Type V: McArdle	Skeletal muscle glycogen phosphorylase	Increased amount of glycogen (normal structure) in **muscle;** cannot be broken down	Painful cramps on strenuous exercise Myoglobinuria	Autosomal recessive
Type VI: Hers	Liver glycogen phosphorylase	Increased amount of glycogen in **liver**	Like type I but milder	Autosomal recessive
Type VII: Tarui	Muscle phosphofructokinase	Increased amount of glycogen (normal structure) in **muscle**	Resembles type V	Autosomal recessive
Type VIII	Phosphorylase kinase	Increased amount of glycogen (normal structure) in **liver**	Mild hypoglycemia Mild hepatomegaly	X-linked

- Glucagon and epinephrine increase glycogenolysis by phosphorylating (activating) *glycogen phosphorylase*. Insulin turns it off.

- Diseases of glycogen storage are listed in Table 1-2. Be familiar with these; particularly **Von Gierke's disease**, **Pompe's disease**, **Cori's disease**, and **McArdle's disease**. Light microscopy of diseased organs might show foamy cytoplasm with PAS-positive staining of the excess glycogen.

Pentose-Phosphate Pathway

The pentose-phosphate pathway, a catabolic glucose pathway, supplies the five-carbon sugars needed for the synthesis of RNA, DNA, and other nucleotides (including ATP, NAD$^+$, NADP$^+$, FAD, and coenzyme A). It is also important as a major supplier of NADPH used in anabolic pathways, such as fatty acid and cholesterol synthesis. Finally, the process can produce or use glycolytic intermediates.

- The pentose phosphate pathway occurs in the cytosol.

- The pathway is made up of an oxidative segment that consists of two irreversible reactions that generate NADPH (Fig. 1-23). This is followed by a nonoxidative segment of many sugar-phosphate interconversions, which can go in many possible directions, depending on the needs of the cell.

- This pathway does not directly use or make ATP.

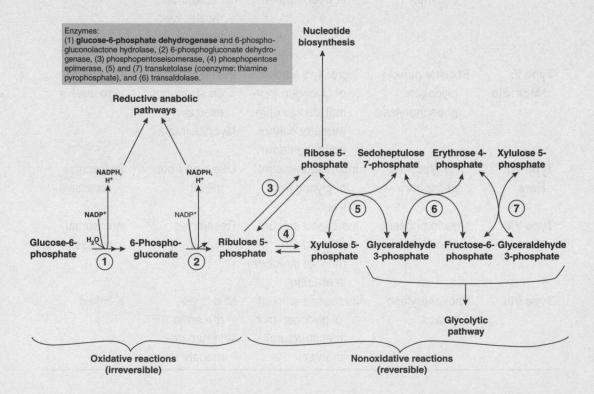

Fig. 1-23. Pentose phosphate pathway (also called *hexose monophosphate* [HMP] *pathway*).

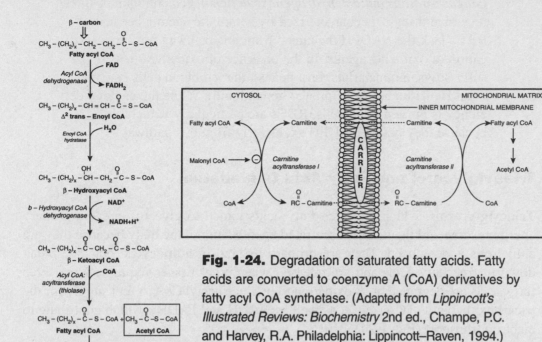

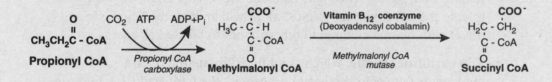

Fig. 1-24. Degradation of saturated fatty acids. Fatty acids are converted to coenzyme A (CoA) derivatives by fatty acyl CoA synthetase. (Adapted from *Lippincott's Illustrated Reviews: Biochemistry* 2nd ed., Champe, P.C. and Harvey, R.A. Philadelphia: Lippincott–Raven, 1994.)

Fig. 1-25. Fatty acids with an odd number of carbons are oxidized as above until only three carbons are left. Then, the three-carbon molecule is converted to succinyl coenzyme A (below) and can enter the tricarboxylic acid cycle.

Fig. 1-26. The catabolism of proteins, carbohydrates, and fats converges at the tricarboxylic acid (TCA) cycle for energy production.

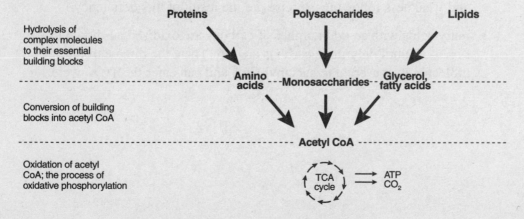

- *Glucose-6-phosphate dehydrogenase deficiency*, a common X-linked recessive disease, is characterized by hemolytic anemia because RBCs lack the NADPH they need from this pathway for the detoxification of oxidizing agents. In the presence of oxidative stress (e.g., sulfa drugs, antimalarials, fava beans), the red blood cells lyse and form Heinz bodies (precipitated hemoglobin). While the enzyme deficiency is present in all cells, RBCs are particularly vulnerable because they obtain NADPH exclusively from this pathway.

Triacylglycerol and Fatty Acid Degradation

Triacylglycerols, which are three fatty acids joined to glycerol, are the primary energy reserve and the most concentrated energy store of the body because they are anhydrous and reduced. They are primarily stored in **adipocytes**, but they break down to free fatty acids and are released when other tissues require energy. Free fatty acids are degraded by β-oxidation to produce acetyl CoA, a fuel supply for the tricarboxylic acid (TCA) cycle, as well as NADH and $FADH_2$, which contribute to electron transport (Fig. 1-24).

- Fatty acid β-oxidation occurs in the mitochondria of most tissues, except nervous tissue (including the brain, which prefers glucose), RBCs, and the adrenal medulla.

- The degradation of triacylglycerols starts with the hormone-sensitive enzyme **lipase**, which removes fatty acid at one end of the glycerol backbone. This enzyme is active when it is phosphorylated (via a cAMP-mediated pathway stimulated by epinephrine) and is inactive (dephosphorylated) when plasma insulin levels are high. Other lipases release the remaining fatty acids, all of which leave the adipocyte and travel with plasma albumin to other tissues to be used as energy.

- The **carnitine shuttle**, which is inhibited by **malonyl CoA** (an intermediate of fatty acid synthesis), transports the fatty acyl CoA into the mitochondrial matrix. There, β-oxidation degrades the molecules two carbons at a time.

- **Carnitine deficiency** (due to defective synthesis) or congenital absence of *carnitine acyltransferase* in skeletal muscle causes an inability to use fatty acids as fuel during exercise. **Myoglobinemia** and weakness following exercise are the result of this deficiency.

- Fatty acids with an odd number of carbons are oxidized as shown in Fig. 1-25 until only three carbons are left. Then, the three-carbon molecule is converted to succinyl CoA and can enter the TCA cycle.

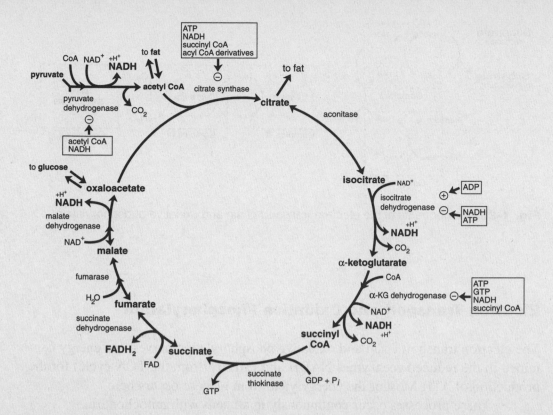

Fig. 1-27. Tricarboxylic acid cycle with important regulatory steps. (With permission from *Basic Concepts in Biochemistry. A Student's Survival Guide*, Gilbert, H.F. New York, Mc Graw-Hill, 1992. p. 122.)

Tricarboxylic Acid Cycle

The **TCA cycle** (also known as the citric acid cycle) oxidizes acetyl CoA to H_2O and CO_2 and is the final common pathway for the degradation of fatty acids, carbohydrates, and amino acids (Fig. 1-26). It provides NADH and $FADH_2$ to the electron transport chain for ATP generation (Fig. 1-27).

- The TCA cycle occurs in all cells with mitochondria. The **pyruvate** from aerobic glycolysis enters the mitochondria after being converted to **acetyl CoA** by the *pyruvate dehydrogenase complex*, which also yields one CO_2 and one NADH. Remember that the *pyruvate dehydrogenase complex* requires five cofactors: **thiamine pyrophosphate**, **lipoamide**, **FAD**, **NAD⁺**, and **CoA**. These cofactors are also required by the TCA cycle enzyme *α-ketoglutarate dehydrogenase*.

- Overall stoichiometry, starting from acetyl CoA, is as follows:

Acetyl CoA + 3 NAD⁺ + FAD + GDP + P_i + 2 H_2O →

2 CO_2 + 3 NADH + $FADH_2$ + GTP + 3 H⁺ + CoA

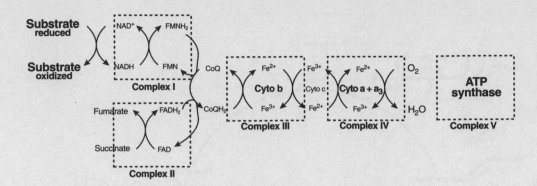

Fig. 1-28. Components of the electron transport chain and oxidative phosphorylation.

Electron Transport and Oxidative Phosphorylation

The electron transport chain and oxidative phosphorylation harvest the energy contained in the reduced coenzymes NADH and $FADH_2$ (from the TCA cycle) for the production of ATP. Most of the energy yield from glucose occurs here.

- These processes occur continuously in all cells with mitochondria. The enzyme complexes are located in the inner mitochondrial membrane.

- The chain consists of four complexes (I-IV), each of which accepts and donates electrons to the next complex in the chain (Fig. 1-28). NADH and $FADH_2$ donate electrons to the chain, and oxygen is the ultimate electron acceptor. This process accounts for the body's greatest oxygen consumption. The free energy released from electron flow does not produce ATP directly; instead it creates a proton gradient in the intermembrane space, which is used by *ATP synthase* (complex V) to produce ATP from ADP (oxidative phosphorylation) (Fig. 1-29). Oxidative phosphorylation is regulated by the level of available ADP.

After electron transport and oxidative phosphorylation, all the energy from glucose has been converted to 30 ATP per glucose molecule (or 32 if the malate-aspartate rather than glycerol-phosphate shuttle is used to transport NADH from the cytosol into the mitochondrion). In contrast, each glucose from anaerobic glycolysis yields 2 ATP (or 3, starting from glycogen). As you can see, the overall energy yield is many times greater in the presence of oxygen.

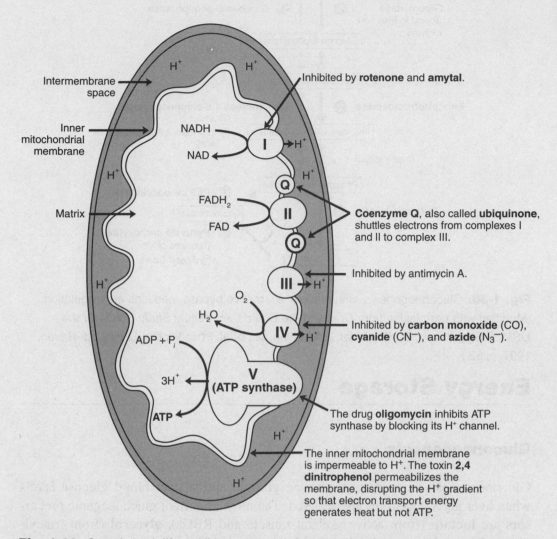

Intermembrane space

Inner mitochondrial membrane

Matrix

Inhibited by **rotenone** and **amytal**.

NADH

NAD

H^+

H^+

I

H^+

Q

FADH$_2$

FAD

II

Q

Coenzyme Q, also called **ubiquinone**, shuttles electrons from complexes I and II to complex III.

III

H^+

Inhibited by antimycin A.

O_2

H_2O

IV

H^+

Inhibited by **carbon monoxide (CO)**, **cyanide (CN⁻)**, and **azide (N₃⁻)**.

ADP + P$_i$

3H$^+$

V
(ATP synthase)

ATP

The drug **oligomycin** inhibits ATP synthase by blocking its H^+ channel.

H^+

H^+

The inner mitochondrial membrane is impermeable to H^+. The toxin **2,4 dinitrophenol** permeabilizes the membrane, disrupting the H^+ gradient so that electron transport energy generates heat but not ATP.

Fig. 1-29. Complexes I, III, and IV create an electrochemical gradient, used by adenosine triphosphate (ATP) synthase for ATP generation. Toxins, drugs, and several site-specific inhibitors hinder ATP production. (Modified with permission from *Crashing the Boards. A Friendly Study Guide for the USMLE Step 1*, Yeh, B., Paydarfar, J.A., Flynn, M., et al. Philadelphia, Lippincott–Raven, 1997. p. 50.)

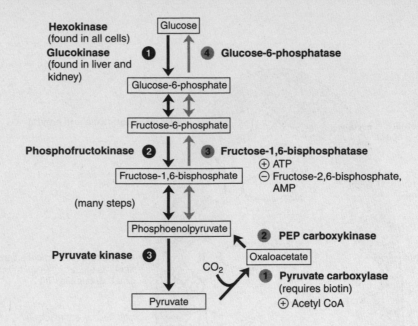

Fig. 1-30. Gluconeogenesis, with the four alternative bypass reactions and regulation. (Modified with permission from *Crashing the Boards. A Friendly Study Guide for the USMLE Step 1*, Yeh, B., Paydarfar, J.A., Flynn, M., et al. Philadelphia, Lippincott–Raven, 1997. p. 52.)

Energy Storage

Gluconeogenesis

Gluconeogenesis is used to synthesize glucose and sustain blood glucose levels when liver glycogen stores are depleted. The most important gluconeogenic precursors are **lactate** (from active skeletal muscle and RBCs), **glycerol** (from triacylglycerol breakdown), and **α-keto acids** (from amino acid breakdown).

• Gluconeogenesis occurs in the liver and kidneys but not in muscle. It takes place in the cell's cytosol, except for the conversion of pyruvate to oxaloacetate, which occurs in the mitochondrion.

• Glucose is produced through a reversal of seven of the ten glycolytic reactions; the remaining three reactions of glycolysis are irreversible and are bypassed by four alternative enzymatic reactions (Fig. 1-30).

• Gluconeogenesis is stimulated by glucagon.

• During starvation, acetyl CoA from fatty acid degradation is the most important allosteric stimulator of gluconeogenesis, and it serves as an activator of *pyruvate carboxylase*.

• The **Cori cycle** describes the conversion of lactate from exercising skeletal muscle into glucose by the liver (Fig. 1-31).

• Overall energy and NADH consumption is as follows:

2 pyruvate + 4 ATP + 2 GTP + 2 NADH + 2 H$^+$ + 6 H$_2$O →

Glucose + 2 NAD$^+$ + 4 ADP + 2 GDP + 6 P$_i$ + 6 H+

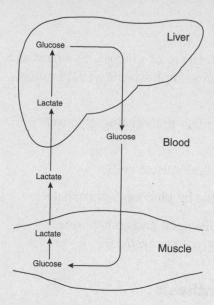

Fig. 1-31. The Cori cycle. Lactate from exercising skeletal muscle is sent via the bloodstream to the liver, where it is converted by gluconeogenesis into glucose for export.

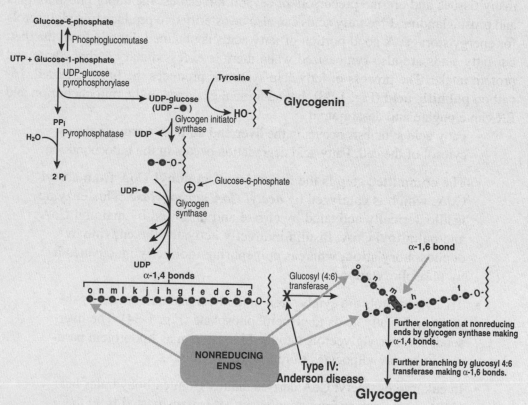

Fig. 1-32. Glycogen synthesis. Uridine diphosphate (UDP)-glucose must be added to a primer, either pre-existing glycogen or the protein glycogenin.

Glycogenesis

Glycogenesis is the synthesis of glycogen, a fuel reserve of glucose. Synthase and branching enzymes build the polymer from uridine diphosphate (UDP)-glucose (Fig. 1-32).

- UDP-glucose must be added to a primer, either pre-existing glycogen or the protein **glycogenin**.

- Synthesis occurs in the cytosol of hepatic and muscle cells.

- *Glycogen synthase* is allosterically activated by glucose-6-phosphate.

- Insulin turns the synthetic pathway on. Glucagon and epinephrine ultimately turn it off by phosphorylating *glycogen synthase*.

Fatty Acid and Triacylglycerol Biosynthesis

Fatty acids are straight-chain hydrocarbons with a polar carboxylic acid group at one end. Fatty acids can be **saturated** (no double bonds) or **unsaturated** (*cis* double bonds, either monounsaturated or polyunsaturated). They can be used as fuel by many tissues and are the precursors of several molecules, including phospholipids and prostaglandins. Free fatty acids can also be esterified to produce triacylglycerols for energy storage. A good portion of fatty acids is obtained directly from the diet, but fatty acids are also synthesized when there is excess dietary carbohydrate and protein intake. The process of fatty acid synthesis produces the fully saturated, 16-carbon **palmitic acid** (Fig. 1-33), but additional enzymes in the mitochondrion and ER can elongate and desaturate it.

- Fatty acid synthesis occurs in the **liver** and **adipose tissue**, in the cytosol of the cell. Fatty acid degradation occurs in the mitochondrion.

- The committed step is the formation of **malonyl CoA** from acetyl CoA, which is catalyzed by *acetyl CoA carboxylase*. This enzyme is allosterically activated by citrate and inhibited by malonyl CoA and palmitoyl CoA. Insulin indirectly activates the enzyme by dephosphorylation, whereas epinephrine indirectly inactivates it by phosphorylation.

- Triacylglycerols are synthesized in the liver and adipocytes by the addition of fatty acids to glycerol phosphate (Fig. 1-34). The liver sends the triacylglycerols into the bloodstream as lipoprotein particles, whereas adipocytes store triacylglycerols.

- In eukaryotes, acetyl CoA derives mainly from carbohydrates but also to some extent from amino acids. It is translocated from the mitochondrion to the cytosol by the **citrate shuttle**, where it is converted to malonyl CoA, which adds two carbons at a time to produce a growing chain. *Fatty acid synthase* controls it all with a single pattern of organic chemistry reactions: condensation, reduction, dehydration, reduction.

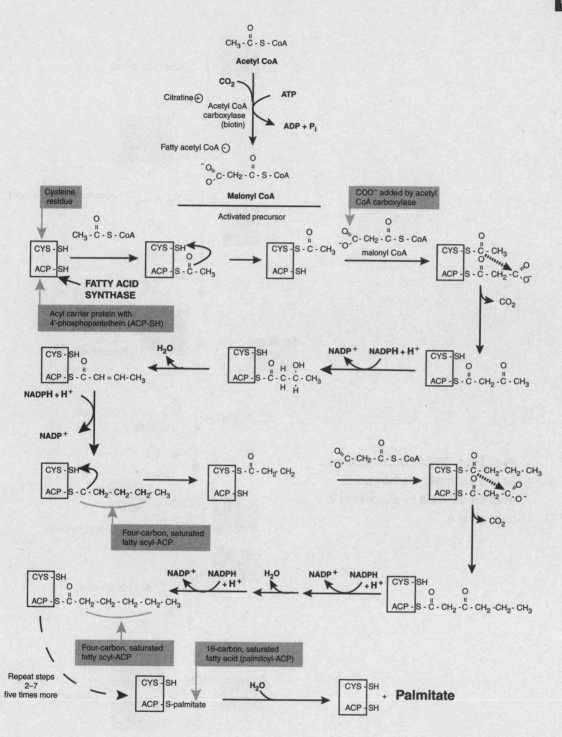

Fig. 1-33. Schematic of palmitate synthesis from acetyl CoA in prokaryotes (very similar to eukaryotes).

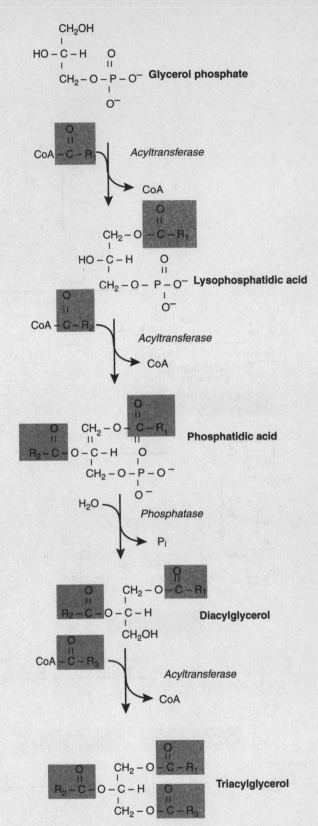

Fig. 1-34. Triacylglycerol synthesis. Before synthesis, the fatty acids must be activated by attachment to coenzyme A.

- Human cells need unsaturated fatty acids with double bonds beyond carbon 9, but humans are not equipped with the proper enzymes to make those double bonds. Consequently, two fatty acids must be acquired in our diet: **linoleic acid** and **linolenic acid**. These are known as **essential fatty acids**.

- Overall stoichiometry for palmitate synthesis is as follows:

8 acetyl CoA + 7 ATP + 14 NADPH + 6 H$^+$ →

Palmitate + 7 ADP + 7 P$_i$ + 14 NADP$^+$ + 6 H$_2$O

Altered Energy Metabolism

Cyanide Poisoning

Cyanide (CN$^-$) is a potent and fast-acting poison. It is a site-specific inhibitor that binds tightly to ferric iron (Fe^{3+}) in *cytochrome oxidase* (complex IV) of the electron transport chain. Electron flow is blocked, and because electron transport and oxidative phosphorylation are closely coupled, ATP production stops. Cyanide poisoning causes hypoxic injury to major organs, including the brain, kidneys, and liver. The antidote for cyanide poisoning is administration of **nitrites**, which convert hemoglobin to methemoglobin. Methemoglobin quickly binds free CN$^-$, preventing it from binding the mitochondrial complex. Also, thiosulfate is simultaneously administered to promote conversion of cyanide to thiocyanate, which is less toxic.

Mitochondrial Myopathies

Mitochondria contain DNA (**mtDNA**), which is maternally inherited. mtDNA codes for some of the enzymes involved in oxidative phosphorylation. Mutations in these genes have adverse effects on the tissues that depend heavily on ATP, such as the CNS, skeletal and cardiac muscle, the kidneys, and liver. **Leber's hereditary optic neuropathy**, which results in neurodegenerative, bilateral loss of central vision, is one example of an mtDNA defect–causing disease. Other syndromes associated with abnormal mitochondria DNA include **MERRF** (myoclonic epilepsy, ragged red fiber syndrome) and **MELAS** (myopathy, encephalopathy, lactic acidosis, and stroke-like episodes).

Ketoacidosis

In addition to glucose, many cells can use amino acids and fatty acids as alternative fuels in starvation. The brain, however, is incapable of using fatty acids for energy in a prolonged fasting state. To compensate for that, **ketone bodies—acetoacetate, acetone**, and **3-hydroxybutyrate**—are made in liver mitochondria from extra acetyl CoA that is left over from fatty acid breakdown or pyruvate oxidation (Fig. 1-35). Ketone bodies are transported via the bloodstream to peripheral tissues, where they are reconverted to acetyl CoA and can enter the TCA cycle. The liver itself cannot use ketone bodies for energy. In diabetics (mainly type I), insulin deficiency and glucagon excess can cause excessive mobilization of fatty acids and the overproduction of ketone bodies. As a result, blood and urine ketone body concentrations are elevated. Ketone bodies in the blood lose protons, acidifying the plasma. In **ketoacidosis**, the excess acetone can often be smelled on the breath.

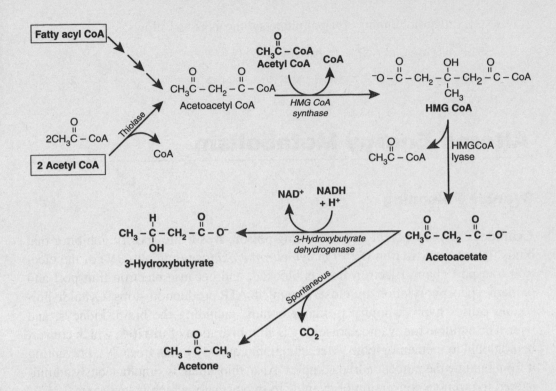

Fig. 1-35. Ketone body synthesis in the liver.

Small Molecule Metabolism

Amino Acid Biosynthesis

Humans are not able to synthesize all of the amino acids needed to make proteins. Those that we can synthesize are called nonessential amino acids, and those required in the diet are essential amino acids. The nonessential amino acids are produced from essential amino acids or from the intermediates of glycolysis and the TCA cycle (Fig. 1-36). (If you know the one-letter abbreviations for amino acids, here is a mnemonic for remembering non-essential amino acids: CANDY Sally Eats Pints Quarts Gallons [cysteine, alanine, asparagine, aspartic acid, tyrosine, serine, glutamic acid, proline, glutamine, glycine].)

Recall that amino acids in the extracellular fluid must be taken into the cell by active transport. One of the most common inherited diseases is **cystinuria**, in which the membrane carrier for the amino acids cysteine, arginine, ornithine, and lysine is defective. In this disease, cysteine precipitation eventually causes kidney stones. (Again, you can remember the affected amino acids by their one-letter abbreviations: CORK [cysteine, ornithine, arginine, lysine]. Picture kidney stones CORKing the cyst (bladder) when you think of cystinuria.)

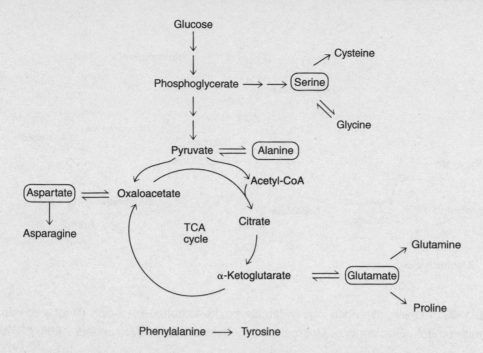

Fig. 1-36. Overview of nonessential amino acid synthesis. (Reprinted with permission from *Biochemistry*, Roskoski Jr., R. Philadelphia, W.B. Saunders, 1996. p. 237.)

Amino Acid Degradation and the Urea Cycle

Excess amino acids are degraded into carbon skeletons that can be used in glucose or ketone body production or as a fuel source for the body, supplementing the energy provided by carbohydrates and triacylglycerols. The nitrogen from amino acids must then be processed by the **urea cycle** for elimination from the body.

- In degradation, first the α-amino group is removed by the processes of transamination and oxidative deamination, yielding nitrogen in the form of **aspartate** or **ammonia**. As you can see, the –NH$_2$ group recipients in transamination are your now-familiar friends from the TCA cycle (Fig. 1-37). The majority of the amino groups are ultimately channeled into the production of glutamate from α-ketoglutarate, since glutamate is the only amino acid that can undergo rapid enzyme-catalyzed oxidative deamination to produce free ammonia. A small portion of the ammonia is excreted in the urine, but most is converted to urea in the **urea cycle**.

- Urea is produced in the liver and transported in the blood to the kidneys for excretion. In the cell, the urea cycle occurs partly in the mitochondrion and partly in the cytosol (Fig. 1-38).

- The rate-limiting step of the urea cycle is catalyzed by *carbamoyl phosphate synthetase I*, which requires the allosteric activator **acetylglutamate**.

- Aspartate and ammonia each provide one of the nitrogen atoms of urea, and CO_2 provides the carbon and oxygen.

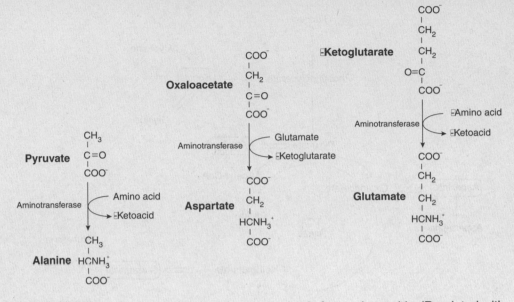

Fig. 1-37. Alanine, aspartate, and glutamate synthesis from α-ketoacids. (Reprinted with permission from *Biochemistry*, Roskoski Jr., R. Philadelphia, W.B. Saunders, 1996. p. 240.)

- The overall reaction of the urea cycle is as follows:

Aspartate + NH_3 + CO_2 + 3 ATP →

Urea + fumarate + 2 ADP + AMP + 2 P_i + PP_i + 3 H_2O

After the amino group is removed, the carbon skeleton of the amino acid is broken down to a product that can be either catabolized by the TCA cycle for energy or used to synthesize glucose or lipids (Fig. 1-39). Amino acids are characterized as either **ketogenic** or **glucogenic**, or both, depending on the product of their degradation (Table 1-3). Glucogenic amino acids produce pyruvate or TCA cycle intermediates, and these molecules can then be converted to glucose and glycogen. The carbon skeletons of ketogenic amino acids are degraded to acetoacetate, which is a ketone body, or its precursor acetyl CoA (Fig. 1-40). Diseases associated with genetic defects of amino acid degradation are listed in Table 1-4. **Phenylketonuria** is a relatively common genetic disorder (1:14,000), but be aware of the others as well.

Table 1-3. Classification of amino acids as glucogenic, ketogenic, or both

Glucogenic		Ketogenic	Glucogenic and ketogenic
Alanine	Glycine	Leucine	Isoleucine
Arginine	Histidine	Lysine	Phenylalanine
Asparagine	Methionine		Tryptophan
Aspartate	Proline		Tyrosine
Cysteine	Serine		
Glutamate	Threonine		
Glutamine	Valine		

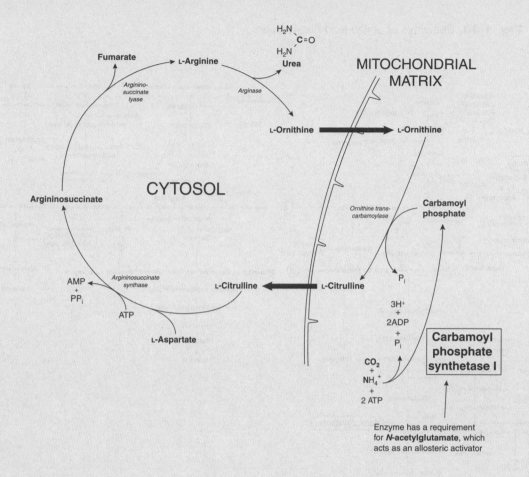

Fig. 1-38. Urea cycle. Aspartate and ammonia each provide one of the nitrogen atoms of urea, and CO_2 provides the carbon and oxygen.

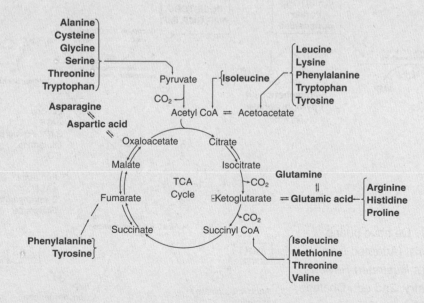

Fig. 1-39. Simplified overview of amino acid degradation.

Fig. 1-40. Pathways of amino acid degradation.

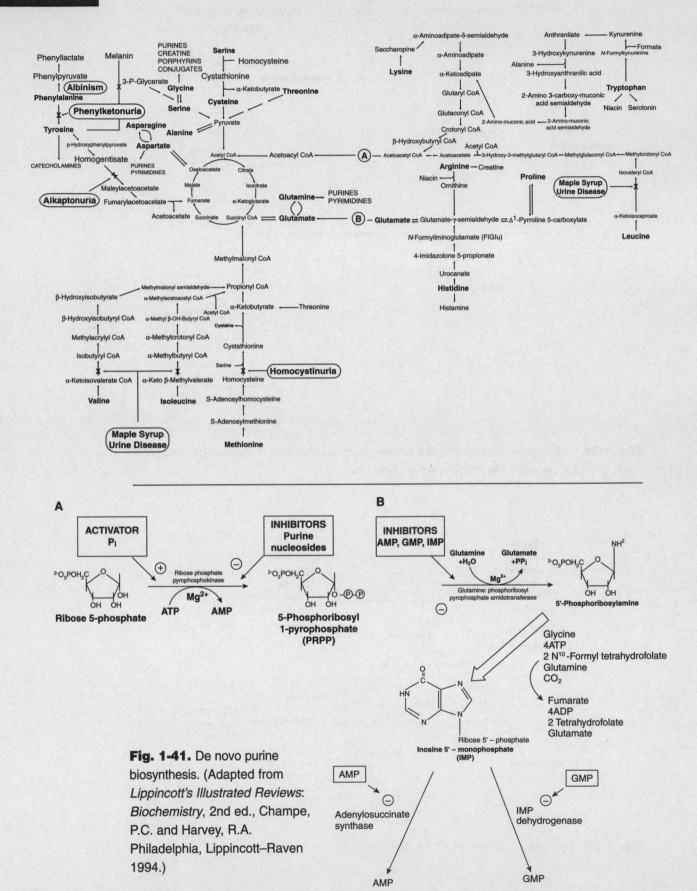

Fig. 1-41. De novo purine biosynthesis. (Adapted from *Lippincott's Illustrated Reviews: Biochemistry*, 2nd ed., Champe, P.C. and Harvey, R.A. Philadelphia, Lippincott–Raven 1994.)

Table 1-4. Diseases associated with amino acid metabolism

Disease	Enzyme deficient	Metabolic effects	Results in	Notes
Phenylketo-nuria	Phenylalanine hydroxylase	Cannot convert phenylalanine to tyrosine	Mental retardation Pigmentation deficiency Eczema Mousy odor	Autosomal recessive Screening performed at birth Treatment: low phenyl-alanine, higher tyro-sine diet
Maple syrup urine disease	Branched-chain α-ketoacid dehydrogenase	Cannot degrade branched amino acids (valine, leucine, iso-leucine)	Severe CNS defects Mental retar-dation High mortality	Urine smells like maple syrup Autosomal recessive "branches of maple tree"
Alkaptonuria	Homogentisate oxidase	Accumulate homo-gentisate	Dark urine Dark connective tissue	Autosomal recessive Benign disease
Albinism	Tyrosinase	Cannot synthesize melanin from tyrosine	Pigmentation deficiency Increased skin cancer risk	
Homocystin-uria	Cystathionine synthetase	Accumulate homo-cysteine (in the urine), cannot produce cysteine	Mental retar-dation Osteoporosis Lens dislocation	Autosomal recessive Treatment: low methionine and cys-teine in diet

Purine Nucleotide Biosynthesis

Purines and **pyrimidines** are the two types of bases found in nucleotides; they can be made de novo or obtained from salvage pathways. Nucleotides are needed for DNA and RNA synthesis but are also used in other important ways: as energy currency (such as ATP and GTP), as carriers of activated intermediates in biosynthesis, and in coenzyme molecules (such as NAD^+ and FAD).

In de novo synthesis, the purines are constructed from the starting molecule ribose 5-phosphate (provided by the pentose-phosphate pathway) (Fig. 1-41). The pathway produces **inosine 5'-monophosphate** (IMP), which can then be converted to AMP or GMP. The monophosphates can then be phosphorylated by kinases to give diphosphates and triphosphates. The pathway makes ribonucleotides, which can be converted to their deoxy forms by the enzyme *ribonucleotide reductase* for use in DNA.

- Purine synthesis occurs in the cytosol.

- The committed step of the de novo pathway is catalyzed by gluta-mine and ***phosphoribosyl pyrophosphate amidotransferase***. The lat-ter is a principal regulatory enzyme that receives feedback inhibition from IMP, GMP, and AMP (the end products of the pathway).

- **Methotrexate**, an antineoplastic and anti-inflammatory agent, inhibits the reduction of dihydrofolate to tetrahydrofolate by inhibit-ing dihydrofolate reductase. Since THF is required for de novo purine and pyrimidine synthesis, decreasing its production slows DNA syn-thesis and is toxic to rapidly dividing cells.

- **Sulfa drugs** target THF production, and ultimately purine synthesis, in bacteria by inhibiting folic acid synthesis. Since humans cannot make folic acid and must rely on external sources, human purine syn-thesis is unaffected by sulfa drugs.

In the salvage pathway, the bases from nucleic acid turnover or dietary intake can be reconverted to nucleoside triphosphates (Fig. 1-42).

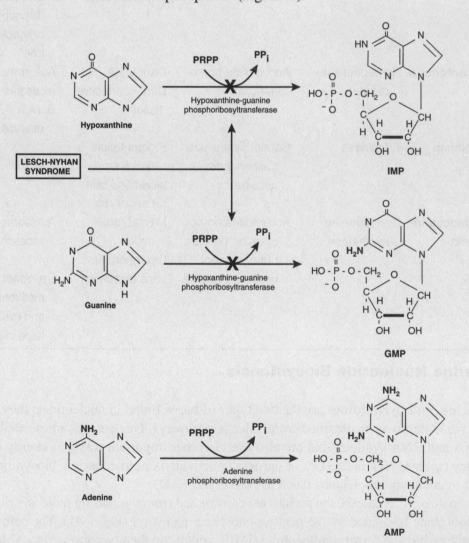

Fig. 1-42. Purine salvage. (Adapted from *Lippincott's Illustrated Reviews: Biochemistry*, 2nd ed., Champe, P.C. and Harvey, R.A. Philadelphia, Lippincott–Raven 1994.)

Table 1-5. Diseases associated with nucleotide metabolism

Disease	Enzyme deficient	Metabolic effects	Results in	Notes
Gout	Many causes, affecting uric acid metabolism (uric acid is the product of purine degradation)	High uric acid levels in serum (hyperuricemia)	Uric acid crystals in joints, causing arthritis	Treatment: allopurinol, which inhibits xanthine oxidase to lower uric acid production
Lesch-Nyhan syndrome	Hypoxanthine-guanine phosphoribosyltransferase (purine salvage)	Accumulation of hypoxanthine and guanine. Excess uric acid production because salvage inhibition increases purine metabolism	Self-mutilation and aggression. Mental and physical retardation. Spastic cerebral palsy	Rare X-linked recessive disease, seen only in males. Sometimes gouty arthritis develops
Adenosine deaminase (ADA) deficiency	ADA (purine degradation)	Accumulation of dATP, which inhibits ribonucleotide reductase (and DNA synthesis)	Severe combined immunodeficiency	Presents in neonatal period. Children die from infection before age 2. Autosomal recessive
Orotic aciduria	UMP synthase complex (orotate phosphoribosyltransferase and OMP decarboxylase; in pyrimidine synthesis)	High urinary orotic acid secretion	Retarded physical and mental development. Megaloblastic anemia	Autosomal recessive

UMP = uridine monophosphate; OMP = orotidine monophosphate.

- The molecule **5-phosphoribosyl 1-pyrophosphate** (PRPP) is used by HGPRT as the donor of ribose 5-phosphate.

- Deficiency of *hypoxanthine-guanine phosphoribosyltransferase* (*HGPRT*) causes excessive uric acid production, which results in a constellation of characteristics (self-mutilation, mental retardation, involuntary movements) known as **Lesch-Nyhan syndrome** (Table 1-5).

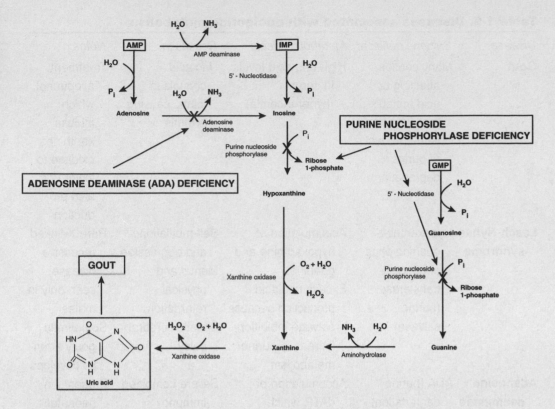

Fig. 1-43. Purine degradation, yielding uric acid. (Adapted from *Lippincott's Illustrated Reviews*: *Biochemistry*, 2nd ed., Champe, P.C. and Harvey, R.A. Philadelphia, Lippincott–Raven 1994.)

Purine Nucleotide Degradation

The product of purine nucleotide breakdown is **uric acid**, which is excreted in the urine (Fig. 1-43).

- **Gout** is a consequence of the overproduction of **uric acid**, which leads to hyperuricemia and arthritic joint inflammation with uric acid crystals (Table 1-5). Elevated uric acid levels may be due to an inborn error of metabolism or may be secondary to other diseases, such as cancer (high cell turnover), chronic renal insufficiency (decreased uric acid excretion), or HGPRT deficiency (inability to salvage purines).

- A deficiency in *adenosine deaminase* (*ADA*) leads to dATP accumulation, which blocks the function of ribonucleotide reductase and, thus, DNA synthesis. The result is **severe combined immunodeficiency** (SCID) and early death from overwhelming infection (Table 1-5).

- Similarly, *purine nucleoside phosphorylase deficiency* leads to deoxynucleotide accumulation and immune dysfunction. In this case, however, dGTP accumulates, leading to dATP overproduction and, consequently, inhibition of ribonucleotide reductase. T cell function is impaired, but B cell function remains normal.

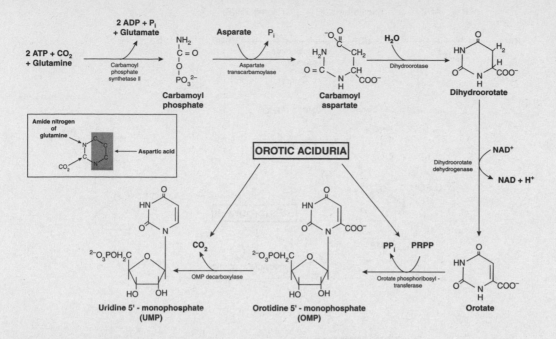

Fig. 1-44. Pyrimidine biosynthesis.

Pyrimidine Nucleotide Biosynthesis

The three main pyrimidines are **uracil**, **cytosine**, and **thymine**. Unlike purine synthesis, the pyrimidine ring is first built from scratch and then attached to a ribose 5-phosphate. The pathway produces uridine 5'-monophosphate (UMP), which can undergo various modifications to produce the other pyrimidine nucleotides. One of the most important conversions is the conversion of UMP to deoxythymidylate, which is used in DNA synthesis (Fig. 1-44). As is true for purine nucleotides, these ribonucleotides can also be converted by *ribonucleotide reductase* to deoxyribonucleotides for use in DNA (Fig. 1-45).

- Pyrimidine synthesis occurs in the cytosol.

- The regulated step in pyrimidine synthesis is different for humans and bacteria. In humans, ***carbamoyl synthetase II*** is the regulated step. It is activated by ATP and PRPP and inhibited by UTP. In bacteria, *aspartate transcarbamoylase* is the regulated step. It is inhibited by cytidine triphosphate. (Don't confuse *carbamoyl synthetase II*, which is located in the cytosol, with *carbamoyl synthetase I*, which is located in the mitochondria and used in the urea cycle.)

- Pyrimidines can also be salvaged by the enzyme *pyrimidine phosphoribosyltransferase*, which recycles the pyrimidines back into nucleotides using the ribose 5-phosphate donor PRPP (as in purine salvage).

Two important drugs, **methotrexate** and **5-fluorouracil**, are used in anticancer therapies because they slow DNA replication. These drugs decrease the availability of nucleotides by inhibiting the conversion of deoxyuridine monophosphate to thymidylate. 5-fluorouracil, a thymine analog, inhibits ***thymidylate synthase***. Methotrexate, as we discussed above, is a powerful competitive inhibitor of ***dihydrofolate reductase***, which prevents tetrahydrofolate regeneration and decreases thymidylate and purine synthesis.

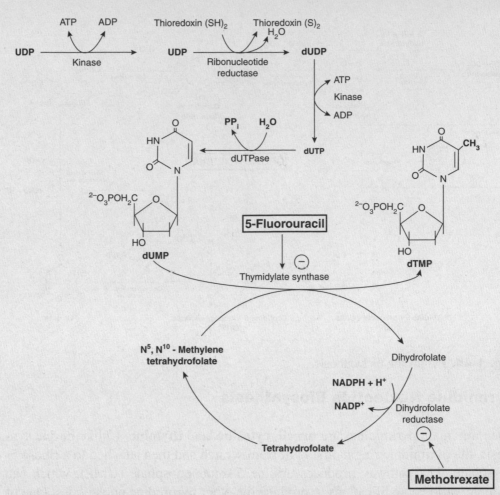

Fig. 1-45. Thymidylate (dTMP) synthesis from uridine 5'-monophosphate (UMP). (Adapted from *Lippincott's Illustrated Reviews: Biochemistry*, 2nd ed., Champe, P.C. and Harvey, R.A. Philadelphia, Lippincott–Raven 1994.)

Pyrimidine Nucleotide Degradation

In contrast to the purine ring, the pyrimidine ring in humans can be totally degraded to metabolic intermediates. Diseases associated with nucleotide metabolism are summarized in Table 1-5.

Cholesterol Biosynthesis and Degradation

Cholesterol is a critical component of cell membranes and also serves as a precursor of steroid hormones, bile acids, and vitamin D. It can be obtained from the diet or synthesized de novo from acetyl CoA (Fig. 1-46).

- Cholesterol is synthesized by most tissues in the body. The main site of synthesis is the liver, and smaller sites include the intestine, reproductive organs, and adrenal cortex. Synthesis occurs in the cytosol of nucleated cells.

- The rate-limiting step in the synthesis of cholesterol is catalyzed by *3-hydroxy-3-methylglutaryl (HMG) CoA reductase*, which receives feedback inhibition from cholesterol. Insulin increases cholesterol synthesis, whereas glucagon decreases it. Also, the cholesterol taken

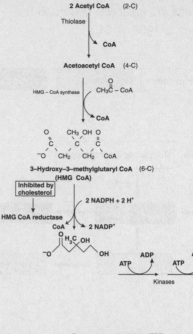

Fig. 1-46. Cholesterol biosynthesis. (Adapted from *Lippincott's Illustrated Reviews*: *Biochemistry*, 2nd ed., Champe, P.C. and Harvey, R.A. Philadelphia, Lippincott–Raven 1994.)

up by cells for lipoprotein metabolism decreases the transcription of HMG CoA reductase, which reduces cholesterol synthesis. The drugs **lovastatin** and **mevastatin** are competitive inhibitors of the enzyme and are used to lower plasma cholesterol levels.

- Cholesterol cannot be catabolized to CO_2 and H_2O to release energy. It is therefore either converted to bile acids or secreted into the bile and excreted via the intestines.

Steroid Hormone Biosynthesis

Steroid hormones are synthesized from cholesterol in the adrenal cortex, ovaries, and testes and are transported through the blood to target tissues. The five types of steroid hormones are **estrogens**, **progestins**, **androgens**, **glucocorticoids**, and **mineralocorticoids** (Fig. 1-47).

- Synthesis of steroid hormones occurs in the cytosol and the mitochondria.

Fig. 1-47. Steroidogenesis in the adrenal cortex (*Blueprints in Pediatrics*, Marino, B.S. Sneed, K.L., McMillan, J.A. Massachusetts: Blackwell Science, 1998. p. 61.)

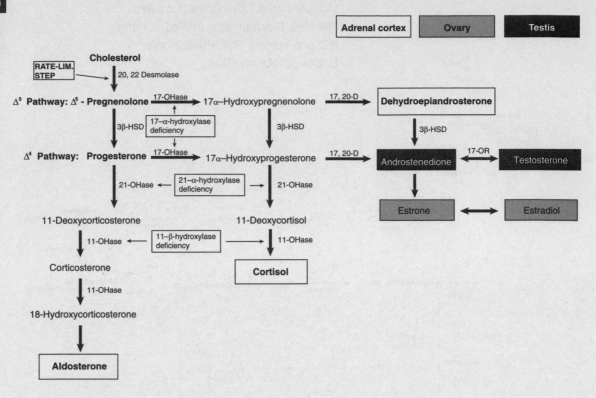

- The rate-limiting step is the conversion of cholesterol to **pregnenolone**, which is catalyzed by the *desmolase* **complex**.

- Defects of steroid synthesis associated with **congenital adrenal hyperplasia** are listed in Table 1-6. As with other enzyme deficiencies, these are prime test material, so know these cold!

Bile Acid Biosynthesis and Degradation

Bile acids, also derived from cholesterol, are steroid carboxylic acids and are one organic component of bile. Because they are amphipathic, they can solubilize dietary lipids for digestion. **Cholic acid** and **chenodeoxycholic acid** are the two most prevalent bile acids.

- The liver produces bile acids and converts them to primary bile salts by **conjugating** them with glycine or taurine before it releases them into the biliary system. The most prevalent of the four primary bile salts is **glycocholate**.

- The first and rate-limiting step is catalyzed by 7-α-hydroxylase, which is inhibited by **cholic acid**.

- In the intestine, bacteria deconjugate some of the bile acids back to bile salts, then dehydroxylate them to form secondary bile acids: **lithocholate** (from chenodeoxycholate) and **deoxycholate** (from cholate). The lithocholate is insoluble and excreted in the stool, and the deoxycholate is reconjugated to form two additional forms of bile salts.

Table 1-6. Defects of steroid hormone synthesis

Enzyme deficient	Metabolic effects	Results in	Notes
3-β-Hydroxysteroid dehydrogenase	No androgens, estrogens, glucocorticoids, or mineralocorticoids	High urinary salt excretion Early death	Autosomal recessive
17-α-Hydroxylase	No sex hormones or cortisol Increased mineralocorticoids	Salt and water retention and hypertension	Autosomal recessive Phenotypically female but maturity is inhibited
21-α-Hydroxylase	Diminished glucocorticoid and mineralocorticoid production	High adrenocorticotropic hormone levels High androgen levels and masculinization due to precursor salt wasting	Autosomal recessive Most common inherited disease of steroid hormone synthesis (90%) Therapy: glucocorticoids
11-β-Hydroxylase	Lower serum cortisol, corticosterone, and aldosterone Higher deoxycorticosterone synthesis	Masculinization High deoxycorticosterone levels leads to water retention and hypertension	Autosomal recessive 5% of CAH cases

- Bile acids and salts are mostly reabsorbed at the distal ileum and delivered to the liver for re-use. The bile acids and salts that are not re-absorbed are excreted in the feces. The excretion of lithocholate is the body's primary means of ridding itself of cholesterol.

Prostaglandin, Thromboxane, and Leukotriene Biosynthesis and Degradation

Prostaglandins, **thromboxanes**, and **leukotrienes** are powerful, short-lived signal compounds that are synthesized from polyunsaturated fatty acids (Fig. 1-48). They cause a variety of physiologic responses, depending on the tissue. Effects include vasoconstriction and vasodilation, smooth muscle contraction and relaxation, and inhibition and promotion of platelet aggregation.

Prostaglandins are synthesized on demand in nearly all tissues and act locally. They are not stored but are catabolized at their site of synthesis to inactive products soon after use.

- The rate-limiting step, generating **arachidonic acid** from phospholipids, is catalyzed by *phospholipase A*.

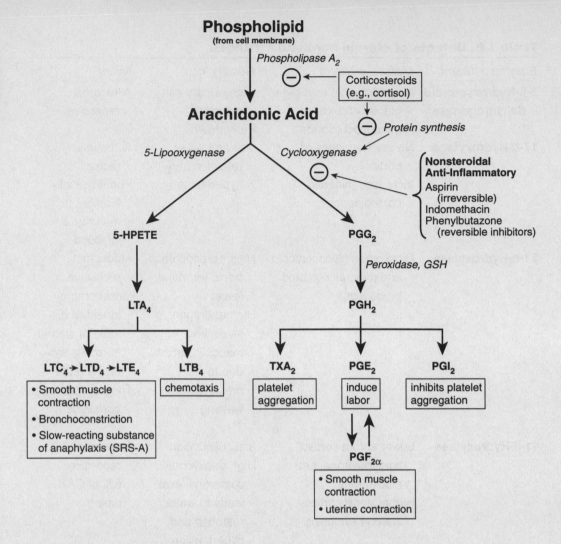

Fig. 1-48. Schematic of prostaglandin and thromboxane synthesis.

- **PGE_2** causes vasodilation and smooth muscle relaxation, and is used to induce labor. **PGI_2** (prostacyclin), which is primarily produced in vessel endothelium, causes vasodilation and inhibits platelet aggregation. **$PGF_{2\alpha}$**, on the other hand, causes vasoconstriction and smooth muscle contraction. It stimulates uterine contractions.

- **Thromboxane A_2**, which is produced primarily by platelets, promotes platelet aggregation, vasoconstriction, and contraction of smooth muscle. It is the target of **aspirin** therapy to prevent thrombosis in patients with angina and chronic atrial fibrillation, and it is used prophylactically to prevent venous thromboses in surgical patients.

- **Leukotrienes C_4, D_4,** and **E_4** cause smooth muscle contraction and bronchoconstriction. They are also components of slow-reacting substance of anaphylaxis (SRS-A). **Leukotriene B_4** is an important chemotactic factor in inflammation.

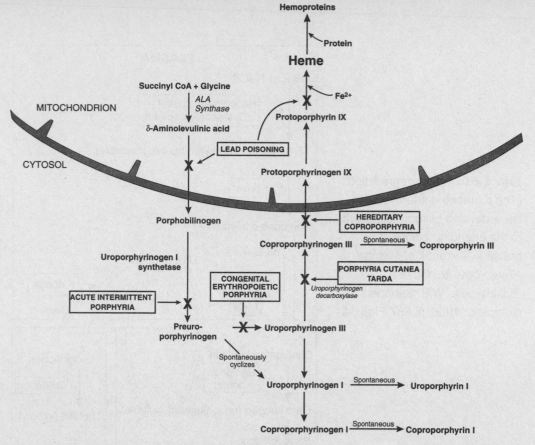

Fig. 1-49. Schematic of heme (and other porphyrin) synthesis and associated diseases. (Adapted from *Lippincott's Illustrated Reviews: Biochemistry*, 2nd ed., Champe, P.C. and Harvey, R.A. Philadelphia, Lippincott–Raven 1994.)

Porphyrin Biosynthesis

Porphyrins are cyclic molecules that can bind metal ions, typically iron. The most abundant metalloporphyrin is **heme**, which is crucial to the function of such proteins as hemoglobin, myoglobin, and cytochromes. All of the carbons and nitrogens in porphyrins come from the amino acid glycine and the TCA cycle intermediate succinyl CoA.

- Heme synthesis takes place in the liver and bone marrow. Synthesis starts with two steps in the mitochondrion, continues for three steps in the cytosol, and is completed in three steps in the mitochondrion (Fig. 1-49). Recall that mature RBCs cannot synthesize heme.

- The first step in the synthesis of porphyrins is rate-limiting and is catalyzed by *δ-aminolevulinate synthase* (*ALA synthase*). Deficiencies in certain other enzymes involved in porphyrin synthesis cause various diseases, which are listed in Table 1-7.

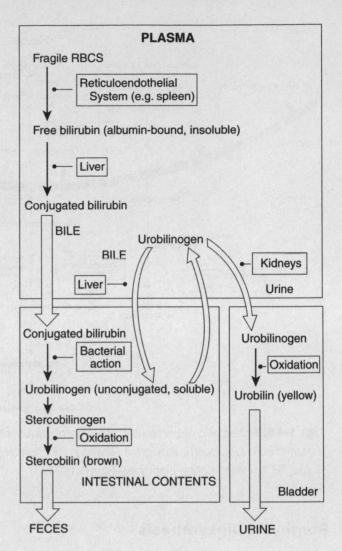

Fig. 1-50. Heme degradation. (The pigmented intermediates biliverdin and bilirubin contribute to the changing colors of a bruise.) (*Textbook of Medical Physiology*, 9e, Guyton, Philadelphia, W.B. Saunders Company, 1996. p. 887 Fig.70-2)

Porphyrin Degradation

RBCs have a lifetime of approximately 120 days. At this point the heme from hemoglobin is degraded. Several organ systems take part in heme degradation. RBCs are initially broken down in the spleen, but the degradative pathway ends with the generation of **bilirubin diglucuronide** (conjugated bilirubin) in the liver, which is secreted into the bile (Fig. 1-50). This molecule is then hydrolyzed and reduced by bacterial enzymes in the large intestine to form **urobilinogen**. Most urobilinogen is converted by bacteria to **stercobilin**, which gives stools their brown color. Some urobilinogen is absorbed by the intestine, transported through the blood and sent to the kidneys, which excrete it as **urobilin**, the yellow pigment that gives urine its color.

Table 1-7. Diseases associated with heme biosynthesis

Disease	Cause	Metabolites accumulated in urine	Results in	Notes
Lead poisoning	Lead inhibits aminolevulinic acid (ALA) dehydrase and ferrochelatase	Coproporphyrin and ALA	Anemia	Advanced toxicity causes neurologic problems
Acute intermittent porphyria	Deficiency of uroporphyrinogen I synthetase	Porphobilinogen and δ-aminolevulinic acid	Symptoms after puberty: acute episodes of abdominal, neurologic, or psychiatric problems	Autosomal dominant ⒶⒹ Latent with acute attacks precipitated by factors such as barbiturates *babies precipitate attacks*
Congenital erythropoietic porphyria	Deficiency of uroporphyrinogen III cosynthetase	Uroporphyrinogen I and coproporphyrinogen I	Photosensitivity Mutilating skin lesions Hemolytic anemia Splenomegaly	Autosomal recessive
Porphyria cutanea tarda	Deficiency of uroporphyrinogen decarboxylase	Uroporphyrin and coproporphyrin	Cutaneous photosensitivity, causing skin lesions	Most common of the porphyrias Congenital or acquired
Hereditary coproporphyria	Deficiency of coproporphyrinogen oxidase	Coproporphyrinogen III and its precursors	Cutaneous photosensitivity	Autosomal dominant ⒶⒹ

Other Macromolecule Metabolism

Glycoprotein Biosynthesis and Degradation

Glycoproteins are proteins that have covalently attached oligosaccharides (sugars), which are usually branched. They serve a number of functions: Glycoproteins in the plasma membrane participate in cell surface recognition and antigenicity, whereas secreted glycoproteins have roles in the extracellular matrix and are present in gastrointestinal and urogenital mucins. The carbohydrate chains are bound to asparagine residues through *N*-glycosidic linkages or to serine and threonine residues via *O*-glycosidic bonds. (The letter refers to the attachment group, *N* for amine, *O* for hydroxyl.)

Only proteins that are translated on ER-bound ribosomes can be glycosylated. Oligosaccharides are initially added to proteins in the ER lumen, and modifications occur as the proteins travel through the ER and then through the *cis*, medial, and *trans* Golgi.

- *O*-linked glycosides are synthesized by the immediate addition of *N*-acetylgalactosamine onto serine or threonine residues. Afterward, additional sugars are added by glycosyltransferases in the ER and Golgi.

- *N*-linked glycosides are synthesized in a different way: A branched core oligosaccharide of 14 sugars is constructed by transferase-catalyzed addition of activated sugar precursors (UDP, GDP, and dolichol pyrophosphate derivatives) onto a dolichol phosphate group. Dolichol is a lipid held in the ER membrane that serves as a temporary foundation for this glucose skyscraper. The activated core oligosaccharide is then transferred to the asparagine residue of a protein by a **protein-oligosaccharide transferase**. Trimming and addition of monosaccharides occur in the ER and Golgi (Fig. 1-51).

- To remember how these glycoproteins are made, think, "*O* grows outward, *N* is *trimmed*."

- Glycoproteins are degraded by hydrolytic enzymes in the lysosome. Generally, sugar units are removed in the reverse order of synthesis.

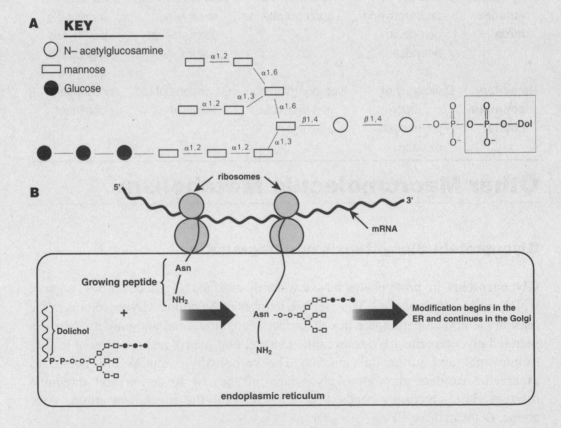

Fig. 1-51. A. *N*-linked glycoside synthesis. (Reprinted with permission from *Biochemistry* 2nd ed., Stryer, L. San Francisco, W.H. Freeman, 1981. p. 715.) **B.** Glycoside modification. (Glc = glucose; Man = mannose; NAcGlc = *N*-acetylglucosamine.)

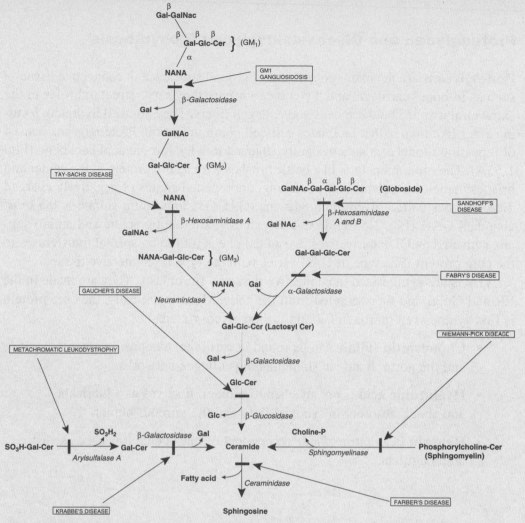

Fig. 1-52. Glycolipid degradation. Glycosphingolipids are endocytosed, and lysosomes contain hydrolytic enzymes that dismantle the molecules in the reverse order of synthesis (like glycoproteins).

Glycosphingolipid Biosynthesis and Degradation

Glycosphingolipids are found in the plasma membranes of all cells and are most prominent in nerve tissue. They are located mainly in the outer layer of the bilayer membrane, and they participate in extracellular interactions. They consist of a sugar attached by an O-glycosidic bond to **ceramide**, which is made up of a fatty acid connected to the aminoalcohol **sphingosine** (Fig. 2-2).

- Glycosphingolipid synthesis occurs in the ER and Golgi.

- Glycosphingolipids are synthesized by the stepwise addition of glycosyl units from activated sugar-nucleotide donors. This addition of sugars to an acceptor molecule is catalyzed by specific glycosyltransferases. The degradation pathways are shown in Fig. 1-52.

- Diseases caused by enzymatic defects in sphingolipid degradation are shown in Table 1-8. Most are autosomal recessive and cause early death. These sphingolipidoses arise from deficiencies in degradative lysosomal enzymes and comprise a portion of the lysosomal storage diseases. If you can recognize that these diseases belong to this group, you're in good shape.

Proteoglycan and Glycosaminoglycan Biosynthesis

Proteoglycans are the major constituent of ground substance in connective tissue—such as in bone, cartilage, and the cornea—where they serve structural roles in the extracellular space between cells and collagen fibers. They are well hydrated, forming a gel-like matrix that facilitates cell-cell communication. Proteoglycans consist of repeating monomers noncovalently attached to a hyaluronic acid backbone (Fig. 1-53A). The monomers look like bottle brushes with a core protein in the center and bristles made of covalently-attached long, unbranched chains of negatively charged disaccharides called glycosaminoglycans (GAGs). Chondroitin sulfate is the most abundant GAG (Fig. 1-53B). In GAG synthesis, alternating acidic and amino sugars, activated as UDP derivatives, are added one at a time by special transferases to the core protein. The type of GAG varies with the type of connective tissue.

GAGs are synthesized in connective tissue by fibroblasts. They are made in the ER and Golgi and then secreted from the cells. More specifically, the core protein is first synthesized on rough ER and is then glycosylated.

- **Chondroitin sulfate** can be found in cartilage, tendons, ligaments, and the aorta. It aids in strengthening collagen networks.

- **Hyaluronic acid** is not attached to protein. It serves as a lubricant and shock absorber in synovial fluid and the vitreous humor.

- **Heparin** is an *intracellular* component of mast cells. It is used as an anticoagulant.

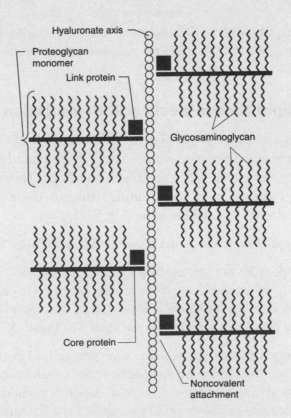

A

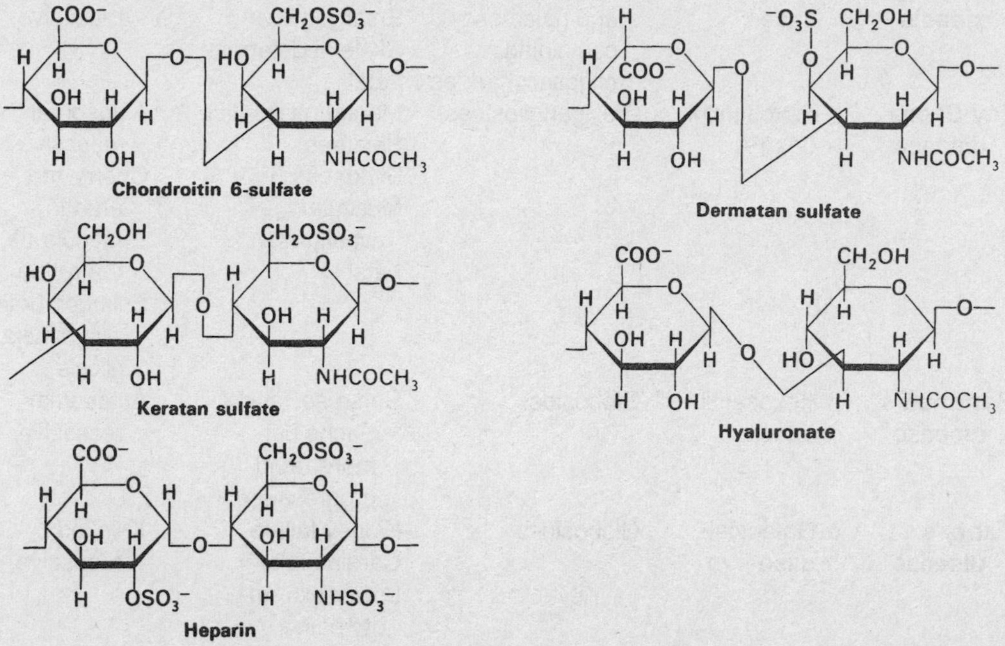

Fig. 1-53. Proteoglycan and glycosaminoglycan architecture. **A.** Overall proteoglycan structure. (Reprinted with permission from *Biochemistry*, Roskoski Jr., R. Philadelphia, W.B. Saunders, 1996. p. 479.) **B.** Structure of the disaccharide unit of common glycosaminoglycans. (Reprinted with permission from *Biochemistry* 2nd ed., Stryer, L. San Francisco, W.H. Freeman, 1981. p. 201.)

Proteoglycan and Glycosaminoglycan Degradation

GAGs, like sphingolipids, are degraded in the lysosome (Fig. 1-54). Enzymatic deficiencies in the catabolic pathways cause some of the lysosomal storage diseases (Table 1-8). The undegraded molecules accumulate in lysosomes and can sometimes be visualized by microscopy.

Table 1-8. Diseases associated with sphingolipid degradation (most are autosomal recessive and cause death, usually early)

Disease	Enzyme deficient	Main metabolite accumulated	Results in	Notes
GM$_1$ gangliosidosis	β-Galactosidase	GM$_1$ gangliosides and galactose-containing oligosaccharides	Mental retardation Enlarged liver Skeletal deformity Fatal	Autosomal recessive
Tay-Sachs disease	β-Hexosaminidase A	GM$_2$ gangliosides	Mental retardation Seizures Blindness Muscular weakness Fatal	Autosomal recessive Cherry-red area in macula of the retina Enlarged brain with diffuse gliosis
Sandhoff's disease	β-Hexosaminidase	Globosides	Same as Tay-Sachs but more rapid progression	Autosomal recessive
Fabry's disease	α-Galactosidase	Globosides	Kidney failure Cardiac failure Lower extremity pain Skin rash	X-linked recessive
Gaucher's disease	β-Glucosidase	Glucocerebrosides	Mental retardation Osteoporosis Hepatosplenomegaly	Autosomal recessive
Metachromatic leukodystrophy	Sulfatide sulfatase	Sulfatides	Mental retardation Demyelination normal at birth Progressive paralysis and dementia Fatal	Autosomal recessive Metachromatic granules (toluidine blue stain)
Krabbe's disease	β-Galactosidase	Galactocerebrosides	Mental retardation Paralysis Convulsions Myelin nearly absent Blindness Deafness Fatal	Autosomal recessive
Farber's disease	Ceramidase	Ceramide	Painful or deformed joints Subcutaneous nodules Fatal	Autosomal recessive
Niemann-Pick disease	Sphingomyelinase	Sphingomyelin	Mental retardation Hepatosplenomegaly Fatal	Autosomal recessive Cherry-red area in macula of retina

toluidine blue

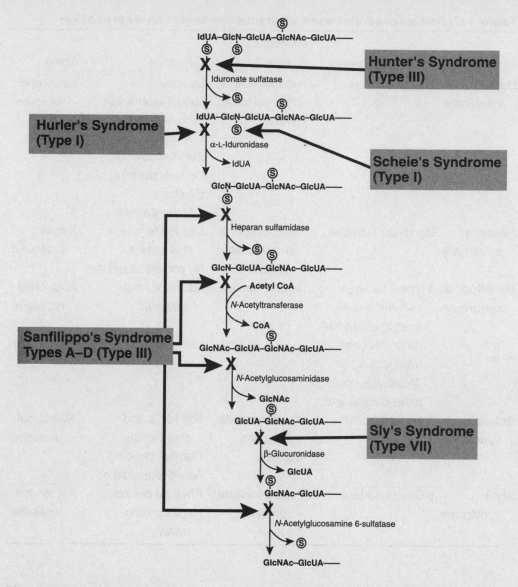

Fig. 1-54. Lysosomal degradation of the glycosaminoglycan heparan sulfate. (IdUA = L-iduronic acid; GlcN = glucosamine; GlcNAc = N-acetylglucosamine.) (Adapted from *Lippincott's Illustrated Reviews: Biochemistry*, 2nd ed., Champe, P.C. and Harvey, R.A. Philadelphia, Lippincott–Raven 1994.)

Table 1-9. Associated diseases of glycosaminoglycan degradation

Syndrome	Enzyme deficient	Metabolites in urine	Results in	Notes
Hurler's syndrome	α-L-Iduronidase	Heparan sulfate and dermatan sulfate	Dwarfism / Mental retardation / Coarse facial features / Skeletal defects / Corneal clouding / Coronary complications	Autosomal recessive
Hunter's syndrome	Iduronate sulfatase	Heparan sulfate and dermatan sulfate	Like Hurler's but less severe / No corneal clouding	X-linked recessive
Sanfilippo's syndrome	4 types: heparan sulfamidase, N-acetylglucosaminidase, N-acetyltransferase, N-acetylglucosamine-6-sulfatase	Heparan sulfate	Severe mental retardation	Autosomal recessive
Scheie's syndrome	α-L-Iduronidase	Heparan sulfate, dermatan sulfate	Stiff joints and claw hands / Corneal clouding / Aortic regurgitation	Autosomal recessive
Sly's syndrome	β-Glucuronidase	Heparan sulfate, dermatan sulfate	Physical deformity / Hepatosplenomegaly	Autosomal recessive

CHAPTER 2

Cell Biology

Cell Membranes

Plasma Membrane

The **plasma membrane** is a selectively permeable barrier that allows for the flow of molecules into and out of cells and is involved in cellular recognition and communication. Cellular organelles are themselves defined by internal membrane systems.

Membranes are composed of lipids and proteins. All lipids are amphipathic: The lipid molecule has a polar hydrophilic ("water-loving") head and a nonpolar hydrophobic ("water-fearing") tail. As such, they are not very soluble in water.

The major class of membrane lipids are **phospholipids**. Those include:

- **Phosphoglycerides**, which consist of a glycerol backbone, two fatty acid chains, and a phosphorylated alcohol (Fig. 2-1)

- Sphingosine-derived phospholipids, such as **glycolipids** and **sphingomyelin** (Fig. 2-2)

- **Cholesterol**, which enhances the mechanical stability of the membrane and regulates membrane fluidity (Fig. 2-3)

The fatty acid chains are usually 14–24 carbons in length and have zero to three *cis* bonds. The physical properties of membranes are determined by the length of their fatty acid chains and the number of their *cis* or *trans* bonds. For example, the melting point of an unsaturated fatty acid (one or more double bonds) is lower than that of a saturated fatty acid (no double bonds). There are more kinks in unsaturated fatty acid chains because of the double bonds, and this prevents them from forming as many van der Waals interactions as do saturated fatty acids. Because saturated fatty acids have more noncovalent interactions, more energy (heat) is required to break them apart.

The two fatty acid side chains of phospholipids allow formation of the membrane bilayer because of the amphipathic nature of the lipids. In biological membranes, the phospholipid bilayer is formed when hydrophobic fatty acid chains huddle in the middle of the bilayer (forming the hydrophobic core) and the

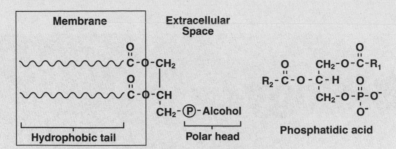

Fig. 2-1. Phospholipid structure.

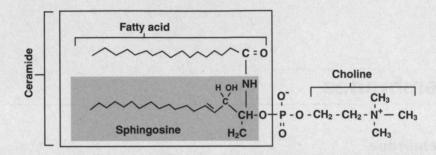

Fig. 2-2. Sphingomyelin structure.

hydrophilic polar heads line the outer and inner surface of the bilayer. Transmembrane proteins cross this bilayer membrane, whereas peripheral proteins bind on its interior or exterior (Fig. 2-4). Oligosaccharide chains are attached to proteins (glycoproteins) on the extracellular surface and participate in cell-cell interactions.

Ion Channels and Pumps

Simple diffusion accounts for the passage across the cell membrane of molecules such as oxygen, CO_2, NO, 2,4-deoxyribonucleoprotein (DNP), and steroids. The movement of the particles follows an electrochemical gradient, and no carrier protein is involved.

Facilitated diffusion is the movement of a compound down its electrochemical gradient through a carrier protein, or pore, in the membrane. Some examples of substances that cross the membrane in this way include glucose, amino acids, fatty acids, and ions (e.g., K^+, Na^+, Ca^{2+}, Cl^-).

Active transport uses the energy stored in adenosine triphosphate (ATP) to unidirectionally "pump" a molecule against its concentration gradient. The Na^+/K^+ and Ca^{2+} pumps are examples of active transport.

Ion channels (facilitated diffusion) are classified into the following categories:

- **Voltage-gated channels** switch between closed and open conformations according to changes in membrane potential. Sodium and potassium channels are voltage-gated and are found in nerve axons and muscle plasma membrane. Electrical stimulation causes an increase

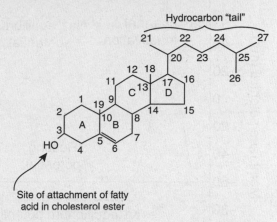

Fig. 2-3. Cholesterol structure.

Site of attachment of fatty
acid in cholesterol ester

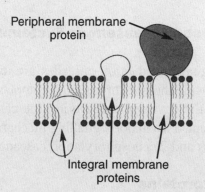

Fig. 2-4. Membrane bilayer. (Reprinted with permission from *Biochemistry* 2nd ed., Stryer, L. San Francisco, W.H. Freeman, 1981. p. 217.)

in Na⁺ conductance of the membrane, which in turn opens additional Na⁺ channels. Sodium ions flow into the cell down their electrochemical gradient (determined by the Nernst equation). Further depolarization due to influx of sodium ions results in a large change of membrane potential (from −60 mV to +30 mV) within 1 msec. The sodium channel is then auto-inactivated. Voltage-gated potassium channels, which open more slowly than sodium channels, remain open during this time. The continuing K⁺ efflux initially causes a hyperpolarization and brings the membrane back to resting membrane potential (Fig. 2-5).

Tetrodotoxin, found in puffer fish (a delicacy in Japan), leads to respiratory paralysis by binding to the sodium channel pore and blocking nerve impulse conduction. **Saxitoxin** is a similar poison produced by dinoflagellates; it is the reason shellfish that feed on dinoflagellates should be avoided during a red tide.

- **Ligand-gated channels** switch between closed and open forms when small molecules or proteins bind to them or when they are covalently modified (e.g., by phosphorylation). One example is the ryanodine-Ca²⁺ receptor, found in heart muscle.

- **Stretch-activated channels** switch between closed and open forms via mechanical displacement.

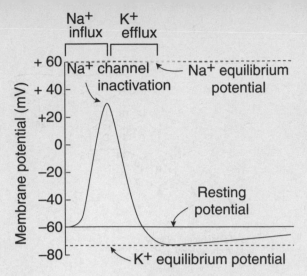

Fig. 2-5. Action potential.

Second Messenger Systems

Signal transduction cascades are used by cells to communicate information from outside the cell through the cytoplasm and to the nucleus so it can react to changes in the environment. During the cascade, signal amplification and integration can occur. Two major signalling mechanisms occur through 1) G protein-coupled receptors and 2) phosphorylation cascades.

G proteins

The binding of a peptide or a molecule, or the absorption of a photon by a special group of seven-helix receptors on the cell surface can activate the G-protein cascade. β-Adrenergic receptors and rhodopsin are classic members of this receptor family.

    Rhodopsin, for instance, contains a light-absorbing molecule called 11-*cis* retinal, which isomerizes to the all-*trans* form after the absorption of light. This conformational change activates a G protein called **transducin**. The binding of epinephrine to the β-adrenergic receptor activates a different G protein.

    G proteins are located inside, very close to the intracellular surface of the plasma membrane. They are composed of three polypeptide chains—α, β, and γ—which are bound to the inner leaflet of the plasma membrane (Fig. 2-6). When the α subunit has a bound guanosine triphosphate (GTP) group, the G proteins are in an active state; hydrolysis of GTP to guanosine diphosphate inactivates the complex. There are different classes of G proteins, including G_t (transducin), G_s (stimulatory G protein), G_i (inhibitory G protein), and G_{olf} (olfactory G protein). G_t hydrolyzes cyclic guanosine monophosphate (cGMP) to GMP, whereas G_s and G_{olf} both activate adenylate cyclase and increase intracellular cyclic adenosine monophosphate (cAMP) concentrations. G_i opens potassium channels and inhibits adenylate cyclase at the same time.

    Muscarinic acetylcholine receptors (unlike the nicotinic acetylcholine receptors, which are ligand-gated ion channels) are members of the seven-helix family. In the 1920s, Otto Loewi discovered that acetylcholine can slow down the heart. It is now known that the binding of acetylcholine to the muscarinic receptor activates G_i, which hyperpolarizes atrial muscle cells by opening potassium channels and slowing the cardiac pacemaker.

Teratogenic Drugs

While the majority of women use medications while pregnant, only a few of the medications have been proven to be teratogenic. These include **thalidomide**, a sleeping pill found to cause total or partial absence of limbs, and **isotretinoin**, a vitamin A analogue used topically for acne and other dermatoses. Antineoplastic agents such as **aminopterin** have also been shown to produce defects.

Antiepileptic agents like **phenytoin**, **valproic acid**, and **trimethadione** cause major malformations. Antipsychotic agents, particularly **lithium** and **phenothiazine**, are suspected to produce congenital malformations, as are antianxiety agents such as **meprobamate**, **chlordiazepoxide**, and **diazepam**. The antidepressant **imipramine** has been linked to limb deformities.

While the anticoagulant **warfarin** is a teratogen, **heparin** is not and is safer to use for pregnant women. **ACE inhibitors** have been shown to produce renal dysfunction, oligohydramnios, growth retardation, and fetal death.

Caution should also be exercised in using antibiotics such as **streptomycin**, which is linked to deafness, and **tetracycline**, which causes tooth and bone abnormalities. **Sulfonamides** have been associated with kernicterus, and **quinine** is linked with deafness.

Finally, abused drugs such as **cocaine** and **alcohol** are strongly associated with birth defects. **PCP** and **marijuana** are less conclusively linked to birth defects, and **LSD** is associated with limb and CNS malformations when used in high doeses.

Types of Mutations

- **Missense mutation**: a base pair point mutation that affects the protein coding sequence.

- **Nonsense mutation**: causes early termination of translation by creating a stop codon. The result is a shortened, often nonfunctional protein.

- **Frameshift mutation**: deletion or insertion of nucleotides, which changes the reading frame of the protein.

- **Amorphic mutation**: complete loss of protein function that is usually inherited in a recessive manner. Example: Type I OI, which presents in early childhood with one or more fractures of long bones (Table 3-2).

- **Hypomorphic mutation**: partial loss of protein function that is usually inherited in a recessive manner. Example: PKU.

- **Hypermorphic mutation**: usually inherited in a dominant manner, it leads to hyperactive enzyme activity. Example: Such mutations in phosphoribosyl pyrophosphate synthase cause heritable forms of gout due to elevations of uric acid in the blood and crystal formation in synovial joints.

- **Antimorphic mutation**: antimorphic gene products (also called dominant negatives) are expressed as proteins that complex with the normal gene product and inactivate it. Example: Type II OI presents at or before birth with multiple fractures, bone deformities, and blue sclera; usually results in death within a few months of birth.

- **Neomorphic mutation**: usually inherited in a dominant manner. The gene product acquires novel characteristics that cause defects ranging from new secretion activity to cellular death. Regulatory gene mutations causing abnormal expression of normal genes are also possible. Example: Huntington's disease, in which cellular death of neurons leads to movement disorders, emotional problems, mental function deficits, and death.

- **Enzyme mutations**: diseases caused by end-product deficiency or substrate accumulation. Example: PKU. The mental retardation and seizures found in PKU are caused by excess phenylalanine: inhibition of neutral amino acid transport across the blood-brain barrier, effects on protein synthesis, and altered neurotransmitter homeostasis during brain development. Because PKU is not caused by end-product deficiency (i.e., lack of tyrosine), decreasing the substrate (phenylalanine) accumulation can provide an effective treatment (i.e., no diet sodas for these pregnant women).

- **Pleiotropy**: Different parts of the body can be affected when absence of end products from inborn errors of metabolism affect the eyes and skin due to defects in melanin synthesis pathways.

Unstable/Dynamic Mutation and Genetic Anticipation

Not all mutations are stably transmitted by the rules of Mendel. For instance, **fragile X syndrome** can be transmitted via a "premutation" by asymptomatic individuals (**unstable mutation**). **Myotonic dystrophy** presents with symptoms at an earlier age with each successive generation (**genetic anticipation**). The basis for these concepts seems to be **trinucleotide repeat expansions** (TREs). TREs are intragenic expansions of triplet repeats in DNA. TRE localization in an untranslated region can lead to loss of function, whereas localization in the coding region may cause gain of function. Other diseases associated with trinucleotide repeat expansions, which have in common loss of motor control and which (with the exception of Friedrich's ataxia) show genetic anticipation, include **Huntington disease, spinocerebellar ataxia type I, X-linked spinal and bulbar muscular atrophy, Friedrich's ataxia, Haw River syndrome**, and **Machado-Joseph disease**.

Penetrance and Variable Expressibility

- **Penetrance**: For some diseases, such as polydactyly and Huntington's disease, not all individuals inheriting the disease-causing allele express the disorder. Hence, these diseases are not fully penetrant.

- **Variable expressivity**: Some diseases are expressed in different degrees in different individuals carrying the responsible allele. One example is OI.

Population Genetics and the Hardy-Weinberg Law

Population genetics describes genetic variations in human populations. It has great implications regarding diagnosis and therapy of human diseases, evolution, and forensic science.

Hardy-Weinberg Law

The genetic variation of a single DNA locus with two alleles, p and q, can be described by the frequency of genotype distribution or the frequency of allele distribution at this locus. The latter can be measured by counting alleles, as the following example illustrates:

Genotypes:

pp = 60 people
pq = 30 people
qq = 10 people
Allele frequency of p = (60 + 60 + 30)/200 = 150/200 = 0.75
Allele frequency of q = (30 + 10 + 10)/200 = 50/200 = 0.25

Note that the sum of frequencies of all alleles at a locus must add up to 1 (i.e., $p + q = 1$). The nomenclature is such that alleles thought to cause a disease are termed q and the normal allele is termed p. The Hardy-Weinberg law allows us to know the frequency of genotypes if we know the allele frequency at a locus. The **Hardy-Weinberg equilibrium** states that after one generation of **random mating**, the genotype frequency, independent of the initial genotype frequency, is as follows:

p^2 = normal allele homozygotes,
$2pq$ = heterozygotes,

q^2 = mutant allele homozygotes,
and that $p^2 + 2pq + q^2 = 1$.

The Hardy-Weinberg equilibrium allows us to predict the frequency of heterozygous carriers if the frequency of the disorder (mutant homozygotes) is known.
Gene frequency in a population, however, can be altered by

- Mutation selection

- Nonrandom mating, such as consanguinity

- Migration into or out of the studied population

- Genetic drift

Table 3-3. Monosomy-associated diseases

Abnormality	Frequency	Characteristics
Turner's syndrome (45,X)	1 in 3,000	Hypogonadism, gonadal streak (remnant tissue), no estrogen or menses, no secondary sex characteristics, webbed neck, short stature, coarctation of aorta, infertility
45,Y	Unknown	Lethal

Table 3-4. Trisomy-associated diseases

Abnormality	Frequency	Characteristics
Klinefelter's syndrome (47,XXY)	1 in 850	Infertile, male phenotype, small testes and penis, tall, lower IQ
Trisomy X (47,XXX)	1 in 1,200	Usualy benign, sometimes sterility or mild mental retardation
Down syndrome (trisomy 21)	1 in 800	Mental retardation, cardiac malformations, close-set, slanted eyes, palmar simian creases, poor immunity
Patau's syndrome (trisomy 13)	1 in 10,000	Mental retardation, cleft lip and palate, microphthalmia, postaxial polydactyly
Edwards' syndrome (trisomy 18)	1 in 6,000	Mental retardation, "rocker-bottom" feet, micrognathia

Table 3-5. Autosomal dominant diseases

Disease	Mutation	Characteristics
Osteogenesis imperfecta	Collagen type I	Fracture-prone bones, dwarfism, blue sclera, death (severe form)
Marfan syndrome	Fibrillin gene (fibrillin acts as a connective tissue "glue")	Retinal detachment, cataracts, floppy cardiac valves (especially mitral and tricuspid), aortic aneurysm
Achondroplasia	Fibroblast growth factor receptor 3	Shortened limbs, normal-size head, dwarfism
Hereditary spherocytosis	Spectrin gene	Chronic hemolytic anemia
Adult polycystic kidney disease	Unknown gene on chromosome 16	Renal failure around age 35 due to bilateral cystic dilations of renal tubules
Huntington's disease	CAG trinucleotide expansion on chromosome 4	Dementia, chorea
Familial hyper-cholesterolemia	Low-density lipoprotein–receptor gene	Hyperlipidemia, xanthomas
Neurofibromatosis type 1	NF-1 gene	Multiple neurofibromas, "café au lait" spots, Lisch noduels
Neurofibromatosis type 1	NF-2	Bilateral acoustic neuromas, "café au lait" spots
Von-Hippel-Lindau disease	VHL gene	Hemangioblastomas, multiple renal cell carcinomas (50%)

Founder Effect

The founder effect is important in small groups in which the founders have a high frequency of carrying an abnormal gene. Under these circumstances, the abnormal gene will be present at high frequencies. The only way for this frequency to be decreased is through some sort of selection against the abnormal gene. Because of the founder effect, South African Afrikaners have the highest frequency of porphyria variegata in the world. One of the original Dutch founders carried the autosomal dominant trait that predisposes an individual to this disease.

Table 3-6. Autosomal recessive diseases

Disease	*Mutation*	*Characteristics*
Albinism	Tyrosinase	Lack of melanin, increased skin cancer risk
Alkaptonuria	Homogentisic oxidase	Dark urine, ochronosis, brittle articular cartilage
Childhood polycystic kidney disease		Collecting duct dilation, rapidly fatal
Cystic fibrosis	Cystic fibrosis transmembrane conductance regulation gene on chromosome 7 (defective chloride pump)	Super-thick secretions, pneumonia, pancreatic insufficiency, death around age 30, diagnosis by sweat electrolyte test
Gaucher's disease	Glucocerebrosidase deficiency	Glucocerebroside accumulation in phagocytes
Tay-Sachs disease	Hexosaminidase A deficiency	Mental deficiencies, blindness
Mucopolysaccharidoses	Mucopolysaccharide accumulation	Neurologic problems, cardiac manifestations
Niemann-Pick disease	Sphingomyelinase	Hepatosplenomegaly, multiple renal cell carcinomas (50%)
Phenylketonuria	Phenylalanine hydroxylase	Mousy odor, mental retardation, eczema, convulsions

Table 3-7. X-linked diseases

Disease	*Mutation*	*Characteristics*
Duchenne's muscular dystrophy	Dystrophin gene	Muscle degeneration, pseudohypertrophy, death in 20s due to respiratory insufficiency
Fragile X syndrome	Defect in *FMR-1* transcription	Mental retardation, oversized jaws and ears, enlarged testes
Hemophilia A	Mutation in factor VIII	Uncontrolled bleeding
Hemophilia B	Mutation in factor IX	Uncontrolled bleeding

Mutation-Selection Equilibrium

Mutation-selection equilibrium explains why some gene frequencies are constant from one generation to another. Abnormal alleles that are lost due to reproductive failure or death can be replaced by new mutations that maintain the frequency, thus establishing the mutation-selection equilibrium.

- In an autosomal dominant disease that can't be passed to the next generation because it causes death or reproductive failure, the mutation frequency is one-half the disease frequency. These mutation frequencies are approximately 10^{-5}.
- An X-linked recessive disease that is lethal or causes sterility in males has a mutation frequency that is about one-third of the disease frequency. The corollary of this statement is that mothers of males who have a genetically lethal X-linked recessive trait have a two-thirds chance of being carriers.

Imprinting

Also called *parent-of-origin effect*, **imprinting** explains one form of non-Mendelian gene expression. Imprinted genes are differentially expressed in offspring depending on the parent they are inherited from. These genes are thought to be differentially expressed due to methylation-chromatin changes that occur during gametogenesis. One of the best examples of imprinting is that of **Prader-Willi** and **Angelman syndromes**. The cytogenetic changes in both syndromes are the same: a small deletion on chromosome 15. However, inheritance of this deletion from the father results in Prader-Willi syndrome and inheritance from the mother results in Angelman syndrome (think "Pater"-Willi and Angel-"mom").

Mosaicism

An individual is a **mosaic** if he or she carries more than one cell line with different karyotypes. Usually, the mosaicism is due to one normal and one abnormal cell line. One cause of mosaicism is chromosome nondisjunction in the early stages of embryogenesis. An example is mosaic trisomy 21. It is estimated that 2% of individuals suffering from Down syndrome are mosaics. Mosaic trisomy 8, 13, and 18 are also possible. Mosaic Turner's syndrome (45, X) is another example.

Chromosomal Abnormalities

Chromosomal abnormalities in which the number of chromosomes has changed are classified as **numeric abnormalities**:

- **Triploidy**: three sets of the haploid genome (69, XXX, XXY, or XYY).

- **Aneuploidy**: The number of chromosomes is increased or decreased from the normal 46, XX or 46, XY complement.

- **Monosomy**: An aneuploid condition in which a chromosome is present in only one copy, resulting in a total of 45 chromosomes (Table 3-3). Autosomal monosomies are almost always incompatible with survival.

- **Trisomy**: An aneuploid condition in which there is an extra copy of one chromosome, resulting in a total of 47 chromosomes (Table 3-4).

Structural chromosomal abnormalities refer to deletions, translocations, and inversions of chromatid parts. An example is **cri du chat syndrome** (46, XX-5p), which results from a deletion in the short arm (p) of chromosome 5. Children with this syndrome are similar to children with Down syndrome and have a characteristic high-pitched cry.

In **autosomal dominant disorders**, the carrying of a dominant genetic mutation predisposes an individual to the disorder even if the normal recessive gene is present (i.e., the individual is a heterozygote). Therefore, autosomal dominant disorders are transmitted to 50% of children of this carrier. Some examples of autosomal dominant diseases are listed in Table 3-5.

Autosomal recessive disorders (Table 3-6) manifest clinical symptoms only if both alleles are of the mutant form.

Table 3-8. Prenatal diagnosis

Diagnostic test	When performed	Risks and other comments	Detected
Ultrasonography	Throughout pregnancy	Minimal	Structural defects
Amniocentesis	At 14–18 weeks of gestation	Risk of spontaneous abortion is 1 in 200	Chromosome abnormalities, neural tube defects, select metabolic diseases
Chorionic villus sampling	At 9–12 weeks of gestation	Risk of spontaneous abortion is < 1%	Chromosome gestation abnormalities, select metabolic diseases
Cordocentesis	After 18 weeks of gestation	Risk of fetal loss is 1–2%	Chromosome abnormalities, hematologic and immune disorders

duchene's
fragile x
hemophilia A + B

X-linked recessive disorders are found in males because the Y chromosome lacks the normal allele counterpart (Table 3-7). Daughters of affected males are asymptomatic carriers because the other X chromosome (from Mom) carries the normal gene, which masks the effects of the mutated gene.

Multifactorial Diseases

Unlike single gene disorders, most human diseases are polygenic in nature. Some diseases with multifactorial causes are described here.

Diabetes Mellitus

Type I (juvenile onset, insulin dependent) is strongly linked to the major histocompatibility complex genes HLA-DR3/4 and results from autoimmune destruction of pancreatic islet cells. However, monozygotic twin studies (50% concordance rates) also indicate that environmental causes, such as certain viral infections, may play a role in the onset of type I diabetes.

Type II (adult onset, non–insulin dependent) has a near 100% concordance rate in monozygous twin studies. The strong genetic predisposition is tempered by environmental factors, such as obesity, which can jump-start the disease manifestations. Hence, controlling obesity can help prevent type II diabetes even if an individual is predisposed.

Atherosclerotic Heart Disease

The leading cause of death in the Western world is coronary artery disease, which has a 65% concordance rate among monozygotic twins. Genetic predisposition is particularly important in patients with premature atherosclerosis (defined as angina or heart attack before age 60). Low-density lipoprotein–receptor gene mutations, as in familial hyperlipidemia, can be one factor contributing to premature atherosclerosis.

Schizophrenia

0.5%

Approximately 0.5% of the U.S. population has schizophrenia. Schizophrenia seems to have a genetic basis, as evidenced by high concordance rates among monozygotic twins.

Bipolar, or Manic-Depressive, Disorder

1.0%

Approximately 1% of the population suffers from bipolar disorder. There is a 20% risk among first-degree relatives of affected individuals. Concordance rates among monozygotic twins are 70%.

Gene Therapy

The aim of gene therapy is the correction of genetic defects.

Principles of Gene Therapy

Screening

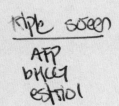

triple screen
AFP
bHCG
estriol

One of the important motivations behind genetic screening is management. For example, PKU screening of newborns allows for dietary management to prevent mental retardation. Likewise, testing of pregnant women via serum triple marker screening and amniocentesis provides the women who test positive with information, so that the parents may choose to either abort the fetus or to prepare for a child with Down syndrome. Many couples request genetic screening because they want to know their odds of having an abnormal child. If the odds are high enough, these couples may opt for adoption or artificial insemination.

Predictive Testing

Predictive testing for certain genetic mutations can now be conducted in the laboratory. When family history of a certain disease is present, predictive testing can inform an asymptomatic member of the family whether or not he or she carries the mutation. Hence, this form of testing can allow an individual to plan for what he or she might face and seek preventive treatment, if possible. One disadvantage of predictive testing is the potential misuse of the information and discrimination by employers and insurance companies.

Genetic Counseling

The goal of genetic counseling is to provide families and individuals with risk assessment for a genetic disease as well as alternatives for dealing with the disease. A recurrence risk is also included in this assessment. Family history is the first step of genetic counseling, followed by clinical examinations and laboratory tests. At the very least, family history should include first-degree relatives, family ethnicity, disease history, and consanguinity information.

Prenatal Diagnosis

One of the objectives of prenatal diagnosis is to allow parents at high risk to have a normal child (Table 3-8). Reproductive options for high-risk parents can include adoption, in vitro fertilization, and artificial insemination. Prenatal diagnosis also gives parents options if the fetus is found to be abnormal—namely, termination of pregnancy or preparation for the child. It is important to note, however, that prenatal diagnosis can't guarantee a normal child because, currently, 98% of abnormalities cannot be detected. Nevertheless, prenatal diagnosis should be strongly considered if any of the following factors are present:

98% of abnormalities cannot be detected

- Family history of a disorder that is testable
- Previous children with chromosomal abnormalities
- Advanced maternal age

Current patterns of anomalies are as follows:

- 3–5% of all pregnancies are at risk for minor birth defects.
- 0.5–1.0% are at risk for major birth defects (defined as compromising life expectancy and requiring intervention such as surgical treatment). If a couple already has a child with a birth defect, there is a 3–5% chance of their next child having the same birth defect.

Methods of Gene Therapy

Many methods of gene therapy are being explored. Some strategies are outlined here:

- **Transplantation** seems to be a promising strategy for treatment of certain genetic disorders. For instance, bone marrow transplantation may be one way to circumvent the immunodeficiency caused by **adenosine deaminase deficiency**. **Parkinson's disease** may be treatable at some point by transplantation of fibroblasts engineered to secrete dopamine. Organ transplantation is also being tested.

- **Somatic gene therapy** attempts to correct the genetic defect at the level of the gene. For example, the normal gene for a defective metabolic enzyme, such as that found in PKU, can be substituted. Excessive gene expression can be blocked by the use of **antisense RNA or DNA**. **Targeted mutagenesis** can be used to correct a genetic mutation. Whereas somatic gene therapy treats the patient only, germline therapy can correct the defect in future generations if successful.

Many neoplasia treatment approaches are being tested that fall under the definition of gene therapy. One approach is the addition of tumor-suppressor genes. Another approach hopes to take advantage of the body's immune system by making the tumor cells more immunogenic.

Pharmacogenetics

Pharmacogenetics is an important consideration because an individual's genetic background can affect his or her response to medications. Genes controlling drug metabolism can have dramatic effects on therapy. **Acetylation**, for instance, is important for removal of many drugs from the body, and the rate of acetylation can affect the dosage needed for effective treatment. For example, an individual whose genes dictate a high rate of acetylation need more of a drug for treatment. Also, there are polymorphisms for genes involved in the **cytochrome P-450 system**, which is also essential for drug metabolism. Approximately 10% of Caucasians in the United States have trouble metabolizing drugs that rely on the P-450 system for clearance from the body. As such, these individuals have high rates of drug side effects at regular doses (e.g., with the β-blocker propranolol). Polymorphisms in the **acetaldehyde dehydrogenase gene** cause the many Asians who lack this gene to be more susceptible to the effects of ethanol.

Pharmacology

CHAPTER 4

Pharmacokinetics

Pharmacokinetics describe what happens to a drug as it passes through the body. The process can be separated into four entities: absorption, distribution, metabolism, and excretion. Clinically, the variability seen in drug effect from patient to patient can be attributed to differences in these processes. Pharmacokinetics are affected by disease states, especially diseases of the major organs involved in drug metabolism and excretion (kidneys and liver). Knowledge of pharmacokinetics is important in determining the dosage intervals of a drug for a patient.

Absorption

Absorption describes how the drug enters the body, either by (1) mouth, (p.o.) usually requiring gastrointestinal (GI) absorption (beware of the first-pass effect; see later), (2) intramuscular (IM) injection, (3) subdermal or intradermal injection, (4) inhalation, (5) sublingual, (6) buccal, (7) rectal, (8) topical, and (9) intravenous (IV) administration. The route of absorption used depends on availability, the need for rapid access, or simply patient ease and compliance. Also, drugs may have to be given by IV because they are broken down in the GI tract. The route of administration affects the drug's bioavailability, or the percentage of the drug that reaches systemic circulation. By definition, IV drugs have 100% bioavailability.

First-pass effect: Drugs absorbed via the GI tract are often significantly metabolized by the liver before reaching the systemic circulation, so only a fraction of the initial amount reaches the serum (recall that venous return from the stomach and bowels travels via the portal circulation through the liver before reaching the systemic circulation). This means that an IV dose required for a particular drug may be smaller than the p.o. dose of the same drug. Liver disease may result in increased bioavailability of these drugs because of decreased drug metabolism by the sick liver.

115

Distribution

Distribution is the transfer of drug from one body compartment to another. Distribution of drugs follows the laws of thermodynamics (mass effect, equilibrium kinetics, reversibility). Many drugs distribute throughout the body, so that the body acts as a reservoir.

Volume of distribution (V_d) is a quantitative measure of how well a drug is distributed.

$$V_d \text{ (in liters)} = D/[C_p]$$

where D = total amount of drug in the body and C_p = concentration of drug in plasma.

The larger the volume of distribution, the more the drug is dispersed outside the intravascular volume. Remember that the volume of distribution has absolutely no anatomic meaning.

Metabolism

Metabolism is the chemical modification of drugs in the body, usually as a first step in the removal of the drug. Drug metabolism usually takes place in the liver, but it also occurs in the kidney, lungs, and bloodstream. Metabolism is particularly important for lipophilic drugs because these are absorbed rapidly and distribute well and would therefore linger and cause toxicity if they were not broken down.

Metabolism usually occurs in two steps: **phase I** (biotransformation) and **phase II** (conjugation).

- **Phase I**, or biotransformation, involves the liver's **cytochrome P-450** system. Phase I involves adding a functional group (e.g., —OH, —NH$_2$) to the drug that increases the water solubility of the drug. After dilution, however, the end products may still be toxic.

There are multiple forms of the P-450 enzymes, each with different substrate specificities. They metabolize both endogenous molecules and exogenous drugs, and they cover a broad range of substrates, so that one drug may compete with the metabolism of another drug. Increasing the burden of drug in the body (e.g., starting a month-long Valium binge) increases the levels of P-450 enzymes due to enzyme synthesis. These enzymes display considerable genetic variability from person to person.

- In **Phase II**, or conjugation, an organic moiety (e.g., glucuronic acid, acetate, glutathione) is added to the drug, so that the drug can be eliminated via the bile or urine.

Excretion

Excretion is the physical removal of drug from the body. It occurs primarily in the kidney but can also occur through the GI tract and skin. Only drugs not bound to plasma proteins can be eliminated by the kidney; in other words, drugs must be hydrophilic or modified to be more hydrophilic for renal excretion. Drugs in the kidney can be passively filtered, actively reabsorbed, or actively secreted. The rate of

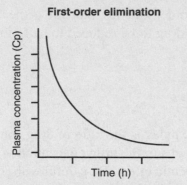
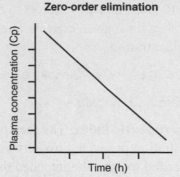

Fig. 4-1. First-order and zero-order kinetics.

renal excretion depends on the glomerular filtration rate. **Elimination**, or removal of active drug molecules from the body, is calculated by the following formula:

Metabolism + excretion = Elimination

Kinetics

Elimination, absorption, and distribution all obey the principles of thermodynamics and are described as either first-order or zero-order kinetics (Fig. 4-1). (There are a few instances of more complicated kinetics in the body's handling of drugs.)

- **First-order kinetics**: A constant fraction of remaining drug is eliminated, distributed, or absorbed. This produces an exponential decay in the concentration of the drug and a **half-life of elimination** that is constant regardless of drug concentration. Most drugs behave in this way in the body.

- **Zero-order kinetics**: A constant amount of drug in the body is eliminated, absorbed, or distributed. Zero-order kinetics occur because the organ or enzyme's ability to process the drug is saturated. For example, a particular drug metabolized by the liver may saturate all the enzymes available to metabolize the drug, resulting in zero-order metabolism kinetics. **Ethanol** is a commonly used example of zero-order kinetics.

- **Clearance**: Conceptually, clearance is the volume of blood completely cleared of drug per unit time. Clearance is described in more detail in chapter 14.

Dosage Intervals

The components of pharmacokinetics (absorption, distribution, elimination) must be considered in designing a dosing regimen for a particular drug. Here are a few key concepts:

- **Half-life**: For drugs subject to first-order kinetics, half-life is the time it takes for a given concentration of drug to be reduced to half of that concentration.

  $t_{1/2} = (0.693 \times V_d)/\text{Clearance}$

  where $t_{1/2}$ = half-life.

- **Therapeutic index**: The therapeutic index is the ratio of drug concentration producing toxicity in patients to the drug concentration required to have the intended therapeutic effect. Be careful with drugs that have a narrow therapeutic index because the dose that grants the desired effect is very close to the dose that causes toxicity.

- **Dosing interval**: The dosing interval depends on drug half-life, therapeutic index, and patient convenience. The interval should be narrow enough that drug's peak concentration is below toxic levels, while the trough levels are at or above the drug's minimum effective concentration.

- **Maintenance dose**: The dose needed for a given dosing interval to maintain a steady-state concentration of drug in the bloodstream.

  Maintenance dose = $C_p \times$ Clearance

- **Loading dose**: When a patient is initially given a drug, the first several doses may have to be higher than subsequent maintenance doses. This is because the initial drug doses fill the body's volume of distribution before reaching high enough levels to produce a therapeutic level in the bloodstream. Once the V_d is filled, a maintenance dose is required to offset the body's elimination of the drug, thus maintaining steady-state serum concentrations.

  Loading dose = $C_p \times V_d$

Individual Factors

- **Age**: Hepatic drug metabolic activity decreases with increasing age. Therefore, drug doses often need to be lowered in older patients.

- **Gender**: There are likely to be differences in hepatic enzyme function and efficacy between men and women, a subject only now being investigated.

- **Disease**: Liver disease reduces drug metabolizing activity, and renal disease reduces excretion. Dosages must be altered according to the clinical situation.

- **Tolerance**: With many drugs, the degree of responsiveness (effect) diminishes with continued administration (tolerance). The mechanism may be at the receptor and cellular level (e.g., down-regulation of receptors) or the result of up-regulation of metabolic enzymes in the liver. Rapid loss of response after a drug is administered is called **tachyphylaxis**. With tolerance, larger doses are needed to achieve the same effect that was previously achieved.

- **Dependence**: Withdrawal of the drug produces symptoms and signs that are often the opposite of the drug's effects. Dependence can be either psychological or physical.

- **Compliance**: Physicians must be aware of the ability and desire of patients to comply with prescribed regimens. Often, side effects are intolerable to the patient, and drugs are discontinued. A common example is β-blockers, which have side effects of general dysphoria—and in men erectile dysfunction—and may be intolerable to many patients.

- **Body weight**: Weight has an obvious effect on the dosing of a drug because a larger mass has a larger absolute volume of distribution.

Pharmacodynamics

Receptors

A receptor is simply any macromolecule in the body to which a drug must bind to achieve its effects. Receptors can be soluble molecules (acetylcholinesterase), cell membrane proteins (ion channels), intracellular organelle proteins (ribosomes targeted by aminoglycoside antibiotics), or nucleic acids (many chemotherapeutic agents).

Structure-Activity Relationships

Binding of drug to receptor is a function of the usual intermolecular forces: hydrogen bonds, van der Waals forces, ionic bonds, and covalent bonds.

Agonists and Antagonists

Agonists are drugs that bind to receptors and stimulate their associated cellular activities. Receptor agonists activate the primary effect of binding of ligand to receptor. **Antagonists** bind to receptors and block their activation.

Agonists are classified into three types. A **full agonist** produces the full response when bound to receptor. A **partial agonist** produces a lower response than a full agonist, even when receptors are fully bound. An **inverse agonist** binds a receptor and produces the opposite effect; this can be seen with beta-carbolines, which elicit anxiogenic and convulsant effects when they bind benzodiazepine receptors.

Efficacy is the relationship between maximum receptor occupancy and pharmacologic effect. Zero efficacy means that even with all receptors bound, the drug has no effect. Partial agonists have lower efficacy than full agonists. **Potency**, on the other hand, is the amount of drug needed to produce an effect. It is usually denoted as EC_{50}, the concentration to achieve half-maximal effect.

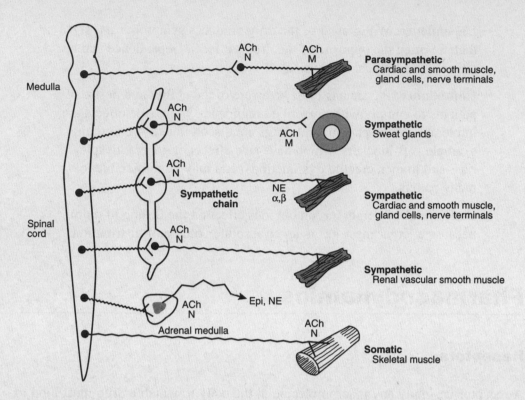

Fig. 4-2. Sympathetic and parasympathetic nerve endings. (ACh = acetylcholine; NE = norepinephrine; Epi = epinephrine, N = nicotinic, M = muscarinic.)

Antagonists are classified as competitive or noncompetitive:

- **Competitive antagonist**: A drug that binds reversibly to the receptor at the same site as the agonist, so that adding more and more antagonist inhibits the binding of agonist by mass effect (i.e., it floods out the agonist). A clinically important example is nondepolarizing muscle relaxants (pancuronium, vecuronium), which compete with acetylcholine at the nicotinic receptor.

- **Noncompetitive antagonist**: A drug that binds to the receptor at a different site than the agonist. It induces a conformational change, so even if the agonist is present, it cannot bind and cannot flood out the antagonist, no matter how high the concentration.

- **Irreversible antagonist**: Once bound to the receptor, it does not fall off. No matter how much of the agonist is available, that receptor is blocked.

Side Effects

Side effects are a key aspect of drugs, not only because physicians pledge, "First, do no harm," but also because the examination tests your knowledge of drug side effects. Toxic side effects are included in drug discussions throughout this chapter and the rest of the book.

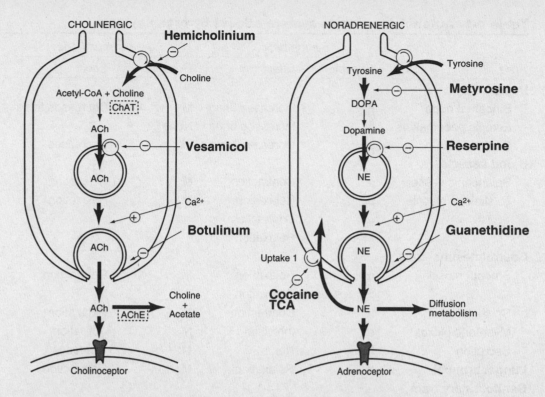

Fig. 4-3. Actions of the sympathetic and parasympathetic systems.

Autonomic Nervous System Pharmacology

The autonomic nervous system (ANS) is concerned with automatic, unconscious, and involuntary bodily activities (Fig. 4-2). The ANS is composed of **adrenergic** (norepinephrine [NE] = primary neurotransmitter), **cholinergic** (acetylcholine = primary transmitter), and **dopaminergic** (dopamine = primary neurotransmitter) synapses. Cholinergic receptors may be **muscarinic** or **nicotinic**. The sympathetic system is the part of the ANS that originates in thoracic and lumbar spinal cord segments (T1-L5). The parasympathetic system originates in the cranial nerves and sacral spinal cord segments. Preganglionic neurons in both the sympathetic and parasympathetic nervous system synapse onto nicotinic acetylcholine receptors. The postganglionic sympathetic neurons release NE as their primary neurotransmitter, while the postganglionic parasympathetic neurons release ACh to muscarinic receptors (Fig. 4-3). The cardiovascular system and the pupillary responses of the eye are two systems demonstrating complex autonomic control. Other actions are described in Table 4-1.

Table 4-1. Autonomic nervous system effects by organ system

Area	Sympathetic		Parasympathetic	
	Receptor	Effect	Receptor	Effect
Heart				
Sinoatrial node	β_1	Increases firing	M_2	Decreases firing
Ectopic pacemakers	β_1	Increases firing	None	
Contractility	β_1	Increases firing	M_2	Decreases
Blood vessels				
Splanchnic vessels	α	Contraction	M_3	Relaxation
To skeletal muscle	β_2	Relaxation	M_3	Relaxation
	α	Contraction		
	M	Relaxation		
Gastrointestinal tract				
Smooth muscle	α_2	Relaxation	M_3	Contraction
	β_2	Relaxation		
Sphincters	α_1	Contraction	M_3	Relaxation
Myenteric plexus	α	Inhibition	M_1	Activation
Secretion	None	None	M_3	Increases
Lungs: bronchi	β_2	Relaxation	M_3	Contraction
Genitourinary tract				
Bladder	β_2	Relaxation	M_3	Contraction
Sphincter	α_1	Contraction	M_3	Relaxation
Uterus	β_2	Relaxation	M_3	Contraction
	α	Contraction		
Penis	α	Ejaculation	M	Erection
Eye				
Radial muscle	α_1	Contraction	None	None
Circular muscle	None	None	M_3	Contraction
Ciliary muscle	β	Relaxation	M_3	Contraction
Skin				
Pilomotor muscles	α	Contraction		
Sweat glands	α (apocrine)	Activation	M (thermo-regulatory)	Activation

Adrenergics

Some drugs act directly at the adrenergic receptor, and others act indirectly by releasing endogenous NE from the presynaptic terminal (e.g., amphetamine requires an intact presynaptic terminal) or blocking synaptic reuptake of NE (e.g., cocaine) (Fig. 4-4). Long-term treatment with receptor or neuronal blockers leads to accommodation, whereby the postsynaptic cell increases the number of receptors and develops enhanced sensitivity to catecholamines. Therefore, abrupt withdrawal of the blocker may be dangerous. Increased catecholamines (e.g., in pheochromocytoma) and increased sympathetic tone (e.g., congestive heart failure) may lead to decreased sensitivity to catecholamines (e.g., through loss of receptors from the cell surface by internalization). Tables 4-2 and 4-3 list the location of various adrenergic receptors and their effects.

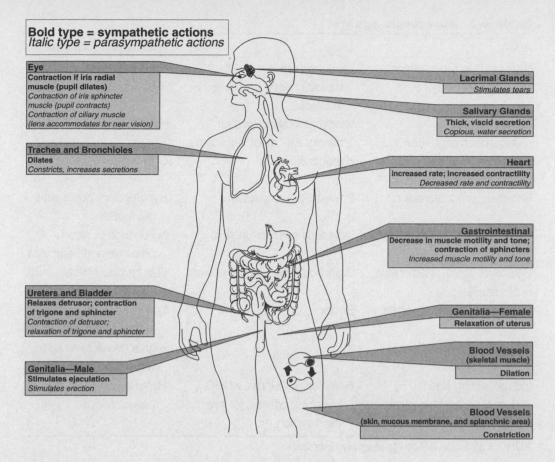

Bold type = sympathetic actions
Italic type = parasympathetic actions

Eye
Contraction if iris radial muscle (pupil dilates)
Contraction of iris sphincter muscle (pupil contracts)
Contraction of ciliary muscle (lens accommodates for near vision)

Lacrimal Glands
Stimulates tears

Salivary Glands
Thick, viscid secretion
Copious, water secretion

Trachea and Bronchioles
Dilates
Constricts, increases secretions

Heart
Increased rate; increased contractility
Decreased rate and contractility

Gastrointestinal
Decrease in muscle motility and tone; contraction of sphincters
Increased muscle motility and tone

Ureters and Bladder
Relaxes detrusor; contraction of trigone and sphincter
Contraction of detrusor; relaxation of trigone and sphincter

Genitalia—Female
Relaxation of uterus

Blood Vessels
(skeletal muscle)
Dilation

Genitalia—Male
Stimulates ejaculation
Stimulates erection

Blood Vessels
(skin, mucous membrane, and splanchnic area)
Constriction

Fig. 4-4. Adrenergic and cholinergic nerve terminals.

Table 4-2. Adrenergic receptors

Receptor	Location	Action
α_1	Vasculature	Contraction
	Glands	Secretion
	Pupil of eye	Dilation
	Pilomotor muscle	Contraction
α_2	Smooth muscle	Contraction
	Nerve endings	Inhibits transmitter release
	Platelets	Aggregation
	Pancreas	Inhibits insulin release
β_1	Cardiac muscle	Increased heart rate
	Kidney	Increased contractility
	Pancreas	Increased renin release
		Stimulates insulin release
β_2	Smooth muscle	Relaxation
	Cardiac muscle	Increased heart rate and force
	Liver	Stimulates glycogenolysis
	Somatic muscle	Tremors
D_1	Smooth muscle	Renal vascular relaxation
D_2	Nerve terminals	Inhibits adenylyl cyclase

Table 4-3. Adrenergic agents

Agent	Uses	Additional comments
Nonselective (epinephrine, norepinephrine)	Vasoconstriction; used to maintain blood pressure in shock	Norepinephrine doesn't bind to β_2 receptors
Selective, $\alpha_1 > \alpha_2$ (e.g., phenylephrine)	Vasoconstriction; used for paroxysmal atrial tachycardia	Hypertension, bradycardia
Selective, $\alpha_2 > \alpha_1$ (e.g., clonidine)	Hypertension	Orthostatic hypotension
Selective, β (isoproterenol)	Prevents bronchospasm	Hypotension, decreased gut motility
Selective, $\beta_1 > \beta_2$ (dobutamine)	Increases cardiac function	No change in blood pressure and heart rate
Selective, $\beta_2 > \beta_1$ (terbutaline, albuterol)	Bronchodilator, uterine relaxant	Few cardiac effects
Dopamine, β_1 and D receptors	Shock	Low doses preserve kidney perfusion Higher doses raise systemic blood pressure
Indirect-acting agents (tyramine, amphetamine, ephedrine)	Narcolepsy, asthma, ADHD, obesity, mydriasis for eye examination	Hypertension, anxiety, hallucinations

ADHD = attention deficit hyperactivity disorder.

Table 4-4. Antiadrenergic agents

Agent	Mechanism	Use	Side effects
α-Adrenergic receptor blocking drugs (ergot alkaloids)	Serotonin antagonist	Migraine	Contraindicated in patients with CAD Do not give in pregnancy
Noncompetitive α-blockers (phenoxybenzamine)	Irreversibly blocks α_1 and α_2 receptors	Pheochromocytoma	Orthostatic hypotension, nausea and vomiting, inhibits ejaculation
Competitive α-blockers (phentolamine, tolazoline, prazosin, yohimbine)	Reversibly blocks α_1 and α_2 receptors	Hypertension, benign prostatic hypertrophy	Reflex tachycardia, angina, nasal stuffiness, postural hypotension, edema
Nonselective β-adrenergic receptor blockers (propranolol, alprenolol, nadolol, timolol)	Blocks β_1 and β_2 receptors	Hypertension, glaucoma, angina, hyperthyroidism	Do not give to asthmatics and diabetics: causes bronchoconstriction and hypoglycemia

Table 4-4 continued

125

Pharmacology

Agent	Mechanism	Use	Side effects
β_1-Selective (metoprolol, atenolol, and esmolol)	Blocks β_1 receptors	Hypertension	Can be given to asthmatics; esmolol is very short acting, given IV
β_2-Selective (butoxamine)	Blocks β_2 receptors	Experimental only	—
Reserpine	Blocks ATP-dependent transport of NE, D, and serotonin into storage granules in PNS and CNS	Hypertension	Sedation, depression, postural hypotension, edema
Guanethidine	Blocks release of stored epinephrine	Hypertension	Diarrhea; interacts with tricyclic antidepressants, amphetamine, and α-adrenergic agonists
Centrally acting agents (inhibition of sympathetic outflow from the CNS), such as α-methyldopa	Converted to α-methyl-NE, used as a neurotransmitter; blocks α_2 receptors	Hypertension in people with renal disease	CNS sedation, dry mouth, sleep disturbances, edema, hemolytic anemia, lupus-like syndrome, hepatitis
Clonidine	Similar to α-methyl-dopa; blocks α_2 receptors	Hypertension	Similar to α-methyl-dopa; withdrawal syndrome of headache, tachycardia, and hypertension may result from abrupt discontinuation

CAD = coronary artery disease; NE = norepinephrine; D = dopamine; PNS = peripheral nervous system.

Antiadrenergic agents work by blocking the release of NE or by blocking post-synaptic adrenergic receptors (Table 4-4).

Cholinergics

Cholinomimetics, or cholinergic-receptor agonists, are either **direct acting** (e.g., acetylcholine) or **indirect acting** (cholinesterase inhibitors, e.g., neostigmine). The direct-acting drugs are divided into muscarinic and nicotinic stimulators. Table 4-5 lists the actions of cholinomimetics.

Table 4-5. Cholinergic effects

Organ	Action
Heart	
Sinoatrial node	Decreases rate
Atrioventricular node	Decreases conduction velocity
Contractility	Decreases contractility
Blood vessels: splanchnic and to skeletal muscle	Dilation
Gastrointestinal tract	
Smooth muscle	Increases motility
Sphincters	Relaxation
Lungs: bronchi	Bronchoconstriction
Genitourinary tract	
Bladder	Contraction
Sphincter	Relaxation
Eye	
Circular muscle	Contraction, causing miosis
Ciliary muscle	Contraction
Skeletal muscle	Contraction
Glands: salivary, sweat, mucous, and lacrimal	Increased secretion

Table 4-6. Cholinergic agonists

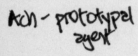

ACh - prototypal agent

Agent	Mechanism	Use	Side effects
Nicotinic agonists (nicotine)	Excites and then leads to a depolarizing blockade of sympathetic and parasympathetic ganglia and skeletal muscle; stimulates release of catecholamines in adrenal medulla	Mild stimulant found in tobacco and some insecticides	Potentially addicting; overdose can lead to paralysis of respiratory muscles and coma
Muscarinic agonists (methacholine, carbachol, bethanechol)	Muscarinic cholinergic receptor agonists	Bethanechol occasionally used to relieve postoperative abdominal distension and in nonobstructive urinary retention	CNS stimulation, miosis, bronchoconstriction, increased gastrointestinal and genitourinary activity (diarrhea, vomiting, salivation, urination), sweating, bradycardia
Cholinomimetic alkaloids (pilocarpine, muscarine, oxotremorine)	Cholinergic receptor agonists	Acute glaucoma	Contraindicated in bronchial asthma, peptic ulcer disease, coronary artery disease, and hyperthyroidism

Table 4-7. Anticholinesterases (produce cholinergic agonist effect)

Agent	Mechanism	Uses
Edrophonium	Binds the anionic site of acetyl-cholinesterase, inhibiting the enzyme; reversible, short acting, competitive	Diagnosis of myasthenia gravis
Carbamates (physostigmine, neostigmine)	Bind the esteratic site of acetyl-cholinesterase, inhibiting the enzyme	Treatment of myasthenia gravis
Organophosphates (parathion, malathion, diisopropylfluoro-phosphonate, dichlorvos)	Irreversibly bind the esteratic site of acetylcholinesterase; very long-acting	Insecticides and nerve gases; produces both neuromuscular blockade and stimulation of the parasympathetic nervous system. **Pralidoxime** is useful for treatment of organo-phosphate poisoning

Table 4-8. Nicotinic antagonists

Agents	Mechanism	Use	Toxicity
Ganglionic blockers (hexamethonium, trimethaphan)	Competitive blockade at autonomic ganglia; inhibits PANS and SANS transmission	Malignant hypertension, controlled hypotension for neurosurgery	Parasympathetic blockade leads to paralysis of accommodation, constipation, and urinary retention. Sympathetic blockade leads to orthostatic hypotension.
Competitive (non-depolarizing) blockers at the skeletal NMJ (tubocurarine, pancuronium, vecuronium, atracurium)	Competitive antagonists of the NMJ	Muscle relaxation in surgery	Vasodilation and hypotension
Noncompetitive (depolarizing) blockers at the skeletal NMJ (decamethonium, succinylcholine)	Agonists that lead to a depolarizing blockade	Muscle relaxation in surgery	Negative inotropic and chronotropic effects (through stimulation of muscarinic receptors)*

PANS = parasympathetic autonomic nervous system; SANS = sympathetic autonomic nervous system; NMJ = neuromuscular junction. ***Malignant hyperthermia** is a rare reaction in patients receiving halothane with succinylcholine. Inability to sequester calcium leads to prolonged skeletal muscle spasm, lactic acid generation, and heat production. Treat with dantrolene.

[handwritten margin notes:]
competitive
· non-depolarizing
noncompetitive
· depolarizing
can have 2
doctae negative

Table 4-9. Nicotinic ganglion blocker effects

Area	Effect
Eye	Mydriasis and cycloplegia
Gastrointestinal tract	Reduced motility, causing constipation
Genitourinary tract	Reduced bladder contraction
	Erectile and ejaculatory dysfunction
Heart	Tachycardia, decreased force
Bronchi	Minimal effect
Vasculature	Vasodilation (arteries and veins)
Glands	Decreased secretion

Table 4-10. Effects of muscarinic blockers

Area	Effects
Eye	Mydriasis and cycloplegia
Gastrointestinal tract	Relaxation, leading to constipation
Genitourinary tract	Relaxation, leading to urinary retention
Heart	Bradycardia, then reflex tachycardia
Bronchi	Bronchodilation
Vasculature	Blocks vasodilation
Glands	Reduced secretion
Central nervous system	Sedation

Table 4-11. Muscarinic antagonists

Agents	Mechanism	Uses	Side effects
Atropine, scopolamine, benztropine, ipratropium	Bind to muscarinic receptors but do not activate them (competitive blockade)	Motion sickness, organophosphate poisoning	Cycloplegia, which can precipitate acute glaucoma Hyperthermia Urinary retention

Table 4-12. Some common opiates

Agent	Uses	Comments
Meperidine	Pain relief	Anticholinergic effects
Morphine	Pain relief	Respiratory suppression
Fentanyl	Anesthetic Sedative	Mast cell histamine release possible with morphine
Heroin	Street drug	Gives a "rush"
Methadone	Opiate withdrawal Long-term pain relief	Long half-life Oral medication
Codeine	Mild pain relief Cough suppressant	Weaker opioid, often combined with acetaminophen
Diphenoxylate	Diarrhea	—

Table 4-13. Benzodiazepines

Agents	Uses	Additional comments
Short-acting (midazolam)	Status epilepticus, anesthesia	—
Intermediate-acting (lorazepam, oxazepam, temazepam, alprazolam)	Anxiety, panic disorder, insomnia, alcohol withdrawal	Alprazolam is also an antidepressant
Long-acting (diazepam, chlordiazepoxide, flurazepam)	Anxiety, panic disorder, insomnia, alcohol withdrawal, anti-convulsant	Chlordiazepoxide has the longest duration of action
Newer agents (zolpidem, zopiclone)	Insomnia	Less potential for addiction and cognitive impairment

Mnemonic: Atropine poisoning: "Dry as a bone, red as a beet, mad as a hatter, blind as a bat, and hot as a pistol."

Direct cholinergic agonists are listed in Table 4-6. Acetylcholine is the prototypic agent, stimulating both nicotinic and muscarinic receptors.

Anticholinesterases inhibit **acetylcholinesterase**, the enzyme that breaks down acetylcholine. These drugs indirectly increase cholinergic activity. They are used in the treatment of atropine poisoning, paralytic ileus, urinary atony, and glaucoma. Their toxicity can be remembered by the mnemonic DUMBELS: Diarrhea, Urination, Miosis, Bradycardia/Bronchoconstriction, Excitation, Lacrimation, Salivation/Sweating. Table 4-7 lists the major anticholinesterases and their effects.

Nicotinic antagonists are specific antagonists at the nicotinic cholinergic receptors. Their effects are listed in Table 4-8. Nicotinic ganglion blocker effects are listed in Table 4-9.

Muscarinic antagonists (Tables 4-10 and 4-11) are specific antagonists at the muscarinic cholinergic receptors. Muscarinic receptors are divided into three groups:

1. M_1 receptors are found on gastric parietal cells and autonomic ganglia.

2. M_2 receptors are located in the heart.

3. M_3 receptors are found on exocrine and smooth muscle cells.

Anesthesia

Endorphins and Opiate Receptors

Opioids, both exogenous and endogenous, have diverse effects and involve almost every organ system (Table 4-12). The opioids bind to opiate receptors on neurons, resulting in presynaptic inhibition. Opiate receptors are found in virtually all parts of the CNS. The effects of opioids include the following:

- Analgesia, sedation, altered consciousness. Pain control is produced due to binding at the spinal cord, brain stem, and limbic system. Opioids *obtund* both the perception of pain and the emotional response to pain.

- Cough suppression, probably not via opioid receptors

- Respiratory depression, an unwanted side effect

- Suppression of release of gonadotropin-releasing hormone

- Miosis: In the emergency room, it's a key sign in diagnosing heroin or opiate overdose (pinpoint pupils).

- Constipation, a useful effect for treating diarrhea, but often an unwanted side effect during pain management

The **opioid receptor** is G-protein coupled and has several subtypes. The **delta** subtype prefers enkephalins, the **kappa** subtype prefers dynorphin, the **epsilon** subtype prefers β-endorphins, and the **mu** subtype prefers exogenous opiates (morphine; think "mu for morphine").

Endogenous opiates are short polypeptides made in the body. The DNA for these proteins is found on three genes:

- Pro-opio-melanocortin has the adrenocorticotropic hormone, β-endorphin, and melanocyte-stimulating hormone genes on one sequence

- Proenkephalin

- Prodynorphin

Opiates have *reinforcing* properties, or feelings of satisfaction that accompany their use. Tolerance and physical dependence then develop. The development of physical tolerance is associated with the mu receptor. An **abstinence syndrome** occurs if their use is stopped, which includes agitation, mydriasis, lacrimation, rhinorrhea, chills, hyperthermia, and diarrhea. **Naloxone** (Narcan) and naltrexone are opioid antagonists used to treat opiate overdose. **Narcotics** is a legal designation drugs that include opioids and cocaine.

Table 4-14. Anesthetics

Class	Agent	Mechanism	Toxicities	Comments
Esters	Procaine (short), cocaine (medium), tetracaine (long), benzocaine (surface-active)	Blocks voltage-dependent sodium channels	Convulsions and coma; all except cocaine are vasodilators; cocaine is a vasoconstrictor and can be cardiotoxic; allergies are common	Used for minor surgeries and local spinal anesthesia
Amides	Lidocaine, bupivacaine, etidocaine, prilocaine	Blocks voltage-dependent sodium channels	Convulsions and coma; all are vasodilators; allergic reactions are less common	Local and spinal anesthesia; lidocaine has the shortest onset (<1 min), bupivacaine has the longest (>10 min)
Inhalational	Nitrous oxide	Unknown	May interfere with oxygen uptake, leading to hypoxia	Used with other agents; 70% is maximal safe concentration
Halogenated inhalational compounds	Halothane, isoflurane, enflurane	Nonselective CNS actions	Hypotension, respiratory depression, renal dysfunction from toxic metabolites	**Malignant hyperthermia** may occur—treat with **dantrolene**
Barbiturates	Thiamylal, methohexital (thiopental)	GABA agonist	Cardiovascular and respiratory depression	Quick onset; used in induction; lowers intracranial pressure
Miscellaneous agents	Propofol	GABA agonist	Hypotension, respiratory depression	Rapid onset; only works with continuous infusion
	Ketamine	Glutamic acid antagonist that inhibits NMDA receptor	Increased sympathetic activity; hallucinations during recovery	Dissociative anesthesia: patient remains conscious but has amnesia and analgesia. Hallucinations during recovery
	Etomidate	GABA agonist	Myoclonus, vomiting, adrenal insufficiency	Quick onset; used in short procedures

GABA = γ-aminobutyric acid; NMDA = N-methyl D-aspartate.

Table 4-15. Stimulants

Agents	Mechanism	Use	Toxicities
Cocaine	Blocks reuptake of nor-epinephrine and dopamine; blocks sodium channels	Vasoconstriction and local anesthetic	Euphoria, cardiac arrhyth-mias, psychosis, halluci-nations In pregnant women, can cause abruptio placen-tae, low birth weight, and respiratory difficulty
Nicotine	Short-acting cholin-ergic agonist at nicotinic acetyl-choline receptors	Mild stimulant; patches used to prevent withdrawal	Tachycardia, vasoconstric-tion, euphoria; can lead to addiction and tolerance
Caffeine	Blocks central adeno-sine receptors	Mild stimulant	Controversial: has been associated with peptic ulcer disease, coronary heart disease, and can-cer
Methylphenidate	Releases stored catecholamines	Attention-deficit hyperactivity disorder, narco-lepsy, obesity	High abuse potential

Treatment of opiate addiction includes

- Detoxification: quitting cold turkey, using alternative approaches (e.g., acupuncture), incarceration, support groups

- Maintenance on a surrogate: **Methadone** is a long-acting opiate with a half-life of approximately 24 hours. The idea is that the half-life of morphine, heroin, and other opiates is so short that an addict's life is wasted with continuous drug-seeking behavior. With methadone, the addict goes into a clinic every morning, gets methadone, and theoreti-cally doesn't crave opiates anymore.

Opiate overdose can produce coma, respiratory depression, and hypotension, a potentially fatal combination. If overdose is suspected, naloxone is administered intravenously. Opioids interact with ethanol, sedative-hypnotics, anesthetics, antipsychotic drugs, TCAs, and antihistamines to produce an additive CNS depres-sant effect.

Benzodiazepines

Benzodiazepines (BZPs) enhance action at the γ-aminobutyric acid (GABA$_A$) receptor (Table 4-13). BZP binding increases the frequency of opening of the GABA-stimulated chloride channel. Effects of all BZPs include amnesia and addic-tion, along with sedation and respiratory depression. Most BZPs are metabolized by the P-450 system. **Flumazenil** is a BZP antagonist used to treat BZP overdose.

Table 4-16. Nondepolarizing agents

Agents	Uses	Toxicities
Short duration (atracurium, mivacurium)	Muscle relaxation; used during anesthesia for easier ventilation and surgical manipulation	Must give slowly to avoid massive histamine release
Intermediate duration (vecuronium, rocuronium)	Same as above	Severe tachycardia, brady-cardia, and atrioventricu-lar block may occur.
Long duration (tubocurarine, pancuronium)	Same as above	Bronchospasm with tubocurarine

see table 4.7 4.8

Table 4-17. Gaseous toxins

Chemical	Source	Symptoms	Treatment
Carbon monoxide	Exhaust fumes, tobacco smoke	Symptoms of hypoxia	100% oxygen
Hydrocarbons	Industrial solvents, cleaning agents	Central nervous system depression, nephro-toxicity, cardiotoxicity	No specific treatment; treat injured organs
Nitrogen oxides	Fires, silos, silage	Eye and nose irritation, chest pain, dyspnea	No specific treatment
Ozone	High-voltage electric equipment, ozone layer	Deep lung irritation, shallow, rapid breathing, dyspnea	No specific treatment
Sulfur dioxide	Combustion of fossil fuels	Eye and mucous mem-brane irritation, bronchospasm	No specific treatment

General and Local Anesthetics

Anesthesia occurs in three stages: (1) **induction** (from waking until complete anesthesia), (2) **maintenance**, and (3) **recovery** (from complete anesthesia until consciousness is regained). **Balanced anesthesia** refers to a mix of inhaled and IV agents used to reduce overlapping toxicities. The agents listed in Table 4-14 are used in various combinations to achieve full anesthesia.

Inhaled anesthetics are classified by their **minimum alveolar concentration** (MAC), which is defined as the concentration of gas needed to anesthetize 50% of patients. The more potent the gas, the smaller the MAC. MAC values are additive, so a combination of gases may be used. The MAC for nitrous oxide is greater than 100%, because even full-concentration nitrous oxide does not provide surgical anesthesia for 50% of patients.

Table 4-18. Heavy metals

Chemical	Source	Symptoms	Treatment
Arsenic	Coal, insecticides, herbicides, semi-conductors, chip manufacturing	Acute: nausea and vomiting, diarrhea, "garlicky" breath Chronic: marrow depression, encephalopathy, neuropathy, death	Dimercaprol or penicil-lamine chelators, gastric lavage, emetic
Iron	Vitamins, iron tablets	Nausea and vomiting, then hyperglycemia, gastroenteritis, shock, acidosis	Deferoxamine chelator, intensive care unit support, emetics, gastric lavage
Lead	Old paint, some pottery glazes, welding fumes	Early: irritability, headache, abdominal pain, constipation Severe: lethargy, ataxia, seizures, coma Chronic: neuropathy, developmental delay in children	Dimercaprol, ethylene-diamine tetraacetic acid
Mercury (Hg)	Thermometers, fungicides, contaminated seafood	Elemental Hg: encephalopathy, gingivitis, pneumonitis, neuropsychiatric symptoms Inorganic Hg: gastroenteritis, acute tubular necrosis, gingivitis, dysarthria Organic Hg: sensory defects, ataxia, uncontrollable crying and laughing	Dimercaprol; 2,3-dimercaptosuccinic acid; supportive care
Radon	Basements of homes (esp. in New Jersey)	Radiation syndrome	Reduce exposure

Table 4-19. Insecticides

Chemical	Source	Symptoms	Treatment
Chlorinated hydrocarbons (e.g., dichlorodiphenyl-trichloroethane)	Pesticides	Tremor, convulsions	No treatment
Cholinesterase inhibitors (e.g., carbamates, organophosphates)	Pesticides, flea collars, crop sprays	"DUMBELS" (see Cholinergics)	Atropine (anticholinergic); **pralidoxime** inhibits organophosphate binding to acetylcholinesterase
Paraquat	Insecticides	Early: gastrointestinal irritation Delayed: pulmonary fibrosis	Gastric lavage and dialysis
Polychlorinated biphenyls (PCBs)	Plasticizers, flame retardants	Dermatologic problems, cancer	No treatment

Table 4-20. Toxicities of certain drugs and chemicals

Chemical	Symptoms	Mechanism	Treatment
Acetaminophen	Initial: nausea, anorexia Late: hepatic necrosis	Saturates the hepatic glutathione detoxification system	N-acetylcysteine
Benzodiazepines	Slurred speech, disinhibition, drowsiness, respiratory depression	Binds GABA receptor	Flumazenil
β-Blockers	Hypotension, bradycardia, atrioventricular block, pulmonary edema, hypoglycemia, hyperkalemia	Competition with β-adrenergic agents for receptor	Glucagon (treat hypoglycemia), for bradycardia, atrioventricular block, atropine, pacemaker
Cyanide	Headache, nausea and vomiting, confusion, collapse	Inhibits cytochrome oxidases in electron transport pathway	Nitrite or hydroxcobalamin
Ethylene glycol (antifreeze)	Metabolic acidosis, acute renal failure	Metabolized to oxalate, which crystallizes all over the body	Ethanol
Heparin	Bleeding	Potentiates antithrombin III effect on factors X, V	Protamine sulfate
Isopropyl alcohol	CNS depression, coma	Metabolized to acetone, causes gap acidosis	Supportive
Methanol	Visual disturbances, headache, dizziness, seizures	Gap acidosis, metabolized to formaldehyde, formic acid	Ethanol
Digoxin or foxglove plants	Anorexia, nausea and vomiting, gastrointestinal disturbance, visual disturbance, arrhythmias	Blocks Na^+/K^+ ATPase	Digoxin-specific antibodies
Salicylates	Nausea and vomiting, tinnitus, hyperventilation, gap acidosis	Direct central nervous system toxicity, cellular respiration inhibition	Gastrointestinal decontamination, charcoal, correct metabolic abnormalities, hemodialysis
Strychnine	Convulsions	Blocks glycine receptor in CNS	None
Thrombolytics (e.g., streptokinase)	Bleeding, esp. gastrointestinal, CNS bleeds	Activates thrombolysis	Stop drug, give fresh frozen plasma, platelets
Tricyclic antidepressants	Anticholinergic effects (dry mouth, urinary retention, tachycardia, agitation)	Anticholinergic, adrenergic blocker effects	Bicarbonate
Warfarin	Bleeding	Inhibits production of factors II, VII, IX, X	Vitamin K, fresh frozen plasma

GABA = γ-aminobutyric acid; ATPase = adenosine triphosphatase.

Table 4-21. Street drugs

Drug	Symptoms	Mechanism	Treatment
Amphetamines	Hypertension, euphoria, seizures, hyperthermia, mydriasis	CNS stimulant	Diazepam, nitroprusside for hypertension, β-blocker for tachycardia, rule out myocardial infarction
Cocaine	Excitement, hypertension, tachycardia, arrhythmias, seizures, myocardial infarction	Na^+ channel blocker	Rule out myocardial infarction protocol, supportive care
Heroin and opioids	Coma, lethargy, pinpoint pupils	Binds opiate receptors in the CNS	Naloxone (Narcan)
Lysergic dimethyl acid (LSD)	Panic reactions ("bad trips")	Uncertain	Barbiturates or benzodiazepines
Polychlorinated biphenyl (PCB)	Bizarre behavior: violent, agitated	Sympathomimetic, hallucinogenic, dissociative agent (like ketamine)	Diazepam, haloperidol
Poisonous mushrooms	Hepatic necrosis: nausea and vomiting, gastrointestinal distress, jaundice	Many contain amatoxin	Find out the type of mushroom, follow and support hepatic function, thioctic acid

Stimulants

Stimulants exhibit direct and indirect sympathomimetic actions with strong central action (more hydrophobic than catecholamines) and a long duration of action (not susceptible to breakdown by enzymes that degrade catecholamines, namely, catechol *O*-methyltransferase and monoamine oxidase). They act directly on dopamine receptors in the CNS. Effects include stimulation, including restlessness, insomnia, tremor, mood elevation, and increased alertness and activity. Anorexic effects are strong but transient, and tolerance develops easily. Some stimulants (Table 4-15) are commonly used, such as caffeine and nicotine. Others are used for the treatment of narcolepsy and attention-deficit hyperactivity disorder. **Ammonium chloride** is an amphetamine antagonist used to treat amphetamine overdoses.

Caffeine withdrawal symptoms include headache and lethargy. Withdrawal from nicotine produces anxiety and mental discomfort. Cocaine and amphetamine withdrawal lead to a period of exhaustion, mental depression, and increased appetite.

Neuromuscular Blocking Agents

Neuromuscular blocking agents are used during surgery and cause respiratory paralysis and autonomic effects. They interact with inhaled anesthetics, by increasing and prolonging the neuromuscular blockade, and with antiarrhythmics, by prolonging the relaxant actions.

Nondepolarizing blockade occurs with pure antagonists of nicotinic receptors. Because the antagonists cause no depolarizations, muscle fasciculations do not occur. Nondepolarizing agents (Table 4-16) can be overcome with high doses of acetylcholine.

Depolarizing blockade occurs when binding of an agonist causes depolarization, resulting in muscle fasciculations. The agonist is released slowly, and the receptor cannot be stimulated by acetylcholine until the depolarizing agonist is released. **Succinylcholine**, the most commonly used depolarizing agent, is used to induce paralysis for surgery. Its use is usually followed by the administration of a nondepolarizing agent. Succinylcholine is metabolized by plasma cholinesterase.

Autacoids and Ergot Alkaloids

The two main autacoids are **histamine** and **serotonin** (5-hydroxytryptamine, or 5-HT). Both are products of amino acid modification (histidine and tryptophan, respectively.) Both also act in multiple organ systems. Antihistamines are used in allergies and peptic ulcer disease (Table 4-22).

Serotonin plays a role in the CNS and enteric nervous system. The 5-HT_2 receptor in brain and peripheral tissues may mediate the effects (diarrhea, flushing, bronchoconstriction) of **carcinoid tumor**. Antagonists of the 5-HT_2 receptor are being tested to block those effects. Antagonism of the 5-HT_3 receptor, located in the brain's vomiting center, by **ondansetron**, helps control postoperative and postchemotherapeutic vomiting.

Sumatriptan, the only drug used for its serotonin agonist effects, binds to 5-HT_{1d} and is administered by injection to treat migraine headaches.

Table 4-22. Autacoid

Receptor subtype	Action	Antagonist	Antagonist side effects
H_1	Bronchoconstriction, vasodilation, capillary endothelium contraction	Diphenhydramine, loratidine, terfenadine	Sedation (less with loratidine, terfenadine)
H_2	Gastric acid secretion, cardiac stimulant	Cimetidine, ranitidine	Antiandrogen effects (cimetidine), reduced hepatic drug metabolism
H_3	Presynaptic modulator	—	—

Table 4-23. Miscellaneous antibiotic agents

Agent	Mechanism	Activity	Uses	Toxicity
Bacitracin	Inhibits dephosphorylation of lipid pyrophosphate	Gram-positive cocci	Topical skin infections Eye infections	Nephrotoxic
Vancomycin	Inhibits transfer of disaccharides during cell wall synthesis	Multidrug-resistant *Staphylococcus aureus* *Clostridium difficile*	A "big gun": Use only when you need it A new *S. aureus*, called VISA is somewhat resistant to it	"Red man" syndrome is histamine release with rapid IV infusion Ototoxic Nephrotoxic
Aztreonam	Inhibits cell wall cross-linking	Gram-negative rods, including *Pseudomonas sp.*	A really big gun!	Same as penicillin
Imipenem	Inhibits cell wall cross-linking	Everything	The last resort!	Same as penicillin Seizures
Chloramphenicol	Binds to the 50S ribosomal subunit	Gram-negatives except *Pseudomonas sp.*	Not used much due to toxicity	Reversible, dose-related bone marrow suppression Irreversible aplastic anemia "Gray baby syndrome"

Table 4-24. Sulfonamides (alone or with trimethoprim or pyrimethamine)

Activity	Uses	Toxicities
Escherichia coli, *Klebsiella sp.,* *Enterobacter sp.,* *Pneumocystis carinii, Shigella sp.,* and *Salmonella sp.*	Uncomplicated urinary tract infection Cystitis *P. carinii* prophylaxis Diarrhea Otitis media	Blood dyscrasias (hemolytic anemia, various "-penias") especially with G6PD deficiency Crystalline aggregates in kidney (must increase fluid intake) Allergic reactions, drug fever, skin reaction more common

G6PD = glucose-6-phosphate dehydrogenase.

Table 4-25. Penicillins

Agents	Activity	Uses	Toxicities
Limited spectrum (penicillin G, penicillin V, potassium)	*Streptococcus pyogenes* *Neisseria meningitidis* *Clostridium sp.* *Treponema pallidum*	Pharyngitis Meningitis (some cases) Syphilis	Allergic reaction in 5% Nephritis Hemolytic anemia
Second generation (ampicillin, amoxicillin)	Same as penicillin G + HEEP	Otitis media Pharyngitis Sinusitis Pneumonia	Diarrhea
Third generation (carbenicillin, ticarcillin)	As above and *Pseudomonas sp.*	Pseudomonal infections	Neutropenia, anemia
Fourth generation (mezlocillin, piperacillin)	As above and better *Pseudomonas sp.* and *Klebsiella pneumoniae*	Pseudomonal and resistant gram-negative infections	Neutropenia Anemia
β-Lactamase resistant (methicillin, nafcillin, dicloxacillin)	Resistant *Staphylococcus* infections	Nephropathy	

HEEP = *Haemophilus influenzae, Escherichia coli,* enterics (*Shigella, Salmonella*), *Proteus.*

Ergot alkaloids

Ergot alkaloids are partial agonists at α-adrenoreceptors and 5-HT receptors. They originate in fungus found in spoiled grain; now there are some semisynthetic derivatives as well. Their functions can be divided into three major groups:

- **CNS: LSD** produces hallucinogenic effects. **Bromocriptine** acts in the pituitary as a dopamine-like inhibitor of prolactin secretion. It is also used to treat Parkinson's disease.

- **Uterus: Ergonovine** and **ergotamine** have an oxytocin-like effect on the uterus, causing it to contract. They can be used to treat postpartum bleeding.

Table 4-26. Cephalosporins

Agents	Activity	Uses	Toxicity
First generation (cefazolin, cephalexin)	Gram-positive cocci (*Staphylococcus aureus* and *Streptococcus sp.*) Some *Escherichia coli, Klebsiella sp., Proteus sp.* strains	Back-up to penicillin for strep and staph Used for prophylaxis before surgery	Cephalosporin allergy seen in 10% of pen-allergic patients Gastrointestinal upset Anemia Nephrotoxicity
Second generation (cefoxitin, cefaclor, cefuroxime)	Gram-positive Mild gram-negative bacteria	Pharyngitis Otitis media Sinusitis Skin infections	Same as above
Third generation (ceftriaxone, cefotaxime, ceftazidime, moxalactam)	Increased gram-negative activity Great for pretty much everything, except it's expensive and less active than first-generation against gram-positives, penetrates CSF well	Gonorrhea Lyme disease Broad coverage when you don't know what they have and they're getting sicker by the hour	Same as above

Table 4-27. Aminoglycosides (gentamicin, tobramycin, streptomycin)

Activity	Uses	Toxicity
Aerobic gram-negative rods, such as *Escherichia coli*, *Klebsiella sp.*, *Pseudomonas sp.*	Severe gram-negative infections Tularemia Plague	Ototoxicity due to loss of cochlear hair cells, results in loss of hearing at high frequencies; irreversible Nephrotoxicity (often reversible)

Table 4-28. Tetracyclines

Agent	Activity	Uses	Toxicity
Tetracycline	Weird and intracellular bugs: *Rickettsia sp.*, *Mycoplasma sp.*, *Chlamydia sp.*	Atypical pneumonia Chronic bronchitis Acne Lyme disease	Gastrointestinal irritation Hepatotoxicity Renal toxicity Discoloration of teeth in children Calcium chelator Photosensitivity
Doxycycline and minocycline	Enteric bugs, diarrhea	Lyme disease Meningococcal carrier state	Less renal toxicity

- **Vessels: Ergotamine** and **methysergide** produce α-adrenergic receptor-mediated vasoconstriction. Ergotamine is used to treat acute migraine attacks, while methysergide and ergonovine are administered prophylactically.

The strong vasoconstrictive effects of ergot alkaloids place patients at risk for ischemia and gangrene. The antidote is **nitroprusside**.

Toxicology

Toxicology is considered part of pharmacology. For our purposes, toxins include gaseous toxins, heavy metals, insecticides, and certain drugs and chemicals. We suggest that you memorize the antidotes listed in Tables 4-17 through 4-21, especially for the drugs: These are common, easy Boards questions!

Anion Gap

A number of toxic substances cause anion gap acidosis. The anion gap is calculated by subtracting the chloride and bicarbonate laboratory values from the sodium value. A normal gap is 8–12 mm. If the value is greater than 12, the patient has an increased anion gap. This gap may be caused by certain disease states (e.g., lactic

Table 4-29. Macrolides

Agent	Activity	Uses	Toxicity
Erythromycin	Community-acquired pneumonia and atypicals, such as *Mycoplasma sp.* and *Legionella sp.* + 2Cs (*Chlamydia sp.*, *Corynebacteria sp.*)	Alternative to penicillin if allergic Pneumonia	Gastrointestinal irritation
Azithromycin	Same as above	Same as above	Fewer gastrointestinal problems than erythromycin
Clarithromycin	Same as above	*Mycobacterium avium* complex	Fewer gastrointestinal problems than erythromycin (especially in AIDS patients)

Table 4-30. Lincosamines (clindamycin, lincomycin)

Activities	Uses	Toxicity
Same as erythromycin plus anaerobic bacteria, such as *Bacteroides sp.* and *Clostridium sp.*	Mixed anaerobic and aerobic infections (such as intra-abdominal infections)	Diarrhea Pseudomembranous colitis

Table 4-31. Fluoroquinolones and quinolones

Agents	Activity	Uses	Toxicity
Ciprofloxacin, ofloxacin, norfloxacin	All the gram-negative rods and *Pseudomonas sp.*, *Mycoplasma sp.*	Urinary tract infection; sexually transmitted diseases; otitis, sinusitis, bronchitis; osteomyelitis	Gastrointestinal discomfort; photosensitive rash
Nalidixic acid	Gram-negative rods except *Pseudomonas sp.*	Urinary tract infection	Gastrointestinal discomfort; photosensitive rash; growth plate toxicity in children

acidosis or diabetic ketoacidosis) or by the ingestion of foreign materials. A mnemonic for the causes of anion gap acidosis is MUDPILES:

Methanol
Uremia (it's really the inorganic anions, not the urea nitrogen)
Diabetic ketoacidosis
Paraldehyde
Intoxication (ethyl alcohol, isopropyl alcohol)
Lactic acid
Ethylene glycol
Salicylates

Table 4-32. Antitubercular agents

Agent	Mechanism	Uses	Toxicity
Isoniazid (INH)	Inhibits synthesis of mycolic acids (part of mycobacterial cell wall)	Tuberculosis (with other drugs for active disease; alone for prophylaxis)	Peripheral neuritis and neurotoxicity from pyridoxine deficiency Rash Hepatotoxicity Inactivated by N-acetylation; eliminated in urine Genetic difference in acetylation: "fast" and "slow" Fast type gives poorer response, and slow type gives toxicity
Rifampin	Binds beta subunit of RNA polymerase: inhibits translation	Tuberculosis, pox virus (different mechanism) Prophylaxis for meningitis in close contacts of sick patients	Tears, urine turns orange in all patients Induces cytochrome P-450 enzymes Hepatotoxicity Hypersensitivity Mutation (RNA polymerase that does not bind rifampin) happens rapidly, so use with other drugs No cross-resistance
Ethambutol	Inhibits mycolic acid transfer to cell wall	Tuberculosis	Optic neuritis (dose-dependent; reversible) Peripheral neuropathy Hyperuricemia
Pyrazinamide	Unknown	Tuberculosis	Irreversible hepatic injury Hyperuricemia

Antibiotics

Antibiotics are probably one of the hardest things to study for the Step 1 examination because it is really hard to remember all the likely organisms and the drugs that cover them unless you use them all the time. We recommend that you know the classic toxicities and coverage of each class of antibiotics, without spending too much time on the details. You are not expected to know dosages. Miscellaneous agents not covered in the sections below are shown in Table 4-23.

Sulfonamides

Sulfonamides are bacteriostatic competitive analogues of para-aminobenzoic acid (PABA) that inhibit DNA synthesis by preventing the synthesis of folic acid (Table 4-24). Sulfonamides inhibit the first step in folic acid synthesis by blocking the enzyme **dihydropteroate synthetase**, preventing the synthesis of dihydropteroic acid from PABA. **Trimethoprim** and **pyrimethamine** block dihydrofolic reductase, which is used to make tetrahydrofolate. **Trimethoprim** and **sulfamethoxazole** are often used together because of their synergism: They attack two separate parts of folic acid synthesis. Resistance develops by these mechanisms:

- Reduced drug uptake

- Increased intracellular PABA

- Lowered affinity in the dihydropteroate synthetase enzyme

Penicillins

Penicillins are bactericidal only to growing bacteria because they interfere with cell wall synthesis, resulting in bacterial cell lysis (Table 4-25). **Penicillin-binding proteins** are proteins used in cell wall manufacture that bind penicillin and contribute to the bactericidal effect of penicillin.

Resistance is usually caused by the presence of **beta-lactamases**, which break the beta-lactam ring found in penicillin. In gram-negative organisms, **plasmids** usually account for resistance and allow the accumulation of beta-lactamases in the periplasmic space, between the membrane and cell wall. Gram-positive resistance can be either chromosomal or plasmid derived. **Clavulanic acid** is a beta-lactam that inhibits beta-lactamases. Given with penicillins, clavulanic acid can broaden the spectrum and increase drug activity. Beta-lactamase–resistant penicillins, such as methicillin, are also used, but resistance to these drugs has already developed.

Cephalosporins

Cephalosporins (Table 4-26) are similar to penicillins in that they are beta-lactam drugs that inhibit cell wall synthesis. The newer generations of cephalorsporins are more effective against gram-negative organisms but are less effective against gram-positive organisms. Many third-generation cephalosporins cross the blood-brain barrier.

Table 4-33. Antivirals

Agent	Mechanism	Uses	Toxicity
Acyclovir	Viral **thymidine kinase** (tk) converts drug to triphosphate nucleoside analogue, which inhibits DNA synthesis and causes chain termination	Oral and genital HSV and zoster	Skin irritation Renal crystal formation if given too rapidly
Ganciclovir	Similar to acyclovir	CMV retinitis and severe CMV infections	Granulocytopenia, thrombocytopenia
Vidarabine	Nucleoside analogue Activated drug inhibits viral DNA polymerase	HSV encephalitis	Flulike symptoms, anorexia, hepatotoxicity, encephalopathy
Iododeoxyuridine	Viral DNA strand breakage; not selective to viral polymerase so only used topically	HSV keratitis	Photophobia, conjunctivitis
Foscarnet	Pyrophosphate analogue: inhibits viral DNA polymerase and reverse transcriptase	CMV retinitis	Renal toxicity, hypocalcemia; anemia; diarrhea; deposits in bone and teeth
Amantadine, Rimantadine	Binds influenza matrix protein and inhibits viral uncoating	Influenza A prophylaxis, parkinsonism	Central nervous system toxicity, depression, congestive heart failure, urinary retention use rimantidine in patients with renal failure
Ribavirin	Unknown	Severe respiratory syncytial virus infection	Decreased pulmonary function
Interferons	Cytokines	Herpes zoster in cancer patients, HBV viremia	GI irritation, fatigue, myalgia, mental confusion, fatigue, CV dysfunction

HSV = herpes simplex virus; CMV = cytomegalovirus; HBV= hepatitis B virus

Table 4-34. Nucleoside analogues

Agent	Additional comments and toxicity
Zidovudine (AZT)	Thymidine analogue
	Headaches, nausea, myalgias, anemia, and neutropenia
Dideoxyinosine (ddI)	Converted to ddATP
	Peripheral neuropathy, pancreatitis, diarrhea, headache
Dideoxycytosine (ddC)	Converted to ddCTP
	Peripheral neuropathy, pancreatitis, bone marrow suppression
Lamivudine (3TC)	Headache, malaise, nausea, pancreatitis
Stavudine (d4T)	Converted to stavudine triphosphate
	Peripheral neuropathy, liver enzyme elevations

ddATP = dideoxy adenosine triphosphate; ddCTP = dideoxy cytosine triphosphate.

Table 4-35. Protease inhibitors

Agent	Additional comments and toxicities
Indinavir	Kidney stones, hyperbilirubinemia, neutropenia, gastrointestinal effects
Nelfinavir	Diarrhea and other gastrointestinal effects
Ritonavir	Gastrointestinal effects; many drug interactions!
Saquinavir	Gastrointestinal effects

Aminoglycosides

Aminoglycosides (Table 4-27), the "–mycin" drugs, are bactericidal drugs that bind bacterial ribosomes at the 30S/50S subunits and inhibit protein synthesis. They are **synergistic** with **beta-lactam antibiotics**, which allow for increased uptake of aminoglycosides. Resistance develops due to altered ribosomal structure or the development of enzymatic deactivation (by **group transferases**) of the antibiotic by the bacteria. Aminoglycosides have little activity against strict anaerobes because they rely on oxygen-dependent transport to enter bacteria.

Tetracyclines

Tetracyclines (Table 4-28) are bacteriostatic drugs that bind the 30S subunit of ribosomes, resulting in decreased protein synthesis. Resistance can develop through decreased uptake by energy-dependent transporters or through the development of a protein "pump" that actively excretes the drug.

Macrolide Antibiotics

Macrolide antibiotics (Table 4-29), the "–ithromycin" drugs, bind the 50S ribosomal subunit and inhibit protein synthesis. Erythromycin also acts as an analogue to motilin, an endogenous hormone that causes increased GI motility, so its ability to cause diarrhea is no surprise.

Table 4-36. Antifungal agents

Agent	Activity	Uses	Toxicity
Amphotericin B	Binds ergosterol in fungal membrane blocking synthesis	Systemic fungal infections Fungal meningitis	Fairly toxic with chills, fever, headache, nausea; renal toxicity; hypokalemia; basal metabolism suppression; anemia; thrombophlebitis
Griseofulvin	Interferes with microtubule function, arresting mitotic activity	Systemic drug for tinea infections	Teratogenic, carcinogenic, gastrointestinal, headache, allergic reactions
Nystatin	Destroys fungal membrane	Topical drug for *Candida sp.* and mixed fungi	Few side effects
Miconazole	Inhibits ergosterol synthesis	Topical drug for *Candida sp.* and mixed fungi	Topical irritation
Ketoconazole	Blocks demethylation of lanosterol to ergosterol and blocks cholesterol synthesis	*Candida sp., Coccidioides sp., Histoplasma sp., Paracoccidioides sp.*	Nausea, vomiting, hepatitis, testosterone suppression; poor CSF penetration
Itraconazole	Inhibitor of fungal P-450, causing membrane damage	*Aspergillus, Histoplasma, Blastomyces sp., Coccidioides sp.,*	Nausea, vomiting, hepatitis; poor CSF penetration
Fluconazole	Similar to itraconazole	*Cryptococcus sp., Candida sp.;* cryptococcal meningitis prophylaxis	Good CSF penetration; gastrointestinal distress
Terbinafine	Inhibits sterol metabolism	Systemic drug for tinea corporis and unguium	Diarrhea, skin irritation
5-Fluorouracil and flucytosine	Incorporated into DNA and inhibits thymidylate synthase	Second-line drug for *Cryptococcus sp., Aspergillus sp.,* and *Candida sp.*	Teratogenic; renal toxicity; hepatotoxicity; myelosuppression, gastrointestinal effects
Potassium iodide	Unknown	*Sporothrix sp.*	Rash, drug fever, paroitis

Table 4-37. Antiparasitic agents

Agent	Mechanism	Uses	Toxicities
Quinine	Unknown	Malaria (*Plasmodium falciparum*)	Cinchonism: headache, tinnitus, nausea; bitter taste; uterine contractions; cardiovascular depressant
Chloroquine	Unknown	Malaria prophylaxis and treatment in nonresistant areas (*P. falciparum*)	Same as above
Mefloquine	Unknown	Malaria prophylaxis and treatment in chloroquine-resistant areas	Weird neuropsychiatric disturbances have been reported
Primaquine	Affects glutathione levels and protein synthesis	Malaria treatment for strains resistant to other medicines, esp. *P. vivax* and *P. ovale*	Hemolytic anemia in people with G6PD deficiency; gastrointestinal effects, CNS effects
Fansidar (sulfadoxine and pyrimethamine)	Affects parasites reductase enzyme	Resistant *P. falciparum*, toxoplasmosis	Anemia
Metronidazole	Binds DNA and inhibits replication	*Giardia sp., Trichomonas sp.,* amebiasis	Metallic taste, nausea, vertigo, leukopenia; must avoid ethanol
Iodoquinol	Unknown	Amebiasis in gastrointestinal tract	Mild gastrointestinal effects
Pyrantel pamoate	Nerve depolarization and paralysis of organism	*Ascaris sp.,* hookworm, *Enterobius sp.*	Gastrointestinal effects, somnolence
Thiabendazole	Inhibits fumarate reductase in parasitic mitochondria	*Strongyloides sp.,* other roundworms	Malaise, hepatitis, dizziness
Mebendazole	Inhibits glucose uptake and microtubule formation	*Trichuris sp.,* other roundworms	Diarrhea, rash, neutropenia, hepatitis
Suramin	Unknown	Roundworms	Vomiting, peripheral neuropathy, proteinuria
Ivermectin	Causes GABA release resulting in tonic paralysis	*Strongyloides sp., Onchocerca sp.*	Rash, edema, visual loss; can be used during pregnancy
Niclosamide	Inhibits glucose uptake, allows worm to be digested	*Diphyllobothrium latum, Hymenolepis nana,* and *Taenia saginata*	Nausea/vomiting, abdominal pain, itching
Praziquantel	Stimulates motility and impairs suckers	*D. latum, H. nana, T. solium,* and *T. saginata*	Cannot operate machinery because >30% get dizziness and headache

GABA = γ-aminobutyric acid; G6PD = glucose-6-phosphate dehydrogenase.

Table 4-38. Alkylating agents

Drug	Mechanism	Use	Toxicities
Chlorambucil	Alkylating agent	CLL	The usual, particularly myelosuppression
Cyclophos- phamide	Alkylating agent	Various hematologic cancers	Hemorrhagic cystitis
Mechlorethamine	Alkylating agent	Prototype nitrogen mustard	Myelosuppression
Carmustine (BCNU)	Alkylating agents, lipophilic, so it crosses the BBB	CNS tumors	Local phlebitis, myelosuppression
Lomustine (CCNU)	Alkylating agents, lipophilic, so it crosses the BBB	CNS tumors	Myelosuppression
Busulfan	Alkylating agent, specific to granu- locyte cells	CML	Pulmonary fibrosis, myelosuppression
Cisplatin	Not an alkylator, but a similar mechanism is purported	Solid cancers, ovarian and testicular cancer	Nephrotoxicity and ototoxicity
Dacarbazine	Not an alkylator, but a similar mechanism is purported	Melanoma, soft- tissue tumors, Hodgkin's disease	Flushing, rash, myelo- suppression
Procarbazine	Not an alkylator, but a similar mechanism is purported	Hodgkin's disease	Photosensitivity, myelosuppression, must avoid tyramine

CLL = chronic lymphocytic leukemia; CML = chronic myeloid leukemia; BBB = blood-brain barrier.

Lincosamines

Lincosamines (Table 4-30) also bind the 50S subunit of ribosomes. The classic toxicity associated with clindamycin use is **pseudomembranous colitis**, in which overgrowth of *Clostridium difficile* causes an invasive colitis. Although this can develop in anyone on long-term antibiotics, clindamycin is the classic drug (and therefore a common test question).

Fluoroquinolones and Quinolones

Fluoroquinolones and quinolones (Table 4-31) are bactericidal drugs that inhibit bacterial **DNA gyrase** (topoisomerase II). Children and pregnant women should not use them because these drugs may cause cartilage erosion. A classic case associated with fluoroquinolone use is the rupture of a tendon (e.g., the Achilles tendon) following a course of antibiotics.

Table 4-39. Antimetabolites

Drug	Mechanism	Use	Toxicities
Methotrexate	Analogue of folic acid, inhibits S phase of cell cycle	Heme cancers, breast cancer	Hepatitis, oral and gastrointestinal ulcers, pulmonary fibrosis, nausea and vomiting
6-Mercaptopurine	Inhibits purine synthesis (analogue of hypoxanthine), inhibits HGPRT-transferase	Acute lymphatic leukemia	Myelosuppression
Thioguanine	Guanine analogue	AML	Myelosuppression
5-Fluorouracil	Noncompetitive inhibitor of thymidylate synthase	Colon and breast cancer	Gastrointestinal and oral ulcers, cardiac arrhythmias
Cytarabine	Competitive inhibition of DNA polymerase (analogue of deoxycytidine)	AML, immunosuppression	Conjunctivitis, pulmonary edema, myelosuppression
Leucovorin	Inhibits methotrexate only in normal cells—malignant cells can't transport leucovorin	Given after methotrexate to protect normal cells	——

HGPRT = hypoxanthine-guanine-phosphoribosyl transferase; AML = acute myeloid leukemia.

Table 4-40. Plant alkaloids

Drug	Mechanism	Use	Toxicities
Vinblastine	From the periwinkle (*Vinca rosea*), binds microtubules	Hodgkin's disease	Leukopenia, neuropathy
Vincristine	From the periwinkle, binds microtubules	Hodgkin's disease, ALL	Peripheral neuropathy, autonomic dysfunction
Etoposide	Blocks topoisomerase II	Small cell lung cancer	Hypotension, alopecia, bone marrow suppression
Taxol	Microtubule binding	Ovarian and breast cancer	Hypersensitivity, flushing, urticaria, bronchospasm, peripheral neuropathy

ALL = acute lymphocytic leukemia.

Tuberculosis Drugs

Because mycobacteria are slow growing, treatments (Table 4-32) are usually very long term. As a result, problems of resistance and patient compliance have emerged.

Table 4-41. Antibiotics

Drug	Mechanism	Use	Toxicities
Doxorubicin (adriamycin)	Intercalates into DNA	Sarcomas, ovary, endometrium, thyroid, metastatic breast cancer, heme cancers	Cardiotoxicity: a constrictive cardiomyopathy Red urine, flushing, conjunctivitis
Daunorubicin	Intercalates into DNA	AML, ALL	Cardiotoxicity: a constrictive cardiomyopathy Red urine, flushing, conjunctivitis
Bleomycin	DNA binding	Squamous cell cancers, lymphomas, breast cancer	Pulmonary fibrosis, stomatitis, hyperpigmentation, cystitis
Dactinomycin	Intercalates into DNA	Wilms' tumor	Myelosuppression
Mitomycin	Alkylating agent	Adenocarcinomas of gastrointestinal tract, squamous cell cancers	Interstitial pneumonitis, alopecia, myelosuppression
Mithramycin	Interacts with osteoclasts, leading to decrease in serum calcium	Hypercalcemia seen in tumor with bone involvement	——

AML = acute myeloid leukemia; ALL = acute lymphocytic leukemia.

Table 4-42. Hormones and antihormones

Drug	Mechanism	Use	Toxicities
Prednisone	Corticosteroid	Heme tumors	Cushingoid side effects
Tamoxifen	Estrogen antagonist	Breast cancer (estrogen-receptor positive)	Hot flashes, thromboembolism
Flutamide	Androgen receptor antagonist	Prostate cancer	Gynecomastia, hepatotoxicity
Leuprolide	Gonadotropin-releasing hormone, luteinizing hormone–releasing hormone analogues, suppresses androgen synthesis	Prostate cancer	——

Granulomatous lesions also pose a problem since they are often difficult to penetrate with drugs. Antimycobacterial drugs are used in combinations (e.g., simultaneous administration of isoniazid, rifampin, and pyrazinamide, with possible addition of ethambutol) in an effort to combat drug resistance.

Antivirals

Common antiviral agents are listed in Table 4-33.

Anti–Human Immunodeficiency Virus Drugs

Human immunodeficiency virus (HIV) is a retrovirus that uses the enzyme reverse transcriptase to convert its RNA genome into DNA. Nucleoside analogues (Table 4-34) are converted to nucleotides in the cell and inhibit reverse transcriptase, which causes DNA chain termination.

Protease inhibitors are the latest addition to the drugs used for HIV treatment (Table 4-35). The protease in HIV is encoded on the *pol* gene and is used to cleave precursor proteins during viral synthesis. Protease inhibitors therefore block viral production. As with tuberculosis, multiple drugs are used simultaneously in HIV to decrease viral load and prevent development of resistance.

Antifungal Agents

Table 4-36 lists antifungal agents.

Antiparasitic Agents

Table 4-37 lists antiparasitic agents.

Antineoplastic Drugs

The underlying rationale for the use of chemotherapy is that cancers are made up of rapidly dividing cells. Therefore, drugs that disrupt various aspects of **cell division** have been the primary modality of most chemotherapy drugs. Likewise, most of the side effects of chemotherapy are the result of disruption of normally dividing cells. As a result, the most chemo-responsive tumors are usually those with a high **growth fraction**—most childhood tumors, acute lymphoblastic leukemia, Hodgkin's disease, and testicular and ovarian germ cell cancers.

The general side effects of antineoplastics affect the following areas:

- Hair follicles, resulting in alopecia
- GI cells, causing stomatitis, nausea and vomiting, and diarrhea
- Marrow and lymphoid cells, causing pancytopenia (anemia, thrombocytopenia, leukopenia)
- Germinal cells of the testis and ovary, impairing fertility

Side effects to be aware of during chemotherapy include the following:

- **Tumor lysis syndrome**: When bulky tumors are effectively killed by chemotherapy, many cells die and lyse. These dead cells flood the body with a load of intracellular debris, which can be fatal if not treated.

- **Hyperuricemia**: Urate is released and can cause renal failure by plugging up the kidneys. Treatment is with allopurinol and aggressive hydration with IV fluids.

- **Hyperkalemia**: This can lead to arrhythmias. Prophylaxis is achieved with IV fluids. Treat high K^+ with glucose/insulin (drives K^+ intracellularly), calcium gluconate (cardioprotection), bicarbonate (drives K^+ intracellularly), a β-agonist (drives K^+ intracellularly), Kayexalate (chelates K^+ in the gut), or Lasix (increases K^+ excretion by kidneys).

Additionally, specific agents have particular side effects that must be monitored (discussed later). One final point to remember about chemotherapy agents: Clinically, most cancers are treated with a combination of several agents because studies have found that various combinations work relatively well.

Alkylating Agents

Alkylating agents (Table 4-38) are **non-cell cycle specific**. They alkylate nucleic acids and lead to DNA cross-linking.

Antimetabolites

Antimetabolites (Table 4-39) are analogues of normal metabolites and block normal metabolic function. They act in the **S phase** of the cell cycle.

Plant Alkaloids

Plant alkaloids (Table 4-40) bind to tubulin in cellular microtubules, so they block **mitosis** during metaphase.

Antibiotics Used to Treat Cancer

In general, antibiotics intercalate between DNA base pairs, leading to DNA breaks. Myelosuppression is common to most of the antibiotics (Table 4-41). They are **non-cell cycle specific** with the exception of **bleomycin**, which acts in the G_2 **phase** of the cell cycle.

Hormones and Antihormones

Table 4-42 lists antineoplastic hormones and antihormones. Hormones and antihormones act by stimulating or blocking, respectively, hormone receptors found on tumor cells, relying on the principle that cell tumor growth is regulated by these hormone receptors.

Regulatory Issues

Most new drugs are found by one of these methods:

- Chemical alteration of a known drug molecule

- Screening of natural products

- Rational drug design based on known physiologic mechanisms

The goal of drug investigation is to produce a "lead molecule," which is a front runner for a possible usable drug.

Initial studies include the following:

- Pharmacologic profiles, which use molecular studies, such as receptor binding and enzyme activity studies

- Cellular studies of the effects on cell function

- Systems and disease models, often using animal models

Preclinical safety testing is performed to evaluate the potential side effects of a new drug (done in the laboratory). This testing encompasses the following areas:

- Acute toxicity

- Chronic toxicity

- Teratogenicity

- Carcinogenicity

- Mutagenicity

- Investigative toxicity

An attempt is also made to determine the **no-effect dose**, the maximal dose at which no toxic effect is seen; the **minimum lethal dose**, the smallest dose needed to kill any animal; and the LD_{50} (lethal dose, 50%), the dose that kills half of the experimental animals.

Limitations to human trials include the following factors:

- The variable natural course of most diseases confounds results.

- The presence of comorbid conditions is difficult to control and eliminate.

- Subject and observer bias, including the placebo response; ideally, this factor is controlled with double-blind studies.

Some drugs designed to treat rare diseases are known as orphan drugs. An amendment in 1983 provides incentives for the development of these drugs.

Before a new drug is approved by the U.S. Food and Drug Administration (FDA), it must undergo three phases of clinical testing:

- In **phase I trials**, the drug is given to healthy volunteers in varying dosages to find out if it is safe.

- **Phase II trials** are performed on patients with the disease. The drug is compared to an older, gold-standard drug or a placebo, and the safety and efficacy of the drug is evaluated.

- Finally, in **phase III trials**, hundreds to thousands of patients are given the drug, and side effects, compliance, and other factors are measured.

After FDA approval, **phase IV** occurs, in which the drug is monitored in actual clinical use and rare side effects are found. A good example of this occurred when the diet drug dexfenfluramine was pulled from the market because it caused rare but potentially fatal pulmonary hypertension and heart valve damage.

CHAPTER 5

Microbiology

General Structure

Bacterial Structure and Composition

The genomic DNA of bacteria is a circle of double-stranded DNA (dsDNA), containing approximately 2,000 genes. Because prokaryotes (e.g., bacteria) have no true nucleus or nuclear membrane, genomic DNA floats in the cytoplasm of the cell. The single cell may have one or more **plasmids** (small, circular dsDNA), which can be replicated independently of genomic DNA. Plasmids may be transmissible (e.g., large plasmids containing genes for synthesis and use of sex pilus) or nontransmissible (e.g., small with a few genes; many copies per cell). Plasmids can confer resistance to antibiotics, heavy metals, and UV light. They can also encode exotoxins and nitrogen fixation enzymes.

Protein synthesis in bacteria uses slightly different machinery than in eukaryotes. The prokaryotic ribosome is 70S (composed of 50S and 30S subunits) as compared to the 80S eukaryotic ribosome (composed of 60S and 40S subunits). This difference allows the selective action of some antibiotics to harm bacterial ribosomes without affecting host ribosomes. Protein synthesis occurs on **polyribosomes** (i.e., many ribosome molecules per RNA strand), which results in parallel production of multiple copies of a given protein. Recall that prokaryotic organelles are not membrane bound.

Bacteria are surrounded by a cytoplasmic membrane composed of a phospholipid bilayer. It is similar to the eukaryotic membrane except that it does not contain sterols. *Mycoplasma sp.* is the exception. An invagination of the cytoplasmic membrane is called a **mesosome**. Surrounding the cytoplasmic membrane is the peptidoglycan cell wall, which is rigid and determines the shape of the cell. **Peptidoglycan** is composed of a sugar backbone with cross-linked peptide side chains. The most commonly encountered shapes include **cocci** (spheres that are often found in pairs, rows, or clusters), **bacilli** (rods), and **spirochetes** (curved or spiral). Between the cytoplasmic membrane and the cell wall is the **periplasmic space**, which may contain enzymes important in bacterial resistance to penicillins (Fig. 5-1). The average bacterial size is 0.2–5.0 μm in diameter.

Gram positive   **Gram negative**

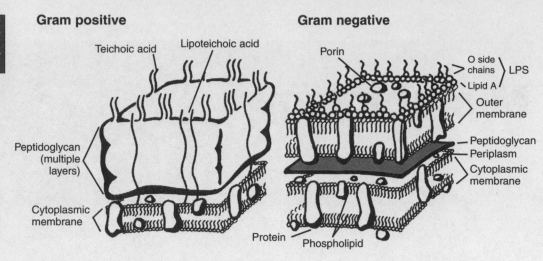

Prokaryotic cell

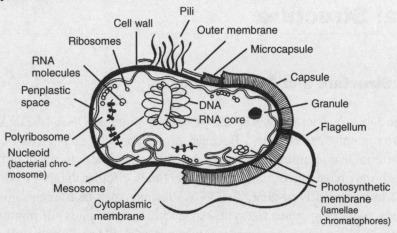

Fig. 5-1. Bacterial structure. (LPS = lipopolysaccharide.)

Gram's stain is frequently used to identify organisms. First, crystal violet and iodine are used to stain all the cells blue. Then the cells are washed with ethanol or acetone. Finally, they are stained with a red counterstain, such as safranin. **Gram-positive** organisms are blue on Gram's stain. These organisms have a thick, multi-layered peptidoglycan layer that absorbs the crystal violet stain well and resists destaining by organic solvents. Some gram-positive organisms have teichoic acid for an outer membrane. **Gram-negative** organisms are red on Gram's stain. These organisms have a thin peptidoglycan layer and a complex outer membrane containing **lipopolysaccharide (LPS)**, which absorbs the crystal violet stain poorly and is easily destained by organic solvent. **Acid-fast bacteria**, such as Mycobacteria, do not change color on Gram's stain but rather stain with carbolfuchsin. Their cell walls have a high lipid content (mycolic acid).

Peptidoglycan, also called *mucopeptide*, is composed of alternating *N*-acetyl-muramic acid and N-acetylglucosamine, with tetrapeptide attachments to muramic acid. The tetrapeptide has D-alanine (most proteins use the L isomeric form), which is important in the cross-linking of chains. Peptidoglycan allows the cell to withstand low osmotic pressure without bursting. Lysozyme is an enzyme found in human secretions that cleaves the sugar backbone of peptidoglycan. If lysozyme-treated bacteria are placed in water, swelling and lysis occur.

LPS is found only in gram-negative organisms. It is also known as **endotoxin**, and it can cause fever and shock. LPS is composed of lipid A (the cause of toxic effects), a core polysaccharide, and an outer polysaccharide. The latter is important in identification of some strains of gram-negative bacteria using the O antigen.

Some bacteria are surrounded by **capsules**, composed of a gelatinous, polysaccharide layer outside of the cell wall. Capsules are used frequently to determine serologic type within a species. The **Quellung reaction** describes the swelling of a capsule due to binding of antibody. Capsules can act as virulence factors and are often immunogenic, allowing them to be used in vaccines. Capsules may be involved in adhesion to human tissues.

Flagella are long, whiplike protrusions made of many subunits of flagellin protein, which are used for motility. Unlike cocci, many rods have flagella, and some spirochetes have an axial filament that is like a flagellum. Bacteria can have one or several flagella, and they are sometimes helpful in bacterial identification using specific antibody tests.

Pili, or fimbriae, are short, hairlike projections composed of subunits of pilin protein. Pili are found mainly on gram-negative bacteria. They mediate the attachment of bacteria to human tissue. The sex pilus is used for conjugation between bacteria (bacteria sex). The **glycocalyx** is a secreted slime layer, made up of polysaccharides, that allows adhesion to certain tissues.

Spores made by genus *Bacillus* and genus *Clostridium* are metabolically inactive forms of bacteria. Spores are highly resistant to heat and chemicals due to a thick, keratinlike coat containing dipicolinic acid (a calcium chelator), which is responsible for resistance to adverse conditions.

Bacterial Metabolism

The nutritional requirements of bacteria vary widely. **Lithotrophs** can use carbon dioxide and minerals for sustenance, whereas **organotrophs** require more complex organic molecules for growth. Some bacteria are known as **fastidious** bacteria because they have complex nutritional requirements.

Most bacteria can take up small molecules but not larger macromolecules; some secrete enzymes to break down complex molecules into products that can be transported into the cell. Methods of transport include facilitated diffusion, group translocation, and active transport. Iron uptake is performed by **siderophores**, which are secreted by the bacteria. The siderophores bind the iron and are then taken up by the bacteria.

Bacteria have the ability to move toward nutrients or away from harmful chemicals. Concentration is sensed by chemoreceptors in the periplasm or in the cytoplasmic membrane, and movement occurs either up or down the concentration gradient.

Bacteria move with their flagella. A counterclockwise rotation of the flagellum results in a straight-line motion; a clockwise rotation results in a "tumbling" or random motion.

Obligate aerobes require oxygen for growth, whereas **facultative anaerobes** can use oxygen if available but otherwise can survive on fermentation. **Obligate anaerobes**, such as *Clostridium* and *Bacteroides* species, can't grow in the presence of oxygen because they do not have the enzymes **catalase** or **superoxide dismutase**, which are important in neutralizing toxic reactive oxygen metabolites.

The four phases of a bacterial growth curve

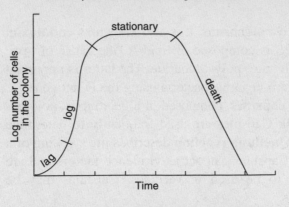

Fig. 5-2. Bacterial growth cycle.

Fermentation describes the combustion of substrate in the absence of oxygen. It uses an incomplete oxidation pathway and results in the accumulation of an end product made to regenerate nicotinamide adenine dinucleotide (NAD). This end product may be useful in the identification of bacteria. *Clostridium* species can use amino acids for fermentation.

In aerobic respiration, the final electron acceptor is oxygen, whereas in anaerobic respiration, the final electron acceptor is an inorganic molecule. Both are used by facultative anaerobes. Other electron acceptors include nitrate, fumarate, sulfate, and carbonate.

Bacteria reproduce via **binary fission**. The **doubling time** can range from 20 minutes (e.g., *Escherichia coli* in ideal conditions) to longer than 24 hours (*Mycobacterium tuberculosis*). Bacterial growth has four phases (Fig. 5-2):

- The **lag phase** consists of little division but lots of internal metabolic activity as the cells prepare copies of everything for duplication.

- The **log phase** is the period of optimal cell division.

- The **stationary phase** occurs when there is nutritional depletion and the number of new cells made equals the number of old cells dying.

- The **death phase** occurs when there is a decrease in the viable cell number due to buildup of toxins and lack of nutrients.

Genetics

Bacteria are haploid—that is, they have only one copy of their genome. As a result, mutations caused by radiation, chemicals, viruses, or transposons are more likely to affect the genome and alter function.

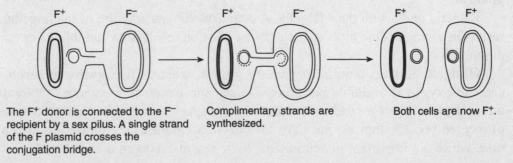

The F⁺ donor is connected to the F⁻ recipient by a sex pilus. A single strand of the F plasmid crosses the conjugation bridge.

Complimentary strands are synthesized.

Both cells are now F⁺.

Fig. 5-3. A F Plasmid conjugation.

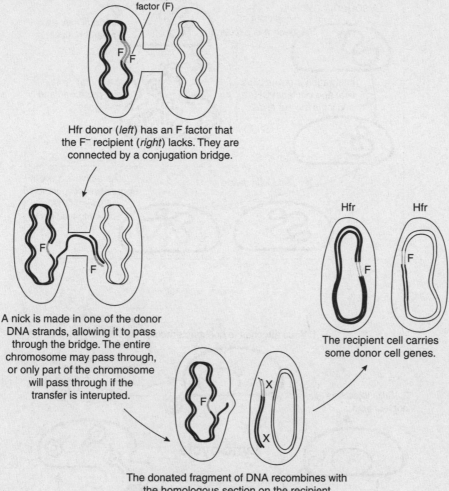

Fertility factor (F)

Hfr donor (*left*) has an F factor that the F⁻ recipient (*right*) lacks. They are connected by a conjugation bridge.

A nick is made in one of the donor DNA strands, allowing it to pass through the bridge. The entire chromosome may pass through, or only part of the chromosome will pass through if the transfer is interupted.

Hfr   Hfr

The recipient cell carries some donor cell genes.

The donated fragment of DNA recombines with the homologous section on the recipient chromosome. The F factor may be incorporated into the recipient's genome. The donor cell synthesizes DNA to replace the single-standed fragment.

Fig. 5-3. B. Hfr conjugation.

Bacterial DNA Transfer

Conjugation, or the "mating" of two cells, is controlled by the **F (fertility) plasmid**. The F plasmid contains information for a sex pilus, which acts as the conjugation tube. During conjugation, the pilus on an F⁺ bacterium binds to a receptor on the F⁻ bacterium. The cells are then in close contact and linked by a conjugation tube (Fig. 5-3A, B). A single strand of the F plasmid DNA is cleaved, and one end goes through the conjugation tube to the F⁻ cell. Complementary strands are then made in both cells, to produce complete, identical plasmids. The resulting cells are both F⁺.

The F plasmid can also be integrated into the host genome so that "mating" can transfer pieces of genomic DNA from one bacteria to another. This is called **high-frequency recombination** (Hfr). (Fig. 5-3B) Approximately 100 minutes is required to transfer the entire genomic DNA, but because the mating complex is unstable, usually only a portion of the genome is transferred. The transferred segment can recombine with the recipient's genomic DNA.

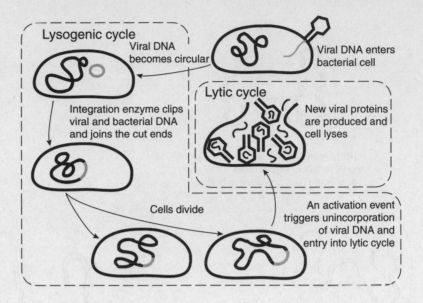

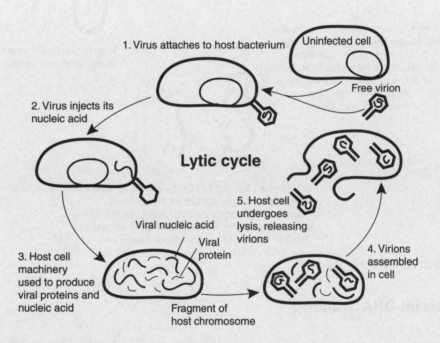

Fig. 5-4. Viral lysogenic and lytic cycles.

Transduction occurs via a **bacteriophage**, a virus that infects bacteria. The bacteriophage can infect bacteria and can enter either lytic or lysogenic cycles (Fig. 5-4). In the **lytic** cycle, the virus replicates in the bacterium and is released with lysis of the bacterium. In the **lysogenic** cycle, the virus is integrated into host genomic DNA and is dormant for some time before entering the lytic cycle. During virus replication, by error some host genomic DNA can be packaged into the phage capsid. When this phage infects another bacterial cell, the new host gets a bonus chunk of bacterial DNA, which can recombine with the host DNA. Generalized transduction occurs when a phage carries away a random piece of bacterial DNA (the cell's DNA is broken into smaller pieces). Specialized transduction occurs when the integrated virus takes along an adjacent piece of bacterial DNA when it enters the lytic cycle. The piece that is taken is specific for each phage because the phage DNA goes into a specific place in the host genomic DNA.

Transformation is the direct uptake of naked DNA. Dying bacteria may release their DNA, which can then be taken up by other bacteria. Although this is probably not an important process in disease, it is often used as a laboratory technique with purified DNA.

Sterilization and Culture Technique

Sterilization occurs when all microorganisms die, including spores (often the hardest organisms to kill!). With sterilization, metabolic activity may still exist, but reproduction is impossible. **Disinfection** is the elimination of pathogenic microorganisms.

The most effective method of sterilization is autoclaving. Moist heat (steam) for 15 minutes at 121°C, under pressure of 15 psi, is sufficient to sterilize an object. Alternatively, dry heat (180°C for 2 hours) can be used. **Radiation** can also be used for sterilization. Ionizing radiation (e.g., X-ray, gamma ray) has good penetration but requires high energy. UV light uses less energy than does ionizing radiation but is less penetrating; it is effective in sterilizing surfaces. **Filtration**, using a 0.22-μm cellulose ester filter, is performed to sterilize heat-labile substances, such as drugs and solutions.

Boiling and chemicals, on the other hand, may be inadequate mechanisms for inactivating the hardy spores. **Chemical agents** show a wide variability in effectiveness. They are compared using the phenol coefficient (i.e., the ratio of concentration of the agent to concentration of phenol needed for the same amount of killing). Chemical agents have three types of effects:

- They may act to disrupt cell membranes; examples include alcohols (e.g., 70 percent ethanol), detergents (e.g., benzalkonium chloride), and phenols.

- They may modify important proteins. Substances that modify proteins include chlorine, iodine, and hydrogen peroxide (oxidizing agents); heavy metals (block enzymatic activity); glutaraldehyde and ethylene oxide (alkylating agents), acids, and alkalis. Alcohols and phenols can also denature proteins.

- They may act to modify DNA, as do the dyes crystal violet and malachite green, as well as glutaraldehyde and ethylene oxide.

Virulence Factors

Virulence factors are the characteristics of the micro-organism that determine its pathogenic potential, both in terms of efficiency (how few or many organisms are required to cause disease) and of symptoms (severity, type of disease, location of infection in the body). Examples of virulence factors are as follows:

- **Adherence** occurs via pili. If the pili are lost, the bacteria are usually nonpathogenic.

- **Invasiveness** is mediated by enzymes secreted by the bacteria that lead to tissue destruction and disease. **Collagenase** and **hyaluronidase** allow spread through subcutaneous tissue. They are important in cellulitis, especially in *Streptococcus pyogenes* infection. **Coagulase**, secreted by *Staphylococcus aureus*, enhances clot formation (fibrin deposition) and may protect bacteria by formation of a fibrin coat. **IgA protease** allows adherence to mucous membranes and is used by *Neisseria gonorrhoeae*, *Haemophilus influenzae*, and *Streptococcus pneumoniae*. **Leukocidins** that are toxic to neutrophils and macrophages can be secreted.

- **Antiphagocytic** traits may allow bacteria to resist destruction. **Capsules** are used by *Neisseria meningitidis* and *S. pneumoniae*. Vaccines for these organisms contain capsular antigens to promote anticapsule-antibody formation. This allows opsonization and subsequent phagocytosis. **Cell-wall proteins** are found in some gram-positive cocci, such as *S. aureus* (**protein A**) and *S. pyogenes* (**M protein**). **Invasins** are seen in intracellular organisms. Invasins bind the integrin-family protein on reticuloendothelial cells, allowing the organism to enter the cell. Other factors prevent digestion of bacteria once inside the macrophage.

Endotoxin causes IL-1 and TNF release.

- **Toxins** present in bacteria may affect pathogenicity. **Endotoxins** (LPS) are found in the cell wall of gram-negative bacteria. They are encoded in the bacterial genome, and **lipid A** is the active component. The toxicity and immunogenicity of endotoxin are low, and it is not used in vaccines. Endotoxin causes fever via macrophage release of interleukin-1 (IL-1) and tumor necrosis factor (TNF); antibodies to TNF can block endotoxin symptoms. The resulting syndrome causes hypotension and septic shock by bradykinin– and nitric oxide–mediated vasodilation. Disseminated intravascular coagulation (DIC), after activation of factor XII, results in thrombosis and ischemia. Endotoxin activates the alternate complement pathway, resulting in inflammation, and activates macrophages and B cells. These manifestations are seen in meningitis (by gram-negative cocci) and sepsis (by gram-negative rods).

Endotoxin-like effects are seen with some cases of gram-positive sepsis (*S. aureus, S. pyogenes*) due to some other component of the cell wall that may activate IL-1, TNF, and other factors.

Exotoxins are a large group of toxins with many effects. The gene for exotoxin is usually encoded on plasmid or phage DNA. The protein is secreted and is usually extremely toxic. Exotoxins are mostly the A-B type (the B subunit is used for entry into the target cell; the A subunit does the damage). They are highly immunogenic and are used in vaccines. Purified, inactivated toxins, known as toxoids, are also immunogenic and are used in vaccines. Examples of exotoxins are given below.

Neurotoxins

- **Tetanus toxin** is made by *Clostridium tetani*. This toxin is encoded by a plasmid and inhibits the release of glycine, an inhibitory neurotransmitter. This results in tetanus, consisting of muscle spasm and lockjaw. The toxin travels from a wound to the anterior horn of the spinal cord in the blood or by retrograde axonal transport.

- **Botulinum toxin** is made by *Clostridium botulinum*. It is encoded by a bacteriophage and blocks the release of acetylcholine at the synapse, resulting in paralysis. It is very toxic: 1 μg is lethal.

Enterotoxins

- **Heat-labile enterotoxin** is made by *E. coli* and encoded on plasmid DNA. In the small intestine, this toxin causes ADP-ribosylation of a stimulatory G protein. This causes the protein to be constitutively active and results in the activation of adenylate cyclase. Cyclic adenosine monophosphate (cAMP) increases and protein kinases undergo increased activation, resulting in increased Cl^- excretion and decreased Na^+ absorption. This ultimately causes increased water and electrolyte loss, resulting in diarrhea. Toxins from *Vibrio cholerae*, *Campylobacter jejuni*, and *Bacillus cereus* act in a similar manner to cause diarrhea.

- **Heat-stable toxin**, which is not inactivated by boiling, is also made by *E. coli* and results in the activation of guanylate cyclase, which leads to increased cyclic guanosine monophosphate and decreased Na^+ absorption, ultimately resulting in diarrhea. *Yersinia enterocolitica* makes a similar toxin.

- **Verotoxin** is made by the 0157:H7 *E. coli* serotype. It acts by removing adenine from 28S ribosomal RNA (rRNA), thus stopping protein synthesis. It is found in undercooked contaminated meat and causes outbreaks of bloody diarrhea. **Shiga toxin**, produced by *Shigella dysenteriae*, also acts by blocking protein synthesis.

- Ingestion of **staphylococcal heat-stable toxin**, produced by *Staphylococcus aureus*, results in diarrhea and vomiting that lasts less than one day. *Bacillus cereus* also produces a heat-stable toxin that results in vomiting that lasts for one day, and limited diarrhea when ingested.

Pyrogenic toxins

- **Erythrogenic toxin**, made by *S. pyogenes*, is encoded by a lysogenized phage. This toxin causes scarlet fever by an unknown mechanism.

- **Toxic shock syndrome toxin** (TSST) is made by some strains of *S. aureus*. It is known as a *superantigen* (SAg). TSST binds major histocompatibility complex class II and stimulates large populations of T cells. These activated T cells release inflammatory cytokines and interleukins, resulting in toxic shock.

Tissue Invasive toxins

- **Diphtheria toxin** is made by *Corynebacterium diphtheriae*. This toxin, encoded by the *TOX* gene of the lysogenized phage, causes adenosine diphosphate (ADP)-ribosylation of elongation factor 2 (EF-2), which inhibits protein synthesis and results in cell death. The diphtheria toxin exhibits specificity for eukaryotic EF-2 by its unique amino acid diphthamide (a modified histidine) and does not inhibit prokaryotic EF-2. EF-2 is found in all cells, and thus there is no toxin-tissue specificity. This toxin is extremely potent: One molecule can kill a cell within hours. **Pseudomonas exotoxin A**, produced by *Pseudomonas aeruginosa*, acts with a similar mechanism to cause liver damage.

- **Pertussis toxin** is made by *Bordetella pertussis*. It activates adenylate cyclase by ADP-ribosylation.

- *Clostridium perfringens* **toxins** cause gas gangrene. Twelve toxins (seven lethal; five enzymes) are secreted. The **alpha toxin** is a phospholipase that hydrolyzes lecithin in the cell membrane, resulting in cell death.

- *Clostridium difficile* produces **toxin A** and **toxin B**, which act in concert to produce pseudomembranous enterocolitis, characterized by colonic inflammation, fever, abdominal pain, and bloody diarrhea.

- **Anthrax toxin**, produced by *Bacillus anthracis*, has three components. **Edema factor** is the A subunit, which increases cAMP levels in phagocytes to inhibit phagocytosis. **Protective antigen** is the B subunit, which allows entry into target cells. **Lethal factor** kills macrophages.

- *Staphylococcus aureus* and *Streptococcus pyogenes* make a number of toxins, including streptokinase, DNases, hyaluronidase, lipases, etc., that result in tissue destruction in the form of abscesses, skin infections, and systemic infections. **Exfoliatin** from *S. aureus*, for example, produces scalded skin syndrome in infants.

Principles of Laboratory Diagnosis

Several culture methods are used for diagnosis of infection. The major types are described here.

Blood cultures are used in the diagnosis of sepsis, endocarditis, meningitis, pneumonia, and osteomyelitis. Three 10-ml samples of blood are drawn over 24 hours and added to 100 ml of growth media. The most commonly grown organisms in blood cultures are gram-positive cocci (*S. aureus* or *S. pneumoniae*) or gram-negative rods (*E. coli*, *Klebsiella pneumoniae*, *Pseudomonas aeruginosa*). Skin flora, such as *Staphylococcus epidermidis*, may grow as a contaminant resulting from the blood draw itself.

Throat cultures are performed in cases of suspected *S. pyogenes* and in cases of thrush (*Candida*), diphtheria, and gonococcal pharyngitis. A swab of the posterior pharyngeal exudate is spread onto a blood agar plate, which is subsequently checked for beta-hemolysis and bacitracin sensitivity.

Sputum cultures are used in the diagnosis of pneumonia, tuberculosis (TB), or lung abscesses. Commonly isolated organisms include *S. pneumoniae* (community-acquired) or *K. pneumoniae* (nosocomial).

An acceptable sputum specimen requires more than 25 leukocytes and fewer than 10 epithelial cells per 100x field. The sputum is gram stained and spread onto a blood agar plate. If TB is suspected, the sample is placed onto special media for 6 weeks, and an acid-fast stain is performed.

Acceptable sputum:
>25 WBCs and
<10 epithelial cells per
100× field.

Spinal fluid culture is done for suspected meningitis (spinal fluid is often negative in cases of encephalitis or brain abscess). Common organisms include *N. meningitidis*, *S. pneumoniae*, and *H. influenzae*. A Gram's stain and Quellung test are performed immediately to identify encapsulated organisms. Cultures on blood and chocolate agar are performed; **hematin** and **NAD (factors X and V)** are added for *H. influenzae* growth. Subacute meningitis usually results from *M. tuberculosis* (identified on acid-fast stain) or *Cryptococcus neoformans* (identified on India ink stain).

H. influenzae requires
factors X and V for growth

Stool cultures are performed in cases of enterocolitis. Usual organisms are *Shigella*, *Salmonella*, and *Campylobacter*. Gram's stain is generally not performed because of the abundance of normal organisms already present in stool. However, methylene blue stain may reveal increased lymphocytes, indicating the possible presence of an invasive organism. Common stool cultures include MacConkey, eosin-methylene blue (EMB), triple sugar iron (TSI), and Skirrow's agar.

Urine culture is performed for suspected urethritis, cystitis, or pyelonephritis. By far the most common organism in urine cultures is *E. coli*, followed by *Enterobacter*, *Proteus*, and *Streptococcus faecalis*. *Staphylococcus saprophyticus* is seen in urinary tract infections (UTIs) in sexually active women. Midstream specimens are used for analysis to avoid contamination with normal flora.

Genital tract cultures are used in the detection of sexually transmitted diseases. Urethral discharge can be gram stained directly and inspected for intracellular diplococci, indicating *N. gonorrhoeae* infection. Discharge from the endocervix or anal canal must be cultured. *Chlamydia trachomatis* is an intracellular organism that must grow on human cells and therefore requires a special transport medium. *Treponema pallidum*, which causes syphilis, cannot be grown in culture. Diagnosis is made by darkfield microscopy (visualizing motile spirochetes) and serology.

Wounds and abscesses may be caused by aerobic or anaerobic organisms or a mixture, depending on the site of the infection. Therefore, both anaerobic and aerobic cultures must be performed.

Immunologic Methods to Identify Known Antigens

The **Quellung reaction** consists of capsular swelling in the presence of homologous antiserum.

A **slide agglutination test** is performed when an antibody to O antigen on *Salmonella* and *Shigella* causes clumping of the organism. A **latex agglutination test** is similarly performed, except the antibodies used are latex coated.

Counter immunoelectrophoresis tests are used to detect the presence of capsular antigens in spinal fluid. The antigen and antibody move toward each other in a gel. Subsequent binding causes precipitation.

Immunologic Methods to Identify Serum Antibodies

A slide or tube agglutination test requires serial dilutions of patient serum with bacterial suspensions to determine the organism and antibody titer. A fourfold rise in serum titer is needed for diagnosis.

Several serologic tests for *T. pallidum* exist. The **VDRL** (venereal disease research laboratory) and **rapid plasma reagin (RPR)** tests use beef antigen (cardiolipin) to detect cross-reactive antibody to *T. pallidum*. These tests are not specific, but they are relatively inexpensive. Laboratory tests using treponemal antigens include fluorescent treponemal antibody-absorbed (**FTA-ABS**) and microhemagglutination-*T. pallidum* (**MHA-TP**).

The **cold agglutinin test** is performed in suspected cases of *Mycoplasma* infection. *M. pneumoniae* infection induces autoantibodies that agglutinate red blood cells (RBCs) at 4°C, but this test is not specific to *M. pneumoniae*.

Immunization

Vaccinations provide active immunity with bacterial antigens to stimulate a protective immune response. They are divided into three types:

- **Capsular polysaccharide vaccines** are composed of the outer capsules of the organisms. The *S. pneumoniae* **vaccine** contains polysaccharide antigens from the 23 most prevalent serotypes. It is given to people older than age 60 and those at high risk of developing pneumonia. The *N. meningitidis* **vaccine** is composed of antigens from four strains. It is given to high-risk individuals and during periods of meningitis outbreaks. The *H. influenzae* **vaccine** is usually given in combination with diphtheria-pertussis-tetanus (DPT) triple vaccine to infants. The *b* polysaccharide is poorly immunogenic, and coupling to diphtheria toxoid increases immunogenicity.

- **Toxoid vaccines** are composed of inactivated toxin. Commonly used toxoid vaccines include *C. diphtheriae* and *C. tetani*.

- **Whole bacteria or protein vaccines** are used for a variety of organisms, including *B. pertussis*, *Salmonella typhi*, *Vibrio cholerae*, and *Yersinia pestis*. The *Bacillus anthracis* vaccine is a purified "protective antigen" vaccine given to populations at risk. The **bacillus Calmette-Guérin (BCG)** vaccine, used outside the United States, consists of live attenuated *Mycobacterium bovis*. It is used for TB vaccination, although its efficacy has not been proved, and those who get the vaccine will later have a positive PPD test.

Vaccines that provide passive immunity consist of preformed antiserum to provide immediate defense against a pathogen. One example is **tetanus antitoxin antibody**, which is given to wound and injury patients who have not been adequately immunized with tetanus toxoid. **Botulinum antitoxin antibody**, derived from horse antisera, is effective against the A, B, and E types of toxin. **Diphtheria antitoxin antibody** is also synthesized in horses, and unfortunately either the botulinum or diphtheria antisera may elicit a hypersensitivity reaction to the horse serum.

Gram-Positive Cocci

(See Fig. 5-5)

Staphylococcus aureus

Staphylococcus aureus is catalase-positive, coagulase-positive, and beta-hemolytic. **Protein A** in the cell wall binds immunoglobulin G (IgG) Fc, thereby preventing complement activation. **Teichoic acid** is present for cell adherence. **Enterotoxin**, classified as types A–F, stimulates the release of IL-1 and IL-2. **Toxic shock syndrome toxin (TSST)** is enterotoxin F and acts as a super antigen. **Alpha toxin** causes skin necrosis and hemolysis and probably works by punching holes in membranes. *S. aureus* is part of normal human flora and is found in the nose and on skin. Transmission occurs via hands and fomites.

Signs & Symptoms

S. aureus can cause multiple diseases, both by an inflammatory pathway and by a toxin-mediated pathway. Inflammatory syndromes include skin infections, abscesses, endocarditis (especially in IV drug users, causing right-sided disease), osteomyelitis and arthritis (especially in children), pneumonia, and empyema. Toxin-mediated diseases include food poisoning (resulting in a short course of vomiting and watery, nonbloody diarrhea), toxic shock syndrome (fever, rash, and hypotension), and scalded skin syndrome (from exfoliation toxin).

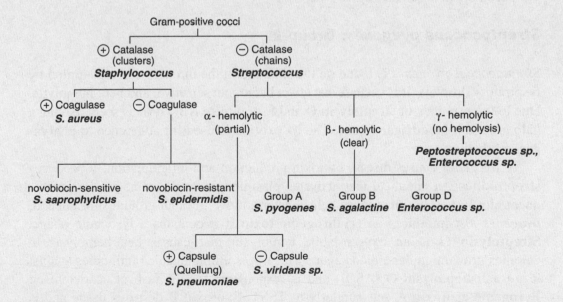

Fig. 5-5. Gram-posotive cocci.

Diagnosis

Gram's stain shows clumps of gram-positive cocci. Cultures reveal yellow colonies ("aureus" means golden) that are coagulase-positive.

Treatment

Most strains are penicillin-resistant because they carry a plasmid-mediated β-lactamase. Drugs of choice include third-generation penicillins, such as nafcillin; some cephalosporins; and vancomycin. An increasingly worrisome strain of *S. aureus*, known as **methicillin-resistant *S. aureus* (MRSA)**, has altered penicillin-binding proteins that make it resistant even to third-generation penicillins. In cases of MRSA, vancomycin is given.

Staphylococcus epidermidis and *Staphylococcus saprophyticus*

Staphylococcus epidermidis and *Staphylococcus saprophyticus* are both coagulase negative. *S. epidermidis* is part of normal human skin flora.

Signs & Symptoms

S. epidermidis causes catheter infections and endocarditis, especially in patients with prosthetic heart valves. *S. saprophyticus* causes UTIs, especially in young, sexually active women.

Diagnosis

Blood or urine culture. The two strains are distinguished by novobiocin sensitivity because only *S. saprophyticus* is sensitive.

Treatment

S. epidermidis is resistant to many antibiotics. If specific sensitivities are not available, treat with vancomycin. *S. saprophyticus* is treated with a quinolone or trimethoprim-sulfamethoxazole (TMP/SMX).

Streptococcus pyogenes: Group A

Streptococcus pyogenes is found on the skin and in the throat and is transmitted by respiratory droplets. It is catalase-negative, bacitracin sensitive, and beta-hemolytic. Due to the presence of **streptolysin O** and **S**, complete RBC lysis is seen, leaving a halo around a blood agar colony. The **M protein** is used for adherence to pharyngeal epithelium.

S. pyogenes causes disease by toxin production and inflammation. It produces **streptokinase**, a chemical that activates plasminogen to plasmin, causing subsequent clot lysis. **Hyaluronidase** helps bacteria move through ground substance. *S. pyogenes* also produces an **erythrogenic toxin** if it contains a lysogenic phage. **Streptolysin O** is an oxygen-labile hemolysin that causes beta-hemolysis in colonies growing under a blood agar surface. It is immunogenic (antibodies against it are antistreptolysin O [ASO]) and is responsible for the rash of scarlet fever. **Pyrogenic exotoxin A** acts similarly to TSST. **Exotoxin B** destroys tissue and is made by the *S. pyogenes* strain, which causes necrotizing fasciitis.

Signs & Symptoms

The most commonly caused clinical syndrome is **streptococcus pharyngitis**. If left untreated, this may develop into otitis, sinusitis, meningitis, and rheumatic fever as well as glomerulonephritis. *S. pyogenes* can also cause **cellulitis** and **necrotizing fasciitis**, a severe superficial infection. **Impetigo**, a skin infection that causes a rash over the arms and trunk, is seen in children.

Rheumatic fever may develop 2 weeks or more after *S. pyogenes* infection. Symptoms include fever, polyarthritis, and carditis, especially damaging the mitral and aortic valves. Manifestations occur due to cross-reactivity between bacterial and self-antigens, causing an autoimmune reaction. Rheumatic sequelae may be prevented by treating the acute infection with antibiotics.

Acute glomerulonephritis occurs approximately 2–3 weeks after skin infection in children. It results from deposition of immune complexes in the glomeruli. Patients develop hypertension, edema of ankles and face, and dark urine.

Diagnosis

On Gram's stain, all streptococci are gram-positive and found in pairs or chains. Smears are performed for wound and skin infections. For suspected pharyngitis, a culture swab is plated on blood agar and colonies are tested for beta-hemolysis and bacitracin sensitivity. ASO antibody titers also help to diagnose a recent *Streptococcus* infection.

Treatment

Penicillin is the drug of choice. Antibiotics are not helpful in the treatment of autoimmune sequelae.

Streptococcus agalactiae: Group B

Streptococcus agalactiae is catalase-negative and beta-hemolytic. It is found in the vagina and transmitted during birth (think B for baby).

Signs & Symptoms

Group B *Streptococcus* causes **neonatal sepsis** and **meningitis**, especially in premature babies.

Diagnosis

Genital tract culture. These streptococci are gram-positive, bacitracin resistant, usually seen as chains, and they hydrolyze hippurate.

Treatment

Penicillin, with the possible addition of an aminoglycoside.

Streptococcus faecalis: Group D

Also known as enterococci, group D *Streptococcus* is found in the colon and occasionally in the genitourinary (GU) tract. It is catalase-negative and has no known virulence factors. (Think D for doo-doo.)

Signs & Symptoms

Group D *Streptococcus* causes **UTIs**, especially in patients with urinary catheters. **Endocarditis**, especially on previously abnormal heart valves, can occur after bacteremia caused by gastrointestinal (GI) or urinary tract surgery.

Diagnosis

Gram's stain and culture of urine or blood. Group D *Streptococcus* grows in hypertonic NaCl (6.5%) and makes a black pigment on bile-esculin agar.

Treatment

Penicillin, with the possible addition of an aminoglycoside. Patients with damaged or prosthetic heart valves should be given ampicillin and gentamicin before GI or GU surgery.

Viridans Streptococci

Streptococcus viridans species, such as *S. mutans* and *S. sanguis*, are found in the oropharynx. They are alpha-hemolytic and catalase-negative. These bacteria use **dextrans** for adherence on teeth.

Signs & Symptoms

S. viridans can cause **infective endocarditis**, characterized by fever, anemia, and a heart murmur. This is especially likely in patients with damaged or prosthetic heart valves who experience bacteremia during a dental procedure.

Diagnosis

Multiple blood cultures are often necessary to detect the organism. Bacteria are seen in chains on Gram's stain. Culture growth is not inhibited by optochin or bile.

Treatment

Penicillin. Prophylactic amoxicillin treatment should be given to high-risk patients before dental procedures.

Streptococcus pneumoniae

Also known as pneumococci, *Streptococcus pneumoniae* are alpha-hemolytic oval diplococci. Up to 50% of people carry *S. pneumoniae* in their oropharynx. Pneumococci have capsular polysaccharides, which can determine serotype. They secrete **IgA protease**, which probably helps in mucosal colonization.

Signs & Symptoms

Pneumococcal pneumonia is the classic "typical" pneumonia, characterized by sudden chill, fever, and rusty sputum. Predisposing factors include alcohol intoxication (which suppresses the cough reflex and can lead to aspiration) and respiratory tract injury from irritants or viral infection. Other infections include **bronchitis**, **otitis media**, and **meningitis**. *S. pneumoniae* is the most common cause of otitis media in young children.

Immunocompromised patients, those who have undergone splenectomy, and sickle-cell patients (self-splenectomized), are at increased risk of infection with encapsulated organisms, especially *Pneumococcus*.

Diagnosis

Gram's stain and Quellung reaction of sputum sample. Organisms are bile-soluble and inhibited by optochin.

Treatment

Penicillin is the treatment of choice, although resistance may be developing. Erythromycin is also used.

Gram-Negative Cocci

Neisseria meningitidis

Also known as meningococci, *Neisseria meningitidis* is seen as kidney bean–shaped diplococci. It is oxidase-positive and has 13 serotypes based on capsular polysaccharides. As with all gram-negative organisms, it has **lipopolysaccharide (LPS)** endotoxin. It is found in the flora of the upper respiratory tract and is transmitted by airborne droplets. Five percent of people become chronic carriers.

The capsule inhibits phagocytosis, and antibodies against the capsule are protective but group specific. Complement activation is important in host defense, so those patients with complement deficiencies are at higher risk for infection. IgA protease is secreted, which helps in adherence to upper respiratory tract membranes. *Meningococcus* is the second most common cause of sporadic meningitis in children ages 6 months to 6 years and is the most common cause of epidemic meningitis.

Signs & Symptoms

Symptoms include fever, headache, and stiff neck. Severe cases may result in a rare form of meningococcemia known as **Waterhouse-Friedrichsen syndrome**, characterized by fever, shock, purpura, disseminated intravascular coagulation, and adrenal insufficiency.

Diagnosis

Gram's stain and latex agglutination tests are performed on cerebrospinal fluid (CSF). Blood or CSF culture is plated on chocolate agar: To differentiate from *N. gonorrhoeae*, remember that meningococci ferments maltose.

Treatment

Penicillin is used because resistance is uncommon. Rifampin prophylaxis is used for close contacts of patients, and patients with suspected meningitis should be in respiratory isolation until *Meningococcus* is ruled out. Prevention of outbreaks is performed with a vaccine made from capsular antigens.

Neisseria gonorrhoeae

Also known as gonococci, *Neisseria gonorrhoeae* is seen as an oxidase-positive diplococci that has no polysaccharide capsule. The organism is serotyped by pilus type, and the more than 100 serotypes are due to antigenic variation in pili from chromosomal rearrangement. It contains lipo-oligosaccharide (LOS) in addition to lipid A. Transmission occurs sexually or to newborns during birth. It is found in the genital tract, anorectal area, and pharynx.

The pili are used for attachment and inhibit phagocytosis; organisms with no pili are usually not virulent. Multiple infections are common because of the antigenic diversity of these pili. IgA protease is also secreted. IgA, IgG, complement, and neutrophils are important in host defense, so deficiencies in any of these arms of the immune system place patients at higher risk of infection.

Signs & Symptoms

Gonorrhea is the most common reportable bacterial disease in the United States. Symptoms in men consist of urethritis with dysuria and purulent discharge. Women can be asymptomatic or experience cervical infection that results in purulent vaginal discharge and bleeding. Ascending infection can cause salpingitis and pelvic inflammatory disease (PID), with the risk of sterility. Disseminated infection includes arthritis and pustules. Anorectal infection can cause proctitis, and oral infection can cause pharyngitis. Neonatal conjunctivitis can occur when the organism is acquired by the newborn during delivery.

Diagnosis

Culture and Gram's stain of the discharge is performed. In men, gram-negative diplococci within neutrophils in the discharge is diagnostic. Culture is performed on Thayer-Martin medium, which has antibiotics to inhibit normal flora. Currently, enzyme-linked immunosorbent assay (ELISA), looking for gonococcal antigens and polymerase chain reaction (PCR) tests for bacterial ribosomal genes are also performed.

Treatment

Ceftriaxone is the treatment of choice, with spectinomycin and ciprofloxacin used if the patient is penicillin allergic. Penicillinase-producing strains have been isolated. If concurrent *C. trachomatis* infection is suspected (and it usually is), tetracycline is given as well. Follow-up culture should be done 1 week after treatment is completed. Neonatal conjunctivitis is preventable with prophylactic erythromycin eye ointment at birth.

Moraxella catarrhalis

Previously called *Branhamella catarrhalis, Moraxella catarrhalis* is seen as a gram-negative diplococcus and is a member of the normal flora of the upper respiratory tract. After *S. pneumoniae* and non-typable *H. influenzae*, it is thought to be a common cause of **otitis media** in young children.

Signs & Symptoms

Children and immunocompromised patients develop otitis, sinusitis, pneumonia, and bronchial infections.

Diagnosis

Gram's stain of sputum or culture.

Treatment

TMP/SMX. Many strains are penicillin resistant.

Gram-Positive Rods

(See Fig. 5-6.)

Bacillus anthracis

Bacillus anthracis is a nonmotile, spore-forming organism. The spores are present in soil, and human infection occurs from spores on animals or animal products. Entry occurs through the skin, mucous membranes, or respiratory tract.

B. anthracis has a unique capsule made of D-glutamate, which inhibits phagocytosis. It produces a toxin composed of three parts: **adenylate cyclase**, **lethal factor**, and **protective factor**. Lethal factor causes death in mice by an unknown mechanism, whereas protective factor facilitates the entry of the other two toxin parts into host cells.

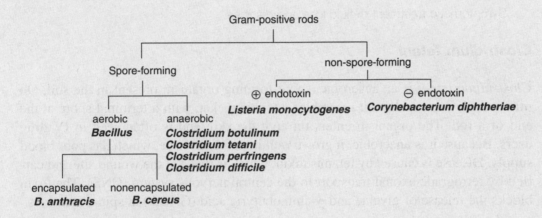

Fig. 5-6. Gram-positive rods.

Signs & Symptoms

The resulting disease is anthrax, seen mostly in animals but sometimes in humans. Symptoms include edema and a black, necrotic painless ulcer known as a malignant pustule. Untreated cases result in bacteremia and death. Inhalation of the spores can cause pneumonia, known as **Woolsorters' disease**.

Diagnosis

Gram's stain shows bacteria in chains.

Treatment

Penicillin. Disease transmission can be prevented by proper disposal of dead animals and sterilization of animal products. Workers at risk should wear masks and protective clothing and can receive vaccination against the disease.

Bacillus cereus

Bacillus cereus is a spore-forming organism that resides on grains and is ingested. The classic test question asks you to associate *B. cereus* with food poisoning after eating reheated fried rice. It has two enterotoxins, which act by unknown mechanisms.

Signs & Symptoms

Persons ingesting the spores develop food poisoning. Two types may occur: a short-incubation type, which develops within 4 hours and is characterized by nausea and vomiting, and a long-incubation type, developing within 18 hours, with associated diarrhea.

Diagnosis

History.

Treatment

Symptomatic treatment of fluid loss and diarrhea.

Clostridium tetani

Tetanus toxin blocks glycine and GABA release.

Clostridium tetani is an anaerobic, spore-forming organism present in the soil. On microscopic examination, it resembles a tennis racket, with a terminal spore at the end of a rod. The organism enters through the skin and is often seen in IV drug users. Because it is anaerobic, it grows well in necrotic tissue, which has poor blood supply. Disease is caused by tetanus toxin, which is made at the wound site and carried by retrograde axonal transport to the central nervous system (CNS). The toxin blocks the release of glycine and γ-aminobutyric acid (GABA) at spinal synapses.

Signs & Symptoms

Tetanus is characterized by violent muscle spasms and lockjaw, in which the mouth cannot be opened. Patients may have exaggerated reflexes and are at severe risk of respiratory failure.

Diagnosis

History of injury. All motor vehicle injuries are presumed to be infected and are treated accordingly.

Treatment

Immediate treatment with immune globulin against the toxin is necessary. The bacteria can be treated with penicillin. Benzodiazepines are used to prevent spasms. Prevention using vaccines with tetanus toxoid booster shots should be performed every 10 years in adults after they have received the initial series of injections in childhood.

Clostridium botulinum

Clostridium botulinum is an anaerobic, spore-forming organism found in soil. These spores can contaminate foods, especially beans, raw honey, mushrooms, and smoked fish, that are improperly sterilized and canned. The bacteria grow in anaerobic conditions and produce preformed toxin, which is then ingested and absorbed into the blood. The toxin travels to synapses in the peripheral nervous system and blocks acetylcholine release.

Signs & Symptoms

Botulism is characterized by weakness and flaccid paralysis, including diplopia, dysphagia, and respiratory failure. Infant botulism, which results in a floppy baby, may develop from ingestion of raw honey, after which the bacteria grows in the gut and secrete toxin.

Diagnosis

A mouse protection assay, in which a mouse is given a sample from the patient and dies if toxin is present, can be performed.

Botulinum toxin blocks ACh release.

Treatment

Immediate antitoxin administration as well as respiratory support are necessary. The toxin is heat labile, so foods should be heated thoroughly before they are eaten.

Clostridium perfringens

Clostridium perfringens is an anaerobic, spore-forming bacteria found in soil and on food. It is also part of normal flora of the colon and vagina. The organism produces **alpha toxin**, which is made by bacteria growing in an infected wound. The toxin damages cell membranes, including hemolysis of RBCs. Gas is produced by other enzymes in the tissue, resulting in **gas gangrene**. Enterotoxin is made in the GI tract during sporulation, resulting in **food poisoning**.

Signs & Symptoms

Gas gangrene occurs in contaminated wounds, resulting in pain, edema, hemolysis, and cellulitis. It is associated with a high mortality rate. Food poisoning occurs by bacterial growth in reheated foods, and causes watery diarrhea 8–16 hours after ingestion, which resolves within 24 hours.

Diagnosis

The organism can be seen on smear of an exudate. Anaerobic cultures and tests for sugar fermentation should be done.

Treatment

Gas gangrene is treated with penicillin and wound debridement. Food poisoning requires only supportive care.

Clostridium difficile

Clostridium difficile is an anaerobic, spore-forming organism that is part of the normal GI flora in up to 30% of hospitalized patients. Transmission route is fecal-oral. The organisms produce exotoxin A, which causes watery diarrhea, and exotoxin B, which causes mucosal damage, resulting in pseudomembrane formation. Exotoxin B functions by ADP-ribosylation of protein r, a G protein that regulates actin. Antibiotic therapy can alter normal flora and allow *C. difficile* overgrowth, resulting in exotoxin formation.

Signs & Symptoms

Pseudomembranous colitis can develop after broad-spectrum antibiotic therapy, especially with clindamycin or aminoglycosides. Patients experience watery, non-bloody diarrhea, and visualization by colonoscopy shows pseudomembranes.

Diagnosis

Exotoxin B can be isolated from stool, and ELISA tests for both exotoxins are available. Because the toxin is difficult to detect, a minimum of three separate stool samples should be analyzed before ruling out *C. difficile* infection.

Treatment

Withdraw causative antibiotic treatment. Treat with metronidazole or vancomycin.

Corynebacterium diphtheriae

Corynebacterium diphtheriae are nonmotile, non–spore-forming, club-shaped rods that are present in the upper respiratory tract. Under the microscope, they appear beaded because of storage granules that display metachromatic staining. Transmission occurs by airborne droplets. **Diphtheria toxin** causes ADP-ribosylation of EF-2, which results in inactivation and cell death. The toxin is produced from a lysogenized bacteriophage; bacteria that do not have the integrated phage are not pathogenic. The host can make antibody to fragment B of the exotoxin. This fragment is necessary for entry into the cell.

Signs & Symptoms

Diphtheria results in a fibrinous, adherent, gray characteristic membrane over the tonsils and throat. Patients also experience fever and cervical adenopathy. Complications include membrane extension, resulting in tracheal obstruction, myocarditis, and recurrent laryngeal nerve palsy.

Diagnosis

Methylene blue stain on smear from a throat swab shows metachromatic granules. The throat swab should be cultured on Löffler's coagulated serum, a tellurite plate (which turns black if organism is present), and blood agar. Toxin production is verified from cultured plates.

Treatment

The antitoxin antibodies neutralize unbound toxin. The antisera is made in horses and may cause hypersensitivity problems in sensitized individuals. Penicillin or erythromycin is used to slow growth of bacteria. Widespread vaccination with inactivated toxoid has resulted in very low incidence of disease.

Listeria monocytogenes

Listeria monocytogenes is a non–spore-forming rod in V or L shapes. It is beta-hemolytic and displays a tumbling motion. It grows preferentially within cells and is found in animals, plants, and soil. *L. monocytogenes* can colonize the GI and female GU tract. Transmission is via contact with animals or feces, contaminated vegetables, and unpasteurized milk and cheese (the classic test question scenario).

Transmission to newborns can occur *in utero* or at delivery. The bacteria produces listeriolysin O, which makes holes in membranes. Suppressed cell-mediated immunity predisposes affected patients to infection.

Signs & Symptoms

Meningitis and sepsis can develop in newborns and immunocompromised patients. Infected mothers are usually asymptomatic.

Diagnosis

Gram's stain and culture. Culture shows small gray colonies on blood agar as well as beta-hemolysis and motile organisms.

Treatment

Ampicillin and gentamicin.

Gram-Negative Rods

Escherichia coli

Escherichia coli is a facultative anaerobe that ferments lactose. It is found in the GI tract, although vaginal colonization may occur. Transmission route is fecal-oral and can occur during birth.

E. coli has **O (cell wall)**, **H (flagellar)**, and **K (capsule)** antigens. More than 1,000 serotypes are possible based on variations in these antigens. Pili are used for attachment to mucosal surfaces. Certain pili types bind receptors on urinary tract epithelium, resulting in uropathic strains of *E. coli*. Some *E. coli* strains invade mucosa and cause bloody diarrhea and mucosal inflammation, with neutrophils present in the feces.

Enterotoxin-producing strains cause watery diarrhea by releasing one or both of the two enterotoxins. **Heat-labile enterotoxin** stimulates adenylate cyclase via ADP-ribosylation of a stimulatory G protein, causing increased cAMP and protein kinase activity. The end result is excretion of electrolytes and fluids. **Heat-stable enterotoxin** stimulates guanylate cyclase. *E. coli* has a capsule that inhibits phagocytosis.

Verotoxin is made by the 0157:H7 strain. Verotoxin removes adenine from 28S rRNA, which inhibits protein synthesis. It causes bloody diarrhea without inflammation (no stool neutrophils). This strain is found in undercooked hamburger meat and can cause life-threatening DIC or hemolytic-uremic syndrome.

Like all gram-negative organisms, *E. coli* also has LPS endotoxin, which causes fever, shock, and DIC.

Signs & Symptoms

E. coli is the most common cause of **UTI**, especially in women, because of the short female urethra and vaginal colonization by fecal flora. Cystitis and pyelonephritis may also result from ascending infection. Sepsis can occur, especially with IV lines. Neonatal meningitis may develop from exposure during birth because approximately 25% of women have vaginal colonization.

Traveler's diarrhea is caused by enterotoxigenic *E. coli* (ETEC) and causes self-limited, watery, nonbloody diarrhea. Bloody diarrhea, with associated abdominal cramping and fever, is caused by enteropathogenic *E. coli*.

Diagnosis

Cultures are performed on blood agar, EMB, and MacConkey agar. *E. coli* produces lactose-fermenting pink colonies that are green on EMB agar.

Treatment

UTIs are treated with TMP/SMX or quinolones. Sepsis is treated with parenteral cephalosporins. Neonatal meningitis is treated with ampicillin and cefotaxime. Diarrhea is usually treated symptomatically; travelers can be given prophylactic doxycycline. Water supplies are routinely tested for the presence of *E. coli* to avoid fecal contamination.

Salmonella typhi

Salmonella
- No lactose fermentation
- Produces H_2S

Salmonella typhi is a facultative anaerobe found in the GI tract. It does not ferment lactose but produces H_2S. *S. typhi* has O (cell wall; type A–I), H (flagellar; phase 1 and 2), and Vi (virulence) antigens. Transmission route is fecal-oral from contaminated sources (e.g., food contaminated by animal feces). Gastric acidity is an important defense mechanism. *S. typhi* enters in the small intestine and multiplies in phagocytes of Peyer's patches. Subsequent spread to the liver, spleen, and gallbladder occur via phagocytes. Three percent of infected persons are carriers (like Typhoid Mary!), with asymptomatic colonization in the gallbladder.

Signs & Symptoms

Typhoid fever consists of slow onset of fever and constipation. About 1 week after exposure, high fever, delirium, and abdominal pain that is either diffuse or mimics appendencitis appear. Spleen enlargement and diarrhea may also develop. "Rose spots" are rare and consist of red macules on the abdomen.

Diagnosis

Gram's stain and culture from blood are performed on EMB and MacConkey agar. Colorless, non–lactose-fermenting colonies are produced. Agglutination tests with antisera for O, H, and Vi antigens are also performed.

Treatment

Ceftriaxone is used, as are ciprofloxacin, ampicillin and TMP/SMX. *S. typhi* can have resistance to chloramphenicol and ampicillin by plasmid-encoded genes. Cholecystectomy can be performed to treat the carrier. Vaccines are available but give limited protection.

Salmonella enteritidis

Salmonella enteritidis is very similar to *S. typhi*. It is a facultative anaerobe in the GI tract, produces H_2S, does not ferment lactose, and has the same antigens. Transmission is fecal-oral from contaminated sources, such as poultry and eggs. Ingestion of at least 100,000 organisms is necessary for disease, and gastric acidity is an important defense mechanism. Disease-causing strains invade the mucosa to the lamina propria, resulting in inflammation and diarrhea. Bacteremia is rare.

Signs & Symptoms

S. enteritidis causes **enterocolitis**. Incubation is 6–48 hours, during which time the patient develops nausea, vomiting, abdominal pain, and diarrhea. It is usually self-limiting. Sepsis with metastatic abscesses can occur, although it is rare. *Salmonella* **osteomyelitis** is seen in sickle-cell patients.

Diagnosis

Gram's stain and culture from stool samples on EMB and MacConkey agar show colorless, non–lactose-fermenting colonies. Agglutination tests can be performed for known antigens.

Treatment

Enterocolitis can be treated conservatively. Severe infection requires ceftriaxone.

Shigella dysenteriae and *Shigella sonnei*

Shigella
- No lactose fermentation
- Does not produce H_2S

Shigella is a nonmotile, facultative anaerobe that is non–lactose-fermenting. It does not produce H_2S. It is found in the GI tract, and the transmission route is fecal-oral by the 4 Fs: fingers, flies, food, feces. It is very virulent: Ingestion of only 10–100 organisms is necessary to cause disease. The cell wall O antigen divides the genus into four groups: A, B, C, D. The organism invades the mucosa of the distal ileum and colon, resulting in inflammation and ulceration. Bacteremia is rare.

Signs & Symptoms

Enterocolitis develops with a 1- to 4-day incubation. Symptoms include fever, abdominal cramps, and bloody diarrhea. Young children and elderly get more severe disease. *S. sonnei* causes mild disease, whereas *S. dysenteriae* causes more severe disease.

Diagnosis

Gram's stain and culture from stool sample on EMB and MacConkey agar show colorless, non–lactose-fermenting colonies. Methylene blue stain of the stool sample reveals neutrophils from the invasive disease.

Treatment

Antibiotics such as ciprofloxacin and TMP/SMX may be used, but resistance to multiple antibiotics is common, and antibiotics may prolong shedding. Otherwise, conservative therapy is used.

Vibrio cholerae

Vibrio cholerae is a comma-shaped, gram-negative rod. It has both human and marine reservoirs and is transmitted via the fecal-oral route by contaminated food, water, or undercooked shellfish. Patients must ingest more than 10^7 organisms for disease to occur. An asymptomatic carrier state exists.

Adherence to the small intestine is dependent on a mucinase enzyme, which dissolves glycoprotein on intestinal cells. The organism then multiplies and makes a toxin known as *choleragen*, which is composed of two subunits. The A subunit ADP-ribosylates G protein, causing chronic activation of adenylate cyclase and increased cAMP, chloride ion, and water secretion. The B subunit binds a receptor on the enterocyte.

Signs & Symptoms

Cholera causes massive **watery diarrhea** ("rice water stools") with no associated blood or abdominal pain. Death occurs from dehydration and electrolyte imbalance if left untreated.

Diagnosis

Colorless colonies are seen on MacConkey agar. *V. cholerae* is oxidase-positive. Agglutination tests with antiserum to O antigen are performed.

Treatment

Fluid and electrolyte replacement is critical. Tetracycline may shorten the duration of illness or eliminate the carrier state. The currently available vaccine is not very effective.

Vibrio parahaemolyticus

This marine organism is transmitted through improperly cooked seafood. *Vibrio parahaemolyticus* makes enterotoxin similar to choleragen from *V. cholera* and is a major cause of diarrhea in Japan due to raw fish consumption.

Signs & Symptoms

Patients develop watery diarrhea, nausea, vomiting, and abdominal cramps. Symptoms are self-limited and typically last 3 days.

Diagnosis

It is distinguished from *V. cholera* by its ability to grow in 8% NaCl.

Treatment

Symptomatic only.

Campylobacter jejuni

Campylobacter jejuni are microaerophilic, motile, comma-shaped rods. Domestic animals and humans are the reservoirs, and transmission is fecal-oral. Pathogenesis is unclear, but some strains make an enterotoxin similar to choleragen. Tissue invasion occurs, resulting in bloody diarrhea.

Signs & Symptoms

Patients develop watery, foul-smelling diarrhea, followed by bloody stools, fever, and abdominal pain. Systemic infection, seen in neonates and adults in poor health, is caused by *C. intestinalis*.

Diagnosis

Stool sample is cultured on a blood agar plate with antibiotics (Skirrow's agar) to inhibit normal flora. Incubation is done at 42°C, 5% O_2, 10% CO_2.

Treatment

Symptomatic therapy. Erythromycin or ciprofloxacin can be given.

Helicobacter pylori

Helicobacter pylori are curved, gram-negative rods that resemble *Campylobacter* in many ways. The natural habitat is the stomach, and transmission is likely oral. *H. pylori* attaches to the gastric mucosa, causing inflammation. It also has a **urease** enzyme, which makes ammonia from urea, resulting in increased pH (i.e., less acidity). The inflammation and ammonia cause mucosal damage.

Signs & Symptoms

H. pylori is a major contributing factor to the development of gastritis and peptic ulcer disease. *H. pylori* infection is also a risk factor for gastric carcinoma.

Diagnosis

Gram's stain and culture of a biopsy specimen. *H. pylori* is urease-positive, unlike *C. jejuni*, which is urease-negative. A radiolabeled urea breath test can also be performed, in which labeled CO_2 is expelled if bacteria are present.

Treatment

Triple therapy with amoxicillin, metronidazole, and bismuth subsalicylate (Pepto-Bismol) is necessary for eradication.

Klebsiella pneumoniae

Klebsiella pneumoniae is an encapsulated, gram-negative rod found in the upper respiratory and GI tracts. Transmission to lungs occurs by aspiration or inhalation, and transmission to the GU tract can occur by ascending infection from fecal flora.

The large capsule has a mucoid appearance and inhibits phagocytosis. Endotoxin is also present in the cell wall.

Signs & Symptoms

Klebsiella usually causes infection in patients who are predisposed to illness and aspiration, such as alcoholics or the elderly. Both community-acquired and hospital-acquired **pneumonia** can occur, productive of thick and bloody "currant-jelly" sputum. Less commonly, UTIs, meningitis, and sepsis can develop.

Diagnosis

Colored, lactose-fermenting colonies grow on EMB or MacConkey agar.

Treatment

Antibiotic resistance is common. Empiric treatment with gentamicin and cefotaxime is given until cultures are tested for specific sensitivities.

Proteus mirabilis and Proteus vulgaris

Proteus mirabilis is a motile, indole-negative, phenylalanine deaminase–positive, urease-positive organism that produces H_2S. Its motility gives a "swarming" effect on agar and may aid in the spread of infection. The organisms are found in soil, water, and the human colon, and **UTI** develops by ascending spread of fecal flora.

The presence of urease results in ammonia production, which causes increased urinary pH. The alkaline urine favors stone formation ("struvites"), resulting in epithelial damage.

Signs & Symptoms

Both community- and hospital-acquired UTIs may develop. Vaginal colonization and urinary catheters predispose to infection. Less common infections include wound infection, pneumonia, and sepsis.

Diagnosis

Colorless, non–lactose-fermenting colonies form on EMB agar. Cultures on blood agar containing phenylethyl alcohol inhibit swarming. Some O antigens cross-react with antigens from Rickettsiae. This is known as the **Weil-Felix reaction** and is used in laboratory screening for antirickettsial antibody.

Treatment

Ampicillin. Most strains are also sensitive to TMP/SMX and aminoglycosides.

Pseudomonas aeruginosa

Pseudomonas aeruginosa is a strict aerobe that can grow in tap water and is very resistant to disinfectants. It is found in soil and water, and 10% of people carry it in the colon, oropharynx, or on the skin. Transmission occurs via respiratory droplets, contact with burned skin, fecal contamination, or aspiration. Its ability to grow in hypotonic solutions allows it to contaminate hospital equipment and fluids easily.

P. aeruginosa synthesizes exotoxin A, which inhibits protein synthesis via ADP-ribosylation of EF-2. It also has a capsule and pili, which inhibit phagocytosis and enhance adherence, respectively. The organism makes the pigments **pyocyanin** (which turns pus blue) and **pyoverdin** (fluorescent under UV light). It also makes a slime layer called **glycocalyx** for adherence to respiratory mucosa.

Signs & Symptoms

P. aeruginosa is an opportunistic pathogen that infects susceptible individuals, including burn victims, cystic fibrosis patients, the immunocompromised, and patients with indwelling catheters. Common infections include UTIs, pneumonia, and wound and burn infections. Sepsis can develop from any of these causes and carries a 50% mortality rate. Other notable infections include osteochondritis of the foot, resulting from puncture wounds through shoes, and corneal infections in contact lens wearers.

Diagnosis

Colorless, non–lactose-fermenting colonies form on EMB and MacConkey agar. *P. aeruginosa* is oxidase-positive and forms a metallic sheen on TSI agar. It is noted for its blue-green pigment and fruity aroma.

Treatment

Ticarcillin and gentamicin. Resistance is common and can arise during therapy.

Bacteroides fragilis

Bacteroides fragilis is the predominant organism in the colon, and 60% of women have vaginal colonization. It is anaerobic and does not form spores. Transmission is endogenous from a break in the GI mucosal surface and requires a predisposing factor for disease, such as surgery or trauma.

Signs & Symptoms

Peritonitis or localized abdominal **abscesses** are the most common infections. Other infections include pelvic or lung abscesses or bacteremia.

Diagnosis

Growth occurs under anaerobic conditions on blood agar plates with kanamycin and vancomycin.

Treatment

Resistance to multiple antibiotics is common. Metronidazole or third-generation cephalosporins are typically used. Aminoglycosides are given to treat mixed infections. Abscesses require drainage. Cefoxitin is often given as prophylaxis before GI surgery.

Haemophilus influenzae

Haemophilus influenzae is an encapsulated coccobacillus with several serotypes. Serotype b is the most pathogenic, causing meningitis in young children. Transmission is by airborne droplets, and the bacteria secretes IgA protease, which helps it attach to respiratory mucosa. *H. influenzae* causes upper respiratory tract illnesses, such as pneumonia, otitis media, and sinusitis. In chronic smokers, it may cause exacerbations of chronic bronchitis. In young children, *H. influenzae* can cause epiglottitis, which may lead to fatal airway obstruction.

Signs & Symptoms

H. influenzae is the leading cause of **meningitis** in children, although this has decreased in recent years due to childhood vaccination. Signs of pneumonia or other respiratory tract infections are common. **Epiglottitis** presents with dysphagia, inspiratory stridor, and excessive drooling.

Diagnosis

Culture and Gram's stain of sputum or CSF is performed; otherwise, it is treated empirically. Growth occurs on chocolate agar supplemented with factors V (NAD) and X (heme). The Quellung reaction is used to ascertain encapsulation, and serotypes are determined by fluorescent antibody and agglutination tests.

Treatment

Common upper respiratory tract infections are treated with ampicillin or TMP/SMX. Meningitis must be treated promptly with a third-generation cephalosporin. If left untreated, the fatality rate exceeds 90%. Current recommendations suggest that all infants less than 1 year of age should receive vaccination with type b antigen coupled with diphtheria toxoid. Epiglottitis is a medical emergency and requires intubation to preserve the airway plus IV cephalosporins.

Legionella pneumophila

Legionella pneumophila are gram-negative rods that do not stain well with Gram's stain or standard hematoxylin-eosin procedures. Transmission occurs through airborne droplets, and their habitat is environmental water sources, such as air conditioners and cooling towers (therefore, person-to-person spread does not occur).

The typical host is usually predisposed by being immunocompromised or having a chronic illness. Elderly men who smoke and drink are also at risk.

Signs & Symptoms

Legionnaire's disease is an atypical pneumonia, which can present with unusual symptoms, such as diarrhea, confusion, and proteinuria. Cough is present but with little sputum.

Diagnosis

Sputum shows neutrophils and few bacteria. Culture grows on blood agar with iron and cysteine added. Diagnosis is made by an increase in antibody titer in convalescing patients or by detection of antigens in the urine.

Treatment

Erythromycin.

Bordetella pertussis

Bordetella pertussis is a small coccobacillus that is transmitted by respiratory droplets. *B. pertussis* makes two toxins. The pertussis toxin causes ADP-ribosylation of an inhibitory subunit of G protein, which blocks inactivation of adenylate cyclase, resulting in increased cAMP. The second toxin is a bacterial adenylate cyclase that is taken up by phagocytes and inhibits their activity.

Currently, pertussis infection is largely prevented by vaccination as part of the DPT vaccine during childhood. Both a killed bacteria and acellular toxoid vaccine are available. The killed bacteria vaccine causes one case of encephalopathy per million injections.

Signs & Symptoms

B. pertussis causes pertussis, or **whooping cough**, primarily in children. Onset is usually mild symptoms, which progress to paroxysmal cough and the production of large amounts of mucus. Symptoms may last for several weeks and can progress to pneumonia, which can be fatal.

Diagnosis

Culture from a nasopharyngeal swab is placed on a Bordet-Gengou agar plate (consisting of 20–30% blood agar). Agglutination and fluorescent antibody test are also performed.

Treatment

Erythromycin decreases the incidence of secondary complications but does not alter disease course because respiratory mucosa is already damaged. Oxygen therapy and frequent suctioning are used as supportive care.

Brucella Species

Brucella species, specifically *B. melitensis*, *B. abortus*, and *B. suis*, are gram-negative rods that can cause undulant fever. They are found in domestic livestock, with *B. melitensis* in goats and sheep, *B. abortus* in cattle, and *B. suis* in pigs. Transmission occurs by ingestion of contaminated milk products or through the skin; the classic patient is an animal handler or a traveler who has consumed unpasteurized milk or cheese products. Infection can be prevented by pasteurization of milk and cheese products and livestock vaccination.

Signs & Symptoms

Undulant fever, or brucellosis, is caused by infection of the reticuloendothelial system, including lymph nodes, spleen, liver, and bone marrow. Patients experience fever, weakness, fatigue, lymphadenopathy, and splenomegaly. The fever "undulates" daily, with a slow rise in temperature through the day, a temperature peak at night, and a return to normal temperature by morning. Symptoms can last from months to years. Complications include osteomyelitis.

Diagnosis

Brucella is cultured in enriched medium and 10% CO_2. Slide agglutination and serum antibody tests are used for diagnosis.

Treatment

Tetracycline and gentamicin.

Francisella tularensis

Francisella tularensis is a pleomorphic, gram-negative rod found in animals such as rabbits, deer, and rodents in most areas of the United States. Transmission occurs between animals by lice, mites, and ticks, especially *Dermacentor* ticks. Transmission to humans occurs from a bite by a vector or contact with the hide of an infected animal. Skin entry leads to lymph node infection, which can cause abscesses or ulceration. Inhalation can cause pneumonia, and ingestion of infected meat can cause GI disease.

F. tularensis infection can be prevented by avoiding contact with wild animals and taking measures to prevent tick bites, such as wearing long sleeves. Persons in high-risk jobs, such as forestry, can be vaccinated against the disease with a live, attenuated vaccine.

Signs & Symptoms

The illness, **tularemia**, can be sudden and flulike or prolonged. There may be an ulcer at the entry site and swollen, painful regional lymph nodes.

Diagnosis

Cultures are not usually done due to the high risk of laboratory worker inhalation. Agglutination test with serum samples and a skin test similar to PPD are performed.

Treatment

Streptomycin.

Yersinia pestis

Yersinia pestis is a small, bipolar-staining organism with a clear central area. It is endemic in wild rodents in Europe and Asia and in prairie dogs in the United States. Transmission occurs with passage between wild rodents and fleas. The rodents are generally asymptomatic carriers from which the fleas obtain the organism after a blood meal. The bacteria then multiply in the flea and are regurgitated during the next meal. Humans are accidental hosts. Transmission via respiratory droplets may also occur if the organism has invaded the bloodstream and causes abscess formation in the lung.

Y. pestis infection can be prevented by avoiding dead rodents. People in high-risk occupations may be vaccinated with a killed bacteria vaccine.

Signs & Symptoms

Y. pestis causes the **bubonic plague**, which is characterized by high fever, myalgias, and painful swollen lymph nodes known as buboes. Septic shock and death develop in more than half of untreated cases. **Pneumonic plague** is characterized by lung abscesses that can develop from inhalation or bacteremia.

Diagnosis

Gram's stain and cultures from blood or a bubo are done. Giemsa or Wayson stain is best for demonstrating bipolar staining. Serology and immunofluorescence are also done.

Treatment

Streptomycin.

Pasteurella multocida

Pasteurella multocida is a short, bipolar-staining organism that is part of the normal oral flora of cats and dogs. Humans are infected by animal bites, which cause localized **cellulitis** or even **osteomyelitis** if the bone is injured during the bite.

Signs & Symptoms

Patients develop wound infection at the site of an animal bite. Sutures may act as a nidus of infection and cause worsened cellulitis.

Diagnosis

Wound culture.

Treatment

Penicillin. Animal bites should not be sutured.

Mycobacteria

Mycobacterium tuberculosis

Mycobacterium tuberculosis is a slow-growing, acid-fast, obligate aerobe that causes tuberculosis. The cell wall contains mycolic acid, and the organism is highly resistant to dehydration.

Isoniazid- and multidrug-resistant (MDR) strains are becoming increasingly common. The resistance is due to mutations of mycolic acid synthase and catalase-peroxidase genes rather than to the acquisition of plasmid-derived genes.

In the United States, most disease occurs from reactivation of previous infection in debilitated or immunocompromised hosts. Primary lesions are usually in the lower lung lobes, but reactivation lesions are typically found in the lung apices, kidneys, brain, and bone. A single, primary lung tubercle is called a **Ghon focus**; after spread to the ipsilateral lymph nodes, the lesions form a **Ghon complex**.

Prior infection is tested with the tuberculin skin test, which detects hypersensitivity to purified protein derivative (PPD). Induration at the site of PPD placement occurs in 48–72 hours if the person has been previously exposed to tuberculosis. Immunocompromised persons require the placement of positive controls, such as *Candida*, because a negative PPD test may indicate anergy rather than lack of previous exposure. Previous immunization with BCG also gives a positive skin test.

Signs & Symptoms

The classic symptoms of pulmonary tuberculosis include fever, fatigue, night sweats, cough, and hemoptysis. Spine infection, known as **Pott's disease**, causes localized pain in the affected areas.

Diagnosis

Acid-fast stains of sputum are performed. It may be grown on Lowenstein-Jensen agar over several weeks. Niacin production is unique for *M. tuberculosis* and may be used to distinguish it from other mycobacteria. Drug sensitivity testing must be performed due to widespread resistance.

Treatment

Multidrug therapy is used to prevent the emergence of resistant strains. Pulmonary TB is treated with isoniazid, rifampin, and pyrazinamide for 6 months. Immunocompromised patients are given ethambutol as well. Isoniazid prophylaxis is given to asymptomatic persons who have developed a newly positive PPD and for close contacts of TB patients. Patients receiving isoniazid should also receive vitamin B_6 (pyridoxine) to avoid the development of peripheral neuropathy.

Mycobacterium leprae

Mycobacterium leprae is an acid-fast organism that grows in the skin and peripheral nerves. The organisms are transmitted through prolonged contact with skin lesions. The disease, known as **leprosy** or Hansen's disease, occurs worldwide, especially in Africa and Asia. In the United States, it is more prevalent in the southwestern areas. Some individuals are more susceptible to infection than others; the reasons for this are unknown.

Signs & Symptoms

Two different forms of leprosy exist: tuberculoid leprosy and the more severe lepromatous leprosy. Most cases are somewhere between the two types.

In **tuberculoid leprosy**, organism growth is limited by cell-mediated immunity, and granulomas form that wall off the organism. Patients develop hypopigmented, macular skin lesions and anesthesia of the skin. Patients with tuberculoid leprosy develop a positive lepromin skin test.

Patients with **lepromatous leprosy** have a poor cell-mediated immune response and develop foamy histiocytes rather than granulomas. The organisms travel in the bloodstream, and patients develop leonine (lionlike) faces and nodular skin lesions. These patients usually have a negative lepromin skin test. Cosmetic disfigurement results from skin anesthesia, which leads to increased trauma to the affected areas and bone resorption, resulting in alteration of features.

Diagnosis

Acid-fast stain or biopsy from a skin lesion.

Treatment

Prolonged dapsone therapy. Dapsone prophylaxis is given to close contacts.

Mycobacterium avium-intracellulare Complex

Mycobacterium avium-intracellulare complex (MAC) is a mixture of two mycobacterial species that are found in the environment. Immunocompromised patients are at particular risk of developing MAC infection.

Signs & Symptoms

Patients may develop a severe pneumonia or systemic infection.

Diagnosis

Sputum and serum cultures take several weeks, so the disease is usually treated presumptively. Affected areas may be biopsied.

Treatment

Resistance is a major problem. Patients may be on as many as six antitubercular drugs at once for treatment. Additional drugs include clarithromycin and rifabutin.

Actinomycetes and Mycoplasmas

Actinomycetes israelii

Actinomycetes are anaerobic, gram-positive rods that form long, branching filaments. They are part of the normal oral flora and are found in the crevices around teeth. Transmission occurs with trauma, such as a dental procedure.

Signs & Symptoms

Actinomycosis is the formation of hard, swollen abscesses on the face, neck, chest, or abdomen.

Diagnosis

Microscopy and culture show filaments and hard, yellow **sulfur granules**, which are not actually sulfur but rather are bacterial microcolonies and cellular debris.

Treatment

Drainage of the abscess and prolonged penicillin course.

Nocardia asteroides

Nocardia are aerobic, weakly gram-positive rods that are acid-fast and form long, branching filaments. They are found in the environment (in the soil) and and are not normal flora. Transmission occurs by airborne droplets.

Signs & Symptoms

Nocardiosis is a pulmonary infection that results in lung abscesses. Immunocompromised patients can develop disseminated disease to the brain and kidneys.

Diagnosis

Microscopy and culture show filaments.

Treatment

TMP/SMX and abscess drainage.

Mycoplasma pneumoniae

Mycoplasma are tiny organisms that have no cell wall. As a result, the organism does not stain on Gram's stain, and antibiotics that inhibit cell wall synthesis, such as penicillin, are not useful in treatment. They are found in the respiratory tract and transmitted by respiratory droplets. They attack by attaching themselves to ciliated respiratory epithelium, which later inhibits ciliary motion and kills the epithelial cells.

Signs & Symptoms

Mycoplasma causes an atypical pneumonia, characterized by the gradual onset of fatigue and cough with scant sputum production. It is the most likely cause of pneumonia in young adults, and outbreaks can occur in closed populations (e.g., the military or college dorms). Symptoms usually resolve spontaneously in a few weeks.

Diagnosis

Cultures are not useful for diagnosis. A **cold agglutinin test** may be positive, and specific complement fixation tests are available. The classic chest X-ray finding is a horrible-looking chest X-ray that is "out of proportion" to the mild symptoms.

Treatment

Erythromycin or tetracycline.

Ureaplasma urealyticum

This member of the *Mycoplasma* family is a member of the normal flora in the majority of healthy sexually active women. It is a good pathogen to keep in mind when thinking of causative agents of **urethritis** (*Neisseria gonorrhoeae* and *Chlamydia trachomatis* are the two other big players). Its claim to fame is its ability to break down urea.

Signs & Symptoms

Ureaplasma-mediated urethritis presents as dysuria (burning on urination) with a possible yellow mucoid discharge.

Diagnosis

Ureaplasma urealyticum grows as tiny colonies that require cholesterol and urea for growth. It can metabolize urea into ammonia and CO_2.

Treatment

Erythromycin or tetracycline.

Spirochetes

See Table 5-1 for a summary of spirochetes.

Table 5-1. Spirochetes

Organism	Disease	Transmission	Diagnosis
Borrelia burgdorferi	Lyme disease	*Ixodes* tick	Clinical + serology
B. recurrentis	Relapsing fever	Human body louse	Blood smear shows organism
Leptospira interrogans	Leptospirosis	Contamination by livestock urine	Clinical + serology
Treponema pallidum	Syphilis	Sexual contact	Serology

Treponema pallidum

Treponema pallidum cannot be grown in culture or Gram stained. It has several antigens that activate an immune response and can be used in diagnosis. Organisms are found in the genital tract, and transmission is by intimate contact with skin or mucous membrane lesions. It can also be transmitted to the fetus across the placenta.

Signs & Symptoms

T. pallidum causes syphilis. **Primary syphilis** is characterized by the formation of a chancre (nontender ulcer) at the site of infection, which heals spontaneously within a few weeks. **Secondary syphilis** develops several months later and causes a maculopapular rash, especially on the palms and soles. **Condylomata lata** (moist papules) develop on the genitals and are very infectious.

Approximately one-third of patients progress to **tertiary syphilis**, which causes skin and bony gummas and CNS and cardiovascular disease. CNS syphilis is known as **tabes dorsalis** and causes **Argyll. Robertson pupils**: pupils that constrict to accommadation but not to light. Cardiovascular lesions include thoracic or abdominal aortic aneurysms (classically in the ascending aorta).

Congenital syphilis can be passed to the fetus. If untreated, it can result in stillbirth or the development of jaundice and rash. Infected newborns develop characteristic "snuffles" due to necrosis of the nasal bone.

Diagnosis

Darkfield microscopy or immunofluorescence can demonstrate the presence of spirochetes in early lesions. Nonspecific serology (VDRL and RPR) are positive, but false-positives can occur in a number of other conditions. Specific tests include fluorescent treponemal antibody-absorbed (FTA-ABS) and microhemagglutination–*T. pallidum* (MHA-TP).

Treatment

Penicillin. A rare complication is the Jarisch-Herxheimer reaction, in which patients with secondary syphilis develop fever, chills, and myalgias from penicillin treatment, which is thought to be due to lysis of spirochetes and the release of toxins.

Borrelia burgdorferi

Borrelia burgdorferi is a motile spirochete that is found in small rodents and other mammals. It is transmitted by tick bites to humans, especially by the *Ixodes* tick. It is found on both East and West coasts, and disease occurs most often in the summer months. Prevention of infection is key, and people who hike or are exposed to ticks should wear long sleeves and inspect the skin for tick bites after possible exposure.

Signs & Symptoms

B. burgdorferi causes **Lyme disease**. The first stage of the disease causes a "target lesion" at the site of the tick bite, accompanied by flulike symptoms. The rash may spread and is known as *erythema chronicum migrans*. Weeks later, patients may develop cardiac abnormalities, such as pericarditis, and neurologic problems, such as meningitis. Finally, months later, patients can develop severe arthritis and worsening CNS disease.

Diagnosis

Cultures are usually not performed. Diagnosis is made by serology or PCR.

Treatment

Doxycycline. Later stages may require ceftriaxone. Suspected exposure should be treated with amoxicillin or doxycycline.

Borrelia recurrentis

Borrelia recurrentis is a spirochete that causes a relapsing fever. It is transmitted by the human body louse (*Pediculus humanis*). As the body develops an antibody response, the organism undergoes an antigenic shift, causing a recurrence of symptoms.

Signs & Symptoms

Patients experience high fever, chills, and headaches, which resolve in 3–6 days with drenching sweats. After an eight–day afebrile period, the cycle begins again.

Diagnosis

Microscopy on blood smear during the febrile period allows visualization of the spirochete.

Treatment

Doxycycline or erythromycin.

Leptospira interrogans

Leptospira is a thin spirochete that is found in domestic livestock, rats, and pets. The animals excrete the organism in their urine, which then contaminates water and soil. The organism can then be ingested or can pass through skin when swimming. Farmers and sewer workers are at particular risk.

Signs & Symptoms

Leptospirosis is a biphasic illness. The initial infection causes high spiking fever, chills, severe muscle aches, and headache, which resolve in about a week. The patient classically has red conjunctiva and photophobia during this time. The second phase, which follows a short afebrile period, is characterized by meningismus and the presence of IgM antibody. A more severe form of leptospirosis, called **Weil's disease**, is characterized by renal failure, hepatitis, jaundice, multi-organ hemorrhage, and mental status changes.

Diagnosis

History and serology are diagnostic. Treatment should be initiated before cultures would be available.

Treatment

Penicillin or doxycycline.

Chlamidiae

Chlamydia trachomatis

Chlamydia is an obligate intracellular organism. It has a cell wall but no peptidoglycan. It is usually found in the genital tract and transmitted by intimate contact or to neonates during birth. Transmission can also occur from finger to eye or from fomite to eye. **Trachoma**, a severe conjunctivitis, is caused by immunotypes A–C. It is common in Africa and Asia and can lead to blindness. Genital tract infections are caused by D–K immunotypes and can lead to infertility in women with severe infections. **Lymphogranuloma venereum** is caused by L1–L3 immunotypes and leads to the development of genital lesions.

Signs & Symptoms

Men develop **urethritis**, and women develop **cervicitis**, which can ascend and cause **PID**. Neonates born to women with genital infection can develop conjunctivitis or pneumonia within a few weeks after birth.

Diagnosis

Giemsa stain shows cytoplasmic inclusions in epithelial cells, and cell cultures are performed. Serology is generally not useful.

Treatment

Erythromycin and other macrolides are used. Intramuscular ceftriaxone followed by oral doxycycline or azithromycin is used to treat urethritis to cover the three major organisms (*Chlamydia trachomatis, Neisseria gonorrhoeae,* and *Ureaplasma urealyticum*). Sexual contacts must also be treated. Erythromycin drops are used to prevent neonatal conjunctivitis. Topical tetracycline is used to treat trachoma to prevent blindness.

Chlamydia psittaci

Chlamydia psittaci is found in birds. Transmission to humans occurs by inhalation of dried bird feces. The disease can be prevented by isolating infected birds and by adding antibiotics to bird feed.

Signs & Symptoms

C. psittaci causes psittacosis. The organism infects lung mucous membranes and can be asymptomatic or cause atypical pneumonia.

Diagnosis

Serology is usually diagnostic. Fluorescent antibody and Giemsa stain may show cytoplasmic inclusions that do not contain glycogen.

Treatment

Tetracycline.

Rickettsiae

Table 5-2. Vector-Borne Rickettsial Diseases

Rickettsia	Disease	Vector
Rickettsia rickettsii	Rocky Mountain Spotted Fever: rash begins on palms, soles, and face, spreads inward	*Dermacentor* tick
Rickettsia akari	Rickettsialpox: vescular rash similar to chickenpox	Mites from house mice
Rickettsia prowazekii	Epidemic typhus: Macular rash sparing palms and soles; epidemic during war or unsanitary conditions	Human lice, fleas from squirrels
Rickettsia typhi	Endemic typhus: Rash and fever similar to epidemic typhus	*Xenopsylla cheopis* flea
Rickettsia tsutsugamushi	Scrub typhus: Rash following 2-week incubation period	Mite larvae (chiggars)

Rickettsia rickettsii

Rickettsia rickettsii are obligate intracellular organisms that are found in animals, such as rodents and dogs. Transmission to humans usually occurs by wood tick bite, especially the *Dermacentor*. It is found on both East and West coasts.

Signs & Symptoms

This organism causes **Rocky Mountain spotted fever**. Within days of the tick bite, patients develop a macular rash on the hands and feet that spreads to the trunk. Patients may also develop a nonspecific flu-like syndrome with myalgias, headache, and fever. This may progress to severe CNS changes, such as delirium and coma. Patients then develop DIC and shock, which may be fatal.

Diagnosis

The Weil-Felix test measures the presence of antirickettsial antibodies, detected by their cross-reactivity to the O antigen of *Proteus vulgaris*. These days, serology is used for diagnosis, and many patients are treated empirically.

Treatment

Tetracycline.

Coxiella burnetii

Coxiella burnetii are obligate intracellular organisms that are found in domestic livestock. The organism is transmitted in urine and other bodily fluids, so milk must be pasteurized at greater than 60°C. *C. burnetii* endospores are present in dried tick feces and on cowhides, and when inhaled they cause lung infection.

Signs & Symptoms

This organism causes Q fever. **Q fever** is characterized by the sudden onset of fever and headache, which may progress to pneumonia and hepatitis. Endocarditis is a rare complication.

Diagnosis

The Weil-Felix test does not work for *C. burnetii* infections. Serology is diagnostic.

Treatment

Tetracycline. A vaccine is available for high-risk individuals, such as farmers.

Viruses

Viruses are obligate intracellular parasites and require host cells to replicate. They consist of nucleic acids surrounded by a protein capsid. The viral genome can be RNA or DNA and can be single- or double-stranded. Viruses usually have a haploid genome (one copy of each gene), except for retroviruses, which are diploid. The capsid is made of repeating subunits of protein, called a **capsomer**. The genome and capsid may be surrounded by a lipoprotein envelope.

Viral lytic and lysogenic cycles are described in Fig. 5-4. Lysogenic viruses are able to integrate their DNA into the host cell for a period of time and then convert to the lytic cycle when ready.

Viruses are usually grown in cell culture. After a period of growth, they produce a **cytopathic effect** (CPE) that causes the cells to deform in a specific way for each virus. Specific tests for viral antigens or viral antibodies are also used for diagnosis. Light microscopy can reveal inclusion bodies (areas of high virus concentration) and **giant cells** (cell fusion caused by the virus). UV microscopy is often used for fluorescent staining.

Vaccinations for viral diseases are made from live, attenuated virus, killed virus, or recombinant viral protein (Table 5-3). Live virus vaccinations result in stronger immune response and longer-lasting memory. The virus can regain virulence within the host, however, causing disease, especially in immunocompromised individuals. A killed virus vaccine induces a weaker immune response but cannot revert to virulence. Passive immunity is provided by immune globulin and is given to exposed persons at high risk for developing disease.

Table 5-3. Viral vaccines

Virus	Type of vaccine
Adenovirus	Live attenuated
Hepatitis A	Killed
Hepatitis B	Recombinant protein
Influenza	Killed
Measles	Live attenuated
Mumps	Live attenuated
Polio	Live (OPV) and killed (IPV)
Rabies	Killed
Rubella	Live attenuated
Smallpox	Live attenuated
Varicella-zoster	Live attenuated
Yellow fever	Live attenuated

OPV = live oral poliovirus vaccine; IPV = inactivated poliovirus vaccine.

Naked nucleic acids (in the absence of viral proteins) from most double-stranded DNA viruses and positive-strand single-stranded RNA viruses are infectious. Exceptions include poxviruses and hepatitis B virus. Since the viral nucleic acids resemble host cell nucleic acids (DNA and mRNA), viral proteins are not needed to transcribe and/or translate the nucleic acids.

Herpesviruses

Herpes Simplex Virus 1

Herpes simplex virus 1 (HSV-1) is a double-stranded DNA virus commonly seen in children. Patients who are infected develop recurrent lesions that can be triggered by sunlight, stress, and other infections. Transmission occurs by contact with the infected vesicle. The virus has the ability to reside in a latent state in sensory ganglia.

Signs & Symptoms

HSV-1 causes herpes labialis, or cold sores, as well as gingivostomatitis and kerato-conjunctivitis. Serious complications include blindness and encephalitis. HSV-1 is the most common cause of viral encephalitis in the United States. Immunocompromised patients may develop disseminated disease.

Diagnosis

Cell culture from the lesion shows CPE and multinucleated giant cells. Tzanck smear is positive in all herpesvirus infections. Serology and immunofluorescence can be used for diagnosis of primary infections.

Treatment

Acyclovir.

Herpes Simplex Virus 2

HSV-2 is a double-stranded DNA virus that is sexually transmitted and causes genital or anal infection. Like HSV-1, recurrences are common, and the virus resides in the sensory ganglia in a latent state.

Signs & Symptoms

HSV-2 causes genital herpes, with painful vesicular genital or anal lesions. Neonatal herpes can develop in the newborns of mothers with active lesions.

Diagnosis

As with HSV-1, cell culture shows CPE, multinucleated giant cells, and a positive Tzanck smear. Serology and fluorescent antibodies are used for viral detection.

Treatment

Acyclovir shortens duration of recurrence and reduces viral shedding.

Varicella-Zoster Virus

Varicella-zoster virus (VZV) is a double-stranded DNA virus that causes **chickenpox** in children and shingles in adults. It is transmitted by respiratory droplets and causes disease, which is generally more severe in older patients. As with other herpesviruses, the virus can remain latent in the sensory ganglia and reactivate later in life, at times of immunocompromise. Exposure to VZV in pregnant women can result in severe congenital birth defects and may cause fetal death. A live, attenuated VZV immunization is now available and is recommended for all children.

Signs & Symptoms

Three weeks after primary exposure, chickenpox develops with fever and malaise, followed by a pruritic vesicular rash that spreads from the trunk to the extremities and face. Severe infections can progress to encephalitis and pneumonia.

Shingles manifests by the development of vesicles along a sensory nerve dermatome, usually on the trunk or face. The lesions may last for several weeks to months and are very painful.

Diagnosis

Clinical inspection. Tzanck smear shows multinucleated giant cells. Serology and immunofluorescent antibodies may also be used.

Treatment

Conservative management, although aspirin should not be given to children because of the possibility of **Reye's syndrome** (a potentially lethal condition that can result in encephalopathy and liver failure). Severe cases of VZV are treated with acyclovir. Pregnant women who are exposed should receive varicella immune globulin.

Cytomegalovirus

Cytomegalovirus (CMV) is a common double-stranded DNA virus that usually causes asymptomatic infection. However, it can be lethal in immunosuppressed populations, such as transplant recipients, newborns, and acquired immunodeficiency syndrome (AIDS) patients. It is transmissible in all bodily fluids and is present in infected donor organs.

Signs & Symptoms

In fetuses and infants, CMV causes cytomegalic inclusion disease. Newborns with the disease have a "blueberry corn muffin" appearance, with jaundice, petechiae, and growth retardation. Mental retardation, blindness, and hearing loss are common sequelae.

In adults, CMV causes heterophil-negative mononucleosis, characterized by fever, lethargy, and abnormal lymphocytes. CMV can also cause pneumonia, hepatitis, and diarrhea. CMV is a common cause of retinitis in AIDS patients.

Diagnosis

Cell culture shows a characteristic CPE. Inclusion bodies have an "owl's-eye" appearance. Fluorescent antibodies and serology are performed, although many people are CMV IgG–positive due to past exposure.

Treatment

Ganciclovir or foscarnet. Immunosuppressed persons should receive CMV-negative blood transfusions.

Epstein-Barr Virus

Epstein-Barr virus (EBV) is a double-stranded DNA virus that is transmitted by saliva. EBV is associated with the development of **Burkitt's lymphoma** in African populations. It has also been associated with **nasopharyngeal carcinoma** and **thymic carcinoma**, although the mechanism is not well understood.

Signs & Symptoms

EBV causes **infectious mononucleosis**, characterized by fever, sore throat, cervical lymphadenopathy, and splenomegaly. It usually resolves within a few weeks but can progress to hepatitis and encephalitis, especially in immunocompromised patients.

Diagnosis

Diagnosis is made with the heterophil antibody test (Monospot test). This test takes advantage of the fact that antibodies against EBV cross-react with and agglutinate sheep RBCs. On blood smear, atypical lymphocytes with a large, lobulated nucleus and basophilic cytoplasm are present.

Treatment

No drug therapy is available.

Human Herpesvirus 6

Human herpesvirus 6 (HHV-6) causes **roseola infantum**, one of the most common causes of infantile febrile seizures. The virus tends to infect infants six months to three years of age.

Signs & Symptoms

After a 10-day incubation period, infants develop an extremely high fever that lasts from three to five days, during which time they are at risk of experiencing a febrile seizure. As the fever subsides, a transient rash develops on the trunk.

Diagnosis

The history of the disease progression is diagnostic.

Treatment

No treatment is available.

Human Herpesvirus 8

Human herpesvirus 8 is putatively linked to **Kaposi's sarcoma**, an AIDS-associated malignancy found predominantly in homosexual men and rarely in elderly white men.

Signs & Symptoms

Kaposi's sarcoma appears as violaceous plaques or nodules on the mucous membranes and skin all over the body. It can spread to the GI tract and lungs. Pulmonary Kaposi's sarcoma can be life-threatening.

Diagnosis

Symptomatic.

Treatment

The underlying immunosupression (HIV, immunosuppressive medication) is treated first. Cryotherapy, intralesional chemotherapy, radiation therapy, or laser surgery can be used to treat individual lesions. Intravenous chemotherapy is used for progressive disease.

Poxviruses

Variola virus

The variola virus is a double-stranded DNA virus that causes **smallpox**. It was eradicated in 1977. It had a single stable serotype, which was the key to its eradication because people were vaccinated with a live, attenuated vaccine (vaccinia virus). Transmission occurred from respiratory droplets or contact with a skin lesion.

Signs & Symptoms

Smallpox was characterized by a sudden fever and rash that began as maculopapular but eventually became vesicular and crusted.

Diagnosis

Cell culture (CPE) or immunofluorescence of fluid from the vesicles.

Treatment

No drug therapy is available.

Molluscum Contagiosum Virus

Molluscum contagiosum virus causes a papular lesion that is transmitted by direct skin contact or sexual contact. It can be an early manifestation of opportunistic infection in HIV.

bq lesions

Signs & Symptoms

The translucent, umbilicated papules can be found on the face and trunk of children. When sexually transmitted, the papules can be found on genitalia.

Diagnosis

Diagnosis is usually made by the characteristic appearance of the lesions.

Treatment

The lesions usually resolve spontaneously in a few years and do not require treatment. Surgery or liquid nitrogen can be used to remove papules.

Hepatitis Viruses

The viruses that cause hepatitis come from different families of virus. All are RNA viruses except for the hepatitis B virus. All five viruses can cause **acute viral hepatitis**; HBV, HCV, and HDV are also responsible for **chronic viral hepatitis**.

Hepatitis A Virus

Hepatitis A is a single-stranded RNA virus of the picornavirus family that causes a form of hepatitis commonly seen in children. Transmission is fecal-oral, and patients usually recover without serious sequelae. There is no chronic carrier state. A killed vaccine is currently available to prevent infection in persons traveling to developing countries.

Signs & Symptoms

Most patients are asymptomatic or develop mild hepatitis symptoms, such as jaundice, nausea, and vomiting, which resolves spontaneously after a few weeks. In less than one percent of cases, fulminant hepatitis develops.

Diagnosis

Clinical history and IgM and IgG serum antibody tests are used for diagnosis.

Treatment

None. Immune serum globulin can be administered within two weeks of exposure to close contacts and travelers to endemic regions. A heat-killed vaccine is also available.

Hepatitis B Virus

Hepatitis B virus (HBV) is a double-stranded DNA virus (member of the hepadnavirus family) that has three important antigens. The s antigen (**HBsAg**) is a surface antigen on the viral envelope that is used in diagnosis. The c antigen (**HBcAg**) is a nucleocapsid core antigen that is also used in diagnosis. The e antigen (**HBeAg**), also a nucleocapsid core antigen, is used as an indicator of transmissibility; high levels indicate that the patient is highly infectious. The presence of anti-HBsAg antibody is a marker of immunity to the virus, and the presence of anti-HBeAG antibody is an indication of low transmissibility of the virus.

HBV is transmitted sexually, via blood, and perinatally. There is a high incidence of HBV infection in Asia, and HBV has been associated with the development of **hepatocellular carcinoma**. Approximately 10% of infected persons become chronic carriers. Healthcare workers and persons at increased risk of exposure should receive the recombinant vaccine. Transfusions are routinely screened for HBV.

Signs & Symptoms

Infection with HBV can be asymptomatic but is usually accompanied by jaundice, fever, anorexia, nausea, and vomiting. Incubation period is approximately 12 weeks. Patients may develop arthritis, vasculitis, and glomerulonephritis due to immune complex deposition.

Diagnosis

Different antigens and antibodies are present at varying times after infection (Fig. 5-7). Serum alanine aminotransferase (ALT) and aspartate aminotransferase (AST) are elevated.

Treatment

Acute hepatitis requires supportive care. Interferon-α is given in chronic infections and may decrease hepatocellular damage. Hepatitis B immune globulin can be

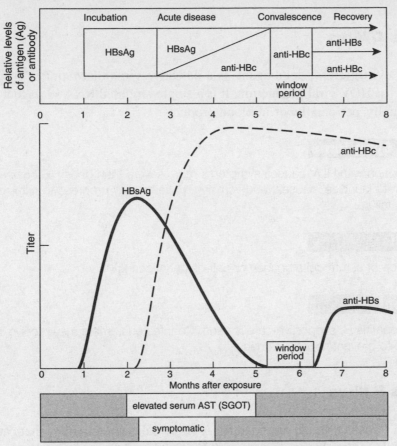

B chronic - 10%.
C chronic - 50%.

(Top) Important tests that aid diagnosis of hepatitis B during the various stages of infection. *(Middle)* The serologic basis for the tests you choose, demonstrating the "window period" during which neither surface antigen nor antisurface antibody can be detected. *(Bottom)* Duration of symptoms and of liver enzyme elevation.

Fig. 5-7. Hepatitis B serologies.

administered soon after exposure to HBV to greatly reduce chances of acquiring symptomatic disease.

Hepatitis C Virus

Hepatitis C virus (HCV) is a single-stranded RNA virus that is transmitted via blood and sexual contact. It is also associated with an increased incidence of **hepatocellular carcinoma**. Approximately one-half of infected patients become chronic carriers. Transfusions are routinely screened for possible HCV infection. A new agent, known as **hepatitis G**, has been linked to HCV infection and may be transmitted similarly.

Signs & Symptoms

As with other hepatitis viruses, patients experience jaundice, nausea, vomiting, and anorexia. Symptoms are usually less severe than with HBV infection, but a higher percentage (> 50%) develop chronic infection.

Diagnosis

ELISA testing is used to detect IgM and IgG antibodies to HCV.

Treatment

Supportive care. Interferon-α may decrease hepatocellular damage in chronic carriers.

Hepatitis D Virus

Hepatitis D virus (HDV, delta agent) is a defective virus that requires co-infection with HBV for HDV viral production. It is a single-stranded RNA virus that is transmitted sexually, perinatally, or in blood products.

Signs & Symptoms

Co-infection with HDV causes symptoms more severe than does HBV alone. In addition to jaundice, nausea, and vomiting, patients may progress to fulminant hepatic failure.

Diagnosis

Detection of serum delta antigen or anti-delta antigen IgM.

Treatment

As in hepatitis B, supportive care is used. Co-infected carriers may receive interferon-α to prevent hepatic damage.

Hepatitis E Virus

Hepatitis E virus is a single-stranded RNA virus (calicivirus family) that causes disease primarily in developing countries. It has fecal-oral transmission, and outbreaks are common. Pregnant women are at increased risk of both fetal and maternal mortality if infected. There is no carrier state.

Signs & Symptoms

Asymptomatic cases are common. Patients who develop the disease experience anorexia, nausea and vomiting, and jaundice after a six-week incubation period. The illness is clinically indistinguishable from HAV infection. In 80% of pregnant women, fulminant hepatitis develops; otherwise, fulminant hepatitis is rare.

Diagnosis

Exclusion of other causes of hepatitis, and serology.

Treatment

No treatment is available.

Single-Stranded DNA Viruses

Parvovirus B-19

Parvovirus B-19 is responsible for **erythema infectiosum**, or Fifth disease, a common infection among young children. The virus, which is spread by respiratory droplets or blood, infects and lyses RBC progenitor cells. This mechanism makes it dangerous to sickle cell patients, who run the risk of an **aplastic crisis** when infected.

Infection of pregnant women can lead to **hydrops fetalis**. Immunocompromised patients may suffer from **chronic anemia**.

Signs & Symptoms

Erythema infectiosum is characterized by a "slapped cheek" red rash on the face followed by a lacy reticular rash on the extremities and trunk. Arthralgia may accompany the infection.

Diagnosis

Presence of IgM B19 antibody in serology assays.

Treatment

No treatment is available.

Double-Stranded DNA Viruses

Adenovirus

Adenovirus is a double-stranded DNA virus that causes both respiratory and enteric infections. Transmission is fecal-oral or by aerosol droplet. Outbreaks in groups living closely together, such as the military, are common, and a live vaccine is available to be given to these groups.

Signs & Symptoms

Some adenoviruses cause respiratory disease with fever, malaise, and pharyngitis. Lower respiratory infection can result in pneumonia. Infantile gastroenteritis with non-bloody diarrhea may also occur. Less common strains can cause conjunctivitis and cystitis.

Diagnosis

Diagnosis is usually made clinically, but cell cultures show CPE, and serology can be performed for definitive diagnosis.

Treatment

No treatment is available.

Human Papillomavirus

Human papillomavirus (HPV) is a double-stranded DNA virus with more than 60 known serotypes. It is transmitted by direct contact and infects squamous epithelium. **Skin warts** are caused by HPV-1 through -4, and **genital warts** are caused by HPV-6 and -11.

Infection with HPV-16, -18, and -31 is associated with the development of **cervical** and **penile carcinoma** (note that these are not the subtypes that cause genital warts). Two genes, known as E6 and E7, may inhibit activity of *p53* and the *retinoblastoma* gene.

Signs & Symptoms

Depending on the subtype, infection can be asymptomatic or can manifest as warts, which are circumscribed, firm, grayish growths on the extremities or genitals. Laryngeal polyposis is an uncommon manifestation.

Pathology

Microscopically, infected cells contain **koilocytes**, cytoplasmic vacuoles that are the hallmark of HPV infection. Koilocytes may be seen in skin biopsies or cervical Papanicolaou smears.

Diagnosis

Clinical inspection. DNA hybridization may be used.

Treatment

Warts are removed with keratolytics such as liquid nitrogen or podophyllin. However, HPV infection is usually lifelong. Genital transmission can be prevented with condoms.

JC Virus

This virus is seen only in immunosupressed individuals, such as HIV patients, leukemics, and transplant recipients. It is responsible for the **progressive multifocal leukoencephalopathy** (PML), a demyelinating disease that is fatal within six months.

Signs & Symptoms

Depending on the site of demyelination, neurological disturbances can include speech impairment, dementia, cognitive dysfunction, motor impairment, loss of vision, and coma.

Treatment

No treatment is available.

Single-Stranded RNA Viruses

Influenza Virus

Influenza virus is a single-stranded RNA that can undergo rapid antigenic drifts due to mutations of its genome; these cause slight changes in the antigenic natures of its surface glycoproteins. Antigenic drift allows the same individual to be reinfected with influenza virus after developing antibodies to the older strain, but the second illness tends to be milder.

Infections occur more commonly in winter and are transmitted by respiratory droplets. Pandemics occur when antigenic shifts produce new, previously unseen viral types. Types A, B, and C are classified by internal capsid proteins. Type A, unlike types B and C, infects both humans and animals. It is responsible for antigenic shifts by swapping RNA segments with animal strains of virus, thus producing influenza strains with antigens very different from those previously seen by human immune systems. Killed vaccines are available for types A and B, but protection is temporary and lasts only a few months. Nonetheless, elderly persons, persons with chronic respiratory disease, and health care workers should receive annual influenza vaccination.

Signs & Symptoms

Influenza A and B cause influenza outbreaks, whereas influenza C causes a mild upper respiratory tract infection. Influenza is characterized by sudden fever, myalgias, and cough that resolve within days or may progress to pneumonia.

Diagnosis

Diagnosis is made clinically. Antibody titers may be used.

Treatment

Supportive care. Children with possible influenza infections should not receive aspirin because they are at risk of developing **Reye's syndrome**, resulting in encephalopathy and liver failure. Amantadine or rimantadine are used to treat infection and to prevent influenza A infection in possible outbreak situations (e.g., nursing homes).

Measles Virus

Measles virus is a single-stranded RNA virus that is transmitted by respiratory droplets. It is very infectious and can cause severe disease in malnourished children and immunocompromised patients. In the United States, all children should receive a live, attenuated vaccine given in conjunction with mumps and rubella vaccine (MMR) at age 15 months. A rare late complication of measles infection is **subacute sclerosing panencephalitis** (SSPE), which can develop years after the primary infection and result in dementia and death.

Signs & Symptoms

Measles (rubeola) develops within 2 weeks of exposure, and begins with fever, photophobia, cough, and **Koplik's spots** on the buccal mucosa, followed by a maculopapular rash, which starts on the face and neck and progresses downward. The lesions are red with a central white dot and frequently appear on the buccal mucosa. Severe infections can progress to pneumonia or encephalitis.

Diagnosis

Diagnosis is made clinically, but serology may be used to assess immunity.

Treatment

None. Persons born before 1980 may require an additional booster vaccination for adequate protection.

Mumps Virus

Mumps is a single-stranded RNA virus that is transmitted by respiratory droplets. A live, attenuated vaccine is given in conjunction with measles and rubella vaccine (MMR) in all children aged 15 months.

Signs & Symptoms

Mumps causes a flulike prodrome for about 3 weeks, followed by the development of tender, swollen parotid glands. Infection can spread to the ovaries, testes, and pancreas. Mumps orchitis can result in sterility.

Diagnosis

Diagnosis is made clinically. Urine or saliva may be cultured. Serology indicates recent infection.

Treatment

No treatment is available.

Respiratory Syncytial Virus

Respiratory syncytial virus (RSV) is a single-stranded RNA virus that is transmitted by respiratory droplets or hand to nose and mouth. It is often responsible for hospital outbreaks of pneumonia. It is prevalent in the winter and spring.

Signs & Symptoms

In older children and adults, RSV causes a mild upper respiratory infection. In infants and young children, RSV causes **bronchiolitis**, which is a severe lower respiratory tract infection that can progress to pneumonia. Children with bronchiolitis exhibit circum-oral cyanosis and a hacking cough.

Diagnosis

Immunofluorescent detection of the virus can be performed from a respiratory epithelium sample. Cultures show multinucleated giant cells. Serology is usually used for diagnosis.

Treatment

Ribavirin is used in hospitalized patients with severe infection.

Parainfluenza Virus

Parainfluenza virus is a single-stranded RNA virus that is transmitted by respiratory droplets. It is responsible for **bronchiolitis** in infants, **croup** in children, and is one of many viruses that can cause the common cold in adults.

Signs & Symptoms

Bronchiolitis is characterized by a hacking cough, hoarseness, and circum-oral cyanosis. Croup, or laryngotracheitis, has a barking cough that may be accompanied by inspiratory stridor and wheezes. In adults, patients experience cough, rhinorrhea, and malaise. Severe cases can progress to pneumonia.

Diagnosis

Clinical diagnosis and serology. Cell cultures show multinucleated giant cells.

Treatment

Respiratory support is given if needed. Inhaled racemic epinephrine may help in severe cases.

Rubella Virus

Rubella is a single-stranded RNA virus that is transmitted by respiratory droplets. Congenital rubella infection, especially in the first trimester, is associated with multiple birth defects, including congenital cataracts, hearing loss, cardiac defects, and mental retardation. Rubella can be prevented with a live, attenuated vaccine, combined with measles and mumps (MMR), that is given at 15 months of age. It should also be given to all unimmunized young women before pregnancy. Although no documented cases of birth defects caused by immunization exist, the vaccine should not be given to pregnant women.

Congenital rubella
- Cataracts
- Hearing loss
- Mental retardation
- Cardiac defects

Signs & Symptoms

About 3 weeks after exposure, patients display a maculopapular rash that starts on the face and spreads downward (**German measles**). The characteristic physical finding is **posterior auricular lymphadenopathy**.

Diagnosis

Diagnosis is performed with serology or ELISA. Antirubella IgM in pregnant women suggests recent infection, and amniocentesis may be done to see if the fetus is infected.

Treatment

No treatment is available.

Rabies Virus

Rabies virus is a single-stranded RNA virus that can infect many mammals. Transmission occurs from the bite of a rabid animal, such as a bat, rodent, or dog, although most domestic animals are immunized against rabies. The bite causes infection of sensory neurons, which spreads to the CNS by axonal transport. Proliferation occurs in the CNS, and the virus travels down the peripheral nerve to the salivary glands, where it can be transmitted by bite. CNS infection causes encephalitis, which can be fatal. Workers at high risk of exposure (e.g., forestry) should receive a killed vaccine for prevention.

Signs & Symptoms

Rabies progresses over several weeks, with patients developing fever, anorexia, confusion, and lethargy. Increased salivation occurs, and patients develop hydrophobia (fear of water) because the throat muscles go into painful spasms when trying to swallow. Symptoms eventually progress to seizures, paralysis, and coma. Death occurs due to vocal cord paralysis and respiratory distress.

Diagnosis

The suspected animal is sacrificed, and brain sections are studied for Negri bodies (cell inclusions) or with antirabies fluorescent antibodies. Infected patients are diagnosed with serology.

Treatment

No treatment is available. Exposed individuals receive a series of rabies immune globulin injections.

Human Immunodeficiency Virus

Human immunodeficiency virus (HIV) is a retrovirus containing single-stranded RNA. It carries reverse transcriptase, an RNA-dependent DNA polymerase, and integrase in its core. The *env* gene encodes gp160, which is cleaved to make the envelope proteins gp120 and gp41. gp120 binds the CD4 receptor, providing its selectivity for T helper cells, and gp41 is involved in fusion with the host cell membrane. The **pol gene** encodes reverse transcriptase, integrase, and protease. The **gag gene** encodes core proteins, of which p24 is the most important and is used in diagnostic tests. The **tat gene** encodes proteins that activate the transcription proteins.

HIV causes **AIDS**, which is associated with an extremely high mortality rate. Transmission occurs by sexual contact, blood, or perinatally. Groups who have been at increased risk of contracting HIV in the United States include homosexual men, IV drug abusers, and hemophiliacs. Around the world, however, HIV infection is seen most commonly in heterosexuals. HIV infection results in the loss of cell-mediated immunity, which predisposes patients to opportunistic infections, lymphoma, and Kaposi's sarcoma.

HIV infections can be prevented through condom use and by not sharing needles. HIV-positive mothers should take zidovudine (AZT) during pregnancy to avoid passing the virus to the fetus. Vaccines are currently being developed but are difficult to produce due to antigenic shifts in the virus.

Signs & Symptoms

The acute phase of HIV infection is associated with fever, lethargy, and lymphadenopathy. Patients are then typically asymptomatic, with normal CD4 counts, although viremia persists. Some patients develop fever, lymphadenopathy, and weight loss with no obvious cause. The late phase of HIV infection (AIDS) is characterized by CD4 counts below 400/mm^3, and patients develop opportunistic infections with agents such as *Pneumocystis carinii*, MAC, and *Candida*.

Diagnosis

Presumptive diagnosis is made by ELISA for antibodies to HIV and HIV proteins. Definitive diagnosis is made by Western blot.

Treatment

HIV-infected individuals are usually given combination therapy with two nucleoside analogues (such as AZT, d4T, and 3TC) and one protease inhibitor (e.g., saquinavir).

Poliovirus

Poliovirus is a single-stranded RNA virus that is transmitted by the fecal-oral route. The virus replicates in the motor neurons of anterior horns in the spinal cord, resulting in motor neuron damage and muscle paralysis.

Widespread vaccination has eradicated poliovirus from the Western hemisphere, although exposure is still common in developing countries. Two vaccines are available. The **Sabin vaccine**, or oral poliovaccine (OPV), is a live, attenuated vaccine that is given orally. It is used commonly in the United States and provides a long-lasting immunity to recipients and contacts through viral shedding. However, this vaccine carries the possibility of viral reversion to wild type, which then causes polio in the recipient. As such, it should not be given to immunocompromised individuals. The **Salk vaccine**, or inactivated polio vaccine (IPV), is a killed vaccine that is injectable.

Signs & Symptoms

The vast majority of infected persons are asymptomatic or develop mild symptoms, such as fever, nausea, and vomiting. Less than 1% go on to develop nonparalytic poliomyelitis, resulting in meningitis, or paralytic poliomyelitis, which leads to muscle paralysis. "Bulbar" poliomyelitis can cause brain stem infection and lead to respiratory paralysis. Exposure as an adult is more likely to lead to symptomatic infection.

Diagnosis

Diagnosis is made with cultures of throat, stool, or CSF. Serology is also useful.

Treatment

No antiviral treatment is available. Physical therapy after infection may limit the extent of disability.

Coxsackievirus

Coxsackievirus is a single-stranded RNA virus that is transmitted by fecal-oral route and respiratory droplets. Infections are more common in the summer and fall. As with poliovirus, it infects the GI tract and travels to the anterior horn motor neurons. Two different types, group A and B, cause different disease entities.

Signs & Symptoms

Group A virus primarily infects skin and mucous membranes, causing fever, sore throat, and tender vesicles in the oropharynx. Children also develop a vesicular rash on the hands and feet, hence the name **hand, foot, and mouth disease**. **Group B** virus infections can cause myocarditis and may be implicated in the development of diabetes mellitus. Both groups can cause mild upper respiratory tract infections.

Diagnosis

Diagnosis is by culture or serology.

Treatment

No treatment is available.

Echoviruses

ECHO stands for enteric cytopathic human orphan viruses. They are single-stranded RNA viruses that are transmitted by the fecal-oral route. The term orphan originally signified that they were not associated with any disease, but it is now thought that echoviruses are the most common cause of **viral meningitis**.

Signs & Symptoms

Echoviruses cause aseptic viral meningitis, upper respiratory tract infections, and diarrhea in infants.

Diagnosis

Cell culture.

Treatment

No treatment is available.

Rhinoviruses

Rhinoviruses are single-stranded RNA viruses that are transmitted by respiratory droplet or from hand contact with the eyes, nose, or mouth. Because they prefer low temperatures, they can infect the nose but are unable to infect the lower respiratory tract. Rhinoviruses cause the common cold, along with adenoviruses, coronaviruses, influenza C virus, and coxsackievirus.

Signs & Symptoms

Symptoms include nasal discharge, fever, sore throat, and headache.

Diagnosis

Clinical diagnosis. Cell cultures from nasal secretions are rare.

Treatment

No treatment is available.

Yellow Fever Virus

Yellow fever virus is a single-stranded RNA virus seen in Africa and South America. There are two types of yellow fever: jungle yellow fever and urban yellow fever. **Jungle yellow fever** is seen in the tropical areas. The reservoir is monkeys, and the vector is the *Haemagogus* mosquito. **Urban yellow fever** has a human reservoir and has the *Aedes aegypti* mosquito as the reservoir. A live, attenuated vaccine is suggested for visitors to endemic areas.

Signs & Symptoms

Yellow fever causes jaundice and fever, accompanied by headache and photophobia. Progression can lead to GI hemorrhage as well as cardiac and renal sequelae.

Diagnosis

Serology or viral culture.

Treatment

No treatment is available.

Dengue Virus

Dengue virus is a single-stranded RNA virus seen in tropical areas, including the Caribbean. The reservoir appears to be humans and other primates, and the vector is the *A. aegypti* mosquito.

Signs & Symptoms

Dengue fever, also known as **breakbone fever**, is characterized by sudden flu-like symptoms accompanied by severe muscle and joint pains. This usually resolves without sequelae. **Dengue hemorrhagic fever**, seen more commonly in South Asia, has the symptoms of breakbone fever, but progresses to GI and skin hemorrhage and shock. It is thought to be caused by immune complex deposition.

Diagnosis

Serology or viral culture.

Treatment

No treatment is available.

Hantavirus

Hantavirus is a single-stranded RNA virus harbored by rodents and transmitted to humans through inhalation of rodent urine and feces. In Europe and Asia, it has been associated with **hemorrhagic fever with renal failure**. In the southwestern states, it is linked to **hantavirus pulmonary syndrome**.

Signs & Symptoms

Hantavirus pulmonary syndrome is characterized by high fever, myalgias, cough, nausea, vomiting, and pulmonary edema. Even with respiratory support, 80% of patients die of the illness.

Treatment

Ribavirin is currently under investigation as a possible treatment.

Double-Stranded RNA Viruses

Rotavirus

Rotavirus is a double-stranded RNA virus that is transmitted via the fecal-oral route. The virus is resistant to stomach acid and is able to infect the small intestine, causing gastroenteritis. Most people are infected in childhood.

Signs & Symptoms

Patients are usually young children who develop nonbloody diarrhea. If fluids are not replaced, this can lead to serious dehydration.

Diagnosis

Diagnosis is made with ELISA or radioimmunoassay of stool sample, or serology.

Treatment

Oral rehydration therapy.

Arboviruses

Arboviruses describe a variety of viruses transmitted by arthropod vector (ArBo = arthropod-borne). Infection in animals or in the arthropod usually does not result in disease, but humans, as accidental hosts, may develop disease. Arboviruses can be classified regionally:

- **Eastern equine encephalitis virus** (EEE) occurs in the Atlantic Coast and Gulf Coast states during summertime. The reservoir is wild birds, and the vector is the *Aedes* mosquito. Humans and horses are accidental hosts that develop severe encephalitis with a high mortality rate. This disease is rare, with less than 10 human cases per year.

- **Western equine encephalitis virus** (WEE) occurs west of the Mississippi. The reservoir is wild birds, and the vector is the *Culex* mosquito. Humans and horses develop a mild encephalitis that is rarely fatal.

- **St. Louis encephalitis virus** is seen in the southern and western United States. The reservoir is wild birds, and the vector is the *Culex* mosquito. The virus can be asymptomatic or cause encephalitis in humans.

- **California encephalitis virus** is seen in the north central states (not California, where it was discovered). The reservoir is small mammals, such as rodents, and the vector is the *Aedes* mosquito. The virus causes a range of symptoms, including (of course) encephalitis, but it is rarely fatal.

- **Colorado tick fever virus** is seen in the Rocky Mountains. The reservoir is wild rodents, and the vector is the *Dermacentor* tick.

Infection in humans cause symptoms such as headache, muscle pain, and fever. This disease is seen in hikers and campers and can be prevented by wearing long sleeves and inspecting skin for tick bites.

Oncogenic Viruses

A number of viruses have been implicated in the development of human cancers. The most commonly associated ones are described here:

- **Human T cell leukemia virus** (HTLV-I and II) preferentially infects CD4 T cells, as HIV does. It causes cutaneous **T-cell lymphoma** and **tropical spastic paraparesis**, an autoimmune disease.

- **HPV** infect squamous epithelium and cause warts. Not all HPV subtypes are associated with cancer development, but HPV-16, -18, and -31 are associated with **cervical** and **penile cancer**.

- **EBV** infects B cells and has been associated with Burkitt's lymphoma in Africa, although cases of **Burkitt's lymphoma** in the United States have not been associated. Nasopharyngeal **carcinoma** in China and **thymic carcinoma** in the United States have also been associated.

- **HSV-2** is seen more commonly in women with cervical cancer, but because both HSV and **cervical cancer** are associated with increased sexual activity, it is unclear whether HSV plays a causative role. In vitro, HSV has shown the ability to transform cells in culture.

- **HBV** and **HCV** are associated with the development of **hepatocellular carcinoma**. Both viruses can cause chronic hepatitis, which may play a role in cancer progression.

- **Human herpesvirus 8** has been detected in **Kaposi's sarcoma** lesions in HIV-infected patients.

Prions

Prions are infectious agents composed only of protein with no nucleic acids. They are highly resistant to heat and chemicals. Prions have been implicated in **Creutzfeldt-Jakob disease** (CJD) and **kuru** in humans as well as **bovine spongiform encephalitis**, or "mad cow" disease, in cattle. CJD is characterized by a spongiform (Swiss-cheese) appearance of brain; patients develop dementia and ataxia, which progress to coma and death. CJD has been transmitted iatrogenically (e.g., during brain surgery or corneal transplant), and kuru has been transmitted through the ingestion of the brains of infected people, done in New Guinea. Kuru patients develop ataxia and tremors but do not develop dementia. **Gerstmann-Straussler-Scheinker syndrome** (GSS) and **Fatal Familial Insomnia** (FFI) are thought to be familial forms of prional diseases. GSS has a long course of illness and is characterized by cerebellar ataxia. FFI does not demonstrate spongiform lesions, but instead is characterized by thalamic atrophy resulting in untreatable insomnia and dysautonomia.

Fungi and Fungal Infections

General Information

Fungi are eukaryotic organisms that have cell walls containing **chitin**, a polymer of *N*-acetylglucosamine. The fungal cell membrane contains **ergosterol** and **zymosterol**, in contrast to animal cells, which contain cholesterol. Fungi can exist as yeasts or molds, but some fungi are **dimorphic**, having the ability to grow as a yeast or mold, depending on environmental conditions.

Yeasts grow as single cells, which reproduce by budding. Some produce **pseudohyphae**, which are buds that do not detach. **Molds** grow as filaments known as **hyphae** and form mats known as mycelium. Septate hyphae form transverse walls and nonseptate hyphae have multinucleate cells. Fungi are typically aerobic. Some fungi reproduce sexually, but most medically important fungi reproduce asexually, forming spores called **conidia**.

The typical host response to fungal infection is a cell-mediated immune response, resulting in granuloma formation. Fungal skin tests are delayed-type hypersensitivity reactions (type IV), but allergies to fungi are mediated by IgE and are type I hypersensitivity reactions.

Laboratory diagnosis is done through microscopy by the identification of characteristic spores and hyphae. Fungal cultures are usually grown on **Sabouraud dextrose agar**, which inhibits bacterial growth. Serology and fungal antigens are also used in diagnosis.

Dermatophytoses

Dermatophytoses are caused by a variety of species, including *Epidermophyton*, *Trichophyton*, and *Microsporum*. These fungi are spread by direct contact and infect superficial structures, such as skin, nails, and hair. **Tinea pedis** (athlete's foot), **tinea cruris** (jock itch), and **tinea corporis** (ringworm) are examples of dermatophytoses.

Signs & Symptoms

Patients develop pruritic papules and vesicles as well as broken hair and thickened nails. Lesions occurring from an allergic response to the infection are known as **dermatophytid** ("id") reactions. These patients develop vesicles on their fingers, although the primary infection is elsewhere.

Diagnosis

Microscopy shows hyphae and conidia. Affected areas fluoresce under UV light.

Treatment

Topical antifungals, such as miconazole, are used. Griseofulvin can be used for severe infections.

Tinea Versicolor

Tinea versicolor is a superficial skin infection caused by *Malassezia furfur* (also known as *Pityrosporum orbiculare*), which occurs frequently in humid climates.

Signs & Symptoms

Patients develop areas of hypopigmentation and scaling on the neck, arms, and upper trunk.

Diagnosis

Microscopy examination of a skin scraping shows hyphae and budding yeast.

Treatment

Topical miconazole.

Sporothrix schenckii

Sporothrix schenckii causes sporotrichosis. The organism grows on vegetation and is transmitted through a thorn prick (classic test question scenario) or other injury.

Signs & Symptoms

Infection causes a localized pustule and lymphadenopathy.

Diagnosis

Microscopy shows cigar-shaped budding yeasts (See Fig. 5-8).

Fig. 5-8 *Sporothrix schenckii* Yeast forms unequal budding.

Treatment

Potassium iodide or itraconazole.

Coccidioides immitis

Coccidioides immitis is a dimorphic fungus that takes the form of a mold in soil but forms spherules within the body. It is present in the soil of the southwestern United States and Latin America. Infection occurs from inhalation of arthrospores, which spread by direct extension or through the circulation to the bone and CNS, where they form granulomatous lesions. People in endemic areas usually have positive skin tests.

Signs & Symptoms

Coccidioidomycosis is a lung infection that is usually asymptomatic but can manifest flulike symptoms, known as **valley fever**. Some people develop arthralgias, and meningitis can develop in immunosuppressed patients. The development of **erythema nodosum**—red, tender nodules on the extensor surfaces of extremities—is due to a delayed-type hypersensitivity response to fungal infection.

Diagnosis

Microscopy of tissue sample shows spherules (See Fig. 5-9). Serology is used for detecting past infection and recovery.

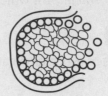

Fig. 5-9 *Coccidioides immitis.*

Treatment

Ketoconazole is given for respiratory symptoms, and amphotericin B is used for disseminated disease.

Histoplasma capsulatum

Histoplasma capsulatum is a dimorphic fungus that forms mold in the soil and yeast in tissue. It is found in the soil in the Ohio and Mississippi River valleys. Infection occurs from inhalation of the spores, which are ingested by macrophages and become yeast. They form granulomas in tissue.

Signs & Symptoms

Histoplasma infection is usually asymptomatic but can also cause pneumonia and produces disseminated disease in infants or the immunocompromised.

Diagnosis

Microscopy shows oval, budding yeast in macrophages (See Fig. 5-10). Cultures and RNA probes are also used.

Fig. 5-10 *Histoplasma capsulatum* in a macrophage.

Treatment

Ketoconazole is given in lung disease and amphotericin B for disseminated disease.

Blastomyces dermatitidis

Blastomyces dermatitidis is a dimorphic fungus that forms mold in the soil and yeast in tissue. It is found in moist soil in both North and South America. Infection occurs from inhalation of the spores.

Signs & Symptoms

Blastomycosis is usually asymptomatic but can form lung granulomas. Disseminated disease causes ulcerated granulomas of the skin and bone.

Diagnosis

Microscopy shows thick-walled yeast with a broad-based bud (See Fig. 5-11). Cultures grow hyphae with conidia. Serology is not performed.

Fig. 5-11 *Blastomyces dermatitidis.*

Treatment

Ketoconazole.

Paracoccidioides brasiliensis

Paracoccidioides brasiliensis is a dimorphic fungus that forms mold in the soil and yeast in tissue. It is found in the soil in South America. Infection occurs from inhalation of the spores.

Signs & Symptoms

Paracoccidioidomycosis is usually asymptomatic but may cause oral lesions, lymphadenopathy, and widespread dissemination.

Diagnosis

Microscopy shows a thick-walled yeast with multiple buds (See Fig. 5.12). Serology is also useful.

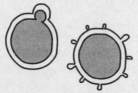

Fig. 5-12 *Paracoccidioides brasiliensis.*

Treatment

Itraconazole or ketoconazole.

Opportunistic Mycoses

Candida albicans

Candida albicans is part of the normal flora of the upper respiratory tract, GI tract, and female genital tract. Candidal overgrowth can occur normally, but diabetics and persons taking antibiotics are predisposed to overgrowth. Candidiasis also occurs commonly in immunosuppressed patients.

Signs & Symptoms

Thrush occurs in the mouth, forming white patches that cannot be easily scraped off. Candidal overgrowth can also cause vaginitis, diaper rash, and intertrigo in skin folds. Immunosuppressed patients can develop esophageal or disseminated candidiasis, and IV drug users can develop endocarditis.

Diagnosis

Microscopy shows budding yeasts and pseudohyphae (See Fig. 5-13).

Fig. 5-13 *Candida albicans.*

Treatment

Mucous membrane infection is treated with fluconazole or ketoconazole. Skin infections are treated with topical antifungal agents.

Cryptococcus neoformans

Cryptococcus neoformans is an encapsulated, oval, budding yeast that grows in soil contaminated with pigeon droppings. Infection occurs from inhalation of the yeast cells.

Signs & Symptoms

Cryptococcosis is usually asymptomatic but can cause pneumonia or meningitis. Immunocompromised persons develop disseminated disease.

Diagnosis

Microscopy; India ink stain reveals yeast with wide unstained area caused by the capsule (See Fig. 5-14). CSF cultures and serology are also performed.

Fig. 5-14 *Cryptococcus neoformans.*

Treatment

Amphotericin B and flucytosine are used to treat meningitis. Fluconazole is given to AIDS patients for long-term meningitis prophylaxis.

Aspergillus fumigatus

Aspergillus fumigatus is a mold that grows on decaying vegetation. Infection occurs by inhalation or contact with airborne spores.

Signs & Symptoms

A. fumigatus can infect wounds and burns, especially in immunocompromised patients. It can infect the lungs and form a fungal ball known as an **aspergilloma**, which causes hemoptysis. Patients can also develop **allergic bronchopulmonary aspergillosis**, which causes asthmatic symptoms.

Diagnosis

Microscopic examination shows septate, branching hyphae (See Fig. 5-15).

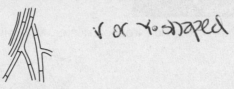

Fig. 5-15 *Aspergillus fumigatus.*

Treatment

Amphotericin B and surgical debridement.

Mucor and Rhizopus

Mucor and *Rhizopus* are molds that are found widely in soil. Infection occurs from inhalation of spores.

Signs & Symptoms

These fungi cause invasive infection in immunocompromised patients, especially persons with diabetic ketoacidosis and burns. Proliferation in the endothelium of sinuses and lungs causes severe tissue necrosis.

Diagnosis

Microscopy shows nonseptate hyphae with right-angle branches (See Fig. 5-16).

Fig. 5-16 *Mucor and Rhizopus spp.*

Treatment

Amphotericin B and surgical debridement.

Parasites

Entamoeba histolytica

Entamoeba histolytica exists in two forms. The **trophozoite** form is motile and exists in lesions and diarrheal stool. **Nonmotile cysts** are found in nondiarrheal stool. Transmission is fecal-oral. Ingestion of the cysts causes colonization of the colon, which can invade through the gut wall and enter the portal circulation, resulting in liver abscesses.

Signs & Symptoms

The vast majority of infected persons are asymptomatic, although the cysts are still shed in the feces. Some develop **amebic dysentery** with bloody, mucus-containing diarrhea. Liver abscesses cause right upper quadrant pain, weight loss, and fever.

Diagnosis

Stool samples show trophozoites or cysts with four nuclei (See Fig. 5-17).

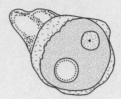

Fig. 5-17 *Entamoeba histolytica* trophozite with one ingested blood cell and one nucleus.

Treatment

Metronidazole and iodoquinol.

Giardia lamblia

Giardia lamblia exists in two forms. The **trophozoite** has a suction disk for attachment to the intestinal wall. **Nonmotile cysts** are found in stool. This is found in wild mammals and humans, and transmission is fecal-oral. The classic case of *Giardia* is a hiker who drinks stream water that is contaminated with infected animal feces.

Signs & Symptoms

Giardiasis causes a foul-smelling, greasy, nonbloody diarrhea. Symptoms can last for several weeks.

Diagnosis

Pear-shaped, flagellated trophozoites and cysts are found in stool. The "string" test is performed by having the patient swallow a string and removing it, with trophozoites adhering to the string.

Treatment

Metronidazole.

Trichomonas vaginalis

Trichomonas vaginalis resides in the human vagina and prostate and is transmitted by sexual contact. Condom use can prevent transmission.

Signs & Symptoms

In women, trichomoniasis causes a thin, malodorous (fishy-smelling), frothy discharge with pruritus. Men may be asymptomatic or can develop urethritis.

Diagnosis

Wet mount of discharge shows motile, pear-shaped, flagellated trophozoites (See Fig. 5-18).

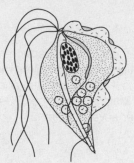

Fig. 5-18 *Trichomonas vaginalis* trophozoite.

Treatment

Metronidazole. Both partners must be treated to prevent reinfection.

Cryptosporidium parvum

Cryptosporidium parvum is transmitted by the fecal-oral route and is a concern in immunocompromised patients because water supplies can become contaminated despite chlorination. The **oocytes** attach themselves to the small intestine and release **trophozoites**, which then become **schizonts** and **merozoites**. The latter make **microgametes** and **macrogametes**, which unite to make an oocyte.

Signs & Symptoms

Cryptosporidiosis causes a copious, watery **diarrhea**, which is more persistent in immunocompromised patients.

Diagnosis

Acid-fast stain of stool sample reveals oocytes.

Treatment

No treatment is available.

Plasmodium Species

Plasmodium species that cause infection in humans are *P. vivax, P. ovale, P. malariae*, and *P. falciparum*. They have a complicated life cycle, with a sexual stage in the *Anopheles* mosquito as vectors and an asexual stage in humans. Briefly, **sporozoites** are introduced into the human bloodstream by mosquito bite and are quickly taken into the hepatocytes, where they infect RBCs and differentiate into **gametocytes**. These are then ingested by the mosquito in a blood meal and reproduce sexually within the mosquito, forming sporozoites. Symptoms occur as the RBCs rupture, which occurs every 72 hours with *P. malariae* and every 48 hours with the other *Plasmodium* species.

Malaria is a global public health problem, causing more than a million deaths per year in developing countries. **Chloroquine resistance** is widespread in southeast

Asia, South America, and East Africa. Mefloquine (Lariam) prophylaxis is recommended for people traveling to endemic areas, but reports of neurologic and psychiatric symptoms in mefloquine users has kept some people from taking the drug.

Signs & Symptoms

Malaria causes abrupt fever, chills, and headaches a few weeks after infection, with a spiking fever pattern. Patients develop splenomegaly, hepatomegaly, and anemia. *P. falciparum* causes the most severe disease and can be life-threatening due to brain and kidney damage. Malaria from other *Plasmodium* species is self-limited but can still cause relapses after several years.

Diagnosis

Microscopy of blood smear shows crescent-shaped or spherical gametes within the blood cells (See Fig. 5-19).

A   B

Fig. 5-19 A. *Plasmodium vivax* signet-ring trophozoite within a red blood cell.
B. *P. vivax* ameboid trophozoite within a red blood cell, with Schüffner's dots.

Treatment

If sensitive, chloroquine is used. Otherwise, mefloquine or quinine plus pyrimethamine-sulfadoxine is used for chloroquine-resistant strains. Primaquine is used to rid the liver of hypnozoites from *P. vivax* and *P. ovale*.

Toxoplasma gondii

Toxoplasma gondii results from eating infected meat or exposure to cat feces that carry *Toxoplasma gondii* cysts. Persistent asymptomatic infection can occur in the cells of brain, muscle, and liver, which can cause disease again when the host is immunocompromised. Transplacental transmission can occur if primary infection occurs during pregnancy. Disease can be prevented by properly cooking meat and avoiding cat litter boxes if pregnant or immunocompromised.

Signs & Symptoms

Toxoplasmosis is usually asymptomatic or causes flulike symptoms. In immunosuppressed patients, the disease can disseminate and cause brain abscesses or encephalitis. Congenital infection can cause growth retardation, seizures, and blindness.

Diagnosis

Serology is used to determine previous or current exposure. Otherwise, biopsy of the affected tissue shows cysts within the cells.

Treatment

Sulfadiazine and pyrimethamine.

Trypanosoma cruzi

Trypanosoma cruzi has two life cycles. The first cycle is within the **reduviid bug**, also known as a kissing bug, in which the insect ingests **trypomastigotes** from a blood meal, which undergo multiplication within the bug and are shed in its feces. If the feces are shed on a host, the trypomastigotes can enter the host's bloodstream by being scratched into the site of a bite or rubbed into a mucous membrane, especially the eyes. They then transform into **amastigotes** and reside in cardiac tissue, glial tissue, and esophageal tissue. Further conversion to trypomastigotes in the bloodstream allows the organism to be spread by the next bug bite. The disease is typically found in Central and South America but is occasionally found in the southern United States.

Signs & Symptoms

T. cruzi causes **Chagas' disease** (American trypanosomiasis). During acute infection, patients develop an edematous **chagoma** at the site of the bite. This progresses to lymphadenopathy, fever, and hepatosplenomegaly. If the feces are rubbed into the eyes, edema of the eyes ensues (called Romaña's sign). Chronic disease is rare and leads to myocarditis and neuronal injury resulting in loss of muscle tone in the colon and esophagus, causing megacolon or mega-esophagus. Death usually occurs from cardiac complications.

Diagnosis

Blood smear, bone marrow, or muscle biopsy reveals the organism (See Fig. 5-20). Serology is also performed.

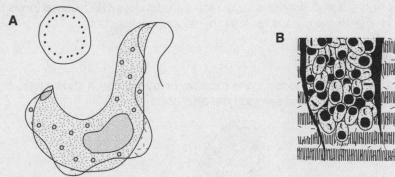

Fig. 5-20 A. *Trypanosoma cruzi* trypomastigote in human blood.
      B. *T. cruzi* amastigotes found in cardiac muscle.

Treatment

Nifurtimox.

Trypanosoma brucei gambiense and Trypanosoma brucei rhodesiense

Trypanosoma brucei gambiense and *T. brucei rhodesiense* have two life cycles. The first cycle occurs in the **tsetse fly**, in which the insect ingests **trypomastigotes** from a blood meal. These multiply in the tsetse fly and infect the host through the insect's saliva at the time of a bite. The organism then infects locally, in the bloodstream, and in the CNS. The organism evades the host immune system by repeatedly varying its surface antigens through **variant surface glycoproteins** (VSGs). The disease is found in Africa.

Signs & Symptoms

African trypanosomiasis causes **sleeping sickness**. Disease from *T. brucei gambiense* is low grade and chronic, but disease from *T. brucei rhodesiense* is rapidly progressive. Patients develop a chancre at the site of the bite, followed by headache and somnolence, which leads to coma and death. **Winterbottom's sign**, or posterior cervical lymphadenopathy, is a common finding.

Diagnosis

Blood and CSF examination shows the organism. Serology is useful in acute infection.

Treatment

Suramin and melarsoprol.

Leishmania donovani

Leishmania donovani has two life cycles. The first cycle in the **sandfly** occurs during ingestion from a blood meal. The organism undergoes multiplication within the bug and is shed in its saliva during a bite. The organism infects the macrophages and reticuloendothelial system, including the spleen, liver, and bone marrow. The disease is found in Asia and Africa.

Signs & Symptoms

Visceral leishmaniasis, or **kala-azar**, causes periodic fevers, weakness, pancytopenia, weight loss, and hepatosplenomegaly. Months later, hyperpigmentation of the extremities and a warty, ulcerative facial rash can develop. The disease tends to be chronic and, if untreated, leads to death by secondary infection.

Diagnosis

Microscopy of the lymph nodes, bone marrow, or spleen tissue shows amastigotes (See Fig. 5.21). Cultures and serology are also done.

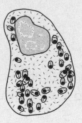

Fig. 5-21 *Leishmania donovani* amastigotes within splenic macrophages.

Treatment

Sodium stibogluconate.

Leishmania braziliensis, L. mexicana, and L. tropica

The life cycle of these organisms is similar to that of *Leishmania donovani*, and the vector is the **sandfly**. However, the infection is limited to the skin and mucous membranes. *L. braziliensis* and *L. mexicana* are found in South America, whereas *L. tropica* is seen in Asia and Africa.

Signs & Symptoms

L. braziliensis causes **espundia**, a mucocutaneous disease that forms ulcers at the bite site and spreads to the nose and mouth, where it can cause total destruction of the nasal cartilage. *L. mexicana* and *L. tropica* cause a localized ulcer and rash at the site of the bite.

Diagnosis

Microscopy of the skin lesion shows amastigotes.

Treatment

Sodium stibogluconate.

Pneumocystis carinii

Although *Pneumocystis carinii* is genetically a fungus, it is considered a parasite because it does not grow on fungal media and is not treated with antifungals. *P. carinii* cysts are ubiquitous in the environment, and transmission occurs by cyst inhalation. Most people are infected during childhood but are asymptomatic and carry the cysts in their lungs until they trigger infection when patients are in an immunocompromised state. HIV-infected patients are placed on TMP/SMX as prophylaxis against *Pneumocystis* infection.

Signs & Symptoms

P. carinii pneumonia (PCP) is common in immunocompromised patients. It is characterized by sudden fever, cough, and dyspnea with bilateral rales and rhonchi.

Diagnosis

Chest X-ray shows a diffuse interstitial infiltrate. Sputum sample from bronchial lavage shows cysts with sporozoites (which appear boat-shaped).

Treatment

TMP/SMX. Pentamidine is used in sulfa-allergic patients.

Cestodes

Taenia solium

Taenia solium is a species of tapeworm that causes disease through the ingestion of undercooked pork. The pig ingests food that has been fecally contaminated with *T. solium* eggs. These form **cysticerci**, larvae that invade muscle tissue (meat), CNS, and the gut. Once in the gut, the cysticerci form worms that release the segmented body parts (**proglottids**) full of eggs.

Signs & Symptoms

Taeniasis or intestinal tapeworm, can be asymptomatic or cause diarrhea and anorexia. It results from eating undercooked pork that contain cysticerci. Disseminated disease is called **cysticercosis** and causes space-occupying lesions in the brain and eyes. It is due to ingestion of eggs (fecal-oral).

Diagnosis

Stool sample shows gravid proglottids with five to ten uterine branches. Cysticerci may be seen on CT scan or X-ray, if calcified.

Treatment

Niclosamide is used for intestinal infection. Cysticercosis is treated with praziquantel or albendazole.

Taenia saginata

Taenia saginata is similar to *T. solium*, except transmission occurs by ingestion of undercooked beef. *T. saginata* does not cause disseminated disease to the CNS.

Signs & Symptoms

T. saginata is asymptomatic or causes postprandial nausea.

Diagnosis

Stool sample shows gravid proglottids with 15–25 uterine branches.

Treatment

Niclosamide.

Diphyllobothrium latum

Diphyllobothrium latum is ingested in raw fish. Patients who harbor *D. latum* can develop **vitamin B$_{12}$ deficiency** because the worm preferentially absorbs it, causing megaloblastic anemia. The fish ingest the larvae or other fish (who have already ingested the larvae). These are ingested by the host, and the tapeworm resides in the small intestine, shedding eggs in proglottids, which eventually contaminate the water and form larvae. *D. latum* can be killed if the infected fish is cooked adequately.

Signs & Symptoms

Diphyllobothriasis is usually asymptomatic but may cause diarrhea.

Diagnosis

Stool sample reveals oval eggs with operculae (small "lids").

Treatment

Niclosamide.

Echinococcus granulosus

Echinococcus granulosus is a parasite of dogs, and humans are a dead-end host. Infected dogs shed the eggs in their feces and humans ingest them through fecal contamination. The larvae hatch in the small intestine and produce cysts in the liver, lung, and brain. *E. granulosus* is endemic to the Mediterranean, Middle East, and western United States.

Signs & Symptoms

Hydatid cysts form in the liver, lung, and CNS. Hypersensitivity can develop due to continual exposure, which can cause anaphylaxis if the cyst ruptures.

Diagnosis

Microscopy of affected tissue and serology.

Treatment

Careful surgical removal of the cyst and treatment with albendazole. The organisms are killed before removal to prevent possible rupture.

Trematodes *praxi or mebendzole*

Schistosoma mansoni and *Schistosoma japonicum*

Schistosomes are blood flukes transmitted by swimming in infected water. Free-swimming **cercaria** penetrate the skin and enter the portal circulation to the liver, where they mature into adults. These then travel through the mesenteric veins into the gut lumen and shed eggs into the feces. The eggs then have a cycle in snails before producing cercaria into the water. *Schistosoma mansoni* is seen in Central and South America, and *S. japonicum* is seen in southeast Asia and Japan. Infection can be prevented by proper waste disposal and avoiding swimming in endemic areas.

Signs & Symptoms

Schistosomiasis is usually asymptomatic or causes pruritus and rash soon after infection. This is followed by fever, chills, and diarrhea. Patients develop a granulo-matous response to the eggs, causing hepatosplenomegaly, portal hypertension, and GI hemorrhage through varices.

Diagnosis

Stool sample reveals eggs with large or small lateral spine (See Fig. 5.22).

Fig. 5-22 *Schistosoma mansoni* ovum with lateral spine.

Treatment

Praziquantel.

Schistosoma haematobium

The life cycle of *Schistosoma haematobium* is similar to that of the other schistosomes, but the adult organism resides in the venous plexus of the bladder and is excreted in the urine. It is endemic to Africa and the Middle East. It is associated with the development of **squamous cell bladder carcinoma**.

Signs & Symptoms

Patients may experience **hematuria** and develop obstructive symptoms if there are too many eggs in the urethra.

Diagnosis

Urine sample shows eggs with a large terminal spine (See Fig. 5-23). X-rays may show calcification of the bladder.

Fig. 5-23 *Schistosoma haematobium* ovum with terminal spine.

Treatment

Praziquantel.

Clonorchis sinensis

Clonorchis sinensis, the Oriental liver fluke, is contracted by ingesting raw fish. The larvae hatch into the small intestine and mature in the bile duct. Eggs are passed into the feces, where they contaminate the water in which the fish live. Snails act as intermediate hosts before the organism encysts onto fish scales and enters the fish muscle. *C. sinensis* is endemic to Japan, China, and southeast Asia. *Clonorchis* infection has been associated with the development of cholangiocarcinoma.

Signs & Symptoms

Clonorchiasis is usually asymptomatic but can cause abdominal pain and hepatomegaly.

Diagnosis

Stool sample shows eggs with operculae.

Treatment

Praziquantel.

Paragonimus westermani

Paragonimus westermani, the lung fluke, is ingested in undercooked crabmeat. The worms hatch in the small intestine and travel to the lung. Eggs are present in sputum and are coughed up or swallowed and shed in feces, where they contaminate water. Snails act as intermediate hosts before the organism encysts onto crabs and enters the meat.

Signs & Symptoms

Paragonimiasis causes a **chronic cough** with bloody sputum, which is similar to tuberculosis.

Diagnosis

Microscopy shows operculated eggs in the sputum or feces.

Treatment

Praziquantel.

Enterobius vermicularis

Enterobius vermicularis causes **pinworm** infection, which usually affects children. The eggs are picked up on the hands and ingested. The eggs mature into worms in the colon and migrate to the perianal area, where they lay eggs that are picked up by direct contact.

Signs & Symptoms

Pinworm causes perianal pruritus.

Diagnosis

Cellophane tape on the perianal region collects eggs, which can be examined microscopically. Worms can be found in the stool.

Treatment

Mebendazole. Reinfection is common.

Trichuris trichiura

Trichuris trichiura, or whipworm, is transmitted via the fecal-oral route. Eggs are ingested from contaminated food or soil, and they hatch and mature in the small intestine. Eggs are then passed in the feces. The disease occurs in tropical areas and in the southern United States.

Signs & Symptoms

Whipworm infection is usually asymptomatic but it can cause diarrhea and prolapsed rectum.

Diagnosis

Stool sample shows barrel-shaped eggs with plugged ends.

Treatment

Mebendazole.

Ascaris lumbricoides

Ascaris lumbricoides is ingested in contaminated food and travels through the gut wall into the bloodstream to the lungs and heart. In the lungs, the organism is coughed up and swallowed and eventually settles in the small intestine. Eggs are then shed in the feces. The disease occurs in tropical areas and in the southern United States.

Signs & Symptoms

Ascariasis is usually asymptomatic, but a heavy worm burden can cause malnutrition. Lung infection causes fever and cough.

Diagnosis

Stool sample reveals oval eggs and occasionally worms.

Treatment

Mebendazole or pyrantel pamoate.

Ancylostoma duodenale **and** *Necator americanus*

Ancylostoma duodenale and *Necator americanus* cause **hookworm**. Contaminated soil carries larvae that enter through the skin and migrate to the lungs, where they are coughed up and swallowed. Maturation occurs in the small intestine and eggs are shed in the feces, where they hatch in moist soil. *A. duodenale* is seen in Africa and Asia, whereas *N. americanus* is seen in tropical areas of South America and the southern United States. Infection can be prevented by wearing shoes.

Signs & Symptoms

Hookworm causes a pruritic papule at the site of infection. Lung infection can cause pneumonia. While the hookworm is in the small intestine, it secretes an anticoagulation factor that causes blood loss and subsequent anemia.

Diagnosis

Stool sample shows eggs and blood cells.

Treatment

Mebendazole or pyrantel pamoate.

Strongyloides stercoralis

Strongyloides stercoralis has two life cycles. It has a free-living cycle in the soil, during which **filariform larvae** can penetrate the skin. It travels into the bloodstream to the lungs, where it is coughed up and swallowed. **Rhabditiform larvae** then develop in the small intestines and are shed in the feces. Disease occurs mainly in the tropics and in the southeastern United States. Autoinfection may occur, when larvae penetrate the gut wall and enter the bloodstream to travel to the lungs. Wearing shoes can prevent infection.

Signs & Symptoms

Strongyloidiasis is usually asymptomatic but causes a pruritic papule at the entry site. Lung infection can cause pneumonia, and gut irritation may cause watery diarrhea. Autoinfection can lead to sepsis from the coentry of enteric bacteria and is especially dangerous in immunocompromised patients.

Diagnosis

Laboratory tests show eosinophilia. Stool sample shows larvae.

Treatment

Thiabendazole.

Trichinella spiralis

Trichinella spiralis is ingested in undercooked pork. The calcified larvae are present in pig muscle, which is ingested, and then they live in the small intestine. **Larvae** are hatched and then migrate to the heart, CNS, and striated muscle. Humans are a dead-end host. The disease can be prevented by not feeding pigs undercooked infected meat.

Signs & Symptoms

Trichinosis causes gastroenteritis followed by fever, muscle pain, and periorbital edema. Cardiac and CNS infection can result in granuloma formation.

Diagnosis

Laboratory tests show eosinophilia. Muscle biopsy shows encysted larvae in cells. Serology is also useful.

Treatment

Thiabendazole or mebendazole.

Wuchereria bancrofti and *Brugia malayi*

Wuchereria bancrofti and *Brugia malayi* are transmitted by the *Anopheles* and *Culex* mosquito. The mosquito deposits larvae during a bite, which then enter the lymphatic system. The larvae mature in the lymph nodes and produce **microfilariae**, which enter the bloodstream and are ingested by a biting mosquito. *W. bancrofti* infection occurs in Africa, South America, and southeast Asia while *B. malayi* is found in Malaysia.

Signs & Symptoms

Filariasis causes inflammation of the lymphatic system, leading to obstruction and edema. Persistent and severe infection causes massive lymphatic obstruction, resulting in **elephantiasis**, usually of the lower extremity and scrotum.

Diagnosis

Blood smears taken at night show microfilariae.

Treatment

Diethylcarbamazine kills microfilariae.

Onchocerca volvulus

Onchocerca volvulus is transmitted by the **blackfly**, which leaves the organism in subcutaneous tissue after a bite. The organisms develop into nodules and spread throughout the subcutaneous tissue, where they are taken up by other biting blackflies. These organisms do not enter the bloodstream, although lesions close to the eye may cause infection and blindness. Most disease is found along rivers in Africa and Central America.

Signs & Symptoms

Onchocerciasis causes a pruritic papule and subsequent nodule development. **"River blindness"** occurs when microfilariae concentrate in retina, cornea, and conjunctiva.

Diagnosis

Skin biopsy reveals microfilariae.

Treatment

Ivermectin. Suramin is used in ocular lesions.

Loa loa

Loa loa is transmitted by the **deerfly** (*Chrysops*), which deposits larvae into the subcutaneous tissues during a bite. The organism spreads to the eyes and the bloodstream during the daytime, when it is ingested by a biting deerfly. It is seen in Africa.

Signs & Symptoms

Loiasis causes transient, nonerythematous swellings on the extremities called **Calabar swellings**. Adult worms may be seen crawling across the conjunctiva.

Diagnosis

Blood smear shows microfilariae.

Treatment

Diethylcarbamazine.

Dracunculus medinensis

Dracunculus medinensis infection is transmitted by **copepods**, tiny crustaceans that can be found in contaminated drinking water. Once ingested, the larvae penetrate the small intestine and enter the subcutaneous tissue, where they travel to the lower extremities and mature. The adults live in the skin but create ulcers for the larvae to pop out of the skin and into the water, where they are ingested by copepods. Disease occurs in Africa, the Middle East, and India, and can be prevented by boiling drinking water.

Signs & Symptoms

Dracunculiasis causes skin ulceration and pruritus at the exit site.

Diagnosis

The head of the adult worm can be visualized in the ulcer.

Treatment

The worm is slowly wound out on a stick over several days. Niridazole or metronidazole may make this easier.

Toxocara canis

Toxocara canis infection occurs in dogs. Eggs are present in infected dog feces, which are ingested by humans. These hatch larvae that enter the small intestine and travel to the liver, CNS, eyes, and other organs. Humans are dead-end hosts. Infection control is performed by treatment of infected dogs.

Signs & Symptoms

T. canis produces **visceral larva migrans**, a creeping eruption caused by granulomatous hypersensitivity to the larvae. It can also cause blindness and encephalitis.

Diagnosis

Serology or tissue microscopy to visualize larvae.

Treatment

Thiabenzadole and steroids.

CHAPTER 6

Immunology

Immunity

Immunity is the ability of the body to limit or block infections. It can be subdivided into two categories: **innate immunity** and **acquired immunity**. Innate immunity is nonspecific and does not require prior contact with an antigen. It includes barrier defenses (skin, mucous membranes, cilia, normal flora), cells (NK cells, phagocytes), and proteins (lysozymes in secretions, interferons, complement). Acquired immunity is specific and requires contact with foreign antigens.

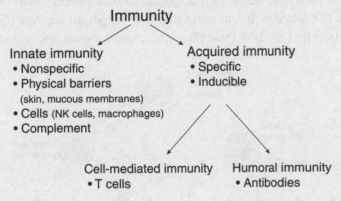

Fig. 6-1. Types of immunity.

Acquired immunity can be classified into two types, depending on whether it is B- or T-cell mediated:

- **Cell-mediated immunity** relies on the activation of T cells. Cell-mediated responses (e.g., delayed hypersensitivity, lymphokine production, cytotoxicity) are directed against
  - Viruses
  - Mycobacteria
  - Fungi
  - Parasites

- Tumors

- Organ transplants

- **Humoral immunity** is mediated by antibody-producing B cells. These antibodies **opsonize** (cover) microorganisms to target them for phagocytosis and neutralize antigens by binding to bacterial and viral receptors. Humoral immunity is directed primarily against the following:

  - Toxin-induced diseases, such as toxic shock syndrome

  - Polysaccharide-encapsulated microorganisms, such as pneumococci

  - Some viruses

Humoral immunity can be **active**, in which the host actively produces an immune response, or **passive**, in which preformed antibodies are transferred to the host. Passive immunity can occur naturally (transplacental transfer of maternal IgG to the fetus) or through injections of preformed antibodies. The advantage of active immunity is that resistance is long term, but it is slow in onset. Passive immunity confers fast availability of antibody, but the antibodies are short lived.

Cells of the Immune System

All blood cells differentiate from pluripotent hematopoietic stem cells, guided by cytokines that stimulate differentiation into the **lymphoid lineage** (lymphocytes) or the **myeloid lineage** (erythrocytes, platelets, granulocytes, and monocytes).

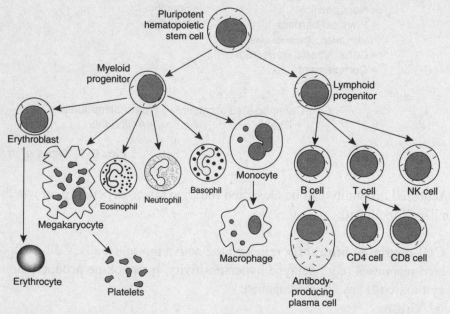

Fig. 6-2 Differentiation of the cells of the immune system. (NK=natural killers)

Granulocytes encompass the three types of polymorphonuclear leukocytes, which differentiate into **neutrophils, eosinophils,** and **basophils** under the regulation of several colony-stimulating factors (CSFs). Approximately 60% of white blood cells are **neutrophils**, and **eosinophils** and **basophils** are minor components (5%). Another 5% of white blood cells are **monocytes**, which also descend from the myeloid lineage. The remaining 30% of white blood cells are **lymphocytes**, which descend from the lymphoid lineage. The ratio of T cells to B cells is approximately 3:1, and natural killer (NK) cells comprise a minor fraction.

Monocytes, macrophages, dendritic cells, and Langerhans' cells are termed **accessory** cells because they facilitate the generation of an immune response through antigen presentation. B cells may also act as antigen-presenting cells, thereby serving an accessory function.

Mononuclear Phagocytes

As the name implies, mononuclear phagocytes have a single nucleus, and their primary function is phagocytosis (i.e., they engulf foreign things). Mononuclear phagocytes first differentiate into **monocytes**, which travel through the blood and migrate into tissues to become **macrophages**. Macrophages have different names according to their location in the tissue. Liver macrophages are called **Kupffer cells**, in the lung they are **alveolar macrophages**, in the central nervous system they are **microglia**, and in connective tissue they are **histiocytes**.

Macrophages function as the principal "scavenger cells" of the body. They have three important functions:

- Phagocytosis

- Antigen presentation

- Cytokine production

Stimulation by interferon-γ (IFN-γ) and other T cell–derived factors up-regulates macrophage function, including release of interleukin 1 (IL-1), which mediates fever and the release of IFN, tumor necrosis factor (TNF), and growth-promoting factors for lymphoid and other cells. Both monocytes and macrophages serve as antigen-presenting cells. Bacteria, viruses, and other foreign particles ingested by phagocytosis are degraded by lysosomal enzymes, and their peptides are presented on MHC class II proteins to CD4 T cells.

Interdigitating dendritic cells are thought to arise from marrow precursors and are related in lineage to mononuclear phagocytes. They are present in the interstitium of most organs, are abundant in T cell–rich areas of lymph nodes and spleen, and are scattered throughout the epidermis of the skin, where they are called **Langerhans' cells**. They are extremely efficient at presenting antigen to CD4 T cells.

Granulocytes

Granulocytes contain abundant lysosomes and cytoplasmic granules of collagenases, proteases, nucleases, lipases, and gelatinases, which facilitate the killing of microorganisms. These cells are also referred to as *inflammatory cells* because they play important roles in inflammation and innate immunity. However, like macrophages, granulocytes are stimulated by T cell–derived cytokines and function mainly as phagocytic cells, engulfing bacteria and other opsonized particles.

Neutrophils are the first leukocytes to arrive at the scene of an injury. They can be activated by cytokines to phagocytose and destroy foreign particles and respond rapidly to chemotactic factors, such as C5a, to migrate to the site of infection.

Eosinophils leave the circulation and reside in areas exposed to the external environment, such as skin, mucosa of the bronchi, and gastrointestinal (GI) tract. They express IgE receptors and bind avidly to IgE-coated particles. Eosinophils are abundant at sites of type I immediate hypersensitivity reactions and are particularly effective at destroying infectious agents, such as helminthic parasites that stimulate the production of IgE.

Basophils also express high-affinity receptors for IgE. When IgE-antigen complexes are bound, the basophilic granules release heparin, histamine, platelet-activating factor, and other allergic mediators.

Lymphocytes

Lymphocytes are responsible for the specificity of the immune response. **Cytotoxic T cells, helper T cells,** and **B cells** form antigen-specific memory cells, which are quickly ready for action when re-exposed to the same antigen.

T-Lymphocytes

The progenitors of T-lymphocytes wander from bone marrow to **thymus**, where T cells are produced throughout life. During passage through the thymus these progenitors differentiate into immunocompetent T cells expressing **CD3** and a unique **T-cell receptor (TCR)**. The TCR is formed by somatic gene rearrangement (in other words, DNA splicing) to produce a diverse range of receptors, such that each T cell has a unique receptor on its surface. T cells recognize foreign protein antigens associated with MHC molecules using their TCR. Activated T cells reproduce themselves to yield large numbers of cells specific to a particular antigen.

Mature T cells can be divided into two main categories based on expression of the CD4 or CD8 surface molecules. Regulatory functions, such as IL production, are mediated primarily by **helper T cells**, which express the CD4 surface molecule. CD4 cells predominate in the thymic medulla, tonsils, and blood. Other functions, such as killing of virus-infected cells, tumor cells, and allografts, are carried out primarily by **cytotoxic T cells**, which express the CD8 surface molecule. CD8 lymphocytes kill either by the release of perforins, which poke holes in cell membranes, or by the induction of programmed cell death (apoptosis). CD8 cells predominate in the bone marrow and gut lymphoid tissue.

B-Lymphocytes

B-lymphoid progenitors mature in the bone marrow before migrating to peripheral lymphoid tissue, where they develop into antibody-producing plasma cells.

The surface receptor of a B cell is a unique immunoglobulin (either IgM or IgD) that is able to bind different types of foreign antigen. Antigen binding stimulates B-cell proliferation and differentiation into clones of plasma cells, which synthesize and secrete antibody with the same antigenic specificity as that carried by the selected B cell. Plasma cells secrete thousands of antibody molecules per second for a few days and then die. Some of these stimulated B cells form **memory cells**, which can hibernate for long periods but respond rapidly on re-exposure to the same antigen. That is why antibody appears so quickly in the secondary response.

B cells also have a separate function as important antigen-presenting cells. Processed peptide antigens bind to class I and class II histocompatibility proteins (HLAs) and are presented to the TCRs of CD8+ and CD4+ T-lymphocytes, respectively.

Natural Killer Cells

NK cells develop from a lymphoid progenitor but lack the specific cell surface markers of T- or B-lymphocytes. They are large granular lymphocytes that play an important role in innate immunity by killing tumor cells and virus-infected cells, and they may also have an important role in recognition of "self" cells. They are called natural killer cells because they are nonspecific and noninducible and they have no immunologic memory. NK cells kill their target cells by secreting cytotoxins similar to those of cytotoxic T cells. Unlike T cells, however, they do not require simultaneous recognition of self MHC proteins for killing. They are also able to destroy antibody-coated target cells by a process called **antibody-dependent cellular cytotoxicity**.

Major Histocompatibility Complex

Secondary response: memory B cells, stronger antibodies

The **major histocompatibility complex (MHC)** is key in the development of acquired immunity. The principal products of the human major histocompatibility complex (MHC) are the **human leukocyte antigens (HLAs)**, which are glycoproteins found on the surface of most cells of the body. T-lymphocytes recognize foreign polypeptide antigens only when they are stuck to an HLA of a self antigen–presenting cell (e.g., macrophage), a phenomenon known as **MHC restriction.**

The human MHC locus is on the short arm of chromosome 6. There are three genes at the class I locus (HLA-A, -B, -C), and three genes at the class II locus (HLA-DP, -DQ, -DR). Between the class I and class II gene loci is a third locus, called class III, which contains genes for some complement components and cytokines expressed in cases of severe illness. The HLA genes are **codominantly** expressed. Therefore, each cell expresses genes from both the paternal and the maternal chromosome, leading to a maximum of six different class I and at least six different class II proteins. (Because class II proteins are made of separate a and b chains, and because a maternal a chain in some cases could pair with a paternal b chain and vice versa, the number of MHC class II proteins is probably greater.) The combination of HLA genes inherited from each parent is known as an **HLA haplotype**. There are many different alleles of the class I and II genes in the population, which encode many unique HLA molecules that can bind just about any antigen. The HLA system then helps to present these antigens to the T-cell receptor (TCR). Transplant donors and recipients must be matched for their HLA antigens to avoid cell-mediated rejection, which is caused by the recipient's T cells' recognition of the donor's HLA antigens as foreign. Some HLA molecules are strongly associated with certain autoimmune diseases. CD8 T cells are HLA class I restricted, and CD4 T cells are HLA class II restricted . (Figure 6.3).

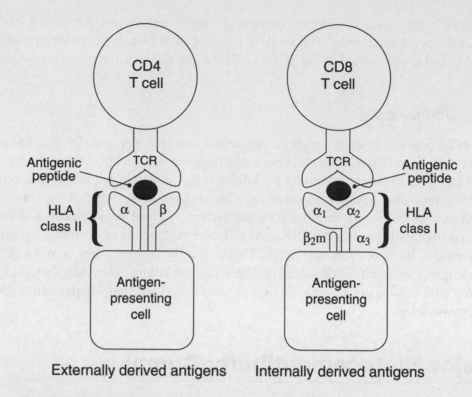

Fig. 6-3. Major histocompatibility complex–restricted antigen presentation to T cells. (TCR = T-cell antigen receptor; β_2m = β_2-microglobulin.)

Class I Human Leukocyte Antigens

Class I molecules consist of a heavy chain covalently linked to β2-microglobulin. Class I HLA molecules are expressed on the surface of all nucleated cells (i.e., all cells except red blood cells). Endogenously derived foreign antigens (e.g., viral proteins), as well as other intracellular proteins, are processed and bind to the class I molecule within the cell. The class I–antigen complex is then transported to the cell surface, where it is recognized by the TCR of CD8 T cells.

Class II Human Leukocyte Antigens

Class II proteins consist of an α chain and a β chain. Class II HLA molecules are expressed on the surface of specialized antigen-presenting cells: macrophages, B cells, dendritic cells in the spleen, and Langerhans cells in the skin. Foreign antigens derived from extracellular microorganisms that have been phagocytized by the antigen-presenting cell (e.g., bacterial proteins) as well as other extracellular proteins are processed and bind to the class II molecule within the cell. The class II–antigen complex is then transported to the cell surface, where it is recognized by the TCR of CD4 T cells.

Tolerance and Clonal Deletion

Tolerance and clonal deletion are processes involved in T-cell maturation, which occurs in the thymus. Overeager T cells that react too strongly with self-proteins are identified by **negative selection** and killed by a system of clonal deletion. Dunce T cells, which do not recognize self MHC proteins, are identified by **positive selection** and are also killed. This positive and negative clonal deletion process produces mature T cells that are selected for their ability to both react to foreign antigens and interact with self MHC proteins (HLA). This requirement for double recognition is known as **MHC restriction**, and it is necessary for T cells to become activated by the TCR.

Tolerance is a state of unresponsiveness to an antigen. Tolerance to self is the result of clonal deletion of self-reactive T-cell precursors during embryonic development. Antigens that were not encountered when the body was immunologically maturing are considered foreign, or nonself, and usually elicit an immunologic response. Tolerance is determined by

- Structure of the antigen

- Dose of the antigen

- Immunologic maturity of the host

- Immunosuppressive drugs

- Cross-reactive antigens (which may terminate tolerance)

Loss of tolerance to self may result in autoimmune disease. Various bacteria, viruses, and drugs are implicated as the source of cross-reacting antigens that trigger the activation of autoreactive T or B cells. **Molecular mimicry** refers to the theory that an environmental trigger capable of stimulating an immune response resembles (mimics) a component of the body enough that an immune attack is directed against the cross-reacting self-component.

The pool of B-lymphocytes also become tolerant to self by clonal deletion of B cells that bear surface immunoglobulins reactive against self-proteins. (Figure 6.4).

$MHC \times CD = 8$
$MHC\ I \times CD8 = 8$
$MHC\ II \times CD4 = 8$

Class I: On all nucleated cells (not RBCs)

Class II: Antigen-presenting cells (e.g., macrophages and B cells)

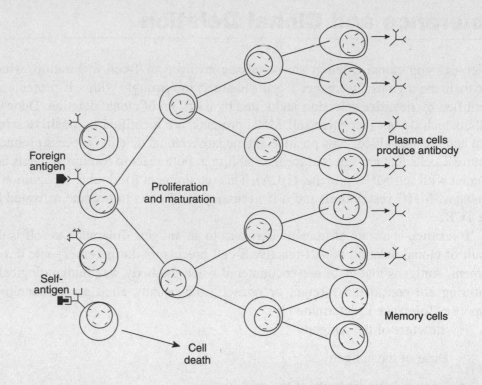

Fig. 6-4. Clonal selection and deletion of B cells.

Such self-reactive B cells are deleted before being able to form antibody-secreting plasma cells. However, tolerance in B cells is less complete than in T cells, an observation supported by the finding that many autoimmune diseases are antibody mediated.

Antibodies

Immunoglobulins, or antibodies, are glycoproteins produced by B cells. They consist of two light (L) polypeptide chains linked by disulfide bonds to two heavy (H) polypeptide chains (Fig. 6-5). Light and heavy chains are subdivided into **variable** and **constant** regions. The variable regions are responsible for antigen binding, whereas the constant regions are responsible for biological functions such as complement activation and binding to cell surface receptors. DNA re-arrangement and RNA splicing of variable and constant gene segments produces the large number of different immunoglobulin molecules.

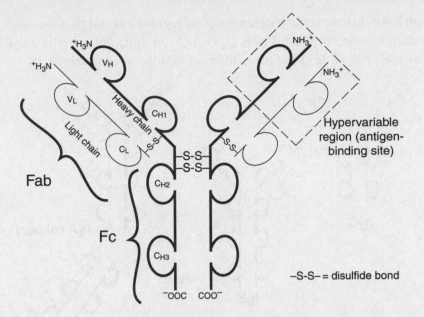

Fig. 6-5. Antibody structure.

Monoclonal antibodies are antibodies that arise from a clone of cells that originated from a single cell. A laboratory trick for making practically unlimited quantities of a monoclonal antibody involves fusing a myeloma cell (an immortal B cell) with the antibody-producing cell to produce a "hybridoma."

Antibodies are remarkably specific, thanks to **hypervariable regions** in both the light and heavy chains. The hypervariable regions form the antigen-binding site. The Y-shaped antibody can be cleaved below the branch-point so that the V-fork forms the **Fab fragment**, which carries the antigen-binding sites ("ab" stands for antigen-binding). The remaining vertical portion forms the **Fc fragment**, which is involved in placental transfer, complement fixation, attachment sites for various cells, and other biological activities ("c" stands for constant region). Antibody diversity depends on

- Multiple gene segments

- Rearrangement of DNA into different sequences

- Combining of different L and H chains

- Mutations, required for affinity maturation

The antigen specificity of the antibody is determined by the re-arrangement in maturing B cells of variable-region DNA that codes for the antibody hypervariable region. The great number of variable-region sequences that can be spliced together to code for antibody hypervariable regions ensures that a diverse repertoire of antibodies will be produced. All of the antibodies expressed on a given B cell have the same hypervariable region, because the rearrangements are on the DNA level.

There are five major classes, or **isotypes**, of immunoglobulins: IgG, IgE, IgM, IgA, and IgD (Fig. 6-6). The constant region of the H chain determines the isotype. All B cells initially carry the IgM isotype. When exposed to their specific antigen, they first produce more IgM antibody. Later, gene re-arrangement permits antibody formation of the same antigenic specificity but of different immunoglobulin classes, in a phenomenon called **isotype (class) switching.** The same heavy-chain variable

Neutrophils are the paramedics of the body— the first on the scene.

Eosinophils, IgE, Type I hypersensitivity, Parasites

region can have different heavy-chain constant regions cut and pasted onto it, so that the immunoglobulins produced later (IgG, IgA, or IgE) are specific for the same antigen as the original IgM but have different biological characteristics.

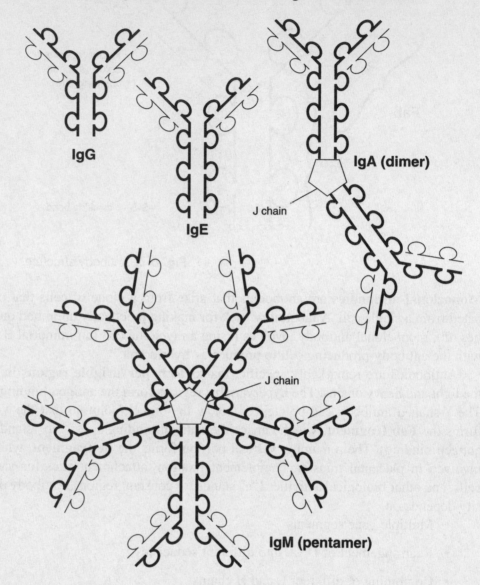

Fig. 6-6. Possible isotype structures.

Isotype-switching to IgD can occur through splicing on the mRNA level without requiring DNA re-arrangement. Isotype-switching to IgG, IgA, or IgE, however, requires a DNA splicing event that permanently removes the section coding for the IgM constant region, thus preventing the cell from ever being able to make IgM again.

Immunoglobulin G

IgG comprises approximately 85% of the serum immunoglobulin in adults and has a major role in the secondary humoral immune response. IgG fixes complement, neutralizes bacterial toxins and viruses, and can opsonize bacteria. IgG is the only antibody able to **cross the placenta** and, therefore, is the most abundant immunoglobulin in newborns.

Immunoglobulin A

IgA comprises 5–15% of the serum antibody pool. In addition to two heavy and two light chains, IgA has a J chain and a secretory component that enables passage to the mucosal surface, where the immunoglobulin dimer is **secreted by mucous membranes**. IgA is present mainly in secretions such as saliva, tears, and colostrum and in respiratory, intestinal, and genital tract secretions.

Immunoglobulin M

IgM comprises 5–10% of the antibodies produced by B cells. It is present in monomeric form on the surface of B cells and has a major role in the primary humoral immune response. In the serum, it takes the form of a **pentamer** composed of two heavy and two light chains, plus a J chain. The IgM pentamer is the most efficient immunoglobulin in **agglutination** and **complement fixation.** IgM is also the major antibody produced by the fetus.

Immunoglobulin D

IgD has no known function. It is present in small amounts in the serum and on the surface of B cells. IgD and IgE together comprise less than 1% of the total serum immunoglobulins.

Immunoglobulin E

IgE is present in trace amounts in the serum, but its level is elevated in response to infection with certain parasites and in immediate **hypersensitivity** reactions. The Fc portion of IgE binds to mast cells and basophils, and after cross-linking with an antigen (known as an **allergen**), these cells degranulate and release mediators, causing allergic responses.

Immune Response

The kinetics of humoral immunity (an important Board topic!) occurs in two phases: the **primary** and **secondary** immune responses (Fig. 6-7). The first encounter with an antigen initiates the primary response, which is characterized by a rise in serum IgM and is detectable within 7–10 days. The serum antibody concentration (usually IgG) continues to rise for several weeks, at which point it declines and may drop to very low levels. In addition, a small clone of B cells and plasma cells specific for the antigen is formed.

After a second encounter with the same antigen, a rapid response occurs within 3–5 days.

This rapid response is attributed to the persistence of antigen-specific **memory cells** produced during the primary response. These memory cells proliferate to form a large clone of specific B cells and plasma cells, which mediate the secondary antibody response. Antibodies produced in the secondary response display **higher avidity**, or chemical attraction, for the antigen. With each succeeding exposure to the same antigen, the antibodies tend to bind more firmly, in a process called **affinity maturation**. Affinity maturation occurs by mutation of the DNA encoding the antigen-binding site. The mutation can result in stronger or weaker binding to antigen. The key is that B cells with mutations that code for higher-affinity antibodies bind more readily to antigen and consequently receive more stimulation to proliferate and produce antibody. Those with mutations that code for weaker-affinity antibodies receive less stimulation and may eventually die off.

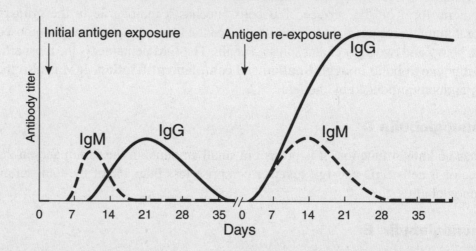

Fig. 6-7. The humoral immune response.

The timing of the T-cell response in cell-mediated immunity follows the same pattern as the antibody response in humoral immunity. Primary exposure to an antigen induces specific T cells to proliferate and form a small clone of antigen-specific cells. Subsequent exposure to the same antigen induces expansion of antigen-specific, memory T-cell clones in a rapid secondary response.

Antigenicity and Immunogenicity

Classic pathway initiated by antigen-antibody complexes

Alternative pathway has nonspecific activation (e.g., endotoxin, cell walls)

Antigens are molecules that react with antibodies, whereas **immunogens** are molecules that induce an immune response. Immunogenic substances are always antigenic, whereas antigenic substances are not necessarily immunogenic. The principal immunogens are proteins and polysaccharides. **Immunogenicity** of a molecule is determined by:

- Foreignness (nonself)

- Molecular size (most potent immunogens are large proteins)

- Chemical structural complexity (a minimum amount is needed)

- Number of epitopes (described below)

- Administration (dosage, route, timing)

Adjuvants are chemically unrelated to the immunogen but can stimulate immunoreactive cells and enhance the immune response to a given antigen. Pertussis toxin, for example, acts as an adjuvant for tetanus and diphtheria toxoids in the DTP vaccine.

Epitopes are antigenic determinant sites. They are small chemical groups on the antigen molecule that can react with an antibody. An antigen can have one or more epitopes and usually has many.

Haptens are nonprotein, antigenic molecules that may become immunogenic when coupled with a carrier protein but not by themselves. They are usually small molecules containing a limited number of epitopes. Many drugs, such as penicillin, act as haptens.

Idiotopes are the antigen binding areas formed by the hypervariable region of an antibody molecule that distinguishes immunoglobulins synthesized from each clone of B lymphocytes. The collection of idiotopes on a given immunoglobulin constitutes the **idiotype** of the antibody. An **anti-idiotype** antibody reacts only with the hypervariable region of the specific immunoglobulin that induced it (Fig. 6-8). Idiotype vaccines comprise antibodies that mimic antigens—that is, the antigen and the anti-idiotype have similar shapes—and they induce immunity specific to the antigens they mimic.

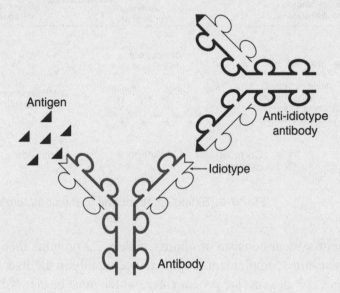

Fig. 6-8. Anti-idiotype antibodies.

Complement

Complement proteins are nonspecific mediators of humoral immunity that assist, or complement, the effects of other components of the immune system. The main biological functions of complement are as follows (Fig. 6-9):

- Cell lysis

- Opsonization to promote phagocytosis

- Generation of anaphylatoxins and inflammatory mediators

- Solubilization of immune complexes

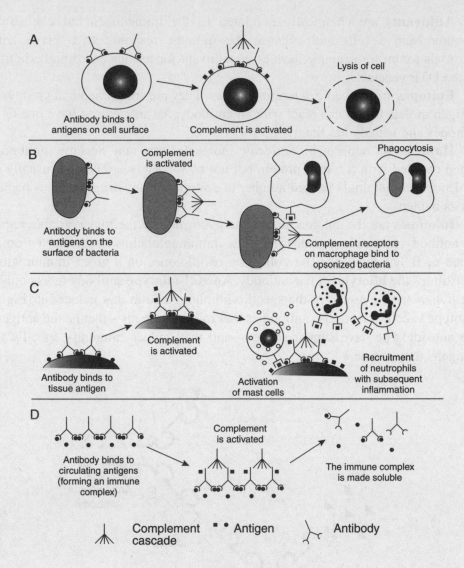

A
Antibody binds to antigens on cell surface
Complement is activated
Lysis of cell

B
Complement is activated
Phagocytosis
Antibody binds to antigens on the surface of bacteria
Complement receptors on macrophage bind to opsonized bacteria

C
Complement is activated
Antibody binds to tissue antigen
Activation of mast cells
Recruitment of neutrophils with subsequent inflammation

D
Complement is activated
Antibody binds to circulating antigens (forming an immune complex)
The immune complex is made soluble

Complement cascade   Antigen   Antibody

Fig. 6-9. Biological functions of the complement system.

The complement system consists of approximately 20 proteins that are present in normal human serum. Complement is synthesized mainly in the liver, although several complement components are proenzymes, which must be cleaved to form active enzymes. Activation of the complement cascade can be initiated either by antigen-antibody complexes via the **classic pathway**, or by a variety of nonimmunologic molecules, such as endotoxin, in the **alternative pathway**. Both pathways lead to the production of C3, which is the central component of the complement system. The proteolytic cleavage products of **C3** have two important functions: opsonization of bacteria and generation of **C5** convertase, the enzyme that leads to the production of the **membrane attack complex** (**MAC**). The classic and alternative pathways include distinct protein components that are activated in different ways to generate the C3 convertases. The cleavage of C3 produces C3b, which binds to the C3 convertase enzymes, changing them to C5 convertases. Once C5 is cleaved, both pathways share the same terminal steps (Fig. 6-10).

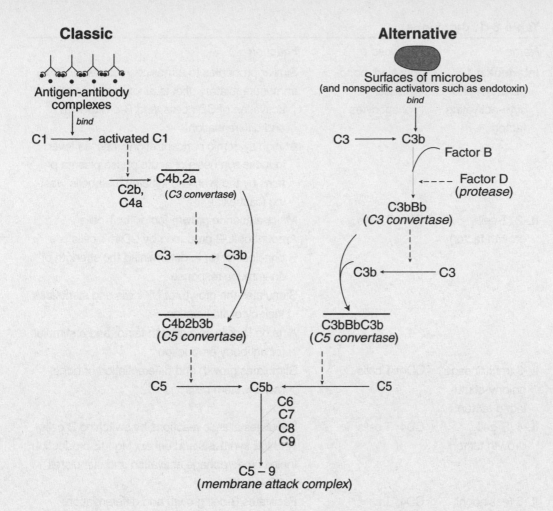

Classic

Antigen-antibody
complexes

| *bind*

C1 ——→ activated C1

—————→ C4b,2a
C2b,   (*C3 convertase*)
C4a

C3 ——→ C3b

C4b2b3b
(*C5 convertase*)

C5 ——————→ C5b
C6
C7
C8
C9

C5 − 9
(*membrane attack complex*)

Alternative

Surfaces of microbes
(and nonspecific activators such as endotoxin)
bind

C3 ——→ C3b
Factor B

┄┄ Factor D
(*protease*)

C3bBb
(*C3 convertase*)

C3b ←—— C3

C3bBbC3b
(*C5 convertase*)

C5

Fig. 6-10. The classic and alternative complement cascades.

The classic pathway is initiated by complexes of antigen with IgG or IgM antibody. Antigen binding to IgG or IgM causes a conformational shift, exposing the complement-binding site on the antibody heavy chain, which allows the C1 component to bind and initiate the cascade. The alternative pathway represents a nonspecific immune defense, which is activated by many unrelated cell surface substances, including bacterial lipopolysaccharides such as endotoxin, fungal cell walls, and viral envelopes.

Immunologic Mediators

Various mediators of immediate hypersensitivity, such as histamine and arachidonic acid metabolites, are released by mast cells or basophils when antigen binds to surface IgE. **Cytokines** are immune system proteins that coordinate antibody and T-cell immune system interactions and amplify immune reactivity (Table 6-1). **Lymphokines** refer to cytokines, such as interleukins, IFN-γ, granulocyte-macrophage colony-stimulating factor (GM-CSF), and lymphotoxin, that are produced mainly by activated T cells and NK cells. **Monokines** are produced by mononuclear phagocytes and include IL-1, TNF, IFN-α, IFN-β, and colony-stimulating factors. Adhesion molecules, which facilitate the interaction of T cells with other cells, and signal-transducing molecules, which help activate T cells, are classified as **accessory molecules**.

Table 6-1. Cytokines

Name	Produced by	Function
Interleukin 1 (IL-1; lympho-cyte-activating factor)	Activated mono-nuclear phagocytes	Similar properties to tumor necrosis factor (TNF) Immunoregulatory effects at low concentrations, activation of CD4 cells, and B-cell growth and differentiation At high systemic concentrations, causes fever, induces synthesis of acute phase plasma proteins by the liver, and initiates metabolic wasting (cachexia)
IL-2 (T-cell growth factor)	CD4$^+$ T cells	Major autocrine growth factor for T cells Amount of IL-2 produced by CD4$^+$ T cells is a principal factor in determining the strength of an immune response Stimulates the growth of NK cells and stimulates their cytolytic function Acts on B cells as a growth factor and a stimulus for antibody production
IL-3 (multilineage colony-stimu-lating factor)	CD4$^+$ T cells	Stimulates growth and differentiation of bone marrow stem cells
IL-4 (B-cell growth factor)	CD4$^+$ T cells	Regulates allergic reactions by switching B cells to IgE synthesis and enhancing IgE production Inhibits macrophage activation and stimulates CD4$^+$ cells
IL-5 (eosinophil differentiation factor)	CD4$^+$ T cells and mast cells	Facilitates B-cell growth and differentiation Stimulates growth and activation of eosinophils and renders them capable of killing helminths
IL-6 (B-cell differ-entiation factor/ B-cell–stimu-lating factor II)	Mononuclear phago-cytes, vascular endothelial cells, fibroblasts, acti-vated T cells, and other cells	Synthesized in response to IL-1 or TNF Serves as a growth factor for activated B cells late in the sequence of B-cell differentiation Induces hepatocytes to synthesize acute-phase proteins, such as fibrinogen
IL-7	Bone marrow stromal cells	Facilitates lymphoid stem cell differentiation into progenitor B cells
IL-8 (neutrophil-activating protein 1)	Macrophages and endothelial cells	Powerful chemo-attractant for T cells and neutrophils
IL-10 (cytokine synthesis inhibitory factor)	T cells, activated B cells, macro-phages, and some nonlymphocytic cell types—e.g., keratinocytes	Inhibits T cell–mediated immune inflammation by inhibiting monokine production and inhibiting the accessory functions of macro-phages in T-cell activation Also inhibits cytokine production and develop-ment of T$_h$-1 cells and drives the system toward a humoral immune response
IL-12	Activated monocytes and B cells	Potent stimulator of NK cells; stimulates the differentiation of CD8$^+$ T cells into function-

Table 6-1. *(Continued)*

Name	Produced by	Function
		ally active CTLs
		Regulates the balance between T_h-1 cells and T_h-2 cells by stimulating the differentiation of naive CD4$^+$ T cells to the T_h-1 subset
IL-13	Produced by activated T cells	Has a pleiotropic action on mononuclear phagocytes, neutrophils, and B cells, which produces an anti-inflammatory response and suppresses cell-mediated immunity
Interferon γ (IFN-γ)	CD4$^+$ T cells, CD8$^+$ T cells, and NK cells	A potent activator of mononuclear phagocytes
		Facilitates differentiation of T and B cells, activates vascular endothelial cells and neutrophils, stimulates the cytolytic activity of NK cells, up-regulates HLA class I expression, and induces many cell types to express HLA class II molecules
TNF-α	Mainly, macrophages stimulated with bacterial endotoxin but also activated T cells, NK cells, and other cell types	Principal mediator of the host response to gram-negative bacteria
		At low concentrations, it stimulates leukocytes, mononuclear phagocytes, and vascular endothelial cells
		At high concentrations, it induces fever, cachexia, and septic shock
TNF-β (lymphotoxin)	Activated T cells	Has similar actions to TNF-α and binds to the same cell surface receptors, although it is usually a locally acting paracrine factor and not a mediator of systemic injury
		Like TNF-α, a potent activator of neutrophils and an important regulator of acute inflammatory reactions
Transforming growth factor β (TGF-β)	Activated T cells and endotoxin-activated mononuclear phagocytes	Acts as an "anticytokine," which antagonizes many responses of lymphocytes
		Inhibits T-cell proliferation and maturation and macrophage activation
		Acts on other cells, such as polymorphonuclear leukocytes and endothelial cells, to counteract the effects of proinflammatory cytokines
		Promotes wound healing, synthesis of collagens, bone formation, and angiogenesis
Granulocyte-macrophage colony-stimulating factor (GM-CSF)	Produced by activated T cells, activated mononuclear phagocytes, vascular endothelial cells, and fibroblasts	Promotes growth of undifferentiated hematopoietic cells and activates mature leukocytes
		Recombinant GM-CSF is administered clinically to promote hematopoiesis

NK = natural killer; T_h = helper T cells; CTL = cytotoxic lyphocyte.

Histamine

Histamine is synthesized and stored in mast cells and basophils by decarboxylation of histidine. It is the principal pharmacological mediator of **immediate (type I) hypersensitivity** in humans and acts by binding to H1 or H2 receptors on target cells. Its release by degranulation causes the following:

- Vasodilation

- Increased capillary permeability

- Smooth-muscle contraction

- Increased secretion by the mucous glands of the nose and bronchial tree

Antihistamines block histamine receptor sites and inhibit the "wheal and flare" response to intradermal allergen or anti-IgE antibody.

Arachidonic Acid Metabolites

Arachidonic acid derivatives are not stored in the cell but rather are synthesized after antigen contact. Membrane phospholipids are broken down to release arachidonic acid, which is converted by enzyme cascades into prostaglandins, thromboxanes, and leukotrienes by either the cyclooxygenase or lipoxygenase pathways (Fig. 6-11).

Live, attenuated vaccines give longer lasting immunity than killed vaccines

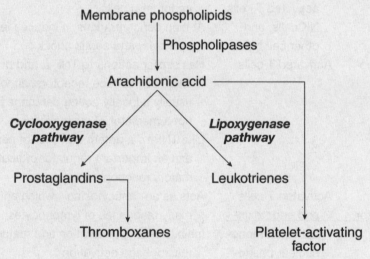

Fig. 6-11. Arachidonic acid metabolites.

Prostaglandins and Thromboxanes

Prostaglandins (PGs) and **thromboxanes (TXs)** are made from the cyclooxygenase pathway. Prostaglandins are a family of biologically active lipids that are grouped according to their five-membered ring structure. **PGD_2** is released during anaphylactic reactions mediated by IgE on mast cells, producing small blood vessel dilation and constriction of bronchial and pulmonary blood vessels. PGD_2 and **PGE_2** prevent platelet aggregation. Thromboxanes are formed from prostaglandins PGG_2 and PGH_2. The term thromboxane refers to thrombus-forming potential. **TXA_2** increases after injury to vessels and stimulates a primary hemostatic response. It is a potent inducer of platelet aggregation, in addition to causing vaso-constriction and smooth muscle contraction. Anti-inflammatory agents, such as aspirin, block prostaglandin and thromboxane synthesis.

Leukotrienes

Leukotrienes (LTs) are formed from arachidonic acid by the lipoxygenase pathway. The name derives from their discovery on leukocytes and their triene chemical structure. The three main mast cell–derived leukotrienes are LTC_4, LTD_4, and LTE_4, which cause increased vascular permeability and smooth muscle contraction. They are the principal mediators in the bronchoconstriction of asthma and are not influenced by antihistamines.

Platelet-Activating Factor

Platelet-activating factor (PAF) forms the third class of lipid mediators (along with prostaglandins-thromboxanes and leukotrienes). It is also produced from fatty acids released by degradation of membrane phospholipids. PAF performs the following actions:

- Accompanies anaphylactic shock

- Direct bronchoconstricting actions

- Transient reduction in blood platelets

- Hypotension and vascular permeability

- *No* effects on contracting smooth muscle

- *No* chemotactic activity

Nitric Oxide

Nitric oxide (NO) is an important mediator made by macrophages in response to the presence of endotoxin, a lipopolysaccharide found in the cell wall of gram-negative bacteria. It is toxic to parasites, fungi, tumor cells, and some bacteria. An inducible form of **NO synthase** is stimulated by IFN-γ and TNF to convert molecular oxygen and L-arginine to NO. In addition to its bactericidal and tumoricidal effects, release of NO causes vasodilation through the activation of guanylate cyclase. Therefore, overproduction of NO has been implicated in septic shock–induced hypotension in humans. Inhibitors of NO synthase show the most promise for clinical use to prevent the hypotension associated with septic shock.

Vaccines

Vaccines provide prophylactic immunization against infectious diseases. Vaccination can induce active or passive immunity, or a combination of both. **Active immunity** is acquired through vaccination with killed or attenuated micro-organisms or their products. Purified antigen vaccines contain a suspension of structural components, such as capsular polysaccharides or inactivated toxins (toxoids). In general, live, attenuated vaccines (which contain live micro-organisms that are unable to cause disease but retain their antigenicity) induce a longer-lasting immunity and produce a more effective cell-mediated response than killed vaccines. Killed vaccines, containing a suspension of inactivated, intact micro-organisms, induce a predominantly humoral response. A successful active vaccine should lead to the production of memory T and B cells. **Passive immunity** is provided by the administration of preformed antitoxin or antiviral antibodies in preparations called immune globulins.

Combined immunization is widely used—for example, the diphtheria-tetanus-pertussis vaccine (purified bacterial antigen vaccine) or the measles-mumps-rubella vaccine (live attenuated viral vaccine). Snake and spider antivenins are equine (horse) immunoglobulins that provide passive immunity.

Tumor Immunology

Many tumor cells develop new antigens on their surface, which can be recognized by T cells or antibodies. These **tumor-associated antigens** and **tumor-specific antigens** may be unique antigens found only on tumor cells, or they may be antigens found on both tumor and normal cells.

Tissue-specific antigens include **S-100** protein expressed by melanoma, common acute lymphoblastic leukemia antigen (**CALLA**) expressed in B-cell leukemia/lymphoma, and **CA-125** and **CA-19-9** glycoproteins expressed by ovarian and pancreatic cancer cells, respectively. **Carcinoembryonic antigen (CEA)** and **α-fetoprotein (AFP)** are proteins that occur normally in fetal tissue but are expressed abnormally in tumor cells of hepatocellular carcinoma and carcinoma of the colon, pancreas, breast, ovary, lung, and stomach.

Macrophages and NK cells respond to tumor cells by releasing TNF-a and lysing cells, respectively. T and B cells may also participate in a more specific immune response. To escape immunosurveillance by cytotoxic T cells, MHC class I expression may be down-regulated in some tumor and virally infected cells.

Tumor immunotherapy is still somewhat experimental. One method is to stimulate the immune system by local injection of killed or irradiated tumor cells together with nonspecific adjuvants (e.g., bacillus Calmette-Guérin mycobacterium) or high-dose administration of cytokines, such as IL-2, TNF-α, IFN-α, and IFN-γ. Passive immunity can also be induced by administering "magic bullets," monoclonal antibodies against tumor-specific antigens, which are linked to toxic molecules, radioisotopes, or drugs to selectively kill tumor cells (a kind of immunologic "Trojan horse"). A modification of this approach is to use hybrid monoclonal antibodies, with one component specific for tumor antigen and the other for the TCR. These heteroconjugates allow activated T cells to confront tumor cells, potentially leading to tumor regression.

Erythrocyte Antigens

All human red blood cells express antigens that vary among individual members of a species. **ABO** and the **Rh (Rhesus)** blood group antigens are the two most important erythrocyte antigen systems.

ABO

The **ABO system** is the basis for blood typing and transfusions. It is based on a glycosphingolipid on the surface of RBCs. Everyone synthesizes the O antigen, which is a sphingolipid attached to a common core glycan. A single genetic locus encoding glycosyl transferase enzymes determines ABO blood type. People with type A and type B blood express enzymes that attach an additional sugar residue — an additional N-acetylgalactosamine on A cells, and an additional galactose on B cells — to the O antigen. People with type O blood lack that enzymatic activity, and express only the basic O antigen scaffold on their RBCs. So, a single extra sugar group determines the ABO blood grouping!

Erythrocytes are typed for their surface antigens, and all blood for transfusions is matched. This is because individuals produce IgM antibodies against whichever ABO antigens they do not express (probably because gut flora bear similar antigens that sensitize the immune system!). Thus, anti-A is carried by group B individuals, anti-B is carried by group A individuals, and anti-A and anti-B are carried by group O individuals (Table 6-2). As you can imagine, **transfusion reactions** result when incompatible donor red blood cells are transfused. Picture a lot of immune complexes forming in the vessels of that unfortunate recipient!

Individuals with blood group O have no A or B antigens on their red cells and are termed **universal donor**s because they can donate blood to all recipients. No one should make antibodies against the O antigen on the transfused RBCs. Donor type O blood does contain anti-A and anti-B antibodies, but a clinically detectable reaction does not occur in the type A or type B recipient because the donor antibody is rapidly diluted below a significant concentration. Individuals with group AB blood have neither anti-A nor anti-B antibodies, and thus are known as **universal recipients**. Red blood cells containing any of the ABO antigens may be transfused to them without inducing a hemolytic transfusion reaction.

Table 6-2. ABO blood group

Blood type	Antigen on surface of RBC	Antibody in serum	Occurrence of phenotype
A	A	Anti-B	40%
B	B	Anti-A	10%
AB (universal recipient)	AB	No antibody	5%
O (universal donor)	No antigens	Anti-A and anti-B	45%

RBC = red blood cell.

Rh Factor

The Rh system is complex, and not all of the Rh alloantigens have been characterized biochemically. The **RhD antigen**, expressed on the erythrocytes of approximately 85% of the human population, is the one of most clinical concern. Unlike the ABO system, anti-Rh antibodies do not occur naturally in the serum. If an RhD– individual is transfused with RhD+ blood, or if an RhD– female has an RhD+ fetus (the D gene being inherited from the father), the RhD antigen stimulates the development of anti-RhD antibodies, which can lead to severe reactions with further transfusions of RhD+ blood. This occurs most often when RhD+ erythrocytes of the fetus leak into the maternal circulation during delivery of an RhD+ child. Subsequent RhD+ pregnancies are likely to be affected by the mother's anti-RhD IgG antibody crossing the placenta and attacking the fetus' RBCs, which can result in hemolytic disease of the newborn (erythroblastosis fetalis). **Erythroblastosis fetalis** can be prevented by administering high doses of anti-RhD antibodies (Rhogam) to the RhD– mother immediately on delivery of her first RhD+ child. These antibodies bind to contaminating RhD+ fetal erythrocytes and prevent the mother from producing her own antibodies (Fig. 6-12).

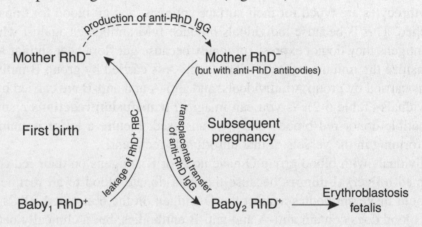

Fig. 6-12. Antibody feedback mechanisms in hemolytic disease of the newborn.

Transfusion Reactions

Transfusion refers to transplantation of circulating blood cells or plasma from one individual to another. **Transfusion reactions** may occur if there are differences between the antigens of the donor and the recipient. Antigens, such as the ABO blood group antigens, which cause an immune response if injected into a genetically dissimilar member of the same species, are called **isoantigens**. Transfusion reactions due to ABO incompatibility result in antigen-antibody binding, complement-dependent lysis of the foreign red blood cells, and anaphylaxis. Symptoms include fever, back pain, nausea, and hypotension. Transfusion reactions can also be induced by:

- Administration of blood to IgA-deficient subjects

- Serum sickness

- Nonimmune mechanisms such as air embolism or bacterial contamination

- Clerical error (the most common cause!)

If a patient experiences symptoms of transfusion reaction, stop the transfusion immediately! Depending on the severity of the reaction, patients may require antihistamines and steroids.

Transplantation

Transplantable organs include kidney, liver, heart, lung, pancreas (including pancreatic islets), intestine, and skin. Bone marrow, bone matrix, cardiac valves, and corneas are also transplanted. In most situations, donors and recipients must be matched for blood group ABO compatibility and HLA antigens to avoid graft rejection. HLA-A, -B, and -DR are the most important HLA antigens to match in transplantation.

Tissue typing by sequence analysis of the HLA genes, or serologic reactions between HLA antigens and specific antibodies, are used to select donors with compatible HLA types. A test called the **mixed leukocyte reaction (MLR)**, which measures the proliferation of recipient lymphocytes in response to donor lymphocytes, can be used to determine if individuals are well matched. There are different categories of transplants, and each has a different success rate. An **autograft** is the transfer of an individual's own tissue (skin, blood), which is always accepted. A **syngeneic graft** is the transfer of tissue between genetically identical individuals (monozygotic twins) and has a low risk of rejection. An **allograft** is the transfer of tissue between genetically different individuals of the same species, which is the most common type of human transplant. Allografts have a high risk of rejection and require long-term immunosuppression of the recipient. **Xenografts** are transplants between different species (human, primates, pigs) and are only experimental in humans.

Transplant Rejection

Transplant rejection is an immune response to an allograft, which occurs when the recipient cells recognize the donor cells as foreign. The immune response to alloantigens may lead to graft failure, necessitating its removal. The severity and rapidity of rejection varies, depending on the degree of HLA differences between the donor and the recipient, the immunocompetence of the recipient, and the type of tissue being transplanted. In cell-mediated rejection, CD8 T cells are activated by recognition of foreign class I alloantigens expressed by cells in the graft, and CD4 T cells are activated by class II alloantigens. Humoral responses against foreign HLA antigens can generate antibodies that target the graft vasculature, causing immune complex deposition and associated tissue injury.

Graft rejection is usually classified as hyperacute, acute, or chronic rejection (Table 6.3). **Hyperacute (white graft) rejection** is mediated by pre-existing antibodies (e.g., anti-ABO antibodies) that bind to endothelium and activate complement. It is characterized by rapid thrombotic occlusion that begins within minutes after vascular anastomosis is complete. **Acute rejection** occurs within days to weeks of transplantation and is characterized by extensive lymphocyte and macrophage infiltration and tissue necrosis. **Chronic rejection** can occur months or years after transplantation and is characterized by fibrosis and loss of normal organ structure. A T cell–mediated reaction is the main cause of rejection of many types of grafts, but antibodies contribute to the rejection of certain transplants, especially bone marrow.

Table 6-3. Graft Rejection Chart

Type of rejection	Onset	Histology	Gross
Hyperacute	Minutes or Hours	Vascular occlusion neutrophils, antibodies	Engorged, cyanotic
Acute	Days to weeks	Molecular cell infiltration necrotizing vasculis	—
Chronic	Months to years	Fibrous, mononuclear infiltration	Fibrosis, shrinkage

Transplant recipients may also display **graft-versus-host (GVH)** reactions if grafted immunocompetent T cells attack host cells. The GVH reaction can be either acute or chronic and is particularly common after bone marrow transplantation. Target organs include the skin, liver, and GI tract. Patients develop skin rash, jaundice, and diarrhea. GVH disease can be minimized by pretransplantation T-cell depletion of donor tissue with drugs or radiation.

Alterations in Immunologic Function

Defects in the immune system lead to immunodeficiency diseases, which can be primary (**congenital**) or secondary (**acquired**) immunodeficiencies. The principal consequences of immunodeficiency are an increased susceptibility to infections and certain cancers. Deficiencies of B cells result predominantly in bacterial infections, particularly encapsulated organisms, whereas T-cell defects result mostly in viral, protozoal, and fungal infections (Fig. 6-13).

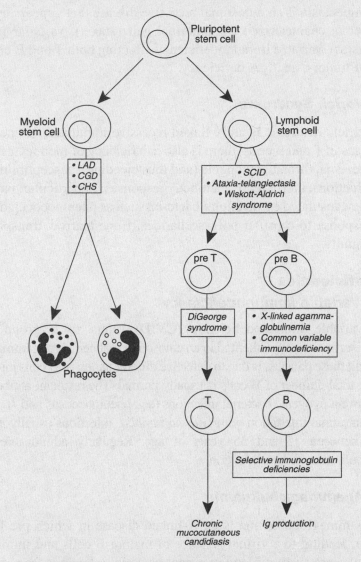

Fig. 6-13. Immunodeficiency diseases caused by congenital defects in lymphocyte and phagocyte development. (CGD = chronic granulomatous disease; CHS = Chédiak-Higashi syndrome; LAD = leukocyte adhesion deficiency; SCID = severe combined immunodeficiency.)

Combined B- and T-Cell Immunodeficiencies
Severe Combined Immunodeficiency

Severe combined immunodeficiency disease (SCID) is a family of congenital X-linked or autosomal diseases that cause impaired B and T cell function due to a defect in the differentiation of B and T cells from stem cell progenitors. Two known causes of SCID are adenosine deaminase (ADA) deficiency and purine nucleotide phosphorylase deficiency. Infants show normal or markedly reduced lymphocyte counts in the thymus, blood, and peripheral lymphoid organs and are deficient in all immune functions. Affected individuals fail to thrive and usually die during the first 2 years of life due to recurrent and overwhelming infections from all varieties of microorganisms. Treatment includes protection from microorganisms (such as living in a "bubble") and avoidance of live viral vaccines. Bone marrow transplant may help restore immunity.

Ataxia Telangiectasia

Ataxia telangiectasia is an autosomal recessive disease that appears by age 2 years. The disorder is characterized by abnormal gait (ataxia), vascular malformations (telangiectasias), variable immunodeficiency affecting both T and B cells, increased incidence of tumors, and IgA deficiency.

Wiskott-Aldrich Syndrome

Wiskott-Aldrich syndrome is an X-linked recessive immunodeficiency. In addition to deficiencies in T and B cells, there is also a deficiency of monocytes and platelets, leading to eczema, thrombocytopenia (and thus bleeding), susceptibility to recurrent bacterial infections, and defective antibody responses. In particular, patients are susceptible to encapsulated extracellular bacteria, such as pneumococci, due to a defective IgM response to capsular polysaccharides. Bone marrow transplant may help restore immunity.

B-Cell Deficiencies

Common Variable Immunodeficiency

Common variable immunodeficiency (CVID) refers to a group of antibody deficiency disorders usually inherited in an autosomal manner. Hypogammaglobulinemia, common to all these patients, is due to defective differentiation of B cells into plasma cells, although the total number of B cells is usually normal. The resultant antibody deficiency leads to recurrent pyogenic bacterial infections (e.g. pneumococcus and *H. influenzae*), in addition to intestinal infestation with *Giardia lamblia*. Infections usually appear in these individuals between 15 and 35 years of age. Regularly administered intravenous immunoglobulin may reduce infection.

Bruton's Agammaglobulinemia

Bruton's agammaglobulinemia is an X-linked disease in which pre-B cells fail to differentiate, leading to a virtual absence of mature B cells and immunoglobulins. Affected males are susceptible to recurrent bacterial infections from 5–6 months of age onward, after the disappearance of maternal IgG. Pooled gamma globulin may be administered to reduce the number of infections.

Selective Immunoglobulin Deficiencies

Selective immunoglobulin deficiencies are diseases characterized by an insufficient quantity of one of the three major immunoglobulins (IgA, IgG, or IgM) or of a subclass of IgA or IgG. **IgA deficiency** is the most common of these and the most frequent immunodeficiency disorder, affecting 1 in 700 individuals of Caucasian descent. IgA-deficient individuals may have an increased incidence of respiratory and GI tract infections and some autoimmune diseases. They should not be transfused with gamma globulin since they may react against the foreign IgA and, by cross-reactivity, deplete their already low stores of IgA. Hyper-IgM syndrome is an X-linked or autosomal dominant disorder characterized by elevated IgM in combination with diminished IgG and IgA. It is caused by failed class switching because of a faulty B cell–CD4 T cell interaction.

T-Cell Deficiencies
DiGeorge Syndrome (Thymic Aplasia)

DiGeorge syndrome is a congenital malformation resulting in absence of the thymus due to the failure of the third and fourth pharyngeal pouch to develop. It is accompanied by hypoparathyroidism, so tetany due to hypocalcemia is often the presenting symptom. Defective maturation and reduction in the number of T cells leads to impaired cell-mediated immunity and dysfunction in delayed-type hypersensitivity. Treatment by fetal thymic transplantation is successful.

Chronic Mucocutaneous Candidiasis

Chronic mucocutaneous candidiasis is a T-cell defect specific for *Candida albicans*, resulting in infection of the skin and mucous membranes. The delayed hypersensitivity skin reaction to *Candida* antigen is negative, but other T- and B-cell functions are normal. This disorder is associated with the development of endocrine dysfunction, particularly Addison's disease.

Deficiencies of Phagocytic Cells
Chronic Granulomatous Disease

Chronic granulomatous disease is inherited as an X-linked or autosomal recessive disease that occurs by the age of 2 years. Lack of NADPH oxidase activity results in decreased intracellular microbial killing by neutrophils. Affected individuals have an increased susceptibility to infections with microorganisms that are normally not pathogenic, such as *Staphylococcus epidermidis* and *Candida* spp. There is also an increased susceptibility to S. aureus, gram-negative enterics, and *Aspergillus fumigatus*, but not viruses or protozoa. T and B cells usually function normally. Diagnosis can be confirmed by the nitroblue tetrazolium dye reduction test.

Chédiak-Higashi Syndrome

Chédiak-Higashi syndrome is an autosomal recessive disorder characterized by failure of lysosomal emptying and presence of giant lysosomal granules in neutrophils, monocytes, and lymphocytes of affected individuals. NK cell function and neutrophil killing is impaired, resulting in recurrent pyogenic bacterial infections, partial albinism, and central nervous system disorders.

Leukocyte Adhesion Deficiency

Leukocyte adhesion deficiency is an autosomal recessive disorder in which most adhesion-dependent functions of leukocytes are abnormal. A defect in the expression of glycoproteins of the β-integrin family produces a disease characterized by recurrent bacterial and fungal infections and impaired wound healing.

Complement Deficiencies

C2 deficiency is the most commonly identified complement deficiency. Deficiencies in the early components of the classic pathway (C2 and C4) are associated with autoimmune diseases (e.g., systemic lupus erythematosus or glomerulonephritis). **C3 deficiency** is associated with frequent, serious, pyogenic bacterial infections that may be fatal. Patients with deficiencies in the terminal components of the complement pathway (C5, C6, C7, C8, or C9) have an increased susceptibility to infections by *Neisseria* spp. **Hereditary angioedema** is an autosomal dominant deficiency in **C1 inhibitor**, leading to edema in the skin and mucosa. Steroids may be helpful in increasing C1 inhibitor concentrations.

Paroxysmal nocturnal hemoglobinuria is a rare disease that causes hemoglobinuria (brownish urine), particularly upon awakening. It is caused by a defect in the ability to attach decay-accelerating factor (DAF) and CD59 to cell membranes. DAF and CD59 are molecules that protect host cells (including RBCs) from activating the alternative complement pathway. Their absence leads to complement-mediated intravascular red blood cell lysis.

Acquired Immunodeficiency

Acquired immunodeficiency is a decrease in the immune response that may occur as a result of another disease process, such as neoplasia, malnutrition, infection, or as a complication of treatment, such as chemotherapy. Drug-induced immunosuppression is used to treat inflammatory diseases and autoimmune diseases and to prevent allograft rejection. **Corticosteroids** and cyclosporin A are the most commonly used immunosuppressive drugs. Corticosteroids cause selective lysis of T cells and lymphoid precursor cells, leading to decreased antibody responsiveness, reduction in phagocytosis by macrophages, and decreased cytokine production. **Cyclosporin A** selectively affects CD4 helper T cells and acts to block the IL-2–dependent growth and differentiation of T cells. Other immunosuppressive drugs include metabolic toxins, such as **azathioprine** and **cyclophosphamide**. Newer medications include **FK506**, which resembles cyclosporin A in its mode of action, and **rapamycin**, which blocks T-cell growth in response to IL-2. Chemotherapeutic drugs and radiation therapy administered to cancer patients are usually cytotoxic to both mature and developing leukocytes.

Acquired immunodeficiency syndrome (AIDS) is caused by the **human immunodeficiency** virus (HIV). HIV infects CD4-expressing cells, which are primarily T-helper cells, but also include macrophages, monocytes, and follicular dendritic cells in lymph nodes. CD4 cells are destroyed by the virus, which leads to loss of cell-mediated immunity and B-cell abnormalities. Patients have increased susceptibility to opportunistic infections, such as *Pneumocystis carinii* pneumonia, and certain tumors, such as Kaposi's sarcoma and lymphoma. Severe neurologic problems, such as dementia or neuropathy, can also arise due to HIV infection of brain monocytes and macrophages or as the result of overwhelming opportunistic infection.

The HIV genome contains the three typical retroviral genes—*gag, env,* and *pol*—that encode the core structural proteins, the envelope glycoproteins, and the enzymes required for viral replication, respectively. HIV enters cells via fusion of the viral envelope with the cell membrane after binding of the virion gp120 envelope protein to the CD4 protein on the target cell surface. The virus integrates into the host genome and may enter a stage of latency that can last for months or years (Fig. 6-14). Initiation of HIV gene transcription and HIV replication appears to be stimulated by the same mechanisms, such as antigen or cytokine stimulation, that promote growth of the host T cell. The virions assemble in the cytoplasm and are released from the cell by budding.

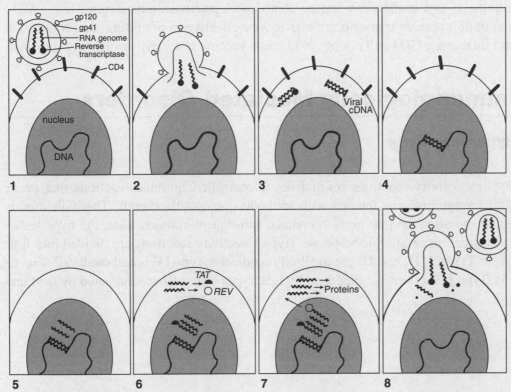

Fig. 6-14. The life cycle of human immunodeficiency virus in CD4 T cells. **(1)** Adherence of viral particle to CD4 molecule on T cell. **(2)** Fusion of viral envelope with cell membrane; entrance of viral genome. **(3)** Copying of viral RNA into double-stranded cDNA by reverse transcriptase. **(4)** Integration of viral cDNA into host DNA; quiescent until T-cell activation. **(5)** T-cell activation; induction of provirus transcription at a low level. **(6)** Multiple splicing of RNA transcripts; translation of early genes (*TAT* and *REV*). **(7)** Amplification of viral RNA transcription by *TAT*; transport of viral RNA to cytoplasm by *REV*. **(8)** Translation of late proteins (*GAG, POL, ENV*) and assembly into virus particles; budding from cell.

The clinical picture of HIV infection can be divided into three stages. The **early, acute stage** usually begins 2–4 weeks after infection and is characterized by a mononucleosis-like picture of fever, lethargy, sore throat, rashes, and generalized lymphadenopathy. A **middle, latent stage** of several years usually follows, during which patients may by asymptomatic or may develop clinical features known as **AIDS-related complex**. The most frequent manifestations of this complex are persistent fevers, night sweats, weight loss, chronic diarrhea, and generalized lymphadenopathy. The **late stage** of HIV infection is AIDS, manifested by a decline in the number of CD4 cells in the peripheral blood, from a normal amount of about 1,000/ml^3 to fewer than 400/ml^3, and an increase in the frequency and severity of opportunistic infections.

Transmission of HIV occurs primarily by sexual contact and by transfer of infected blood. Perinatal transmission from infected mother to neonate also occurs, either at birth or, infrequently, via breast milk. Preliminary diagnosis of HIV infection is made by the detection of antibodies by enzyme-linked immunosorbent assay (ELISA) and is confirmed by Western blot analysis. Antibodies to HIV typically appear 2–3 months after infection, but polymerase chain reaction (PCR) can be used to directly detect viral presence before this time. **Protease inhibitors**, such as saquinavir and indinavir, when combined with **nucleoside analogues** (e.g., AZT) that inhibit reverse transcriptase activity, are effective in inhibiting viral replication and increasing CD4 cell counts. No human vaccine is widely available at this time.

Immunologically Mediated Disorders

Hypersensitivity

Hypersensitivity reactions result from uncontrolled immune reactions that occur after foreign antigens interact with antibodies or sensitized cells. The individual is sensitized after the first antigen contact; subsequent contacts elicit the hypersensitivity reaction or allergic response. Hypersensitivity reactions are divided into four types: **Types I, II,** and **III** are **antibody mediated**; **type IV** is cell mediated (Fig. 6-15). Type I reactions are mediated by IgE; types II and III are mediated by IgM and IgG.

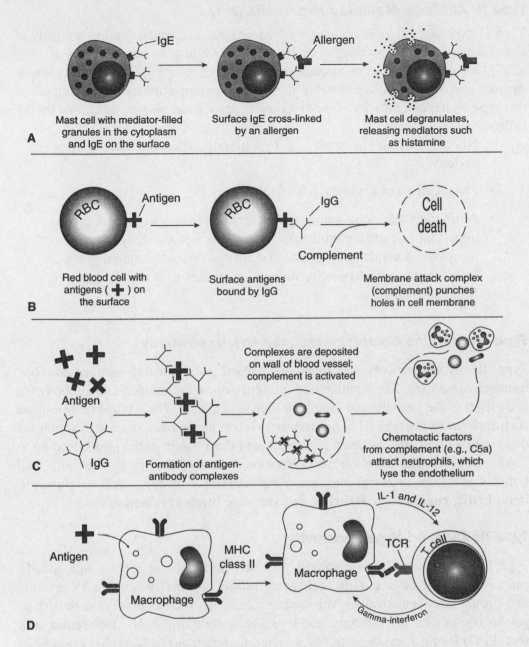

Fig. 6-15. The four types of hypersensitivity reactions. **A.** Type I, immediate/anaphylactic hypersensitivity. **B.** Type II, antibody/complement-mediated cytotoxic hypersensitivity. **C.** Type III, immune complex–mediated hypersensitivity. **D.** Type IV, delayed hypersensitivity.

Type I: Immediate Hypersensitivity

Type I is an **immediate hypersensitivity**, or anaphylactic, reaction, which occurs within minutes after re-exposure to an antigen. Cross-linking of **antigen-bound IgE** on the surface of sensitized mast cells or basophils leads to cellular degranulation and release of pharmacologic mediators, such as histamine, prostaglandins, thromboxanes, and leukotrienes. Symptoms of anaphylaxis include erythema, urticaria (hives), asthma, rhinitis, conjunctivitis, and eczema. Injection of protein antigens, such as antitoxins or drugs (particularly antimicrobial agents, such as penicillin), can cause systemic anaphylaxis leading to severe bronchoconstriction and hypotension.

Type II: Antibody-Mediated Hypersensitivity

Type II hypersensitivity is induced by IgM or IgG. Antibodies bind to antigens of the cell membrane, activating complement and leading to target cell lysis. The anti–glomerular basement membrane antibody that develops in **Goodpasture's syndrome**, and antibodies that develop during **Rh incompatibility**, are examples of this type of hypersensitivity. Type II hypersensitivity can also be generated by the following:

- NK cells, which kill target cells by antibody-dependent cellular cytotoxicity.

- Phagocytosis of antibody-coated target cells.

- Antibodies that cause pathologic effects by binding to functionally important cell surface molecules. Antibodies against acetylcholine receptors in **myasthenia gravis** and against thyroid-stimulating hormone receptors in **hyperthyroidism** are examples of this kind of type II hypersensitivity.

Type III: Immune Complex–Mediated Hypersensitivity

Type III hypersensitivity reactions are caused by persisting antigen-antibody immune complexes. The simultaneous presence of excess antigen and antibody (or IgG) leads to the formation of soluble immune complexes. The **Arthus reaction** and **serum sickness** are type III hypersensitivity reactions. In the tissues, the complexes deposit mainly in arteries, renal glomeruli, and the synovia of the joints, leading to complement fixation and neutrophil activation. Subsequent vasculitis, nephritis, and arthritis associate immune complexes with clinical disorders, such as **glomerulonephritis**, **rheumatoid arthritis**, and **systemic lupus erythematosus**.

Type IV: Delayed Hypersensitivity

Type IV is a form of hypersensitivity resulting from antigen contact with specifically sensitized T cells and macrophages. **Contact sensitivity** is a type IV reaction that occurs after sensitization with simple chemicals, such as plant materials (e.g., poison ivy, poison oak), metals, and topically applied drugs. The **tuberculin skin test** (PPD) for prior exposure to Mycobacterium tuberculosis is another example of a delayed, type IV reaction. In both instances, the response is delayed and may take 24–48 hours to appear.

Autoimmune Disorders

Autoimmunity results from a breakdown in the mechanism of self-tolerance. Immunologic diseases produced by humoral or cell-mediated reactions against self-antigens constitute autoimmune diseases. Multiple interacting factors contribute to the development of disease, which may be systemic or organ specific. There is a strong association of some diseases with certain HLA specificities (e.g., **HLA-DR4** with **rheumatoid arthritis**, and **HLA-B27** with **ankylosing spondylitis**), indicating some genetic predisposition. Exposure to an agent that triggers a cross-reacting immune response against normal tissue may also be a contributing cause to autoimmune disease. For example, antibodies against group A streptococci cross-react with cardiac muscle to cause rheumatic fever. These diseases are usually chronic and irreversible. A list of common autoimmune diseases is provided in Table 6-4.

Table 6-4. Some autoimmune diseases

Disease	HLA association	Cause
Idiopathic thrombocytopenic purpura	—	Antibody-mediated platelet destruction
Pernicious anemia	—	Antibody-mediated faulty absorption of vitamin B_{12}
Myasthenia gravis	DR3, B8	Antibody-mediated disruption of neuromuscular junctions
Graves' disease	DR3, B8	Antibody-mediated overproduction of thyroid hormone
Insulin-dependent diabetes mellitus	DR3, DR4	Cell- and antibody-mediated inability to synthesize insulin
Rheumatoid arthritis	DR4, DR1	Cell- and antibody-mediated inflammatory joint disease
Systemic lupus erythematosus	DR2, DR3	Antibody-mediated systemic inflammatory disease
Sjögren's syndrome	DR3	Cell- and antibody-mediated destruction of exocrine glands

Diagnostic Tests

Antigen-antibody reactions reflect physical characteristics of the antigen or antibody. **Affinity** refers to the strength of the attraction between a single antigenic epitope and the antibody binding site. **Avidity** refers to the strength of the interaction between multivalent antigens and complementary antibodies. Diagnostic tests determine the presence of unknown antigen or antibody in patient serum by complementarity with specific standard antigens or antibodies.

Table 6-5. Antigen-antibody diagnostic tests

Test	Description	Representative example
Agglutination	Particulate antigen (e.g., bacteria) combines with specific antibody and forms an aggregate	Widal test to diagnose enteric *Salmonella* infection
Hemagglutination inhibition	Antiviral antibody-inhibition of red blood cell agglutination	Diagnosis of viral infections
Precipitation	Soluble antigen combines with specific antibody and forms an aggregate	Serum test for antibody to diphtheria toxoid
Double diffusion (Ouchterlony technique)	Precipitation reaction in agar, leading to visible lines of precipitate	Diagnosis of hypersensitivity pneumonitis (e.g., pigeon breeder's lung)
Immunoelectrophoresis	Precipitation in agar with an electric field identifies antigens by charge, size, and specificity	Diagnosis of selective globulin immunodeficiencies
Antiglobulin	Visible aggregation due to bridging of antibody-coated cells by anti-γ globulin	Coombs' test for erythroblastosis fetalis
Radioimmunoassay (RIA)	Antigen bound to specific antibody is quantitated by comparison to radio-labeled antigen standards competitively bound to the same antibody	Detection of antibodies to hepatitis B surface antigen
Enzyme-linked immunosorbent assay (ELISA)	Similar to RIA, but antigen-antibody binding is quantitated by colorimetric detection of an enzyme substrate	Human immunodeficiency virus antibody screening
Immunofluorescence	Microscopic detection of fluorescently labeled antigen or antibodies in histologic tissue sections	Identification of antinuclear antibodies in systemic lupus erythematosus
Western blot	Antigenic proteins separated by electrophoresis are blotted to a membrane and detected by reaction with labeled antibodies	Confirmatory test for HIV
Complement fixation	Complement is added to identify either partner in an antigen-antibody complex if the other is known: hemolysis constitutes a negative reaction	Wasserman test for syphilis
Mixed lymphocyte culture	Responder T cells proliferate and/or lyse irradiated target cells in response to foreign human leukocyte antigens	Test of transplant donor and recipient compatibility
Fluorescence-activated cell sorting (FACS)	Blood cell enumeration by laser detection of fluorescently labeled monoclonal antibodies directed against cell surface markers	CD4$^+$ T cell counts in HIV patients

CHAPTER 7

Hematology

Erythropoiesis

The site of red blood cell (RBC) synthesis varies with age. RBCs containing fetal hemoglobin are initially synthesized in the **yolk sac** from gestational week 2 through week 10; the liver takes over from week 6 until birth. By week 20, RBC production in the skeleton (vertebrae, ribs, sternum, pelvis, scapulae, skull, and extremities) has begun. In adulthood, the primary location for erythropoiesis is the **axial skeleton** and the proximal humerus and femur.

RBCs arise from pluripotent stem cells that progress to become **proerythroblasts**. Under the influence of **erythropoietin (EPO)**, hemoglobin synthesis begins, and after about 5 days, the cell spits out its nucleus and becomes a **reticulocyte**. Although reticulocytes do not have nuclei, they continue to have ribosomes, RNA, and mitochondria, which stain slightly bluish on a blood smear. This allows them to be distinguished from mature RBCs. After about 2 days, the cells become mature RBCs.

RBCs have an average life span of about 120 days. Aged cells are removed from the circulation after going through the spleen, a virtual RBC obstacle course. Cells that cannot bend and squeeze through get eaten by macrophages. Patients with certain RBC defects have cells that cannot deform easily; these cells have a much shorter life span and are destroyed faster than they can be synthesized, resulting in hemolytic anemia.

EPO is a hormone secreted by the juxtaglomerular apparatus in the kidney. EPO secretion is triggered by tissue hypoxia, which can be due to anemia, cardiopulmonary disease, or high altitudes. EPO causes

- Development of erythroid precursors from stem cells

- Development of proerythroblasts into RBCs

- Shortened RBC maturation time

- Release of reticulocytes into the bloodstream

Hemoglobin

Normal adult hemoglobin is composed of a tetramer of two α globin chains and two β globin chains, each of which carries a heme group. Fetal hemoglobin, which has a highTreatmentr affinity for oxygen, is composed of two α chains and two γ chains and is known as **hemoglobin F**. At birth, γ chain production decreases and β chain production increases, until about age 6 months, when all γ chains are usually gone. Abnormalities in the α or β chains cause abnormal hemoglobin syndromes, known as thalassemias (described in more detail later in this chapter).

Dissociation Curves

Hemoglobin must pick up oxygen in the lungs and carry it to the tissues, where it is released. Oxygen pressure and other factors can affect how easily the oxygen can be "dropped off" in the tissues. This is expressed in the classic **hemoglobin-oxygen dissociation curve** (Fig. 7-1).

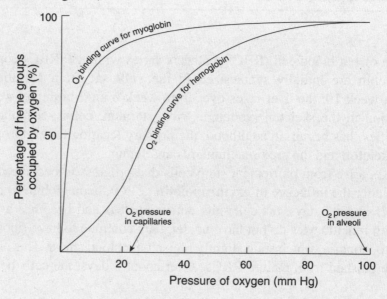

Fig. 7-1. Hemoglobin-oxygen dissociation curve.

Several physiologic situations cause the curve to shift to the right (Fig. 7-2). This shift means that oxygen's attachment to hemoglobin is weaker, and it can be dropped off more easily in the oxygen-hungry tissues. The following states cause a rightward shift, and you may be able to remember them more intuitively if you think about what happens at the tissue level during exercise:

- Increased acidity (this is known as the **Bohr effect**)

- Increased CO_2

- Increased temperature

- Increased 2,3-diphosphoglycerate—a result of increased glycolysis

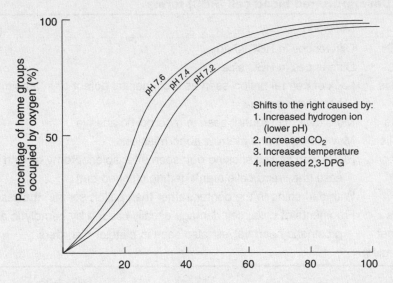

Fig. 7-2. Hemoglobin-oxygen dissociation curve shifts with different substrates. (2,3-DPG=2,3-diphosphoglycerate.)

Oxygen that is dropped off in muscle tissue is picked up by **myoglobin**, a similar protein that has a higher affinity for oxygen than hemoglobin and can therefore grab it away when needed.

Laboratory Evaluation

$Hct = RBC \times MCV$

Three measures are directly determined from a blood sample. **Hemoglobin levels** indicate the amount of hemoglobin in a quantity of blood, usually measured in grams per deciliter. **RBC count** is the number of RBCs in a specific quantity of blood (usually measured in millions per milliliter). Finally, **mean corpuscular volume** (**MCV**) measures the average volume of each RBC, expressed in femtoliters (fl).

From these values, other important indices are calculated. The most widely used is the hematocrit (Hct), calculated by multiplying the RBC count by the MCV. The **hematocrit** is the percentage of RBCs in the blood and is normally 35–45 in women and 40–55 in men (don't bother to memorize these values; more accurate ones are available in the table of normal values during the test). Hematocrit levels are commonly used as a measure of anemia; however, other factors, such as dehydration, can affect hematocrit levels and should be taken into account. Other, less commonly used calculated values are the mean corpuscular hemoglobin (MCH) and the mean corpuscular hemoglobin concentration (MCHC), which are measures of the amount of hemoglobin in each RBC.

The MCV is used to classify anemias by describing the relative size of the RBC. Normal MCV is 80–100 fl. Less than 80 fl constitutes **microcytosis**, whereas more than 100 is **macrocytosis**. If a patient has a mixed microcytosis and macrocytosis, however, the laboratory equipment averages out the size and may report it as normal. In that case, one more measurement, the **red cell distribution width** (**RDW**), is used. The RDW is basically a measure of the "spread" of values around the mean. If the RDW is high, there's a lot of variability in cell size, and you may be dealing with a mixed picture.

Table 7-1. Descriptive red blood cell (RBC) terms

Term	Definition
Poikilocytosis	Differences in RBC shape
Anisocytosis	Differences in RBC size
Spherocytosis	Lack of central pallor; seen as a congenital defect or in autoimmune hemolytic anemia
Elliptocytosis	More oval than round; seen in macrocytic anemia
Teardrop cells	May indicate bone marrow abnormalities
Acanthocytes	RBCs with spikes sticking out; seen after splenectomy or with liver disease (the weird cells aren't getting cleaned out)
Target cells	With darkening in the center, rather than pallor; seen in thalassemias
Schistocytes (e.g., helmet cells, triangles)	Fragments of cells; cell damage usually caused by hemolytic anemia or prosthetic heart valves; also seen in platelet disorders

Other laboratory tests of importance include the following:

- **Reticulocyte count:** A measurement of how many reticulocytes are floating around in the bloodstream. Increased levels during anemia are appropriate.

- **Peripheral blood smear:** Examination of the blood may show abnormalities in RBCs and WBCs that are specific for different conditions. A list of terms used to describe RBCs is provided in Table 7-1.

- **Ferritin:** This protein is the most rapidly accessible iron storage unit. Generally, if levels are high, so are iron levels—but beware! Ferritin is also an acute phase reactant, which means that levels go up inexplicably when people are sick.

- **Serum iron:** This measurement of iron available in the bloodstream does not represent iron stores in the liver or marrow.

- **Transferrin saturation:** Transferrin is the main protein carrier of iron in the blood, along with albumin (by contrast, ferritin is a storage protein). Transferrin saturation (expressed as a percentage) tells you how full these carrier proteins are with iron.

- **Total iron binding capacity (TIBC):** Iron is carried by several proteins in the blood, including transferrin and albumin. This measurement simply tells you how much carrier capacity is out there.

- **Hemosiderin:** This iron storage protein is present in the bone marrow. Bone marrow samples obtained from biopsy are stained for hemosiderin to assess iron stores; this is usually only done in difficult-to-diagnose cases.

Platelet Production

Platelets are tiny chips of **megakaryocytes** (large, multinucleated cells produced in the bone marrow) that float around and plug up any holes or other damage to the endothelium. Platelets love to party: Whenever a few get together (after being activated by binding to damaged epithelium), they tend to send out factors that attract other platelets. The average platelet lives for about 10 days, so when it is "poisoned" (e.g., a patient takes aspirin), it takes about 10 days before the platelets are functional again.

Platelets contain three types of secretory granules:

- **Lysosomes**, which contain acid hydrolases

- **α-Granules**, which carry platelet growth factors

- **δ-Granules**, which contain adenosine triphosphate (ATP), calcium, and serotonin

About 40% of platelets are stored in the spleen and can be released when needed at times of stress and trauma. Platelet aggregation occurs in conjunction with the coagulation cascade, a chain reaction that helps regulate hemostasis.

Hemostasis

When vascular injury occurs, a blood clot forms to stop the bleeding. As simple as that sounds, a number of different responses must occur in sync for proper plug formation and healing to occur:

- Platelet plug formation

- Coagulation

- Antithrombotic mechanisms

Platelet Plug Formation

The four steps of platelet plug formation are 1) adhesion, 2) aggregation, 3) secretion, and 4) procoagulant activity.

Adhesion occurs when the platelets deposit on the subendothelial matrix. This is mediated by the binding of platelet surface receptor glycoprotein **GPIb-IX** to **von Willebrand factor (vWF)**, a sticky protein found in the subendothelial matrix. Endothelial cells are responsible for producing vWF, which they release into the circulating plasma and deposit into the subendothelial matrix. When the subendothelial matrix is exposed by injury, the vWF lures platelets into sticking to the damaged site.

Aggregation, or platelet-platelet cohesion, occurs via the platelet's surface fibrinogen receptor, the **GPIIb-IIIa** complex. When a platelet is stimulated (e.g., by collagen, thrombin, or ADP), its GPIIb-IIIa undergoes a conformational change that allows it to bind **fibrinogen**. Fibrinogen is a divalent, symmetrical molecule, so one stimulated platelet can bind it at one end, and another stimulated platelet can bind the other end; in other words, fibrinogen serves as a bridge between two platelets. It's a good thing that the GPIIb-IIIa of unstimulated platelets does not bind fibrinogen, since that would cause platelets to aggregate uncontrollably throughout our circulating blood! Certain **snake venom** peptides, and the drug abciximab (see end of chapter), prevent platelet aggregation by targeting GPIIb-IIIa.

Secretion refers to the release of granule contents by stimulated platelets. A number of factors that aid in aggregation are released (e.g., ADP, serotonin, thrombospondin, and thromboxane). Growth factors, such as **platelet-derived growth factor (PDGF)**, are also released and may help in mediating tissue repair.

Finally, the activated platelets demonstrate **procoagulant activity**. The platelets produce **factor V**, a component of the coagulation cascade (described below). When activated, the platelets release factor V and bind it to their surfaces. The activated version of factor V (factor Va) serves to bring factor Xa and prothrombin in close proximity, which speeds up thrombin formation and ensures that coagulation occurs at the site of the platelet clot.

Platelet count, platelet morphology, and **bleeding time** are used to assess platelet function.

Coagulation

The coagulation cascade is a series of molecular events that transforms a soluble blood protein, **fibrinogen**, into an insoluble one, called **fibrin**. This can occur by two pathways (Fig. 7-3).

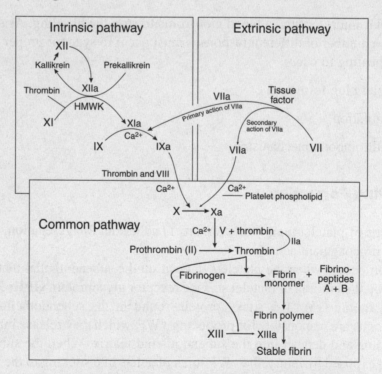

Fig. 7-3. Coagulation cascade. (HMWK = high-molecular-weight kininogen.)

The **extrinsic pathway** (tissue factor $\longrightarrow$ VII $\longrightarrow$ X $\longrightarrow$ II $\longrightarrow$ fibrin) occurs when tissue thromboplastin is released during tissue injury and complexes with circulating factor VII, resulting in its activation. This activates factor X, which then activates factor II (**prothrombin**) to make **thrombin**. Thrombin then cleaves fibrinogen to fibrin, and clotting occurs. In the midst of all this, platelets and calcium also get into the act and enhance activation many thousandfold. Thrombin also activates factor XIII, which cross-links and strengthens the fibrin clot.

The triggers for the **intrinsic pathway** $\longrightarrow$ XI $\longrightarrow$ IX $\longrightarrow$ X $\longrightarrow$ II $\longrightarrow$ fibrin) are less clear but may be related to collagen exposure. The pathway gets its name from the fact that all the substrates needed for clotting are present in, or intrinsic to, the circulating blood. The trigger activates factor XII, which then transforms prekallikrein to kallikrein. Kallikrein feeds back to make more factor XII, and activates factor XI, which activates factor IX. Factor IX activates factor X, which then activates prothrombin and follows the rest of the pathway listed above.

Coagulation tests that are used to assess the pathways include the following:

- **Prothrombin time (PT)** is used to assess the extrinsic pathway and depends on the concentrations of factors II, V, VII, and X. Prolongation of the PT is seen with warfarin use, vitamin K deficiency, and liver disease (since those affect the production of factors II, VI, IX, and X).

- **Partial thromboplastin time (PTT)** is used to assess the intrinsic system. It depends on functionality of factors XII, HMWK, prekallikrein, XI, IX, and VIII. It is prolonged during heparin use, in hemophilia A, B, and von Willebrand's disease. Activated PTT (aPTT) is prolonged by the lupus anticoagulant (LA).

- **Specific factor assays** (e.g., factor VIII) are used to confirm isolated deficiencies, as in the case of hemophilia.

- **D-Dimer** is an assay used to assess possible intravascular clotting. D-Dimer is a cleavage product of fibrin and is elevated in disseminated intravascular coagulation (DIC), in thromboembolic events, and after surgery.

- **Fibrin split products** are also remnants of clotting. They are increased in DIC, after surgery, or in cases of liver or renal failure, when clearance of the products is poor.

Anti-Thrombotic Mechanisms

While the clotting mechanisms are great for preventing uncontrolled bleeding and encouraging vessel repair, other mechanisms are required to ensure that the clotting does not get out of hand and lead to thromboses. These antithrombotic mechanisms include:

- **Regulation of the coagulation cascade:** antithrombin III (ATIII), protein C and protein S, tissue factor pathway inhibitor (TFPI)

- **Modulation of vascular and platelet reactivity: prostacyclin (PGI2)**, endothelium-derived relaxing factor (EDRF)/ nitric oxide (NO)

- **Fibrinolysis:** tissue plasminogen activator (tPA), plasmin

All of the above mechanisms are anchored on endothelial cells.

Regulation of the coagulation cascade

Antithrombin III (ATIII) inhibits thrombin and factor Xa. It can be found circulating in the plasma. Binding of ATIII to the proteoglycan **heparan sulfate** on endothelial cells induces a conformational change that accelerates the action of ATIII greatly. Intravenous **heparin** and subcutaneous **low molecular weight heparin (LMWH)** also augment ATIII activity and are used to treat deep venous thrombosis and pulmonary embolism.

Protein C is a vitamin K-dependent plasma protein that degrades factors Va and VIIIa. The endothelium is key to its activation. First, the binding of thrombin to **thrombomodulin**, an endothelial cell-surface protein, converts the thrombin to an activator of protein C. Once protein C is activated, it binds **protein S**, an endothelium-derived cofactor, and chews up factors Va and VIIIa.

Tissue factor pathway inhibitor (TFPI) is a circulating plasma protein. Half of the circulating TFPI is associated with lipoprotein, particularly LDL. TFPI may also be associated with heparan sulfate on the endothelial surface, which may explain why TFPI levels increase after intravenous heparin administration. TFPI binds to and inhibits factor Xa. After binding factor Xa, it undergoes a conformational change that allows it to inhibit factor VIIa–tissue factor activity as well.

Modulation of vascular and platelet reactivity

Prostacyclin (PGI2) is an arachidonic acid derivative produced by endothelial cells. Its production is induced by cell perturbation (e.g., by thrombin, shear stress, or inflammatory cytokines) leading to the release of arachidonic acid from the cell membrane by phospholipase A_2. PGI_2 induces vasodilation and inhibits platelet activity.

Nitric oxide (NO), known also as **endothelium-derived relaxing factor (EDRF)**, is also released by the endothelium. Because hemoglobin rapidly destroys it, its function is mainly local. It produces vasodilation by relaxing the underlying vascular smooth muscle, and it inhibits platelet adhesion and aggregation.

Fibrinolysis

The key players in fibrinolysis are **tissue plasminogen activator (tPA)** and **plasmin.** When endothelial cells are perturbed (as would happen during vascular injury), they release tPA. tPA converts **plasminogen** to plasmin, which munches on fibrin.

Both tPA and plasminogen have an affinity for fibrin, so they home in on fibrin clots. That's pretty convenient, since the fibrin brings the two into close proximity to each other, facilitating plasmin generation just where plasmin is needed most.

What happens if plasmin is released into the general circulation? **α2-antiplasmin** comes to the rescue. It rapidly inactivates circulating plasmin, thus preventing it from degrading plasma proteins in a generalized and uncontrolled fashion. Bleeding problems occur in those rare patients with congenital deficiency of α2-antiplasmin.

And, to stop tPA activity from going unchecked, **plasminogen activator inhibitor-1 (PAI-1)**, the major physiologic inhibitor of tPA, is released from platelets and endothelial cells. Bleeding disorders in patients with PAI-1 deficiency have been reported.

Histology

- **Erythrocytes (RBCs)** are biconcave disks packed with hemoglobin (Fig. 7-4). They do not have nuclei and do have an area of central pallor, which makes them look like donuts. **Basophilic** stippling of cells occurs in β-thalassemia and **lead poisoning.**

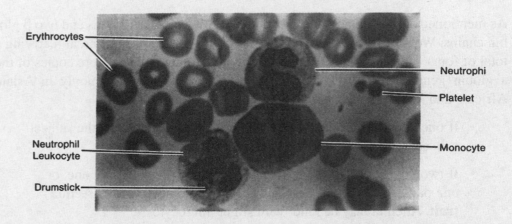

Erythrocytes

Neutrophi

Platelet

Neutrophil
Leukocyte

Monocyte

Drumstick

Fig. 7-4. Cell types. (Reprinted with permission from WJ Krause. *Essentials of Human Histology* [2nd ed]. Boston: Little, Brown, 1996;91, 92.)

- **Reticulocytes** look like RBCs except that they are slightly larger, do not have central pallor, and when stained, show little blue flecks in the cytoplasm, which are the remnant ribosomes that have not yet deteriorated.

- **Neutrophils** are the most common WBC. They feature a multilobed nucleus with pink granulated cytoplasm (the granules are lysosomes). Three to four nuclear lobes are normal; more lobes can indicate underlying disease.

- **Eosinophils** are less common than neutrophils. They are full of bright pink and purple granules and have a large bilobed nucleus. The granules are full of hydrolytic enzymes.

- **Basophils** are small, deep purplish blue cells with bilobed nuclei that are fairly rare. They contain histamine, heparin, and other vasoactive peptides that participate in allergic reactions and anaphylaxis.

- **Lymphocytes** (B and T cells) are small and have big round nuclei that take up most of the cell. They are irregularly shaped in **infectious** mononucleosis.

- **Monocytes** (macrophages) are big, pinkish stained cells with a horse-shoe-shaped nucleus. They are present in the blood and in tissues.

- **Platelets** are little specks of purplish cells that are often clumped together in a blood smear.

A blood smear or two is not unusual on the USMLE, so you might want to glance at a histology book to get a feeling for what the normal proportions of things are on a regular smear—the abnormalities will then be easier to spot.

Congenital Defects

α-Thalassemia

As mentioned earlier, hemoglobin is made up of two α globin chains and two β globin chains. We receive two copies of the a globin gene from each parent (carrying a total of four). α-Thalassemia is the result of a deletion of one or more copies of the a globin gene. Both α- and β-thalassemia are seen more commonly in Asian, African, and Mediterranean populations.

- If one copy of the a gene is deleted (leaving three copies), the subject is usually an **asymptomatic carrier** of α-thalassemia.

- If two copies are deleted (either by each parent giving only one, or one parent giving none), the subject is said to have **α-thalassemia trait**. Anemia may be mild, with slight microcytosis.

- If three copies are deleted, the subject has **Hb-H** disease. These patients have a microcytic anemia. The extra β chains form **tetramers** called *hemoglobin H*. The cells have extra membrane, giving them a **target cell** appearance. Also, they are destroyed faster than normal RBCs, resulting in **hemolysis**.

- Having all four copies deleted is incompatible with life and is called **hydrops fetalis**. Infants are stillborn or barely surviving because they still have g chains, which form tetramers called **Hb Bart**. However, this is not enough for long-term survival.

Diagnosis

Patients suspected of α-thalassemia should undergo hemoglobin electrophoresis to document the extent of disease. This is especially important for genetic counseling and to avoid unnecessary iron therapy because some doctor in the future may see the microcytosis and think it means an iron-deficiency anemia.

There are about 10 published formulas on quick ways to tell iron deficiency from thalassemia. The general rule of thumb is that patients with thalassemia have microcytosis out of proportion to the anemia, meaning that the MCV is much lower than would be expected with a normal or slightly low hematocrit. A more objective method is calculation of the Mentzer index:

$$\text{Mentzer index} = \frac{MCV}{RBC\ count}$$

If the Mentzer index is less than 13, it is usually thalassemia rather than iron-deficiency anemia.

Treatment

No treatment exists, other than genetic counseling to avoid hydrops fetalis births.

β-Thalassemia

β-Thalassemia results from defective β globin chains rather than gene deletion, as in a-thalassemia. Unlike a globin genes, we receive only one copy of the β globin gene from each parent.

If one of the two copies is bad, the patient has **β-thalassemia minor.** This is usually asymptomatic with microcytic anemia and target cells seen on blood smear. These patients also have **basophilic stippling** of their RBCs. They produce small amounts of δ or γ globin chains, which can pair with the a chains and make functional hemoglobin.

If both copies are bad (**β-thalassemia major**), the body is not able to produce enough alternate chains to pair with the a globin chains. The extra a chains precipitate, causing hemolysis. These patients are usually transfusion dependent and have a life expectancy of about 20 years.

Diagnosis

Hemoglobin electrophoresis.

Treatment

No treatment exists. Genetic counseling is important. Patients with β-thalassemia major are usually iron overloaded from hemolysis and transfusions and may need iron chelation therapy with deferoxamine.

Sickle Cell Anemia

Sickle cell anemia is caused by a structural defect in the β globin gene. A base change from GAG to GTG results in a change of the sixth amino acid from glutamic acid to valine. This produces hemoglobin that becomes insoluble and polymerizes when deoxygenated or in low pH. This, in turn, causes RBCs to take on a sickle shape, giving the disease its name. Sickle cell anemia is seen almost exclusively in people of African descent.

If patients carry only one copy of the abnormal β globin gene, they are said to have **sickle-cell trait** and are usually asymptomatic or may have hematuria. Also, it has been noted in a few studies that these patients are more likely to experience sudden death in times of intense physical stress.

If both copies are bad, full-blown **sickle-cell disease** is present, which is manifested by the following:

- **Hemolytic anemia:** Patients develop **jaundice** and **scleral icterus** because of excess unconjugated bilirubin, which also leads to hyper-pigmented gallstones. They may also have **folate deficiency**, from a constant high-production state of RBCs, and **iron overload** because they usually have too much iron from Hb breakdown and from trans-fusions.

- **Destruction of the spleen and increased risk of infection:** The spleen becomes enlarged from all the hemolysis, and parts of it become ischemic (known as **autosplenectomy**). These patients are therefore at greater risk for infection from **encapsulated bacteria**, especially **Streptococcus pneumoniae**, and they tend to develop other unusual infections, such as *Salmonella* osteomyelitis.

- **Painful sickle crises:** These come on with dehydration, stress, and illness and are caused by tissue vaso-occlusion. Pain can be anywhere but is typically along the back and arms. During crises, patients are hospitalized, hydrated, and given narcotics until the pain lessens.

- **Physical abnormalities and decreased life expectancy:** Patients have bone and cardiac abnormalities as well as delayed sexual development. Life expectancy is around 40 years.

All of the above notwithstanding, the genetic story behind sickle cell anemia is interesting. The current theory is that this gene survived because heterozygotes (those with sickle-cell trait) are more resistant to contracting malaria than people without the gene. This apparently conferred an advantage (known as **heterozygote advantage**) on these people and selected for the gene, although the occasional child with sickle-cell disease was born.

Glucose-6-Phosphate Dehydrogenase Deficiency

Glucose-6-phosphate dehydrogenase (G6PD) is an enzyme of the pentose phosphate pathway, used to create the reduced form of nicotinamide-adenosine dinucleotide phosphate (NADPH). When the RBCs of people with this enzyme deficiency are exposed to oxidizing substances, the cells cannot generate reduced glutathione to protect themselves from the oxidative damage. The hemoglobin in the RBCs becomes oxidized and denatures, causing it to precipitate and forming **Heinz** bodies, which damage the cell membrane. The damaged cells are then chewed up by the spleen, which causes a hemolytic anemia. There are many different G6PD deficiency variants, but the most common are X-linked and affect Mediterranean and African populations. Offending substances include quinine derivatives, sulfa drugs, dapsone, aspirin, isoniazid, and fava beans.

Signs & Symptoms

Hemolysis occurs 1–3 days after ingesting the substance. The patient may become jaundiced and produce dark urine.

Diagnosis

Enzyme assay of cells reveals the deficiency. The assay may not show an enzymatic defect soon after a hemolytic episode in individuals with less severe cases of G6PD, because the newly generated, undamaged cells may have near-normal enzymatic activity. Spherocytes and bite cells are seen on peripheral smears during an episode of hemolysis. Heinz bodies may be seen by crystal violet stain.

Treatment

Patients must avoid possible offending substances. Patients undergoing a hemolytic episode should receive hydration, supportive care, and transfusions.

Hereditary Spherocytosis

Hereditary spherocytosis is an autosomal dominant disorder of cell membrane proteins, specifically spectrin and ankyrin, that results in more fragile RBCs, which are prone to destruction within the spleen.

Signs & Symptoms

Patients are often asymptomatic but may develop signs of hemolysis, including jaundice, scleral icterus, and gallstones.

Diagnosis

In addition to a blood smear, an osmotic fragility test aids in diagnosis.

Treatment

Splenectomy is basically curative of the hemolytic anemia. Patients should receive folic acid supplementation.

Anemia

General Approach to Anemia

Anemia is defined as a deficiency in RBCs or hemoglobin. It occurs as a result of one of three situations:

- **Decreased RBC production:** This includes iron, vitamin B_{12}, and folate deficiencies, as well as functional problems, such as anemia of chronic disease (ACD).

- **Increased RBC destruction:** This occurs in hemolytic anemias and other genetic abnormalities.

- **Blood loss:** In young women, this is commonly due to menstrual blood loss. In older women and men, gastrointestinal (GI) tract blood loss (due to peptic ulcer disease or malignancy) is often suspected.

The MCV or the RBC size is the most important value to know when searching for the cause of an anemia. Assuming that the cell population is not mixed (see earlier discussion of RDW under Laboratory Evaluation), the differential diagnosis is shown in Table 7-2.

In addition to the MCV, other tests that assess iron stores and RBC production are then helpful in making a final diagnosis. Table 7-3 shows a comparison of these tests.

The classic symptoms of anemia are **weakness, fatigue**, and **dyspnea on exertion**. Depending on the type of anemia, patients may also exhibit other symptoms.

Table 7-2. Differential diagnosis for anemia

Microcytic (<80 fl)	Normocytic (80–100 fl)	Macrocytic (>100 fl)
Iron-deficiency anemia	Anemia of chronic disease	Vitamin B$_{12}$ or folate deficiency
Thalassemias	Mild iron-deficiency anemia	Liver disease
Lead poisoning	Hemolytic anemia	Hemolytic anemia
Sideroblastic anemia	Anemia following rapid blood loss	Hypothyroidism

Table 7-3. Laboratory tests in selected anemias

Laboratory test	Iron deficiency	Anemia of chronic disease	Thalassemia	Sideroblastic anemia
Serum iron	Low	Low–normal	Normal–high	High
Ferritin	Low	High	Normal–high	High
Transferrin saturation	Low	Low–normal	Normal–high	High
Total iron-binding capacity	Normal–high	Low–normal	Normal	Low–normal
Hemosiderin	None–low	Normal–high	Normal–high	High

Iron-Deficiency Anemia

Iron-deficiency anemia is the most common cause of anemia worldwide. Besides menstruating women, pregnant women and babies (no iron in breast milk) are at increased risk of developing iron deficiency. In men, the GI tract is the first place to look for blood loss.

Signs & Symptoms

Depending on the severity, patients may be asymptomatic or have the classic symptoms. Iron deficiency is also associated with brittle fingernails, smooth tongue, stomatitis, and pica (the desire to eat non-nutritive substances, such as dirt).

Diagnosis

Blood and iron studies show microcytic or normocytic anemia with increased central pallor of the RBCs. Serum iron and ferritin are low, transferrin saturation is low, and TIBC is normal to high. Bone marrow smears show no hemosiderin, revealing a lack of iron stores.

Treatment

Ferrous sulfate supplementation for several months to correct the anemia and rebuild iron stores. Side effects of therapy include constipation and GI distress, making compliance a big issue. Postpartum women should continue to take prenatal vitamins (which are high in iron) to restore blood losses during delivery. Breast-fed babies require iron supplementation as well.

Anemia of Chronic Disease

ACD is the most common anemia in hospitalized patients. For some unknown reason, the presence of a chronic illness, such as malignancy, causes granulocytes to produce **lactoferrin**, which binds iron and sequesters it away. The bone marrow is also less responsive to EPO, resulting in anemia. ACD takes about 1 month to develop, so it is unlikely in acutely ill patients.

Signs & Symptoms

Patients are usually asymptomatic but have some other underlying illness.

Diagnosis

Anemia is usually mild. Iron studies show low iron, high ferritin, low transferrin saturation, and low TIBC.

Treatment

Treatment of the underlying disease. Do not give iron supplementation!

Sideroblastic Anemia

Sideroblastic anemia refers to a group of acquired disorders in which the heme group cannot become part of hemoglobin due to metabolic problems. It is typically seen in cases of lead poisoning, isoniazid toxicity, and chronic alcoholism. As a result, iron collects in the mitochondria, and Prussian blue staining of the cells shows a circle of iron in the cell.

Signs & Symptoms

Similar to other forms of anemia. The symptoms of lead poisoning are discussed in chapter 4.

Diagnosis

MCV may be low, normal, or high. Iron studies show elevated iron and transferrin saturation levels. In cases of lead poisoning, RBCs show basophilic stippling. Definitive diagnosis is made by bone marrow biopsy, which shows erythroid hyperplasia but poor hematopoiesis.

Treatment

The offending agent is removed, if possible. Iron chelation therapy may be useful.

Megaloblastic Anemias

Megaloblastic anemias develop when DNA synthesis is disrupted in the bone marrow. The two most common causes are deficiencies of **vitamin B$_{12}$** and **folate**, although toxic drugs such as **methotrexate** can cause it as well. Megaloblastic anemias are characterized by the following:

- **Macrocytic cells**, known as macro-ovalocytes

- **Pancytopenia**, due to effects on DNA of all three cell lines

- **Hypersegmented neutrophils**, with more than five nucleus lobes

- **Decreased reticulocyte** count

Folate deficiency is the most common cause of megaloblastic anemia, because humans typically carry only a few months of folate stores. Deficiency is seen in anyone who does not get enough leafy, green vegetables (alcoholics, poor or elderly people) or has poor absorption (sprue or Crohn's patients). Pregnant women require increased folate intake because lack of folate is associated with fetal neural tube defects.

Vitamin B_{12} deficiency develops over several years, so it is usually caused by problematic absorption rather than poor intake. As you will see in chapter 13, vitamin B_{12} binds to **intrinsic factor (IF)**, which is produced by gastric parietal cells. The complex is then taken up by the terminal ileum. Any disruption in this process (e.g., gastrectomy, ileectomy, sprue) can cause vitamin B_{12} deficiency. The most common cause is **pernicious anemia**, an autoimmune disorder in which patients have antibodies to IF and parietal cells, resulting in atrophic gastritis and achlorhydria. Other less common (but always testable!) causes of vitamin B_{12} deficiency include bacterial overgrowth (competing for vitamin B_{12}) and infection with the fish tapeworm *Diphyllobothrium latum.*

Signs & Symptoms

In addition to the anemia, folate deficiency is characterized by mouth soreness and a smooth, beefy red tongue. Vitamin B_{12} deficiency is similar but is associated with neurologic defects, such as ataxia, paresthesias, and loss of vibration sense and proprioception. These symptoms are reversible if caught early but may become permanent.

Diagnosis

Folate levels are most accurately checked against RBC folate levels because serum folate reflects recent intake and can be affected by hospital diet. Serum vitamin B_{12} levels are low.

To determine the cause of vitamin B_{12} deficiency, a **Schilling test** must be performed. First, give the patient an intramuscular injection of high-dose vitamin B_{12} to saturate the B_{12} carrier protein, **transcobalamin**. Then, give the patient an oral dose of radiolabeled B_{12}. The radiolabeled B_{12} has no available carrier proteins, so it floats in the blood and is excreted by the kidney. Therefore, if the urine has low levels of B_{12}, you know that it is not being absorbed from the gut; if there's lots of radiolabeled B_{12} in the urine, absorption is normal.

If GI absorption of vitamin B_{12} is poor, you must determine whether it is due to a lack of IF (pernicious anemia) or other causes, such as bacterial overgrowth. When you perform the test again, give the patient a dose of IF to swallow. If urinary excretion of vitamin B_{12} is now normal, the patient has an IF deficiency. If B_{12} urinary excretion is still low, other causes, such as bacterial overgrowth or that gluttonous fish tapeworm, must be considered.

Treatment

Vitamin B_{12} and folate supplementation. Folate deficiency is corrected in several weeks. Depending on the cause, patients with vitamin B_{12} deficiency usually need daily, weekly, then monthly injections to replenish stores and avoid recurrence.

Hemolytic Anemia

Hemolytic anemias can be congenital or acquired, and they result from three basic defects:

- Defects in the circulating environment

- Defects in the RBC membrane

- Defects in the hemoglobin and enzymes

The third type has already been discussed: It includes G6PD deficiency and hemoglobinopathies.

Patients with hemolytic anemias develop hallmarks of hemolysis: jaundice, scleral icterus, dark urine, and gallstones. This is a result of increased serum levels of unconjugated bilirubin derived from heme breakdown. Patients also develop splenomegaly. Serum LDH is elevated, and free plasma **haptoglobin** (a protein that binds heme and takes it to the liver) is low because the haptoglobin is all bound to extra heme in the serum.

Microangiopathic hemolytic anemia is a defect of the circulation. In this disease, things like prosthetic valves or weird endothelial abnormalities (e.g., aneurysms) cause RBC damage. Patients develop the typical signs of hemolytic anemia. Treatment is aimed at the underlying cause, with vitamin supplements and transfusions until then.

Autoimmune hemolytic anemia occurs when antibodies and complement bind to the RBC membrane. In the typical scenario, C3b and Fc fragments cover the RBCs, which allows macrophages to nibble off little bits of plasma membrane. The resulting cell reseals and becomes spherical due to this loss of surface area. The RBCs then get trapped in the spleen and microvasculature. Autoimmune hemolytic anemia can be caused by the following:

- **Warm-reacting antibodies**, which cling to RBCs best at body temperature. This type comprises 90% of autoimmune hemolytic anemias. It is seen in systemic lupus erythematosus patients and persons with malignancy. It is treated with steroids and splenectomy.

- **Cold-reacting antibodies**, which cling at temperatures between 0° and 5°C. Symptoms occur when the extremities get cold, resulting in vaso-occlusion and cyanosis in the fingers, toes, nose, and ears. It is treated by keeping extremities warm and giving steroids.

- **Drug-induced hemolysis**. Some drugs can act as haptens (such as penicillin), whereas others form immune complexes (such as quinidine). Still others can induce antibodies long after the drug has been cleared (such as L-dopa).

Diagnosis

Coombs' test is used to diagnose autoimmune hemolytic anemia. It is performed by mixing Coombs' reagent (antibodies to complement and antibodies to human Igs) with the patient's RBCs. If agglutination occurs, the test is positive.

Treatment

In addition to the measures listed above, treatment for severe cases includes cyto-toxic drugs and plasmapheresis.

Aplastic Anemia

Aplastic anemia is bone marrow failure, with little or no production of RBCs, WBCs, and platelets, resulting in pancytopenia. Causes include the following:

- Drugs, such as chloramphenicol, chlorpromazine, thiouracil, gold compounds, or sulfonamides; or chemotherapeutic agents

- Chemicals, such as benzene (a solvent)

- Radiation

- Infections, particularly hepatitis C

- Congenital anomalies (e.g. Fanconi's aplastic anemia)

- Autoimmune disorders

Signs & Symptoms

Patients develop symptoms characteristic of the loss of each blood cell line. Anemia causes fatigue, dyspnea, and syncope. Neutropenia results in increased infections, particularly bacterial. Thrombocytopenia causes easy bleeding, bruising, and petechiae. Fanconi's aplastic anemia would be associated with other congenital anomalies, such as skeletal malformation and hyperpigmentation. You would not expect splenomegaly or lymphadenopathy in aplastic anemia; the presence of those should point you to other causes, such as leukemia, lymphoma, or myeloid metaplasia.

Diagnosis

Complete blood count (CBC) shows diminishing counts. Bone marrow reveals empty marrow with fatty replacement.

Treatment

Depending on the cause, steroids, granulocyte colony–stimulating factor (G-CSF), and bone marrow transplantation are used if removal of the offending agent is not enough.

Red Cell Aplasia

Unlike aplastic anemia, RBC aplasia is characterized by reticulocytopenia and normocytic anemia in the presence of normal levels and production of leukocytes and platelets. Causes include:

- Parvovirus B19 infection of individuals with chronic hemolytic anemia (e.g., sickle cell anemia, hereditary spherocytosis, acquired immune hemolytic anemia)

- Parvovirus B19 infection of individuals with immunodeficiency (primary, or secondary to AIDS or chemotherapy)

- Transient erythroblastopenia of childhood (TEC)

- Diamond-Blackfan syndrome

- Acquired pure red cell aplasia (PRCA) in adults, associated with hematologic malignancy, autoimmune diseases, and various drugs

Signs and Symptoms

In addition to symptoms of anemia, patients may have symptoms of their underlying disease process. TEC is often preceded by a viral infection (not parvovirus) in a child 0-4 years of age. Patients with Diamond-Blackfan syndrome may have other anomalies, such as a malformed thumb or short stature.

Diagnosis

Bone marrow reveals normal myelopoiesis, normal thrombocytopoiesis, and a markedly reduced presence of erythroid precursors. Diamond-Blackfan syndrome can be differentiated from TEC by markedly elevated erythropoietin levels, macrocytic anemia presenting in the first six months of life, "i" antigen, and increased fetal hemoglobin content.

Treatment

Parvovirus B19-associated erythroid aplasia in patients with chronic hemolytic anemia resolves on its own after a few days. Likewise, spontaneous recovery from TEC occurs over a few weeks, and no treatment is required other than a single RBC transfusion. Intravenous gamma globulin (which contains anti-B19 antibodies) may be helpful in immunodeficiency-associated red cell aplasia. Diamond-Blackfan syndrome is treated with corticosteroids, RBC transfusions, and bone marrow transplantation. Removal of possible instigating drugs, evaluation for thymoma, and treatment of underlying disease is the primary course of action for patients with PRCA. Next, immunosuppression with steroids and other drugs may help achieve remission.

Cythemias

Polycythemia

Polycythemia is an increase in RBCs. In addition to polycythemia vera, a myeloproliferative disorder discussed later, a number of other causes are associated:

- **Spurious polycythemia** occurs when a patient is dehydrated and the CBC looks as if the RBC count is too high. It is corrected with fluids.

- **Blood doping**, or induced erythrocythemia, refers to the transfusion of packed red blood cells or whole blood, often drawn and stored weeks in advance, into an athlete one to seven days before competition. The athletes believe the increased oxygen-carrying capacity improves endurance. This practice is banned by both the International Olympic Committee and the National College Athletic Association. Alternatively, athletes might use recombinant erythropoietin, also classified as a blood doping agent by the International Olympic Committee, to increase oxygen-carrying capacity. Unlike blood transfusions, EPO can be taken in private, without medical personnel. The danger of blood doping in these athletes is that the initially elevated hematocrit, in combination with the spurious polycythemia that occurs during an intense athletic event (secondary to dehydration), may cause the final hematocrit to be as high as in the 60s, increasing the danger of impaired blood flow, thrombosis, infarction, and pulmonary embolism.

- **Secondary polycythemia** is caused by increased EPO secretion. Other than in patients with tumors, this is most often seen in patients who are hypoxic (e.g., smokers with chronic obstructive pulmonary disease and people living at high altitudes). Cardiac shunting and pulmonary hypertension can also cause polycythemia.

- **Stress polycythemia** refers to increased RBCs, possibly from the spleen, at times of physical stress.

Polycythemia Vera

Polycythemia vera is a neoplastic disorder seen in older patients: Mean age at diagnosis is 60. Complications relate to hyperviscosity (from lots of extra cells clogging the works) and include stroke, pulmonary embolus, and deep vein thrombosis. Peptic ulcer disease is more likely, resulting from GI hypoxia with subsequent loss of bicarbonate production and the cytoprotective barrier.

Signs & Symptoms

Signs and symptoms include headache, weakness, and dizziness. There may be generalized itching, particularly after taking a warm shower or bath. Nosebleeds are common, as is splenomegaly. Weight loss, shortness of breath, and joint symptoms are also seen.

Diagnosis

Diagnosis is made by CBC, which shows an elevated hematocrit with normal red blood cell morphology and often shows increased WBCs and thrombocythemia as well. EPO level is decreased due to feedback inhibition. Arterial oxygen saturation is normal.

Treatment

Phlebotomy ("bleeding" the patient—some things never change in medicine!) and chemotherapy. You cannot give the RBCs to other people in transfusions because the RBCs from the patient are cancerous, and about 15% of polycythemia vera patients go on to develop acute myeloblastic leukemia (AML). Survival is about 10 years, and thrombotic complications are common.

Myelofibrosis

Myelofibrosis is the fibrous replacement of bone marrow tissue. The cause is unknown, and it develops in older patients. Fetal sites of erythropoiesis (e.g., liver, spleen) are reactivated. On blood smear, patients have **teardrop-shaped RBCs** and **giant platelets**. Immature WBCs are also seen. Bone marrow aspirate is usually dry. Treatment includes transfusions, splenectomy, and bone marrow transplantation.

Platelet Disorders

Thrombocytopenia

Thrombocytopenia is a decreased number of platelets. Besides the thrombocytopenic disorders discussed below, causes include bone marrow invasion and replacement in leukemia and other malignancies. Thrombocytopenia can also occur in the setting of pancytopenia caused by lack of nutrients (e.g., vitamin B_{12} and folate) or drug reactions. Infectious agents, such as cytomegalovirus and human immunodeficiency virus (HIV), are associated with thrombocytopenia. Consumptive processes, such as DIC, may also decrease platelets. Treatment is typically aimed at the cause, with platelet transfusions given until then. Platelet transfusions are not helpful in consumptive processes and should not be given.

Idiopathic Thrombocytopenia Purpura

Idiopathic thrombocytopenia purpura (ITP) is an autoimmune disorder in which IgG antibodies to platelets are made. ITP in children typically has an abrupt onset after a viral infection and is self-limited. ITP in adults has a more chronic course and is seen more often in women than men.

Signs & Symptoms

Patients experience nosebleeds, menorrhagia, bruising, and mucosal bleeding. Splenomegaly is seen in children.

Diagnosis

Platelet counts are usually less than 10,000/ml. Platelets appear enlarged on blood smear. Platelet-associated IgG assay is often diagnostic.

Treatment

Steroids, splenectomy, and other immunosuppressives are used. Platelet transfusions are not helpful because donor platelets are also destroyed by the autoimmune process.

Thrombotic Thrombocytopenia Purpura

Thrombotic thrombocytopenia purpura (TTP) is a rare disease that is seen in adults. It has five major characteristics:

- Fever

- Thrombocytopenia

- Microangiopathic hemolytic anemia

- Neurologic abnormalities, such as headaches and aphasia

- Renal insufficiency

TTP has been associated with estrogen use and HIV disease, although the exact etiology is unknown.

Diagnosis

In addition to the characteristics listed above, patients have anemia and reticulocytosis. On blood smear, schistocytes and other chewed-up cells are present.

Treatment

Plasmapheresis and steroids are used. Splenectomy can be performed if plasmapheresis is ineffective. The disease course is waxing and waning, with spontaneous remissions.

Hemolytic-Uremic Syndrome

Hemolytic-uremic syndrome is seen in infants and children and frequently occurs after *Salmonella*, *Shigella*, or *Escherichia* coli 0157:H7 infection. It has most of the same characteristics as TTP, although it may present with diarrhea, and there are no neurologic effects. The syndrome is usually self-limited and requires supportive care.

Other Platelet Dysfunctions

- **Glanzmann's thrombasthenia** is a rare, autosomal recessive disease in which patients have abnormal platelets that are unable to aggregate because they are deficient in GPIIb–IIIa. Laboratory tests show normal platelet numbers and morphology. Treatment is with platelet transfusions.

- **Bernard-Soulier disease** is a rare, autosomal recessive disease in which platelets lack receptors for von Willebrand's factor (vWF). On smear, platelets appear large, and are often present in low numbers. Treatment is with platelet transfusions.

- **Storage pool disease** is an autosomal dominant disease seen primarily in women, in which platelets are normal in size and shape but have decreased δ-granule content. Symptoms are usually mild and treatable with platelet transfusions.

- **Aspirin** and other nonsteroidal anti-inflammatory drugs affect platelets through acetylation of cyclooxygenase, a factor in platelet aggregation. This effect basically "poisons" the platelet for its life span, so that patients have an increased bleeding tendency for about 10 days, until new platelets are released.

- **Uremia** affects platelet aggregation, although the mechanism is not well understood. Platelet transfusions are not helpful, although dialysis and cryoprecipitate may help.

Coagulopathies

Hemophilia A and B

Hemophilia A is an X-linked recessive deficiency in factor VIII that affects about 1 in 10,000 males. **Hemophilia B** is an X-linked recessive deficiency of factor IX that is less common than hemophilia A, affecting 1 in 100,000 people. The two diseases are clinically indistinguishable and are differentiated only by laboratory tests. Most hemophiliacs are HIV-positive because of tainted plasma supplies in the 1970s and 1980s.

Signs & Symptoms

Patients begin experiencing spontaneous bleeding shortly after birth. Bleeding often occurs in the joints and soft tissues but may occur anywhere, including the urinary tract, GI tract, and central nervous system.

Diagnosis

Prolonged PTT is seen. Definitive diagnosis is made with a factor VIII or IX assay, which reveals the deficiency. Bleeding time (a standardized test in which a person is given a small cut and timed for spontaneous clotting) is normal, as this is a disorder of coagulation, not platelet plug formation (compare with von Willebrand's disease, discussed later).

Treatment

Coagulation factor and plasma replacement. The antidiuretic hormone analogue deamino-8-D-arginine vasopressin (ddAVP) may increase factor VIII production.

von Willebrand's Disease

von Willebrand's disease is an autosomal dominant disease in which patients have a deficiency of vWF, which is needed for platelet adhesion to endothelial tissue. They also have a functional deficiency of factor VIII activity, since vWF is a carrier protein for circulating factor VIII.

Signs & Symptoms

Bleeding from the skin and mucous membranes is common, including easy bruisability, nosebleeds, and menorrhagia. Bleeding into the joints is uncommon.

Diagnosis

Prolonged PTT is due to effect on factor VIII function. Bleeding time is prolonged due to effect on platelet plug formation. Assays of factor VIII and vWF show deficiency.

Treatment

Replacement of factor VIII and vWF.

Protein C and Protein S Deficiencies

Protein C and protein S are vitamin K–dependent proteases that inactivate factors V and VIII. Deficiency of one or both of these proteins is usually autosomal dominant. Patients with this deficiency who are started on warfarin may experience a precipitous drop in what low levels of proteins C and S they have, resulting in hypercoagulability and skin necrosis. Therefore, it is standard to keep patients on heparin until warfarin levels are therapeutic and confirmed by a prolonged PT.

Antithrombin III Deficiency

Patients with ATIII deficiency, an autosomal dominant deficiency, have a clinical presentation similar to patients with protein C and protein S deficiency. The first thrombosis usually occurs in the second or third decades and is usually venous. Thrombosis is treated with heparin, with or without ATIII administration, and patients are kept on life-long warfarin therapy.

Factor V Leiden

Factor V Leiden is caused by a single amino acid substitution at the activated protein C cleavage site of factor V, rendering it ten times less susceptible to degradation by protein C. Heterozygotes have a ten-fold greater risk for venous thromboses, and homozygotes have a 50- to 100-fold greater risk. This mutation has a high prevalence in the Caucasian population.

Disseminated Intravascular Coagulation

DIC occurs when the coagulation system goes completely haywire. Increased activation of the entire clotting system occurs, resulting in microthrombi and infarction. This causes an overconsumption of platelets and clotting factors, so that even though patients are clotting, they start bleeding to death. The cause is unknown but may be related to the release of a tissue factor into the circulation. It is seen most commonly after obstetric complications, severe infections, and massive injury.

Signs & Symptoms

Patients may experience bleeding, infarction, or both. Organs that are often affected include the kidneys, lungs, and brain. Convulsions and coma are seen in the final stages.

Diagnosis

Laboratory tests show low fibrinogen, low platelets, and elevated D-dimer and other fibrin split products.

Treatment

Treatment depends on whether patients are bleeding or infarcting. Heparin (for infarctions) or fresh frozen plasma (for bleeding) is often given. Treatment of the underlying disease is crucial.

Lymphomas

Hodgkin's Disease

Hodgkin's disease (HD) causes 40% of all lymphomas and has a bimodal distribution, affecting young adults as well as older adults. Patients with immune deficiency, either congenital or acquired (e.g., from HIV), are at greater risk of developing HD. HD may also have a genetic predisposition.

Signs & Symptoms

The classic presentation is a painless, rubbery lymph node in the neck (can also be mediastinal or para-aortic) accompanied by constitutional symptoms, such as weight loss and night sweats. The disease often spreads contiguously to adjacent lymph nodes.

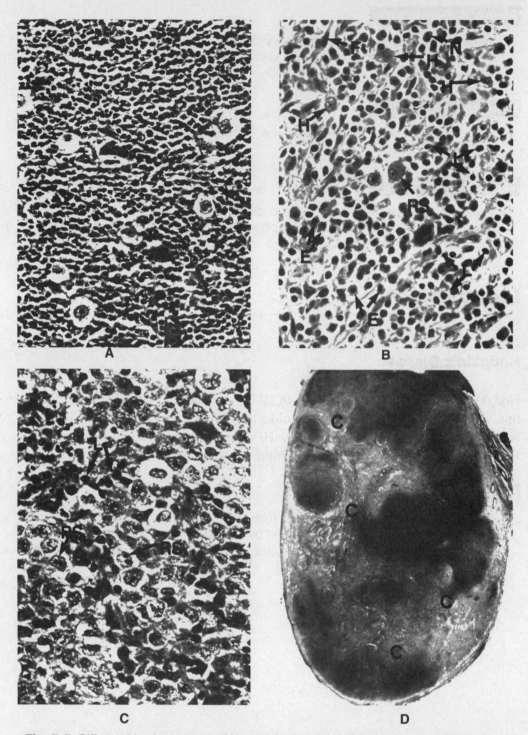

Fig. 7-5. Different histologic types of Hodgkin's disease. **A.** Lymphocyte-predominant pattern. **B.** Lymphocyte-depleted pattern. **C.** Mixed cellularity pattern. **D.** Nodular sclerosing pattern. (RS = Reed-Sternberg cells; C = collagen.) (Reprinted with permission from PR Wheater, HG Burkitt, A Stevens, JS Lowe. *Basic Histopathology: A Colour Atlas and Text* [2nd ed]. Edinburgh: Churchill Livingstone, 1991;165.)

Diagnosis

Lymph node biopsy reveals **Reed-Sternberg (RS) cells** (they look like a pair of owl's eyes), which confirms the diagnosis (Fig. 7-5). There are four main types of HD:

- **Nodular sclerosing HD** (75%) is slowly progressive and has an associated fibroblastic response with collagen production. It occurs more often in women and in adolescents and young adults. The prognosis is good.

- **Mixed cellularity HD** (20%) can be localized or widespread and has an intermediate progression rate. It is characterized by plasma cells and granulocytes mixed with RS cells. It is often symptomatic, and the prognosis is intermediate.

- **Lymphocyte-predominant HD** (5%) is slowly progressive and tends to be localized and asymptomatic. It is characterized by few RS cells relative to the abundant lymphocytes. It tends to occur in younger individuals (<35 years old). Prognosis is excellent.

- **Lymphocyte-depleted HD** (<1%) is aggressive and characterized by mostly RS cells. It tends to occur in older patients and is asymptomatic with widespread involvement. The prognosis is poor.

Treatment

Radiation and chemotherapy. The cure rate is generally excellent, with a 10-year survival averaging more than 75%. Stage is the most important prognostic factor.

Non-Hodgkin's Lymphoma

Non-Hodgkin's lymphoma (NHL) is a mixed group of disorders of lymphocytic cancers found in tissues. NHL is seen in people over age 50 and is more common in males. The lymphomas that are included in this classification are listed in Table 7-4.

NHL has been associated with a number of factors:

- Some forms of NHL are associated with viral infections. In Africa, Burkitt's lymphoma is associated with Epstein-Barr virus (although the virus has not been associated with North American forms).

- Immune deficiency by HIV or congenital causes is associated with NHL.

- Increased rates of NHL are seen in people exposed to herbicides.

Signs & Symptoms

Painless lymphadenopathy and constitutional symptoms. Many forms are found in the abdomen and are not diagnosed until dissemination and bone marrow involvement has occurred.

Table 7-4. Non-Hodgkin's lymphoma

Disease	Notes
Low-grade	
Small lymphocytic	Bone marrow involvement
	Older patients
	Overlaps with chronic lymphoblastic leukemia
Small cleaved cell	B cells (look larger with cleaved nucleus)
	Bone marrow involvement
	Translocation (14:18)
Small cleaved and large cell	Like small cleaved
	Rare
Intermediate-grade	
Follicular large cell	Rare
	Many mitotic figures
	Poor prognosis
Diffuse small cleaved cell	More common in males
	Aggressive
	Translocation (11:14)
Diffuse mixed cell	Cells are 4× size of regular lymph nodes
Diffuse large cell	Acts like a high-grade lymphoma
High-grade	
Immunoblastic	Cells are 5× size of regular lymph nodes
	Mostly B cells
	Spread to central nervous system, gastrointestinal tract, **Waldeyer's ring** (nodes around mouth)
Small noncleaved (including Burkitt's)	Burkitt's associated with Epstein-Barr virus
	B cells express IgM
	Frequently affects jaw and abdomen
Lymphoblastic	Thymus involvement
	Usually in childhood; aggressive

Diagnosis

Lymph node biopsy reveals the diagnosis. If disseminated, "blast" cells may be found in the bloodstream, in which case the distinction between lymphoma and

Diagnosis

Lymph node biopsy reveals the diagnosis. If disseminated, "blast" cells may be found in the bloodstream, in which case the distinction between lymphoma and leukemia is difficult to make.

Treatment

Radiation and chemotherapy, but the prognosis is grim, with median survival of about 1–3 years.

Leukemias

Acute Lymphoblastic Leukemia

Acute lymphoblastic leukemia (ALL) is most often seen in pediatric groups, with peak ages at 3–7 years. ALL comprises 80% of all childhood leukemia. It occurs due to clonal overproliferation of lymphoblasts, which crowd out all other cell types in the bone marrow. About 60% of cases display a B-cell antigen known as the common antigen, or CALLA.

Signs & Symptoms

Kids develop fatigue, anorexia, and frequent nosebleeds over a period of a few weeks. Lymphadenopathy and hepatosplenomegaly are present.

Diagnosis

CBC shows pancytopenia, and bone marrow biopsy is full of lymphoblasts with aneuploid chromosomal abnormalities.

Treatment

Chemotherapy with vincristine and doxorubicin is often followed by bone marrow transplantation. In young patients, prognosis is very good, with long-term survival exceeding 60%.

Acute Myeloblastic Leukemia

AML is a disease of adults and is seen with slightly increased frequency after age 40. AML causes 20% of all childhood leukemias. It is caused by the proliferation of pluripotent hematopoietic stem cells, which can cause overgrowth of immature cells in any myeloid line, including monocytes, granulocytes, and megakaryocytes. Translocation (t 15:17) is associated with AML.

Signs & Symptoms

Patients develop anemia, neutropenia, and thrombocytopenia over a period of a few months. Severe fatigue, recurrent infections, and gingival bleeding are common. Splenomegaly is seen, although hepatomegaly is uncommon.

Diagnosis

CBC shows pancytopenia. Bone marrow biopsy shows an increase in myeloblast cells, which contain rodlike inclusions known as **Auer rods.**

Treatment

Chemotherapy with cytarabine or daunorubicin. Prognosis is poor, with a 20% 5-year survival rate. However, bone marrow transplant has good results in patients under 30 and may bring the survival up to 65%. Death usually occurs due to infection.

Chronic Lymphocytic Leukemia

Chronic lymphocytic leukemia is seen in adults over age 35. It appears to have a familial tendency, unlike other leukemias. Abnormal proliferation of lymphocytes occurs in the bone marrow, lymph nodes, and spleen.

Signs & Symptoms

Most patients are asymptomatic, and diagnosis occurs when a CBC is done for other medical problems. Fatigue, weight loss, and lymphadenopathy are seen.

Diagnosis

CBC shows a mildly elevated WBC count with increased absolute lymphocyte count to about 8,000/ml. Surface antigen testing of the lymphocytes is done for diagnosis. Bone marrow biopsy is rarely necessary but shows infiltration with well-differentiated lymphocytes.

Treatment

Treatment may not be beneficial until the patient is symptomatic and there is evidence of bone marrow infiltration, which may take several years. Once the disease becomes more active, chemotherapy to reduce lymphocyte mass is used. Survival depends on the stage of diagnosis but is usually at least 2–4 years, and death occurs due to infection.

Chronic Myeloid Leukemia

Chronic myeloid leukemia (CML) is typically seen in patients over age 20. It is like AML, except that the leukemic cells tend to be more mature cells, often with megakaryocytes. CML is associated with the **Philadelphia chromosome**, a reciprocal translocation between **chromosomes 9** and **22**. The proto-oncogenes *abl* and *bcr* are pasted together to form a fusion gene.

Signs & Symptoms

Long, insidious development of fatigue, easy bruisability, and early satiety. Splenomegaly is almost always seen. After a number of years, the patient's disease may accelerate into a blastic phase, with symptoms similar to AML.

Diagnosis

CBC shows WBC count greater than 20,000/ml and possibly up to several hundred thousand! Increased basophils and eosinophils are common. Bone marrow biopsy shows overgrowth of granulocyte and megakaryocyte precursors. Cells in metaphase almost always have the Philadelphia chromosome. Normal erythropoiesis may continue, although it is reduced.

Treatment

Chemotherapy with busulfan or hydroxyurea. Interferon-a is also used and may cause elimination of the Philadelphia cell clone. Survival can exceed 10 years, but median survival is about 3–5 years. Once the blastic phase starts, survival is usually less than 6 months.

Hairy Cell Leukemia

Hairy cell leukemia is a rare B-cell leukemia seen in older men. The cells contain tartrate-resistant acid phosphatase, and the cells have hairlike cytoplasmic projections, which give the disease its name. Patients present with pancytopenia and splenomegaly. Survival is 3–4 years with treatment.

Plasma Cell Dysfunction

Multiple Myeloma

Multiple myeloma is cancer of the plasma cells seen in older adults. The cells produce a single monoclonal antibody (usually IgG or IgA, rarely IgD or IgE). It is seen more commonly in radiation-exposed people and in people of African descent. It is associated with the c-myc translocation.

Signs & Symptoms

Patients typically have back pain and bone pain where the disease causes lytic lesions. Symptoms of anemia and infections due to neoplastic overgrowth of hematopoietic centers are also common.

Diagnosis

Pathologic fractures and **punched-out lesions** are seen on X-ray, and patients have **Bence Jones proteins** (immunoglobulin light chains) in their urine. Hypercalcemia due to lytic lesions and renal disease may develop. Definitive diagnosis is made with serum electrophoresis, which shows a monoclonal spike.

Treatment

Palliative treatment. Persistent back pain may be a sign of spinal cord compression and requires radiation or surgery. Patients should receive vaccinations for encapsulated organisms, such as *S. pneumoniae* and *Haemophilus influenzae*.

Waldenström's Macroglobulinemia

Waldenström's macroglobulinemia is a B-cell malignancy of IgM production seen in elderly persons.

Signs & Symptoms

Patients develop a hyperviscosity syndrome with neurologic changes and visual impairment. The proteins may precipitate at low temperatures and cause sluggish circulation in the extremities.

Diagnosis

Monoclonal IgM spike is seen on serum electrophoresis. Coombs' test may be positive.

Treatment

Plasmapheresis and chemotherapy. Survival is usually a few years.

Pharmacology

Table 7-5 lists the most commonly used anticoagulant drugs.

Table 7-5. Anticoagulant drugs

Agent	Mechanism	Uses	Toxicity
Heparin	Binds antithrombin III and inhibits activation of factor X and thrombin	Deep vein thrombosis Myocardial infarction Pulmonary embolism Deep vein thrombosis prophylaxis	Risk of hemorrhage Antidote is protamine sulfate Monitor partial thromboplastin time
Warfarin (Coumadin)	Vitamin K antagonist Decreases synthesis of factors (II, VII, IX, and X)	Deep vein thrombosis Myocardial infarction Pulmonary embolism Atrial fibrillation	Teratogen, can cause fetal hemorrhage Monitor prothrombin Antidote is vitamin K and fresh frozen plasma P-450 drugs can decrease effect

Table 7-6 lists some common antiplatelet drugs.

Table 7-6. Antiplatelet drugs

Agent	Mechanism	Uses	Toxicity
Aspirin	Irreversibly binds cyclooxygenase, preventing thromboxane formation and platelet aggregation	Stroke prophylaxis Myocardial infarction prophylaxis	Gastrointestinal effects (gastritis, peptic ulcer disease)
Ticlopidine	ADP inhibition, preventing platelet aggregation	Stroke prophylaxis	For people who can't tolerate aspirin Neutropenia Gastrointestinal upset
dipyridimole	Not understood, possibly increases platelet cAMP concentration	Thrombosis prevention in patients with heart valves	Angina pectoris, EKG changes
Abciximab (ReoPro)	Fab fragment of monoclonal antibody to GPIIb-IIIa receptor blocks platelet aggression	Antithrombotic agent in high risk patients undergoing coronary artery balloon angioplasty (PCTA)	Bleeding, hypertension thrombocytopenia

Table 7-7 lists the most commonly used thrombolytic agents.

Table 7-7. Thrombolytic drugs

Agent	Mechanism	Uses	Toxicity
Tissue plasminogen activator (tPA)	Binds to fibrin and converts plasminogen to plasmin, which digests fibrin clots	Emergency treatment of coronary artery and treatment of multiple pulmonary emboli	Bleeding, downstream emboli
Streptokinase	Derived from bacterial-cultures, converts plasminogen to plasmin	Emergency treatment of coronary artery thrombosis (acute myocardial infraction), treatment of multiple pulmonary emboli and deep venouss thrembosi	Bleeding, downstream emboli, fever, usually avoid giving to patients twice because antibodies may form after first administration
Urokinase	Derived from cultured, human kidney cells, converts plasminogen to plasmin	Treatment of multiple pulmonary emboli; locally injected for treatment of arterial and venous thromboses (not usually used for myccardial infraction	Bleeding, downstream emboli

Certain drugs and gases can damage the ability of hemoglobin to carry oxygen to tissues. **Carbon monoxide** binds to hemoglobin with 250 times the affinity of oxygen. Low levels of CO can cause symptoms of headache, nausea, and dizziness, while high levels can lead to confusion, dyspnea, syncope, or even seizures and coma. Treatment consists of 100% oxygen delivered at high flow.

Methemoglobinemia occurs when the iron in hemoglobin is oxidized to its ferric state, producing methemoglobin. Drugs capable of causing this reaction include benzocaine, nitrites, nitrous oxide gas, and dapsone. Methemoglobin is incapable of carrying oxygen. Individuals with methemoglobinemia, like those with carbon monoxide poisoning, may have experience dizziness, headache, nausea, or confusion, or they may suffer from seizures or coma. The patient may appear cyanotic due to the "chocolate brown" color of methemoglobin (which retains this dark color even when the blood is exposed to room air), but the PO_2 obtained by arterial blood gas will appear normal. Treatment includes administration of high-flow oxygen and intravenous administration of methylene blue, which converts the methemoglobin to hemoglobin.

Of note, for victims of **cyanide poisoning**, you actually *want* to induce methemoglobin production, usually through administration of **amyl nitrite**. Cyanide, as you may recall, has a predilection for poisoning mitochondria, which can cause a lot of damage to a lot of vital organs. Methemoglobin has a higher affinity for cyanide than hemoglobin, so by inducing methemoglobinemia, you have a better chance of sequestering the cyanide away from the mitochondria. The temporary loss of some RBC functionality is a small price to pay to keep those vital organs alive!

CHAPTER 8

Neurology and Neuroanatomy

Embryonic Development

The complex human nervous system forms from a simple, ectodermal tube. During week 3 of development, the neural plate forms from a thickened area of ectoderm. This invaginates and forms the **neural tube**. Parts of ectoderm are pinched off and joined to form the **neural crest** that overlies the tube (Fig. 8-1).

Central Nervous System Development

Neural tube derivatives include most of the central nervous system (CNS): brain, brain stem, and spinal cord. The hollow center of the tube becomes the ventricular system of the brain.

The tube closes first in the cervical area. Closure then occurs both rostrally (toward the head) and caudally (toward the buttocks). Disorders occur when closure fails (discussed later). The rostral opening closes by mid-week 4. The caudal neuropore closes about 2 days later.

During the fourth week of development, the tube's gray matter differentiates into a ventral **basal plate** and dorsal **alar plate** (Fig. 8-2). The basal plate becomes the anterior horn of the spinal cord. Motor neurons develop in the anterior horn and extend out of the spinal cord to innervate skeletal muscles. This basal plate–motor relationship holds true in the brain stem as well.

Similarly, the **alar plate** becomes the posterior horn of the spinal cord. Sensory neurons, in the periphery, derive from neural crest cells. Their processes end mainly in the posterior horn and synapse with neurons that ascend to the brain. The same alar-sensory relationship holds true in the brain stem (Fig. 8-3). The only difference is that instead of dorsal, the sensory nuclei are pushed laterally in the rostral medulla and caudal pons by the fat fourth ventricle. Superior to the brain stem, the entire cerebrum is thought to derive from the alar plate.

In addition to the ventral motor horn and the dorsal sensory horn, a group of neurons gathering between them forms a small intermediate horn with mainly sym-

Basal plate becomes the anterior horn, with motor neurons.

Alar plate becomes the posterior horn, with sensory neurons.

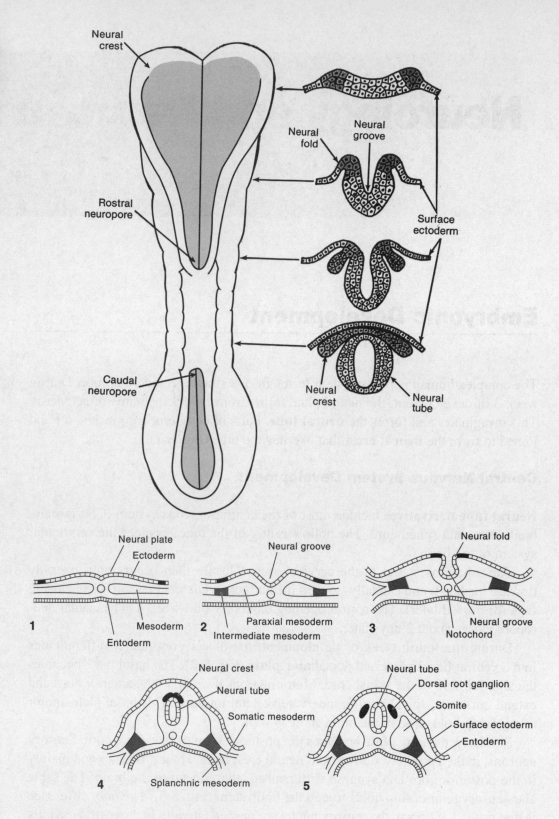

Fig. 8-1. Neural tube development.

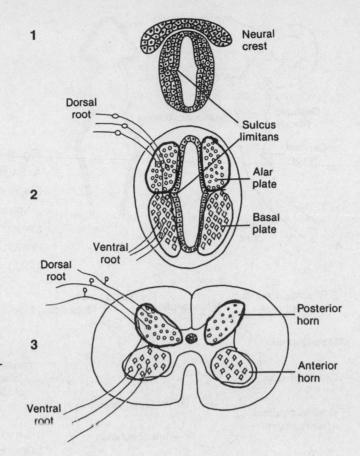

Fig. 8-2. Basal and alar plates. (Reprinted with permission from J Nolte. *The Human Brain: An Introduction to Its Functional Anatomy* [3rd ed]. St. Louis: Mosby, 1993.)

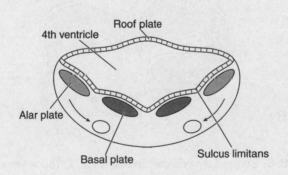

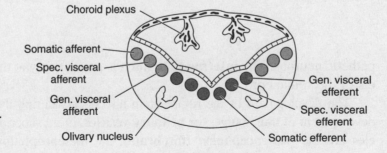

Fig. 8-3. Basal and alar plates in the brain stem.

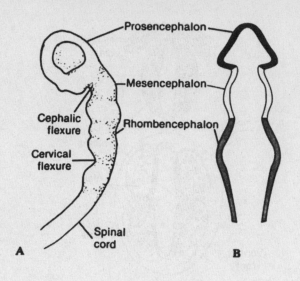

Fig. 8-4. Primary vesicles (week 4). **A.** Sagittal view. **B.** Coronal view. (Reprinted with permission from J Nolte. *The Human Brain: An Introduction to Its Functional Anatomy* [3rd ed]. St. Louis: Mosby, 1993.)

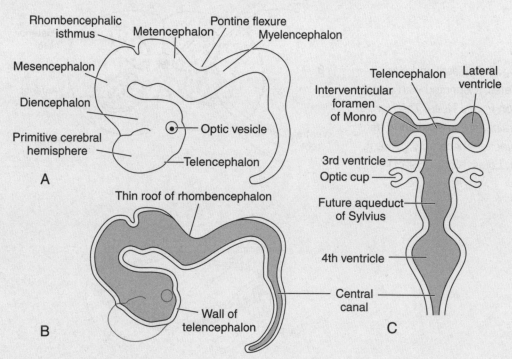

Fig. 8-5. Secondary vesicles (week 6). **A.** Exterior view. **B.** Sagittal view. **C.** Coronal view.

pathetic neurons. The **intermediate horn** is present only at thoracic and L2–L3 levels of the spinal cord.

The development of the future brain also occurs during the fourth week with the development of three bulges, or **primary vesicles**. From superior to inferior, these vesicles are the **prosencephalon (forebrain)**, the **mesencephalon (midbrain)**, and the **rhombencephalon (hindbrain)** (Fig. 8-4). Two of these then divide into **secondary vesicles** (week 5; Fig. 8-5), which develop into various brain and brain stem areas. Each secondary vesicle retains a cavity that becomes part of the ventricular system (Table 8-1).

The rostral end of the neural tube undergoes intense cell replication and complex folding. Once the basic shape of the brain is established, cell division continues in

Table 8-1. Neural tube derivatives

Primary vesicle	Secondary vesicle	Neural tube derivatives	Cavity
Prosencephalon	Telencephalon	Cerebral hemispheres	Lateral ventricles
	Diencephalon	Thalamus, hypothalamus	Third ventricle
Mesencephalon	Mesencephalon	Midbrain	Cerebral aqueduct
Rhombencephalon	Metencephalon	Pons and cerebellum	Fourth ventricle
	Myelencephalon	Medulla	Fourth ventricle and central canal

regions found along the lining of the ventricular system (**germinal zones** or matrices). Neurons and glia must migrate to their appropriate targets. The shape of the ventricular system mimics that of the rostral end of the brain. The **cerebellum** arises from the roof of the rhombencephalon and is covered over by the expansion of the cerebrum.

Two separate cerebral hemispheres are joined by the **corpus callosum** and form a central **brain stem** and **thalamus**. The spiral growth of the cerebral hemisphere results in formation of the temporal, parietal, occipital, and frontal lobes surrounding an area of cortex known as the **insula**. During the second half of pregnancy and after birth, myelination and development of dendrites, axons, and synapses continues.

There is a long period of continued neuronal and glial growth, and an even longer period during which neurons elaborate dendritic and axonal branches. In fact, rearrangement and development of new structural connections may continue throughout life. Postnatal growth of the brain is likely due to glial proliferation, myelin formation, and dendritic or axonal growth rather than generation of new neurons. There is probably no postnatal neuron genesis in humans.

Myelination promotes more rapid axonal conduction and accompanies the onset of sophisticated motor and sensory abilities. Spinal cord nerve fibers are myelinated by **oligodendroglia**. This also begins during the fourth month of intrauterine life and continues postnatally. Peripheral nerves are myelinated by **Schwann cells**, which originate from the neural crest and wrap themselves around the axons. This occurs around the fourth month of fetal life.

CNS myelination by oligodendroglia

Peripheral nerves are myelinated by Schwann cells.

Peripheral Nervous System Development

Neural crest derivatives include most of the peripheral nervous system (PNS). Cell types include sensory neurons of the spinal and cranial nerve ganglia, postganglionic neurons of the autonomic nervous system, Schwann cells, and satellite cells of the PNS. Other types include pigment cells, odontoblasts, meninges, and mesenchyme of the branchial arches. The neural crest cells of the sympathetic system invade the medial aspect of the developing adrenal gland, giving rise to its medulla (**chromaffin cells**). Failure of the neural crest cells to migrate into the wall of the colon results in lack of parasympathetic ganglia in this region. The resulting absence of the myenteric plexus causes the congenital megacolon of **Hirschsprung's disease**, characterized by fecal retention and abdominal distention.

In the autonomic nervous system, the sympathetic system is located in the thoracolumbar region and the parasympathetic system is found in the cervical and sacral regions.

Histology

Cells proliferate rapidly after the neural tube closes. When a cell is destined to stop dividing, the postmitotic neuron migrates to its intended position in the CNS. In a few regions, neuroblasts may divide after migrating. However, the vast majority of neurons are formed by the time of birth and must last a lifetime.

Differentiation of cell types occurs as follows:

- **Nerve cells**: Neuroepithelial cells divide to form neuroblasts. These cells lose their ability to divide. They migrate and develop **axons** and **dendrites**, eventually becoming neurons.

- **Glial cells**: Neuroepithelial cells divide to form glioblasts, too (after they're finished producing neuroblasts). **Astrocytes** and **oligodendroglia** are thought to come from glioblasts. However, **microglia** (CNS macrophage-like cells) likely derive from mesenchyme cells.

- **Ependymal cells**: When the neuroepithelial cells cease producing neuroblasts and glioblasts, they finally differentiate into **ependymal cells**, which line the ventricles.

Fetal Nervous System Development

The development of neurons, axon projections, and synaptic connections depends on molecular cues. At a later stage of development, however, the fine-tuning of synaptic connections depends on electrical activity and neuron use. For example, the development of normal vision relies on visual experience.

An overabundance of neurons is produced, and up to 50% ultimately die during normal development. This may occur by way of a programmed cell death (**apoptosis**). A neuron survives or dies depending on whether it forms appropriate target connections.

Neuroanatomy

Figure 8-6 shows a cross section of the major regions of the developed brain. Remember, the spinal nerves C1–C7 all travel above their corresponding vertebrae. The rest of the spinal nerves travel below the vertebrae (except C8, which passes beneath the C7 vertebra).

The entire brain and spinal cord are encased in **meninges**. This protective covering has three layers. The innermost is the **pia** (soft) mater, middle is the **arachnoid**, and most exterior is the **dura** (hard) mater. The pia mater adheres closely to the brain and spinal cord. The arachnoid is a weblike intermediate layer. Cerebrospinal fluid (CSF) flows in the subarachnoid space. The dura mater forms the tough outer covering of the CNS.

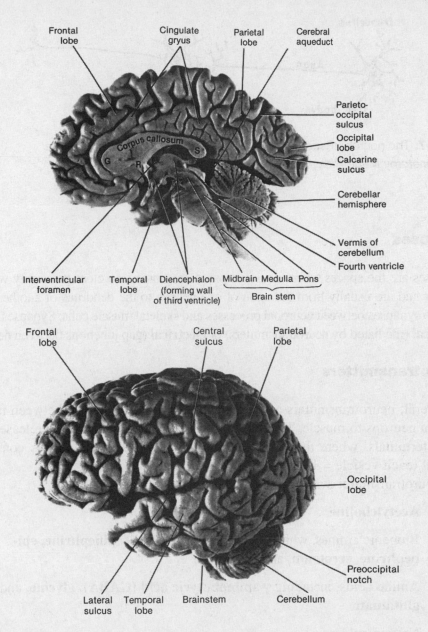

Frontal lobe
Cingulate gryus
Parietal lobe
Cerebral aqueduct
Corpus callosum
G
S
R
Parieto-occipital sulcus
Occipital lobe
Calcarine sulcus
Cerebellar hemisphere
Vermis of cerebellum
Fourth ventricle
Interventricular foramen
Temporal lobe
Diencephalon (forming wall of third ventricle)
Midbrain
Medulla
Pons
Brain stem

Frontal lobe
Central sulcus
Parietal lobe
Occipital lobe
Preoccipital notch
Lateral sulcus
Temporal lobe
Brainstem
Cerebellum

Fig. 8-6. Regions of the cerebral cortex. (Reprinted with permission from J Nolte. *The Human Brain: An Introduction to Its Functional Anatomy* [3rd ed]. St. Louis: Mosby, 1993.)

Neurons and Neurotransmitters

Neurons

Neurons are the basic unit of communication in the nervous system. They are composed of cell bodies, axons, and dendrites, and they communicate with other neurons at synapses (Fig. 8-7). Neurons with a common function tend to be grouped together in the brain (**nuclei**) or outside the brain (**ganglia**).

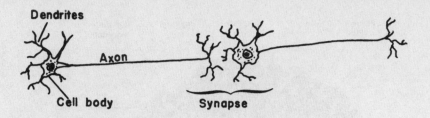

Fig. 8-7. The neuron. (Reprinted with permission from S Goldberg. *Clinical Neuroanatomy Made Ridiculously Simple*. Miami: MedMaster, 1997;4.)

Synapses

Synapses are the spaces where neuronal processes come into close proximity with one another and are usually from the axon of one neuron to the dendrites of another. There are also synapses between neuronal processes and skeletal muscle cells. Synapses may be **chemical** (mediated by neurotransmitters) or **electrical** (gap junctions between neurons).

Neurotransmitters

In general, neurotransmitters are chemicals that serve as signals between neurons or from neurons to muscle. They are synthesized in the neurons and released from nerve terminals, where they are concentrated in vesicles. Release is considered quantal (each vesicle = 1 quantum).

Neurotransmitter systems include the following:

- **Acetylcholine**

- Biogenic amines, which include **dopamine, norepinephrine, epinephrine, serotonin,** and **histamine**

- Amino acids, including **γ-aminobutyric acid (GABA), glycine,** and **glutamate**

- Neuropeptides

There is more than one type of receptor for each neurotransmitter, and therefore, a single neurotransmitter may have a variety of effects on the postsynaptic cell. The neurotransmitter signal terminates either through reuptake (e.g., catecholamines), breakdown (e.g., acetylcholine), or diffusion away from the synapse (e.g., neuropeptides).

Spinal Cord

The spinal cord is part of the CNS, connecting peripheral nerves to the brain stem and performing basic sensory and motor processing. Damage to the spinal cord is generally irreversible and may cause significant neurologic impairment. Meninges encase the spinal cord, with CSF contained in the subarachnoid space.

The spinal cord contains central gray matter and peripheral white matter. The **gray matter** consists of neuronal cell bodies and synapses. The **white matter** con-

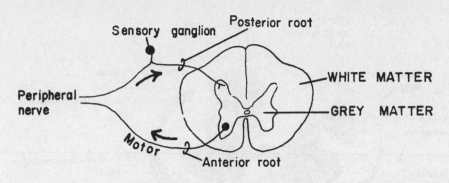

Fig. 8-8. Basic anatomy of spinal cord and nerve roots. (Reprinted with permission from S Goldberg. *Clinical Neuroanatomy Made Ridiculously Simple.* Miami: MedMaster, 1997;19.)

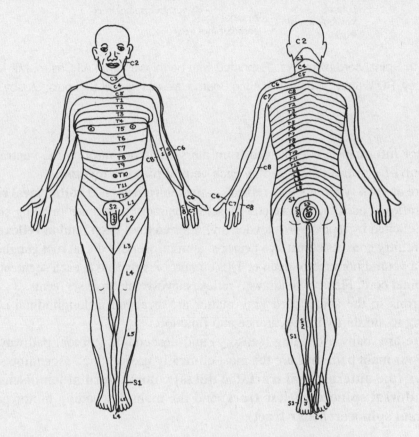

Fig. 8-9. Dermatomes. (Reprinted with permission from S Goldberg. *Clinical Neuroanatomy Made Ridiculously Simple.* Miami: MedMaster, 1997;74.)

tains ascending sensory axon tracts and descending motor axon tracts organized in various pathways (discussed later).

The spinal cord has 31 segments, each giving rise to a pair of spinal nerves: 8 cervical, 12 thoracic, 5 lumbar, 5 sacral, and 1 coccygeal. The spinal cord terminates between the L1 and L2 vertebra (thus lumbar puncture is generally performed at L4–L5 interspace to avoid penetration of the cord). Sensory information is conveyed to the spinal cord through the peripheral nerves into the dorsal roots (Fig. 8-8). The area of skin innervated by a single dorsal root is known as a **dermatome** (Fig. 8-9).

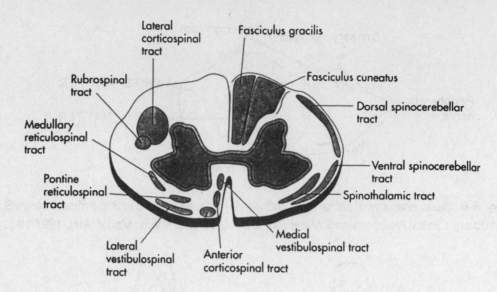

Fig. 8-10. Spinal cord pathways. (Reprinted with permission from AJ Castro, MP Merchut, EJ Neafsey, RD Wurster. *Mosby's Ace the Boards: Neuroscience.* St. Louis: Mosby, 1996.)

Motor information is conveyed from the spinal cord through the ventral roots. The group of muscles innervated by each ventral root is a **myotome**.

There are two types of spinal reflexes—**stretch reflexes** and **withdrawal reflexes**. Stretch reflexes occur when skeletal muscles contract in response to being stretched (usually elicited by tapping on a tendon and referred to as **deep tendon reflexes**). The reflex circuitry consists of just two neurons: a proprioceptive dorsal root ganglion neuron and a ventral horn motor neuron. This circuitry is repeated at each segmental level of the spinal cord. Flexor (withdrawal) reflexes involve multiple segments.

Neurons in the spinal cord gray matter are arranged in longitudinal columns according to similarity in appearance and function.

There are many ascending (sensory) and descending (motor) pathways (Fig. 8-10). Four main pathways are the most clinically useful: three ascending sensory pathways (the **anterolateral tract**, the **dorsal column–medial lemniscus tract**, and the **dorsal spinocerebellar tract**) and the main descending motor pathway (the **dorsal spinocerebellar tract**).

Dorsal Column–Medial Lemniscus Pathway

Dorsal columns mediate light touch, vibration, and proprioception.

Nucleus gracilis = sensation from legs. Nucleus cutaneous = sensation from arms.

The dorsal column–medial lemniscus pathway mediates conscious perception of light touch, vibration, and proprioception (Fig. 8-11). The first-order neuron in the dorsal root ganglion transmits a stimulus to the second-order neuron in the posterior column of the ipsilateral medulla. **Nucleus gracilis** carries sensations from the legs; **nucleus cuneatus** does the arms. Fibers cross the midline to form the **medial lemniscus** and to form a synapse with the third-order neuron in the ventroposterolateral nucleus of the thalamus. These fibers project to the somatosensory cortex of the postcentral gyrus.

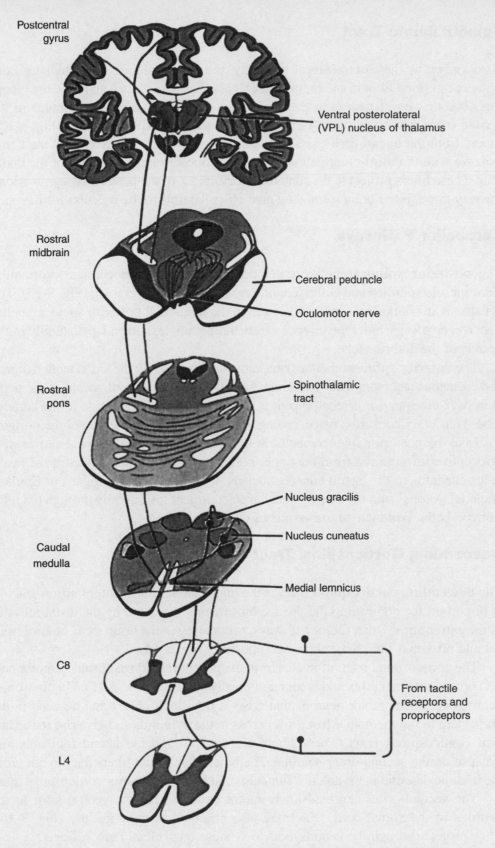

Fig. 8-11. Dorsal column pathway. (Reprinted with permission from J Nolte. *The Human Brain: An Introduction to Its Functional Anatomy* [3rd ed]. St. Louis: Mosby, 1993.)

Spinothalamic Tract

The spinothalamic tract
mediates pain and
temperature.

Also known as the **anterolateral pathway**, the spinothalamic tract mediates conscious perception of pain and temperature. It also has some touch and pressure receptors. The first-order neuron in the dorsal root ganglion transmits a stimulus to the second-order neuron in the dorsal horn of the spinal cord gray matter (Fig. 8-12). Fibers from the dorsal horn cross the midline, forming the spinothalamic tract, and synapse with the third-order neuron in the ventroposterolateral nucleus of the thalamus. These fibers project to the somatosensory cortex of the postcentral gyrus. Along the way through the brain stem, they give off collaterals to the reticular formation.

Cerebellar Pathways

The **posterior spinocerebellar tract** carries mainly proprioceptive information from muscle spindles and Golgi tendon organs of the ipsilateral leg (Fig. 8-13). The synapse is in Clarke's nucleus. Fibers run in the ipsilateral posterior spinocerebellar tract (no crossing), enter the inferior cerebellar peduncle, and end ipsilaterally in the vermis of the anterior lobe.

The **anterior spinocerebellar tract** carries afferents from the Golgi tendon organs and cutaneous receptors. They cross immediately in the spinal cord, ascend to the pons, loop over the superior cerebellar peduncle, and recross in the vermis of the anterior lobe. Thus, the fibers cross twice, ending in the cerebellum on the side of their origin.

Like the posterior spinocerebellar tract, the **cuneocerebellar tract** carries proprioceptive information from the upper body (e.g., arm). Fibers travel in the fasciculus cuneatus to the lateral cuneate nucleus of the medulla (analogous to Clarke's nucleus). Axons from the cuneocerebellar tract project ipsilaterally through the inferior cerebellar peduncle to the vermis of the cerebellum.

Descending Corticospinal Tract

The corticospinal tract
controls fine motor
movements.

The **descending corticospinal tract** is the major descending motor outflow tract. It is important for controlling the precise movements mediated by the distal muscles of the extremities. Other motor pathways, originating in the brain stem, control truncal and proximal limb musculature and posture (Fig. 8-14).

The corticospinal tract originates from the **precentral gyrus** (primary motor cortex) of the cerebral cortex and is somatotopically arranged (Fig. 8-15). The first-order neurons are upper motor neurons that arise in the motor cortex and descend in the brain stem to the medulla. Most (90%) cross in the pyramids and give rise to the **lateral corticospinal tract**. These fibers descend through the lateral funiculus and synapse on the second-order neurons. The other 10% of the fibers that do not cross the midline descend in the anterior funiculus and form the anterior corticospinal tract.

The second-order neurons (lower motor neurons) are the ventral horn motor neurons in the spinal cord, which are also arranged somatotopically (Fig. 8-16). They project through the ventral roots to synapse on skeletal muscle fibers.

Muscle weakness can occur as a result of damage to the upper motor neurons or lower motor neurons:

Upper motor neuron:

Increased muscle tone

Hyperactive reflexes

Babinski sign

- **Upper motor neuron** damage results in increased motor tone (resistance to passive movements) and hyperactive reflexes. There is a

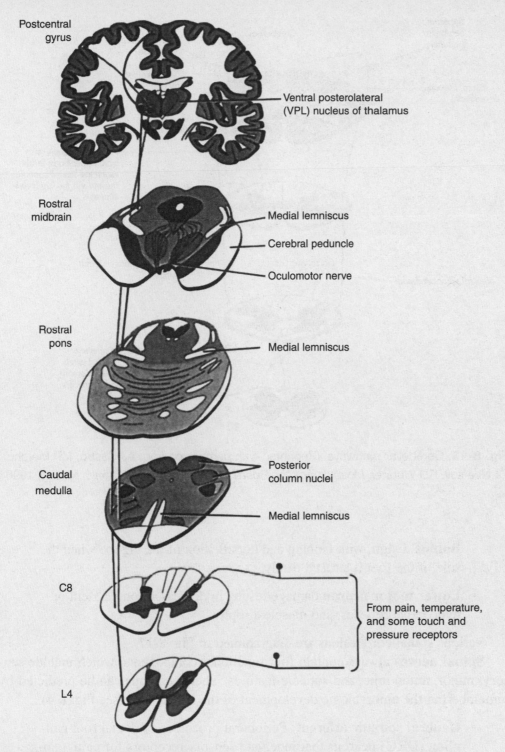

Postcentral gyrus

Ventral posterolateral (VPL) nucleus of thalamus

Rostral midbrain

Medial lemniscus

Cerebral peduncle

Oculomotor nerve

Rostral pons

Medial lemniscus

Caudal medulla

Posterior column nuclei

Medial lemniscus

C8

From pain, temperature, and some touch and pressure receptors

L4

Fig. 8-12. Spinothalamic tract. (Reprinted with permission from J Nolte. *The Human Brain: An Introduction to Its Functional Anatomy* [3rd ed]. St. Louis: Mosby, 1993.)

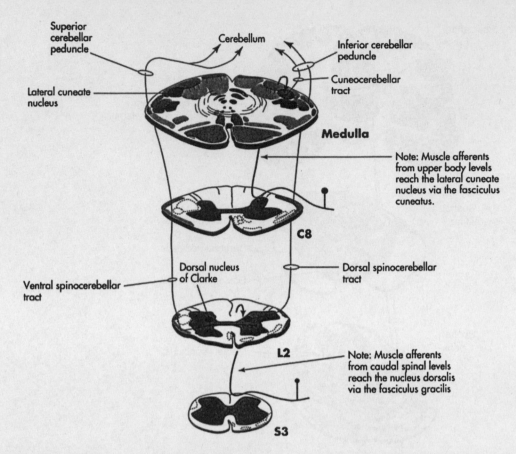

Fig. 8-13. Cerebellar pathways. (Reprinted with permission from AJ Castro, MP Merchut, EJ Neafsey, RD Wurster. *Mosby's Ace the Boards: Neuroscience.* St. Louis: Mosby, 1996.)

Babinski sign, with fanning and dorsiflexion of the big toe when the sole of the foot is stroked firmly.

Lower motor neurons

Decreased muscle tone

Absent/reduced reflexes

Muscle atrophy

- **Lower motor neuron** damage results in decreased tone, absent or hypoactive reflexes, and muscle atrophy.

Various spinal cord lesions are diagrammed in Fig. 8-17.

Spinal nerves always contain four functional components, which include sensory, motor, autonomic, and somatic features. Their positions can be predicted by remembering the embryologic development of the spinal cord (see Fig. 8-4):

- **General somatic afferent**: Peripheral processes of dorsal root ganglion (DRG) neurons that innervate sensory receptors for pain, temperature, touch, and proprioception.

- **General visceral afferent**: The peripheral processes of DRG neurons that innervate sensory receptors in viscera.

- **General visceral efferent**: The motor axons of preganglionic autonomic neurons that innervate glands and visceral muscle.

- **General somatic efferent**: The motor axons of lower motor neurons that innervate skeletal muscle.

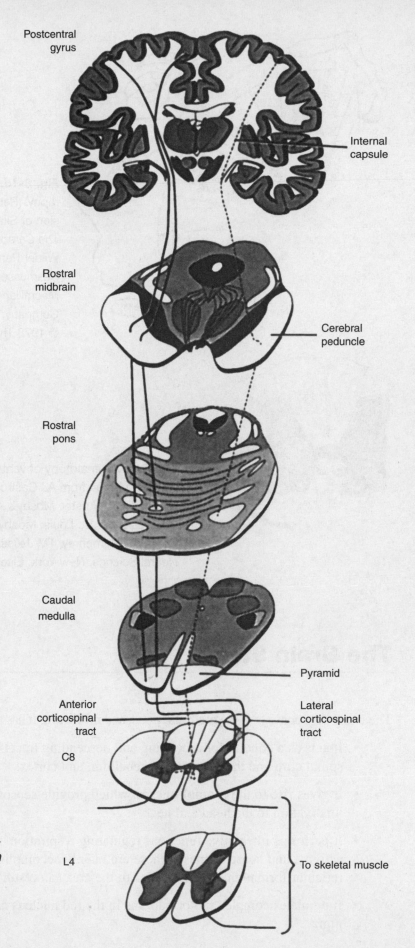

Postcentral
gyrus

Internal
capsule

Rostral
midbrain

Cerebral
peduncle

Rostral
pons

Caudal
medulla

Pyramid

Anterior
corticospinal
tract

Lateral
corticospinal
tract

C8

L4

To skeletal muscle

Fig. 8-14.
Corticospinal tract.
(Reprinted with per-
mission from J Nolte.
*The Human Brain: An
Introduction to Its
Functional Anatomy*
[3rd ed]. St. Louis:
Mosby, 1993.)

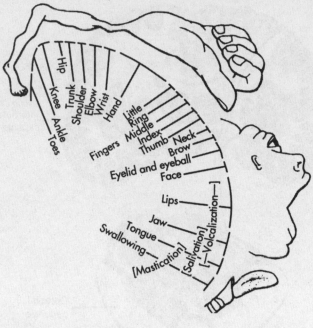

Fig. 8-15. Motor cortex topography. (Reprinted with permission of Simon & Schuster from *The Cerebral Cortex of Man* by Wilder Penfield and Theodore Rasmussen. Copyright 1950 Macmillan Publishing Company; copyright renewed © 1978 Theodore Rasmussen.)

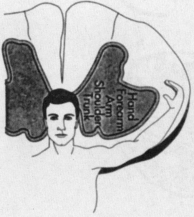

Fig. 8-16. Somatotopy of ventral horn. (Reprinted with permission from AJ Castro, MP Merchut, EJ Neafsey, RD Wurster. *Mosby's Ace the Boards: Neuroscience.* St. Louis: Mosby, 1996; and EC Crosby, T Humphrey, TM Jessell. Principles of Neural Science. New York: Elsevier, 1991.)

The Brain Stem

The brain stem consists of the **medulla, pons,** and **midbrain**. It has four major functions:

- It acts as a conduit for ascending and descending tracts between the spinal cord and the thalamus, cerebellum, and cortex.

- It gives rise to the **cranial nerves**, which provide sensory and motor innervation to the head and neck.

- It performs integrative functions regulating respiration, cardiovascular activity, and consciousness. These are mainly accomplished by the reticular formation. Small injuries to the area can result in coma.

- It regulates complex motor patterns in the red nucleus and substantia nigra.

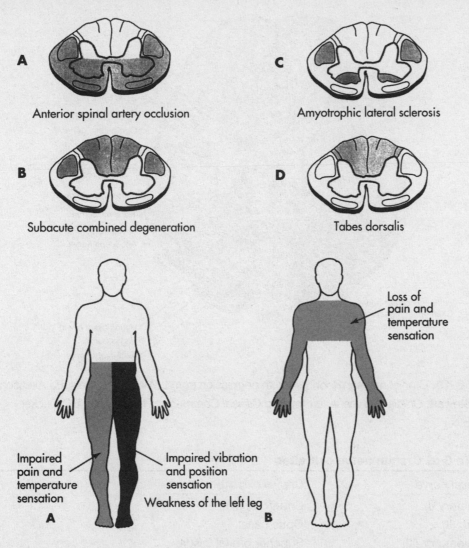

Fig. 8-17. Spinal cord lesions. (Reprinted with permission from AJ Castro, MP Merchut, EJ Neafsey, RD Wurster. *Mosby's Ace the Boards: Neuroscience.* St. Louis: Mosby, 1996.)

Cranial Nerves

Ten of the twelve cranial nerves are located in the brain stem (Fig. 8-18). Table 8-2 summarizes their sites of exit from the cranium. The functions of the cranial nerves include the following:

- Providing motor and sensory innervation to skin, muscles, and joints of the head and neck

- Relaying information from the special senses (vision, hearing, olfaction, and taste) to the brain

- Carrying parasympathetic innervation that controls visceral functions, including breathing, heart rate, blood pressure, coughing, and swallowing

The cranial nerves and their projections are summarized here:

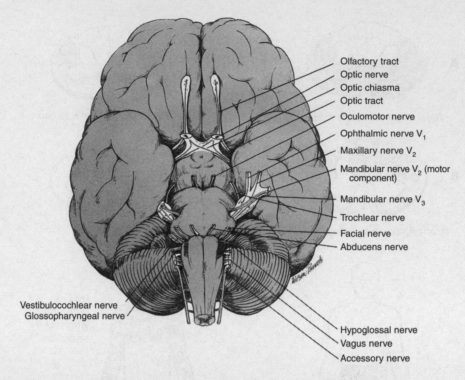

Fig. 8-18. Cranial nerves. (Reprinted with permission from L Wilson-Pauwels, EJ Akesson, PA Stewart. *Cranial Nerves: Anatomy and Clinical Comments.* Philadelphia: BC Decker, 1988;ix.)

Table 8-2. Cranial nerve exit sites

Cranial nerve	Cranial exit site
Olfactory (I)	Cribriform plate
Optic (II)	Optic canal
Oculomotor (III)	Superior orbital fissure
Trochlear (IV)	Superior orbital fissure
Trigeminal (V)	V_1: Superior orbital fissure
	V_2: Foramen rotundum
	V_3: Foramen ovale
Abducens (VI)	Superior orbital fissure
Facial (VII)	Stylomastoid foramen
Auditory (VIII)	Internal acoustic meatus
Glossopharyngeal (IX)	Jugular foramen
Vagus (X)	Jugular foramen
Accessory (XI)	Jugular foramen
Hypoglossal (XII)	Hypoglossal canal

- **CN I**—olfactory; derives from cerebral cortex
  Sensory: smell
  Motor: none

- **CN II**—optic; derives from diencephalon
  Sensory: sight
  Motor: none

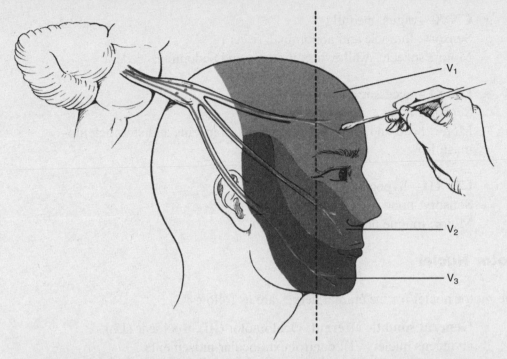

Fig. 8-19. Divisions of trigeminal nerve (V). (Reprinted with permission from L Wilson-Pauwels, EJ Akesson, PA Stewart. *Cranial Nerves: Anatomy and Clinical Comments.* Philadelphia: BC Decker, 1988;69.)

- **CN III**—oculomotor; midbrain
  Sensory: none
  Motor: eye movements (superior, inferior, and medial rectus muscles) and pupil and lens function

- **CN IV**—trochlear; midbrain
  Sensory: none
  Motor: eye movements (superior oblique muscles)

- **CN V**—trigeminal; pons (Fig. 8-19)
  Sensory: facial sensation and tongue sensation (except taste)
  Motor: chewing

- **CN VI**—abducens; pons
  Sensory: none
  Motor: eye movements (lateral rectus muscle)

- **CN VII**—facial; pons
  Sensory: taste (anterior two-thirds of tongue)
  Motor: facial expression; branches are the *t*emporal, *z*ygomatic, *b*uccal, *m*andibular, and *c*ervical

- **CN VIII**—vestibulocochlear; pons
  Sensory: hearing, equilibrium
  Motor: none

- **CN IX**—glossopharyngeal; medulla
  Sensory: taste (posterior third of tongue)
  Motor: swallowing

Mnemonic for CN VII motor branches: "*To Zanzibar By Motor Car.*"

- **CN X**—vagus; medulla
  Sensory: thoracic and abdominal viscera
  Motor: speech, swallowing; thoracic and abdominal viscera

- **CN XI**—accessory; medulla
  Sensory: none
  Motor: head and shoulder movements (trapezius and sternocleido-mastoid)

- **CN XII**—hypoglossal; medulla
  Sensory: none
  Motor: tongue movements

Motor Nuclei

The motor nuclei for the cranial nerves are as follows:

- **General somatic efferent**: Oculomotor (III), trochlear (IV), abducens nuclei (VI); control extraocular movements.

- **Special visceral efferent:**
  The motor nucleus of trigeminal (V) controls mastication.
  The motor component facial nucleus (VII) controls facial expression.
  The **nucleus ambiguus** (IX, X) controls striated muscle in larynx and pharynx.
  The spinal accessory nucleus (XI) controls the sternocleidomastoid and trapezius.

- **General visceral efferent**: Parasympathetic preganglionic neurons **Edinger-Westphal nucleus** (III) controls pupillary constriction and ciliary muscle. The superior and inferior salivatory nucleus (VII, IX) controls the salivary and mucous glands. The dorsal motor nucleus of the vagus (X) innervates the heart, lungs, and gut.

The lower muscles of facial expression are controlled by the upper motor neurons on the contralateral side, whereas the upper muscles of facial expression are controlled by the upper motor neurons from both sides. Therefore, an upper motor neuron defect produces a defect in the contralateral lower quadrant. A lower motor neuron defect affects ipsilateral upper and lower quadrants (Fig. 8-20). This is a common test question!

Various brain stem lesions lead to different respiratory patterns (Fig. 8-21).

Sensory Nuclei

The sensory nuclei for the cranial nerves are as follows:

- **General visceral afferent and special visceral afferent**: Solitary nucleus (VII, IX, X)—carotid body, larynx, pharynx, heart, lungs, gut

- **Special somatic afferent**: Cochlear nucleus (VIII)—hearing
  Vestibular nucleus (VIII)—balance

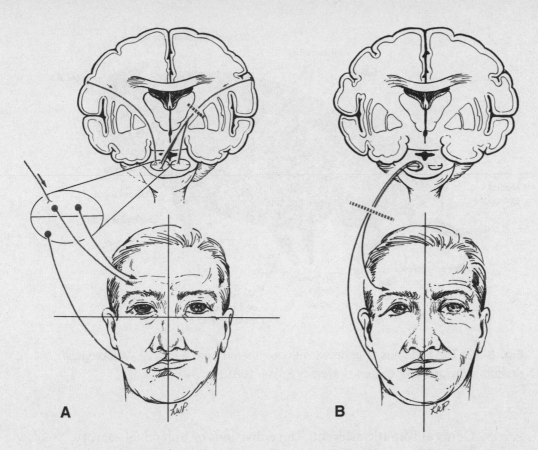

Fig. 8-20. Facial nerve (VII) lesions. **A.** Upper motor neuron lesion—characterized by loss of voluntary control of lower facial muscles (expression). **B.** Lower motor neuron lesion— characterized by loss of function of all facial muscles. This causes Bell's palsy. (Reprinted with permission from L Wilson-Pauwels, EJ Akesson, PA Stewart. *Cranial Nerves: Anatomy and Clinical Comments.* Philadelphia: BC Decker, 1988;89.)

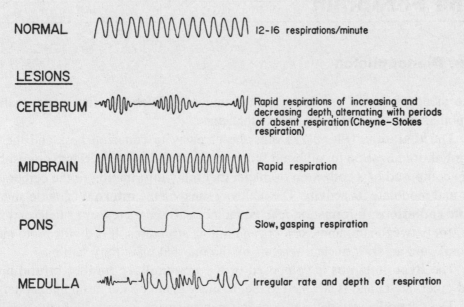

Fig. 8-21. Respiratory patterns with central nervous system lesions. (Reprinted with permission from S Goldberg. *Clinical Neuroanatomy Made Ridiculously Simple.* Miami: MedMaster, 1997;59.)

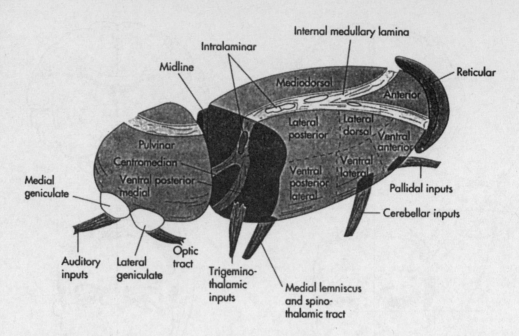

Fig. 8-22. The thalamus. (Reprinted with permission from A Brodal. *Neurological Anatomy.* Oxford, UK: Oxford University Press, 1981.)

- **General somatic afferent**: Three divisions of trigeminal sensory nuclei (V).
  Mesencephalic nucleus; proprioception in jaw
  Main sensory nucleus; touch in head and neck
  Spinal trigeminal nucleus; pain and temperature in head and neck

The Forebrain

The Diencephalon

The diencephalon is just rostral to the midbrain. There are four parts: thalamus, hypothalamus, epithalamus, and subthalamus.

The **thalamus** (Fig. 8-22) runs the gateway to consciousness and the focal point of organization for all brain functions mediated by the cerebral hemispheres. It is composed of a collection of nuclei that relay information to the cerebral cortex and modulate its activity. The pathway runs via the **internal capsule** and **thalamic radiations**. Information relayed includes all senses (except smell) and motor control between autonomic centers and limbic structures. It is divided into medial, lateral, and anterior nuclear regions by the internal medullary lamina.

The **hypothalamus** is composed of the **mammillary bodies**, **infundibulum**, and other nuclei and is attached to the pituitary gland by the infundibular stalk.

The **preoptic area** secretes gonadotropin-releasing hormone into the capillaries of the hypothalamo-hypophyseal portal system. It likely plays a role in sexual arousal and temperature regulation.

The **supraoptic area** contains several nuclei, including the following:

- The **paraventricular nuclei** perform several functions. The medial division secretes corticotropin-releasing factor, thyroxin-releasing hormone, somatostatin, and dopamine into the hypothalamo-hypophyseal portal system capillaries. The intermediate division projects directly into the posterior pituitary and releases oxytocin and vasopressin.

- The **suprachiasmatic nuclei** play a role in circadian rhythm.

- The **supraoptic nuclei** sends projections (along with the paraventricular nuclei) to release oxytocin and vasopressin into posterior pituitary capillaries.

The **mammillary nuclei** receive hippocampal projections and project to the reticular formation and the anterior nuclei of the thalamus. They may be involved in memory and are damaged by alcohol in the **Wernicke-Korsakoff syndrome**. The posterior nucleus activates heat-generating mechanisms, such as shivering and vasoconstriction.

The **pituitary gland** is the regulator of the endocrine system. It is divided into anterior and posterior lobes. The posterior lobe (neurohypophysis) secretes vasopressin and oxytocin into the bloodstream (produced in the hypothalamus). The anterior lobe (adenohypophysis) secretes pituitary hormones into the bloodstream, including adrenocorticotropic hormone, follicle-stimulating hormone, luteinizing hormone, growth hormone, thyroid-stimulating hormone, and melanocyte-stimulating hormone. It is regulated by hypothalamic releasing factors, which circulate in the hypothalamo-hypophyseal portal system. The pituitary gland is discussed in more detail in chapter 16.

Epithalamus and Subthalamus

The **epithalamus** consists of the pineal gland, habenula, and two commissures (habenular and posterior). The **pineal gland** is neurosecretory. It receives input from sympathetic neurons and the visual system (by way of the hypothalamus). It produces melatonin and may function in circadian rhythm and neuroimmunologic interactions. It often calcifies with age, providing a useful radiologic landmark.

The **subthalamus** contains mostly white matter tracts going to the thalamus.

The Telencephalon

The telencephalon includes the **cerebral cortex, basal ganglia, hippocampus,** and **amygdala**.

Cerebral Cortex

The cerebral cortex processes signals concerned with the senses, limb movement, eye and head movement, higher brain functions, and autonomic and endocrine control.

Anatomically, the cerebral cortex is divided into several lobes (Fig. 8-23).

Paraventricular nuclei release CRF, TRF, somatostatin, dopamine, oxytocin, and vasopressin.

Supraoptic nuclei release oxytocin and vasopressin.

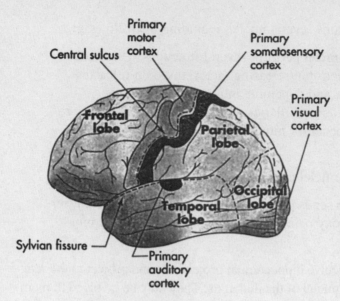

Fig. 8-23. Cortical areas. (Reprinted with permission from AJ Castro, MP Merchut, EJ Neafsey, RD Wurster. *Mosby's Ace the Boards: Neuroscience.* St. Louis: Mosby, 1996.)

- The **parietal lobe** is involved with somatosensory perception, discrimination, and integration of visual and auditory information.

- The **temporal lobe** controls auditory perception and discrimination, learning and memory, and limbic functions.

- The **occipital lobe** controls visual perception and recognition.

- The **frontal lobe** is involved in the initiation and control of voluntary movement, language expression, and higher functions.

- The **insular area** (not shown) controls taste, somatosensory, and limbic functions.

The Basal Ganglia

The basal ganglia consists of a related set of nuclei in the telencephalon, diencephalon, and midbrain. The basic anatomy includes the **caudate, putamen, globus pallidus, substantia nigra,** and **subthalamic nucleus** (Fig. 8-24).

The basal ganglia function with the cerebellum as part of the extrapyramidal motor system in modulating motor information. Complex interconnections are found between cortex, basal ganglia, and thalamus.

The key principle of basal ganglia function is **double inhibition**. Basal ganglia output exerts an inhibitory influence on motor structure. Therefore, movements are facilitated by transiently removing this tonic inhibition (i.e., inhibiting the inhibition). The two major pathways are the direct pathway and the indirect pathway.

The **direct pathway** facilitates movement. Basal ganglia output from the globus pallidus (GP) and substantia nigra (SN) inhibits motor structures. To facilitate a movement, the cortex transiently excites neurons in the striatum (caudate and putamen), which then transiently inhibit the GP/SN. Disorders in which there is too much tonic inhibition from GP/SN to motor structures leave patients stiff and unable to initiate movements (e.g., **Parkinson's disease**).

The **indirect pathway** inhibits movements. The subthalamic nucleus, by exciting the GP, is responsible for the tonic activity of the inhibitory GP neurons. The

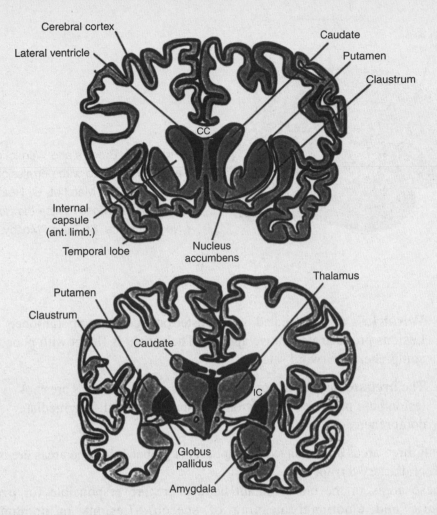

Labels in figure:
- Cerebral cortex
- Lateral ventricle
- Caudate
- Putamen
- Claustrum
- CC
- Internal capsule (ant. limb.)
- Temporal lobe
- Nucleus accumbens
- Thalamus
- Putamen
- Claustrum
- Caudate
- IC
- Globus pallidus
- Amygdala

Fig. 8-24. The basal ganglia. (Reprinted with permission from AJ Castro, MP Merchut, EJ Neafsey, RD Wurster. *Mosby's Ace the Boards: Neuroscience.* St. Louis: Mosby, 1996.)

destruction of the subthalamic nucleus leads to the hyperkinetic movement disorder known as **hemiballismus** (wild and unpredictable contralateral limb movements). In **Huntington's disease**, the enkephalin-containing neurons of the neostriatum are destroyed. The subthalamic nucleus is then inhibited, which leads to the movement disorders, of **chorea** and **athetosis** (rhythmic and writhing movements).

Higher Functions of the Forebrain

Language is the ability to communicate by means of symbols. It includes elements of comprehension and expression. **Aphasia** refers to the disturbance of previously intact language function. The left hemisphere is dominant for language in 99% of right-handed people but only 50% of left-handed people.

- **Broca's area** is located in the posterior inferior frontal lobe (Fig. 8-25). Lesions produce an expressive aphasia. The patient is nonfluent but has good comprehension. This aphasia usually occurs together with right hemiparesis (because Broca's area is near the primary motor cortex).

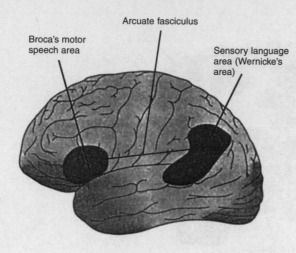

Arcuate fasciculus

Broca's motor
speech area

Sensory language
area (Wernicke's
area)

Fig. 8-25. Broca's and Wernicke's areas. (Reprinted with permission from AJ Castro, MP Merchut, EJ Neafsey, RD Wurster. *Mosby's Ace the Boards: Neuroscience.* St. Louis: Mosby, 1996.)

- **Wernicke's area** is located in the posterior superior temporal lobe. Lesions produce a receptive aphasia. The patient is fluent with poor comprehension (word salad).

- The **arcuate fasciculus** connects Broca's and Wernicke's areas. A lesion here produces conduction aphasia (fluent with intermediate comprehension).

If all three areas are damaged, the aphasia is global. All three areas are in middle cerebral artery territory.

These areas in the nondominant hemisphere are responsible for **prosody** (semantic and emotional meaning of speech). Lesions in nondominant Wernicke's area leads to receptive aprosody (loss of understanding of emotional tone of words spoken by others). Lesions in nondominant Broca's area lead to expressive prosody.

Memory is a complex function with components of registration, storage, and retrieval. Studies of patients with memory disorders suggest a role for the hippocampus and related structures (e.g., dorsomedial nucleus of the thalamus) in short-term memory processing. Long-term memory (retrieval of previously learned information) may be stored in diffuse regions of cerebral cortex.

The Limbic System

The limbic system forebrain structures form a rim (Latin, *limbus*) around the brain stem and have extensive bidirectional connections to hypothalamus and neocortex (Fig. 8-26). The limbic system is composed of the **amygdala, hippocampal formation, cingulate cortex, septal nuclei, nucleus accumbens,** and **parts of the thalamus** (i.e., mediodorsal nucleus).

The limbic system is associated with emotional expression and attention. Lesions of septal nuclei increase rage and aggression. The limbic system is also associated with motivation and reward. Animals work for a reward with stimulation of the septal region and parts of the lateral hypothalamus. A dopaminergic pathway

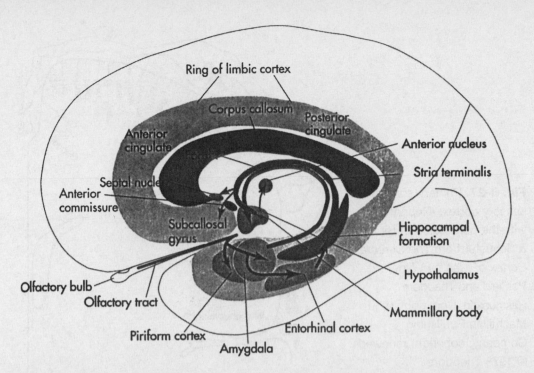

Fig. 8-26. The limbic system. (Reprinted with permission from AJ Castro, MP Merchut, EJ Neafsey, RD Wurster. *Mosby's Ace the Boards: Neuroscience.* St. Louis: Mosby, 1996.)

involved in cocaine, amphetamine, and perhaps opiate reinforcement may be a projection from the ventral tegmental area to the nucleus accumbens.

Sleep and Circadian Rhythms

Sleep

The recording of electrical potentials to characterize sleep is known as **polysomnography**. Sleep is composed of **rapid eye movement (REM)** and **nonREM** states. NonREM sleep precedes REM sleep and is composed of four stages. REM sleep is associated with dreaming. It occupies more than 50% of sleep time in newborns, decreasing to 20–25% of sleep from age 2 onward.

The quality of sleep is manifested in the level of sleepiness or alertness on the subsequent day. The average latency to sleep is decreased in people with sleep deprivation. Sleep deprivation impairs cognition, and prolonged sleep deprivation impairs physiologic function, ultimately resulting in death.

Several brain regions are involved in control of sleep and wakefulness. The brain stem contains the **reticular activating system** (wakefulness) and the **medullary raphe nuclei** and **nucleus tractus solitarius** (sleep onset). The pons alone is necessary to generate REM sleep.

In addition, the basal forebrain and hypothalamus appear to be implicated in sleep control. The **suprachiasmatic nucleus** plays a major role in timing sleep and wakefulness.

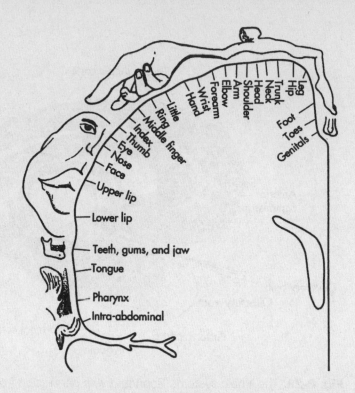

Fig. 8-27. Primary somatosensory cortex. (Reprinted with the permission of Simon & Schuster from *The Cerebral Cortex of Man* by Wilder Penfield and Theodore Rasmussen. Copyright 1950 Macmillan Publishing Company; copyright renewed © 1978 Theodore Rasmussen.)

Circadian Rhythms

Humans exhibit endogenous rhythms. Circadian rhythms have periods around 24 hours long. They are set by environmental variables, such as light exposure, temperature, food availability, and social interaction.

The circadian pacemaker is localized in the suprachiasmatic nucleus of the hypothalamus. Afferent stimuli come from the retina and midbrain raphe nuclei. Efferent output goes to the hypothalamus and thalamus. The suprachiasmatic nucleus provides sympathetic input to the pineal gland, with peak melatonin concentrations occurring at night. Conversely, the suprachiasmatic nucleus contains melatonin receptors, suggesting that melatonin may set circadian rhythms (thus the interest in melatonin as a potential "jet-lag pill" to hasten adjustment of the biological clock after intercontinental flights).

Sensory Systems

Transduction

Sensation begins with the somatosensory receptors, which are nerve endings in skin and deep tissues that respond to somatic stimuli. Innervation of the deep tissue occurs by a number of pathways. Muscle spindle afferents conduct proprioceptive stimuli. Golgi tendon organs are activated by tension on the tendon, and the signal is carried by large Ib afferent axons. Joint receptors also have endings in ligaments around joints.

The somatosensory pathway contains a topographic map of the body surface (Fig. 8-27). Body surface representations are distorted to reflect innervation density

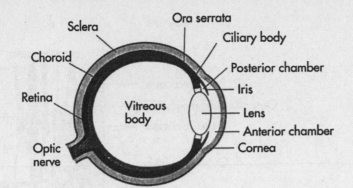

Fig. 8-28. Eye anatomy. (Reprinted with permission from AJ Castro, MP Merchut, EJ Neafsey, RD Wurster. *Mosby's Ace the Boards: Neuroscience.* St. Louis: Mosby, 1996.)

over different surfaces (e.g., fingers are magnified versus the thorax). Precise topography in the somatosensory cortex resembles an inverted torso with the lower limb hanging over the medial convexity of the hemisphere.

Several cortical areas are involved in somatosensory processing:

- **Primary somatosensory cortex (SI):** This is located in the postcentral gyrus of the parietal lobe. Information comes from medial lemniscal, spinothalamic, and trigeminothalamic tracts, which transmit information from cutaneous tactile receptors and joint and muscle spindle receptors. The primary somatosensory cortex has a precise topography. Lesions lead to contralateral deficits with inability to discriminate size, texture, and shape from tactile stimuli as well as deficits in position and movement sense of body parts.

- **Secondary somatosensory cortex (SII):** This is located caudal to SI in the upper bank of the lateral sulcus (sylvian fissure). Inputs are from SI and thalamic nuclei. This has a less precise somatotopy, and lesions do not cause well-defined disorders.

Vision

The histologic layers of the eye are shown in Fig. 8-28. The external layer consists of the **sclera** and **cornea**. The middle layer consists of the **iris, choroid,** and **ciliary body**. The inner layer is the **retina**.

The anterior and posterior chambers contain **aqueous humor**, whereas the vitreous body contains **vitreous humor**. Aqueous humor flows through the pupil from posterior chamber to anterior chamber, where it is reabsorbed in the **canal of Schlemm**. If aqueous production surpasses reabsorption rate, intraocular pressure rises. "Floaters" are caused by large protein molecules in the vitreous humor coming into focus near the retinal surface. Loss of lens transparency results in **cataracts**.

Pupillary constriction is accomplished by constriction of the circular smooth muscle (innervated by postganglionic parasympathetic nerve fibers from the ciliary ganglion). **Pupillary dilation** occurs with activation of radial smooth muscle (innervated by postganglionic sympathetic fibers from the superior cervical ganglion).

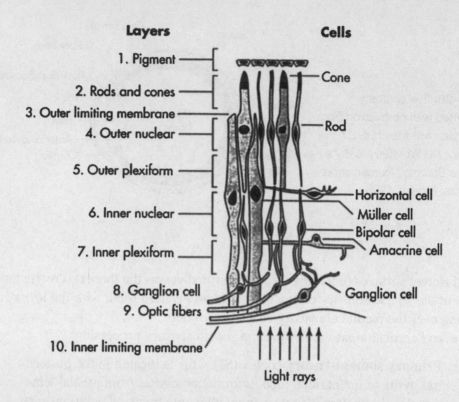

Layers

1. Pigment
2. Rods and cones
3. Outer limiting membrane
4. Outer nuclear
5. Outer plexiform
6. Inner nuclear
7. Inner plexiform
8. Ganglion cell
9. Optic fibers
10. Inner limiting membrane

Cells

Cone
Rod
Horizontal cell
Müller cell
Bipolar cell
Amacrine cell
Ganglion cell

Light rays

Fig. 8-29. Retinal layers. (Reprinted with permission from AJ Castro, MP Merchut, EJ Neafsey, RD Wurster. *Mosby's Ace the Boards: Neuroscience*. St. Louis: Mosby, 1996.)

The cornea and lens are responsible for the optical power (bending of light) of the eye. The lens can vary its optical power to focus objects at different distances from the eye (**accommodation**). This is controlled by the ciliary muscles.

Myopia, or nearsightedness, occurs when objects are focused in front of the retina. This is corrected by a negative-diopter (concave) lens. **Hyperopia**, or farsightedness, occurs when objects are focused behind the retina. Hyperopia is corrected by a positive-diopter (convex) lens. **Presbyopia** (literally, "old vision") describes the loss of elasticity of the lens after roughly age 40. This leads to insufficient thickening of the lens during accommodation for near vision and is corrected by positive-diopter reading glasses.

Astigmatism describes the condition of light passing through the eye in various planes without focusing on the same point. Astigmatism is corrected by the use of spherical lenses with different optical power in one plane than in another.

The retina is composed of outer and inner layers (Fig. 8-29). **Photoreceptors** are the rods and cones that are activated by light and send information to horizontal and bipolar cells. **Rods** contain **rhodopsin** photopigment. They are highly sensitive to light and are used in low light conditions. The ratio of rods to bipolar cells is high. The three types of **cones** contain three photopigments (red, green, and blue). The ratio of cones to bipolar cells is low, which leads to high-acuity vision. Cones are responsible for color sensitivity in bright light conditions.

The optic nerve and ophthalmic artery and vein enter the eye in the optic disc on the medial, posterior side of the retina. This results in a blind spot (**scotoma**) in the upper, lateral visual field. The area of the highest visual acuity is the **macula**.

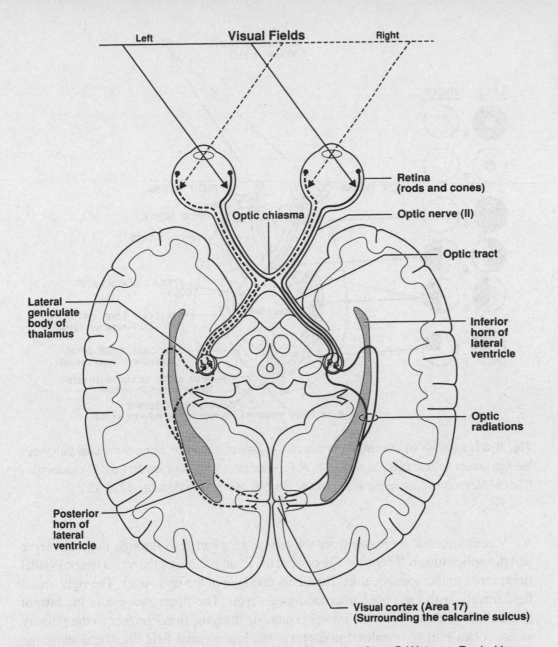

Fig. 8-30. The visual pathways. (Reprinted with permission from C Watson. *Basic Human Neuroanatomy: An Introductory Atlas* [5th ed]. Boston: Little, Brown, 1995;32.)

Horizontal cells receive input from photoreceptors and feed back to them. **Bipolar cells** receive input from photoreceptors and excite **amacrine** and **ganglion** cells. **Müller cells** are glia in the retina that regulate the ionic and neurotransmitter environment.

Light strikes the photosensitive pigments, which contain opsin and retinal. During this photostimulation, retinal isomerizes from *cis* to *trans*. Activated retinal activates **transducin** (a G-protein), which activates cyclic guanosine monophosphate (cGMP) phosphodiesterase, turning cGMP into GMP. Light causes cGMP-dependent sodium channels to close, leading to photoreceptor hyperpolarization and inhibition of the release of the neurotransmitter **glutamate**.

The left side of the visual field is focused on the right side of the retina (and vice versa), as shown in Fig. 8-30.

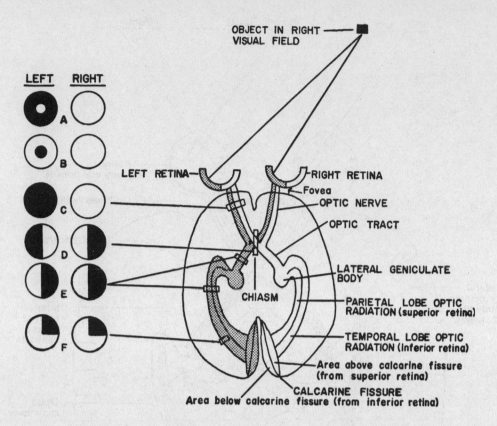

Fig. 8-31. Lesions of the visual pathways. Lesions at each site along the visual pathways lead to visual field losses, as shown in A–F. (Reprinted with permission from S Goldberg. *Clinical Neuroanatomy Made Ridiculously Simple.* Miami: MedMaster, 1997;45.)

Visual information passes from the retinal ganglion cells through the optic nerve and the optic chiasm. There, the fibers from the nasal portion of the retina (lateral visual field) cross to the opposite side. The fibers continue in the optic tract: The right visual field travels in the left optic tract (and vice versa). The fibers synapse in the **lateral geniculate nucleus**. From the lateral geniculate nucleus, fibers project to the primary visual cortex (striate or **calcarine cortex**). The lower visual field fibers end above the calcarine sulcus; the upper visual field fibers end below the calcarine sulcus (**Meyer's loop**). The effects of various lesions of the visual pathway are shown in Fig. 8-31.

The **light reflex** occurs when one eye is exposed to light and both pupils constrict (Fig. 8-32). This reflex depends on the pretectal area of the brain. Each eye projects bilaterally to the pretectal area (after the optic chiasm, each optic tract is composed of fibers from both eyes). The left and right pretectal areas project to the Edinger-Westphal nucleus, which innervates the pupillary constrictor muscles of each eye via parasympathetic relays through the ciliary ganglia.

The **doll's eyes phenomenon** is a test of brain stem function. On turning the head suddenly to one side, the eyes should lag behind in patients with a normal brain stem.

The pathways governing conjugate eye movements are shown in Fig. 8-33.

Auditory System

The ear is divided into three parts (Fig. 8-34). The **outer ear** includes the pinna, external auditory meatus, and tympanic membrane. The **middle ear** contains

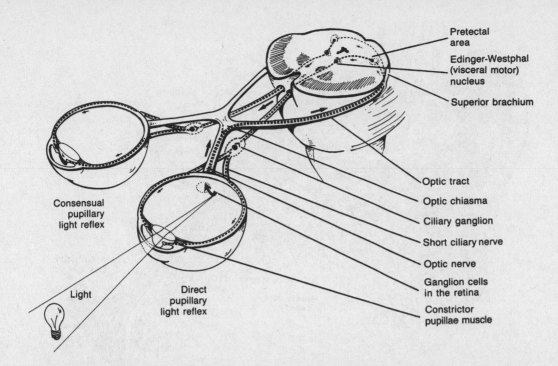

Fig. 8-32. The pupillary light reflex. (Reprinted with permission from L Wilson-Pauwels, EJ Akesson, PA Stewart. *Cranial Nerves: Anatomy and Clinical Comments.* Philadelphia: BC Decker, 1988;35.)

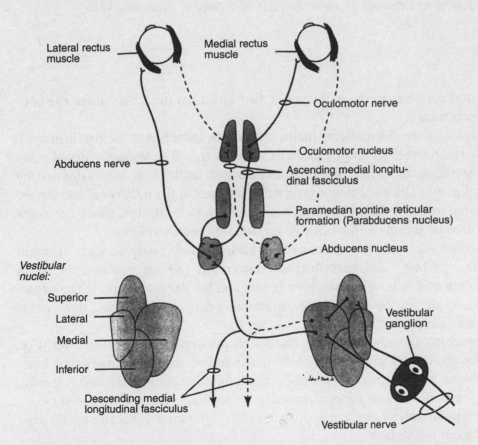

Fig. 8-33. Conjugate eye movement pathways. (Reprinted with permission from AJ Castro, MP Merchut, EJ Neafsey, RD Wurster. *Mosby's Ace the Boards: Neuroscience.* St. Louis: Mosby, 1996.)

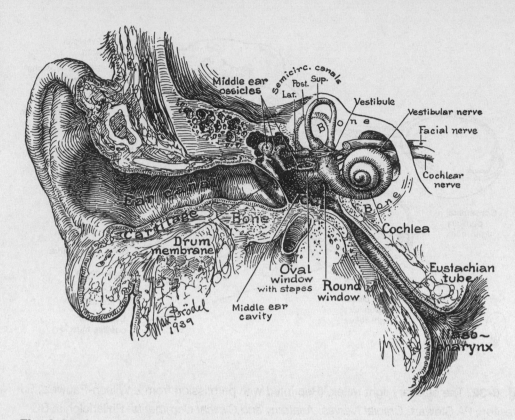

Fig. 8-34. Anatomy of the auditory system. (Reprinted with permission from M Brödal. *Three Unpublished Drawings of the Human Ear*. Philadelphia: Saunders, 1946.)

ossicles and connects to the pharynx via the eustachian tube. The **inner ear** contains the cochlea.

The ossicles are the **malleus, incus,** and **stapes** (attached to the oval window). These are responsible for amplification of sound energy. The **tensor tympani muscle** (connected to the walls of the middle ear and malleus) is innervated by the trigeminal nerve. The stapedius, connected to the wall of the middle ear and stapes, is innervated by the facial nerve. Loud sound leads to its activation, which decreases amplification of sound oscillations (the **acoustic stapedius reflex**).

The inner ear includes the **bony labyrinth** (which contains scala tympani and scala vestibuli) and **membranous labyrinth** (which contains the scala media, organ of Corti, vestibular membrane, and basilar membrane). The **organ of Corti** sits on the basilar membrane and contains one inner and three outer rows of hair cells.

The **cochlea** is a closed system filled with **perilymph** and **endolymph** (Fig. 8-35). The oscillatory movements of the oval window are transmitted to the basilar membrane, which causes a to-and-fro shearing movement of the hair cell cilia. The hair cells depolarize or hyperpolarize, depending on the direction they are moved. Depolarization leads to neurotransmitter (glutamate) release, which activates cochlear nerve fibers.

The hair cells are arranged tonotopically. Hair cells near the oval window respond better to high frequencies, and hair cells nearer to the helicotrema (center of the spiral cochlea) respond better to lower frequencies.

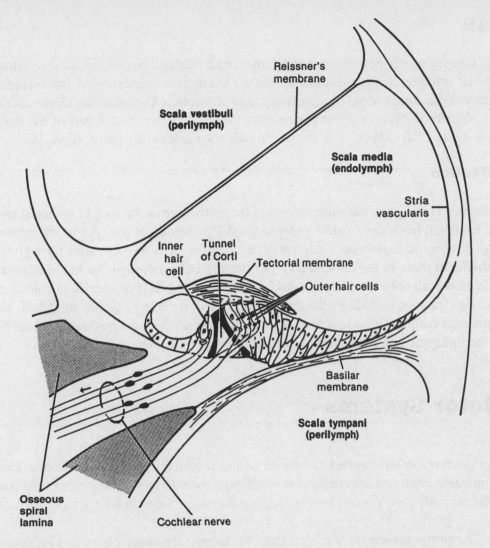

Fig. 8-35. Cochlear anatomy. (Reprinted with permission from J Nolte. *The Human Brain: An Introduction to Its Functional Anatomy* [3rd ed]. St. Louis: Mosby, 1993.)

Sound stimuli are carried by the cochlear nerve to the cochlear nuclei, which then project to the ipsilateral and contralateral superior olivary nuclei in the pons. These send signals via the lateral lemniscus to the **inferior colliculus**, which connects to the **medial geniculate nucleus** of the thalamus, and finally the auditory projections arrive at the auditory cortex (transverse temporal gyrus).

Decreased ability to hear is evaluated by air and bone conduction testing and audiometry. Categories include **conduction deafness** (impaired transmission of vibrations to basilar membrane), **nerve deafness** (often associated with hair cell damage), and **central deafness** (a rare form of deafness caused by a CNS lesion).

The vestibular area of cortex is thought to be located in the superior temporal gyrus near the auditory cortex. Disordered vestibular function is associated with nystagmus and gait ataxia.

Labyrinthitis causes vertigo, nausea, and vomiting and resolves over days to weeks. **Meniere's syndrome** is associated with swelling and rupture of the membranous labyrinth, leading to progressive vertigo, tinnitus, and deafness.

Taste

The sensory supply of the tongue is described under Cranial Nerves, earlier in the chapter. The complex arrangement stems from the fact that the tongue derives from separate embryologic components. The gustatory area of cortex is located at the inferior end of the postcentral gyrus. Afferents arise from the ventroposteromedial part of the thalamus, which relays inputs from the rostral **solitary nucleus** (the gustatory nucleus).

Olfaction

Olfactory (smell) receptors are located in the epithelium in the roof of the nasal cavity. Each cell has a preferential response to odor molecules of one type by the expression of specific membrane receptors. The olfactory cells project axons through the **cribriform plate** of the ethmoid into the olfactory bulb; these synapse in the olfactory bulb glomeruli onto dendrites of mitral cells. The mitral cells project via the olfactory tract onto targets, including olfactory tubercle, piriform cortex, medial amygdala, and entorhinal cortex. These structures also form synapses with the mediodorsal nucleus of the thalamus and ventromedial nucleus of the hypothalamus.

Motor Systems

The **primary motor cortex** is located in the precentral gyrus of the frontal lobe. Stimulation from this area leads to simple flexion or extension movements of the contralateral body part. Lesions lead to spastic paralysis of the contralateral face, arm, and leg.

The **premotor cortex** sends efferents to the primary motor cortex and influences corticospinal tract output. It receives afferents from sensory association cortices and ventrolateral thalamus. It is somatotopically arranged. Lesions in this area lead to spasticity.

The **supplementary motor cortex** is involved in coordinating posture and complex bilateral movements. This area becomes active before a movement occurs.

The cerebellum and basal ganglia correct ongoing movements based on afferent feedback information.

The **lower-level control system** for muscle is composed of alpha and gamma motor neurons, spindle receptors, Golgi tendon organs (supplying an inhibitory stimulus), spinal reflex circuits, and the muscle and its load.

Autonomic Nervous System

The autonomic nervous system functions to innervate smooth muscle, cardiac muscle, gland cells, fat cells, and immune cells. It is composed of the sympathetic and parasympathetic systems. The basic structure includes a **preganglionic cell** (neuronal body in brain stem or spinal cord), which projects by way of thinly myelinated axons or B fibers to autonomic ganglia. There, the preganglionic fiber releases **acetylcholine** to excite the postganglionic cell body via **nicotinic receptors**. The postganglionic neuron sends unmyelinated axons (C fibers) to its target. At the target, neurotransmitters are released.

The Parasympathetic System

The preganglionic cell bodies are located in the **brain stem** or **sacral spinal cord**. Their axons project all the way to a ganglion close to the effector organ (i.e., long preganglionic axons, short postganglionic axons). Acetylcholine is the main transmitter, activating **muscarinic receptors** on effector organs.

The Sympathetic System

The preganglionic cell bodies are located in the intermediolateral cell column from **T1 to L2 spinal cord levels**. They synapse in sympathetic ganglia, including paravertebral ganglia (associated with spinal nerves or stellate ganglion) and prevertebral ganglia (celiac, superior mesenteric, and inferior mesenteric). Short preganglionic and long postganglionic fibers are characteristic, and the main neurotransmitter is norepinephrine.

The enteric system includes the submucosal (Meissner's) plexus and the myenteric (Auerbach's) plexus.

Metabolism of the Nervous System

Neurons rely on glucose for their energy needs. This molecule must cross two membranes by way of glucose transporters to enter neurons: the capillary membrane (blood-brain barrier) and the cell membrane. Neurons do not store glucose to any great extent and so must rely on such uptake to supply their needs. Glucose uptake can limit the rate of energy metabolism on rare occasions (e.g., status epilepticus, hypoglycemia).

Cerebral Circulation and the Blood-Brain Barrier

Blood flows to the brain through the internal carotids anteriorly and the vertebral arteries posteriorly (Fig. 8-36). These supply systems feed into the **circle of Willis**, which has multiple anastomoses: Blood can flow either way, which can help protect against ischemic damage as a result of occlusion (Fig. 8-37). There is significant variation from person to person in circle of Willis anatomy. Blood drains into the sinuses and down through the jugulars (Fig. 8-38).

The brain is a protected space. The blood-brain barrier limits what molecules can get into the brain from the blood. Only lipid-soluble substances with specific endothelial transporters (glucose, amino acids) can cross the barrier easily. The barrier is composed of astrocyte foot processes that wrap around CNS capillaries and form tight junctions.

CSF is secreted by the **choroid plexus** into ventricles. The system includes two lateral ventricles (one on either side) feeding through the interventricular foramina into the third ventricle, through the aqueduct of Sylvius to the fourth ventricle, then through the lateral foramen of Luschka and the medial foramen of Magendie to bathe the spinal cord. CSF is taken up by arachnoid villi and dumped into the superior sagittal sinus.

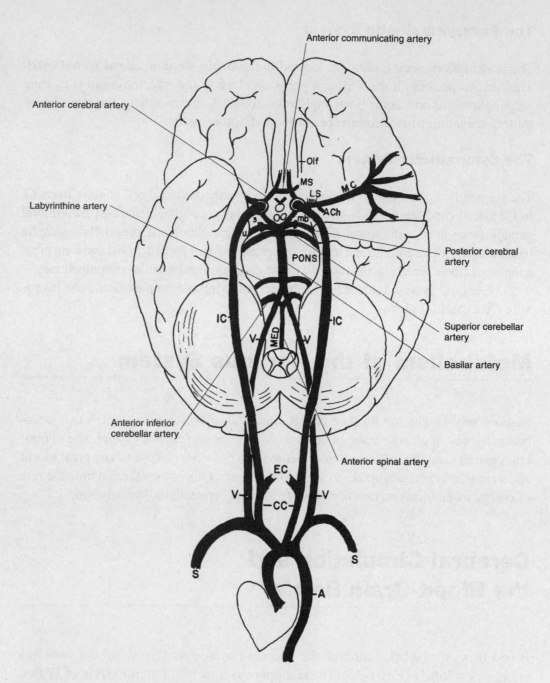

Fig. 8-36. Vascular supply of the central nervous system. (Olf = olfactory bulb; MC = middle cerebral artery; IC = internal carotid artery; V = vertebral artery; EC = external carotid artery; CC = common carotid artery; S = subclavian artery; A = aorta.) (Modified with permission from S Goldberg. *Clinical Neuroanatomy Made Ridiculously Simple.* Miami: MedMaster, 1997;11.)

Repair and Regeneration

In general, injured peripheral nerve axons regenerate, whereas injured central axons in the brain and spinal cord do not. Many millions of people are disabled by head and spinal cord trauma and stroke when neurons of the CNS die.

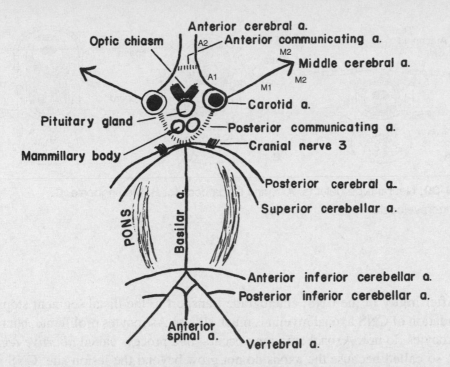

Fig. 8-37. The circle of Willis. (Reprinted with permission from S Goldberg. *Clinical Neuroanatomy Made Ridiculously Simple.* Miami: MedMaster, 1997;12.)

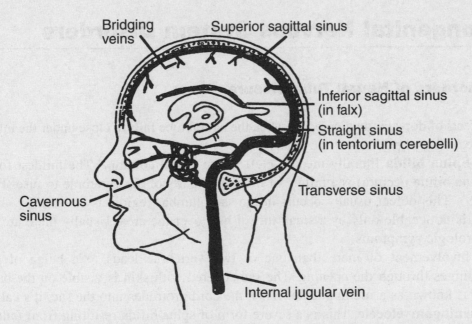

Fig. 8-38. Venous drainage of the central nervous system. (Reprinted with permission from S Goldberg. *Clinical Neuroanatomy Made Ridiculously Simple.* Miami: MedMaster, 1997;14.)

In the PNS, nerve injury leads to **Wallerian degeneration**, a degradation of the distal axon and myelin. Within a few hours of peripheral nerve damage, fine sprouts protrude from the proximal stump and grow at 3–4 mm per day. Growth is mediated by neuronal cell adhesion molecules, integrins (which bind laminin, fibronectin, and collagen), and neurotrophins (nerve growth factors).

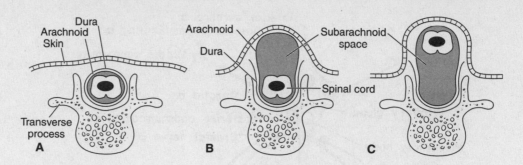

Fig. 8-39. Neural tube defects. **A.** Spina bifida occulta. **B.** Meningocele. **C.** Meningomyelocele.

After injury in the CNS, anterograde transport to the distal segment stops, but degradation of CNS axonal myelin is much slower. Astrocytes proliferate, but oligodendrocytes do not. Axonal sprouting occurs, in a process called *abortive regeneration*, so called because the axons do not grow beyond the lesion site. CNS nerve cell bodies and their proximal axons survive for many weeks to months but fail to produce cell body responses appropriate for regeneration.

Congenital Nervous System Disorders

Disorders of Neural Tube Closure

Defects of dorsal induction occur when the neural tube fails to close under the influence of dorsal portions of the embryo.

Spina bifida literally means "cleft in the spinal column." The mildest form (spina bifida occulta) is a failure of the dorsal parts of the vertebrae to fuse (Fig. 8-39). This defect usually occurs in the sacrolumbar region, is covered by skin, and is noticeable only by a small tuft of hair over the area. Usually there are no neurologic symptoms.

Involvement of more than one or two vertebrae leads to a bulge of the meninges through the opening. The sac covered with skin is visible on the back and is known as a **meningocele**. When the cord protrudes into the sac, it's called a **meningomyelocele**. This is a severe form of spina bifida resulting from failure of the caudal neuropore to close. For unknown reasons, this entity is accompanied by the **Arnold-Chiari malformation**, in which the caudal brain stem and cerebellum elongate and push down into the foramen magnum. This frequently obstructs the flow of CSF, resulting in hydrocephalus.

Anencephaly results from failure of the rostral neuropore to close. Much of each cerebral hemisphere is absent, and this is obviously fatal.

Trisomy 21 (Down Syndrome)

Down syndrome is one of the best-known disorders causing mental retardation.

Signs & Symptoms

Characteristic facial and limb features, including almond-shaped eyes, slanted palpebral fissures; round face; transverse palmar creases; and short, stubby digits. Other non-neurologic anomalies include duodenal atresia, an atrioventricular septal defect, and congenital hypothyroidism.

Neurologic problems include impaired mental function (ranging from profound retardation to near-normal intelligence), oral-facial-lingual dyskinesia, sensorineural hearing loss, autistic features, seizures, and the nearly inevitable development of Alzheimer's dementia beginning in the fourth decade.

Pathology

Presence of an extra chromosome 21. Neuronal proliferation, differentiation, and organization are affected. The brain is small, with progressive dendritic atrophy in early childhood.

Diagnosis

Many cases are diagnosed in utero by amniocentesis in women known to be at risk. There is an increased risk of occurrence in women bearing children at older ages.

Treatment

Early intervention to maximize the child's learning potential is believed to be helpful. There has been an increase in popularity of plastic surgery to alter the characteristic trisomy 21 appearance and lead to better social acceptance of the affected individuals.

Huntington's Disease

Huntington's disease is an autosomal dominant disorder characterized by progressive development of chorea and dementia. It progresses to death in about 15 years. The disorder is caused by a recently cloned unstable trinucleotide repeat on chromosome 4, although the exact mechanism is unknown.

Signs & Symptoms

Symptoms tend to develop in the fourth or fifth decade and begin with abnormal movement or intellectual changes. These slowly progress to dementia and chorea.

Pathology

Patients develop degeneration of the striatum, cerebral cortex, and other areas. The movement disorder is thought to be due to striatal degeneration. In particular, GABA-containing neurons projecting from caudate and putamen to the globus pallidus are lost.

Diagnosis

The presence of the above signs and symptoms along with family history, genetic testing, and computed tomography (CT) scan or magnetic resonance imaging (MRI) showing atrophy of cerebral cortex and caudate nucleus.

Treatment

There is no cure or treatment for the dementia. Dopamine-receptor blockers (e.g., haloperidol or chlorpromazine) and drugs that deplete dopamine (e.g., reserpine) may ameliorate the movement disorder.

Prevention

Offspring of affected patients have a 50% chance of inheriting the disease. Therefore, genetic counseling is important in Huntington's disease families. Presymptomatic genetic testing is now available.

Inflammatory Disorders

The CNS is a privileged place, protected by the blood-brain barrier and thus from most infections. However, certain viruses, bacteria, fungi, and parasites may infect the CNS, particularly in the immunocompromised patient.

Meningitis

Meningitis is inflammation of the meninges due to infection of the subarachnoid space or due to the presence of blood or foreign material. Meningitis may be due to infection with a variety of organisms, including bacteria, viruses, fungi, and parasites. Tuberculosis and syphilis may also cause meningitis.

Bacterial meningitis may be severe and potentially fatal but can be treated early and aggressively with antibiotics. Viral meningitis, although not treatable, is usually milder and resolves spontaneously. Other forms of meningitis tend to occur in immunosuppressed, malnourished, or elderly patients and tend to be chronic and milder. These require specific antibiotics.

Complications of meningitis include **hydrocephalus** (CSF flow blockage), inflammation of the cortex (**meningoencephalitis**), infarction due to thrombosis of blood vessels, and postmeningitic deafness (especially in children).

Signs & Symptoms

Patients develop fever, nausea and vomiting, headache, and lethargy. They may develop a decreased level of consciousness, neck stiffness, and meningeal irritation. **Kernig's sign** refers to the inability to straighten the lower extremity while the thigh is flexed, and **Brudzinski's sign** is flexion of the hips when the neck is flexed. Both signs indicate meningeal irritation.

Diagnosis

Clinical signs and symptoms plus CSF findings lead to diagnosis. Bacterial meningitis is characterized by increased polymorphonuclear neutrophils, low glucose, and high protein in the CSF. Demonstration of bacteria by Gram's stain or culture is diagnostic.

Treatment

Suspected bacterial meningitis should be treated empirically with antibiotics immediately. Distant sources of infection that may have seeded the meninges should be sought and treated. Babies should begin receiving *Haemophilus influenzae* type b vaccination at 2 months of age to prevent the development of meningitis. Meningococcal vaccine is also available for persons traveling abroad or living in close quarters (e.g., military).

Encephalitis

Encephalitis is infection or inflammation of the brain. It is usually viral and may include viruses transmitted by arthropods (ticks, mosquitoes), which tend to be seasonal. Polio, rabies, and herpes simplex virus can also cause encephalitis, and untreated cases have a high mortality rate. Encephalitis is also caused by prion proteins ("slow viruses," e.g., Creutzfeldt-Jakob disease), which cause a more chronic picture, taking months to years to evolve and frequently resulting in dementia and death.

Signs & Symptoms

Patients experience fever, headache, changes in consciousness or behavior, seizures, or focal deficits. The presentation may be similar to meningitis, along with seizures and focal deficits.

Pathology

Pathology shows neuronal loss, tiny hemorrhages, viral inclusions, edema, and patchy demyelination. In Creutzfeldt-Jakob disease, inclusions or spongiform changes are present.

Diagnosis

Lumbar puncture is performed to obtain CSF. MRI may be performed to rule out trauma and to establish the presence of inflammation. Herpes simplex DNA may be detected in the CSF with polymerase chain reaction. Serum antibody titers for suspected viruses may be helpful. In severe cases, as in Creutzfeldt-Jakob disease, brain biopsy is performed.

Treatment

Acyclovir for herpes simplex encephalitis. Other forms have no effective treatment. Supportive care is provided to treat symptoms such as agitation, seizures, increased intracranial pressure, and associated metabolic disorders.

Neurologic Complications of HIV Infection and AIDS

In addition to its other systemic manifestations, acquired immunodeficiency syndrome (AIDS) is characterized by a variety of neurologic disturbances, including dementia, myelopathy, neuropathy, stroke, and acute confusional states. Neurologic complications occur in roughly 30–65% of adults and 50–90% of children with AIDS.

Virtually every level of the nervous system can be involved, except the neuromuscular junction. Pathogenesis of the disorders is thought to result from one or more of the following: direct viral infection of the nervous system, damage by substances released when infected cells are lysed, or autoimmune attack against nervous system cells. Immune suppression leads to the development of CNS lymphoma and opportunistic infections.

Major neurologic diseases in human immunodeficiency virus (HIV) infection include the following:

- Cryptococcal meningitis
- Tubercular meningitis

- CNS lymphoma

- Cerebral toxoplasmosis

- Cytomegalovirus retinitis and encephalitis

- Peripheral neuropathy

- Progressive multifocal leukoencephalopathy (PML)

- AIDS dementia

Signs & Symptoms

Vary widely, depending on the disease and the patient's ability to mount an inflammatory response.

Diagnosis

CSF analysis, CT or MRI, and brain biopsy are all performed.

Treatment

Combinations of nucleoside reverse transcriptase inhibitors (NRTIs), non-NRTIs, and protease inhibitors may delay the onset of pathology directly related to HIV. Specific infections are treated with appropriate antibiotics.

Demyelinating Disorders

Multiple Sclerosis

Multiple sclerosis is a common neurologic disorder, with its highest incidence in young adulthood (peaks between ages 20 and 40). Women are somewhat more often affected than men. The cause is unknown but appears to be an immune mechanism against myelin antigens. There is a strong association with HLA-DR2.

Signs & Symptoms

Patients present with a variety of symptoms, most commonly the transient onset of focal weakness, numbness, tingling, unsteadiness in a limb, optic neuritis (vision loss in one eye), diplopia, disequilibrium, and bladder dysfunction. Patients may also present with acute or gradually progressive spastic paraparesis and sensory deficit. Over the course of the illness, there is a relapsing-remitting pattern of symptoms and disability. Relapses can be triggered by infection and after childbirth.

Pathology

Includes development of focal scattered areas of demyelination followed by reactive gliosis. Lesions occur in white matter of the brain, spinal cord, and optic nerve.

Diagnosis

CSF is frequently abnormal, revealing a mild lymphocytosis and protein elevation. Electrophoresis shows oligoclonal bands in the immunoglobulin G region. MRI or CT scan may detect demyelinating lesions.

Treatment

β-Interferon reduces relapse rate. Corticosteroids may be used for acute symptoms. Cytotoxic drugs (cyclophosphamide, azathioprine) are also used for short-term therapy. Plasmapheresis has a questionable role. Cyclosporine may prevent disease progression but has high toxicity.

Myasthenia Gravis

Myasthenia gravis is an immune disorder in which antibodies are directed against acetylcholine receptors, leading to sustained activation and desensitization, blocking neuromuscular transmission. It is characterized by fluctuating weakness and easy fatigability of voluntary muscles. It particularly affects extraocular muscles and facial muscles and may affect respiratory and limb muscles. It can occur at any age and is more common in females than males.

Signs & Symptoms

Patients present with ptosis, diplopia, difficulty chewing or swallowing, nasal speech, respiratory difficulties, or weakness of the limbs. Sustained up-gaze can lead to increased ptosis, with increased power after a brief rest. Sensation and reflexes are normal.

Exacerbations occur during infection and pregnancy or before menses. Certain drugs can worsen symptoms. The disease is slowly progressive, with relapses, remissions, and diurnal variations.

Myasthenia gravis differs from **Lambert-Eaton (myasthenic) syndrome**. Lambert-Eaton syndrome spares extraocular muscles, and power increases (rather than decreases) if a contraction is maintained.

Diagnosis

The edrophonium (Tensilon) test is performed. Edrophonium, an anticholinesterase drug, is injected, and diagnosis is confirmed if there is temporary improvement in the strength of weak muscles. Atropine should be immediately available to counteract muscarinic cholinergic side effects.

Electromyography and other electrophysiologic studies may be performed. Serum acetylcholine-receptor antibody levels are increased in 80–90% of patients. A chest X-ray or CT scan may reveal a coexisting thymoma.

Treatment

Anticholinesterase drugs, such as neostigmine, are used. Thymectomy is often performed in patients under 60 years of age. Corticosteroids and azathioprine are used for patients responding poorly to anticholinesterase drugs but may initially exacerbate weakness. Plasmapheresis is used for temporary improvement (e.g., before surgery).

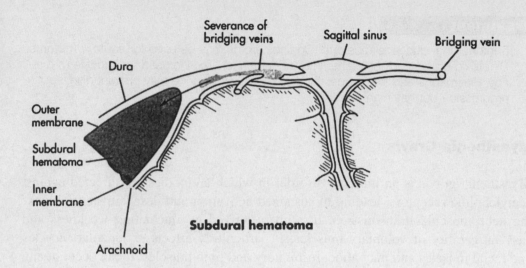

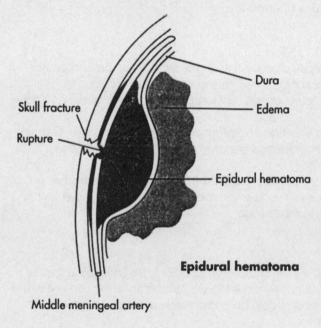

Fig. 8-40. Subdural and epidural hematomas. (Reprinted with permission from AJ Castro, MP Merchut, EJ Neafsey, RD Wurster. *Mosby's Ace the Boards: Neuroscience.* St. Louis: Mosby, 1996.)

Traumatic Disorders

Subdural Hematoma

Subdural hematoma is a supratentorial mass lesion usually caused by trauma (Fig. 8-40). Older age makes patients more susceptible due to increased risk of falls and easier rupture of bridging veins.

Signs & Symptoms

Headache and altered consciousness are common, but symptoms can be variable and even absent. Waxing and waning signs and symptoms are classic. If present, hemiparesis is usually contralateral to the lesion, with ipsilateral pupillary dilation.

Diagnosis

CT or MRI scan. Lumbar puncture is not diagnostic.

Treatment

Neurosurgery to evacuate the blood if symptoms are severe.

Epidural Hematoma

Epidural hematoma usually results from severe head trauma associated with lateral skull fracture and tearing of the **middle meningeal artery** and vein (see Fig. 8-40).

Signs & Symptoms

Patient may be fine for several hours and then progress to headache, vomiting, obtundation, seizures, focal neurologic signs, and coma. Epidural hematoma may also occur in the spinal cord (e.g., following lumbar puncture) with back pain, paresis, sensory disturbances, and bowel and bladder dysfunction.

Diagnosis

CT or MRI scan.

Treatment

Rapid surgical evacuation of hematoma is essential.

Hydrocephalus

Normal-pressure hydrocephalus (NPH) is known as a **communicating hydrocephalus** because the flow of CSF between ventricles is not obstructed. Rather, the increased fluid is likely due to impaired CSF absorption from arachnoid granulations. NPH may be idiopathic or secondary to conditions that interfere with CSF absorption (e.g., meningitis, subarachnoid hemorrhage).

Noncommunicating or **obstructive hydrocephalus** is caused by blockade of CSF circulation in the ventricular system (e.g., by tumor). It is associated with increased CSF pressure, headache, and papilledema.

Signs & Symptoms

Dementia, gait apraxia (unsteadiness on standing and difficulty initiating walking), and incontinence develop over weeks to months.

Diagnosis

Fundoscope examination may show hazy outlines of the optic disk. Lumbar puncture reveals normal or low opening pressure. CT or MRI scan shows enlarged lateral ventricles without increased prominence of cortical sulci (which is seen in Alzheimer's).

Treatment

Shunting of CSF benefits some patients (especially those with hydrocephalus from meningitis or subarachnoid hemorrhage) but has a high complication rate caused by infection, subdural hematoma, and shunt malfunctions.

Peripheral Neuropathy

Peripheral nerve lesions, or neuropathies, may be subdivided into the following categories: **mononeuropathy** (one nerve affected) and **polyneuropathy** (numerous peripheral nerves are affected, classically causing distal and symmetric deficits with loss of tendon reflexes).

There are multiple causes, including inflammatory, infectious (HIV), vasculitic, ischemic, neoplastic, toxin- or drug-induced, hereditary, birth-related, metabolic (diabetes) and entrapment-related etiologies; although many cases are idiopathic.

Signs & Symptoms

May include sensory disturbances (usually paresthesias in a "stocking-glove" distribution, motor deficits, altered tendon reflexes, and autonomic disturbances, such as postural hypotension. Enlarged nerves are rarely noted on examination but may be seen in cases of leprosy.

Diagnosis

Diagnosis is based on time course and other coexisting medical conditions. Studies include electromyography, nerve conduction studies, and histopathology. Work up for systemic causes (e.g., toxins in blood, vitamin B_{12} levels, syphilis tests, rheumatoid factor) should also be performed.

Treatment

Treat the underlying cause. Nursing care is provided to prevent decubitus ulcers, contractures, and additional nerve damage. Analgesics are used. If they are ineffective, lancinating pain may be treated with phenytoin, carbamazepine, mexiletine, or amitriptyline. It is crucial that extremities with sensory loss be protected from repeated minor trauma.

Neoplastic Disorders

Brain tumors may be primary (arising from glia, neurons, or meninges) or metastatic (spreading to CNS from non-CNS source). Primary brain tumors almost never spread to other areas of the body. In the brain, even benign tumors (those that do not metastasize and tend to grow slower) can be fatal due to their mass effect and involvement of critical brain structures. Tumors are usually infratentorial in children (cerebellar medulloblastoma or astrocytoma) and supratentorial in adults.

The most common brain neoplasms are described here:

- **Meningioma**: The most common benign primary brain tumor. Meningiomas arise from the arachnoid and grow slowly over several years. On CT scan, they are often calcified and accompanied by bony reaction (hyperostosis) of adjacent skull and brain edema. Histologically, they appear as whorls or sheets of cells with **psammoma bodies**. Depending on tumor location, they are often resectable and have the best prognosis of all brain tumors.

- **Astrocytoma**: Malignant tumors arising from astrocytes. Higher grade (including **glioblastoma multiforme**) indicates worse prognosis, with survival in weeks to months for adults.

- **Metastatic cancer**: Metastatic lesions are the most common tumors in the brain. They tend to be multiple and are often present at the gray-white subcortical junction. They most commonly arise from cancers of the lung, breast, colon, and kidney as well as melanoma and sarcoma. Although systemic lymphoma can spread to brain, primary CNS lymphomas may also occur, particularly in patients with AIDS.

A single brain metastasis may be excised and then treated with radiation therapy, which has a better survival rate than multiple metastases treated with radiation therapy alone. Steroid treatment is often beneficial.

The spread of cancer cells throughout the CSF is known as **meningeal carcinomatosis**. This causes cranial neuropathies, radiculopathies, changes in mental status, and headache.

Signs & Symptoms

Symptoms are variable and tend to evolve slowly over time. These include seizures, headache, nausea and vomiting, drowsiness, focal deficits, and mental impairment.

Diagnosis

CT or MRI scan. Biopsy is performed for definitive diagnosis.

Treatment

Surgical excision, radiation therapy, and chemotherapy. Steroids decrease edema around the tumor, thus reducing neurologic symptoms.

Neurodegenerative Disorders

Excitatory amino acids (EAAs), **nitric oxide**, and **calcium** play a critical role in neuronal death and dysfunction. EAAs, such as glutamate and aspartate, are neurotransmitters that are released by presynaptic neurons and bind to specific EAA receptors on postsynaptic cells. These receptors transmit signals into the cells using second messenger systems. In the case of the N-methyl-D-aspartate glutamate receptor, the binding of EAAs leads to opening of the receptor channel and calcium flow into the cell.

Under normal circumstances, ATP is used to actively transport calcium back out of the cell or into storage compartments in the cell. However, when there is an increase in EAAs or a decrease in cellular energy reserves there may be excess calcium floating in the cell. This may lead to multiple detrimental effects, such as increased free radical formation and lipase activation, which damage the cell. Nitric oxide may play a role in modulating the receptor. In epilepsy, the repetitive firing of neurons leads to increased stimulation of EAA receptors. In Alzheimer's disease and Parkinson's disease, there may be deficient ATP production and increased intracellular calcium.

Dementia

Dementia refers to an acquired, global disorder of cognitive function. It affects the content, rather than the level, of consciousness. Its incidence increases with age (affecting roughly 5–20% of people over 65). Dementia must be differentiated from acute confusional states (delerium) and **pseudodementia** (cognitive loss produced by depression).

Alzheimer's disease is the most common cause of dementia (60%), followed by multi-infarct dementia (15%), and then other causes, such as alcohol related, metabolic, neoplastic disease and NPH, Parkinson's disease, and Huntington's disease. Treatable causes of dementia include NPH, intracranial mass lesions, vitamin B_{12} deficiency, hypothyroidism, and neurosyphilis.

Alzheimer's Disease

Alzheimer's disease is the most common cause of dementia. The incidence increases with age and occurs equally in both sexes. Patients experience a progressive loss of cognitive function. Toxic substances may play a role in Alzheimer's disease pathogenesis.

Most cases of Alzheimer's disease are sporadic with unknown cause, but a minority of cases have a genetic basis. These include trisomy 21 (Down syndrome), in which nearly all patients develop the disease, and autosomal dominant familial Alzheimer's disease, which may have an early-onset pattern. The genetic mutations responsible for familial Alzheimer's vary and include mutations on chromosomes 21 and 14, among others.

Signs & Symptoms

The disease begins with impairment of recent memory, followed by disorientation to time and place. Aphasia, anomia (inability to name things), and acalculia (inability to calculate) may develop. Depression occurs early and may give way to agitation and restlessness. Apraxias and visuospatial disorientation then occur, and patients become lost easily. Primitive reflexes are commonly found.

In later stages, psychiatric symptoms may occur, including psychosis, hallucinations, or delusions. The patient becomes mute, incontinent, and bedridden. Death generally occurs 5–10 years after symptom onset.

Pathology

The disease is marked pathologically by the presence of neuritic plaques and neurofibrillary tangles in the brain. β-Amyloid is found in neuritic plaques and the cerebral blood vessels. There are also changes in several neurotransmitter systems, particularly acetylcholine. Degeneration of the **nucleus basalis of Meynert** (the origin of cortical cholinergic innervation) often occurs.

Diagnosis

There are no laboratory tests. CT or MRI scan often shows cortical atrophy and enlarged ventricles, which may be seen in normal elderly patients. It is important to rule out other diseases, particularly potentially reversible causes of dementia.

Treatment

Tacrine, an acetylcholinesterase inhibitor, may improve cognitive function via cholinergic replacement. Liver function enzymes must be followed to monitor for hepatotoxicity.

Korsakoff Amnestic Syndrome

Korsakoff amnestic syndrome is caused by **thiamine deficiency** and occurs in chronic alcoholism and other malnourished states. It is marked by the inability to form new memories, leading to particularly severe impairment of short-term memory. It is also frequently marked by confabulation. The patient generally has one or several episodes of **Wernicke's encephalopathy** (confusion, ataxia, and ophthalmoplegia) before developing Korsakoff's syndrome. Treatment is prompt administration of thiamine, which may prevent progression but is not likely to improve the existing amnesia. In a patient with Wernicke's encephalopathy who has not yet developed Korsakoff's syndrome, thiamine may prevent the development of amnesia.

Parkinsonism and Parkinson's Disease

Parkinsonism is a syndrome of tremor, bradykinesia, rigidity, and abnormal gait and posture. It has a prevalence of 1–2 in 1,000 in the United States and western Europe, with males and females approximately equally affected.

Parkinson's disease is the name for parkinsonism of unknown etiology. However, other forms of parkinsonism exist. For example, drug- or toxin-induced parkinsonism is becoming increasingly common. It is caused by therapeutic drugs, such as phenothiazines, butyrophenones, metoclopramide, reserpine, and tetrabenazine. Drug-induced cases are often reversible. Toxins such as MPTP, manganese dust, carbon disulfide, and carbon monoxide poisoning are irreversible causes of parkinsonism. MPTP was previously synthesized as a street drug and led to parkinsonism in drug users. Its metabolite, MPP, blocks oxidative metabolism and selectively destroys dopaminergic neurons in the substantia nigra and adrenergic neurons in the locus ceruleus.

Signs & Symptoms

Patients have a characteristic tremor, which is most evident at rest and decreases with voluntary activity. It may involve one or more limbs. Patients also exhibit **cogwheel rigidity**, with increased resistance to passive movement. Patients tend to stand flexed and have difficulty initiating movement and may walk with tiny steps to prevent falls (**festinating gait**).

Bradykinesia, or slowness of voluntary movement and decreased automatic movement (such as less swinging of arms while walking), is also characteristic. Patients may also have a "**masklike faces**": an immobile face with fixed expression and decreased blinking. They tend to have small handwriting (micrographia) and low volume when speaking.

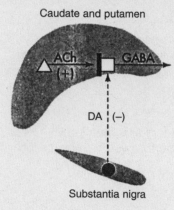

Caudate and putamen

Substantia nigra

Fig. 8-41. Neurotransmitters in Parkinson's disease. (Ach = acetylcholine; GABA = γ-aminobutyric acid; DA = dopamine.) (From DA Greenberg, MJ Aminoff, RP Simon. *Clinical Neurology* [2nd ed]. Norwalk, CT: Appleton & Lange, 1993.)

Pathology

In Parkinson's disease, there is loss of pigmentation and cells in the **substantia nigra** and other brain stem centers, cell loss in the **globus pallidus** and **putamen**, and the presence of eosinophilic intraneural inclusion granules (**Lewy bodies**) in the basal ganglia, brain stem, spinal cord, and sympathetic ganglia. The loss of dopaminergic cells in the nigrostriatal system leads to unopposed acetylcholine activation of striatal GABAergic neurons (Fig. 8-41). This is thought to lead to the motor symptoms.

Diagnosis

The above signs and symptoms support the diagnosis.

Treatment

Drugs such as L-dopa or carbidopa are used. Pallidotomy or thalamotomy are often helpful when patients are not responsive or cannot tolerate medication. Fetal tissue transplantations to the adrenal medulla or substantia nigra are being studied.

Patients benefit from physical therapy and speech therapy. Quality of life may be improved by providing aids such as rails, banisters, nonslip table mats, and even chairs that help eject the occupant.

Epilepsy

Seizures occur due to abnormal excitability of cerebral cortex neurons, leading to paroxysmal discharges in groups of neurons. Depending on where the process begins, a seizure may be restricted to one area of the brain or spread to other areas.

Epilepsy is a condition characterized by recurrent, unprovoked seizures. More than 10% of the U.S. population will have a seizure during their lifetime, but only 1–2% of the population develop epilepsy.

The risk of developing epilepsy is increased after traumatic brain injury, hypoxia, encephalitis, and structural lesions, such as tumors and arteriovenous malformations (AVMs). In children, epilepsy may arise secondary to improper development of brain regions (cerebral dysgenesis). Epilepsy may also affect the elderly as a result of cerebrovascular disease, neoplasms, metabolic derangements, and head trauma. Epilepsy may be described by types of seizures (e.g., complex partial seizures) and by types of epileptic syndrome (e.g., temporal lobe epilepsy).

Febrile seizures occur during a high fever and affect 2–4% of children younger than 5. Most children who experience febrile seizures do not develop epilepsy, and usually their seizures are not treated. **Status epilepticus**, continuous or repeated seizures lasting more than 30 minutes, is a medical emergency and must be treated rapidly.

Signs & Symptoms

Partial seizures consist of focal motor signs, which are somatosensory or special sensory symptoms over a discrete anatomic region. If the patient also loses consciousness, it's a **complex seizure**. If not, it's a **simple seizure**. Complex partial seizures may display automatisms (involuntary, semipurposeful movements).

Generalized seizures are always associated with loss of consciousness and are divided into two types. **Tonic-clonic** (or grand mal) seizures are characterized by convulsions and loss of bowel or bladder control. **Absence** (or petit mal) seizures are usually seen in children and characterized by a blank stare, eyelid fluttering, and fine mouth and hand movements.

Diagnosis

Electroencephalography shows characteristic changes during seizures and frequently shows background epileptiform abnormalities even in the absence of seizure. MRI is useful for identifying structural epileptogenic lesions.

Treatment

Antiepileptic drugs are described in more detail at the end of this chapter. Medically intractable patients may be candidates for surgical ablation of hyperactive neurologic foci.

Blindness and Visual Disorders

Visual disturbances have a myriad of causes. Multiple sclerosis may involve the optic nerve or brain stem. Atherosclerosis, hypertension, and diabetes can cause vascular disorders of the eye, cranial nerves, and brain visual pathways. Hyperthyroidism can cause ocular myopathy with exophthalmos (bulging of the eyes). Cancer or connective tissue disease can affect the visual system. Malnutrition can decrease visual acuity. Vitamin B_{12} deficiency leading to Wernicke's encephalopathy may manifest as ophthalmoplegia. Many drugs (e.g., ethambutol, isoniazid, digitalis, clioquinol) are toxic to the visual system.

Monocular Disorders

- **Amaurosis fugax**: Also known as *transient retinal artery occlusion*, this condition causes a transient loss of vision that develops over seconds and resolves over minutes. It frequently results from carotid artery emboli, and people who experience it are at increased risk of subsequent stroke.

- **Optic neuritis**: Optic neuritis is inflammation of the optic nerve. Visual impairment (usually a central scotoma or blind spot) occurs over hours to days. It is associated with headache and eye pain. It may be the presenting symptom of multiple sclerosis or may be postviral, idiopathic, or due to a variety of other less common causes. Treatment with steroids is controversial because it may actually lead to a higher recurrence rate.

- **Temporal arteritis**: Also known as *giant cell arteritis*, this condition may cause infarction of the optic nerve, resulting in sudden vision loss that is usually unilateral but may be bilateral. Patients may complain of a headache over the temporal poles and jaw claudication. It is diagnosed with an elevated sedimentation rate and temporal artery biopsy. Treatment is with corticosteroids.

Binocular Disorders

- **Papilledema**: Papilledema is bilateral disk swelling associated with increased intracranial pressure. It may be caused by intracranial mass, meningitis, or **pseudotumor cerebri** (usually idiopathic; most common in obese women of childbearing age). Vision loss is variable and associated with headache, nausea, and vomiting. On funduscopic examination, disk swelling may be seen.

- **Optic chiasm lesions**: These lesions can include pituitary tumors and aneurysms. They cause **bitemporal hemianopsia** (loss of the lateral visual field of each eye).

- **Optic tract lesions**: Lesions of the optic tract and lateral geniculate body are usually due to infarction. They cause **homonymous hemianopsia** (loss of the same visual field in each eye).

- **Optic radiation lesions**: Lesions of the optic radiations also cause congruous **homonymous field deficits**. Damage to the temporal lobe by optic radiation affects the upper visual fields, whereas parietal damage affects the lower ones.

- **Occipital cortex lesions**: These lesions cause **homonymous hemianopsias** affecting the contralateral visual field. They frequently have macular sparing due to dual blood supply and cortical representation. Posterior cerebral artery infarctions are the most common cause. Bilateral occipital lobe involvement results in cortical blindness.

Narcolepsy

Narcolepsy is a disease in which REM sleep occurs at inappropriate times. It appears to have a genetic basis.

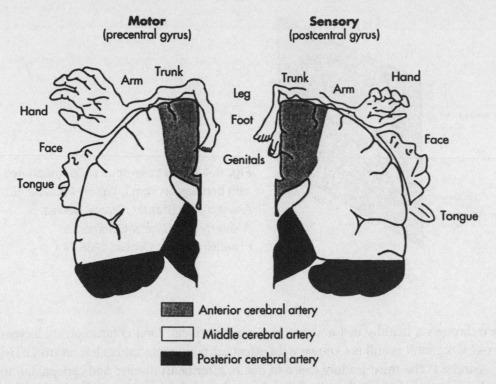

Fig. 8-42. Distribution of cerebral artery branches. (From DA Greenberg, MJ Aminoff, RP Simon. *Clinical Neurology* [2nd ed]. Norwalk, CT: Appleton & Lange, 1993.)

Signs & Symptoms

Inappropriate sleep attacks. **Cataplexy** is loss of muscle tone prompted by emotional stimuli. Patients may also experience sleep paralysis (the transient feeling of paralysis on waking) and hypnagogic hallucinations (vivid dreams that occur when falling asleep).

Diagnosis

Sleep latency tests show early onset of REM sleep.

Treatment

Medications include stimulants and REM suppressants.

Vascular Disorders

Stroke

Stroke is a focal neurologic abnormality due to a disturbance in blood flow to the brain by any cause; it is generally of sudden onset and fails to resolve completely in 24 hours. A **transient ischemic attack (TIA)** is a focal neurologic dysfunction that resolves within 24 hours.

Avoidable risk factors for stroke include **hypertension, smoking, obesity, cocaine use, excess alcohol,** and **use of oral contraceptives.** Prevention of coronary artery dis-

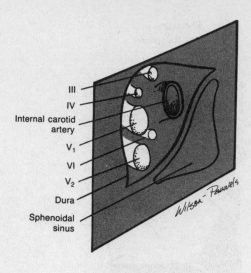

III

IV

Internal carotid
artery

V₁

VI

V₂

Dura

Sphenoidal
sinus

Fig. 8-43. The cavernous sinus. (Reprinted with permission from L Wilson-Pauwels, EJ Akesson, PA Stewart. *Cranial Nerves: Anatomy and Clinical Comments.* Philadelphia: BC Decker, 1988;74.)

ease through a healthy diet and exercise is also critical. Oral contraceptives increase stroke risk, but it is still not known what effect estrogen replacement has on stroke risk.

Stroke is the third leading cause of death, after heart disease and cancer, and the leading cause of long-term disability in the United States. **Ischemic stroke** may result from an embolus released from a plaque in the carotid artery or cerebral vasculature. **Hemorrhagic stroke** occurs when the ischemic cerebral infarct starts to bleed, resulting in the formation of a hematoma. This may cause ischemia in surrounding tissues by mass effect.

Signs & Symptoms

Depending on the location of blood flow disturbance, symptoms may include changes in motor function, sensation, sleep and arousal, speech, mood, intellect, and behavior. The pattern of blood supply to various parts of sensory and motor cortex is shown in Fig. 8-42. From this you can deduce, for example, that hemiplegia with weakness of the face and arm would suggest a middle cerebral artery stroke.

Diagnosis

Diagnosis is based primarily on clinical syndrome, examination, and history. Changes on CT or MRI scan generally do not occur for at least 12 hours. However, immediate CT scan is obtained to rule out hemorrhage and look for previous infarct or neoplasm. Carotid duplex scanning and angiography should be done to evaluate the carotids.

Treatment

Thrombolytic agents, such as tissue plasminogen activator, are now approved for use in the first few hours after a stroke. Otherwise, anticoagulant therapy with heparin and warfarin is begun, once intracerebral hemorrhage is ruled out by CT scan.

In patients with known carotid artery atherosclerosis, antiplatelet agents (e.g., aspirin and ticlopidine) and anticoagulants (e.g., warfarin) may be used to decrease the risk of embolic stroke. Carotid endarterectomy may help prevent stroke in patients with carotid artery stenosis.

Cavernous Sinus Thrombosis

Cavernous sinus thrombosis may result from inflammatory lesions and hypercoagulable states. In particular, because the wall of the cavernous sinus surrounds the sphenoid sinus, sphenoid sinusitis can result in cavernous sinus thrombophlebitis. Other lesions of the cavernous sinus may be caused by tumors or carotid aneurysms. Structures traversing the sinus include the third, fourth, and sixth cranial nerves; the first two divisions of the fifth nerve; sympathetic fibers supplying the pupil; and the carotid artery (Fig. 8-43).

Signs & Symptoms

Patients experience palsies of cranial nerves III, IV, or VI; proptosis; and orbital chemosis.

Diagnosis

CT or MRI scan.

Treatment

Antibiotics are used if an infectious cause is suspected. Drainage of the area and sphenoid sinus may be necessary.

Multi-Infarct Dementia

Multi-infarct dementia is the second most common cause of dementia after Alzheimer's disease. Patients with this diagnosis have either multiple large cortical infarcts from occlusion of major cerebral arteries or several smaller infarcts (known as *lacunar infarcts*). As with all strokes, hypertension is a risk factor.

It is not known how strokes are related to dementia. Patients may be accumulating infarcts over a period of time while remaining functionally intact, and then an additional infarct may tip the balance to cause the development of dementia.

Signs & Symptoms

There is a progression of deficits with relatively acute onset of dementia and focal neurologic symptoms and signs. **Pseudobulbar palsy** is common, along with dysarthria, dysphagia, and pathologic emotionality, focal motor and sensory deficits, ataxia, gait apraxia, hyperreflexia, and extensor plantar response.

Diagnosis

CT or MRI scan. An additional search for causes of multiple infarctions includes looking for a possible embolic source or hypercoagulable state.

Treatment

No treatment exists for the infarcts. Hypertension or other possible causes should be controlled to prevent further ischemic damage.

Vascular Malformations

Cerebral arterial aneurysms and **arteriovenous malformations** (AVMs) cause most cases of spontaneous subarachnoid hemorrhage. **Berry aneurysms** are outpouchings at arterial bifurcations that enlarge, with increasing risk of rupture over time. They are found most commonly in the anterior circle of Willis. Ten percent to 30% of patients have multiple aneurysms.

AVMs are developmental abnormalities that cause defective communication between arteries, capillaries, and veins, resulting in a network of tortuous blood vessels. If the walls are too thin, these vessels are prone to rupture. Shunting of blood may produce an ischemic state in the neighboring brain. Depending on the structure and location of the AVM, seizures, focal neurologic deficits, infarction, or bleeding into the subarachnoid space or brain tissue may occur.

Signs & Symptoms

Prodromal symptoms of berry aneurysms include third-nerve palsy, sixth-nerve palsy, posterior cervical pain, and pain behind the eye or in the low temple. The initial presentation is usually an acute major subarachnoid hemorrhage with the sudden onset of a severe headache ("worst headache of my life"). Vomiting, neck stiffness, and loss of consciousness may occur. Milder headaches in the weeks leading up to the event are common, and probably relate to small "sentinel" hemorrhages.

AVMs may cause a migraine-like or diffuse headache unassociated with bleeding. Seizures occur in about 30% of patients. In half of the cases, AVMs present as intracerebral hemorrhage that ranges from massive to small. AVM hemorrhage is usually intraparenchymal, with a small amount of spillage into the subarachnoid space.

Diagnosis

CT scan shows recent hemorrhage. In subarachnoid hemorrhage, look for blood in basal cisterns. Lumbar puncture may indicate minor hemorrhage even if the CT scan is normal. Contrast CT or MRI scan may show channels of AVM before rupture.

Treatment

Angiography and surgery.

Neuropharmacology

Anticonvulsants

Anticonvulsants are usually used individually at increased dosages until seizures are controlled or toxicity becomes overwhelming (Table 8-3). Additional agents increase the risk of toxicity and drug interactions. Almost all anticonvulsants are teratogenic and can cause craniofacial abnormalities (cleft lip and palate), heart defects (e.g., ventricular septal defect), and neural tube defects (e.g., spina bifida).

Antiparkinson Drugs

Two strategies are used in the treatment of parkinsonism (Table 8-4). The first method is to increase dopaminergic transmission; the second is to decrease muscarinic cholinergic transmission in the striatum.

Table 8-3. Anticonvulsants

Agent	Mechanism	Uses	Toxicities
Phenytoin (Dilantin)	Regulates sodium transport Affects second messenger systems (calmodulin and cyclic nucleotides)	Partial and generalized seizures	Ataxia, nystagmus, incoordination Long-term complications include gingival hypertrophy, hirsutism, and acne Inhibits P-450 enzyme
Carbamazepine (Tegretol)	Similar to phenytoin Membrane stabilization effects	Partial and generalized seizures	Same as phenytoin Also has gastrointestinal and bone marrow effects
Phenobarbital	Unknown	Partial and generalized seizures Second-line agent	Sedation, irritability, depression, nystagmus, ataxia, and abnormal collagen deposition leading to Dupuytren's contracture
Ethosuximide	Thalamic inhibition by reduction of calcium currents	Absence seizures	Gastrointestinal effects, photophobia, bone marrow suppression
Valproic acid (Divalproate)	Increased GABA concentrations in CNS	All generalized seizures, including absence seizures	Gastrointestinal effects, weight gain, tremor, platelet dysfunction Inhibits cytochrome P-450 system Rare fatal hepatic necrosis
Benzodiazepine (clonazepam)	Potentiates GABA-mediated neuronal inhibition, increasing chloride permeability	Partial and generalized seizures Second-line drug	Sedation and CNS effects Efficacy wears off after 6 months
Gabapentin	GABA analogue	Partial seizures	Somnolence and fatigue, but less so than other agents
Lamotrigine	Affects voltage-sensitive calcium channels	Partial and generalized seizures	Rash, dizziness, ataxia, somnolence Interaction with valproic acid

GABA = γ-aminobutyric acid.

Table 8-4. Antiparkinson drugs

Agent	Mechanism	Uses	Toxicities
L-Dopa	Decarboxylated to dopamine in the striatum	Treatment for akinesia and rigidity	Nausea and vomiting, orthostatic hypotension, dyskinesia, hallucinations, paranoia, depression
Decarboxylase inhibitors (e.g., carbidopa)	Inhibits peripheral decarboxylation of L-dopa	Given with L-dopa	—
Anticholinergics (e.g., benztropine)	Weak cholinergic stimulation Dopamine uptake inhibitor	Used with L-dopa Reduces parkinsonism produced by antipsychotic drugs	Dry mouth, blurred vision, dizziness, constipation, drowsiness, urinary retention
Dopaminergics (e.g., bromocriptine, pergolide, lisuride)	Stimulation of D2 receptors, with lesser effects at D1 receptors	Parkinsonism and hyperprolactinemia	Nausea, hypotension, hallucinations Bromocriptine is a D2 agonist and D1 antagonist.
MAO inhibitors (e.g., selegiline)	Inhibits MAO-B and decreases breakdown of dopamine	Given with L-dopa May also be given early and delays L-dopa therapy	No interaction with tyramine, unlike classic MAO inhibitors
Amantadine	Stimulates dopamine release, inhibits dopamine reuptake, some anticholinergic activity	Given with L-dopa Synergistic effects	Like anticholinergics

MAO = monoamine oxidase.

CHAPTER 9

Skin and Connective Tissue

The major function of the skin is to act as a barrier between the environment and the rest of the body. Additional functions include regulating fluid loss and temperature and receiving information about touch (Table 9-1).

The external surface of the skin is a keratinized, stratified, squamous epithelium called the epidermis. The **epidermis** grows outward from an innermost germinal layer (basal cell layer) to an outer keratinized layer that is shed continuously. Stages of growth are represented by five morphologic layers (Table 9-2, Fig. 9-1). Other epidermal cells are listed in Table 9-3.

Table 9-1. Skin structures and their functions

Structure	Function
Epidermis	Barrier
	Vitamin D synthesis
Stratum corneum	Physical barrier
Melanocytes	Light barrier
Langerhans' cells	Immunologic barrier
Blood vessels and eccrine sweat glands	Temperature regulation
Nerves	Touch sensation
Subcutaneous fat	Insulation from cold and trauma
	Calorie reservoir
Sebaceous glands	Unknown

Table 9-2. Epidermal structure

Layer	Description
Stratum germinativum or basale (basal cell layer)	Single-cell germinal layer adjacent to the dermis and separated from it by a basement membrane
Stratum spinosum (prickle cell layer)	Cells containing fine tonofibrils that are in the process of growth and early keratin synthesis
Stratum granulosum (granular layer)	Cells with keratohyaline granules, which contribute to keratinization
Stratum lucidum (clear layer)	Cells between the granulosum and the corneum; found only in thick (glabrous) skin (e.g., on the heel)
Stratum corneum (horny layer)	Flattened, fused cell remnants filled with keratin

TIP: To remember the layers from the bottom up: Boys Still Give Cookies= Basalis; spinosum; granulosum; lucidum; corneum.

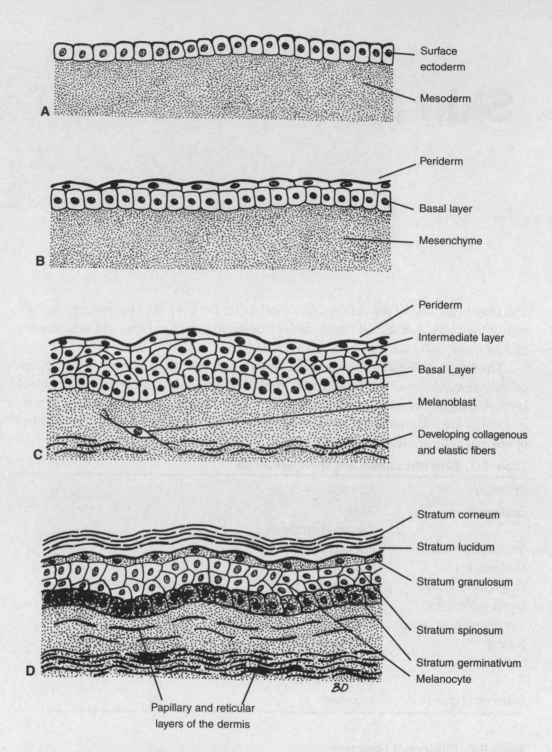

Fig. 9-1. Skin Development. a. Ectoderm. b, Two months gestational age. c. Four months gestational age. d. At birth.

Table 9-3. Other epidermal cells

Cell type	Description
Melanocytes	Cells in the basal layer that protect the skin from UV radiation by producing a pigment
	Dendrites extend into the stratum spinosum and extrude pigment granules (**melanosomes**) filled with **melanin**, a **tyrosine** derivative
	Everyone has the same number of melanocytes; darker-skinned people have larger and more numerous melanosomes
	Responsible for suntans
Langerhans' cells	Cells from the bone marrow that present antigens to lymphocytes (identical to tissue macrophages)
	Important component of the immunologic barrier of skin

Living on the surface of the skin and within hair follicles are organisms that constitute the skin's **normal flora**. The predominant organism is *Staphylococcus epidermidis*. Less predominant organisms include *Staphylococcus aureus*, *Corynebacterium*, some streptococci, and *Pseudomonas aeruginosa*. Anaerobic organisms such as *Propionibacterium* and *Peptostreptococcus* can be found hanging around in low-oxygen areas, such as the deeper follicles in the dermis. The yeast *Candida albicans* can also be found on the skin. The normal flora is an important part of our defense against infection; it prevents the growth of more pathogenic organisms.

The epidermis is supported and nourished by dense, fibroelastic connective tissue called the **dermis**. The dermis is highly vascular and contains many sensory receptors. The dermis is attached to underlying tissues by a layer of loose connective tissue called the **hypodermis**, which contains variable amounts of adipose tissue. **Skin appendages** include hair follicles, sweat glands, sebaceous glands, and nails (Figure 9.2, Table 9-4). Except for the nails, the appendages are downgrowths of epidermal epithelium that settle into the dermis and hypodermis.

Blood is supplied to the skin by arteries located deep in the hypodermis. These arteries give rise to multiple branches that rise to the skin and form two anastomosing plexuses. The deeper plexus, the **cutaneous plexus**, is located at the junction between the hypodermis and the dermis. Branches from this plexus supply the hypodermis, the deep dermis, the hair follicles, and the deep sweat and sebaceous glands. The more superficial plexus, the **subpapillary plexus**, is located just beneath the dermal papillae (those fingers of dermis that poke up and make the base of the epidermis look wavy). This plexus supplies the upper dermis and superficial appendages and sends capillary loops into the dermal papillae. Venous drainage is organized in a similar manner.

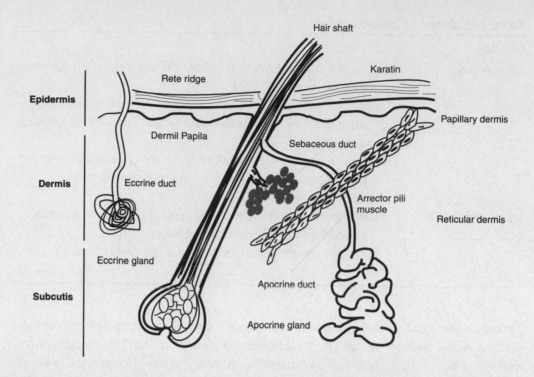

Epidermis
Dermis
Subcutis

Hair shaft
Karatin
Rete ridge
Papillary dermis
Dermil Papila
Sebaceous duct
Eccrine duct
Arrector pili muscle
Reticular dermis
Eccrine gland
Apocrine duct
Apocrine gland

Fig 9.2. Sectional View.

Table 9-4. Skin appendages

Appendage	Description
Eccrine sweat glands	Help regulate temperature by secreting sweat, which is initially isotonic to plasma but becomes hypotonic by the time it reaches the surface (by a process of ductal reabsorption of electrolytes)
Apocrine sweat glands	Secrete an odorless sweat that becomes smelly when bacteria act on it
	Located at the midportion of hair follicles, mainly in the axillae and anogenital areas
Sebaceous glands	Produce oily substances called *sebum*, mostly made of triglycerides, that drains into the hair follicle
	Fatty acid of sebum have antimicrobial activity
	Part of the pilosebaceous unit
	Located in the dermal layer
	Most prominent on the scalp and face and moderately prominent on the upper trunk
	Size and activity are under androgen control
	The cells are wholly secreted (**holocrine secretion**)
Hair follicle	Distributed over the whole body surface except the palms and soles
	Cells at the bottom (**hair bulb**) actively divide and then differentiate, forming a keratinous hair shaft
	Hair bulb projects into the hippodermus
	Melanocytes in the matrix contribute pigment
	There is an associated **arrector pili muscle**, which causes the hair to stand up, resulting in "goose bumps"

Nail	Like hair, made of keratin formed from a matrix of dividing epidermal cells
	The matrix produces the **nail plate** (the hard part)
	The **proximal nail fold** helps protect the matrix and produce the cuticle
	The nail bed produces a minimal amount of keratin, which adheres tightly to the bottom of the nail plate

A number of different receptors mediate sensory information from the skin (Table 9-5.)

Table 9-5. Touch Receptors

Cell type	Description
Meissner's corpuscles	Small encapsulated sensory receptors found in the dermal papillae of the palms, soles, and digits
	Responsible for light discriminatory touch
Pacinian corpuscles	Large encapsulated sensory receptors in the deep layers of the dermis at the ligaments, joint capsules, serous membranes, and mesenteries
	Responsible for pressure, coarse touch, vibration, and tension sensations
Free Nerve Endings	Found throughout the body along the dermo-epidermal junction. Resposible for temperature, touch, and pain.

Embryology

The epidermis derives from **ectoderm**, originally a single layer of cells. At 2 months, ectoderm divides into the **periderm** and a **basal layer.** At 4 months, the basal layer divides into an **intermediate layer** and a basal layer. After 4 months, the periderm divides into the granular layer (**stratum granulosum**) and the horny layer (**stratum corneum**), the intermediate layer becomes the spinous layer (**stratum spinosum**), and the basal layer remains the basal layer (**stratum basale** or **germinativum**) (Figs. 9-1).

The dermis derives from mesenchyme. In the third and fourth months, dermal papillae project upward, toward the epidermis. The papillae contain small capillaries or sensory nerve end organs. Deeper layers of dermis contain large amounts of fatty tissue.

Sensory fibers to skin appear as early as 5 weeks of gestation. **Neural crest cells,** which will become **melanocytes**, migrate to the epidermis within the first 3 months. Hair follicles, sebaceous glands, and sweat glands develop at about 3 months.

The next few pages list the most-often tested dermatologic conditions on the USMLE Step 1. See Table 9-6 for definitions of clinical terms.

Table 9-6. Clinical terms related to dermatologic conditions

Term	Definition
Macule	Flat, colored lesion <0.5 cm in diameter
Patch	A macule >0.5 cm in diameter
Papule	Small, raised skin lesion <0.5 cm in diameter
Plaque	A plaque >0.5 cm in diameter
Nodule	Solid, round lesion
Vesicle	Small fluid-filled blister
Bulla	Large fluid-filled blister
Pustule	Pus-containing blister
Cyst	Fluid- or semifluid-filled round lesion
Scale	Thickened stratum corneum, dry and usually whitish
Ulcer	A loss of epidermis and dermis in pathologically altered skin (leads to scarring)
Wheal (hives)	Plaque or papule of dermal edema, often with central pallor and irregular borders
Keloid	Hypertropic, elevated, progessively enlarging scar
Miliune	Tiny epidermal cyst presenting as a keratin-untaining papule

Congenital and Metabolic Disorders

Epidermolysis Bullosa

Epidermolysis bullosa refers to a group of congenital disorders that result in bulla formation at points of pressure or trauma. There are several types, all having different causes, including auto-immune and genetic disorders. **Epidermolysis bullosa dystrophica** can be inherited as an autosomal recessive or dominant disorder and results in scarring. **Epidermolysis bullosa** simplex is an autosomal dominant disorder that is more common in males, in which lesions heal without scarring. It results from basal cell degeneration in the epidermis.

Signs & Symptoms

Patients generally have multiple blisters as well as scars, keloids, milia, and thickened skin on the palms and soles. Severe scars on the digits of the hands and feet may be noted.

Pathology

Varies depending on the cause. Excessive immunoglobulin G (IgG) and C3 within the skin layers have been noted in some cases. Others may show abnormal collagen.

Diagnosis

Made clinically and with skin biopsy.

Treatment

Protective padding in areas of repeated trauma. Prenatal diagnosis can be performed with fetal skin biopsy.

Ehlers-Danlos Syndrome

Ehlers-Danlos syndrome refers to a group of disorders caused by a genetic defect in collagen synthesis that results in either reduced collagen production or the production of defective collagen (especially types I and III). Defective copper metabolism has also been implicated. Although skin manifestations are common, the biggest concern in these patients is the possibility of arterial or colonic rupture, both of which may be fatal.

Signs & Symptoms

Patients have fragile skin, abnormal joint laxity, and easy bruising. Arthritis, joint dislocations, and poor wound healing are common.

Pathology

Microscopically, collagen fibrils may appear large and irregular. Arterial walls and skin may appear thinner than normal.

Diagnosis

Family history combined with skin biopsy, if necessary. Prenatal diagnosis can be performed with fetal skin biopsy.

Treatment

Prolonged wound protection is needed to allow proper healing. Ascorbic acid is used in some cases.

Albinism

Different degrees of **hypopigmentation** occur in albinism, depending on the genetic cause. Autosomal dominant and autosomal recessive forms exist. The hair may be white, the skin pink-white, and the iris and pupil red. **Tyrosinase** activity may be absent or present. Individuals with albinism are much more susceptible to skin cancer and should avoid exposure to sunlight.

Scurvy

Scurvy is a disease of abnormal collagen synthesis due to **vitamin C deficiency**. Vitamin C (ascorbic acid) is a reducing agent used in the hydroxylation of collagen alpha chains. The hydroxylation of **proline** and **lysine** residues is critical in the cross-linking of these chains; without it, the resulting collagen has reduced tensile strength and increased fragility.

Signs & Symptoms

Early signs include weakness and fatigue. As the course progresses, patients develop perifollicular hemorrhages, bleeding gums, petechiae, and joint hemorrhages. Late stages express nervous system abnormalities, such as neuropathy and cerebral hemorrhages.

Diagnosis

History and skin lesions, along with a reduced plasma ascorbic acid level.

Treatment

Ascorbic acid supplementation.

Hypervitaminosis A

Vitamin A (retinol) is important in epithelial cell growth and differentiation, and in normal wound healing. In excess, however, it can be very toxic, with skin, GI, and CNS manifestations.

Signs & Symptoms

Excess intake of β-carotene, the plant precursor of vitamin A, leads to yellow staining of the skin, especially the palms and soles. Otherwise, excess β-carotene is benign. Acute excessive vitamin A intake (e.g. massive vitamin supplement overdose, polar bear liver consumption) causes GI symptoms (nausea, vomiting, abdominal pain) as well as CNS symptoms (headache, lethargy, papilledema). Chronic over-ingestion of vitamin A causes dry, scaly skin and hair loss, in addition to mouth sores, anorexia, and vomiting. Hepatomegaly and symptoms of elevated intracranial pressure may also occur.

Diagnosis

History and elevated serum vitamin A levels.

Treatment

Remove vitamin A from diet.

Infectious Disorders

Herpes Simplex Infection

Infection with herpes simplex virus (HSV) causes a vesicular eruption that is characteristically followed by recurrent attacks because the latent HSV survives in the dorsal root or autonomic ganglia. HSV type 1 (HSV-1) typically causes oral lesions, whereas HSV-2 usually causes genital disease. Primary infections with HSV-1 usually occur in childhood. HSV-2 infection is usually due to sexual contact, producing acute vulvovaginitis or penile lesions.

Signs & Symptoms

Primary HSV-1 infections are subclinical or may manifest as acute gingivostomatitis. Primary infections with HSV-2 are frequently accompanied by fever, malaise, myalgias, headache, and regional adenopathy. Recurrences are common, and the lesions can be very painful. Patients often describe a prodrome of burning or itching sensation before blisters appear.

Diagnosis

Made clinically and confirmed with a Tzanck smear, which shows multinucleated giant cells. Viral culture and an enzyme immunoassay are also performed.

Treatment

Acyclovir or valacyclovir (synthetic purine nucleoside analogues) are often used. Treatment does not prevent recurrence but may lengthen the remission time between episodes. Neonatal herpes may develop in children born to mothers with HSV-2, especially those with active herpetic lesions.

Viral Skin Manifestations

Skin manifestations of viral illnesses are often accompanied by fever, malaise, and other nonspecific symptoms. Some of the most common viruses are as follows:

- **Rubeola** and **rubella** cause a maculopapular rash that begins on the face and spreads to the trunk and extremities. Desquamation occurs after a few days.

- **Enterovirus** can cause a maculopapular or purpuric rash that is similar to rubella. **Coxsackievirus** A is responsible for **herpangina,** which appears as fever, sore throat, and red-based vesicles in the back of the throat. It also causes **hand, foot,** and **mouth disease,** in which vesicles appear on the hands, feet, and mouth.

- **Exanthem subitum,** or **roseola infantum,** is caused by **HHV-6.** Its clinical course is usually a very high fever which, upon dissipation, is immediately followed by the appearance of red papules surrounded by white halos on the trunk and neck.

- **Erythema infectiosum,** or **"fifth disease,"** is caused by **parvovirus B19.** Patients have a red, "slapped-cheek" rash and lacy maculopapular lesions on the extremities.

- **Measles virus** causes **Koplik's spots** (tiny, bright red lesions with a grayish white center) on the buccal mucosa. This is often accompanied by a maculopapular rash that starts on the face or palms and soles and progresses downward, turning brown after several days.

- **Varicella-zoster virus** causes the vesicular lesions of chickenpox in children (spread over the whole body) and shingles in adults (dermatomal distribution). The lesions of chickenpox characteristically appear in "crops," so that on a given part of the body there appear to be vesicles at different stages of resolving. The vesicles are typically described as "dewdrops on a rose petal" in appearance.

- **Warts,** or verrucae, are caused by several viruses in the **HPV** family. They are discussed in more detail later in this chapter.

- **Molluscum contagiosum** is caused by a DNA poxvirus and produces small, umbilicated pink lesions similar to warts. It is a contagious viral disorder occurring most often in children and adolescents.

Skin Conditions Associated with Human Immunodeficiency Virus

The most common skin conditions that develop in infection with human immunodeficiency virus (HIV) are those associated with immunocompromised patients. *Candida* infections and **folliculitis** are frequently seen. In addition, HIV-positive individuals may develop frequent recurrences of **HSV-1, HSV-2**, and **varicella-zoster virus**, which can lead to disseminated infection. **Kaposi's sarcoma** causes violaceous flame-shaped lesions along the extremities and is caused by **human herpesvirus 8 (HHV-8)** infection. Finally, patients with HIV more frequently develop viral skin lesions, such as warts, caused by **human papillomavirus (HPV).**

Cellulitis

Cellulitis refers to infection of the subcutaneous connective tissue, resulting in localized inflammation. It can be caused by a number of organisms, depending on the method of infection. It is most commonly caused by group A streptococci and *Staphylococcus aureus*. **Erysipelas** is a form of cellulitis that is caused by group A streptococci and causes an "orange peel" appearance, usually on the face. **Necrotizing fasciitis** is a severe form of cellulitis caused by a mixed aerobic and anaerobic infection. It is characterized by rapid progression, crepitus, and local cutaneous anesthesia. It can be rapidly fatal if left untreated. **Fournier's gangrene** is necrotizing fasciitis around the male genital area.

Signs & Symptoms

Localized swelling and redness are seen in the affected area. It is associated with pain, fever and a history of local trauma. Necrotizing fasciitis displays blistering and discoloration of the affected skin. Contact dermatitis may be confused with cellulitis, but a good history and the presence of itching rather than pain with contact dermatitis help to differentiate the two.

Diagnosis

History and physical examination.

Treatment

Third-generation penicillins and cephalosporins are used. Surgical debridement may be necessary, especially in cases of necrotizing fasciitis.

Impetigo

Impetigo is a vesicular or bullous disorder of the skin caused by group A *Streptococcus* or *Staphylococcus aureus*. The lesions tend to occur on the face and other exposed areas. Because it is contagious and autoinoculable, contact with the lesions should be avoided. Glomerulonephritis may follow skin infections with group A streptococci.

Signs & Symptoms

Itchiness and crusted, honey-colored lesions often seen at the angle of the mouth and around the nares. Removal of the crusts reveals denuded red areas.

Diagnosis

Culture positive for staphylococci and streptococci. May be confused with contact dermatitis (see below), which is culture negative, and Herpes simplex infection.

Treatment

Antibiotics.

Bacterial skin manifestations

- **Lyme disease,** an infection by *Borrelia burgdoferi* following a tick bite, results in **erythema chronica migrans**, an expanding bull's eye lesion that appears 3 to 32 days later at the site. Secondary lesions will develop that have the same annular appearance but are smaller than the primary lesion.

- **Rocky Mountain Spotted** Fever, caused by *Rickettsia rickettsiae*, produces a red macular rash that begins peripherally on the wrists and ankles and spreads centrally. It is also transmitted by tick bite.

- **Scarlet fever** is a red, sandpapery rash that can accompany *Streptococcus pyogenes* pharyngitis.

- **Staphylococcal scalded skin syndrome** presents as bullae and denuded areas of skin in children due to infection with *Staphylococcus aureus. S. aureus* will grow out on blood culture.

- **Furuncles** and **carbuncles** (multiple furuncles coalesced together) are infections of the hair follicle and surrounding subcutaneous tissue, usually caused by *Staphylococcus aureus,* that lead to abscess formation. Incision and drainage and a course of systemic antibiotics are indicated.

Mycoses

Many fungi cause skin infections. The most common ones are as follows:

- **Dermatophytoses** are fungal infections of keratinized skin. They are caused by *Trichophyton*, *Microsporum*, and *Epidermophyton* spp. The specific disease is named by location, as in tinea pedis (athlete's foot), **tinea cruris** (jock itch), **tinea capitis** (head), and **tinea corporis** (trunk, proximal arms and legs; also called ringworm). Nail (**onychomycosis**) and hair (**trichomycosis**) infections are also seen. Diagnosis is by history and by potassium hydroxide preparation, which shows multiple, septate, tubelike structures (hyphae or mycelia) and spores. Topical antifungals, such as clotrimazole or miconazole, are used for treatment.

- **Tinea versicolor**, caused by *Malassezia furfur,* may be confused with vitiligo because patches of skin may not tan (or they may be hyper-pigmented). The KOH prep should reveal a "spaghetti and meatballs" appearance to the fungus.

- **Cutaneous *Candida*** infections include infections of the body folds (**intertrigo**), genitals, and mucosa. Patients at increased risk are diabetics, immunocompromised patients, and severely obese persons, who may develop increased moisture in skin folds. Treatment is with topical antifungals, such as clotrimazole.

- **Sporotrichosis** is caused by *Sporothrix schenckii*, a soil fungus. Infection usually develops after puncture with contaminated thorns or splinters. The organism forms an ulcerated nodule at the inoculation site and can cause regional lymphadenopathy. Potassium iodide and ketoconazole are used as treatment.

Parasitic arthropods

- **Scabies**, an infestation by *Sarcoptes scabiei*, is characterized by intensely itchy small linear burrows in the finger webs, wrists, elbows, anterior armpit folds, and intertriginous areas. In infants, the head, neck, palm, and soles may be affected. Family members are often affected. The mites and eggs can be see on KOH preparation of skin scrapings.

- **Head lice**, or *Pediculus capitis*, cause severe itchiness of the head. Eggs (nits) can be found on the hair, and adults may be seen on the head.

- **Body lice**, or P*ediculus corporis,* are related to poor hygiene and are associated with homelessness. Severe itchiness may result, and eggs or adult lice may be seen on the body and clothing.

- **Crab lice**, or *Phthirus pubis*, are transmitted by sexual contact but may also appear on the facial hair. Eggs are seen on pubic hair. The lice cause severe itchiness.

- **Flea** bites by *Pulex* may produce a local pruritic wheal due to sensitization.

Inflammatory Skin Disorders

Contact Dermatitis

Contact dermatitis can be due to irritants, such as chemicals that directly injure skin, and allergens that act as antigens in type IV cell-mediated hypersensitivity. Contact dermatitis is one of the most common occupational illnesses; the work environment and pattern of symptoms may provide helpful information. The most common culprits are detergents and soaps. Other causes include poison oak and poison ivy, topical drugs, latex, hair dyes, and adhesive tape.

Signs & Symptoms

Patients develop blisters, redness, and itching at the affected site.

Diagnosis

Clinical history and examination. Patch testing is sometimes used.

Treatment

Topical or systemic steroids and removal of the offending agent.

Acne

Acne refers to inflammation of the follicles, which may result in the formation of pustules and cysts. They are found in areas with numerous sebaceous glands, usually the face and upper trunk. Incidence and severity is usually worst in teens, but it may continue into the third and fourth decades (much to the dismay of adults everywhere).

Although the cause is unknown, a number of factors have been implicated. Increased androgenic hormones during puberty may cause enlargement of the sebaceous glands and increased sebum production. Obstruction during follicular development may prevent sebum from draining freely to the skin surface. Finally, infection of the follicle with *Propionibacterium acnes* has been associated with the development of acne.

Signs & Symptoms

The characteristic erythematous pustules can develop anywhere on the body, but most typically on the face, neck, and trunk.

Diagnosis

Clinical inspection and history.

Treatment

Topical drying agents, such as benzoyl peroxide, are used. Topical and oral antibiotics, such as tetracycline, may also be useful. Systemic retinoids such as isotretinoin (Accutane), a potent vitamin A analogue, are used in severe cystic acne and cause decreased follicular keratinization, sebum production, and intrafollicular bacterial counts. However, caution must be exercised in prescribing retinoids to fertile women, as they are teratogenic.

Mechanical Disorders

The nature of a skin wound determines how it heals. A clean surgical wound heals by **first intention**. Relatively few epithelial and connective tissue cells, only those along the incision site, are damaged. As a result, the incision space can quickly fill with fibrin-clotted blood, and the opposed edges are quickly bridged by fibroblasts (in the subepithelial areas) and epithelial cells (in the epidermis). Neutrophils appear in the wound on day 1, granulation tissue and mononuclear cells take over in the next couple of days, and increasing amounts of collagen accumulation and fibroblasts appear over the next few weeks to bridge the subepithelial space, producing a blanching of the scar. The epidermal separation is filled in by mitosis of epithelial cells. Remodeling of collagen over the next several months strengthens the scar.

In larger wounds with more extensive cell loss, healing by secondary intention occurs. In this process, a greater amount of necrotic tissue and fibrin must be cleared out of the wound. The large defect is filled in with greater quantities of granulation tissue, causing greater amounts of scarring. Wound contraction, or shrinking of the resulting scar, is characteristic of secondary healing and is attributed to myofibroblasts in the wound site.

Child and Elder Abuse

It is important for physicians to recognize signs of abuse. In children, multiple bruises and lesions, especially on the back, may signify intentional injury. Burns are often clearly demarcated (e.g., cigarette burns or scalding injuries) if intentional; accidental burns are accompanied by splash marks. In the elderly, the above signs as well as indications of neglect, such as poor skin turgor (indicating dehydration) and malnutrition, may be present. A history incompatible with the nature of the injury should give rise to suspicion.

Burns

Burns are classified as follows:

- **First-degree burns** affect the epidermis only. They appear erythematous and are painful.

- **Second-degree burns** damage the epidermis and part of the dermis. They may blister and appear red and swollen. They are painful.

- **Third-degree burns** involve epidermal and full dermal thickness injury. These burns appear white or charred and are numb due to nerve ending destruction. Epidermal regrowth cannot occur in these areas because of loss of hair follicles, which serve as epithelial cell reservoirs.

Burns may become easily infected, especially by *Pseudomonas aeruginosa*.

Diagnosis

History and physical examination.

Treatment

Sulfadiazine is used topically. Aggressive replacement of fluid losses is also important. Third-degree and deep second-degree burns require skin grafting.

Decubitus Ulcers

Decubitus ulcers, or pressure sores, are caused by continual pressure and shearing forces in certain areas. They are usually found in bedridden or wheelchair-bound patients unable to ambulate. Commonly affected areas include the sacral and coccygeal areas, ischial tuberosities, and greater trochanters. Diabetics and persons with sensory neuropathies are also at increased risk.

Signs & Symptoms

The sores begin as irregular, ill-defined, reddish, indurated areas that resemble abrasions. If left unprotected, full-thickness skin defects develop, with extension into the subcutaneous tissue and ultimate penetration into the deep fascia and muscle.

Diagnosis

History and examination.

Treatment

Padding and bandages are placed to protect affected areas. Skin should be kept clean and dry, and the patient's position should be changed frequently.

Ultraviolet Light Effects

Natural ultraviolet light (sunlight), especially ultraviolet B (**UVB**), is strongly associated with the development of skin cancer. It is thought that UV light causes the formation of **pyrimidine dimers**, resulting in DNA mutation. It is unclear if UV radiation causes optic damage. Other effects of UV light include sunburns and hyperpigmentation.

The adverse effects of sun exposure can be prevented by using sunscreens. The strength of sunscreen is measured by a number called a sun protective factor (SPF), which is the ratio of the amount of time required to produce skin redness with sunscreen over the time required to produce redness without sunscreen. Sunscreens include chemical agents, such as para-aminobenzoic acid (PABA) esters, salicylates, and benzophenones, as well as physical agents, such as zinc oxide and talc.

A number of drugs produce **photosensitivity**, an increased sensitivity to ultraviolet light. Tetracycline is a classic example, but other drugs include sulfonamides, thiazide diuretics, furosemide, sulfonylureas, phenothiazines, amiodarone, NSAIDs, and indomethacin.

Positive effects of UV radiation include vitamin D production and phototherapy of cutaneous disease. Psoriasis, pityriasis rosea, pruritus of uremia, vitiligo, and mycosis fungoides all respond to UV radiation alone or in combination with photosensitizing drugs (e.g., tar in treatment of psoriasis). High-intensity UVA fluorescent bulbs combined with psoralens plus UVA (**PUVA**) are used to treat psoriasis, vitiligo, mycosis fungoides, and alopecia areata.

Tattoos

Tattoos are the intentional or unintentional deposition of pigment in the dermis. The pigment is taken up resident macrophages, which are unable to break down the particle. Permanent discoloration of the area is the result. The current treatment for tattoo removal uses lasers. It is believed that the lasers may break the pigmented particles into smaller pieces that can be broken down more easily by macrophages. It is also thought that lasers cause some of the pigment to be released transepidermally.

Neoplastic Disorders

Warts

Also known as **verrucae vulgaris**, warts are benign epidermal papillomas caused by HPV. Different subtypes of HPV prefer different sites of infection, but all are transmissible by skin contact. The most common subtypes associated with skin warts are HPV-1 through HPV-4. Genital warts are associated with HPV-6 and -11. HPV-16 and -18 are associated with dysplasias and cancers of the female genital tract, the penis, and the anorectal region.

Signs & Symptoms

Patients develop small, demarcated tumors on the hands, genitals, and plantar areas.

Pathology

Microscopically, warts are characterized by vacuolated cells (koilocytes) in the granular cell layer of the epidermis.

Diagnosis

History and examination.

Treatment

Liquid nitrogen and salicylic acid are used topically. Surgical removal is possible.

Moles

Also known as *nevocellular nevi*, moles are benign tumors derived from melanocytes and include three subtypes, which represent progressive developmental stages:

- **Junctional nevi**, which represent the earliest developmental stage, are confined to the epidermal-dermal junction.

- **Compound nevi** occur at the epidermal-dermal junction and in the dermis. They represent downgrowths of junctional nevi into the dermis.

- **Intradermal nevi** are confined to clusters in the dermis and are often unpigmented. They are believed to be the final developmental stage of pigmented nevi.

Nevocellular nevi may appear during childhood (common acquired nevi) or may be congenital. They are common and benign, but larger congenital forms may present an elevated risk of malignant melanoma.

Variant forms of pigmented nevi include **blue nevi**, which are present at birth and are characterized by a blue external appearance, and **Spitz nevi**, which are red-pink nodules that are common in children and often confused with hemangiomas.

Dysplastic nevi are atypical, irregularly pigmented lesions with disorderly proliferation of melanocytes, dermal fibrosis, and often adjacent dermal lymphocyte infiltration. They may transform into malignant melanoma and should be inspected regularly. They can be inherited as part of the **dysplastic nevus syndrome** in an autosomal dominant pattern.

Signs & Symptoms

Nevocellular nevi tend to be uniformly pigmented and elevated with well-demarcated borders. Dysplastic nevi tend to have more variable borders and are less uniform in their pigmentation. Their surface is quite pebbly in appearance, and, unlike nevocellular nevi, they occur on both sun-exposed and non-sun-exposed skin. Any change in the color, size, or appearance of a nevocellular or dysplastic nevus should prompt further studies because the lesion may in fact be malignant melanoma.

Diagnosis

Clinical inspection. Histology of common acquired and congenital nevocellular nevi reveals nests of melanocytes with uniform, rounded nuclei and minimal mitotic activity. The cells of malignant melanoma, unlike those of nevocellular nevi, do not undergo maturational stages from superficial and pigment-producing to deeper and unpigmented. Blue nevi consist of nodular foci of dendritic, highly pigmented melanocytes in the dermis. Spitz's nevi represent fascicular growth of spindle and epithelioid cells. Dysplastic nevi consist of intradermal nests of melanocytes demonstrating cytologic atypia.

Treatment

Surgical excision.

Malignant Melanoma

Malignant melanoma arises from pigment-forming cells, melanocytes, and nevus cells. It is associated with excessive exposure to sunlight and is more common in fair-skinned persons.

There are four types of malignant melanoma. **Superficial spreading melanoma** is the most common type, with an irregular border and variegated pigmentation. It occurs most frequently on the trunk and extremities and has the best prognosis because metastasis is less common. (Other types of melanoma can metastasize aggressively and are therefore associated with poorer prognosis.)

The depth of vertical invasion determines the likelihood of metastasis. Spread is both lymphatic and hematogenous, with metastases frequently found in not only regional lymph nodes but in the liver, lungs, and brain.

Signs & Symptoms

The most important sign is the change in size, color, or texture of a mole. Lesions may become itchy and ulcerate. The appearance of a new pigmented lesion in adult life is also a red flag. The "ABCDs" of moles—asymmetry, irregular borders, color change, or increasing diameter—are associated with malignant transformation.

Pathology

Microscopically, the melanocytes are irregular and eosinophilic in appearance.

Diagnosis

Biopsy.

Treatment

Surgical excision and adjunctive chemotherapy.

Seborrheic Keratosis

Also called **senile keratosis**, seborrheic keratoses are very common benign neoplasms of the elderly. They appear as sharply demarcated raised papules or plaques with a typical "pasted-on" appearance and represent areas of basaloid cell growth with hyperkeratosis. They are most frequently found on the head, trunk, and extremities. Seborrheic keratoses require no treatment except excision for cosmetic reasons unless the lesions change in appearance. They rarely progress to become squamous cell carcinoma.

Actinic Keratosis

Actinic keratoses are premalignant epidermal lesions caused by excessive chronic exposure to sunlight. They are characterized by rough, scaling, poorly demarcated plaques on the face, neck, upper trunk, or extremities. Some produce so much keratin that a "horn" develops. Histology reveals atypical cells in the lower epidermis that may be due to basal cell hyperplasia. Because these lesions have the potential of progression to malignancy, they should be surgically excised.

Hemangioma

Hemangiomas are benign tumors composed of blood vessels. They may appear as "port-wine" stains or "strawberry" hemangiomas. Hemangiomas may occur as part of **von Hippel–Lindau disease**, an autosomal dominant disease with multiple vascular tumors and other adenomas of the liver, kidneys, and pancreas. This disease is associated with an increased incidence of renal cell carcinoma. Hemangiomas may also occur as part of **Sturge-Weber syndrome**, characterized by a port-wine stain of the face, ipsilateral glaucoma, vascular lesions of ocular choroid, and extensive hemangiomatous involvement of meninges. Severe symptoms include convulsions, mental retardation, and retinal detachment.

Basal Cell Carcinoma

Basal cell carcinoma is the most common skin cancer and the most common malignancy overall. It is caused by sun exposure and is found in sun-exposed areas, such as the head and neck. It is usually seen in fair-skinned, blue-eyed individuals with blonde or red hair. Sun-damaged skin and the presence of actinic keratosis are risk factors. Basal cell cancer can be locally aggressive but almost never metastasizes.

Signs & Symptoms

The lesion presents as a pearly papule with ulceration and telangiectactic vessels.

Pathology

Characterized by clusters of cells with large blue nuclei, resembling the basal layer of epidermis, with a typical palisade arrangement of nuclei at the periphery of the tumor. *palisading nuclei*

Diagnosis

Biopsy.

Treatment

Surgical excision or radiation.

Squamous Cell Carcinoma

Like basal cell carcinoma, squamous cell carcinoma is associated with fair skin and sun exposure, most frequently affecting the sun-exposed areas. It is locally invasive, however, and about 2% of lesions metastasize. They often originate from pre-existing actinic keratosis and are also associated with chemical carcinogens, radiation exposure, and a family history of skin cancer.

Signs & Symptoms

Usually presents as a scaling, indurated plaque or nodule that can bleed or ulcerate.

Pathology

Microscopically, it is characterized by invasion of the dermis by sheets and islands of neoplastic epidermal cells, often with **keratin pearls**, and by hyperkeratosis and atypical keratinocytes in the epidermis.

Diagnosis

Biopsy.

Treatment

Surgical excision.

Keratoacanthoma

Be aware that a keratoacanthoma can resemble squamous cell carcinoma both clinically and histologically, and should be treated like a squamous cell carcinoma. It favors sun-exposed areas and occurs in men more than in women.

Mycosis fungoides

Mycosis fungoides, or cutaneous T cell lymphoma, is a slowly progressive malignancy that remains in the skin for many years. Based on its presentation, it can be confused with psoriasis, leprosy, eczematous dermatitis, a drug eruption, or tinea corporis. The diagnosis is made by histology.

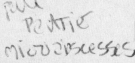

Signs & Symptoms

Itchy, scaling patches or plaques (>5 cm), usually located on the trunk. Tumors and lymphadenopathy are late findings.

Pathology

The epidermis and upper dermis are infiltrated by neoplastic T cells, which may have cerebriform nuclei.

Diagnosis

Biopsy.

Treatment

Topical steroids, PUVA, and topical mechlorethamine ointment for local lesions; radiation therapy, systemic retinoids and chemotherapeutic agents for advanced disease. Early aggressive treatment has not been shown to be curative.

Autoimmune and Vasculitic Disorders

Skin Manifestations of Systemic Lupus Erythematosus

The most commonly known skin manifestation of systemic lupus erythematosus (SLE) is the **malar butterfly rash**, which is an erythematous, purplish rash along the bridge of the nose and cheeks. **Alopecia** (hair loss) is also seen, both as a manifestation of lupus and as a side effect of treatment. **Oral** and **vaginal mucosal ulcers** may be present. Stigmata of vasculitis, such as **purpura** and **splinter hemorrhages,** are possible.

Another common manifestation of SLE is **discoid lesions**. Although about 10% of individuals with SLE have **discoid lesions**, only a small percentage (5%) of patients with discoid lesions have SLE. Individuals with discoid lesions but not systemic disease are said to have discoid lupus erythematosus. The discoid lesions tend to occur in sun-exposed areas and begin as red, well-demarcated plaques, which can progress to hypopigmentation and permanent hair loss. The disease is chronic but rarely progresses to SLE. It is treated with antimalarials.

Psoriasis

Psoriasis is a chronic inflammatory process that can present alone or in association with severe rheumatoid arthritis–like symptoms (**psoriatic arthritis**). Pathogenesis is unknown, but it may be autoimmune. It is associated with HLA-B27 and a family history of psoriasis.

Signs & Symptoms

Psoriasis is characterized by nonpruritic erythematous papules and plaques with characteristic silvery scaling and sharply demarcated borders. They are most often found on the extensor surface of the elbows and knees as well as the scalp and sacral area.

Pathology

Microscopically, epidermal proliferation is seen accompanied by acanthosis (epidermal hyperplasia), parakeratosis (persistent nuclei in the stratum corneum), and neutrophilic abscesses (Munro abscesses) in the stratum corneum.

Diagnosis

Clinical inspection.

Treatment

Topical tar and UV light are used, as well as corticosteroids, methotrexate, and nonsteroidal anti-inflammatory drugs.

Skin Manifestations of Vasculitis

Several vasculitides have associated skin lesions that aid in diagnosis:

- **Erythema** nodosum is associated with tender, red nodules along the arms and legs. It is associated with certain drugs and infections, such as coccidioidomycosis and Salmonella infection.

- **Henoch-Schönlein syndrome** is accompanied by characteristic palpable purpura across the buttocks and the extensor surfaces of the extremities. It is thought to be caused by an allergic vasculitis resulting in IgA immune complex deposition in the superficial vessels and is associated with an IgA nephropathy.

- **Amyloidosis** can cause bruising and periorbital purpura after minor skin contact. The deposition of amyloid in the superficial vessels causes increased skin fragility.

- **Livedo** reticularis is a fishnet-pattern discoloration (lacy cyanotic areas around central pale areas) that is seen on the thighs and forearms and worsens in cold environments. Although the pathogenesis is unknown, it is associated with the presence of cryoglobulins.

- **Raynaud's disease** causes cyanosis and pallor of the hands and feet from arterial constriction in response to cold temperatures and emotional distress. If the manifestation is secondary to another disease such as lupus, atherosclerosis, or rheumatic disease, it is known as **Raynaud's phenomenon** . See Chapter 12 for more details.

Pemphigus

Pemphigus is an autoimmune disease characterized by flaccid bullae that occur in crops. It tends to affect older adults. Autoantibodies to adhesion molecules in the epidermis cause epidermal cells to separate from each other.

Signs & Symptoms

Flaccid bullae. In pemphigus vulgaris, lesions tend to occur in the mouth and become erosive and painful. The scalp is also a commonly affected site.

Pathology

Acantholysis (cell separation within the epidermis) is seen by light microscopy. Immunofluorescence shows IgG deposition in the epidermis in a honeycomb pattern (at cell-cell junctions).

Diagnosis

Histology.

Treatment

Systemic steroids and immunosuppressive agents. Secondary infections are treated with antibiotics, and electrolyte disturbances from skin losses are corrected.

Bullous pemphigoid

Bullous pemphigoid is characterized by *tense* bullae that tend to form in the flexural areas of the elderly. Like pemphigus, it is an autoimmune disease, but in this case the autoantibodies attack the dermal-epidermal junction.

Signs & Symptoms

Pruritis and bullae. Urticaria and swelling may precede the appearance of blisters.

Pathology

Separation at the dermal-epidermal junction.

Diagnosis

Biopsy and immunofluorescence showing IgG and C3 at the dermal-epidermal junction.

Treatment

Steroids. Tetracycline or erythromycin, plus nicotinamide may be used. Methotrexate or azathioprine can be used if the other approaches do not work.

Miscellaneous Skin Findings

Xanthomas

Xanthomas are clusters of foam cells, or macrophages filled with intracellular cholesterol. **Eruptive xanthomas** are red-yellow papules seen, often on the buttocks, on patients with extremely high chylomicron or VLDL levels (triglycerides >1000 mg/dL).

In patients with high LDL secondary to a genetic hyperlipidemia, xanthomas usually appear on Achilles tendon, patellar tendon, or the back of the hand. **Xanthelasmas,** or yellowish plaques along the nasal portion of the eyelids, may also be present.

Hyperpigmentation

There are many causes of hyperpigmentation, including:

- **Pigmented nevi**

- **Ephelides,** or juvenile freckles

- **Lentigenes,** or senile freckles

- **Mongolian spots**

- **ACTH excess** in Addison's disease or after bilateral adrenalectomy to treat Cushing's disease

- **Melasma (chloasma),** a facial hyperpigmentation (upper lip, forehead, malar eminences) seen in pregnancy and in women taking oral contraceptives

- **Acanthosis nigricans** in Addison's disease, insulin resistance, obesity, malignancy, thyroid dysfunction, and polycystic ovaries

- **Neurofibromatosis,** with axillary freckling and café au lait spots

- **Hemochromatosis**

- **McCune-Albright syndrome,** with café au lait spots and bone and endocrine abnormalities

- **Skin damage,** either unintentional (e.g. burns, abrasions, allergies, infection) or intentional (e.g., chemical peels, liquid nitrogen, dermabrasion)

- **Postinflammatory hyperpigmentation,** such as after acne

- **Berloque hyperpigmentation**, a hyperpigmentation secondary to phototoxic responses to essential oils and perfumes (beware the rinds of limes and other citrus fruits and celery)

- **Drugs**, including minocycline, amiodarone, chloroquine, and chlorpromazine

Hypopigmentation

Causes of hypopigmentation include:

- **Vitiligo**, a destruction of melanocytes that is often associated with hyper- or hypothyroidism, diabetes mellitus, Addison's disease, or pernicious anemia

- **Albinism**

- **Piebaldism**, an autosomal dominant trait that results in a white forelock; it is associated with hypopigmented ash leaf spots in tuberous sclerosis

- **Other skin disorders**, such as atopic dermatitis, discoid lupus, lichen planus, and psoriasis, which can cause *leukoderma*

- **Systemic diseases** such as syphilis, myxedema, or thyrotoxicosis

- **Skin damage** (as with hyperpigmentation)

Skin Changes with Aging

As people age, their skin undergoes certain changes that begin to become apparent by the age of 30 to 35.

- **Thinning**: The epidermis thins, making it more fragile.

- **Inelasticity**: A gradual loss of elastic fibers, as well as blood vessels, fat, and dermal collagen, occurs. Fine wrinkles result from the loss of elasticity.

- **Loss of appendages**: The density of hair follicles, sweat ducts, and sebaceous glands decreases. Sebum and sweat production decrease.

In addition to the changes of normal aging, the skin undergoes changes due to **photoaging,** or repeat exposure to the sun.

- **Elastosis**: The skin coarsens and becomes yellowish in color from deposition of a yellow elastotic material that cannot function as elastic fibers.

- **Deep wrinkles**: Unlike the fine wrinkles of normal aging, the deep wrinkles of photoaging do not disappear with stretching. The wrinkles form a criss-cross pattern on the back of the neck.

- **Irregular pigmentation**: Freckles, lentigenes, and other areas of irregular hyperpigmentation and hypopigmentation form on the sun-exposed areas.

- **Vascular changes**: Skin is easily bruised, following minor trauma occurs on the sun-exposed areas of the arms and hands, but not in the unexposed areas (thus differentiating the bleeding from platelet dysfunction).

- **Neoplasms**, both benign and malignant, can occur. They are described in a previous section.

Pharmacology

See Table 9-7 for a list of medications commonly used for skin conditions.

Table 9-7. Drugs used in skin conditions

Drug	Mechanism	Uses	Toxicities
Topical steroids (hydrocortisone, triamcinolone)	Unknown; anti-inflammatory effects	Several dermatologic conditions (e.g., contact dermatitis)	Skin atrophy and acne when used on the face; promote fungal infections on the skin and retard wound and ulcer healing
Retinoic acid, isotretinoin	Decreases epidermal cell adhesion, allowing desquamation	Acne	Possible teratogen; dryness, itching
Methotrexate	Inhibition of dihydrofolate reductase leading to decreased DNA production	Psoriasis	Bone marrow suppression, renal, hepatic, and gastrointestinal toxicity
Keratolytics (salicylic acid, podophyllum)	Unknown; epithelial cell destruction	Condylomata removal	Local damage, central nervous system effects possible
Emollients (skin lotions)	Lipid absorption, lubrication	Dry skin	Few

CHAPTER 10

Musculoskeletal System

The Upper Extremity

The Shoulder

The shoulder joint (i.e., **glenohumeral joint**) is the convergence of three bones and many muscles, all enclosed in a capsule and cushioned by several bursae. **Bursitis** is an inflammation of these fluid-filled sacs, often due to overuse. Because the shoulder requires such a broad range of motion, it is not as bound by ligaments as the more stable hip joint. Much of the stability of the shoulder is provided by the **rotator cuff**, a ring of four muscles (the "SITS" muscles: supraspinatus, infraspinatus, teres minor, and subscapularis) that is frequently strained or torn with overuse, particularly in older individuals.

Besides stabilizing the shoulder, the rotator cuff helps with movement. For example, the supraspinatus assists the deltoid with the initiation of arm abduction. If the deltoid is paralyzed due to axillary nerve injury, the supraspinatus becomes the primary abductor. On the flip side, a torn supraspinatus tendon results in limited arm abduction with a characteristic shoulder shrug during the attempted abduction.

The Brachial Plexus

The brachial plexus is the source of nerves for the upper limb as well as the source of nightmares for the first-year medical student. Fortunately, the number of USMLE questions involving this labyrinth of axons is likely to be small. You may remember that the **anterior primary rami** (roots) from C5 through T1 come together and form a Los Angeles freeway system of roots, trunks, divisions, cords, and nerves. This is far less important than what happens to the nerves after they leave the plexus. Table 10-1 summarizes the motor innervation of the arm and hand.

Mnemonic:
Robert **T**aylor **D**rinks **C**old **B**eer = Brachial plexus: **R**oots, **T**runks, **D**ivisions, **C**ords, and **B**ranches of nerves

Table 10-1. Upper extremity motor innervation

Region	Action	Nerve
Posterior arm	Shoulder extension	Radial Nerve
	Forarm extension	
Posterior forearm	Wrist extension	Radial nerve
	Metacarpophalangeal joint extension	
	Supination	
Anterior arm	Shoulder flexion	Musculocutaneous nerve
	Forearm Flexion	
	Supination	
Anterior forearm	Wrist flexion	Median nerve
	Finger flexion	Ulnar nerve
	Pronation	
Interosseous muscles		
Dorsal	Finger abduction ("DAB")	
Palmar	Finger adduction ("PAD")	
Adductor pollics	Thumb adduction	
Lumbricals	Metacarpophalangeal joint flexion	1 & 2: Median nerve
	Distal interphalangeal (PIP) proximal interphalangeal (PIP) joint extension	3 & 4: Ulnar nerve
Thenar eminence (thumb)	Abduct, flex, and oppose little finger	Median nerve
Hypothenar eminence (pinky)	Abduct, flex, oppose thumb	Ulnar nerver

- The **axillary nerve** (C5–C6) swings around the humerus right at the surgical nec, where it is vulnerable to fractures and dislocation of the humerus. A dislocated humerus interferes with abduction of the arm (deltoid) and causes numbness over the dome of the shoulder.

- The **musculocutaneous nerve** (C5–C6) supplies the arm flexors (biceps, brachialis) and cutaneous innervation to the lateral forearm.

- The **radial nerve** (C5–T1) is essentially the nerve to the back of the arm. It travels in the spiral groove on the back of the humerus, so midshaft fractures demonstrate deficits in the radial nerve's functions: triceps, forearm extensor compartment, brachioradialis, and cutaneous innervation of the back of the arm, forearm, and hand. **Wrist-drop** describes the characteristic flaccid hand flexion from radial nerve injury.

- The **median nerve** (C5–T1) supplies the flexors of the forearm before passing under the **flexor retinaculum** (a fibrous wristband) and supplying the **thenar muscles** (that big lump of muscle at the base of the thumb) and a couple of the intrinsic hand muscles near the thumb. Stress and swelling of the flexor retinaculum impinges on the median nerve and causes numbness or pain over the thumb side of the palm as well as weakness of the thenar muscles (**carpal tunnel syndrome**). Slashing of the wrists may also cause median nerve damage that results in loss of use of the thumb.

- The **ulnar nerve** (C8–T1; notice how the further down the arm you go, the further down the spine you go) gets a couple of forearm muscles (anything with the word **ulnaris**), most of the intrinsic hand muscles, and some sensation over the pinkie side of the hand. Slam your funny bone on your chair. This is the ulnar nerve. Note the tingling in your pinkie and the medial half of your ring finger: This is the cutaneous distribution of the ulnar nerve. Feel free to do this during the USMLE if you forget. Ulnar nerve damage can occur with fractures of the medial epicondyle of the humerus. **Clawhand** describes the characteristic appearance of the hand due to ulnar nerve injury.

You can map out the distribution of radial, median, and ulnar nerve sensations and of spinal root sensations (its **dermatome**), and it is clear that they're not the same but they do overlap (Fig. 10-1). That is because everything gets mixed up in the brachial plexus.

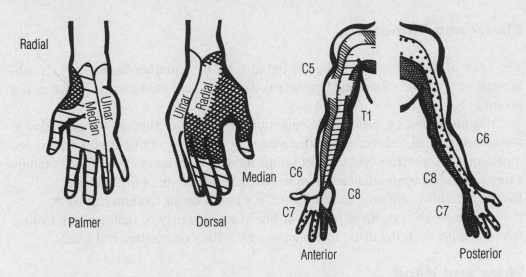

Fig. 10-1. Cutaneous distributions of the nerves and of the spinal roots.

Although these are the five principal nerves coming off the end of the brachial plexus, a few minor nerves branch off much earlier, including the pectoral nerves (supplying the pectorals) and the **long thoracic nerve**, which supplies serratus anterior. This muscle holds the scapula down onto the chest wall; if the nerve is accidentally cut, as in a surgical dissection of the axilla, scapular "winging" results. In addition to individual nerve injuries, the brachial plexus itself may be stretched and injured. For example, a difficult delivery in which the baby's neck gets wrenched to the side may traumatize the upper roots, causing a "waiter's-tip sign" (also called **Erb-Duchenne palsy**; Fig. 10-2).

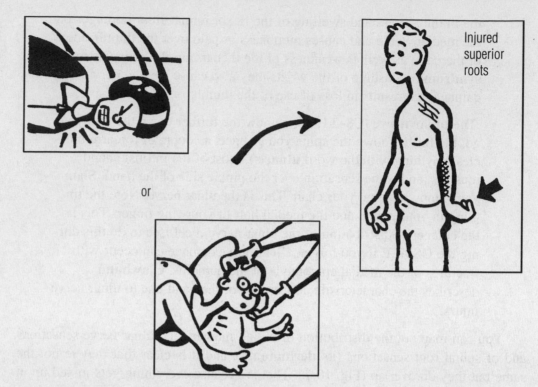

Fig. 10-2. Erb-Duchenne palsy.

Elbow and Forearm

The head of the radius is strapped to the ulna by the **annular ligament**. In a sub-luxated or "pulled" elbow, the ligament is damaged, and the radius is pulled out of position.

You know that pronation and supination are the act of flipping the palm down-ward and upward, respectively. What you may not know is that if you do this too much, or too forcefully, you can get **tennis elbow**, an inflammation of the common extensor tendon where it attaches on the lateral epicondyle of the humerus.
Biceps brachii is not only an arm flexor, it's also a major forearm supinator.
If you or someone you know likes to in-line skate, you may be familiar with Colles' fracture, a break in the distal radius caused by falling on outstretched hands.

Wrist and Hand

There are quite a few **carpal** bones in the wrist, but only three articulate with the radius to form the wrist joint. Those are the **scaphoid**, the **lunate**, and the **tri-quetrum**. The ulna does not articulate with any carpal bones.

The scaphoid is the most commonly fractured wrist bone. It is located in the "anatomic snuffbox" on the thumb (lateral) side of your hand. A fracture results from falling on outstretched arms. It can cause pain, but may not be visible on ini-tial X-ray; 10 days later, when some bone resorption has occurred, the fracture becomes visible. The scaphoid does not have a great blood supply, so a fractured scaphoid may undergo **avascular necrosis**.

Both the radial and ulnar arteries traverse the wrist and supply the hand. They actually arc around in the hand and connect. Thus, if one is compressed, the other can still supply the hand (demonstrated by the **Allen test**). The radial artery is really quite deep, and people who try to kill themselves by severing this artery may end up cutting only flexor tendons. It is often accessed for arterial blood gas sampling. Dupuytren's contracture is a thickening of the palmar fascia, causing the fourth and fifth digits to flex.

Blood Supply to Upper Limb

Blood supply to the arm (Fig. 10-3) begins with the **subclavian artery**, which branches off the **brachiocephalic trunk** on the right side and directly off the aorta on the left side. The subclavian artery becomes the **axillary artery** after crossing the first rib; that, in turn, becomes the **brachial artery** at the posterior edge of the teres major muscle. After crossing the elbow joint, the brachial artery splits into the **radial** and **ulnar arteries**.

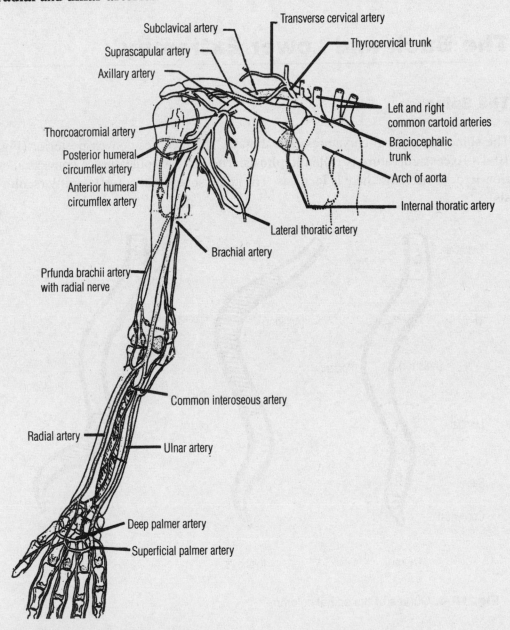

Fig. 10-3. Upper Limb blood suppy

Collateral circulation occurs in the shoulder between the **subscapular artery** (off the axillary artery) and the **suprascapular artery** (off the thyrocervical trunk, which branches early off subclavian artery). Consequently, a surgical ligature could be placed on the subclavian or axillary artery, between the two arteries. Collateral circulation also occurs around the elbow, due to anastomoses between the profunda brachii artery and radial recurrent artery laterally, and the ulnar collateral arteries and ulnar recurrent arteries medially. It is therefore acceptable to place a surgical ligature on the brachial artery **distal to the inferior ulnar collateral artery**. Collateral circulation also occurs in the hands, due to the **superficial palmar arch** (from the ulnar artery) and the **deep palmar arch** (from the radial artery). As long as this collateral circulation is functional (which you assess with the Allen test), you can access blood from the radial artery with less fear of accidentally cutting off all blood supply to the hand.

The Back and Lower Extremity

The Spine

The spine has normal curvatures. The thoracic spine curves convex posterior (Fig. 10-4). Excess curvature is called **kyphosis**. The lumbar spine curves convex anterior. Excess curvature here is **lordosis**. The spine should not curve laterally (**scoliosis**).

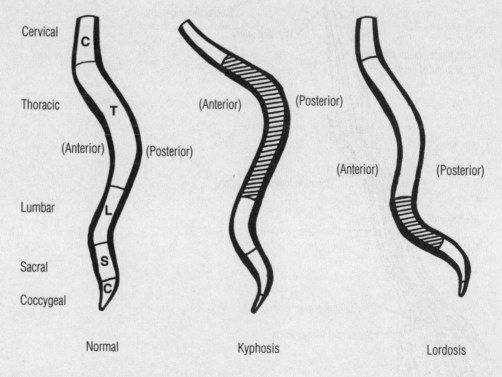

Fig. 10-4. Curves of the spinal column.

Humans have about 33 vertebrae (some of which are fused in the sacrum and coccyx) and 31 pairs of spinal nerves. The spinal cord ends around L1 or L2, and the remaining nerves dangle down as the **cauda equina**. Lumbar punctures can be done at the L4–L5 or L5–S1 level without lancing the spinal cord.

Lumbosacral Plexus

The lumbosacral plexus is an intimidating network of nerves that does for the lower limb what the brachial plexus does for the upper. Memorizing the entire plexus is not particularly high yield, but a few important facts are mentioned here. Table 10-2 highlights the motor innervation of the thigh and leg.

Table 10-2. Lower Extremity motor innervention

Region	Action	Nerve
Gluteal region		
Gluteus maximus	Thigh Extension	Inferior gluteal nerve
Gluteus medius and minimus	Thigh abduction	Superior gluteal nerve
Posterior thigh (Hamstrings)	Hip extension Knee flexion	sciatic nerve (tibial division)
Anterior thigh (Quadriceps)	Hip flexion Knee extensions	Femoral nerve
Posterior leg	Foot plantar flexion and inversion Toe flexion	Tibial nerve
Anterior leg	Foot dorsiflexion and inversion Toe extension	Deep peroneal nerve (Branch of common peroneal nerve)
Lateral leg	Foot eversion	Superficial peroneal nerve (Branch of common peroneal nerve)

The lumbar part consists of nerves branching from T12 to L4; the sacral involves L5–S4. They innervate the pelvis and legs. Sacral nerves S2–S4 also supply some parasympathetic fibers.

Among the nerves emanating from the lumbar plexus are the **femoral nerve** (supplying the quadriceps and important for hip flexion and lower leg extension) and the **lateral femoral cutaneous nerve**, which may be compressed by prolonged sitting in tight jeans. The **iliohypogastric** and **ilioinguinal nerves** swing around the flank down into the pubic region. The **obturator nerve** supplies the thigh adductors.

The largest offshoot of the sacral plexus is the **sciatic nerve** (L4–S3), which runs down the back of the leg and gives off the **common peroneal** and the **tibial nerves**. It can be avoided during gluteal intramuscular injections, by giving the shots in the upper outer buttocks. The common peroneal wraps around near the top of the fibula. It's very susceptible to injury here, resulting in foot drop (because it innervates the anterior leg muscles). The tibial nerve supplies the posterior leg muscles and the sole of the foot. Other nerves of the sacral plexus include the **superior**

gluteal nerve, which innervates muscles of thigh abduction (gluteus medius and minimus), and the **inferior gluteal nerve**, which innervates the gluteus maximus (hip extension, e.g., climbing stairs, jumping, rising from seated position).

Hip and Thigh

The head of the femur may be dislocated from the **acetabulum** of the pelvis either congenitally or by injury. Femoral neck fractures are common and potentially deadly in older people, who may succumb to pulmonary embolism or some other complication during recovery. Total hip replacement helps to prevent the development of recurrent fractures and degenerative joint disease.

The Knee

Ligamentous damage to the knee is a very common athletic injury. A classic triad of knee injury is damage to the **medial collateral ligament**, the **medial meniscus,** and the **anterior cruciate ligament** (ACL) after a blow to the lateral side of the knee. Because the ACL limits hyperextension of the knee, you can diagnose an ACL injury with the "drawer test," pulling the tibia forward with respect to the femur (Fig. 10-5).

TIP From lateral to medial at the leg crease, you have the NAVEL structures: femoral nerve, artery, vein, empty space, lymphatics.]

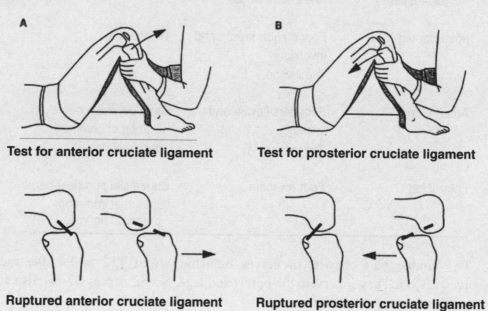

Test for anterior cruciate ligament   **Test for prosterior cruciate ligament**

Ruptured anterior cruciate ligament   **Ruptured prosterior cruciate ligament**

From the middle of the sarcomere, the order of the levels is "**M**any **H**appy **A**nimals **I**n the **Z**oo." (**M**-line, **H**-band, **A**-band, **I**-band, **Z**-line)

Fig. 10-5. The drawer Test. A. Ruptured anterior cruciat ligament. B. Rubtured poserior cruciate ligament. From RW Dudek. *High-Yield Gross Anatomy*. Baltimore: Williams & Wilkins, 1997; 115.

The Ankle

The ankle, like the wrist, is made up of a lot of bones, called **tarsal bones.** The important bone to know in the ankle is the **talus**; it articulates with the tibia superiorly and medially, and the fibula laterally. The ankle joint allows dorsiflexion (foot up) and plantar flexion (toes pointed). Inversion and eversion take place not at the ankle joint but at the **subtalar (talocalcanean) joint** in the foot.

The ankle is notable for its propensity to be sprained. The most common ankle injury is an **inversion sprain**, which runs the risk of causing an avulsion of the lateral malleolus (the fibula) and the proximal end of the fifth metatarsal. **Pott's fracture** results from the less common **eversion sprain**, which causes an avulsion of the medial malleolus (the tibia) because the medial ligament is strong and unlikely to tear. A fracture of the fibula follows due to lateral movement of the talus.

Blood Supply to Lower Limb

See Figure 10-6.

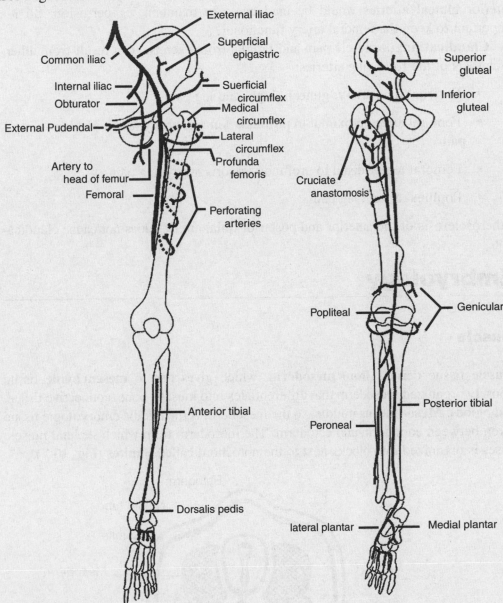

Fig. 10-6. Lower extremity arterial supply. A. Anterior view. B. Posterior view. From RW Dudek. *High-Yield Gross Anatomy*. Baltimore: Williams & Wilkins, 1997; 109.

The bottom of the aorta splits in two to become the **common iliac arteries**. Those two promptly divide in the pelvis to become the **external iliac artery**, the main blood supplier to the leg, and the **internal iliac artery**, whose only contributions to the leg's arterial supply are the **obturator artery** (adductor muscles and head of femur) and the **inferior gluteal artery** (the gluteal region).

The femoral artery is the continuation of the external iliac artery. It travels under the inguinal ligament, midway between the anterior superior iliac spine and the symphysis pubis, where it can be palpated.

After branching off quite a bit, the femoral artery travels through the adductor hiatus to become the **popliteal artery**. That, in turn, gives rise to the **genicular arteries**, which supply the knee and the **anterior** and **posterior tibial arteries.**

If blood supply to the leg were cut off due to trauma to the **femoral artery**, (e.g. during a car accident), the collateral blood supply provided by the obturator and inferior gluteal arteries would be inadequate to maintain leg perfusion. So it's important to keep the femoral artery functional!

Claudication, or muscle pain and fatigue from exercise, can result from atherosclerosis of the following arteries:

- External iliac artery: gluteal, thigh, and leg pain

- Femoral artery proximal to profunda femoris artery: thigh and leg pain

- Femoral artery distal to profunda femoris artery: leg pain

- Popliteal artery: leg pain

Atherosclerosis of the anterior and posterior tibial arteries does not cause claudication.

Embryology

Muscle

> **TIP:** From lateral to medical at the leg crease, you have the NAVEL Structures: femoral nerve, artery, veun, empty space, lymphatics.

> Vitamin **C** **C**ross-links **C**ollagen.

Muscle tissue derives from **mesoderm**, which gives rise to **mesenchyme** tissue (loosely organized mesoderm that differentiates into muscle, bone, connective tissue, and blood). **Meso-** means middle, so the mesoderm is the middle embryologic tissue layer, between endoderm and ectoderm. The mesoderm from which skeletal muscle arises is organized into blocks next to the notochord called **somites** (Fig. 10-7).

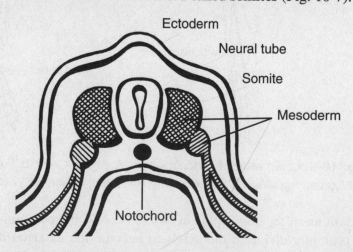

Fig. 10-7. Mesoderm and somites in cross section of embryo.

Most skeletal muscle is formed before birth or within the first year of childhood. Growth of skeletal muscle occurs by the formation of more microfilaments, which increase the diameter of the muscle fibers. Muscle builds up by **hypertrophy**, not hyperplasia.

Smooth muscles (e.g., abdominal organs) derive from the mesenchyme, which surrounds the endoderm of the primitive gut. Cardiac muscle develops from **splanchnic** (visceral) mesoderm surrounding the primordial heart tube. Cardiac muscle cells develop from single cells, whereas skeletal muscle cells develop through the fusion of many cells. Some cardiac muscle cells differentiate into highly specialized conducting fibers, such as Purkinje cells.

Cartilage and Bone

Bony tissue, including cartilaginous structures, develops from mesodermally derived mesenchyme as well. Mesenchyme develops into bone in two ways. The first is **intramembranous ossification**, in which the bone forms spontaneously in the mesenchyme. Flat bones, such as those of the skull and face, typically form this way. The second method of bone development is **endochondral ossification**, which, as its name suggests, involves the formation of a cartilaginous model that is subsequently converted into bone (Fig. 10-8).

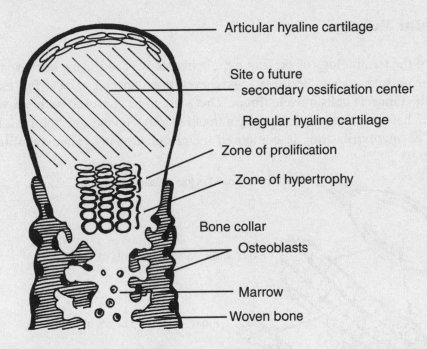

Fig. 10-8. Endochondral ossification.

The limbs, ribs, and other long bones grow by endochondral ossification. First, a **hyaline cartilage** model is formed by condensation of mesenchyme around blood vessels. An **epiphyseal plate** forms at each end of the bone as a factory for elongation. In the epiphyseal plate, the **chondrocytes** (cartilage cells) proliferate in the appropriately named **zone of proliferation**, which allows bone lengthening. Nearby, cells in the future metaphysis differentiate into **osteoblasts**, which produce a hard matrix of calcium and phosphate called **hydroxyapatite**.

The bony collar of calcified matrix in the metaphysis cuts off nutrient supply to the chondrocytes, which first swell (**zone of hypertrophy**) and then die, leaving a marrow cavity. The cartilage keeps on proliferating, with the bony collar following close behind until puberty arrives, after which the epiphyseal plates fuse and only thickening of bone (**appositional growth**) is possible. That's why excess growth hormone causes **gigantism** (long bones) in youth and **acromegaly** (thick bones) after puberty.

Eventually all cartilage is replaced by bone, except for the **articular cartilage**, which remains at the end of the bone and facilitates smooth joint mobility.

Limbs develop in the growing embryo by **tissue induction** by overlying ectoderm, which causes budding.

The development of the skeletal system is far from complete at birth. The deciduous teeth are late and rather temporary arrivers, emerging during the first 2 years and being replaced by permanent teeth starting in the sixth year. Skull morphology also undergoes some changes: The sinuses grow and the face lengthens, causing the eustachian (auditory) tubes to descend from nearly horizontal to about 45 degrees. As a result, bacteria have a much harder time venturing into the middle ear as we get older, and the incidence of otitis media plummets.

Histology

Skeletal Muscle

Much of the terminology of skeletal muscle histology is confusing because the pioneers of muscle science needlessly gave everything special names. For example, they called muscle cells **muscle fibers**. That's not to be confused with a **myofibril**, which is basically one of the many contractile strings bound into the muscle fiber rope. The myofibril string is composed mainly of proteins called **myofilaments** (Fig. 10-9).

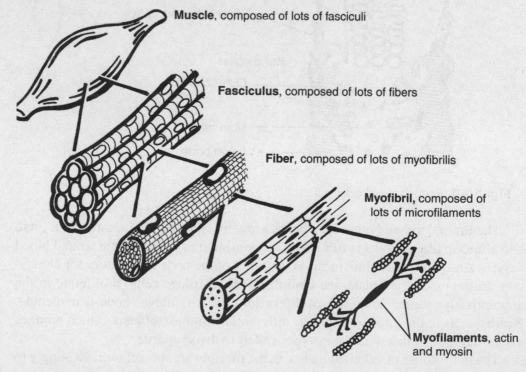

Muscle, composed of lots of fasciculi

Fasciculus, composed of lots of fibers

Fiber, composed of lots of myofibrilis

Myofibril, composed of lots of microfilaments

Myofilaments, actin and myosin

Fig. 10-9. Muscle structure

The two myofilaments are **actin** and **myosin**. The **muscle fasciculus** is a collection of multiple muscle fiber ropes covered by **perimysium**. A bunch of fascicles is surrounded by the **epimysium** ("around the muscle"), which is that tough fibrous coat you may remember trying to cut through in Gross Anatomy.

The common cellular structures even have special names in the muscle cells:

- **Sarcoplasm** for cytoplasm

- **Sarcolemma** for plasma membrane

- **Sarcoplasmic reticulum** for smooth endoplasmic reticulum

Each muscle fiber (or cell) is the product of many different mesenchymal cells fusing to form a long, cylindrical **syncytium**. Thus it has many nuclei. The cells are chock-full of myofibrils, which are long, contractile threads composed of subunits called sarcomeres. The **sarcomere** is the fundamental unit of muscle contraction.

Take a look at the structure of the sarcomere (Fig. 10-10). Notice the many different bands and lines and the arrangement of actin and myosin. The details of muscle contraction are discussed under Physiology.

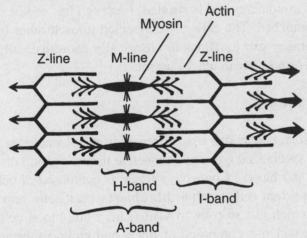

Fig. 10-10. The sarcomere

Smooth Muscle

Smooth muscle is found in the walls of hollow organs (e.g., gut, uterus, bladder, bronchioles) and blood vessels. Unlike syncytial skeletal muscle, smooth muscle cells have only one nucleus, and they are connected electrically by gap junctions (Fig. 10-11).

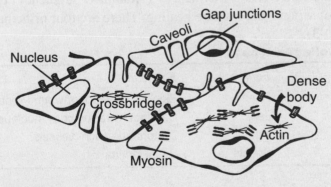

Fig. 10-11. The smooth muscle.

Smooth muscle gets its name from its lack of striations, which are visible as myofibrils lined up in skeletal and cardiac muscle. Smooth muscle has actin and myosin, but they are not arranged in sarcomeres. Instead, the actin is anchored onto **dense bodies,** which are the equivalent of Z-bands.

Smooth muscle is under autonomic control. There are three basic types. **Multiunit** smooth muscle features electrically uncoupled cells (few or no gap junctions), all supplied by nerves. Thus it is under neural control. Examples include the iris, ciliary muscle of the lens, and the vas deferens. In contrast, **unitary** smooth muscle mostly acts autonomously, with only minor modulation by neurotransmitters. Unitary muscle is the more common type and is found in the GI, bladder, uterus, and ureter. It has lots of gap junctions so all the cells can work together, propelling food or babies or liquids. **Vascular** smooth muscle is kind of a combination of both, having coordinated contractions, but it is also under substantial neural control.

Cardiac Muscle

Cardiac muscle combines features of skeletal and smooth muscle. Like skeletal muscle, it contains sarcomeres and is striated. Each cell has one or two nuclei, and the cells may be branched. The cells are connected to each other by **intercalated discs**, which have many gap junctions to electrically coordinate all the cells. Like smooth muscle, it is under involuntary control.

Connective Tissue

Like bone and muscle, connective tissue derives from mesenchyme. (In fact, bone is one of the many specialized types of connective tissue, a group that also includes cartilage, adipose, and blood.) Connective tissue is composed of cells and matrix. The cells may be **resident cell**s (such as **fibroblasts**, mast cells, and adipocytes) or **immigrant cells**, which just stop by to visit (e.g., white blood cells). Fibroblasts secrete the **matrix**, which is composed of fibers and ground substance and fills in all the gaps between cells. The major components of ground substance are **proteoglycans**, which are sugar chains on a protein backbone.

The fibroblast also secretes fibers, principally **collagen** and **elastin**. Elastin comes in handy in structures that get stretched and always return to their original shape (e.g., lung, face, arteries, bladder). Collagen is a versatile and ubiquitous protein (the most common protein in the animal kingdom) made from bundles of **tropocollagen** triple helices. Unless the fibers are cross-linked by **vitamin C**, however, they are unstable. That's why scurvy (vitamin C deficiency) causes capillary rupture and poor wound and fracture healing. There are four principal forms of collagen (Table 10-3).

Table 10-3. Collagen types

Collegen type	Form	Found in
I	Rope	Skin, bone, tendon, wound repair
II	Jelly	Cartilage, vireous body, nucleus pulposus
III	Net	Lymphnode, skin, vessels
IV	Sheets	Basal lamina

Cartilage

Cartilage, a specialized form of connective tissue, comes in several types. The features common to all types are **chondrocytes** (cells that lie in lacunae and secrete matrix), collagen, and ground substance. **Hyaline cartilage** ("glassy cartilage") is by far the most common type. With lots of type II collagen, hyaline cartilage is found in the developing skeleton (as the model for the bone), on articular surfaces, and in the trachea and larynx.

Elastic cartilage has elastin fibers in addition to type II collagen. It is found in the epiglottis and the pinna of the ear. **Fibrocartilage** has lots of type I collagen, making it very tough. It is found in the **annulus fibrosus** of the intervertebral disks (the part that surrounds the nucleus pulposus) and where tendons insert onto bones.

Bone

When you study the skeleton hanging in the corner of your Gross Anatomy class, it's easy to underestimate how complex and dynamic this tissue really is. Only about 60% of the bone is inorganic matter, primarily **hydroxyapatite** crystals of calcium and phosphate. This calcified material gives bone its rigidity and strength, allowing the skeleton to offer mechanical support and protection. However, the cellular components perform the really interesting function: acting as a calcium buffer for the rest of the body.

Bone is covered by a well-innervated connective tissue sheet called **periosteum**, which receives tendinous insertions and is remarkably sensitive when you get kicked in the shin. On the inner surfaces of the bone, lining the canals of compact bone and the trabeculae of cancellous bone, is **endosteum**. Both the endosteum and the periosteum contain many of the cells that are responsible for forming and continuously remodeling the bone over the life of the bone (Fig. 10-12).

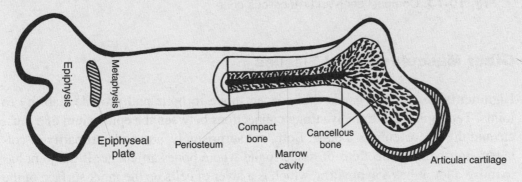

Fig. 10-12. Bone anatomy.

Osteoblasts derive from osteoprogenitor cells. The osteoblasts synthesize **osteoid** (the organic part of the extracellular matrix) from type I collagen and proteoglycans. The osteoid quickly becomes calcified. The osteoblasts are so good at secreting matrix that they eventually encase themselves in osteoid, after which they are called **osteocytes**. Osteocytes are the major mature cell in bone. They feature little cytoplasmic telephone lines that extend through bone **canaliculi** and allow chemical communication with other osteocytes via gap junctions.

The osteocyte's job is to replace any matrix that gets reabsorbed by the third important bone cell: the **osteoclast**. In contrast to osteoblasts and osteocytes, osteoclasts derive from fusion of cells of the monocyte-macrophage lineage, which means that they're multinucleate and they're hungry. They resorb the calcium by dissolving it with acids and allowing it to get into the blood.

When bones are first made, the collagen is laid down somewhat randomly. This **woven bone** (or primary bone) is then remodeled into **lamellar bone** (or secondary bone), in which the collagen is organized into layers (**lamellae**). The two types of lamellar bone are **compact** (dense) **bone** and **cancellous** (spongy) **bone**. Compact bone is made of concentric, cylindrical lamellae arranged around a central canal that contains blood vessels. The whole apparatus is called a **Haversian system,** or an **osteon.** These long columns of mineral along the bone axis are very strong. Cancellous bone consists of networking spicules of lamellar bone with lots of space in between for bone marrow (Fig. 10-13).

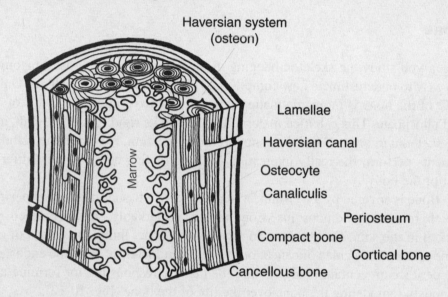

Fig. 10-13. Compact bone and cancellous bone.

Other Musculoskeletal Tissues

Ligaments are fibrous bands that connect bone to bone and provide stability to joints. **Tendons** are extremely strong connections between the epimysium of a muscle and the periosteum of a bone. Both, not surprisingly, are made primarily of collagen. **Joints** are collections of tissue found where bones articulate. If the joint has to move a lot, it has a **synovium**, which is a layer of cells on the inner surface of the joint capsule that secretes lubricating **synovial fluid.**

Many joints that do not move much (e.g., the sutures in your skull or the pubic symphysis) do not have a synovium. The intervertebral joint is a special joint in which the bodies are connected by a disk and the arches articulate via synovial joints. The disk has a gelatinous, central **nucleus pulposus** (derived from the notochord) and a cartilaginous, outer **annulus fibrosus.** If this fibrous ring is weakened by age or injury, the nucleus pulposus can herniate out and impinge on a spinal nerve (**disk herniation** or "slipped disk") (Fig. 10-14).

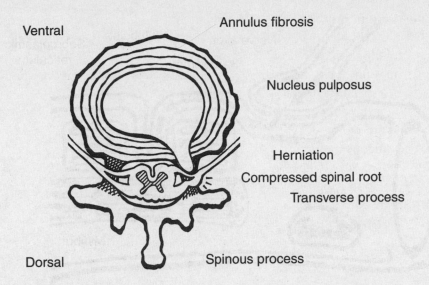

Ventral

Annulus fibrosis

Nucleus pulposus

Herniation

Compressed spinal root

Transverse process

Dorsal

Spinous process

Fig. 10-14. Intervertebral

Physiology

Excitation-Contraction Coupling

A number of physiologic processes must be coordinated perfectly for controlled muscle movement. For example, consider what's required to lift a finger:

- The premotor and primary motor cortices in the frontal lobe generate the command to lift the finger. The signal travels down the axons, through the posterior limb of the internal capsule, through the brainstem and into the spinal cord, where it synapses on a neuron that sends an axon out into the radial nerve. Here the signal finally travels down to the motor end plate of the neuromuscular junction.

- When the nerve terminus depolarizes, calcium channels open, and calcium flows in, causing exocytosis of acetylcholine-containing vesicles.

- The acetylcholine diffuses across the synaptic cleft and binds to acetylcholine-gated ion channels on the muscle cell membrane (sarcolemma), causing sodium to enter the muscle cell (fiber).

- This new action potential travels down the sarcolemma until it reaches a cell membrane invagination (called a **T-tubule**), at which point it dives down toward the interior of the muscle fiber (Fig. 10-15).

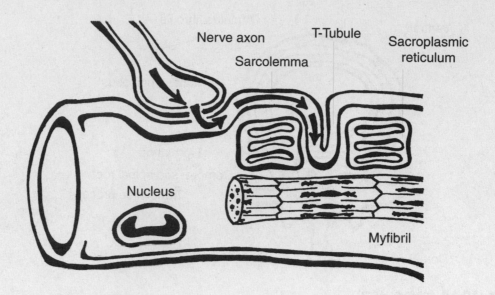

Fig. 10-15. Path action potential.

- The T-tubule (short for **transverse tubule** because it is perpendicular to the sarcolemma) abuts the **sarcoplasmic reticulum** (smooth endoplasmic reticulum), which contains a lot of calcium ions.

- There is a protein on the sarcoplasmic reticulum called the **ryanodine receptor**; it acts as a gatekeeper, allowing the stored calcium to be freed. In skeletal muscle the ryanodine receptor is hooked on to the T-tubule, so that it undergoes a conformational change when the T-tubule is depolarized, spilling the calcium out. In cardiac muscle, the ryanodine receptor is not hooked to the T-tubule; instead, it requires extracellular calcium ions to diffuse in after a depolarization and force it to release its sequestered calcium (Fig. 10-16). That's why the heart depends on a good supply of extracellular calcium.

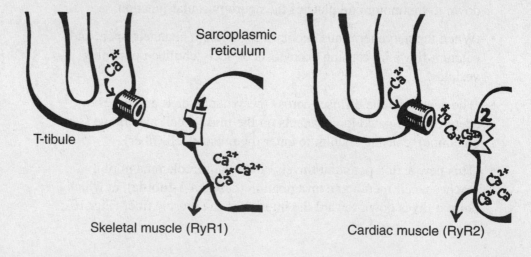

Fig. 10-16. The ryanodine receptor.

- The calcium ions released from the sarcoplasmic reticulum then bind to **troponin C** (C for calcium). Troponin C is one of the proteins on the actin filament, along with **tropomyosin** and **troponins T** (interacts with tropomyosin) and I (inhibits actin-myosin interaction, along with tropomyosin). Actin is a double-stranded chain of protein that has binding sites for another chainlike molecule, myosin. When calcium binds to troponin C, a conformational change occurs in which tropomyosin shifts out of the way and allows myosin to bind actin (Fig. 10-17).

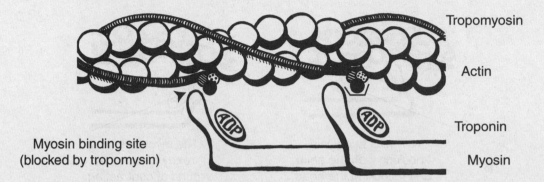

Fig. 10-17. Actin, troponin, and tropomyosin.

- The actin microfilaments are anchored to the Z-lines at the end of the sarcomere (think **a**ctin = **a**nchored). The sarcomere shortens (and the muscle contracts) when myosin pulls an actin and brings the Z-lines close together, shrinking the width of the H band and I band (Fig. 10-18). The A band width remains unchanged.

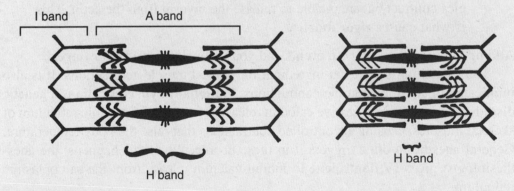

Fig. 10-18. Contraction of a sarcomere. Notice: The H-band and I-band shorten while the A-band does not change.

The myosin microfilaments lie in the center of the sarcomere (think **m**yosin = **m**iddle). The myosin has a light-chain tail and a mobile heavy-chain head, which carries a molecule of adenosine diphosphate (ADP). When the head binds to the actin (as described earlier), the ADP falls off and the head swings down. This causes the actin to move relative to the myosin (Fig. 10-19A).

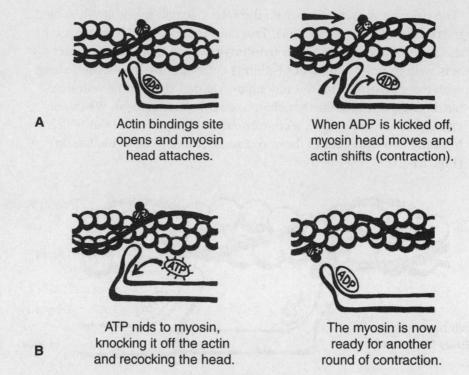

A — Actin bindings site opens and myosin head attaches.

When ADP is kicked off, myosin head moves and actin shifts (contraction).

B — ATP nids to myosin, knocking it off the actin and recocking the head.

The myosin is now ready for another round of contraction.

Fig. 10-19. A. Action of myosin. B. Release and recockong of myosin.

- The Z-bands have now moved a little bit closer together. To continue contracting, however, the band of actin must be released. To release the actin, the myosin requires the binding of adenosine triphosphate (ATP). The hydrolysis of ATP to ADP (which stays bound) causes the head to recock (Fig. 10-19B). Without ATP (i.e., in death), the muscles contract but are unable to release the myosin from the actin. This is what causes **rigor mortis.**

Add up a few million of these events and you've finally moved your finger!

Thus, calcium is a crucial ingredient for normal muscle contractions. It is also implicated in abnormal muscle contractions. **Malignant hyperthermia** is a genetic disorder that results in excessive calcium release from the sarcoplasmic reticulum of skeletal muscles, causing uncontrolled contractions that raise the body temperature. General anesthesia often triggers it in these people. When this happens, the anesthesiologist gives IV **dantrolene** to inhibit calcium release from the sarcoplasmic reticulum.

Smooth Muscle Contraction

Many of the components of smooth muscle are the same as those for skeletal muscle, including actin, myosin, and tropomyosin, but now the actin is anchored to dense bodies. **Calmodulin** also plays an important role in muscle contraction.

The action potential (either from a nerve or from a neighboring smooth muscle cell via gap junctions) opens up calcium channels on the cell membrane. The calcium enters the cell, finds the sarcoplasmic reticulum, and releases more calcium. The calcium binds to calmodulin, which activates a protein kinase whose job is to phosphorylate myosin, allowing the myosin head to bind to actin and contract. Dephosphorylation by another enzyme lets it relax.

The myosin head stays attached to the actin much longer than it does in skeletal muscle. It still requires ATP to reset, but because it resets so infrequently, smooth muscle uses much less energy than its skeletal counterpart. This is great because it allows smooth muscle to stay contracted all day (convenient for maintaining blood pressure), whereas skeletal muscles would tire in a fraction of the time.

Fast and Slow Muscle Fibers

Just as the cells of your blood have specialized roles, so do the cells of your skeletal muscles. One type of muscle fiber, called a **fast-twitch fiber**, is specialized for rapid and powerful contractions. Fast-twitch fibers are large and have many glycolytic enzymes and glycogen stores but relatively few mitochondria because the work they do requires only a short burst of energy. In contrast, **slow-twitch fibers** have lots of mitochondria and lots of blood vessels. They appear red (fast-twitch looks more white). Slow-twitch muscle is specialized for endurance, so it is present in postural muscles.

If you are a sprinter, you need a lot of fast-twitch fibers. You need rapid forceful contractions for only a brief time, and anaerobic metabolism will suffice. If you run marathons, you have to have many mitochondria and a high degree of vascularization in your muscles. Training your muscles won't switch the ratio of fibers you have, but the hypertrophy you attain from weight training will assist your sprinting. The extra mitochondrial enzymes and vascularization from daily jogging will get you through that marathon.

Muscle Metabolism

Muscle needs ATP, but it's only got enough on hand to sustain maximal contractions for a second or two. When it runs out, the first place muscle turns is **phosphocreatine**, which has some high-energy phosphate bonds that can be converted to ATP. This lasts 7 or 8 seconds. Next, muscle turns to glycogen for ATP, snipping off stored glucose residues and converting them to lactic acid and pyruvic acid. This provides a minute of contractions at the expense of a little lactic acidosis. If you want to go further, you need **oxidative metabolism**, which gets as much ATP as possible from various carbohydrates, proteins, and fats through electron transport.

Growth Hormone

Growth hormone (GH, **somatotropin**) has many effects in the body, most visibly on the musculoskeletal system. Naturally, it promotes growth. Kids with GH deficiency (or deficiencies in GH-releasing hormone, insulin-like growth factors, or GH receptors) have **dwarfism** (short stature, delayed puberty, and obesity). An excess of GH causes **gigantism** (long bones) before puberty and **acromegaly** (thick bones) after the epiphyses have fused. GH promotes production of chondrocytes and osteogenic cells. It causes fat to be broken down and protein to be synthesized, resulting in more muscle.

GH is inhibited by **somatostatin**, which is used for treatment of acromegaly.

Repair and Regeneration

Damaged muscle and bone do not regenerate, but they can repair. When you fracture a bone, the osteoblasts in the bone and periosteum leap into action, laying down new bony matrix. The osteoprogenitor cells start churning out even more osteoblasts. Soon, a **callus** composed of cells and matrix forms at the fracture site. Over time, the osteocytes and osteoclasts get involved, remodeling the bone so that it looks as good as new.

Congenital and Metabolic Disorders

Congenital Dislocation of the Hip

Congenital hip dislocation is seen more commonly in females and in infants with a family history of hip dislocation. The cause is unknown, but it may be related to ligamentous laxity or positioning in utero. Examination for hip dislocation is part of the standard newborn examination.

Signs & Symptoms

If dislocation is unilateral, the affected leg appears shorter. On examination, complete abduction of the affected lower extremity with flexion at the hip and knee is not possible, and a "clunk" may be heard as the hip joint slips back into normal position.

Diagnosis

Ultrasound or X-rays may be used to confirm the diagnosis.

Treatment

Treatment includes braces and splints during growth or surgical correction in severe cases.

Osteogenesis Imperfecta

Osteogenesis imperfecta is a disease of abnormal bone fragility caused by a qualitative or quantitative disorder of **type I collagen** formation. The most serious type is osteogenesis imperfecta congenita, which is often fatal in infancy due to trauma during delivery. Patients develop hearing loss due to abnormal formation of the ossicles and abnormally short extremities (dwarfism) due to frequent fractures.

Signs & Symptoms

Newborn infants have multiple limb fractures, soft skull, and a bluish tint to the sclera. The skull feels like a "bag of bones" when palpated. A history of multiple fractures should lead a health care provider to suspect child abuse.

Pathology

Microscopically, the bony tissue is osteopenic and displays abnormally thin cortices and trabeculae.

Diagnosis

Radiologic studies are diagnostic.

Treatment

No treatment currently exists.

Chondrodysplasia

Chondrodysplasia refers to a group of disorders associated with abnormal bony and cartilaginous development. The most commonly known is **achondroplasia**, in which patients experience retarded endochondral bone formation resulting in abnormally short bones and dwarfism. Most cases are acquired mutations, although a small percentage are hereditary and may be autosomal dominant, recessive, or X-linked. **Type II collagen** defects have been implicated in a small number of cases.

Signs & Symptoms

Bones appear short but have normal width. The spine and skull appear normal. Fingers may appear stubby, and the patient generally looks bow-legged.

Diagnosis

History and radiographic findings.

Treatment

Surgical hip replacement may be helpful. Due to abnormal cervical spine formation, care must be taken during neck hyperextension (as during intubation) or spinal cord compression may result.

Muscular Dystrophy

Muscular dystrophy refers to a group of genetic disorders that result in muscle wasting. There are several different types, transmitted as autosomal or X-linked mutations. The most commonly known is **Duchenne's muscular dystrophy**, an X-linked recessive disease that occurs during childhood, particularly in males. This disease has been linked to the absence of the gene for **dystrophin**, a protein that is usually found in the sarcolemma.

Signs & Symptoms

The typical patient is a 5-year-old boy who experiences frequent falls and difficulty climbing stairs, due to proximal muscle weakness. Gower's sign refers to the characteristic use of arms to compensate for hip extensor weakness when rising from a supine to standing position. Pseudohypertrophy of the calves is seen, and cardiac involvement is common.

Pathology

Cardiac and skeletal muscle biopsy show necrosis and fatty replacement of muscle tissue.

Diagnosis

Serum creatine kinase is markedly elevated. Electromyography and nerve conduction studies are also performed.

Treatment

None. Patients are usually wheelchair-bound by age 12, and life expectancy is about 20 years. Patients who have a family history of muscular dystrophy should receive genetic counseling before planning a pregnancy.

Rhabdomyolysis

Rhabdomyolysis is skeletal muscle injury that results in the presence of muscle cell contents in the circulation. It can be caused by overexertion, seizures, and hypoxia. Drugs such as cocaine are also causative factors. **Myoglobin**, the carrier of oxygen in muscle tissue, is a nephrotoxin and can cause renal failure. The mechanism is unclear, but it may be due to intratubular precipitation of myoglobin, causing obstruction, or the concomitant release of proteases from the muscle cells.

Signs & Symptoms

Patients with rhabdomyolysis have myalgias and pain in the affected muscles, with a "doughy" feeling of the muscle masses. Patients also develop dark brown urine (myoglobinuria) from excess myoglobin excretion.

Diagnosis

Creatine phosphokinase and aldolase levels are elevated, and myoglobin is found on urinalysis. Patients are hyperkalemic and hyperphosphatemic due to release from injured muscle. Calcium may be low due to calcium deposition in the injured tissues.

Treatment

Aggressive hydration.

Osteomalacia and Rickets

Osteomalacia in adults and **rickets** in children produce defective mineralization of the bone. This is caused by **vitamin D deficiency**, which may result from poor dietary intake, malabsorption, lack of exposure to sunlight, or renal disease.

Signs & Symptoms

Children may have bowed legs, and infants with the disease may have reduced skull mineralization, known as **craniotabes**. Costochondral beading, known as **rachitic rosary appearance**, and kyphoscoliosis may be present. Adults may be asymptomatic.

Pathology

Microscopically, osteomalacia has thickened trabeculae but deficient mineralization of cartilaginous material. Contrast with osteoporosis.

Diagnosis

Serum vitamin D levels are low.

Treatment

Vitamin D supplementation.

McArdle's Disease

McArdle's disease is caused by a genetic deficiency of **glycogen phosphorylase** in skeletal muscle, resulting in an inability to break down glycogen.

Signs & Symptoms

Cramping and skeletal muscle weakness after exercise.

Diagnosis

Muscle biopsy shows absence of glycogen phosphorylase with increased amount of glycogen. Exercise does not cause a rise in lactate level.

Treatment

Severe exertion should be limited.

Osteoporosis

Osteoporosis is decreased bone mass despite the presence of normal bone, resulting in an increased risk of bone fracture. It develops in postmenopausal women due to lack of estrogen needed to help replace bone. Patients on chronic corticosteroid treatment are also at risk. Asian and Caucasian women are at increased risk, whereas African-American women are at decreased risk. Smoking may also contribute to osteoporosis development.

Several measures have been found to decrease bone loss and delay the development of osteoporosis, including calcium supplementation in the diet, exercise, and estrogen replacement therapy.

Signs & Symptoms

Patients may be asymptomatic or develop kyphosis. The classic fractures associated with osteoporosis are hip, vertebral, and Colles' fractures.

Pathology

Bone tissue appears normal, although the number and size of trabeculae are reduced.

Diagnosis

Bone density studies show decreased bone mass.

Treatment

Estrogen replacement therapy should be considered in all women at risk. If the patient has a uterus, she also needs progestin therapy in conjunction with the estrogen to prevent the development of endometrial cancer. Bisphosphonates (e.g., pamidronate) may also be used to preserve bone. Regular exercise should be encouraged.

Gout

Gout is a form of arthritis caused by the deposition of **uric acid** crystals in the joint. Patients may inadequately excrete uric acid due to renal disease or overproduce uric acid, as with **Lesch-Nyhan syndrome** (a nucleic acid metabolic deficiency).

Pseudogout is caused by **calcium pyrophosphate** deposition in the joints. Etiology is not clear, but trauma is commonly associated with the disease.

Signs & Symptoms

Arthritis affecting the big toe (known as podagra) is classic. Patients may also develop tophi (uric acid deposition in the tissues), especially on the ear.

Diagnosis

Uric acid levels may be normal during the gouty attack. Joint aspiration shows negatively birefringent crystals, as opposed to pseudogout, which has positively birefringent ones.

Treatment

Nonsteroidal anti-inflammatory drugs (NSAIDs) and low-dose colchicine are used in acute attacks. High-dose colchicine, allopurinol, and uricosuric agents (e.g., probenecid) should be started after the attack has resolved.

Inflammatory Diseases

Rheumatoid Arthritis

Rheumatoid arthritis is an autoimmune disease seen predominantly in women. It appears to have a genetic association with the HLA-DR4 haplotype. It usually affects the hand joints, especially the wrist, proximal interphalangeal (PIP), and metacarpophalangeal joints. Joint involvement is usually symmetric.

Signs & Symptoms

Patients develop morning stiffness for at least 1 hour after waking. The affected joints show subluxations (incomplete dislocations) and limitation of movement. Patients may develop rheumatoid nodules on bony prominences or extensor surfaces, such as the elbow.

Diagnosis

Sedimentation rate and serum rheumatoid factor are elevated. X-rays may show erosion of the joint space.

Treatment

Pain relievers such as NSAIDs are used. Corticosteroids (both oral and local injection) and other drugs, such as methotrexate, gold salts, and hydroxychloroquine, may induce remission of symptoms.

Septic Arthritis

Septic arthritis is caused by bacterial infection of the joint space. *Staphylococcus aureus* is a common cause after trauma. However, other predisposing factors may indicate likely infection. For example, young, sexually active persons are more likely to develop gonococcal arthritis, whereas IV drug users may have gram-negative rod infections. Persons with prosthetic joints are at high risk of developing septic arthritis from common skin or oral flora. Also, systemic diseases, such as Lyme disease (*Borrelia burgdorferi*) and hepatitis B, may cause joint symptoms. **Pott's disease** is a tubercular infection in the joint spaces of the spine.

Signs & Symptoms

The ensuing arthrit   ly affects only one or a few joints and is associated with fever and pai   ococcal arthritis may be associated with a pustular rash or genital sympto   yme disease is associated with "target lesions" at the bite site and is discus   in more detail in chapter 5.

Diagnosis

Drainage of the joint fluid shows many white blood cells (usually neutrophils). Gram's stain may reveal an organism.

Treatment

Appropriate antibiotic treatment. Surgical drainage may be necessary.

Spondyloarthropathies

Ankylosing spondylitis is the prototypical spondyloarthropathy highly associated with **HLA-B27**. It is a chronic arthritis that affects the spine and sacroiliac joints, ultimately leading to a rigid spine from bone fusion ("bamboo spine").
Other HLA-B27-associated spondyloarthropathies include:

- **Reiter's syndrome**: Conjunctivitis, urethritis, and arthritis, often following sexually transmitted urethritis or diarrhea from a bacterial intestinal infection. The arthritis is asymmetric and commonly affects the ankles, knees, and feet.

- **Psoriatic arthritis**: Affects approximately 10% of individuals with psoriasis.

- **Spondylitis with inflammatory bowel disease**: A complication of Crohn's disease and ulcerative colitis.

The spondyloarthropathies share a number of common features. They are associated with HLA-B27, and frequently involve the sacroiliac joint in addition to peripheral joints. Unlike rheumatoid arthritis, they occur in the absence of rheumatoid factor (RF), and the pathologic changes begin not in the synovium, but rather in the ligamentous attachments to bone.

Osteomyelitis

Osteomyelitis, or bone infection, can result from direct trauma, localized infection, or hematogenous spread. *S. aureus* is a common causative organism, especially in children. Patients with sickle cell anemia are at increased risk of the development of *Salmonella* osteomyelitis.

Signs & Symptoms

Patients have fever and localized pain at the affected bone.

Pathology

Microscopic examination shows inflammation followed by necrosis and fibrotic replacement. Sequestrum refers to an area of necrotic bone without vascular supply, and involucrum is new periosteal bone formation in response to the infection that surrounds the inflammatory area.

Diagnosis

X-rays are often normal but may show "mottling." Nuclear bone scans show increased white blood cell concentrations in the affected areas.

Treatment

Antibiotics are directed at the causative organism, and surgical drainage may be required in severe cases.

Polymyalgia Rheumatica

Polymyalgia rheumatica is a syndrome of joint pain affecting individuals over age 50. Etiology is unknown, and it may be a diagnosis of exclusion in some cases. It is considered an autoimmune disease but has not been definitively linked to any HLA types.

Signs & Symptoms

Patients complain of pain and stiffness in the neck, shoulders, upper arms, and hips that lasts at least a month. Morning stiffness and symmetric joint involvement is common.

Diagnosis

Sedimentation rate is elevated, but other laboratory tests are normal.

Pathology

Muscle biopsies are normal. Joint examination may reveal mild inflammation.

Treatment

Low-dose prednisone is usually curative.

Osteochondritis Dessicans

Osteochondritis dessicans occurs when a portion of subchondral bone undergoes **avascular necrosis**. The affected bone segment breaks off and floats in the joint space. It commonly affects the knees (the lateral portion of the medial femoral condyles is most common site), hips, elbows, and ankles. The cause is unknown, and it is seen primarily in young male adults.

Signs & Symptoms

Patients experience pain and stiffness that worsen with activity. The joint may lock if the fragment becomes completely detached.

Diagnosis

X-rays are diagnostic.

Treatment

Weight is kept off joints with crutches for several months to promote healing. Surgery is often necessary.

Osgood-Schlatter Disease

Osgood-Schlatter disease is an inflammatory disorder that involves the tibial tuberosity at the insertion of the patellar tendon. It is characteristically seen in active children 10 to 17 years of age and is believed to be caused by repetitive stress and trauma.

Signs & Symptoms

Knee pain aggravated by vigorous exercise.

Diagnosis

X-ray reveals irregularity of the tubercle contour, with possible haziness of the adjacent metaphyseal border.

Treatment

Rest and stretching of the hamstrings and quadriceps. In severe cases, casting for up to 6 weeks may be required.

Degenerative Disorders

Osteoarthritis

Osteoarthritis, also known as DJD, is very common in aging and obese populations. It is a noninflammatory arthritis caused by collagen breakdown and chondrocyte injury. Commonly affected joints include the distal interphalangeal (DIP), PIP, spine, hips, and knees, and distribution is usually asymmetric. History of repetitive injury in a particular joint may predispose to the development of osteoarthritis.

Signs & Symptoms

Gradual onset of joint pain, with little or no morning stiffness. DIP and PIP bony protuberances are common.

Diagnosis

History and examination. X-rays show joint space narrowing, with flaking of cartilage. Areas of excessive smoothness, known as eburnation, may form at contact points.

Treatment

NSAIDs, muscle strengthening, and joint protection.

Carpal Tunnel Syndrome

Carpal tunnel syndrome is caused by compression of the median nerve in the carpal tunnel, which also contains the flexor tendons of the fingers and thumb. In addition to repetitive motion injuries, patients with hypothyroidism and rheumatoid arthritis are predisposed to carpal tunnel syndrome.

Signs & Symptoms

Numbness and tingling in the first three fingers, especially the index finger. Wrist swelling may be present.

Diagnosis

Phalen's test—where the dorsal surfaces of the hands are pressed together with wrist flexion—reproduces the pain. **Tinel's sign** is present when tapping on the median nerve at the wrist reproduces the pain.

Treatment

NSAIDs, wrist splints, and steroid injections of the carpal tunnel.

Scoliosis

Scoliosis is lateral curvature of the spine. It is usually idiopathic, although there may be a genetic predisposition. Teenage girls are most often affected.

Signs & Symptoms

Patients may complain of one shoulder or hip appearing higher than the other. Back pain is a later manifestation.

Diagnosis

Having the patient bend over and touch her toes may reveal the curvature more prominently. X-rays are confirmatory.

Treatment

Casts and back braces are used in mild cases. Surgical correction is performed in more severe cases.

Osteitis Deformans

Also known as **Paget's disease**, osteitis deformans is caused by osteoclastic over-activity followed by abnormal bone deposition. Patients usually develop the disease in middle age, and it is usually diagnosed incidentally, when the patient receives X-rays for another medical problem. Patients with Paget's disease are at increased risk of developing osteosarcoma. It's believed Beethoven may have had Paget's disease.

Signs & Symptoms

Patients are often asymptomatic but may develop gait abnormalities or abnormal bone swelling, especially of the skull. Back pain may develop from malformation of the articular facets, and hearing loss may occur from destruction of the ossicles.

Diagnosis

Serum alkaline phosphatase is elevated, and X-rays show a characteristic mosaic appearance with lytic lesions. Urine hydroxyproline levels are increased because the hydroxyproline and hydroxylysine from the destroyed bone is not used in the manufacture of new bone.

Pathology

Lamellar bone is replaced by woven bone, and the trabeculae are thickened. A mosaic pattern is present microscopically as well.

Treatment

Calcitonin and etidronate may be used to preserve bone.

Slipped Capital Femoral Epiphysis

The typical presentation of slipped capital femoral epiphysis is a painful limp or knee pain in an overweight teenage boy. The cause is a growth disturbance of the proximal femoral growth plate that causes the femur to rotate externally under the capital epiphysis. This phenomenon is rarely seen in prepubescent children. Etiology is unknown.

Signs & Symptoms

Limb shortening and limited internal rotation may also be present.

Diagnosis

X-ray taken in the frog-leg and lateral positions.

Treatment

Pin fixation prevents further misalignment. Osteotomy is required in chronic cases.

Legg-Calve-Perthes Disease

Legg-Calve-Perthes disease is characterized by avascular necrosis of the femoral epiphysis due to unknown cause. Like slipped capital femoral epiphysis, a limp is often the presenting complaint, although in this case the limp tends to be painless. It is seen more commonly in boys than girls and tends to occur in a younger age group (children 4-8) than does slipped capital femoral epiphysis. It can be bilateral.

Signs and Symptoms

Limp, usually without pain. Pain, if present, is referred to the knee. Range of motion is limited upon internal rotation, abduction, and flexion.

Diagnosis

The femoral head is flattened. The initial X-ray may be normal, with later studies revealing epiphyseal radiolucency.

Treatment

Young children with minimal involvement may be observed. Older children with more femoral head changes require orthotic bracing or surgery to protect the fragile femoral head and maintain normal range of motion. Prognosis depends on the amount of ischemic damage. Long-term disability results from abnormal or asymmetric growth.

Injuries

Fractures

Fracture healing occurs in three stages:

- During the **inflammatory phase**, a hematoma forms at the fracture site. Neovascularization occurs, and the formation of a soft **procallus** begins with the presence of pluripotent stem cells that differentiate into osteoclasts and osteoblasts.

- In the **intermediate phase**, the procallus becomes a fibrocartilaginous callus with the removal of necrotic tissue by the osteoclasts and the deposition of new material by the osteoblasts.

- The **remodeling phase** occurs when the fibrocartilaginous tissue is replaced by osseous tissue. This may continue for months after clinical improvement because woven bone is replaced by lamellar bone more suitably oriented for weight bearing. Restoration of the medullary cavity also occurs during this phase.

Complications of fractures include the following:

- **Neurologic** and **vascular damage** can occur through laceration or excessive traction. These are surgical emergencies.

- **Compartment syndrome** occurs when bleeding or swelling occurs within a closed fascial space. The resulting pressure can compress the vascular supply, resulting in tissue necrosis. This occurs most commonly in the forearm or leg. The signs of compartment syndrome are the **six Ps**: **p**ain, **p**allor, **p**ulselessness, **p**aresthesia, **p**oikilothermia, and **p**aralysis. Surgical fasciotomy relieves the pressure.

- **Disuse atrophy** and **joint contractures** are common. These can be prevented with early physical therapy, including range-of-motion exercises.

- **Deep venous thrombosis** may occur due to the prolonged immobilization combined with previous trauma. Breakage of the clot may cause a fatal pulmonary embolus, so all patients should be on deep venous thrombosis prophylaxis, with pneumatic compression boots or subcutaneous heparin injections daily.

Fractures are a common cause of morbidity in elderly patients, and about 20% of cases lead to death from prolonged immobility. Osteoporosis in elderly women predisposes to the development of fractures after a fall. The most common fractures in the elderly are hip, spine, and distal forearm (Colles') fractures. Hip fractures often occur after a fall, and Colles' fractures occur on an outstretched hand. Vertebral fractures may occur gradually and may be asymptomatic or cause varying degrees of back pain.

The following are characteristicly found in certain fractures:

- **Clavicle**: Fractures most commonly occur in the middle one-third of the clavicle, resulting in elevation of the proximal fragment due to the sternocleidomastoid muscle and downward displacement of the lateral fragment due to the deltoid muscle and gravity.

- **Rib**: Fractures result in local pain and tenderness, which can be distinguished from soft-tissue injury by increased pain at the fracture site by compressing the chest anteroposteriorly (simultaneously pressing on the sternum and thoracic spine); this maneuver should not elicit increased pain in the tender site in soft tissue injury. Lower rib fractures should lead to suspicion of possible kidney, liver, or spleen damage.

- **Humerus**: Fracture of the surgical head of the humerus can cause axillary nerve and posterior circumflex humeral artery damage. A mid-shaft fracture can cause radial nerve and profunda brachii artery damage. Once a fracture occurs, the muscles inserted on the humerus (e.g., rotator cuff muscles, pectoralis major, latissimus dorsi, teres major, deltoid, biceps brachii, triceps brachii, and common flexor tendon of the forearm) can pull the pieces of the humerus in different directions, depending on the location of the fracture relative to the insertion sites.

- **Femur**: A fracture at the neck of the femur results in shortening and lateral rotation of the leg (compared to hip dislocation, which produces shortening, **medial** rotation, and flexion of the leg). Fractures in other parts of the femur can pull the pieces in different directions, depending on the relative locations of the fracture site and the muscles attached to the femur.

Sprains

Sprains are injuries to a joint ligament or joint capsule. Common sites are the wrist and the ankle. Ankle sprains are usually caused by hyperinversion or eversion of the foot with foot plantar flexion. The anterior talofibular, calcaneofibular, and the deltoid ligaments are often involved.

Signs & Symptoms

Patients give a history of injury with pain and swelling at the affected site.

Diagnosis

Routine X-rays are usually performed to rule out "hidden" fractures, such as navicular, hook of hamate, or avulsion fractures. A common avulsion fracture is the proximal end of the fifth metatarsal by the peroneus brevis tendon during an inversion sprain of the foot.

Treatment

The mnemonic is "RICE"—rest, ice or heat application, compression (as with an Ace bandage), and elevation. Serious ligamentous injuries may require surgical correction.

Dislocations

Dislocations are disruptions in joint continuity. The most frequently dislocated joints are shoulder, elbow, hip, and knee, although any joint can be dislocated.

- **Shoulder dislocations** are either glenohumeral or acromioclavicular injuries caused by a fall or direct blow to the shoulder. Glenohumeral dislocations can be anterior or posterior; possible axillary nerve damage should be assessed in anterior dislocations. Patients have tenderness and swelling over the joint with fullness of the affected shoulder or elevation of the outer portion of the clavicle.

- **Posterior dislocations** of the elbow occur due to a fall on an outstretched hand. Avulsion fractures of the medial epicondyle and distal radial (Colles') fractures are associated. Another common form of elbow dislocation is the **subluxation of the head of the radius** and tearing of the annular ligament when a parent forcefully pulls or yanks on the arm of a child. Pronation and supination are markedly restricted in this case.

- **Hip dislocations** are usually posterior and often occur during an automobile accident, as the body flies forward and the hip joint hits the steering wheel or dashboard. Fracture of the acetabulum often accompanies this injury. Patients hold their legs in flexion, adduction, and internal rotation. The affected leg appears shorter than the non-affected leg. Avascular necrosis of the femoral head is a common complication that can be prevented if reduction of the dislocation occurs within 6 hours. Possible damage to the sciatic nerve should be assessed. Patients with hip dislocations may demonstrate a positive Trendelenburg's sign, a downward tipping of the pelvis on the opposite side from the stepping leg, due to faulty hip abduction on the side of the stepping leg. This is also seen in superior gluteal nerve injury and fracture of the neck of the femur.

- **Knee dislocations** may occur due to congenital defects in the lateral femoral condyles or may be caused by trauma. Lateral dislocation of the patella is the most commonly seen deformity.

Diagnosis

Patients should always receive X-rays to assess for accompanying fractures.

Treatment

After reduction, slings, splinting, and casts are used.

Bone Neoplasms

Osteosarcoma

Osteosarcomas (osteogenic sarcomas) are the most common primary malignant bone tumors. Malignant cells arise directly from the osteoid. Cases occur in teens and the elderly. Osteosarcoma is associated with the familial retinoblastoma gene, Paget's disease, *p53* mutations, and history of irradiation. These lesions frequently metastasize by hematogenous spread to the lungs, liver, and brain.

Signs & Symptoms

Most cases occur in the metaphyses of long bones, particularly the proximal tibia and distal femur, and have associated pain and swelling.

Pathology

Lesions may be lytic or blastic, depending on the cells involved.

Diagnosis

X-rays show periosteal elevation (**Codman's triangle**). A characteristic "sunburst" appearance due to periosteal inflammation may also be seen on X-ray. Serum alkaline phosphatase is elevated two- to threefold. Biopsy is diagnostic. A CT of the chest should be performed to detect pulmonary metastases.

Treatment

Combination surgery, radiation, and chemotherapy lead to 5-year survival rates of about 60%.

Ewing's Sarcoma

Ewing's sarcoma is a malignant tumor that tends to occur in boys under 15 years of age, unlike osteosarcoma, which is more common in teenage years. In addition to pain and localized swelling, it presents with the systemic symptoms of fever, weight loss, and fatigue, all of which are again rarely seen in osteosarcoma. It is a primitive round cell tumor believed to be of neurogenic origin.

Signs & Symptoms

Pain and swelling locally, along with fever, weight loss, and fatigue. The tumor tends occur in the diaphyseal regions of long bones and in flat bones. Common sites include the midproximal femur and the bones of the pelvis.

Diagnosis

Biopsy is diagnostic. Radiographs reveal a lytic bone lesion with "onion-skin" periosteal elevation (due to calcifications).

Treatment

Chemotherapy.

Osteochondroma

Osteochondroma, the most common benign tumor of the bone, occurs most commonly is males under 25 years of age. It consists of a bony growth covered by a cap of cartilage that projects from the surface of a bone. The growth tends to emerge from the metaphysis, near the growth plate of long bones. Its progression is slow, and growth tends to stop when normal skeletal growth is complete, which lends credence to the belief that it is a malformation rather than a neoplasm.

Usually an osteochondroma is asymptomatic, and the main concern is cosmetic deformity. Pain can result if the growth impinges on a nerve or if its stalk is fractured.

Giant Cell Tumors

Giant cell tumors, or **osteoclastomas**, are the second-most common benign tumor of the bone. They have the distinction of occurring more often in females than in males, and usually between the ages of 20 and 40. Giant cell tumors have the striking histologic finding of multiple large multinucleated giant cells that resemble osteoclasts.

Signs & Symptoms

Presentation is usually localized pain that can be mistaken for arthritis because the tumors tend to occur at the epiphyseal ends of long bones, such as the proximal tibia, distal femur, proximal humerus, or distal radius.

Diagnosis

Biopsy is diagnostic. X-ray reveals a characteristic "soap bubble" appearance.

Treatment

Currettage. Local recurrences are common. Malignant transformation is rare.

Metastatic Bone Disease

Most metastatic bone lesions come from primary tumors in the prostate, breast, kidney, and lung. Most lesions are lytic, and don't forget that multiple myeloma can cause similar bone lesions.

Signs & Symptoms

Bone pain may be the presenting symptom of the primary cancer, particularly in prostate cancer.

Diagnosis

X-rays and nuclear bone scans are useful.

Treatment

Because these lesions represent distant metastasis, prognosis is poor. Local irradiation of the lesion may provide palliative relief.

Soft Tissue Tumors

Lipoma

The most common soft tissue tumor, a **lipoma** is a benign, solitary, sporadic growth that can appear anywhere on the body, usually in the subcutaneous tissue of adults. It tends to be well-circumscribed. Excision is the cure.

Malignant Fibrous Histiocytoma

The most common soft tissue sarcoma of adults, **malignant fibrous histiocytoma** tends to occur in the deep muscular tissues of the extremities or retroperitoneally. It is usually found in adults between 50 and 70 years of age. It appears as a gray-white, encapsulated mass, but is highly infiltrative and very aggressive, with frequent local recurrence. Metastases occur in half of patients.

Rhabdomyosarcoma

Rhabdomyosarcoma is a tumor of childhood, usually occurring in the first decade of life. It is the most common soft tissue sarcoma of childhood. The presentation is variable, ranging from the grape-like **sarcoma botryoides** that arise near mucosal surfaces of the genitourinary tract and in the head and neck, to a less well-defined, infiltrating mass. This tumor is differentiated from other small round cell tumors of childhood by the presence of sarcomeres in electron microscopic examination or the presence of muscle-associated antigens in immunocytochemical preparations.

Pharmacology

Anti-Inflammatory Agents

See Table 10-4 for information about some common anti-inflammatory agents.

Table 10-4 Anti-inflammatory agents

Drug	Mechanism	Use	Toxicity
Aspirin	Irreversibly inhibits cyclooxygenase, leading to decreased synthesis of prostaglandins and thromboxane	Low dose (<300 mg/day): reduces platelet aggregation. Intermediate dose (300–2,400 mg/day): antipyretic and analgesic effects. High dose (2,400–4,000 mg/day): anti-inflammatory	Adverse effects include gastrointestinal disturbances and increased risk of bleeding. Bronchospasm. Higher doses cause tinnitus, vertigo, hyperventilation, respiratory alkalosis, metabolic acidosis. **Reye's syndrome** (hepatic fatty degeneration and encephalopathy) occurs when aspirin is given to children with viral infections
Ibuprofen, indomethacin, nap-	Reversibly inhibit cyclooxygenase. Ibuprofen has lower	Dysmenorrhea, inflammation (rheumatoid arthritis, gout), patent	Indomethacin has increased toxicity

Drug	Mechanism	Use	Toxicity
roxen	potency and shorter action Naproxen has longer action Indomethacin has high potency	ductus arteriosus in premature infants	
Slow-acting antirheu-matic drugs (methotrex-ate, gold mar-compounds, hydroxy-bances chloroquine, penicilla-mine)	Unknown	Benefits may require several months to manifest Used for patients with rheumatoid or other immune complexes in their serum Controversial	**Methotrexate**: bone marrow depression, hepato-toxicity, teratogenic fetal damage, or abortion **Gold**: dermatitis, bone row depression, gas-trointestinal distur- **Hydroxychloroquine**: der-matitis, bone marrow depression, retinal degeneration **Penicillamine**: renal dam-age, aplastic anemia
Cortico-steroids ing,	Enter cell, bind to receptors in cytosol and translocate to nucleus Alter gene expression Decrease lymphocytes, eosinophils, basophils, and monocytes Inhibit migration of leukocytes Suppress production of prostaglandins and leukotrienes due to inhibition of phospho-lipase	Autoimmune disorders	Fat deposition, protein catabolism, skin wast- osteoporosis, growth inhibition (in children) Immunosuppressive Large doses for long peri-ods may cause behav-ioral disturbances; may increase risk of ulcer for-mation
Acetamino-phen	Inhibitor of prostaglandin synthesis, but exact mechanism unknown	Minor musculoskeletal pain	Rash Overdose can cause fulmi-nant hepatic failure

Muscle Relaxants

Skeletal muscle relaxants are discussed in chapter 4. These include drugs (e.g., curare derivatives and succinylcholine) that block nicotinic receptors at the motor end plate; they are used for muscle relaxation during surgery. The drugs listed in Table 10-5 are used for less complete muscle relaxation.

Table 10-5. Muscle relaxants

Drug	Mechanism	Use	Toxicity
Baclofen	Acts on GABA receptors in the central nervous system	Decreases pain in spastic patients	Somnolence, increased seizure activity
Dantrolene	Blocks calcium release from the sarcoplasmic reticulum	Muscle spasticity, malignant hyperthermia	Generalized weakness, sedation, hepatitis
Valium and other benzodiazepines	Bind GABA receptors to cause increased firing frequency	Mild muscle spasm, patients with spinal cord injury	Sedation, ataxia, addictive potential

GABA = γ-aminobutyric acid.

Gout Medications

See Table 10-6 for information about some common gout medications.

Table 10-6 Gout medications

Drug	Mechanism	Use	Toxicity
Colchicine	Inhibits microtubule assembly, decreasing WBC actions	Acute gouty arthritis	Gastrointestinal effects; liver and kidney damage
Allopurinol	Inhibition of xanthine oxidase, an enzyme in uric acid synthesis	Recurrent renal stones; chronic gout	Not to be given in acute gout attack; gastrointestinal upset; peripheral neuropathy
Uricosuric drugs (probenecid, sulfapyrazine)	Inhibits uric acid reabsorption in the kidney	Chronic gout	May worsen acute attacks; can also block renal secretion of penicillin
Phenylbutazone	Prostaglandin inhibitor	Pain relief in acute gout	Aplastic anemia

WBC = white blood count.

Bone Homeostasis

See Table 10-7 for information about drugs that affect bone homeostasis.

Table 10-7 Drugs that effect Bone Homeostasis.

Drug	Mechanism	Use	Toxicity
Bisphosphonates (etidronate, pamidrone, alendronate)	Binds hydroxyapatite crystal and prevents bone resorption and formation	Postmenopausal oseoporosis hypercalcemia, Paget's disease, bone metastases	Hypocalcemia leukemia, lymphopenia
Calcitonin (salmon)	Decreases bone resorption and serum calcium and phosphate by osteoclasts inhibition	Acute treatment of Paget's disease and hypercalcemia	Flushing, GI distress
Estrogen	Prevents or delays loss in postmenopausal women, possibly by inhibiting PTH-induced bone resorption by osteoclasts	Postmenopausal osteoporoosis prophylaxis	Breast tenderness discomfort headaches

CHAPTER 11

Respiratory System

Anatomy

The Upper Airway

Along the path that air travels from the nose and mouth down to the lungs are several distinct regions that form a continuum (Fig. 11-1):

- After dust particles are filtered by the hairs in the nose, air travels back to the **nasopharynx**. Important structures are pharyngeal tonsils and eustachian tube openings.

- The **oropharynx** is continuous with the oral cavity and the nasopharynx at the level of the soft palate and hard palate. The palatine tonsils and uvula are found here.

- The **oral cavity** includes mainly the tongue and teeth (and lots of bacteria!).

- The **hypopharynx** (laryngopharynx) starts below the oropharynx, at the level of the epiglottis, leading directly into the larynx.

- The **epiglottis** is cartilage that closes off the trachea during swallowing (to prevent aspiration).

- The **vallecula** is the nook in front of the epiglottis and behind the tongue. It is medically important because it is the landmark for placing a laryngoscope when performing intubation.

- The vocal cords and arytenoids are found in the **glottis**, or **larynx**, which continues down to the **cricoid cartilage**.

- The **cricothyroid membrane** is the anteromedial space below the thyroid cartilage (Adam's apple) and above the cricoid cartilage. This is where a catheter, scalpel, or even a hollow ball point pen shaft (it's been done!) can be inserted to establish an emergency surgical airway.

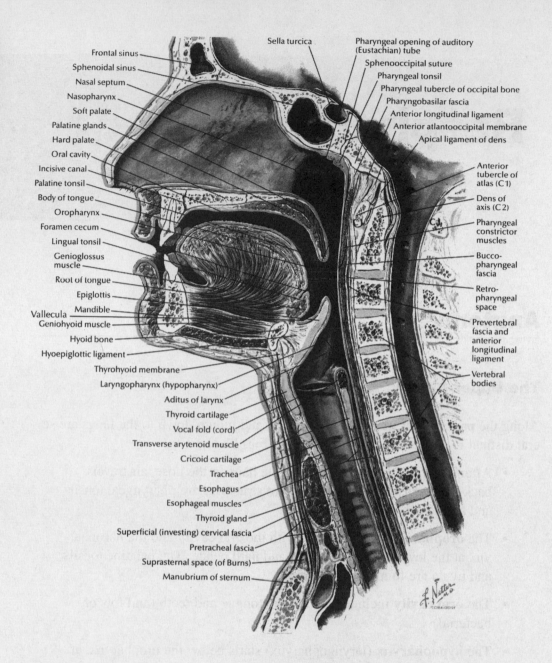

Frontal sinus
Sphenoidal sinus
Nasal septum
Nasopharynx
Soft palate
Palatine glands
Hard palate
Oral cavity
Incisive canal
Palatine tonsil
Body of tongue
Oropharynx
Foramen cecum
Lingual tonsil
Genioglossus muscle
Root of tongue
Epiglottis
Mandible
Vallecula
Geniohyoid muscle
Hyoid bone
Hyoepiglottic ligament
Thyrohyoid membrane
Laryngopharynx (hypopharynx)
Aditus of larynx
Thyroid cartilage
Vocal fold (cord)
Transverse arytenoid muscle
Cricoid cartilage
Trachea
Esophagus
Esophageal muscles
Thyroid gland
Superficial (investing) cervical fascia
Pretracheal fascia
Suprasternal space (of Burns)
Manubrium of sternum

Sella turcica
Pharyngeal opening of auditory (Eustachian) tube
Sphenooccipital suture
Pharyngeal tonsil
Pharyngeal tubercle of occipital bone
Pharyngobasilar fascia
Anterior longitudinal ligament
Anterior atlantooccipital membrane
Apical ligament of dens
Anterior tubercle of atlas (C1)
Dens of axis (C2)
Pharyngeal constrictor muscles
Bucco-pharyngeal fascia
Retro-pharyngeal space
Prevertebral fascia and anterior longitudinal ligament
Vertebral bodies

Fig. 11-1. Upper respiratory anatomy. (Reprinted with permission from FH Netter. *Atlas of Human Anatomy.* Summit, NJ: CIBA–GEIGY, 1989.)

- The tracheal cartilage rings are C shaped and open in the back, except the **cricoid cartilage**, which is the only ring that completely encircles the trachea. This means that firm pressure anteriorly here during intubation closes off the esophagus posteriorly and prevents aspiration.

- **Swallowing (deglutition)**: From a respiratory tract perspective, as food is propelled back in the oral cavity, the soft palate is raised (levator veli palatini) and tensed (tensor veli palatini), closing off the nasopharynx—unless someone makes you laugh, in which case the food comes out the nose. Simultaneously, the whole larynx is elevated and meets the epiglottis, closing off the opening so that food goes down the correct tube.

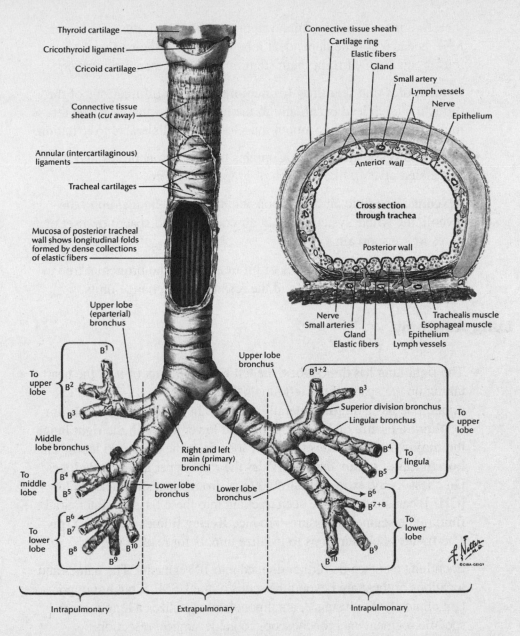

Thyroid cartilage
Cricothyroid ligament
Cricoid cartilage
Connective tissue sheath (cut away)
Annular (intercartilaginous) ligaments
Tracheal cartilages
Mucosa of posterior tracheal wall shows longitudinal folds formed by dense collections of elastic fibers

Connective tissue sheath
Cartilage ring
Elastic fibers
Gland
Small artery
Lymph vessels
Nerve
Epithelium

Anterior wall

Cross section through trachea

Posterior wall

Nerve
Small arteries
Gland
Elastic fibers

Trachealis muscle
Esophageal muscle
Epithelium
Lymph vessels

Upper lobe (eparterial) bronchus

B^1

To upper lobe $\{$ B^2 B^3

Middle lobe bronchus

To middle lobe $\{$ B^4 B^5

To lower lobe $\{$ B^6 B^7 B^8 B^9 B^{10}

Right and left main (primary) bronchi

Lower lobe bronchus

Upper lobe bronchus

B^{1+2} B^3
Superior division bronchus
Lingular bronchus
B^4 B^5

To upper lobe

To lingula

Lower lobe bronchus

B^6 B^{7+8} B^{10} B^9

To lower lobe

Intrapulmonary | Extrapulmonary | Intrapulmonary

Fig. 11-2. Lower respiratory anatomy. (Reprinted with permission from FH Netter. *Atlas of Human Anatomy*. Summit, NJ: CIBA–GEIGY, 1989.)

Lower Respiratory Tract

- **Trachea**: Below the cricoid cartilage, the larynx becomes the trachea proper (Fig. 11-2).

- **Mucociliary escalator**: Traps and propels phlegm back up.

- **Carina**: The bifurcation of the trachea into the right and left main stem bronchi.

- **Bronchi**: The left main stem bronchus branches off at a sharp angle and sits above the heart. The right main stem bronchus is almost a straight shot downward compared to the left main stem. Aspiration is therefore more common on the right, specifically in the right upper lobe, because it's the dependent lobe in supine patients. For the same reason, inadvertent right main stem intubation is a common error.

- **Bronchioles and terminal bronchioles**: Further bifurcations of the bronchi, which lead eventually to the lung's functional unit, the terminal respiratory unit. Smooth muscle in the walls reacts to irritation.

- **Terminal respiratory unit**: Contains terminal bronchioles and their associated alveoli, like a bunch of grapes on a stem.

- **Alveolus**: The little air sac responsible for gas exchange; up to the alveoli, the whole system is a big air conduit (dead space) or a set of pipes to transport air.

- It takes about **16 generations** of bifurcations in the bronchial tree to reach terminal bronchioles and the respiratory exchange units.

Lung Anatomy

- The right lung has three **lobes**, the left has two (think of it as the heart taking up the space of the left lung's third lobe) (Fig. 11-3). The left upper lobe has a **lingula** (literally, tongue). In the left lung, the **major** or **oblique fissure** divides the upper and lower lobes. In the right lung, the **major fissure** divides the lower lobe from the other two lobes. The **horizontal** or **minor fissure** divides the right upper and middle lobes. On chest X-ray, extra pleural fluid (e.g., from congestive heart failure [CHF]) can sometimes be seen tracking into these fissures. Interstitial fluid in the segmental fissures produce **Kerley B** lines on chest X-ray. The fissures help surgeons to localize tumors for resection.

- Each lung can then be further divided into 10 segments. The names and locations of these are beyond the scope of the USMLE but are important clinically. For instance, a pulmonologist localizes a lung mass to a specific segment via bronchoscopy to guide surgical resection.

- Each lung is anchored at the **hilum** (plural = hila), which is where all the lung's plumbing comes in and out (this is a common anatomic theme: nerves, arteries, veins, lymphatics, and other conduits conveniently tend to travel together). Lymph nodes are found here, too.

- Like most other internal organs, the lung is encased in a **visceral pleura**, which is contiguous with the **parietal pleura** that lines the chest wall. The pleural space is a potential space between the two pleural layers. This is the space that pathologically fills with air (in a pneumothorax), or fluid (in CHF).

Blood Supply

- **Pulmonary circulation**: Pulmonary arteries carry unoxygenated blood through the lungs for air exchange in the capillary bed, after

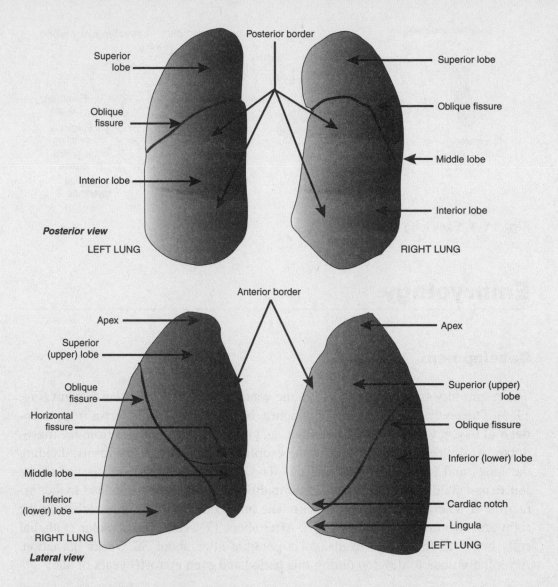

Fig. 11-3. Lung lobes and fissures.

which it leaves through the pulmonary veins. Unlike most other arterial vessels, the pulmonary arterial system is thin walled and more elastic than muscular. This quality, along with the vast branching of pulmonary arteries into capillaries, makes for a low-resistance circuit.

- **Bronchial circulation**: The bronchial arteries are small branches that come directly off the aorta to supply oxygenated blood to the pleura and airway walls. Some of this blood returns to the heart via the pulmonary veins, so some unoxygenated blood is dumped into the systemic circulation, resulting in a **shunt** (described later, under Physiology).

- **Lymphatics**: Important for staging cancers of the lung because most lung tumors spread via lymphatics.

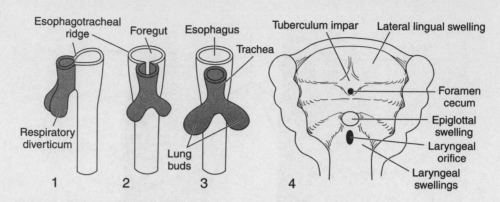

Fig. 11-4. Early lung development.

Embryology

Development

The respiratory system develops from the ventral wall of the primitive **foregut** (Fig. 11-4). The epithelium of the larynx, trachea, bronchi, and alveoli derive from **endodermal** tissue, whereas the cartilaginous and muscular tissue comes from the **mesoderm**. At 4 weeks of development, the **esophagotracheal septum** forms, dividing the lungs and trachea from the foregut. The larynx is formed from tissues of the fourth and sixth branchial arches. Abnormalities in development can lead to the formation of **tracheoesophageal fistulas**. The lung buds form into three lobes on the right and two on the left (Fig. 11-5). After about 17 weeks, the alveolar epithelial cells begin to form. Gas exchange is possible after about 32 weeks' gestation. Alveoli continue to develop during this period and even up to 10 years of age!

Fetal Maturation and Perinatal Changes

In the developing fetus, blood flow through the pulmonary vessels is minimal because the collapsed lungs form a high-resistance circuit. **Surfactant**, the substance that decreases surface tension and prevents collapse of the alveoli, is not produced until approximately 24–26 weeks' gestation. Babies born earlier than this develop **neonatal respiratory distress syndrome** (RDS), discussed later in the chapter.

In the newborn, clamping the umbilical cord (containing the umbilical artery and veins) leads to dramatic changes in the circulation. Blood flow increases markedly in the pulmonary circulation, which now becomes a low-resistance circuit after lung expansion and the baby's first breaths.

Histology

The upper airway cells undergo a gradual transition from the tall, pseudostratified columnar, ciliated cells (larynx, trachea) required for the mucociliary escalator, to

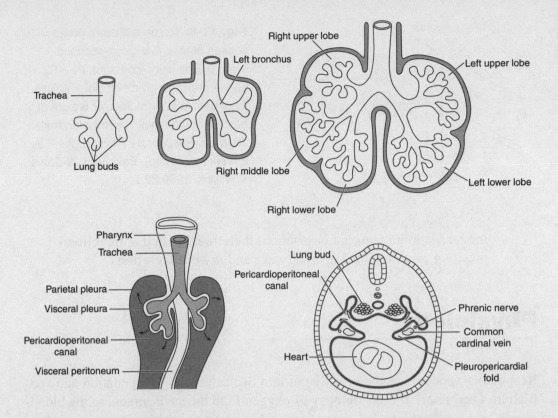

Fig. 11-5. Later lung development.

simple cuboidal cells (terminal bronchioles). The cell types found in the lower airway are as follows:

- **Type I pneumocytes**: The alveolar lining cells that form part of the gas diffusion barrier.

- **Type II pneumocytes**: Thicker, granulated cells that secrete surfactant.

- **Fenestrated endothelial cells** of the capillary wall.

- **Alveolar macrophages (dust cells)**: These cells, like other monocyte-derived cells, phagocytize debris nearby.

- **Smooth muscle**: Found in the mucosal layer, it becomes more prominent as the airway diameter decreases. It is thought that spasm in the smooth muscle is a major factor in **reactive airway disease** (RAD), asthma, and **chronic obstructive pulmonary disease** (COPD). Sympathetic tone (e.g., during stress or exercise) activates β-adrenergic receptors in these cells, leading to smooth muscle relaxation and airway opening for greater air movement. This is why inhaled β-agonists, such as albuterol, are given to wheezing asthmatics and patients with COPD. Cholinergic activity

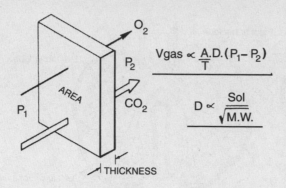

Fig. 11-6. Tissue diffusion. (Vgas = volume of gas; A = cross-sectional area; D = diffusion constant; $P_1 - P_2$ = partial pressure gradient; Sol = solubility of gas; M.W. = molecular weight of gas.) (Reprinted with permission from JB West. *Respiratory Physiology—The Essentials* [4th ed]. Baltimore: Williams & Wilkins, 1990;22.)

induces smooth muscle constriction; therefore, inhaled anticholinergics (e.g., ipratropium) open airways and dry out secretions.

Physiology

Respiratory function can be broadly put into two categories: oxygenation and ventilation. **Oxygenation** is the delivery of oxygen from the environment to the bloodstream and eventually to end-organ tissues. **Ventilation** is the bulk exchange of air that allows the elimination of CO_2 produced by metabolically active tissue.

Diffusion in the Lung

Air moves by bulk flow from the nose to terminal bronchioles. After that, air moves by **diffusion**.

Diffusion is described by **Fick's law** (Fig. 11-6):

$$\text{Rate of diffusion} = (k \times A)/T \times D \times (P_1 - P_2)$$

where k = constant, A = cross-sectional area, T = thickness, D = diffusion constant, and $P_1 - P_2$ = partial pressure gradient.

In the lung, the total surface area is huge (50–100 m^2) and the thickness is very small, optimizing diffusion. If the pressure gradient is large, the rate of diffusion increases because more gas is "pushed" across the gas exchange barrier. The diffusion constant, D, depends on the solubility and molecular weight of a particular gas. Even though CO_2 and O_2 have similar molecular weights, CO_2 diffuses 20 times faster than O_2 because it is much more soluble.

Once an oxygen molecule arrives at an alveolus, it must pass through the gas exchange interface (Fig. 11-7), which includes

- Surfactant fluid layer

- Alveolar epithelium

- Interstitial space

- Capillary endothelium

- Blood plasma

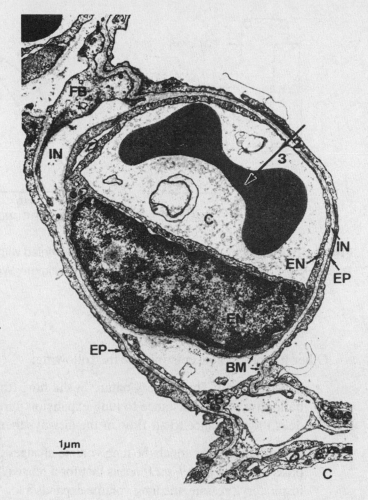

Fig. 11-7. The pulmonary capillary. (FB = fibroblast; IN = interstitial space; C = capillary lumen; EP = alveolar epithelium; EN = capillary epithelium; BM = basement membrane.) (Reprinted with permission from JB West. *Respiratory Physiology—The Essentials* [4th ed]. Baltimore: Williams & Wilkins, 1990;3.)

- Erythrocyte membrane

After all this, the O_2 finally reaches the hemoglobin molecule!

The **interstitial space** is drained via lymphatics. Thickening of this space by either fluid (e.g., CHF) or fibrosis (e.g., interstitial lung disease) increases the gas diffusion barrier.

Mechanics of Breathing

The lung is an elastic entity that expands as a result of the negative pressure gradient generated by diaphragmatic contraction. **Expiration** is a passive event at rest. That's why it takes longer to exhale than to inhale (the normal inspiration-to-expiration ratio is greater than 1:2). During exercise and stress, expiration is in part active, with the abdominal muscles and internal intercostals taking part.

The components of chest wall mechanics include the

- **Diaphragm**: innervated by the phrenic nerve

- **External intercostals**: stiffen the chest wall, preventing collapse of the chest wall during inspiration

- **Accessory muscles** of respiration: scalenes, sternocleidomastoids

Innervation of diaphragm: "C3, C4, C5 keep the diaphragm alive."

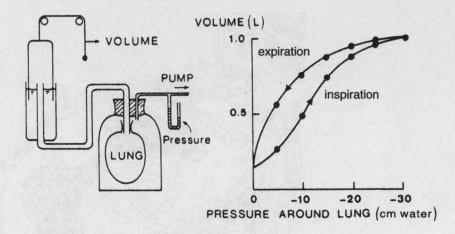

Fig. 11-8. Pressure-volume curve of the lung. (Reprinted with permission from JB West. *Respiratory Physiology—The Essentials* [4th ed]. Baltimore: Williams & Wilkins, 1990;90.)

Other important concepts include the following:

- **Elastic recoil**: The rubbery nature of the lung (think of blowing up a balloon) creates resistance to lung expansion during inspiration, as does the resistance to air flow of the airways themselves.

- **Compliance**: How much the lung volume changes for a given change in pressure. *High compliance* means that for a relatively small increase in inspiratory pressure, the lung volume expands a lot. *Low compliance* implies "stiff" lungs. Emphysematous lungs, with lots of interstitial tissue loss, are highly compliant, whereas the fibrotic lungs of interstitial lung disease have low compliance. Elastance is the reciprocal of compliance.

- **Surfactant**: Decreases surface tension, which tends to collapse alveoli. Surfactant is an amphipathic phospholipid.

- **Hysteresis**: As in Fig. 11-8, the lung's pressure-volume curve is different for inspiration than for expiration. On expiration, at any given pressure, the lung volume is greater than on inspiration, implying that more alveoli are open. This is a result of surfactant's effect on reducing surface tension.

- Airway resistance peaks in the segmental bronchi (about the fifth generation of divisions). Resistance through a tube with laminar flow is determined by **Poiseuille's law**, discussed in chapter 12.

Lung Volumes

- **Tidal volume** (V_T): The volume of air inspired and expired during a normal breath, approximately 6–8 ml/kg body weight at rest (Fig. 11-9).

- **Anatomic dead space** (V_D): The volume of air that does not participate in gas exchange, including air in the conducting airways. About 150 ml, or 2 ml/kg body weight.

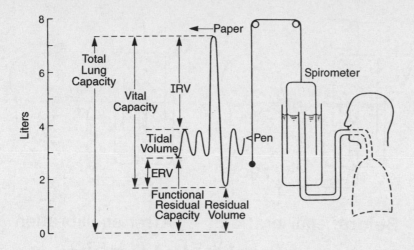

Fig. 11-9. Lung volumes and capacities. (IRV = inspiratory reserve volume; ERV = expiratory reserve volume.) (Reprinted with permission from JB West. *Respiratory Physiology—The Essentials* [4th ed]. Baltimore: Williams & Wilkins, 1990;13.)

- **Inspiratory reserve volume** (IRV): After a normal inspiration, the amount of additional air that can be sucked in.

- **Expiratory reserve volume** (ERV): The volume that can be expired after a normal expiration, usually about 1,100 ml.

- **Residual volume** (RV): After exhaling all that can be exhaled, the volume of air remaining in the lungs. This volume cannot be measured directly by spirometry; a helium dilution technique or plethysmography must be used.

Lung Capacities

The term *capacity* refers to the sum of two or more volumes.

- **Functional residual capacity** (FRC): FRC = ERV + RV. The volume left in the lungs after normal expiration.

- **Inspiratory capacity** (IC): IC = V_T + IRV. The amount of air that can be sucked in after a normal expiration.

- **Vital capacity** (VC): VC = ERV + V_T + IRV.

- **Total lung capacity** (TLC): The whole shebang. TLC = RV + ERV + IRV + V_T.

Respiratory rate (RR) is usually described as breaths per minute (normal, 8–12). Minute ventilation (V_E) = RR × V_T is the total volume of air exchanged per minute (normal, 4–6 liters/minute).

Pulmonary Function Tests

Pulmonary function tests (PFTs) are done to measure lung volumes and are used clinically to diagnose a variety of pulmonary diseases, including obstructive, restrictive, and reactive airway disease. Because the lung cannot completely empty its air (the

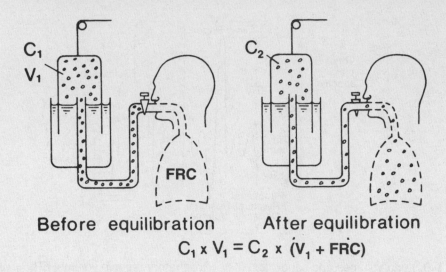

Before equilibration   After equilibration

$$C_1 \times V_1 = C_2 \times (V_1 + FRC)$$

Fig. 11-10. Helium dilution technique. (Reprinted with permission from JB West. *Respiratory Physiology—The Essentials* [4th ed]. Baltimore: Williams & Wilkins, 1990;13.)

RV remains after complete exhalation), **spirometry**—in which the patient sucks and blows into a tube—cannot be used alone to measure FRC and TLC. Instead, one of two techniques must be used:

- **Helium dilution technique** (Fig. 11-10): The patient is hooked up to a spirometer. A known concentration of helium is introduced at the end of expiration (remember, the remaining volume is the FRC) and is breathed in by the patient (helium is not absorbed into the blood-stream, so the given quantity is constant). The helium mixes with the air in the patient's lungs and is diluted. The following equation, with the old and new concentrations of helium (C_1, C_2), gives the volume (V_2) in the patient's lungs:

$$C_1 \times V_1 = C_2 \times (V_1 + FRC)$$

- **Body plethysmography** (Fig. 11-11): Remember **Boyle's law**? It states that in a closed system, pressure (P) times volume (V) is a constant: $P_1 \times V_1 = P_2 \times V_2$. In this technique, the patient sits in an air-tight booth and takes in a big breath against a closed mouthpiece. The lungs expand slightly, increasing lung volume and decreasing lung (intrapleural) pressure. As a result, the pressure increases as the volume of air in the box decreases slightly. These changes can be measured and plugged into Boyle's law, giving us the lung volume.

Other PFTs are used to determine various characteristics of ventilation:

- **Dead space**: The fraction of tidal volume taken up by dead space (and not involved in ventilation) can be calculated using the **Bohr equation**:

$$V_D/V_T = (\text{Paco}_2 - \text{Peco}_2)/\text{Paco}_2$$

where Paco_2 = partial pressure of arterial CO_2 (an approximation of alveolar CO_2), and Peco_2 = partial pressure of mixed expired CO_2,

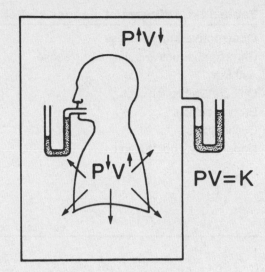

$$PV = K$$

Fig. 11-11. Body plethysmography.
(P = pressure; V = volume; K = constant.)
(Reprinted with permission from JB West.
Respiratory Physiology—The Essentials [4th
ed]. Baltimore: Williams & Wilkins, 1990;14.)

which is always less than Pa_{CO_2} because air in the dead space has not
had a chance to accumulate CO_2 from the alveoli and is mixed with
alveolar air during expiration.

- **Forced expiration**: The subject inhales maximally (unlike Bill Clinton)
  and then exhales as hard as possible. The **forced expiratory volume** in
  one second (FEV_1) is then measured. The ratio between the FEV_1 and
  the **forced vital capacity** (FVC) (usually slightly less than the actual
  VC) is then calculated. A normal FEV_1/FVC is 0.8–1.0. In **restrictive**
  lung disease, both FEV_1 and FVC are decreased, so the ratio is normal
  or slightly increased (often with smaller volumes, it's easier to blow all
  the air out in 1 second). In **obstructive** lung disease, the FEV_1 is
  markedly reduced because the airway's resistance is increased (from the
  obstruction), whereas the FVC is decreased to a lesser extent. This
  makes the FEV_1-to-FVC ratio low in obstructive disease. Obstructive
  and restrictive lung diseases are described in Table 11-1.

  Flow-volume curves provide a way to assess lung disease during
  PFTs (Fig. 11-12). Inspiration and expiration are measured and plotted
  as flow versus lung volume. In restrictive disease, the flow pattern
  shows small flows and volumes, whereas in obstructive disease, the
  overall lung volume is large (due to chronic air trapping), but expiration ends prematurely. In addition, a scalloped appearance (coving) of
  the non–effort-dependent portion of expiration is usually seen.

  The forced expiratory flow in the middle of the expiratory loop
  ($FEF_{25-75\%}$) can also be measured. A decrease in the $FEF_{25-75\%}$ is a
  more sensitive indicator of obstructive disease (Table 11-2).

  Another important component of PFTs is bronchodilator response.
  RAD responds to bronchodilators, and as airways open up in response
  to bronchodilators, FEV_1 increases, thereby raising the FEV_1-to-FVC
  ratio. Values before and after bronchodilator use are compared.

- **Diffusion capacity**: The normal transit time for an RBC through the
  pulmonary capillaries is about 0.75 seconds. CO_2 rapidly diffuses into
  the bloodstream, so its transfer is limited by how fast the blood gets

Normal FEV_1/FVC =
0.8–1.0
Restrictive disease causes
a normal or increased
ratio.
Obstructive disease
causes a decreased ratio.

Table 11-1. Differential diagnosis of obstructive and restrictive lung diseases

Obstructive lung disease	Restrictive lung disease
Chronic obstructive pulmonary disease	Parenchymal disease, including
Asthma	Interstitial lung disease
Obliterative bronchiolitis	Pulmonary edema
Bronchiectasis	Pneumonia
Cystic fibrosis	Sarcoidosis (can also be obstructive)
Upper airway obstruction	Pleuritis
	Chest wall disease, including
	Neuromuscular disease (e.g., paralysis)
	Thoracic cage defects (e.g., scoliosis)
	Obesity

pumped through the capillaries (**perfusion-limited**), whereas carbon monoxide (CO) gradually diffuses into the bloodstream, so its transfer is **diffusion-limited**. Oxygen is normally perfusion-limited, but in disease states that impair diffusion (e.g., interstitial pulmonary edema) O_2 transfer becomes diffusion-limited. In PFTs, diffusion of carbon monoxide (DL_{CO}) is often measured to assess the diffusion capacity of the lungs.

Alveolar Gas Exchange

Room air at sea level has a barometric pressure of 760 mm Hg. Air is 21% O_2, and the partial pressure of O_2 (PO_2) is simply this percentage multiplied by the barometric pressure after water vapor pressure has been subtracted. Because the lungs exchange both O_2 and CO_2 through the same airways and alveoli, the oxygen-rich inspired air mixes with the CO_2-rich air already in the alveoli at the end of expiration. Also, the air is humidified with H_2O, taking up space that O_2 cannot occupy (the partial pressure of H_2O [PH_2O] at body temperature is 47 mm Hg). With all these compounding factors, the **alveolar gas equation** determines how much O_2 actually ends up in the alveoli:

$$PAO_2 = (\text{Atmospheric pressure} - PH_2O) \times [FIO_2 - (PACO_2/RER)]$$
$$= (760 - 47) \times [FIO_2 - (PACO_2/RER)]$$

where FIO_2 = fraction of inspired air that is oxygen, and RER (respiratory exchange ratio) = $\dot{V}CO_2/\dot{V}O_2$, which basically says that given normal metabolism, there is a constant ratio between the amount of O_2 consumed and CO_2 produced by the body, which is factored into the amount of CO_2 found in the alveoli. The RER depends on the primary fuel being used for metabolism; if the fuel source is carbohydrate, the RER is 1.0; if the fuel source is fat, the RER is 0.7. The normal diet RER is estimated to be 0.8.

If we know the inspired O_2 content, the PAO_2, and if we simultaneously measure arterial O_2, the PaO_2 (via an arterial blood gas measurement), we can calculate the **alveolar-arterial O_2 gradient**—(A–a)O_2. This gradient, normally less than 15 mm Hg, is used clinically to determine how well a patient is able to deliver oxygen to the bloodstream.

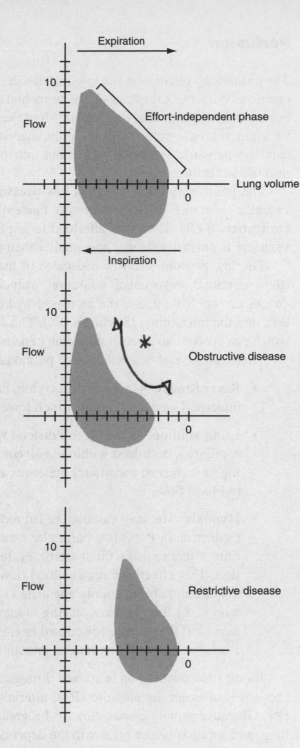

Fig. 11-12. Flow-volume loops.

Table 11-2. Lung volumes in obstructive and restrictive lung states

Disease pattern	FEV_1	FVC	FEV_1/FVC	$FEF_{25-75\%}$	TLC
Normal	—	—	~0.8	—	—
Restrictive	↓	↓	— or ↑↑	↓	↓↓
Obstructive	↓↓	↓	↓↓	↓↓	— or ↑

FEV_1 = forced expiratory volume in 1 second; FVC = forced vital capacity; $FEF_{25-75\%}$ = forced expiratory flow mid-expiratory loop; TLC = total lung capacity.

Perfusion

The pulmonary circulation is a low-resistance circuit, in contrast to the systemic circulation. With the exception of the bronchial arteries, vessels are thin walled and elastic and not particularly muscular. Mixed venous blood (low O_2, high CO_2) from the right ventricle pumps into the pulmonary arterial system, eventually to a large capillary network. The blood then drains into the four pulmonary veins, which dump into the left atrium.

The pulmonary circulation is a **low-pressure system**. Note that the pulmonary vascular resistance (PVR) is normally markedly lower than the **systemic vascular resistance** (SVR). The lower afterload facing the right heart explains why the right ventricle is normally thinner and smaller than the left ventricle (LV).

The low pressure and low resistance of the right side mean that if the LV fails (fluid overload, myocardial infarction, valvulopathy), the pulmonary circulation "backs up" with fluid, and the increased hydrostatic pressure gradient causes fluid leak into the interstitium (Starling's law). This leads to interstitial pulmonary edema, which can evolve into alveolar pulmonary edema, impairing pulmonary gas exchange.

There are several determinants of pulmonary vascular resistance:

- **Recruitment**: As pressures increase, capillary beds that are normally underperfused start filling, which lowers the resistance.

- **Lung volume**: As the alveoli distend with more and more air, the capillaries imbedded within the alveolar walls are pulled taut, resulting in increased transmural pressures and therefore higher resistance to blood flow.

- **Hypoxia**: The lung vasculature is unique in that local hypoxia (reduction in P_{AO_2}) in a particular area of the lung triggers constriction of that region's small arterioles, termed **hypoxic vasoconstriction**. This effectively draws blood flow away from areas of the lung that are not able to supply adequate O_2 (pretty efficient!). In other words, the lung is always trying to maximize ventilation and perfusion ($\dot{V}/\dot{Q}$) matching (discussed later). The mechanism is likely to be a local mediator acting on the smooth muscles of the arterioles.

Blood flow distribution is uneven throughout the lungs, and it depends on three pressures: alveolar air pressure (PA), arterial pressure (Pa), and venous pressure (Pv). Because gravity causes flow to be greater in the dependent portions of the lung, and aeration is also greater in the dependent portions of the lung, the relationship between these three pressures varies from top to bottom in the lung. The lung can therefore be divided into three distinct zones of perfusion (Fig. 11-13):

- **Zone 1**: Alveolar pressure dominates, blood flow is low (PA > Pa > Pv).

- **Zone 2**: Alveolar pressure is in the middle, therefore blood flow is determined by the difference between arterial and alveolar pressures (Pa > PA > Pv).

- **Zone 3**: Alveolar pressure is small compared to both arterial and venous pressures, and blood flow is determined only by arterial and venous pressures (Pa > Pv > PA).

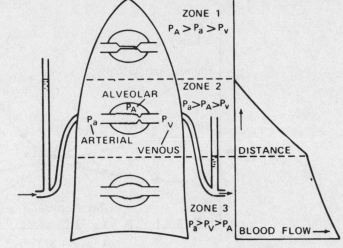

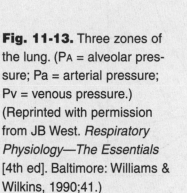

Fig. 11-13. Three zones of the lung. (PA = alveolar pressure; Pa = arterial pressure; Pv = venous pressure.) (Reprinted with permission from JB West. *Respiratory Physiology—The Essentials* [4th ed]. Baltimore: Williams & Wilkins, 1990;41.)

To remember the zones, realize that the relationship Pa > Pv always holds, but where PA fits in determines the appropriate zone. Clinically, this is important because, when using a pulmonary artery (Swan-Ganz) catheter, pulmonary capillary wedge pressure (PCWP) is an accurate estimate of left ventricular end-diastolic pressure (LVEDP) only in lung zone 3.

To measure pulmonary blood flow, the **Fick method** can be used:

$$\dot{Q} = \dot{V}o_2/(Cao_2 - C\bar{v}o_2)$$

where $\dot{Q}$ = blood flow, $\dot{V}o_2$ = O_2 consumption, Cao_2 = arterial O_2 concentration, and $C\bar{v}o_2$ = mixed venous O_2 concentration.

A **shunt** is defined as blood flow through parts of the lung that are not ventilated. There are two important normal physiologic shunts:

- **Bronchial arteries**: These supply the bronchi and pleura with blood but don't participate in gas exchange.

- **Thebesian vessels**: Coronary venous blood that directly dumps into the LV.

Abnormal sources of shunt include the following:

- Anatomic intracardiac shunts (e.g., atrial or ventricular septal defects)

- Intrapleural shunts (atrioventricular malformations, unventilated but perfused lung due to disease)

In the clinical setting, the differential diagnosis of a low Pao_2 (hypox*emia*) found on arterial blood gas (ABG) includes hypox*ia* (low delivery of O_2 to the blood) and a shunt that prevents some blood from reaching the alveoli. These two possibilities can be distinguished by having the patient breathe 100% O_2. With pure hypoxia, the hypoxemia can be corrected, whereas in a significant shunt, the hypoxemia cannot be completely corrected (the shunted blood never sees the 100% O_2).

A clinically important concept is the ratio between ventilation and perfusion in the lung. The lungs are constantly trying to maintain an ideal ratio of $\dot{V}/\dot{Q}$ ($\dot{V}/\dot{Q}$ **matching**). If $\dot{V}/\dot{Q}$ is too high, it implies that blood flow to ventilated lung is inadequate

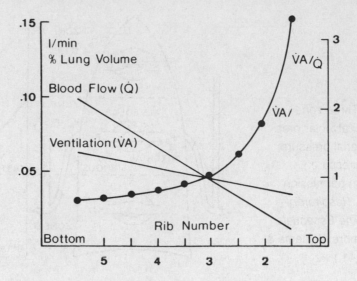

Fig. 11-14. Ventilation and perfusion distribution. (Reprinted with permission from JB West. *Respiratory Physiology—The Essentials* [4th ed]. Baltimore: Williams & Wilkins, 1990;61.)

(increased dead space), whereas a $\dot{V}/\dot{Q}$ that's too low indicates underventilated yet perfused lung (shunt). The $\dot{V}/\dot{Q}$ ratio also depends on the region of lung being examined.

Note that both blood flow and ventilation decrease toward the top of lung, but blood flow changes more rapidly with lung position, resulting in a higher $\dot{V}/\dot{Q}$ ratio at the lung apex and a lower $\dot{V}/\dot{Q}$ at the bases (Fig. 11-14).

Gas Transport and the Bloodstream

Oxygen is transported in two forms: dissolved and bound to hemoglobin. The contribution of dissolved oxygen to total blood oxygen is very small. The relationship of oxygen bound to hemoglobin is described by the O_2 **dissociation curve** (Fig. 11-15). Remember, the P_{O_2} can decrease to approximately 60–70 mm Hg while the O_2 saturation remains greater than 90%.

A right shift in the curve implies that at any given P_{O_2}, less O_2 is bound to hemoglobin, whereas a left shift implies that hemoglobin binds more tightly to O_2 at any given P_{O_2}. A right shift occurs in the setting of increased temperature, increased 2,3-diphosphoglycerate, increased P_{O_2}, or decreased pH (Fig. 11-16).

Essentially, the hemoglobin prefers to unload its O_2 more easily to the peripheral tissues in stressful situations (e.g., exercise, fever, chronic hypoxia).

The concentration of oxygen in the blood can be calculated as follows:

$$O_2 \text{ content of blood} = (1.39 \times Hg \times O_2\text{sat}/100) + 0.003 \times P_{O_2}$$

where Hb = hemoglobin concentration, O_2 sat = percentage of hemoglobin bound to O_2 (as measured by ABG or pulse oximetry), P_{O_2} = O_2 partial pressure (in mm Hg), 0.003 = solubility of O_2 in blood, and 1.39 = a fudge factor.

A **pulse oximeter** is a simple little Band-Aid–like sensor attached to the patient's finger that reads out O_2 saturation and pulse rate. It uses two wavelengths of infrared light, which are modified by the amount of oxygenated or deoxygenated hemoglobin and used to calculate the O_2 saturation.

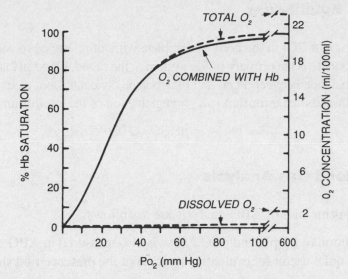

Fig. 11-15. Oxygen dissociation curve. (Reprinted with permission from JB West. *Respiratory Physiology—The Essentials* [4th ed]. Baltimore: Williams & Wilkins, 1990;70.)

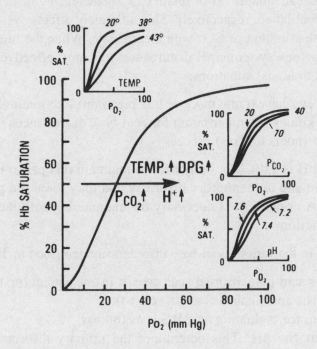

Fig. 11-16. Changes in the oxygen dissociation curve. (Reprinted with permission from JB West. *Respiratory Physiology—The Essentials* [4th ed]. Baltimore: Williams & Wilkins, 1990;73.)

CO_2 is transported in three forms: dissolved, as bicarbonate, and bound to proteins. CO_2 is 20 times more soluble than O_2; therefore, 10% of CO_2 is found in dissolved form. Bicarbonate is formed via the reaction $CO_2 + H_2O \leftrightarrow H_2CO_3 \leftrightarrow H^+ + HCO_3^-$. This reaction is catalyzed by **carbonic anhydrase**.

Hemoglobin bound to O_2 can chelate H^+ ions, thereby allowing more bicarbonate to form from CO_2; in other words, increased O_2 facilitates the blood's CO_2-carrying capacity. This is known as the **Haldane effect**.

Acid-Base Equilibrium

No discussion about CO_2 in the body is complete without reference to acid-base status. Because bicarbonate is the primary buffer system in the blood, blood pH is largely determined by the balance between P_{CO_2} and bicarbonate concentration, as expressed in the **Henderson-Hasselbalch equation** (pK_a = negative log of the equilibrium constant):

$$pH = pK_a + \log[HCO_3^-/0.03(P_{CO_2})]$$

Arterial Blood Gas Analysis

Some general principles of ABG analysis are as follows:

- In addition to the pH and pCO_2, P_{aO_2} is also measured in ABG analysis and is quite useful for evaluating hypoxia or the presence of a shunt.

- Two organ systems account for the maintenance of acid-base status in the body: the **lungs** and the **kidneys**.

- The lungs can breathe off or retain CO_2 by increasing or decreasing minute ventilation, respectively. This ultimately affects systemic pH through the titration of CO_2 with bicarbonate. When the lung is compensating for a systemic pH disturbance, it is most effective in acute (minutes to hours) situations.

- The kidneys can excrete more or less bicarbonate to maintain body pH. The kidney's compensation for acid-base disturbances is largely a chronic (hours to days) process.

- Normal pH is 7.40. The body tries to maintain this pH in the face of metabolic and or respiratory disorders that may force the pH from normal. A normal pH is necessary for maintaining cellular metabolic functions.

- Changes in the various acid-base disorders are described in Table 11-3.

Simultaneous acid-base disorders can coexist in one patient (up to three because respiratory acidosis and alkalosis cannot coexist).

The algorithm for evaluating an ABG is as follows:

First, **look at the pH**: This determines the primary disorder (<7.40 means acidemia, >7.40 means alkalemia).

Second, **look at the CO_2**: Is the primary disorder respiratory? For respiratory acidosis, P_{aCO_2} >40 because CO_2 is retained; for respiratory alkalosis, P_{aCO_2} <40 because CO_2 is blown off. Otherwise, the primary process is metabolic. A pH of 7.40 in the presence of an abnormal CO_2 or bicarbonate implies multiple acid-base disorders because the body cannot completely compensate and bring pH back to normal.

Acute respiratory acidosis can be caused by the following:

- Obstruction

- Aspiration

- Central nervous system (CNS) injury

Table 11-3. Arterial blood gas analysis in acid-base disorders

Condition	pH	P_{CO_2} (mm Hg)	HCO_3^- (mmol)
Normal	7.40 (7.38–7.42)	40 (35–45)	24 (22–26)
Respiratory acidosis	<7.40	>40	Compensated
Metabolic acidosis	<7.40	Compensated	<24
Respiratory alkalosis	>7.40	<40	Compensated
Metabolic alkalosis	>7.40	Compensated	>24

- Narcotic overdose

- Suffocation

Chronic respiratory acidosis may be a result of COPD or chronic lung disease. Hyperventilation leads to **respiratory alkalosis**.

Third, **look at the anion gap** (AG): $AG = Na^+ - (Cl^- + HCO_3^-)$. Normal anion gap is less than 12. Increased anion gap implies an **anion gap metabolic acidosis**.

The way to remember causes of metabolic acidosis with an anion gap is with the mnemonic MUDPILES:

Methanol

Uremia

Diabetic ketoacidosis

Para-aldehyde

Intoxication (ethanol)

Lactate (tissue hypoxia)

Ethylene glycol (antifreeze)

Salicylates (aspirin)

If there's no increased anion gap in the presence of metabolic acidosis, then it's a **nongap metabolic acidosis**. It can be caused by

- Diarrhea (lost HCO_3^-)

- Overzealous administration of normal saline (which is hyper-chloremic and displaces HCO_3^-)

- Renal tubular acidosis

Finally, **metabolic alkalosis** may be caused by

- Vomiting (lost H^+)

- Overzealous bicarbonate administration

- Contraction alkalosis (with diuresis, distal tubule tries to compensate for lost volume by actively reabsorbing excreted Na^+ via an Na^+/H^+ exchanger, so H^+ is lost in the urine)

These determinations are made frequently on the wards, especially in the intensive care unit (ICU), and they factor into treatment decisions, so it's a real help to have a systematic approach to ABG analysis.

Physiologic Response to Exercise, Stress, and High-Altitude Physiology

Minute ventilation increases from 4–6 liters/minute at rest up to 100 liters/minute at maximal exertion on exercise, an increase of nearly 20 times! As a result, $Paco_2$ usually decreases slightly, Pao_2 stays about the same, and pH stays the same or falls slightly from anaerobic lactate production.

With increased cardiac output, there is decreased transit time for the blood passing through the pulmonary circulation. Unless pulmonary disease is present, this shortened transit time is still adequate for maximal oxygenation.

Regulation of Respiratory Function

Control of Respiration

There are both local and central controls of respiration:

- **Local**: Hypoxia promotes pulmonary vasoconstriction to optimize the $\dot{V}/\dot{Q}$ ratio.

- **Central**: The brain stem contains the respiratory centers, where respiratory drive is thought to originate, specifically in the **reticular formation** of the medulla. The pneumotaxic center in the **pons** is thought to fine-tune the respiratory rate and tidal volume. It's easy to induce voluntary hyperventilation but much harder to induce voluntary hypoventilation (try holding your breath as long as possible!) because central stimuli to breathe related to hypercarbia and hypoxia take over.

Sensors of Respiration

There are both peripheral and central sensors of respiration:

- **Peripheral chemoreceptors**: The carotid body (as opposed to the carotid sinus, which senses carotid artery pressure) and the aortic body sense Pao_2 and $Paco_2$, leading to increased minute ventilation with hypoxemia, and to a lesser extent, in response to hypercarbia and acidemia. Overall, central chemoreceptors respond more to $Paco_2$, whereas peripheral chemoreceptors respond more to Pao_2.

- **Central chemoreceptors**: These are located in the medulla, surrounded by cerebrospinal fluid (CSF), and highly sensitive to H^+ concentration (i.e., pH). Increased blood CO_2 allows CO_2 to cross the blood-brain barrier (via diffusion), lowering CSF pH as the CO_2 is converted to H^+ and HCO_3. This increased H^+ concentration is sensed at the central chemoreceptors, which stimulate the drive to breathe. With chronic hypercarbia, as seen in COPD, this central chemoreceptor can shift its "set point" so that increased respiratory drive occurs at higher blood CO_2 concentrations.

Pulmonary Mechanoreceptors

- **Stretch receptors**: Located in smooth muscle, stretch receptors respond to lung parenchymal distention. The signal travels via the vagus (X) nerve. Inflation leads to decreased respiratory rate and increased expiratory time (the Hering-Breuer reflex).

- **Irritant receptors**: Stimulated by noxious substances (e.g., smoke, gases, dust, cold air). These impulses also travel via the vagus nerve. They cause bronchoconstriction and hyperpnea.

- **J-receptors** (juxtacapillary): Stimulated by pulmonary capillary engorgement, leading to rapid, shallow breathing. They are likely responsible in large part for the sensation of dyspnea in CHF and pulmonary edema patients.

Integrated Responses

- **CO_2**: Normally, Pa_{CO_2} is the most important factor in determining minute ventilation. Reducing Pa_{CO_2} below normal effectively diminishes the drive to breathe. Sleep, age, chronic hypercapnia, and drugs (e.g., opiates, barbiturates) suppress the CNS response to Pa_{CO_2}.

- **O_2**: Pa_{O_2} can be reduced markedly (down to ~50 mm Hg) without stimulating the respiratory drive. The exception is in chronic CO_2 retention (e.g., COPD). As discussed earlier, the central CO_2 (more accurately H^+) chemoreceptors of these patients have been reset to higher CO_2 levels, so that Pa_{O_2} becomes their primary stimulus to breathe. This is why COPD patients on high oxygen concentrations can often become apneic.

- **pH**: Can be a strong stimulus to breathe, as seen in diabetic ketoacidosis patients who undergo Cheyne-Stokes breathing (rapid, deep breaths followed by periods of apnea).

Additional Lung Functions

The lung does much more than exchange gases. Some other functions include the following:

- **Immune**: protection against inhaled toxins and pathogens; IgA secretion; protection by pulmonary alveolar macrophages

- **Fibrinolytic system**: clot lysis

- **Metabolic and synthetic function**:

    Angiotensin-converting enzyme: converts angiotensin I to angiotensin II, the active form

    Inactivates bradykinin, serotonin, prostaglandin E, prostaglandin F, norepinephrine, and possibly histamine

    Synthesis of factor VIII

    Synthesis of surfactant

- **Filter**: filters debris from venous return and prevents CNS and end-organ embolic events

- **Blood reservoir**: as a low-resistance circuit, the pulmonary circulation acts as a blood reservoir

Disorders of the Upper Respiratory Tract

Otitis Externa

Otitis externa (OE) is infection of the external auditory canal. OE usually begins as a pustule or folliculitis. Common organisms include skin flora, including *Staphylococcus* and *Streptococcus sp*. OE is also associated with hot tubs, where it is usually caused by *Pseudomonas*.

Diabetics are at risk for **malignant otitis**, an aggressive form due to *Pseudomonas*. If not treated early, malignant otitis can rapidly invade the surrounding bone, soft tissue, and even brain, leading to death.

Signs & Symptoms

Ear pain, which can be severe, and itching.

Diagnosis

Otoscopic examination.

Treatment

Topical antibiotics if there is no associated cellulitis; systemic antibiotics (e.g., dicloxacillin, erythromycin) are required if there is. Malignant otitis requires surgical debridement.

Otitis Media

Otitis media (OM) is an infection of the middle ear. This is the pediatrician's bread and butter, but it is occasionally seen in adults. It is often caused by common upper respiratory tract infection (URI) pathogens, with plugging of the eustachian canals, leading to engorgement in the middle ear. Preschoolers are at greatest risk for OM because the anatomy of the eustachian tube is more horizontal, which prevents drainage.

Common organisms include *Streptococcus pneumoniae*, *Haemophilus influenzae*, *Moraxella catarrhalis*, and viruses. Complications include mastoiditis, meningitis, and brain abscess. Chronic OM can cause tympanic membrane (TM) scarring and diminished hearing.

Signs & Symptoms

Ear pain, fever, vertigo, and tinnitus. In young kids, there may not be localizing symptoms, just irritability.

Diagnosis

Otoscopic examination shows an inflamed TM. Decreased mobility of the TM with air insufflation is the most sensitive and specific test.

Treatment

Antibiotics. Good choices are amoxicillin or trimethoprim-sulfamethoxazole (TMP/SMX). Kids with recurrent OM can have drainage tubes placed to open the eustachian tubes.

Rhinitis

Rhinitis is a very common disorder that involves inflammation or infection of the nasal cavity. The most common pathogens are viral and may be associated with pharyngitis or conjunctivitis. Rhinitis can also be caused by hypersensitivity states, such as allergic rhinitis (hay fever), which can predispose patients to developing sinusitis.

Signs & Symptoms

Itchy, red nose with watery discharge. Patients with allergic rhinitis often have a horizontal skin crease at the bridge of the nose caused by repeated rubbing of the nose. With trauma or CNS surgery, a runny nose may indicate a CSF leak, not nasal inflammation.

Diagnosis

Wet preparation of nasal secretions shows eosinophils in allergic rhinitis but not in infectious rhinitis. It is rarely performed.

Treatment

Because of the viral etiology, infectious rhinitis should not be treated with antibiotics. Patients may get subjective relief with symptomatic cold medications, such as decongestants and antihistamines.

Sinusitis

Infection of the normally air-filled sinuses in the skull is called sinusitis. Common organisms include *S. pneumoniae* and *H. influenzae*. Anaerobes are less common. Complications include meningitis, brain abscess, and subdural empyema.

Signs & Symptoms

Headache, stuffiness, pain, and pus in the turbinates.

Diagnosis

Transillumination of the sinuses shows opacity. Sinus X-rays or computed tomography (CT) scan show opacification and air-fluid levels.

Treatment

Antibiotics, such as amoxicillin or TMP/SMX, and nasal decongestants.

Stomatitis

Stomatitis is inflammation of the mouth, and it can have a variety of etiologies. **Thrush** is caused by *Candida* and is seen in infants, immunocompromised patients (e.g., cancer, AIDS), and patients receiving broad-spectrum antibiotics. **Aphthous stomatitis** (canker sores) are painful, discrete, flat ulcers. These sores are benign and are treated symptomatically. **Herpes simplex virus (HSV-1)** causes lesions on the vermilion border of the lips and oral mucosa. It is treated with acyclovir. Finally, **vitamin deficiencies** may cause stomatitis and angular cheilosis.

Pharyngitis

Pharyngitis, or "sore throat," is an extremely common disease and is often caused by respiratory viruses (e.g., rhinovirus, influenza, parainfluenza, Epstein-Barr virus [EBV]) or *Streptococcus pyogenes*, with most cases occurring in winter. Nonrespiratory causes of sore throat are very uncommon, including atypical angina, dissecting aortic aneurysm, and infectious thyroiditis.

Signs & Symptoms

Usually associated with cold symptoms: rhinorrhea, fever, myalgias, and cough. EBV may cause infectious mononucleosis, with enlarged lymph nodes and pharyngeal erythema.

Diagnosis

Based on clinical symptoms. *Streptococcus* must be ruled out because of the potential complications (rheumatic fever). Rapid *Streptococcus* antigen test kits are quickly replacing the throat culture. The monospot test for EBV antibodies is also available.

Treatment

Symptomatic. Strep throat responds to penicillin (or erythromycin if patient is allergic to penicillin).

Epiglottitis

Epiglottitis is a potential emergency usually seen in young children and is caused by *H. influenzae*. Infection of the epiglottis leads to upper airway obstruction, stridor, and potentially death. Young children in contact with known cases should receive rifampin prophylaxis.

Signs & Symptoms

Sore throat with difficulty swallowing, copious secretions, severe throat pain, and stridor. These patients characteristically lean forward to prevent complete obstruction of the epiglottis.

Diagnosis

Examination (patient is kept sitting up to minimize laryngospasm), lateral X-rays of the neck, and indirect laryngoscopy.

Treatment

Antibiotics. Airway management (intubation) if necessary. This disease has become exceedingly rare thanks to widespread *H. influenzae* vaccinations.

Disorders of the Lower Respiratory Tract

Infectious Bronchiolitis

Infectious bronchiolitis is most often seen in young children and is probably the most common reason for admission to a pediatrics ward. It is often seen in winter months and must be differentiated from pneumonia or URI. The most common causative pathogen is respiratory syncytial virus (RSV), but it is also caused by parainfluenza, influenza, and adenovirus. It is usually seen in 6 month olds to 3 year olds: At that size, the bronchioles are more likely to obstruct with secretions when infected. There is an increased rate of infection in ex-preemies, particularly those with bronchopulmonary dysplasia (discussed later).

Signs & Symptoms

Cough, fever, irritability, and audible wheezes.

Diagnosis

Wheezes on examination; CXR shows hyperinflation, air bronchograms, and patchy, migrating atelectasis, with possible consolidation.

Treatment

Bronchodilators, supplemental O_2, and chest therapy to mobilize secretions. Antibiotics are not needed. Intubation with mechanical ventilation is used in severe cases, and ribavirin may be beneficial.

Pneumonia

Pneumonia is a huge part of internal medicine, accounting for about 10% of adult medicine admissions. It is caused by pathogens (viruses, rickettsiae, mycoplasmas, chlamydiae, bacteria, protozoa, fungi, parasites) entering the lung by either

(1) inhalation of aerosolized particles, (2) aspiration of oropharyngeal secretions—the most common cause, (3) hematogenous spread, or (4) local spread of infection.

Signs & Symptoms

History is crucial. Determine whether the pneumonia is community acquired or nosocomial, the age group, possible unique exposures, and time course. Viral, pneumococcal, and mycoplasmal pneumonia are usually acute (hours to days), whereas tuberculosis (TB), anaerobes, and fungi take longer to evolve. A URI prodrome suggests mycoplasma or viral pneumonia. Diarrhea is associated with *Legionella*.

Common symptoms include cough, fever, tachypnea, tachycardia, and sometimes pleuritic pain. Respiratory distress (increased tachypnea, use of accessory muscles, cyanosis) indicates severe disease. Chest examination shows signs of consolidation: rales, bronchial breath sounds, or decreased breath sounds if pleural effusion is present. Egophony and tactile fremitus may be elicited.

Diagnosis

CXR is warranted. CXR in *Mycoplasma* pneumonia classically looks much worse than the patient appears clinically, with significant, bilateral patchy opacities. *Pneumocystis carinii* infection is the opposite: The CXR often looks better than the patient. Realize that a "negative" CXR does not rule out pneumonia because radiographic signs may lag behind the infection by many hours. Bacterial pneumonia classically demonstrates lobar consolidation. Chronic lung disease patients often show no radiographic signs of pneumonia. Interstitial involvement may suggest a viral etiology. TB can look like absolutely anything on CXR but is classically seen as an upper lung nodule or tiny disseminated (miliary) nodules. Pleural effusion is common.

On laboratory tests, the CBC shows an elevated WBC with left shift. Sputum smear and culture are an essential part of the diagnosis and management. A sputum specimen is considered adequate if it has (1) none to few epithelial cells and (2) polymorphonuclear neutrophils (PMNs).

Treatment

The general treatment principle for suspected pneumonia is initial broad empiric treatment based on a clinical judgment about the likely organism. Antibiotics are then tailored to the organism, as determined from the sputum. *Mycoplasma* is usually treated on an outpatient basis, but the majority of pneumonia patients require hospitalization. Issues of importance include oxygenation status (provide supplemental O_2), systemic complications (sepsis), and management of secretions.

Persistent infection suggests antibiotic resistance, whereas recurrent infections in the same part of the lung suggest **postobstructive pneumonia**. **Empyema** is simply pus that gets into the pleural cavity. Pleural effusion in a febrile patient must be examined via thoracentesis. Pneumococcal and influenza pneumonia can be prevented in susceptible patients (e.g., immunocompromised, postsplenectomy, elderly) with vaccination.

Tuberculosis

The causative organism is *Mycobacterium tuberculosis*, an acid-fast bacillus. TB is intertwined with history, having claimed the lives of such figures as Frederic Chopin, John Keats, and Robert Louis Stevenson. Until the advent of antibiotics, patients were sent to sanitoriums, and as recently as 40 years ago, patients were subjected to such desperate measures as pleuroplasty, where the chest and lung were permanently surgically collapsed in an effort to starve the organisms of oxygen. Today, TB is on an upsurge after decades of control in the United States, mainly because of immigration from endemic parts of the world and the association of TB with AIDS.

- **Primary infection**: Results from an exposure to an actively contagious host, spread via aerosolized particles. It is usually self-limited, with the only manifestation being a conversion to positive purified protein derivative (PPD). Sometimes primary infection leads to respiratory symptoms (cough, fever), and CXR may show patchy infiltrates. Hematogenous dissemination can seed all over the body, leading to sites that can become sources of latent reactivation. About 5–15% of infections lead to active disease. Risk factors include immunosuppression, older age, infancy, diabetes, and other preexisting parenchymal lung disease. Progressive primary TB occurs when the disease progresses at an early stage, often leading to hematogenous spread, or **miliary TB**, in which the lung is full of many tiny TB foci, resembling millet seeds.

- **Reactivation** is the most common presenting form of the disease. After the bugs have remained dormant in some part of the body, the patient begins to experience fever, night sweats, and hemoptysis. CXR shows cavitary lesions with consolidation classically in the posterior segment of the upper lobes or in the superior segments of the lower lobes.

- **Extrapulmonary TB**: Important entities include genitourinary TB, bone and arthritic TB, and meningeal TB. HIV patients often present with disseminated TB, and patients are often PPD-nonreactive (controls are also unreactive, due to overall anergy).

Diagnosis

The diagnosis relies on (1) history, (2) PPD (may be false-positive in those who received bacillus Calmette-Guérin [**BCG**] vaccination, an ineffective vaccine), (3) positive CXR, and (4) sputum samples for smear and culture (culture takes 4–6 weeks). With high clinical suspicion, bronchoscopy is indicated if the sputum smears are negative. Smears reveal acid-fast bacilli (**red snappers**).

Treatment

Because of public health concerns, the first step is **respiratory isolation** for patients with active disease. Given the possibility of resistant strains, drug therapy uses multiple drug regimens. The standard full-course treatment is **four-drug therapy**: **isoniazid** (INH), **rifampin**, **ethambutol**, and **pyrazinamide** for 2 months, and then only isoniazid and rifampin for another 4 months, for a total of 6 months of treatment. Treatment may be longer if resistant strains are suspected.

Household and intimate contacts of actively infected patients must be treated with isoniazid prophylaxis for 6–12 months (or full treatment if they also have disease).

Obstructive Lung Disease

This class of respiratory disease encompasses bronchitis and emphysema (collectively called COPD), asthma, cystic fibrosis (CF), and bronchiectasis. These diseases are characterized by increased airway resistance, which is the result of several pathologic mechanisms: bronchiolar smooth muscle constriction (asthma and COPD), inflammation (bronchiectasis, asthma, and COPD), loss of elastic recoil (COPD), or mucus plugs (CF). The increased resistance and obstruction of the airways leads to decreased peak expiratory flow rates, decreased flow volumes, air trapping, and increased TLC, RV, and FRC. The hyperinflation that results also helps to keep the overly collapsible airways open, a physiologic compensatory mechanism. The altered mechanics and parenchyma results in $\dot{V}/\dot{Q}$ mismatch and decreased oxygenation. The impaired ventilation leads to CO_2 retention. Eventually, the CO_2 set point in the medulla shifts to accept higher baseline Pa_{CO_2} values. This set point shift may be so prominent as to blunt the respiratory drive response to hypercapnia. Therefore, in many COPD patients, Pa_{O_2} has become their primary trigger to breathe. This can be seen when COPD patients are placed on supplemental oxygen, which suppresses their drive to breathe, leading to hypopnea or apnea.

Asthma

Asthma is characterized by airway obstruction that results from hyperreactivity of the inflammatory response of the airways, leading to bronchospasm. The disease is subdivided into several categories, listed in Table 11-4. The classification is important in educating the patient about avoiding triggering substances.

Signs & Symptoms

Intermittent dyspnea, wheezing, and sometimes dry cough may be the only symptoms. Symptoms are often worse at night, possibly due to circadian variations. Specific triggers can often be identified (e.g., exercise, cold, URI).

Diagnosis

CXR shows hyperinflation when symptomatic; PFTs show obstruction with significant bronchodilator response. Alternatively, the asthma may be triggered by administering histamine, cold air, or methacholine.

Treatment

Inhalers, including beta-agonists and anticholinergics for smooth muscle hyperreactivity, cromolyn for mast cell stabilization, and steroids for inflammation. Methylxanthines (theophylline, aminophylline) are bronchodilators with an uncer-

Table 11-4. Categories of asthma

Classification	Etiology
Extrinsic	External allergens leading to mast cell degranulation
Intrinsic	Unknown
Exercise or humidity induced	Mediator release triggered by alterations in airway temperature
Adult onset	Unknown
Aspirin sensitive	Aspirin and nonsteroidal anti-inflammatory drugs
Occupational	Various triggers (e.g., dust)
Allergic aspergillosis	Hypersensitivity to *Aspergillus*

tain mechanism of action; use is controversial given potential toxicity (anxiety, tremor, arrhythmias, seizures). Avoidance of triggers is crucial, and in severe cases, systematic desensitization (allergy shots) to stimulants may be beneficial.

Status asthmaticus is an acute, severe asthma attack that is unresponsive to routine therapy. It is a medical emergency. Pao_2 progressively falls, and $Paco_2$ initially falls with hyperventilation but then gradually rises with impaired ventilation. Intubation may be necessary, along with aggressive bronchodilator and steroid treatment.

Chronic Obstructive Pulmonary Disease

COPD is a progressive disease that results in airway obstruction, dyspnea, and hypoventilation. The tempo of the disease is one of slow progression, often punctuated by acute exacerbations requiring hospitalization. Classically, this is a disease of middle-aged to elderly smokers. Worsening disease is accompanied by increased hypoventilation, increased pulmonary vascular resistance (a result of hypoxic vasoconstriction leading to vascular remodeling and parenchymal tissue destruction) leading to right heart failure, and often acute respiratory failure. Classically, COPD has been subclassified as emphysema (thin, cachectic patients—**pink puffers**) or chronic bronchitis (edematous, cyanotic patients— **blue bloaters**). With the current understanding, the disease is thought to encompass three overlapping components: emphysema, chronic bronchitis, and reactive airways disease (RAD). A particular patient has some combination of the three entities (Fig. 11-17).

- **Emphysema**: Destruction of the alveolar walls, possibly by overactive proteases, leads to enlargement of the air spaces. There is a loss of elastic recoil and increased compliance. Cigarette smoke is thought to trigger this cascade by increasing the neutrophil and macrophage inflammatory response. Laboratory findings peculiar to emphysema include hyperlucency on CXR that corresponds to bullae and increased airways space, attenuation of pulmonary vasculature secondary to the destructive process, and decreased DL_{CO} on PFTs, a result of destruction of pulmonary capillaries.

- **Chronic bronchitis**: Persistent cough with sputum production. Cigarette smoke is the major cause of disease, leading to bronchospasm, mucus

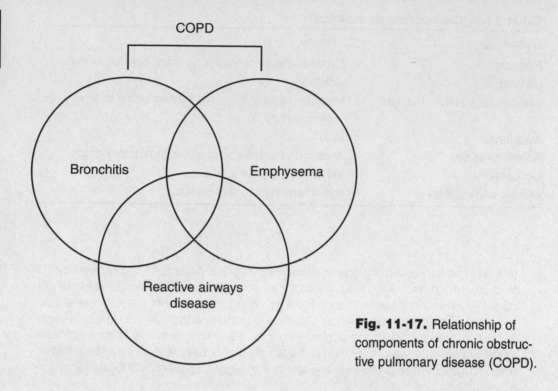

Fig. 11-17. Relationship of components of chronic obstructive pulmonary disease (COPD).

plugging, and associated emphysema. Chronic bacterial colonization occurs, commonly with *S. pneumoniae*, *H. influenzae*, and *Moraxella*.

- **RAD**: Small airways are irritated, with smooth muscle hyperreactivity and eventual fibrosis leading to obstruction.

COPD exacerbations are usually triggered by an infection, as the altered airway immunoprotection (cough, impaired clearance of secretions, hypoxia) leads to colonization of the airways by pathogens.

Signs & Symptoms

Presenting symptoms include dyspnea on exertion, wheezing, and productive cough. Tobacco use is often associated.

Diagnosis

Examination may demonstrate wheezing. CXR shows hyperinflation (increased anteroposterior diameter, flattened diaphragm, increased diaphragmatic excursion), loss of pulmonary vasculature, and perhaps an enlarged right heart. In severe disease, bullae (large air spaces left after destruction of the lung parenchyma) may be seen. Electrocardiography (ECG) and echocardiography may show right heart enlargement, consistent with increased pulmonary artery pressures. PFTs are characteristic. Bronchodilator response is usually modest.

Treatment

The armamentarium is similar to that for asthma: beta-agonists, anticholinergics, steroids, cromolyn, and methylxanthines. Patients with documented chronic hypoxemia (Pao_2 <55 mm Hg) require home supplemental oxygen. In COPD exacerbations, empiric antibiotic treatment is often initiated. Smoking cessation is an obvious preventative measure.

Bronchiectasis

Bronchiectasis is widening of the bronchi with loss of structural integrity, usually the result of severe or recurrent bouts of infection, especially severe necrotizing infection. Predisposing factors include immune deficiency states, CF, and defective ciliary motility (e.g., Kartagener's, Young's syndromes). Chronic colonization usually occurs, with *S. pneumoniae*, *Pseudomonas*, *H. influenzae*, *Staphylococcus*, or atypical mycobacteria.

Signs & Symptoms

Persistent cough, sometimes hemoptysis and foul-smelling sputum. Examination may show cyanosis, clubbing, and crackles over the affected lung area. CXR may be unremarkable or may show linear atelectasis and bronchial thickening. Patients may present with massive hemoptysis.

Diagnosis

Made with CT scan, demonstrating widened, thickened bronchi. PFTs are consistent with obstructive disease, although a restrictive component may also be present.

Treatment

Antibiotics are used for acute exacerbations and sometimes prophylactically. Chest physical therapy (vigorous percussion) is also helpful.

Cystic Fibrosis

The CF gene has been localized to the long arm of chromosome 7, occurring in about 1 in 2,500 live births in Caucasians. Mutations in a **chloride transporter** gene result in defective exocrine gland secretory function. This results in thick mucus plugs in the respiratory and gastrointestinal (GI) tracts, impaired mucociliary transport, recurrent infections, bronchiectasis, and inflammation. *Staphylococcus aureus* in childhood and *Pseudomonas aeruginosa* (and to a lesser extent *H. influenzae* or *Pseudomonas cepacia*) in adulthood colonize the respiratory tract, leading to recurrent infection. The resultant inflammation and damage leads to progressive respiratory failure.

Signs & Symptoms

CF usually presents in childhood with a broad range of symptoms, from recurrent respiratory infection and irritation, to GI symptoms (e.g., steatorrhea, constipation, pancreatic insufficiency) from mucus plugs.

Diagnosis

Made with a sweat chloride test, which is elevated.

Supportive care throughout childhood has improved mean survival to 29 years. Antibiotics for infections, frequent pulmonary toilet, and bronchodilators are used. Newer approaches include gene therapy to introduce the CF gene into the respiratory epithelial cells and treating with viscosity-reducing substances. Advanced disease necessitates evaluation for lung transplantation.

α_1-Antitrypsin Deficiency

α_1-Antitrypsin deficiency is an autosomal inherited disorder characterized by destruction of elastic components in the lung as well as the liver. The normal gene for α_1-antitrypsin is the PiM, the mutant gene is PiZ; whereas heterozygotes (MZ) exhibit attenuated disease. The loss of this inhibitory enzyme leads to destruction of lung parenchyma and emphysematous changes. The approach to treatment is similar to that for emphysema.

Chronic Bronchiolitis

Chronic bronchiolitis is an inflammation of the small airways leading to fibrosis. Two general processes are seen: (1) Inflammation and scarring leads to luminal narrowing, producing an obstructive disease process, such as constrictive bronchiolitis, and (2) the inflamed small airways plug up, and the inflammation spreads into adjacent parenchyma, resulting in **bronchiolitis obliterans with organizing pneumonia (BOOP)**. BOOP shows parenchymal consolidation on CXR and a restrictive pattern on PFTs. Bronchiolitis is a pulmonary end point of several disease processes, including recurrent or severe infection, toxin inhalation, and connective tissue disease (particularly rheumatoid arthritis). Chronic rejection in lung transplantation may result in BOOP, and graft-versus-host disease in bone marrow transplant patients is also a cause. Treatment is with bronchodilators. Recurrent infections are treated with antibiotics and pulmonary toilet.

Diffuse Parenchymal Lung Disease

These diseases include alveolar and interstitial disorders and the pneumoconioses, and the etiology of many of these diseases remains obscure. The pathologic mechanism may be either (1) direct toxicity (gases, radiation), (2) damage secondary to an inflammatory response, or (3) immune-mediated injury (e.g., Ag-Ab complex deposition, complement activation). Some of the more common ones are:

- **Pneumoconioses**: Inhalation of substances as a result of occupational or environmental exposure. Asbestos exposure can cause pulmonary fibrosis but is also associated with bronchogenic carcinoma and malignant mesothelioma. Coal worker's pneumoconiosis ("black lung") and silicosis are also seen. Acute silicosis increases the risk of TB infection.

- **Hypersensitivity pneumonitis**: An abnormal sensitivity to an extrinsic allergen leads to an allergic alveolitis. Reticulonodular infiltrates are seen on CXR. Resolution occurs with removal of the offending agent. **Farmer's lung** is hypersensitivity to *Actinomyces*, found in moldy hay.

- **Sarcoidosis**: An enigmatic disease characterized pathologically by noncaseating, noninfectious granulomas. The disease predominantly affects the lung but can also involve the liver, spleen, lymph nodes, joints, muscles, skin, eyes, and CNS. Classically, the disease presents in the third or fourth decade of life in women more than men, in African-Americans more frequently than others. Hypercalcemia and hypercalcuria may be present.

- **Idiopathic pulmonary fibrosis (IPF)**: A diagnosis of exclusion. Patients are usually middle-aged and present with progressive dyspnea. The disease course can be rapid, culminating in death within months, or progress more slowly. Treatment usually results in a moderate response to steroids, and lung transplantation is the definitive therapy in severe disease. In untreated patients, death usually occurs within 2 years. IPF is also known as usual interstitial pneumonitis, to differentiate it from desquamative interstitial pneumonitis (DIP; see below).

- **DIP**: DIP is interstitial pneumonitis in which the primary pathology involves mononuclear aggregation in the alveoli, presumably from a desquamation process. The cause is unknown, and many patients respond to steroids. The current belief is that DIP may be an early stage of IPF rather than a distinct disease entity.

- **Connective tissue disease**: Many of the collagen-vascular diseases have pulmonary manifestations. Most commonly, a chronic interstitial fibrosis process (e.g., IPF) is seen. Pulmonary manifestations of **rheumatoid arthritis** include pleurisy, interstitial lung disease, intrapulmonary nodules, Caplan's syndrome (an association between rheumatoid nodules with coal worker's pneumoconiosis), pulmonary hypertension, bronchiolitis obliterans, and upper airway obstruction. In systemic lupus erythematosus (SLE), the most common pulmonary manifestation is pleuritis with or without effusion. In Sjögren's syndrome, patients may have lymphocytic interstitial pneumonitis and bronchiolitis obliterans.

Signs & Symptoms

Progressive dyspnea, cough with or without sputum, fever, occasionally hemoptysis, and systemic symptoms if the disease is part of a systemic disease (e.g., SLE). It is critical to elicit the patient's work history, home situation, medication history, and medical history to document possible exposures and associated risks. The onset is usually insidious.

Diagnosis

Lung examination reveals dry crackles, often bibasilar. Look for systemic signs of disease: skin changes, arthropathy, ocular changes. CXR is normal in more than 10% of patients. The classic appearance is diffuse reticulonodular opacities, often with upper lung zone predominance. Hilar lymphadenopathy, pleural involvement, increased lung volumes, calcifications, or even pneumothorax may be evident, depending on the particular disease. CT scan is extremely informative in characterizing the process. PFTs often demonstrate a restrictive pattern with reduced compliance (the lungs become more snappy with the parenchymal disease). DL_{CO} may be decreased because of the loss of air exchange surface area and $\dot{V}/\dot{Q}$ mismatch. Some diseases (e.g., sarcoidosis, hypersensitivity pneumonitis, eosinophilic lung disease) can also show a superimposed obstructive process with airway involvement. Bronchoscopy is performed to rule out infection or malignancy and to make a diagnosis. Lung biopsy (fiberoptic bronchoscopy, thoracoscopy, or open lung biopsy) usually makes the diagnosis.

Diffuse Alveolar Hemorrhage

Diffuse alveolar hemorrhage is bleeding into the alveolar airspace secondary to damage to the pulmonary capillary epithelium. Causes include the following:

- Immune-mediated damage: Goodpasture's syndrome, SLE, vasculitides

- Direct chemical- or radiation-induced damage

- Physical trauma (contusion)

- Coagulopathy

- Increased capillary pressure (e.g., CHF, mitral stenosis)

Presentation includes hemoptysis, dyspnea, and abnormal CXR with diffuse, patchy opacities. Diagnosis is made with bronchoscopy, which demonstrates frank bleeding that persists. The treatment involves correcting the underlying disorder and usually steroids.

Eosinophilic Pneumonias

The eosinophilic pneumonias are as follows:

- **Acute eosinophilic pneumonia**: due to an inhaled antigen.

- **Löffler's**: an ephemeral form of eosinophilic pneumonia.

- **Churg-Strauss**: a systemic eosinophilic disease, with a polyarteritis picture in which small- to medium-sized vessels are affected. Asthma and rhinitis are seen.

- **Pulmonary eosinophilic granuloma** (histiocytosis X): a disease with a benign course and diffuse reticulonodular pattern on CXR.

Signs and symptoms include dyspnea, fever, night sweats, and weight loss. Asthma occurs concomitantly in 50% of cases. CXR shows peripheral interstitial opacification—the "photographic negative" of pulmonary edema (this is pathognomonic). CBC shows eosinophilia, high erythrocyte sedimentation rate, and anemia. Bronchoalveolar lavage shows eosinophils. Treatment is with steroids, often long term.

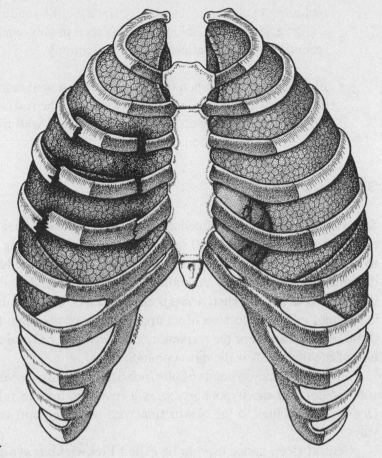

Fig. 11-18. Flail chest.

Disorders in the Control of Breathing

This is a class of diseases in which either a peripheral (mechanical) or central mechanism (CNS) causes a decrease in the ability to ventilate properly. It includes the following:

- **Neurologic disease**: Lesions in the brain stem can result in abnormal breathing patterns, including neurogenic hyperventilation, apneustic breathing (sustained pauses in the inspiratory part of the respiratory cycle), and Cheyne-Stokes breathing (regular cycles of rapid breathing separated by periods of apnea). Central sleep apnea can also occur (described later).

- **Neuromuscular disease**: Ineffective use of the diaphragm or accessory muscles of breathing. Causes include stroke, inflammatory neuropathies, amyotrophic lateral sclerosis, myasthenia gravis, and polio. On examination, the abdominal muscles can be seen to involute rather than expand during inspiration (paradoxical motion). Treatment may require mechanical ventilation.

- **Bellows dysfunction**: Includes diaphragmatic disease and chest wall anatomic defects that can impair proper chest wall bellows motion, including kyphoscoliosis, obesity (fat acts like sandbags on the chest wall), respiratory muscle fatigue (as seen in chronically ill patients or recently extubated patients), and thoracotomy.

- **Flail chest** occurs when trauma to the chest wall results in a part of the chest wall that moves freely away from the rest of the chest wall (Fig. 11-18). As a result, that part of the chest wall moves paradoxically during respiration.

Sleep Apnea

Sleep apnea syndrome is defined as repeated episodes of apnea (i.e., no air flow in the nose and mouth for at least 10 seconds) and hypopnea during sleep. Severe obstructive sleep apnea can result in hundreds of such episodes a night. The sequelae include daytime fatigue, irritability, and falling asleep at work and on the road. The syndrome is classified as (1) **obstructive sleep apnea** (OSA), in which the diaphragm contracts but cannot move air because of an upper airway obstruction; (2) **central apnea**, the result of dysfunction of the respiratory drive center; or (3) **mixed apnea**, a combination of the two. OSA is the most common form.

The most common points of obstruction in OSA are the velopharynx (behind the soft palate) and the hypopharynx, as a result of muscle relaxation during sleep. Obesity contributes to the obstruction with increased soft tissue in the upper airways.

Central sleep apnea used to be called **Pickwickian syndrome** after Pickwick, the Dickens character, who has the typical body habitus of the patient with central apnea: obese, male, and often short in stature. It is now clear that not all patients with central apnea have this habitus. Dysfunction of the central respiratory drive center results in apnea during sleep.

Signs & Symptoms

Most often seen in obese, older males but also seen in postmenopausal women. Much of the sleep history can be obtained from the patient's spouse. Patients present with daytime somnolence, disturbed sleep, and excessively loud snoring. The inadequate sleep leads to poor job performance, automobile accidents, and deterioration of relationships. The continued apnea and associated hypoxia leads to hypoxic vasoconstriction of the pulmonary vasculature and pulmonary hypertension. Hypoxia can also lead to arrhythmias and stroke.

Diagnosis

A sleep study is performed to diagnose sleep apnea syndrome. The patient's sleep pattern, O_2 saturation, air flow, and ECG are monitored overnight, and the episodes of apnea and desaturation are monitored.

Treatment

The first step is encouraging weight loss, but success with this strategy is predictably low. Nasal decongestants (including mechanical devices such as "Breathe Right" nasal dilating adhesive strips have variable benefit. Patients should avoid sedative-hypnotics and alcohol at bedtime. With severe daytime somnolence, cardiovascular manifestations, and frequent apnea, the next step in

Table 11-5. Causes of transudates and exudates

Transudates	Exudates
Congestive heart failure	Infection
Nephrotic syndrome	Malignancy (primary or metastatic)
End-stage liver disease	Rheumatologic diseases
Abdominal fluid leakage (ascites, postperitoneal dialysis)	Pulmonary embolism
	Abdominal processes (pancreatitis)

like plasma   *like blood*

intervention is continuous positive airway pressure (CPAP) during sleep. Positive pressure throughout the respiratory cycle keeps the airways open, but it's not well tolerated by patients. The final step in intervention is surgery.

Pleural Disease

Pneumothorax

Pneumothorax is a potentially life-threatening condition. Air can get to the pleural space by several routes: (1) direct injury of the chest wall, (2) damage to alveoli, leading to air in the interstitial space (pulmonary interstitial emphysema, seen often in mechanically ventilated patients, especially newborns with neonatal RDS), which can rupture through into the pleural space. Air enters the mediastinum, tracking into the interstitium, then out into the pleura.

Causes of pneumothorax can be classified as follows:

- **Spontaneous**: Emphysema, interstitial lung disease, eosinophilic granuloma, CF, asthma, cancer, or idiopathic. Idiopathic pneumothorax is often seen in lanky, tall, Caucasian males. The cause is unknown.

- **Traumatic**: Penetrating chest trauma, nonpenetrating trauma, esophageal perforation, and iatrogenic causes.

A pneumothorax should be evacuated if it consists of greater than 15% of airspace on chest X-ray, causes significant dyspnea or respiratory compromise, causes hypoxemia, recurs, is secondary to pulmonary disease, or is a tension pneumothorax.

In a **tension pneumothorax**, enough air gets into the pleural space to produce positive pressure, leading to displacement of the mediastinal compartment to the contralateral side (mediastinal shift). This is a true emergency because this air pressure can reduce blood return to the heart and lead to hemodynamic collapse.

Table 11-6. Fluid composition of transudates and exudates

Pleural fluid	Transudate	Exudate
Protein	<3 g/dl	>3 g/dl
Ratio of pleural protein to serum protein	<0.5	>0.5
LDH	<200 IU/liter	>200 IU/liter
Ratio of pleural to serum lactate dehydrogenase	<0.6	>0.6

Pleural Effusion

There is normally an undetectable, very small amount of fluid in the pleural space. Anything more than 200 ml of fluid (which is abnormal) can be detected on CXR as blunting of the costophrenic angle. Pleural fluid is classified as either transudate or exudate (Table 11-5). **Transudate** results from increased net pressure for fluid to "filter" out of the vasculature into the pleural space, according to Starling's law (due to increased hydrostatic pressure or decreased oncotic pressure). As a result, transudate has the characteristics of an "ultrafiltrate" of plasma. **Exudate** results from loss of integrity of the vascular barrier or from frank production of fluid locally within the pleural space. An exudate has chemical characteristics closer to blood.

Pleural fluid can be classified according to overall fluid composition. A **hydrothorax** is just fluid (Table 11-6). A **hemothorax** is frank blood, with a hematocrit of the fluid greater than 20; it implies cancer, trauma, or pulmonary embolism (PE) with infarction. A **chylothorax** is chylous lymph that appears milky, with high triglyceride content.

Treatment

An effusion that affects ventilation or oxygenation needs to be evacuated. This can be done by one-time thoracentesis or chest tube placement. Parapneumonic effusions may require antibiotics and thoracentesis drainage. Loculated fluid (pockets of fibrin-bound fluid) requires chest tube placement and instillation of thrombolytics.

Pulmonary Vascular Disease

Pulmonary Hypertension

Pulmonary hypertension is persistent elevation of the pressures in the pulmonary circulation (mean PAP >20 mm Hg). Pulmonary hypertension can be caused by intracardiac shunts, left ventricular failure, obliteration or obstruction of the vasculature, or prolonged hypoxia.

Persistently elevated pressures lead to many hemodynamic changes:

- **In the heart**: Increased afterload on the right heart leads to right ventricular hypertrophy, right atrial enlargement, and eventually signs of right heart failure (elevated jugular venous pressure, pedal edema, but normal left ventricular function). With severe hypertension, the right ventricle fills more than normal, pushing the interventricular septum into the LV and thereby impairing left ventricular function (septal bulge).

- **In the lungs**: With persistent hypertension, remodeling of the pulmonary vasculature occurs, leading to thick-walled vessels. Mild hypoxemia is seen secondary to loss of the capillary circulation and worsened $\dot{V}/\dot{Q}$ match.

Pulmonary Embolism

Pulmonary embolism (PE) can occur from the embolization of clot, fat, marrow, air, or other materials into the pulmonary vasculature. The most common cause of PE is the embolism of a deep venous thrombosis (DVT), most commonly found in the calf. The embolus can then act as a nidus for clot extension, which can be fatal if massive or left untreated. Postsurgical and postpartum patients are at increased risk for developing PE.

Signs & Symptoms

Patients may experience sudden dyspnea and hypoxia.

Diagnosis

Made by $\dot{V}/\dot{Q}$ scan, which can often have ambiguous results. Doppler ultrasound of the legs is done to search for a likely source. The gold standard is pulmonary angiography, in which dye is squirted into the main pulmonary arteries and X-rays are taken. The risks are significant, including nephrotoxicity from dye, dye anaphylaxis, and bleeding

Treatment

The mainstay of therapy is anticoagulation. Remember that anticoagulation prevents new clot formation and does not dissolve old clot, but anticoagulation shifts the balance between clot formation and lysis toward lysis. Proven DVTs are treated with 6 weeks of anticoagulation if the result of a known brief insult (e.g., surgery, trauma), and 6 months or longer otherwise. Heparin is started first, with the goal of a partial thromboplastin time (PTT) at 1.5–2.5 times normal. Warfarin is then overlapped to achieve an international normalized ratio (INR) of 2.0–3.0. The two are overlapped because of the theoretical consideration that warfarin first depletes proteins C and S before depleting factor VII, then factors II, IX, and X, and persons with protein C and S deficiency will then be in a hypercoagulable state. The recent trend has been toward treating with low–molecular-weight heparin because, with it, PTT does not need to be checked. Severe PE with hemodynamic compromise or significant respiratory compromise may require thrombolysis (e.g., with streptokinase or tissue-type plasminogen activator). Massive PE is usually fatal, but experimental therapeutic strategies include surgical thrombectomy. Recurrent embolism from known DVT may be prevented by instillation of a caval interruption filter, which is placed percutaneously in the inferior vena cava, with the intent of catching floating emboli before they get to the lungs. Inferior vena cava filters are also an option for patients with contraindications to anticoagulation (e.g., CNS bleed, recent surgery, severe GI bleed).

Aspiration

Aspiration refers to a solid or liquid entering the airways. Aspiration can cause a chemical pneumonitis (gastric secretions), pneumonia (oral or GI flora), or airway obstruction with foreign objects. Obstruction with foreign objects is important in children, who tend to inhale hot dogs, grapes, peanuts (the peanut oils also cause a chemical pneumonitis), and various small objects. Risk factors include chronic illness, loss of gag reflex, vomiting, and altered mental status. Treatment is supportive, with endoscopic removal of foreign objects and appropriate antibiotic coverage if pneumonia is expected.

Trauma

Remember that *a*irway and *b*reathing are the A and B of the ABCs of resuscitation. Maintaining a patent airway and ventilating a patient are perhaps the most useful skills to have in managing a code situation (usually the job of the anesthesiologist). Airway can be maintained with several maneuvers, including

- Positioning
- Clearing the airway
- Mask ventilation
- Oral airway insertion
- Laryngeal mask airway
- Endotracheal tube
- Cricothyrotomy or tracheostomy

Neoplasms

The important point to remember is that the most common tumors found in a particular region of the airway originate from the most common cell type found in that region. For example, squamous cell carcinoma is the most common tumor in the upper airways.

Nose, Sinus, and Nasopharyngeal Neoplasms

These include lymphoid tumors (plasmacytomas), olfactory neuroblastomas—highly malignant papillomas (occurs in the nose and paranasal sinuses, benign but locally invasive), and carcinomas (squamous cell carcinoma is the most common). Nasopharyngeal squamous cell carcinoma is associated with EBV infection, is particularly common in Southeast Asians, is locally invasive, and metastasizes rapidly. It is highly radiosensitive, however, and the 5-year cure rate is up to 80%.

Oral Cavity Neoplasms

Leukoplakia is a white raised plaque with up to a 15% transformation rate to malignancy. **Erythroplasia** is red, velvety, and not raised; it has up to a 50% transformation rate to malignancy. **Hairy leukoplakia** is associated with HIV infection and is seen on the lateral surface of the tongue. It is associated with human papillomavirus (HPV) and EBV; it usually contains a *Candida* superinfection and is not precancerous.

Squamous cell carcinoma comprises 95% of all oral cavity tumors. Alcohol, smoking, and chewing tobacco are all risk factors. It spreads via the submandibular nodes to distant sites. The 5-year survival rate is 85–90% for lip cancers, 25–65% for floor of the mouth cancers, with the difference due to earlier metastasis in the latter. It is treated by surgical resection.

Laryngeal Neoplasms

Benign laryngeal polyps are smooth, round, sessile polyps often found on the vocal cords. The polyps can ulcerate, leading to a strong inflammatory response. They occur mostly in males and smokers. Papillomas are small (<1 cm), friable, stratified squamous epithelium surrounding a fibrous core. They may be multiple and rarely transform to malignant form.

Squamous cell carcinoma accounts for 95% of all laryngeal carcinomas. It is more common in males than females, and there is increased incidence in smokers, older age, and people with asbestos exposure. They are usually found directly on vocal cords. Patients present with hoarseness, stridor, odynophagia, and hemoptysis.

Diagnosis

Laryngoscopy and biopsy.

Treatment

Surgical excision with radiation therapy. The 5-year survival rate exceeds 50%. Tumor spreads directly, can invade vital structures (airway, major vessels), and then spread via lymphatics.

Lung Neoplasms

Benign lung neoplasms include

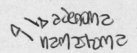

- **Bronchial adenoma**: the most common centrally located benign tumor of the lung.

- **Hamartoma**: the most common peripherally located benign tumor of the lung. On CXR, it typically shows up as a popcorn-shaped calcification.

Carcinoma of the lung is currently the leading cause of cancer deaths in the United States in both men and women (having surpassed breast cancer in women). The primary risk factor is tobacco exposure. Lung cancer rarely affects patients younger than 35 years of age and is most common in the fourth and fifth decades of life. Lung carcinoma is divided into four major histologic classifications:

- Small cell carcinoma (20–25%)

- Adenocarcinoma, including bronchoalveolar carcinoma (32–40%)

- Squamous cell carcinoma (20–25%)

- Large cell carcinoma (8–16%)

Clinically, it is appropriate to think of lung carcinoma in terms of **small cell** versus **non–small cell** (all the others) because this is the primary determinant of prognosis and management. A general rule is that non–small cell carcinoma is evaluated for resectability (surgical intervention), and small cell carcinoma is primarily managed with chemotherapy. This is because non–small cell carcinoma often presents as a distinct parenchymal lung mass with or without lymph node involvement, whereas small cell carcinoma usually presents as diffuse lung disease with or without metastases, and small cell carcinoma often metastasizes early.

Signs & Symptoms

Patients often present with an asymptomatic abnormal CXR, or they may present with symptoms related to the tumor's effect on the airways, including dyspnea, cough, hemoptysis, or recurrent infection. Sometimes patients present with symptoms of paraneoplastic syndrome, Pancoast tumor, or Horner's syndrome (described later).

- **Paraneoplastic syndrome**: Because lung carcinoma cells are dysplastic, they often secrete abnormal hormones, leading to unusual symptoms and signs.

- **Pancoast tumor**: Lung tumors located in the apices of the lung may lead to compression of the brachial plexus. Involvement of the inferior cervical ganglion may lead to **Horner's syndrome** (ptosis, miosis, anhidrosis).

Obstruction of a bronchus may lead to recurrent infections in the affected segment or lobe, called *postobstructive pneumonia*. Compression of the superior vena cava leads to facial and upper extremity edema, headache, and other symptoms associated with increased intracranial pressure. Involvement of the recurrent laryngeal nerve, which loops under the aorta by the ligamentum arteriosum, leads to hoarseness. Spread to the pleura leads to pleural effusion.

Diagnosis

The key is obtaining tissue for diagnosis. Start with a CXR, and compare it to old CXRs to assess interval changes. A CT scan is useful for (1) assessing the details of the primary lesion—calcifications, spiculations, satellite lesions—all of which point to malignancy, (2) determining the presence of additional intrapulmonary lesions, (3) staging—evaluating the presence of hilar, mediastinal, or distant lymphadenopathy; pleural effusion; and involvement of the pleura or chest wall. Remember that the advantage of CT scan over CXR is not resolution (plain films have better resolution) but contrast enhancement. Sputum samples can be evaluated for cytology, although sensitivity is low (50%). The next step is obtaining tissue. Bronchoscopy with or without transbronchial biopsy is indicated for centrally located lesions. One option for evaluation of peripheral lesions is fine-needle aspiration under CT guidance. Most clinicians agree to proceed directly to surgery if the patient is a reasonable candidate.

Treatment

Treatment options include surgery, chemotherapy, and, to a limited extent, radiation therapy. The general rule is that non–small cell carcinoma is treated with surgery (if feasible), and small cell carcinoma is treated with chemotherapy. A small number of small cell carcinoma patients present with limited lung involvement and may benefit from combined modality therapy: chemotherapy plus radiation to shrink the tumor followed by surgery. Unfortunately, overall 3-year survival for small cell carcinoma is less than 5%.

Other Tumors of the Lung and Thorax

- **Carcinoid of lung**: Bronchial carcinoid makes up about 1–5% of all lung tumors. Histologically, the cells contain dense secretory granules. Patients present with wheezing, dyspnea, cough, hemoptysis, and obstructive pneumonia. Many carcinoid tumors secrete vasoactive substances, particularly **serotonin**, leading to signs and symptoms of **carcinoid syndrome**: warmth, flushing, cyanosis, and diarrhea. Carcinoids rarely metastasize and are therefore amenable to resection. The 5- to 10-year survival is 50–95%.

- **Lymphoma**: Non-Hodgkin's lymphoma and Hodgkin's disease may present with mediastinal or hilar lymphadenopathy. These diseases are described in more detail in chapter 7.

- **Benign mesothelioma**: Also known as a *pleural fibroma*, it can be very large, but it is always confined to the pleural surface. There is no association with asbestos exposure.

- **Malignant mesothelioma**: These are fortunately rare tumors but are associated with asbestos exposure. In shipping and industrial areas, up to 90% of mesotheliomas have associated asbestos exposure. There is a long latency to development of mesothelioma after exposure (20–50 years), and there is no increased risk with concomitant smoking. Note that in asbestos-related bronchogenic carcinoma, there is a markedly increased risk of cancer when a patient is both a smoker and has asbestos exposure. Prognosis is poor.

Critical Care Medicine

Respiratory Failure

Respiratory failure is defined as one of the following:

- Poor oxygenation: Pa_{O_2} <55 mm Hg
- Poor ventilation: Pa_{CO_2} >50 mm Hg

These criteria are based on normal individuals. Patients with chronic, partially compensated respiratory disease (e.g., COPD, pulmonary hypertension, shunt) may have relatively poor oxygenation and ventilation as a baseline.

Respiratory failure is an indication for intubation and mechanical ventilatory support. Other indications include altered mental status with inability to protect the airway, apnea, neuromuscular paralysis, pulmonary hemorrhage, and therapeutic hyperventilation for increased intracranial pressure.

Neonatal Respiratory Distress Syndrome

Premature newborns born before week 24 of gestation cannot adequately produce surfactant. As a result, their lungs cannot expand, pulmonary vascular resistance remains high, and respiratory failure ensues. Pregnant women who appear to be at risk of premature labor are given corticosteroids because these appear to hasten lung development. After birth, treatment consists of mechanical ventilatory support until the baby can make its own surfactant as well as the use of a new, artificial surfactant. Common complications include pulmonary interstitial emphysema resulting from high pressures of mechanical ventilators and easily damaged lungs, leading to pneumothorax. With eventual recovery, a significant portion of patients develop **bronchopulmonary dysplasia**, characterized by abnormal CXR, showing areas of bronchiectasis and fibrous scarring, a tendency to recurrent RSV infection, and RAD.

Adult Respiratory Distress Syndrome

Pathologically, it is believed that a primary event somewhere in the body leads to the release of systemic factors, including cytokines, which then lead to leaky capillary membranes. This results in interstitial edema, hypoxemia, and respiratory distress—adult RDS (ARDS). This entity was first described in 1967 by physicians treating Vietnam War soldiers in various states of trauma and infection leading to respiratory failure. Respiratory failure occurs, usually in a hospitalized patient, necessitating mechanical ventilation.

Major criteria for ARDS are as follows:

- Opacities in all four quadrants of the lung fields on CXR

- Poor oxygenation (defined as Pao_2/Fio_2 <200)

- Normal pulmonary capillary wedge pressure (PCWP) (to rule out cardiogenic causes)

Minor criteria for ARDS are as follows:

- Reduced lung compliance

- Clinical picture of sepsis or multiorgan failure syndrome

- Large amount of PEEP required (PEEP is *p*ositive *e*nd-*e*xpiratory *p*ressure, which keeps the alveoli open and improves oxygenation.)

Mortality with ARDS approaches 40–50%. Treatment options are limited. Support in the ICU is necessary. Investigational treatments, including specific alterations in the means of delivering mechanical ventilation, delivering antibodies to various inflammatory mediators, giving inhaled nitric oxide (to improve oxygenation via vasodilation), and placing the patient in a prone position (because ARDS affects dependent portions of the lung more, and so the prone position may improve $\dot{V}/\dot{Q}$ match in the relatively disease-free zones of lung). Steroids are not beneficial.

Pharmacology

Table 11-7 lists drugs used to treat respiratory disorders.

Table 11-7. Drugs used in respiratory disorders

Agent	Mechanism	Use	Toxicities
Antihistamines Diphenhydramine Chlorpheniramine Loratadine Fexofenadine Astemizole Cetirizine	Histamine-receptor antagonist	Allergic rhinitis, urticaria, anaphylaxis	Sedation, antimuscarinic effects (dry mouth, blurred vision)
Cough suppressants Codeine Dextromethorphan	Central cough suppression	Symptomatic relief of cough	Sedation, tolerance, and dependence with codeine
Beta-agonists Albuterol Terbutaline Metaproterenol	Selective for β_2-receptors, causing smooth muscle relaxation	Acute asthma attacks, COPD maintenance and exacerbations	Tremor, tachycardia, palpitations, arrhythmias
Anticholinergics Ipratropium	Reverses acetylcholine-induced bronchoconstriction	Acute asthma attacks, COPD maintenance and exacerbations	Dry mouth, urinary retention, tachycardia, agitation
Cromolyn	Stabilizes mast cells and prevents degranulation, inhibiting histamine release	Asthma and COPD	Dry mouth, throat irritation
Methylxanthines Theophylline Aminophylline Theobromine	Unclear; appears to inhibit phosphodiesterase, leading to increased cellular cAMP Increases respiratory drive, mucociliary clearance, and diaphragm contractility	Asthma and COPD	Mild: anorexia, nausea and vomiting, headache, anxiety, gastrointestinal distress Severe: arrhythmias and seizures Levels must be checked regularly
***N*-Acetylcysteine**	Reduces sulfur bridges in proteinaceous secretions	Also used for acetaminophen overdose	Increases respiratory tract mucus

COPD = chronic obstructive pulmonary disease; cAMP = cyclic adenosine monophosphate.

CHAPTER 12

Cardiovascular System

Anatomy

The Heart and Pericardium

The heart is a muscular structure encased in a pericardial sac. The **pericardium** consists of two layers: a fibrous parietal pericardium, which is anchored to the sternum, diaphragm, and mediastinal pleura; and a visceral pericardium, which is adherent to the heart. A small quantity of pericardial fluid serves as lubrication between the two layers.

The heart has four chambers: the left atrium and ventricle (LA and LV) and the right atrium and ventricle (RA and RV) (Fig. 12-1). The LV has thick walls (9-11 mm) because it pumps blood to the body at high pressures against relatively high resistance, whereas the RV has thinner walls (1/3 the thickness of the LV) because it pumps blood to the lungs under low pressures and against a low resistance. The interventricular (IV) septum separates the LV and RV—the upper part has little muscle tissue and is known as the membranous septum; the lower part is the muscular septum.

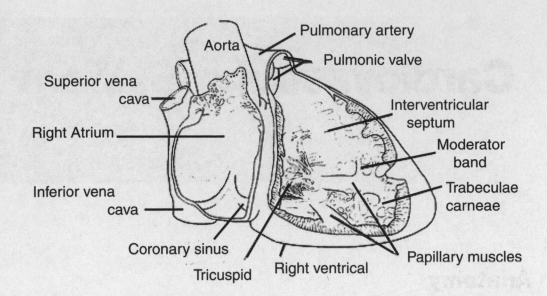

Fig. 12-1. L.S Lilly, edPathophysiology of Heart Disease [2nd Edition]. Baltimore: Williams and Wilkins, 1988; 4,6. **A**. Right atrium and right ventrical. **B**. left atrium and left ventrical. **C**. Valves of the heart.

The Valves

The heart has four valves (Fig. 12-1C)

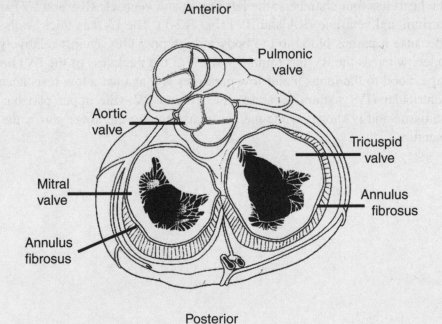

- **Tricuspid valve**: A three-leaflet valve that separates the RA and the RV. When the RV contracts, the tricuspid valve closes and prevents blood from flowing back into the RA. Note that there is no functional valve between the RA and the vena cavae.

- **Pulmonic valve**: A three-leaflet valve that separates the RV and its outflow tract, the pulmonary artery. This valve closes as the RV fills with blood (while the tricuspid valve is open) so that the RV can fill and blood in the pulmonary artery doesn't flow back into the RV. Once the RV contracts, the pulmonic valve opens and allows blood to be expelled forward.

- **Mitral valve**: A bicuspid (two-leaflet) valve that separates the LA from the LV. As the tricuspid does for the right heart, the mitral valve opens to allow blood to flow from the LA to the LV. It then closes when the LV contracts to prevent regurgitation back into the LA.

- **Aortic valve**: This three-leaflet valve separates the aorta from the LV. It's closed during diastole to allow the LV to fill and to prevent regurgitation from the aorta. The aortic valve is open during systole to allow the LV to expel blood into the aorta.

Coronary Circulation

At the bases of the three aortic valve leaflets are the sinuses of Valsalva. The two most anterior sinuses are called the *coronary sinuses* because the roots of the right and left coronary arteries are here. The **right coronary artery** (RCA) travels along the atrioventricular (AV) groove and supplies the RV, RA, and sinus node (Fig. 12-2). In 85% of the population, the RCA reaches the posterior IV groove, where it supplies the posterior IV septum and the AV node via the **posterior descending artery** (PDA). These patients have a right-dominant circulation. In 10% of patients, the circumflex artery from the left reaches posteriorly and supplies the posterior IV septum; this is known as left-dominant circulation. The remaining 5% or so have codominant circulation.

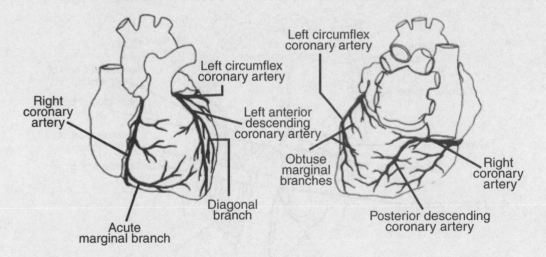

Fig. 12-2. Coronary circulation. L.S Lilly, edPathophysiology of Heart Disease [2nd Edition]. Baltimore: Williams and Wilkins, 1988; 9.

The left main coronary artery splits into the **left anterior descending artery (LAD)**, which travels in the anterior IV groove, and the **left circumflex artery**, which travels in the AV groove toward the back of the heart. The LAD supplies the anterior wall and anterior two-thirds of the IV septum, including the apex. The circumflex supplies the lateral and posterior LV. An occlusion in the LAD is often called a "widow-maker" lesion because the LAD supplies a huge fraction of the myocardium. The LAD sends off several branches: **diagonals** (think "D" for LA**D** and **d**iagonal) and **septal perforators**. The left circumflex artery sends off **obtuse marginal** (OM) branches. Coronary anatomy is highly variable. Venous return from the myocardium flows into various coronary veins, eventually ending in the **coronary sinus**, which dumps into the RA.

Conduction System

All myocardial cells are electrically active and can automatically fire periodically on their own (**automaticity**). Normally, electrical impulses arise from the **sinoatrial (SA) node**, located along the junction between the superior vena cava (SVC) and the RA (Fig. 12-3). Depolarizations initiated at the SA node move outward to stimulate contraction of the LA and RA. As long as the very first site of depolarization is in the SA node, the heart's electrical activity is called **sinus rhythm.**

The depolarization passes from the atria to the ventricles through the atrioventricular (AV) node. After passing through the **AV node**, the wave of depolarization enters and rapidly passes through the ventricular conduction system. This includes, in order of depolarization sequence, the **bundle of His**, the **left** and **right bundle branches**, and, finally, the actual myocytes of the ventricles. The rapid conduction system (bundle of His, left and right bundle branches) is known as the **Purkinje system** (because they're made of Purkinje fibers). Contraction initiates on depolarization but continues well after depolarization is complete—it takes longer to mechanically contract than it does to conduct an electrical impulse.

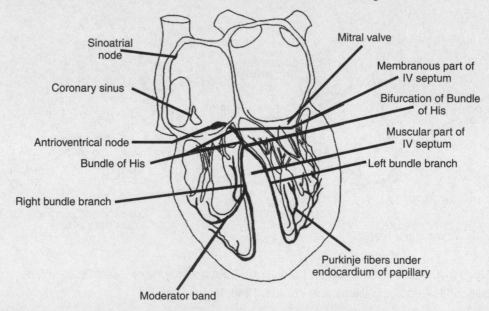

Fig. 12-3. Cardiac conduction system. L.S Lilly, edPathophysiology of Heart Disease [2nd Edition]. Baltimore: Williams and Wilkins, 1988; 7.

Blood Flow

- The SVC, inferior vena cava (IVC), and coronary sinus empty into the RA, which empties through the tricuspid valve into the RV, then out the pulmonic valve into the pulmonary trunk, which eventually goes to the lungs (Fig. 12-4).

- Blood returning from the lungs enters the LA through the four pulmonary veins. The LA empties into the LV through the mitral valve. The LV pumps blood into the aorta through the aortic valve. Note that the LA and RA contract more or less simultaneously, and the LV and RV also contract more or less simultaneously, but there are important physiologic differences in timing (discussed later).

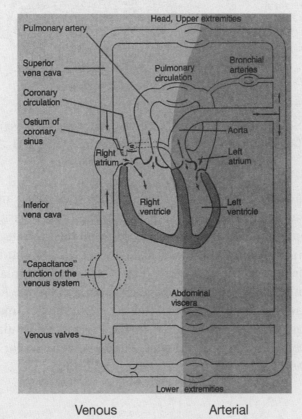

Fig. 12-4. The circulatory system. (Reprinted with permission from TE Andreoli, JC Bennett, CCJ Carpenter, et al. *Cecil Essentials of Medicine* [3rd ed]. Philadelphia: WB Saunders, 1993;3.)

Embryology

Development of the heart

A distinct cardiovascular system can first be discerned at 2–3 weeks' gestation. The myocardial cells of the heart originate from **mesenchymal cells** in the **splanchnic mesoderm**. The heart tube forms from tissue near the prochordal plate (Fig. 12-5).

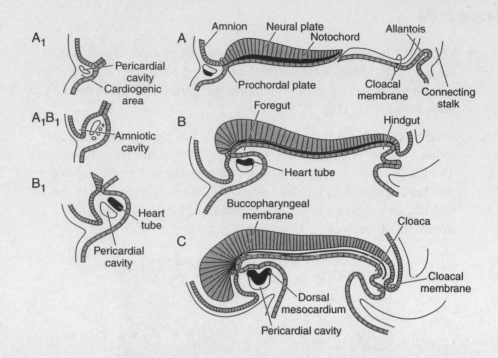

Fig. 12-5. Early cardiac development. The cardiogenic area starts ventral to the pericardial cavity (A_1) then rotates to a dorsal position. **A.** 18 days; **B.** 21 days; **C.** 22 days.

At first, the heart takes the form of a tube, which then twists in the process of forming the eventual adult heart (Fig. 12-6). Once the heart's basic structure is in place, the major septa of the heart are formed between days 27 and 37 of development. Two masses of tissue, the **endocardial cushions**, grow toward each other and eventually meet. The endocardial cushions play a key role in cardiac development. They form the membranous portion of the ventricular septum, the lower part of the atrial septum, the atrioventricular canals, and the aortic and pulmonary channels. Consequently, abnormalities in endocardial cushion formation result in many of the cardiac malformations, including **atrial septal defects**, **ventricular septal defects**, **transposition of the great vessels**, and **tetralogy of Fallot**.

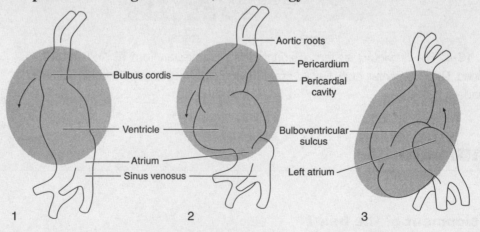

Fig. 12-6. Continued cardiac development. **A.** 22 days. **B.** 23 days. **C.** 24 days.

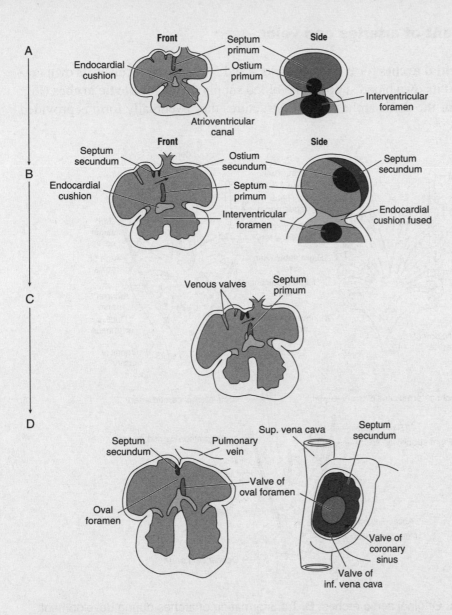

Fig. 12-7. Septal development at **A**. 30 days **B**. 33 days **C**. 37 days **D**. and newborn.

In the atrium, an initial growth forms the **septum primum** (Fig. 12-7). The initial hole left between the septum primum and the endocardial cushions is the **ostium primum**. The ostium primum closes off as it is filled in by extensions of the endocardial cushions. Before the ostium primum is fully obliterated, however, perforations caused by cell death (apoptosis) in the upper portion of the septum primum coalesce to form the **ostium secundum**, which continues to allow communication between the atria. Eventually, a second mass of tissue grows; the **septum secundum**. The passageway through these two membranes is the foramen ovale, which is closed off in the newborn as increased LA pressures push the valve of the foramen ovale against the septum secundum.

The aorta and pulmonary trunk form from the division of a common trunk into two intertwined tubes by a septum. **Tetralogy of Fallot** results when the septum is anteriorly displaced, shortchanging the pulmonary artery and creating an overriding aorta over a ventricular septal defect, the result of which is right ventricular hypertrophy, due to excessive right-sided pressures. **Persistent truncus arteriosus** occurs when the septum fails to connect with the interventricular septum. **Transposition of the great vessels** results from failure of the septum to spiral properly.

Development of arteries and veins

As the **branchial arches** form during weeks 4 and 5, each arch receives its own cranial nerve and its own blood supply. The blood supply forms the **aortic arches** (Fig. 12-8). A list of the aortic arches and the structures they eventually form is provided in Table 12-1.

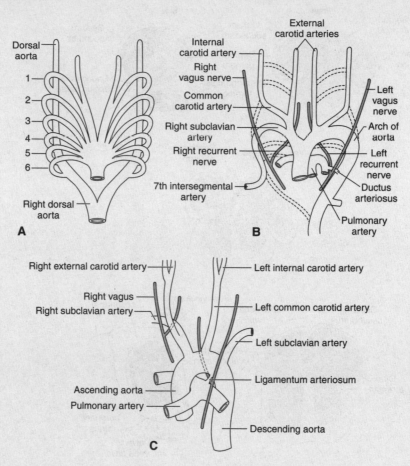

Fig. 12-8. A. Original aortic arches. **B.** Transformation of arches during development. **C.** Adult structures. Note difference in the positions of the right and left recurrent larygeal nerves.

Table 12-1. Aortic arch derivatives

Aortic arch	Structure
1	Maxillary artery
2	Hyoid and stapedial arteries
3	Common carotid artery External carotid artery Internal carotid artery (first portion)
4	Left: aortic arch Right: proximal subclavian artery
5	Transient, no final structure
6 (the lung bud)	Left: ductus arteriosus Right: proximal right pulmonary artery

Because the neck grows as the heart develops, the heart gets pulled caudally during development. As a result, the **recurrent laryngeal nerves** are pulled along, looping around the innominate artery on the right and the aortic arch distal to the ductus arteriosus on the left. The **vitelline arteries** eventually become the celiac artery and the superior and inferior mesenteric arteries. The **umbilical arteries** (there are two) become the internal iliac and superior vesicular arteries proximally and the obliterated medial umbilical ligaments distally.

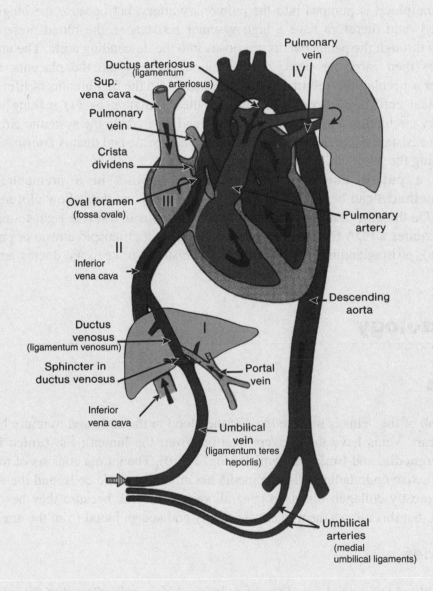

Fig. 12-9. Fetal circulation. Adult structures in parenthesis.

Changes at Birth

In the fetal circulation, the pulmonary and systemic circulations are basically in parallel. Oxygenated blood comes from the **umbilical vein** (from the placenta) and passes through the portal venous system into the IVC and enters the RA (Fig. 12-9). The oxygenated blood preferentially passes through the patent foramen ovale into the LA and LV. The coronary arteries are perfused, as are the upper body and upper trunk. Meanwhile, deoxygenated blood returning from the SVC enters the RA, but because of the flow pattern, it passes through the tricuspid valve into the RV. The blood is pumped into the pulmonary artery, but because the lungs aren't inflated (and therefore have a high vascular resistance), the blood preferentially passes through the patent ductus arteriosus into the descending aorta. The umbilical arteries then carry the deoxygenated blood back toward the placenta and the mother's circulation. At birth, the lungs expand with the first breaths of life, and the umbilical cord is clamped. This changes the circulation by (1) making the pulmonary circulation a low-resistance circuit and (2) making the systemic circulation a high-resistance circuit. As a result, the foramen ovale and ductus arteriosus close, initiating the adult circulation.

If a **patent ductus arteriosus (PDA)** persists in a premature baby, **indomethacin** can be used to decrease PGE1 levels and thus allow closure of the PDA. On the other hand, if a congenital defect results in a severe right-to-left shunt that requires a PDA for blood to reach the lungs (e.g., tricuspid atresia or pulmonic atresia), prostaglandins (PGE1) can be administered to keep the ductus arteriosus open.

Histology

Veins

The job of the veins is to store most of the blood in the body and to return blood to the heart. Veins have three layers (starting from the lumen): the **tunica intima**, **tunica media**, and **tunica adventitia** (Fig. 12-10). The intima consists of metabolically active endothelial cells, the media has smooth muscle cells, and the adventitia is mostly collagen fibers. In general, veins are weak because they have a thin media, but this allows them to expand easily and accept blood from the arteries.

Arteries

Once blood is pumped out of the heart by the LV, it is distributed to the rest of the body via the arteries. There are three major types of arteries, but they are all basically composed of the same three layers: tunica intima, tunica media, and tunica adventitia.

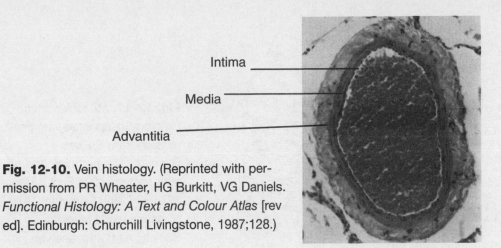

Intima

Media

Advantitia

Fig. 12-10. Vein histology. (Reprinted with permission from PR Wheater, HG Burkitt, VG Daniels. *Functional Histology: A Text and Colour Atlas* [rev ed]. Edinburgh: Churchill Livingstone, 1987;128.)

Elastic Arteries

The **aorta** and its major branches are **elastic arteries**. A thick media makes these arteries strong so that they don't tear when they receive each high-pressured bolus of blood from the LV (Fig. 12-11). These arteries are also very compliant, thanks to the elastic fibers in the intima and media, so that the bolus is easily propelled to the rest of the arterial tree.

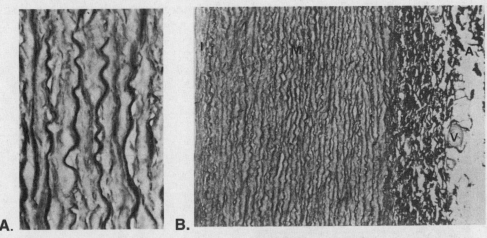

A. B.

A. High-magnification of elastin stain. B. Cross-section of a wall.

Fig. 12-11. Elastic artery histology. (I = intima; M = media; A = adventitia; V = vasa vasorum.) (Reprinted with permission from PR Wheater, HG Burkitt, VG Daniels. *Functional Histology: A Text and Colour Atlas* [rev ed]. Edinburgh: Churchill Livingstone, 1987;121.)

Remember that arteries are composed of active cells and require their own oxygen and nutrients. These are conveniently delivered via small blood vessels in the adventitia called **vasa vasorum.**

Muscular Arteries and Arterioles

Muscular arteries are the most abundant type in the body. They are very similar to elastic arteries, with the exception that all the elastic tissue is compressed into two layers, called the **internal** and **external elastic lamina** (Fig. 12-12).

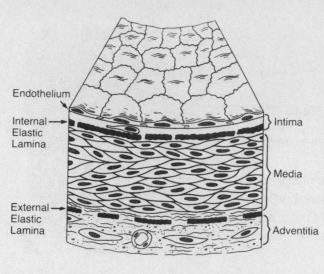

Fig. 12-12. Muscular artery histology. (Reprinted with permission from R Ross, I Glomset. The pathogenesis of atherosclerosis. *N Engl J Med* 1976;295:369. Copyright 1976 Massachusetts Medical Society. All rights reserved.)

Arterioles are simply small muscular arteries with fewer than six layers of smooth muscle cells in the tunica media. This is the level of the vascular tree where most of the peripheral resistance is controlled (i.e., by vasoconstriction or vasodilation).

Capillaries

Capillaries are usually a single endothelial cell layer thick and rest on a basement membrane (Fig. 12-13). They act as a selective barrier between the vessels and surrounding tissues.

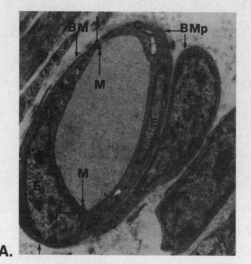

A.

Continous capillary

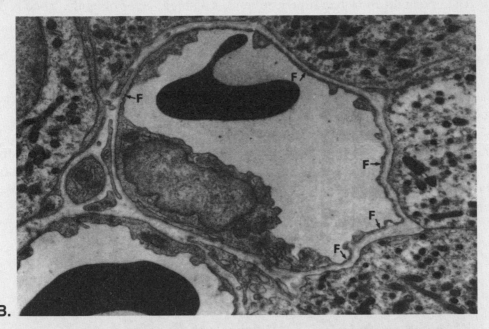

Fig. 12-13. Capillary endothelium. **A.** Continuous capillary. **B.** Fenestrated capillary. (BM = basement membrane; E = endothelial cells; F = fenestration; J = tight junction.) (Reprinted with permission from PR Wheater, HG Burkitt, VG Daniels. *Functional Histology: A Text and Colour Atlas* [rev ed]. Edinburgh: Churchill Livingstone, 1987;124, 125.)

Continuous capillaries are the most common capillary type. They have an uninterrupted barrier that allows only small molecules to pass through. They are found in nervous tissue, muscle, connective tissue, exocrine glands, the brain (blood-brain barrier), and testes (blood-testes barrier).

Fenestrated capillaries have large pores (fenestrations) in the endothelium and can exchange fluids rapidly. The basement membrane remains continuous (no pores). In most fenestrated capillaries, the pores are bridged by a thin **diaphragm**, the function of which is unknown. Fenestrated capillaries tend to be more permeable than continuous capillaries. They can be found in the GI tract, endocrine glands, and exocrine glands.

Discontinuous capillaries not only have multiple fenestrations, they also have some patches without any endothelial lining at all. This type is found only in the liver sinusoids.

Leukocytes that are commuting to work via the blood vessels must first squeeze between endothelial cells in the capillary wall. This process is called **diapedesis**.

The Heart

The heart has three layers just like the rest of the circulation, only more pumped up.

The **endocardium** lines the cardiac chambers and consists of a thin layer of epithelial cells. The endocardium is continuous with the endothelium of incoming and outgoing vessels.

Myocardium is the actual heart muscle and is composed of specialized cardiac myocytes.

The **epicardium** (visceral pericardium) is a single layer of epithelial cells that hugs the heart like a body suit and is continuous with the parietal pericardium.

Cardiac Myocytes

Cardiac myocytes are specialized muscle cells that depolarize and contract with impeccable timing and coordination, ejecting blood into the lungs and aorta.

Cardiac myocytes have sarcomeres like regular muscle cells, but they are also branched and tightly connected to each other at regions called **intercalated discs** (Fig. 12-14). The intercalated discs are composed of cell-cell junctions called **fascia adherens** and **desmosomes**. Other regions have gap junctions, which allow the action potential to spread quickly between cells.

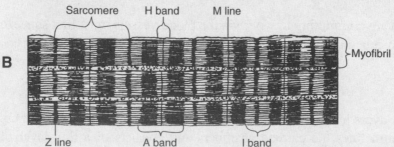

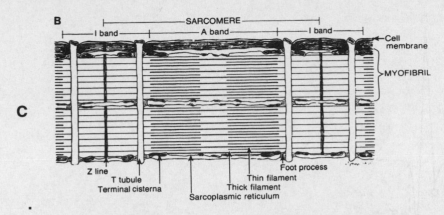

Fig. 12-14. A. Cardiac muscle. (Mi = mitochondria; FA = fascia adherens; N = gap junctions; SR = sarcoplasmic reticulum; G = glycogen granules.) (Reprinted with permission from PR Wheater, HG Burkitt, VG Daniels. *Functional Histology: A Text and Colour Atlas* [rev ed]. Edinburgh: Churchill Livingstone, 1987;94.). **B.** The myofibril. **C.** A close-up view of single sacromere.

Purkinje cells are modified cardiac myocytes that conduct electrical stimuli from the AV node to the myocardium and coordinate the relentless cycles of contraction and relaxation.

T-tubules are found at Z-lines ("TAZ"). They are invaginations of the cell membrane that facilitate the conversion of electrical impulses (depolarization) to physical muscle contractions. The **sarcoplasmic reticulum** (SR) stores calcium in the cell and is located near the T-tubules. The SR is instrumental in facilitating contraction of cardiac myocytes. Cardiac myocytes require an extraordinary amount of energy in the form of adenosine triphosphate (ATP), which is provided by numerous mitochondria. Cardiac muscle cells are described in more detail in chapter 10.

Normal Physiology

The Electrocardiogram

On the electrocardiogram (ECG), the **P wave** represents atrial depolarization (LA and RA together) (Fig. 12-15). Atrial repolarization occurs at the same time as the QRS complex and is not seen.

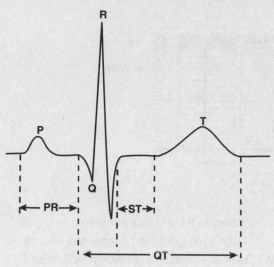

Fig. 12-15. Normal electrocardiogram.

The **PR interval** is the conduction delay between atrial and ventricular depolarization. The stimulus passes through the AV node, left and right bundle branches, and the Purkinje system. The ventricles need this extra time so that they can fill with blood. If the PR interval is prolonged (greater than 0.2 sec, or 5 mm), there is most likely a conduction delay through the AV node (**AV block**).

The **QRS complex** represents ventricular depolarization. If the complex is too wide, there is abnormal conduction through the ventricles.

The **ST segment** is the interval in which the ventricles are completely depolarized. ST segment depression suggests reversible myocardial ischemia; ST segment elevation suggests myocardial infarction (MI).

The **T wave** represents ventricular repolarization. In some circumstances, inverted T waves (pointing downward) suggest myocardial ischemia.

The **QT interval** is the complete period of systole (ventricular contraction). Prolongation may suggest drug toxicity (e.g., quinidine) or electrolyte disturbances (e.g., hypocalcemia).

Know these ECG terms cold—they are high-yield material!

Cardiac Action Potentials

The function of the heart is exquisitely dependent on the balance of intracellular and extracellular ions that make up the heart's resting potential and action potential. At rest, the concentrations of sodium and calcium are higher outside the cell than inside, and the concentration of potassium is higher inside than outside. Ion channels in the cell membrane allow a small constant leak of ions down their concentration gradient (Na^+ and Ca^{2+} flow in, K^+ flows out). Counteracting these leaks are ATP-driven Na^+-K^+ exchange pumps that move Na^+ out of the cell and K^+ into the cell to maintain the resting concentration gradient (Fig. 12-16). Ca^{2+} is moved out of the cell by a Na^+/Ca^{2+} exchanger and, to a lesser degree, by an ATP-driven Ca^{2+} pump.

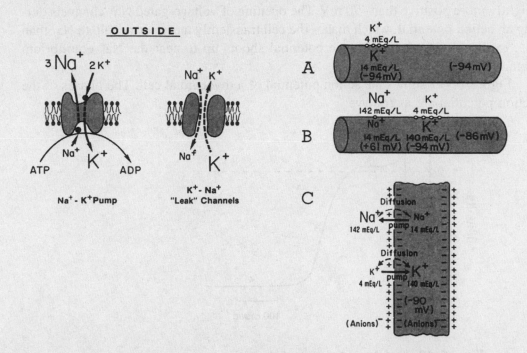

Fig. 12-16. Sodium-potassium pump and membrane potentials. **A, B.** Intracellular and extracellular concentrations of K⁺ and Na⁺. **C.** Flow of Na⁺ and K⁺ across membrane. (Reprinted with permission from AC Guyton. *Textbook of Medical Physiology* [7th ed]. Philadelphia: WB Saunders, 1986;105.)

The potential of a cell at rest and during activation depends on three factors: 1) the concentration of ions inside the cell, 2) the concentration of ions outside the cell, and 3) the relative permeability of the cell to the different ions.

The **Nernst equation** uses the first two factors to determine the equilibrium membrane potential for each ion:

$$Vx = -(RT/zF) \log [X]in/[X]out$$

where $(RT/zF) = 62$, Vx = equilibrium potential of ion X, and $[X]$ = concentration of ion X.

Let's use K⁺ as an example. The concentration of K⁺ inside the cell is much greater than the concentration outside the cell. If all the K⁺ channels opened, K⁺ would rush out of the cell. If K⁺ were not an ion and did not have a charge, it would simply flow down its concentration gradient until the intracellular concentration was equal to the extracellular concentration. But K⁺ is positively charged, and thus when it flows out the cell it leaves a net negative charge inside. The V_{K^+} is the equilibrium membrane potential at which the outward forces drawing K⁺ down its concentration gradient are exactly matched by the electrostatic forces drawing the positively-charged K⁺ into the negatively-charged cell (Fig. 12-16). When you plug and chug the numbers, $V_{K^+} = -90$ mV.

This equation explains why the cell (and its membrane potential) becomes negative with K⁺ efflux from the cell and positive with Na+ or Ca2+ influx. The membrane potential of the cell at any given moment depends on the relative permeability of the cell to the various ions. At rest, Na⁺ channels are leaking much more slowly than are the K⁺ channels, which explains why the resting membrane potential is only slightly more positive than –90 mV. The opening of voltage-gated Na⁺ channels during an action potential, which makes the cell transiently more permeable to Na⁺ than K⁺, explains why the membrane potential shoots up to near the Na⁺ equilibrium potential.

Figure 12-17 shows the action potential of a myocardial cell. The phases of the action potential are as follows:

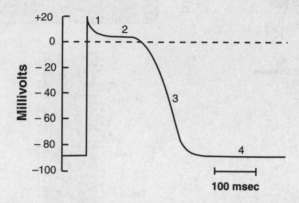

Fig. 12-17. Myocyte action potential.

- Phase 0 is called the *rapid upstroke*. Voltage-gated Na⁺ channels open, Na⁺ flows in, and the cell depolarizes, bringing the cell potential closer to the Na⁺ equilibrium potential.

- Phase 1 is initial repolarization caused by the opening of slow voltage-gated K⁺ channels followed by K⁺ efflux. At the same time, phase 0 Na⁺ channels become inactivated.

- **Phase 2** is called the plateau phase. Voltage-gated Ca²⁺ channels open, causing Ca²+ influx. The Ca²⁺ influx balances K+ efflux, so there is no change in the membrane potential. Ca2+ influx is also important because it drives the contraction of the myocytes via actin and myosin interactions.

- **Phase 3** is rapid repolarization. The Ca²⁺ channels close, and the K⁺ channels are now open without opposition, causing a relatively massive K⁺ efflux. This brings the cell membrane potential back to the resting potential. Repolarization allows the Na⁺ channels to recover from inactivation so that they're ready for the next action potential.

- **Phase 4** is the resting state (resting membrane potential). The resting K⁺ channels are open, allowing K⁺ efflux and bringing the cell close to the K⁺ equilibrium membrane potential (–90 mV).

Pacemaker Cells

The cells of the SA node, AV node, and His-Purkinje system all have pacemaker activity. The SA node normally controls the heart rate, but if it fails, the AV node takes over, followed by the His-Purkinje system.

Figure 12-18 shows the action potential of a pacemaker cell. The phases of the action potential are as follows:

- **Phase 0** is the slow upstroke. Slow Ca^{2+} channels open, causing Ca2+ influx. Resting K^+ channels close due to this depolarization.

There is no phase 1 because voltage-gated Na^+ channels are not involved in phase 0! In pacemaker cells, the resting membrane potential is more positive than normal, therefore the Na+ channels never recover from their inactive state.

- **Phase 3** is repolarization caused by Ca^{2+} channels closing and K+ channels opening, which allows unopposed K^+ efflux (hence, no phase 2).

- **Phase 4** is considered diastolic depolarization (or automaticity). This is caused by the slow closure of K^+ channels and by Na^+ channels letting Na^+ leak into the cell. (These Na+ channels are different from the fast sodium channels responsible for phase 0 cardiac cell depolarization.) The membrane potential gradually becomes more positive until it reaches a threshold and results in an action potential (and heartbeat).

The phase 4 slope determines the heart rate and is controlled by the sympathetic and vagal tone. Catecholamines or $\beta1$-agonists increase the slope by increasing Na^+ influx, so the threshold is reached faster and the heart rate increases (Fig. 12-18).

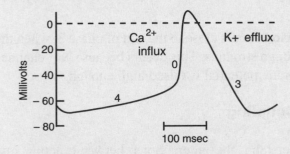

Fig. 12-18. Node cell action potential.

Conduction through the AV node is also faster because of increased Ca^{2+} influx during phase 0 and a steeper phase 0 slope. This is reflected on the ECG by a shorter PR interval. Acetylcholine or muscarinic agonists increase K^+ efflux, lowering the phase 4 slope, prolonging the time to reach threshold and ultimately lowering the heart rate. Conduction velocity through the AV node is slowed, and the PR interval is prolonged.

Refractory periods are part of normal pacemaker activity. The **absolute refractory period** occurs when the cell absolutely refuses to depolarize no matter how much stimulus you give it starting from phase 1 and extending into phase 3 (Fig. 12-19). This inability to depolarize is caused by the temporary mechanical inactivation of voltage-gated channels.

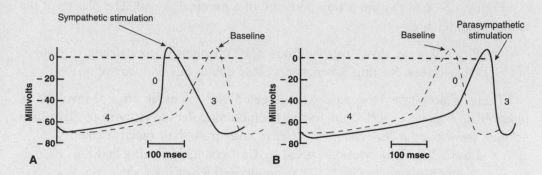

Fig. 12-19. Node cell action potential with (**A**) sympathetic stimulation and (**B**) parasympathetic stimulation.

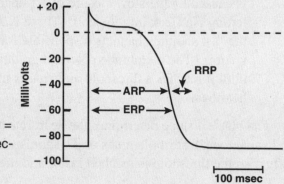

Fig. 12-20. Refractory periods. (ARP = absolute refractory period; ERP = effective refractory period; RRP = relative refractive period.)

The **relative refractory period** occurs close to the end of phase 3, when the cell can depolarize early if given enough stimulus. This occurs because Na$^+$ channels are able to open again if the membrane potential is raised high enough.

Excitation-Contraction Coupling

Refer to chapter 10 to understand the interactions between actin, myosin, tropomyosin, and troponin.

After membrane depolarization, Ca2$^+$ influx occurs during phase 2. Ca^{2+} binds to ryanodine receptors on the SR, which causes them to open, releasing even more Ca^{2+} in the cell (Fig. 12-21). The available intracellular Ca^{2+} leads to sarcomere contraction.

For the myocyte to relax, Ca^{2+} must be removed from the cell. This is done in two ways. The SR has an ATP-dependent Ca^{2+} pump, which brings Ca^{2+} into the SR. If the amount of Ca^{2+} stored in the SR is increased, then the subsequent contractions are even more vigorous. This energy of contraction is called **contractility**.

The other calcium removal mechanism is an N^{a+}-Ca^{2+} exchanger. It depends primarily on the Na$^+$ gradient across the membrane, so that if there's very little Na+ inside, three Na$^+$ can move into the cell quickly in exchange for one Ca^{2+} pushed out. This is important for understanding the effects of digitalis.

Because *digitalis* poisons the Na$^+$/K$^+$ ATPase, Na$^+$ accumulates in the myocyte and decreases the Na$^+$ gradient (Na$^+$ isn't as interested in rushing into the cell because there's already enough Na$^+$ inside). Ultimately, the N^{a+}-Ca^{2+} exchanger doesn't work as well as the calcium pump, Ca^{2+} accumulates in the cell and is stored in the SR, and the muscle contracts more vigorously on subsequent beats (Fig. 12-22). Therefore, digitalis increases contractility and is called a **positive inotrope**.

Extracellular

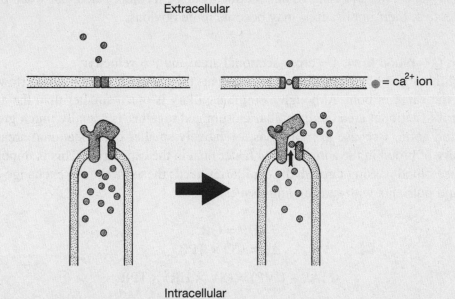

$= ca^{2+}$ ion

Intracellular

Fig. 12-21. Cardiac muscle contraction.

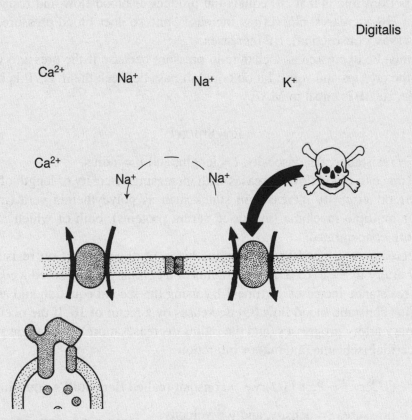

Digitalis

Ca^{2+} Na^+ Na^+ K^+

Ca^{2+}

Na^+ Na^+

Fig. 12-22. Effect of digitalis on cardiac muscle contraction.

The Physics of Circulation

At first glance, the equations in this section may seem complicated, but when put in perspective, their implications may become more obvious.

$$Q = Av$$

where Q = blood flow, A = cross-sectional area, and v = velocity.

Think about blood flow in the aorta versus the capillaries. Total blood flow has to be the same in both. Although a single capillary is much smaller than the aorta, the cross-sectional area of all capillaries summed together is actually much greater than the aorta. Because the aorta has a relatively smaller cross-sectional area, the velocity of blood in the aorta is much faster than in the capillaries. This is important because blood passing through the capillaries needs the extra time to exchange oxygen and nutrients with surrounding tissues.

$$BP = QR$$
$$\Delta P = CO \times TPR$$

$$(MAP - CVP) = (SV \times HR) \times TPR$$

where Q = cardiac output, CO = blood flow, BP = blood pressure = ΔP = mean arterial pressure (MAP) – central venous pressure (CVP), TPR = total peripheral resistance, SV = stroke volume, and HR = heart rate.

The bottom line is that BP equals the product of blood flow and resistance. If the SV or HR increases, blood flow increases, and so does blood pressure. If TPR increases (vasoconstriction), BP increases.

BP must be expressed as a change in pressure because if the pressure were the same in the arteries and veins, blood couldn't pass between them. CVP is basically negligible, so BP is equal to MAP.

$$R = 8\eta l/\pi r^4$$

where R = resistance, η = viscosity, l = length, and r = radius.

Resistance to blood flow increases with increasing viscosity or length of a blood vessel. Blood viscosity increases in states such as polycythemia vera (increased RBCs) or multiple myeloma (increased serum proteins), both of which make the blood more concentrated.

A decrease in a blood vessel's radius has a profound effect on resistance. In coronary artery disease (CAD), if the radius of a coronary artery is reduced by half, then the resistance increases 16 times! By using the second equation and assuming BP remains constant, blood flow (Q) decreases by a factor of 16. If the occlusion in the coronary artery progresses (and the radius decreases more), the patient may suffer myocardial ischemia (angina) or infarction.

$$P_1 + (1/2)rv_1^2 = P_2 + (1/2)rv_2^2 = \text{constant (called \textbf{Bernoulli's equation})}$$

where P = pressure, r = density, and v = velocity.

Unfortunately, this one isn't intuitive. If pressure increases, velocity decreases and vice versa. For example, if you put your thumb over the end of a garden hose, the water shoots out faster, but the water velocity inside the hose is slower, causing pressure to increase behind your thumb. The importance of this will become apparent shortly.

$$s = Pr/w$$

where s = wall stress, P = pressure, r = radius, and w = wall thickness.

The wall stress of an artery increases if the pressure within the artery increases, if the radius of the artery increases, or if wall thickness decreases.

Abdominal aortic aneurysms are a good example of how all these equations come together. They occur when a region of the vessel wall becomes weak and distends. Because the radius increases, the cross-sectional area increases, and the velocity of blood in this region decreases ($Q = Av$). Bernoulli's equation says that if velocity decreases, then pressure increases. And if pressure increases, wall stress increases, which leads to even more distention of the region. Things go from bad to worse! This cycle progresses until the aorta tears and the patient dies or the physician hears an abdominal bruit and saves the day.

The **Starling equation** is as follows:

$$F = k[(P_{cap} - P_{int}) - (\pi cap - \pi int)]$$

where F = transcapillary flow, k = filtration constant, P_{cap} = capillary hydrostatic pressure forcing fluid out of the capillary, P_{int} = interstitial hydrostatic pressure forcing fluid out of the interstitium, π_{cap} = capillary oncotic pressure pulling fluid into the capillary, and π_{int} = interstitial oncotic pressure pulling fluid into the interstitium.

F is simply the amount of fluid that leaks out of the capillary into the interstitium. In **congestive heart failure** (CHF), blood is not ejected efficiently from the LV, and pressure within the LV increases. This increase in pressure is felt within the LA and the pulmonary capillaries. When the pressure within the pulmonary capillaries increases, more fluid leaks into the interstitium, causing **pulmonary edema (PE)**.

Patients with **nephrotic syndrome** lose an enormous amount of protein through their urine. As a result, π_{cap} decreases, F increases, and more fluid leaks into the interstitium.

The Cardiac Cycle

Figure 12-23 illustrates events that occur in the aorta, LA, and LV but could also be used to describe events within the pulmonary artery, RA, and RV. The only difference is that the maximum pressure on the y-axis would be approximately 20 mm Hg in the right-sided circulation.

Atrial systole comes right after the P wave (depolarization of the atria). It is seen in the venous pulse as the **a wave**, and in patients with LV hypertrophy, an S_4 is heard.

Isovolumetric contraction comes right after the QRS complex (depolarization of the ventricles) and causes the mitral valve to close (tricuspid valve on the right side) when LV pressure is greater than LA pressure. This closure corresponds to S1. Because the aortic valve is also closed, no blood is ejected from the ventricle.

Rapid ejection occurs when the LV pressure is greater than the aortic pressure. This is when most of the stroke volume is ejected. The **c wave** corresponds to RV contraction and the tricuspid valve bulging into the RA.

Reduced ejection occurs as blood continues to be ejected slowly from the ventricle. Ventricular pressure begins to decrease (from ventricular repolarization), and aortic pressure starts to fall as blood quickly flows into the smaller arteries.

Isovolumetric relaxation comes right after the T wave. When LV pressure drops below aortic pressure, the back-flow of blood causes the aortic valve to close (pulmonic valve on the right side), which is heard as S_2. The atria continue to fill against a closed tricuspid (and mitral) valve, causing the pressure to increase in the RA (and LA). This is seen as the **v wave** of the jugular venous pressure (JVP). When the aortic valve closes, the transient increase in aortic pressure is called the **dicrotic notch.**

Rapid ventricular filling occurs when LV pressure drops below LA pressure and the mitral valve opens. An S_3 may be heard in normal children but is also heard in patients with dilated CHF.

Reduced ventricular filling (diastasis) is marked by a slower increase in ventricular volume. Diastasis ends with the onset of atrial contraction.

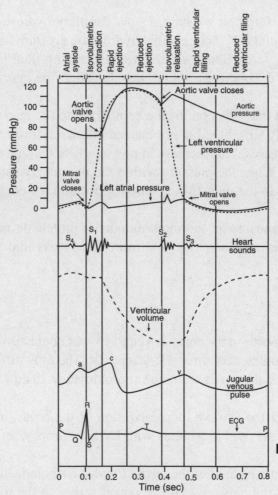

Fig. 12-23. The cardiac cycle.

Cardiac Output

Cardiac output (CO) depends on four parameters: **preload, afterload, heart rate (HR),** and contractility. It is essential to understand these interactions.

Preload is the amount of blood in the ventricle at the end of diastole (end-diastolic volume [EDV]). Preload increases with exercise, transfusion, and sympathetic stimulation (venous constriction). It decreases with hypovolemia (dehydration) or venous dilation (nitroglycerin).

When preload increases, the ventricle fills with more blood, and the sarcomeres in the myocyte are stretched. This increases the number of actin-myosin cross-bridges and facilitates a more vigorous contraction of the myocyte. This is reflected on the **Frank-Starling curve** (Fig. 12-24).

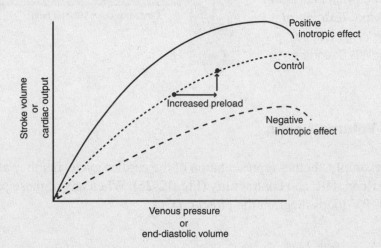

Fig. 12-24. Frank-Starling curves. Increased preload moves the individual from point A to point B on the curves. Positive inotyopes shift the curves up; negative inotypes shift the curve down.

As preload increases, the SV increases, which means that CO increases (CO = SV × HR).

Contractility was described earlier and is basically a reflection of the amount of Ca^{2+} stored in the SR. Contractility can be increased (positive inotropic effect) by sympathetic stimulation, digitalis, catecholamines, O_2, increased muscle mass, increased myofibril number, decreased extracellular Na_+, or an increase in HR. As HR increases, the myocyte is stimulated more times per minute, so more Ca^{2+} is released from the SR each minute, leading to increased contractility. As the curve shows, an increase in contractility leads to an increase in CO at any EDV.

Contractility is decreased (negative inotropic effect) by myocardial damage (e.g., infarction, heart failure), decreased extracellular Ca^{2+}, β-adrenergic receptor blockade, hypoxia, acidosis, or decreased HR.

Afterload is essentially the aortic pressure, but it is a reflection of the TPR (regulated at the level of the arterioles). As afterload increases, the ventricle must eject blood in the face of a higher aortic pressure, resulting in a decreased SV and CO.

Afterload increases with sympathetic stimulation, α1-agonists (phenylephrine), coarctation of the aorta, and aortic valve stenosis. Afterload decreases with vasodilation (angiotensin-converting enzyme [ACE] inhibitors, nifedipine).

CO can be calculated by using the Fick principle, as described earlier (Fig. 12-25). It derives from the fact that oxygen delivered to the tissues is equal to oxygen returning from the tissues plus the amount of O_2 that was consumed by the tissues. All you need is an arterial blood draw, a venous blood draw, and a test that measures expired air for a known period of time; then plug and chug.

Fig. 12-25. The Fick principle. (CO = cardiac output; $\dot{V}o_2$ = O_2 consumption; CaO_2 = arterial O_2 content; CvO_2 = venous O_2 content.) (Reprinted with permission from AC Guyton. *Textbook of Medical Physiology* [7th ed]. Philadelphia: WB Saunders, 1986;284.)

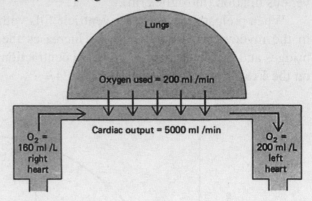

Pressure-Volume Loops

PV loops are simply another representation of the cardiac cycle, but they also reflect preload, afterload, HR, and contractility (Fig. 12-26). When any of these parameters are changed, PV loops diagram the effect on CO.

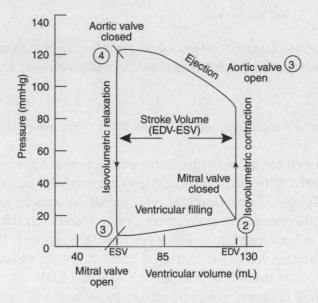

Fig. 12-26. Pressure-volume loop. Numbers correspond to text.

- 1 → 2: Ventricular filling begins once LV pressure drops below LA pressure and the mitral valve opens. The ventricular volume increases, and pressure increases slightly as the ventricular wall is passively stretched by blood. EDV is a reflection of preload.

- 2 → 3: Isovolumetric contraction occurs after the QRS complex, on closure of the mitral valve. LV pressure increases, but ventricular volume doesn't change because both the aortic and mitral valves are closed.

- 3 → 4: Ventricular ejection occurs once the LV pressure is greater than aortic pressure, forcing the aortic valve to open. As blood is ejected into the aorta, ventricular volume decreases. The stroke volume is thus the difference between the EDV and the end-systolic volume (ESV). Ejection fraction is SV/EDV and should be 60–80%. The point at which the aortic valve opens is a reflection of the afterload.

- 4 → 1: Isovolumetric relaxation occurs after the T wave, when LV pressure drops below aortic pressure, and the aortic valve closes. Because both the aortic and mitral valve are again closed, ventricular volume doesn't change as the pressure falls.

The size of the PV loop is also determined by two intersecting lines, E_{es} (**elastance at end systole**) and E_a (**arterial elastance**). The slope of E_{es} describes how tight the ventricle can get at the end of systole and is a reflection of *contractility*. The slope of E_a describes how tight the arterioles can get and is related to TPR. The intersection occurs at the end-systolic pressure and ESV point. E_a intersects the x-axis at the EDV point. E_{es} intersects the x-axis at the point where the ventricle is filled with the maximum amount of blood before ventricular pressure increases (V_0).

If preload increases, the EDV increases on the loop (Fig. 12-27). We already know that the SV increases with increased preload, according to the Frank-Starling relationship (from increased formation of actin and myosin cross-bridges), but now we can see it on the PV loop. If everything else stays constant, the Ea line shifts (in parallel) to a new EDV, and the resulting loop demonstrates an increased SV.

Remember that if SV increases, CO and BP increase (also demonstrated on the loop by an increased diastolic blood pressure [DBP] and systolic blood pressure [SBP]).

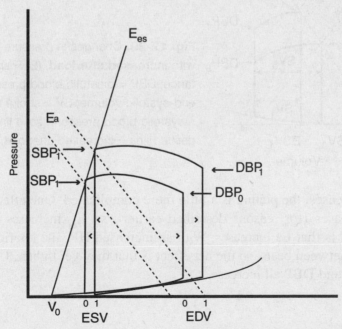

Fig. 12-27. Changes in pressure-volume loop with **increased preload**. (E_a = arterial elastance; DBP = diastolic blood pressure; SBP = systolic blood pressure; EDV = end-diastolic volume; SV = stroke volume.) Afterload and contractility are held constant. 1 represents increased preload, or end-diastolic volume. Note the increased preload.

If contractility increases while everything else remains constant, the slope of the Ees line increases (Fig. 12-28). The new PV loop again demonstrates an increased SV, DBP, and SBP. Intuitively, remember that if the ventricle squeezes harder (increased contractility), SV and CO increase.

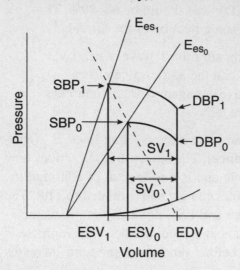

Fig. 12-28. Changes in pressure-volume loop with **increased contractility**. (E_{es} = elastance at end systole; DBP = diastolic blood pressure; ESV = end-systolic volume; EDV = end-diastolic volume; SV = stroke volume; SBP = systolic blood pressure; solid line = baseline.)

If afterload increases while everything else is constant, the slope of the Ea line increases (Fig. 12-29). In this case, the SV decreases (because the LV is now trying to eject blood against a greater aortic pressure), but DBP and SBP increase. This relationship also corresponds to the equation that shows that BP increases when TPR increases (BP = CO x TPR).

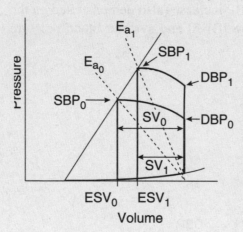

Fig. 12-29. Changes in pressure-volume loop with **increased afterload**. (E_a = arterial elastance; DBP = diastolic blood pressure; ESV = end-systolic volume; SV = stroke volume; SBP = systolic blood pressure; solid line = baseline; dashed line = increased afterload.)

If HR increases, the picture is a little more complicated. One effect is that contractility increases (for reasons described earlier), so E_{es} increases (Fig. 12-30). Another effect is that Ea increases. With an increased HR, the arterioles have less time to relax between beats, so the net effect is that they get tighter. Ultimately, the SV, CO, SBP, and DBP all increase.

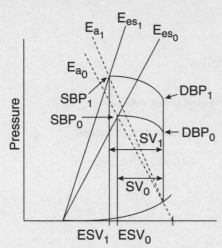

Fig. 12-30. Changes in pressure-volume loop with **increased heart rate**. (E_{es} = elastance at end systole; E_a = arterial elastance; DBP = diastolic blood pressure; ESV = end-systolic volume; EDV = end-diastolic volume; SV = stroke volume; solid line = baseline; dashed line = increased heart rate.)

Although it may seem like overkill, the same information can be presented on *venous return curves* (Fig. 12-31). It's important to be familiar with all these formats because any of them may pop up on the test.

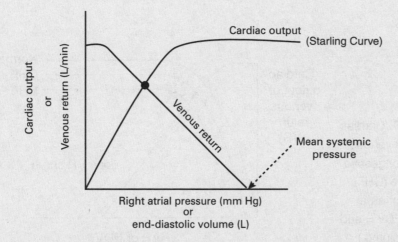

Fig. 12-31. Venous return curve.

The important point is that when the right atrial pressure (RAP) reaches 7 mm Hg, there is no venous return (VR) to the RA. This means that the pressure in the veins (the mean circulatory pressure [MCP]) is also equal to 7 mm Hg. Remember that there must be a change in pressure for blood to flow.

What's cool about this curve is that you can superimpose a Starling curve as well (RAP is another reflection of preload) (see Fig. 12-31). VR has to equal CO because the circulation is a closed system (what goes into the heart must come out). The intercept of the two curves is the value at which CO = VR.

With hemorrhage, the VR curve shifts down and to the left. Because less blood is returning to the heart, the maximum RAP is lower, and CO is lower. If this patient were overtransfused, VR and CO would increase, and the maximum MCP would be higher (Fig. 12-32).

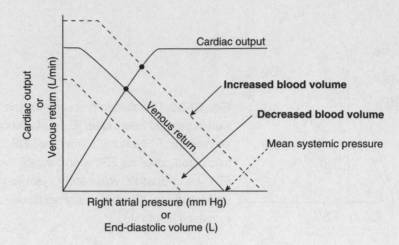

Fig. 12-32. Changes in cardiac output and venous return with transfusion.

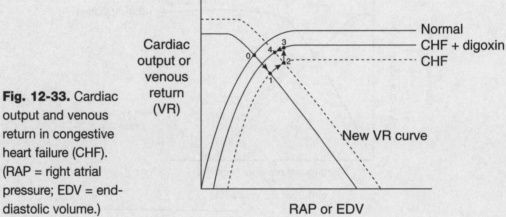

Fig. 12-33. Cardiac output and venous return in congestive heart failure (CHF). (RAP = right atrial pressure; EDV = end-diastolic volume.)

Let's say we have a patient with CHF. The first problem is that the heart is unable to contract the way it normally does. This translates as a decrease in contractility and a shift to a lower Starling curve (point 0 to 1, Fig. 12-33). The body tries to compensate by saving salt and water and increasing preload, which moves the patient up and along the same Starling curve (point 1 to 2—CO also increases a little). You then try to increase the patient's contractility and CO with digoxin (positively inotropic). An increase in contractility shifts the patient to a higher Starling curve (point 2 to 3). Now that the heart is ejecting blood better, there is less congestion in the heart and a lower RAP (point 3 to 4). Although shifting down this Starling curve may lower CO a tiny bit, this measure is ultimately beneficial because it prevents overcongestion and further dilation of the heart.

Regulation of Mean Arterial Pressure

The body is extremely smart and is capable of compensating for a BP that is either too high or too low. The fast response is mediated by the nervous system, and the slower one is mediated by the kidneys.

Consider the example of a patient who has an acute hemorrhage and consequent drop in BP (Fig. 12-34). The decrease in MAP is sensed by baroreceptors in the aortic arch and the carotid sinus. This message is relayed to the medulla via the vagus and glossopharyngeal nerves. The ultimate effect is to decrease stimulation of the vagal center (and decrease parasympathetic outflow) and increase stimulation of sympathetic outflow. Both mechanisms serve to increase the MAP by increasing HR, contractility, VR, and TPR (vasoconstriction).

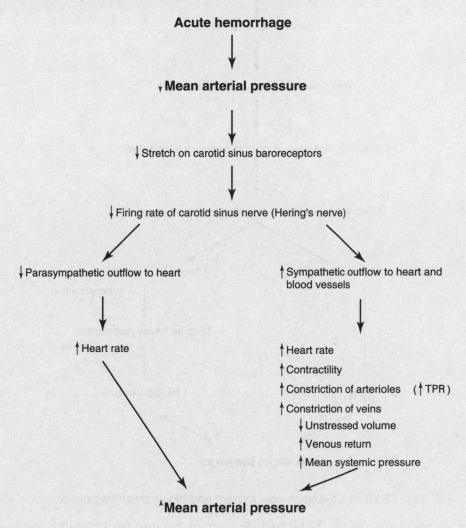

Fig. 12-34. Baroreceptors and fast blood pressure control.

A second, slower method of increasing MAP is via the renin-angiotensin-aldosterone system (Fig. 12-35). The decrease in MAP is sensed by the juxtaglomerular (JG) cells, which then release renin into the blood. Renin converts angiotensinogen to angiotensin I, then angiotensin-converting enzyme (ACE) modifies angiotensin I to angiotensin II in the lungs. Angiotensin II is a potent vasoconstrictor and causes an increase in TPR; it also leads to aldosterone release from the zona glomerulosa of the adrenal cortex. Aldosterone works at the level of the nephron—more specifically, at the distal collecting tubules—to increase retention of Na^+ and water. This increases plasma volume, preload, SV, CO, and ultimately BP.

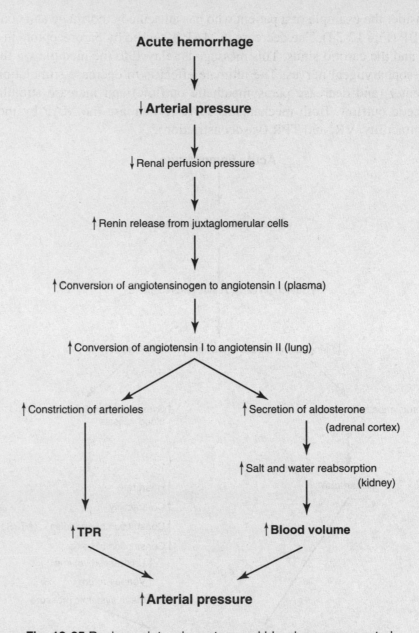

Acute hemorrhage

↓**Arterial pressure**

↓ Renal perfusion pressure

↑ Renin release from juxtaglomerular cells

↑ Conversion of angiotensinogen to angiotensin I (plasma)

↑ Conversion of angiotensin I to angiotensin II (lung)

↑ Constriction of arterioles   ↑ Secretion of aldosterone
                                              (adrenal cortex)

                                          ↑ Salt and water reabsorption
                                              (kidney)

↑**TPR**   ↑**Blood volume**

↑**Arterial pressure**

Fig. 12-35 Renin-angiotensin system and blood pressure control.

Other regulators of the MAP include chemoreceptors peripherally (aortic and carotid bodies) and centrally (the brain). When MAP decreases, less O_2 is delivered to these receptors and blood Pco_2 decreases. The aortic and carotid bodies respond mostly to an increase in Pco_2 (and the resulting decrease in blood pH) but can also respond to a decrease in Po_2. The central receptors do not respond directly to $Po2$. The cumulative effect is to help increase sympathetic tone and decrease vagal tone.

A decrease in MAP also stimulates the posterior pituitary to release antidiuretic hormone, which increases water absorption at the collecting tubules.

On the other hand, if MAP increases, everything works in reverse to lower it. In addition, the elevated MAP stretches the atria, which release atrial natriuretic peptide. This peptide inhibits vasoconstriction (TPR decreases), increases Na^+ and water excretion by the kidney, and inhibits the JG cells from releasing renin. The resultant decrease in TPR and blood volume causes a decrease in MAP.

Table 12-2. Cardiac output to various organ systems

Circulation	% of Resting cardiac output	Control	Vasoactive metabolites
Coronary	5%	Local metabolic	Hypoxia, adenosine
Cerebral	15%	Local metabolic	CO_2, H^+
Muscle	20%	Metabolic and sympathetic	Lactate, adenosine, K^+
Pulmonary	100%	Local metabolic	Hypoxic vasoconstriction
Renal	25%	Local metabolic	—
Skin	5%	Sympathetic	—
Liver	29%	Local metabolic	—

Circulation to Specific Organs

Organs are very selfish by nature and try to preserve their blood flow despite what's going on in the rest of the body (Table 12-2).

- The heart is able to extract a huge amount of O_2 from the blood (large arteriovenous [AV] O_2 difference). If more O_2 is needed (e.g., if HR increases), the only way the muscle can get it is if coronary blood flow increases; it cannot increase O_2 extraction.

- The control of blood flow to skeletal muscle depends on its activity level. At rest, sympathetic fibers stimulate a1-receptors, leading to vasoconstriction and increased TPR. If the muscle is actively exercising, however, local metabolites override sympathetic control and cause vasodilation of local blood vessels, which increases blood flow (and O_2) to the hard-working muscle.

- Skin is one of the few team players. If there is sympathetic stimulation, blood vessels to the skin constrict so that blood can be supplied to more critical organs (i.e., brain and muscle) during a "fight-or-flight" response.

- Kidneys receive the largest amount of blood flow per gram of tissue.

- The lungs must accept the entire CO with each beat. Their circulation is discussed in chapter 11.

- The liver accepts the largest percentage of the systemic CO.

- The GI tract also acts as a martyr during a sympathetic response and diverts blood away by constricting splanchnic vessels.

Responses to Standing

The behavior of blood during postural change is the perfect example that gravity works on fluid, even when the fluid is in blood vessels. Because veins are not muscular structures, blood pools in leg veins when a person moves from a lying to standing position. If more blood remains in the legs, there's less blood to return to the heart, so VR decreases, as does CO and BP. If the body doesn't respond to this drop in CO, the patient may feel light-headed or faint outright. This is called orthostatic hypotension. Most of the time, though, the body responds promptly to maintain BP by increasing sympathetic stimulation, which raises HR and TPR.

Responses to Aerobic Exercise

Exercise is extremely complicated physiologically, but a few generalizations can be made. Sympathetic tone increases, which increases HR and contractility. VR increases from muscle contraction (which "milks" venous blood back to the heart) and from venoconstriction (decreases blood pooled in the veins). CO increases mostly from increased HR but also from increased SV and contractility. TPR increases in nonexercising tissues but decreases in active muscles (from local metabolite-induced vasodilation) to give a net decrease in TPR. The AV O_2 difference increases because muscles are consuming more O_2. All these factors serve to increase BP slightly.

Hypertension

Essential hypertension (95% of hypertensive patients) occurs when no cause can be attributed to persistently elevated BP. **Secondary hypertension** has several possible causes, including the following:

- **Estrogen** in birth control pills causes hypertension in about 5% of women taking the oral contraceptive.

- **Renal diseases** are associated with hypertension, probably due to dysfunction in the renin-angiotensin-aldosterone system.

- **Renovascular hypertension**, or renal artery stenosis, is caused by a thickening of the renal artery wall. It results in the juxtaglomerular apparatus sensing a decrease in renal blood flow, which revs up the renin-angiotensin-aldosterone system.

- **Hyperaldosteronism** and **Cushing's** syndrome often lead to hypertension and are usually due to adrenal adenomas.

- **Pheochromocytoma** is a rare adrenal tumor that secretes epinephrine and norepinephrine.

- **Coarctation** of the aorta causes hypertension and presents in newborns and infants.

Signs & Symptoms

Most patients are asymptomatic. Patients with significant hypertension might show signs of the end-organ damage caused by the disease: blindness, aneurysm, CNS injury (stroke), or coronary artery disease (CAD).

Diagnosis

Patients are diagnosed with elevated BP on at least three separate occasions. White coat fear (i.e., fear of visiting the doctor's office) leading to increased BP must be ruled out. Hypertension is defined as either systolic BP greater than 140 or diastolic BP greater than 90 on three occasions.

Treatment

There are a myriad of drugs to manage hypertension, including β-blockers and diuretics. β-Blockers are contraindicated in chronic obstructive pulmonary disease (COPD), diabetes, and CHF. Other options include ACE inhibitors (useful in diabetics because they decrease diabetic nephropathy), calcium channel blockers, nitrates, direct-acting agents (e.g., hydralazine and minoxidil), and α-adrenergic blockers, such as terazosin, which are useful in male patients with benign prostatic hypertrophy.

Ischemic Heart Disease

Coronary Artery Disease

CAD is a huge cause of morbidity and mortality in our sedentary, hamburger-and-fries-eating, overweight society. The following terms are helpful in understanding CAD:

Atherosclerosis is plaque formation in the arteries. The steps in plaque formation are as follows:

1. Fatty streak (at the intima)

2. Simple plaque formation

3. Fibrin deposition and calcification

4. Complicated plaque

5. Thrombosis, which can lead to occlusion

Ischemic heart disease is thought to be a direct result of atherosclerosis of the coronary arteries. **Angina** is transient chest pain, often described by patients as crushing, suffocating, or "like an elephant sitting on my chest." It is substernal, often with radiation to the left arm, neck, or jaw. It can usually be brought on by exercise (hence the use of treadmill tests for diagnosing cardiac disease). It is relieved by nitrates (e.g., sublingual nitroglycerin) and rest. The pathology of angina is temporary occlusion of the coronary vasculature, either by thrombosis, vasospasm, or embolism.

Several classifications of angina exist. **Stable angina** occurs with a well-specified amount of exertion, regularly, and in an unchanging pattern. **Unstable angina** is angina that is new; that is increasing in frequency, duration, or intensity; or that occurs at rest. **Variant (Prinzmetal's) angina** is caused by coronary vasospasm. It occurs at rest, is relieved by calcium channel blockers, and is thought to be triggered by cold and factors other than exercise.

Myocardial Infarction

Myocardial infarction (MI) is occlusion of a coronary artery lasting long enough to result in ischemia to the myocardium. This can then lead to infarction and necrosis of the involved myocardium. The pathologic changes during an MI are as follows:

Day 1: infarct, necrosis begins

Days 2–4: inflammation, hyperemia, neutrophilic infiltration

Days 5–10: granulation tissue, macrophages, neutrophils

Day 10–6 weeks: completion of scar

Several complications may occur after an MI, including

- Arrhythmias

- CHF, pulmonary edema

- Cardiogenic shock

- Ventricular wall rupture, ventricular aneurysm, papillary muscle rupture

- Pericarditis (known as Dressler's syndrome)

- Sudden cardiac death, usually due to arrhythmia

Signs & Symptoms

Angina, dyspnea, fatigue, diaphoresis, nausea, and vomiting (from vagal stimulation).

Diagnosis

ECG. It's always best to have an old ECG for comparison. Specifically, look for:
- Signs of ischemia—T wave peaking or inversion
- Signs of injury—ST elevations or depressions in consecutive leads
- Signs of infarction—wide and deep Q waves in consecutive leads

Laboratory tests in MI include the following:
- Creatine kinase (CK). Look for a peak in CK levels. CK isoenzymes should be determined. The MB isoenzyme has a cardiac source. Other isoenzymes include MM (skeletal muscle) and BB (CNS source).
- Lactate dehydrogenase (LDH).
- AST. Aspartate aminotransferase.
- Troponin I: a new test
- Homocysteine. High serum levels have recently been found to have an extremely high correlation with the risk for CAD.

Chest X-ray (CXR) may show signs of CHF, such as pulmonary edema.

Treatment

The standard therapy for angina and possible MI (known popularly as a "rule-out MI" protocol) has been determined with extensive clinical investigative trials, and includes the following:
- **β-Blockers**. These reduce myocardial oxygen demand by decreasing inotropy and HR and cause minimal peripheral vasodilation, leading to some decrease in afterload.
- **Aspirin**. Several studies have shown the benefit of aspirin in unstable angina. It acts as an antiplatelet factor as well as a possible antioxidant.
- **Nitrates**. Nitroglycerin acts directly on endothelial cells to cause vasodilation, resulting in decreased preload and somewhat decreased afterload. Coronary vasodilation leads to relief of pain.
- **Supplemental oxygen**. The myocardium, which may be ischemic, benefits from improved oxygen delivery.

- **Pain and anxiety relief.** Opiates and benzodiazepines not only improve the patient's comfort but also decrease myocardial demand by relaxing the patient.
- **ACE inhibitors**. After a significant MI, ACE inhibitors are thought to improve cardiac "remodeling."

Arrhythmias need to be treated, but studies show no benefit to prophylaxis against arrhythmias after MI. The biggest risk for sudden death after MI is from arrhythmias, particularly within 48–72 hours of the event.

Once it has been determined that a patient is likely experiencing ischemia, further investigation or intervention must be initiated, including CK levels and special studies. These studies include the following:

- **Treadmill stress test**: It can uncover stress-induced ischemia, or be used for prognostication. After MI, a treadmill test can determine the patient's likely functional status.
- **Dipyridamole (Persantine)-thallium stress test**: Radiolabeled thallium is an analogue of K^+, so it's taken up by metabolically active myocardial tissue. Dipyridamole causes coronary vasodilation in normal coronaries, so that ischemic areas receive even less blood (a steal phenomenon), thereby unmasking ischemia.
- **Echocardiography**: This is ultrasound imaging of the heart, used to study ventricular wall motion, valve defects, and heart size. It can be performed with dobutamine infusion as a stress test.
- **Cardiac catheterization**: This allows direct examination of the coronary anatomy, looking for areas of occlusion and stenosis. A catheter is inserted in the femoral artery and threaded retrograde to the aortic root, where it's inserted into the right coronary artery and left coronary artery sequentially. Dye is injected, and the coronary blood flow is filmed with fluoroscopy. A right-heart catheter (e.g., Swan-Ganz, PA catheter) can also be inserted to look at the PA pressure, pulmonary capillary wedge pressure (PCWP), and CO. With access to the coronary arteries, there are several options for intervention, such as percutaneous transluminal coronary **angioplasty** (PTCA) or stent placement.
- **Angioplasty**: PTCA involves inserting a catheter through the coronary arteries to the site of an occlusion and dilating a balloon to open up the occlusion. Alternatively, a stent—a device that props open the coronary vessel—can be inserted. Large trials have shown the benefit of PTCA in CAD. Studies comparing PTCA and coronary bypass surgery show that both are efficacious, but bypass lasts longer.
- **Thrombolytics**: Tissue plasminogen activator (tPA) and streptokinase directly lyse clots and are indicated in acute MI, as an alternative to PTCA. They are contraindicated if the patient is at risk for significant bleeding. (See table 7-7).

Prevention of ischemic heart disease includes risk factor reduction:

- Smoking cessation
- Exercise
- Weight loss
- Cholesterol lowering through diet and/or pharmacologic means
- Blood pressure lowering
- Aspirin prophylaxis in men with at least one risk factor and no contraindications
- Folic acid supplementation (1 mg/day), along with vitamins B_6 and B_{12} in pations with elevated plasma homocysteine levels

Congestive Heart Failure

Chronic injury to the myocardium through ischemia or other causes leads to decreased contractility, remodeling of myocardium, and inability of the heart to adequately pump blood. Causes include ischemic injury (MI) and cardiomyopathy (ethanol, viral, toxic, idiopathic).

There are several ways of thinking about CHF: (1) forward versus backward failure, (2) LV versus RV failure, or (3) systolic versus diastolic dysfunction.

- **Forward failure**: The heart can't adequately perfuse the rest of the body, leading to cyanosis, fatigue, and end-organ damage (e.g., renal failure, altered mental status, angina, elevated liver enzymes). **Backward failure**: The heart can't keep up with the volume of blood presented to it (preload), leading to pulmonary edema, dyspnea on exertion, paroxysmal nocturnal dyspnea, orthopnea, distended neck veins, hepatosplenomegaly, and pedal edema. Compensatory mechanisms include increased sympathetic activity: HR increases, contractility increases slightly, fluid is retained (the body tries to maximize Starling forces by increasing preload). **Myocardial hypertrophy** is the dreaded "remodeling" of myocardium. Remodeling is partially thwarted by ACE inhibitors.

- **LV failure** is primarily manifested in pulmonary edema and elevated left atrial pressures (measured through pulmonary capillary wedge pressure with a Swan-Ganz catheter). **RV failure** is manifested primarily through increased jugular venous pressure (JVP), pedal edema, and hepatosplenomegaly.

- **Systolic failure**: A dilated, baggy heart can't contract efficiently during systole. **Diastolic failure**: A stiff, noncompliant heart can't relax fully and therefore can't fill completely with blood, leading to reduced preload and insufficient cardiac output.

Cor pulmonale refers to enlargement of the RV due to pulmonary hypertension. The most common underlying pulmonary disorder is reduction of the lung vascular bed. COPD is the most common cause of cor pulmonale. See chapter 11 for details on diagnosis and treatment.

Signs & Symptoms

Signs of either forward failure or backward failure. These may present with syncope, or even sudden death. Arrhythmias are common.

Diagnosis

ECG may show atrial or ventricular hypertrophy, or both, and possibly conduction abnormalities. Echocardiogram shows depressed myocardial function and may show mural thrombus (from stasis of flow). **Ejection fraction** (EF) can be estimated from Doppler flow studies on echocardiography. An EF less than 20% reveals severe dysfunction (an EF above 50% is considered normal). Coronary catheterization is performed to rule out ischemic causes of cardiomyopathy.

Treatment

Treatment is based on whether the pathology is primarily systolic or diastolic dysfunction. In systolic dysfunction, the plan is to improve CO, limit symptoms, and anticoagulate to prevent embolism from mural thrombus. CO can be enhanced with digoxin, and symptoms of backward failure and resulting fluid overload can be improved with ACE inhibitors and diuretics. β-Blockers and calcium channel blockers are contraindicated because of their negative inotropic effects.

Diastolic dysfunction causes impaired relaxation, which makes the patient's CO highly dependent on preload. If preload is decreased too much, the ventricle inadequately fills, and the patient becomes hypotensive. If the preload is too high (high PCWP), the patient can easily develop pulmonary edema. The key is gentle diuresis and relaxation of the diastolic phase with calcium channel blockers. Nitrates are contraindicated because of their effect on preload.

Cardiomyopathies

Dilated Cardiomyopathy

A big, baggy heart with very little functional myocardium leads to mostly systolic dysfunction. Causes include ischemic heart disease, ethanol, viral causes, and drugs (e.g., adriamycin).

Signs & Symptoms

Signs of CHF, peripheral edema, fatigue, dyspnea on exertion, paroxysmal nocturnal dyspnea, cyanosis, clubbing, S_3 and S_4, and elevated neck veins.

Diagnosis

Echocardiography is diagnostic. ECG, CK levels, LDH, and troponin may be used to rule out MI. Cardiac catheterization is also indicated to rule out ischemic causes that can be treated.

Treatment

Similar to that of CHF.

Hypertrophic Cardiomyopathy

An abnormally thickened myocardium, particularly within the IV septum, leads to primarily diastolic dysfunction. Causes include autosomal dominant inheritance (most cases are familial), athlete's heart, and thick IV septum. This condition is also known as *hypertrophic-obstructive cardiomyopathy* (HOCM) or *idiopathic hypertrophic subaortic stenosis* (IHSS).

Signs & Symptoms

History of sudden death in the family, fatigue, and signs of forward heart failure and backward failure. A murmur is best appreciated in situations that decrease preload (e.g., standing) or decrease afterload (e.g., amyl nitrite infusion). It decreases in situations that increase preload (e.g., squatting) or increase afterload (e.g., hand grip). Note that the opposite is true of murmurs of aortic stenosis. An S4 is common.

Diagnosis

Echocardiography, cardiac catheterization, and PA catheter placement.

Treatment

Because of the risk of sudden death, an implantable defibrillator is strongly advised. The patient's CO is highly dependent on preload, so fluids must be controlled closely. See Congestive Heart Failure, earlier.

Restrictive Cardiomyopathy

Thickened or rigid pericardium prevents the heart from filling properly. Causes include radiation, amyloidosis (described later), sarcoidosis, Löffler's syndrome (transient pulmonary infiltrates, cough, fever, and peripheral blood eosinophilia), and Fabry's disease (α-galactosidase A deficiency).

Signs & Symptoms

Dyspnea on exertion, fatigue, signs of right heart failure, elevated JVP, Kussmaul's sign (neck vein elevation on inspiration), S_3, and S_4.

Diagnosis

ECG, echocardiography, cardiac catheterization, and tissue biopsy to make the specific diagnosis. It is important to rule out ischemia and tamponade.

Treatment

No treatment for the cardiomyopathy, only management of the heart failure. Pacemakers are indicated given the propensity for involvement of the conduction system.

Amyloidosis

Amyloidosis is a disease characterized by deposits of an extracellular protein called *amyloid*. The amyloid can accumulate in any tissue of the body but is most commonly found in the joints, subcutaneous tissue, the solid organs (heart, liver, kidney), lungs, brain, nervous tissue, and bowel. In **primary amyloidosis**, the amyloid protein is an immunoglobulin light chain (AL). The disease is associated with multiple myeloma. In **secondary amyloidosis**, serum amyloid (SAA) is the responsible protein, which deposits mainly in the kidneys, liver, spleen, and adrenals.

Signs & Symptoms

Depends on the organ involved. For example, cardiac involvement can result in restrictive cardiomyopathy or conduction abnormalities.

Diagnosis

Biopsy reveals characteristic apple-green birefringence under polarized light.

Treatment

Radiation therapy for bony involvement and chemotherapy (vincristine, melphalan). Treatment of cardiomyopathy.

Hemochromatosis

Hemochromatosis is characterized by a genetic defect in the metabolism of iron. As a result, iron deposits all over the body. The disease is autosomal recessively inherited, with manifestations usually in the third decade of life. The disease is more common in men because menstrual blood loss can offset the iron accumulation in women. Because it is treatable and can result in significant end-organ damage if not treated, it is an important diagnosis to make.

Signs & Symptoms

The classic triad seen is **hepatic cirrhosis**, **diabetes mellitus** (from pancreatic deposition), and **bronze pigmentation** of the skin. Cardiac involvement leads to restrictive cardiomyopathy.

Diagnosis

Liver biopsy is the diagnostic test of choice. Serum iron studies (total iron-binding capacity, transferrin, ferritin) all indicate iron overload.

Treatment

Intense phlebotomy therapy to unload the body of iron works pretty well. End-stage liver disease requires liver transplantation. Cardiomyopathy should be treated accordingly.

Arrhythmias

Arrhythmias are caused by abnormalities in the heart's electrical conduction system. In normal sinus rhythm, conduction originates at the sinus node. Specific arrhythmias are discussed below.

- **Sinus tachycardia or bradycardia**: A fast or slow heart rate that still originates at the sinus node, which may be a normal physiologic response (exercise, stress) or a response to underlying disease (e.g., infection, shock, pulmonary embolism, thyroid storm).

- **Atrial arrhythmias**: These include premature atrial beats, wandering pacemaker, and sick sinus syndrome.

- **Atrial fibrillation**: Abnormal conduction through the atria is then conducted through to the ventricles, leading to an *irregularly irregular rhythm* and tachycardia. The disorganized contractions of the atria predispose to formation of mural thrombi, which can then dislodge and embolize to the brain, mesentery, or extremities (all bad news). Treatment involves rate control, anticoagulation, and conversion back to normal sinus rhythm if possible.

- **Conduction blocks** are the slowing of normal conduction though the heart's conduction system. Entities include first-degree block (prolonged PR interval), second-degree block (Mobitz I and II, characterized by dropped QRS waves at regular intervals), and third-degree or complete block (complete AV dissociation). Mobitz I is also known as Wenckebach. AV dissociation is a complete lack of communication between the supraventricular and ventricular conduction systems.

- **Supraventricular tachycardia** is a fast beat originating anywhere above the ventricles.

- **Pre-excitation**: Pre-excitation is characterized by a PR interval that is shortened because conduction occurs through an accessory pathway that conducts more rapidly than the AV node. Two forms of pre-excitation exist. Wolff-Parkinson-White (WPW) syndrome is characterized by a shortened PR interval with an upward-ramping QR segment (*delta wave*). This abnormality is the result of an accessory conduction pathway, usually between the atrium and ventricle of one side (the accessory pathway is the bundle of Kent). The QRS complex with a delta wave is the fusion of the electrical impulse travelling through the accessory pathway and the impulse travelling through the AV node. The accessory pathway can lead to a re-entrant rhythm. This condition is treated with ablation of the accessory pathway. The other form of pre-excitation, **Lown-Ganong-Levine (LGL)** syndrome, is like WPW, except that the accessory pathway is *intranodal*. Consequently, you still see the shortened PR interval, but there is no QRS complex widening or delta wave.

- **Long QT syndrome**: The term is self-descriptive. It can be either acquired (drugs, electrolyte abnormalities), or inherited, a rare form of the disease. The inherited form is caused by mutations in either an inward-rectifying K^+ channel or a Na^+ channel. The important sequela is that certain events (e.g., hypokalemia) can cause progressive lengthening of the QT interval, eventually leading to an arrhythmia called torsades de pointes. In torsades de pointes, there is a wide, complex, undulating ventricular conduction pattern that is often hemodynamically unstable. This can lead to frank ventricular fibrillation.

- **Ventricular tachycardia (v-tach)**: Electrical activity originating in the ventricles. So-called sustained v-tach is a dire sign, and it usually means that the ventricles are not happy (e.g., after an MI), often leading to v-fib.

- **Ventricular fibrillation (v-fib)**: Disorganized electrical activity in the ventricles, which is invariably fatal if not converted (by drugs or shocks).

- **Asystole** (cardiac arrest): No electrical activity at all.

Signs & Symptoms

When an arrhythmia is suspected, determine if there is any possible underlying cardiac or systemic disease. For example, arrhythmias are common after MI, with hyperthyroidism, or with electrolyte abnormalities. Common symptoms include signs of CHF or MI, palpitations, syncope (critical to elicit!), presyncope, or possibly fatigue. On examination, irregular heart rhythm may be noted (note whether it's irregularly irregular or regularly irregular), with AV dissociation. Intermittent cannon a waves (as the RA contracts against a closed tricuspid valve) may be noted on the JVP.

Diagnosis

ECG may be diagnostic. If the symptoms appear episodic, the next step is 24-hour ambulatory ECG monitoring (Holter monitor). The next step is invasive electrophysiologic studies. Catheters are introduced into the heart via venous puncture to study the conduction system and therapeutically ablate arrhythmogenic foci if indicated. Pharmacologic or physiologic (e.g., carotid sinus massage) manipulations can sometimes be used to induce arrhythmias to make a diagnosis. This is contraindicated if the patient has evidence of carotid plaques. Head-up tilt-table testing, in which a patient is strapped to a tilting table, can be useful in assessing autonomic function in response to the sympathetic stimulation of standing up. This test is excellent for diagnosing autonomic dysfunction and neurogenic syncope, believed to be a result of an exaggerated vagal response (neurocardiogenic syncope).

Treatment

First, determine if the arrhythmia needs to be treated. Symptomatic disease with hemodynamic compromise needs to be treated. Patients with underlying impaired CO may not tolerate the added insult of the arrhythmia and thus may require treatment. There are two general treatment modalities:

- Drugs: There are lots of antiarrhythmic drugs (discussed under Pharmacology, later).
- Electrical intervention: DC cardioversion (shocking the heart) is used for arrhythmias that lead to hemodynamic compromise, especially when acute. Patients at risk for intracardiac thrombus (atrial fibrillation, valvular heart disease, CHF) may need to be anticoagulated first because the newly synchronous contractions of the heart after cardioversion may lead to thrombus dislocation and embolization.

Cardiac pacemakers can be either permanently implanted devices or temporary devices. The electrodes that deliver pacing currents can be located in the intravascular space (usually in the RA and RV), in the epicardial space (usually placed temporarily after cardiac surgery), or on the skin (usually placed in an emergent setting).

Valvular Heart Disease

The valves of the heart are amazingly durable, given how much mechanical stress they undergo. Any of the four valves (tricuspid, pulmonic, mitral, and aortic) can malfunction. In general, valve disease is thought of as **stenosis**, narrowing of the valve orifice or decreased mobility of the valve leaflets leading to limitation of outflow, or **regurgitation**, a valve that leaks backward when closed, also known as **insufficiency**.

The common causes of valve disease include congenital defects, infections (endocarditis), inflammatory or autoimmune disease (rheumatic heart disease), and mechanical loss of integrity (dilation of the ventricle with CHF leads to an incompetent mitral valve).

- **Mitral stenosis** and **mitral regurgitation** are usually due to rheumatic fever. **Mitral valve prolapse** is the result of a floppy valve. Mitral valve prolapse is a common finding that may have no hemodynamic consequences.

- **Aortic stenosis** is most commonly caused by a congenital bicuspid valve that gradually thickens throughout life, becoming symptomatic in the later years. Aortic regurgitation is most often caused by rheumatic fever.

- Tricuspid and pulmonic valve disease is much less common than the aortic and mitral valve problems. **Tricuspid disease** is most often caused by rheumatic fever. **Pulmonic disease** is most often congenital (see Congenital Heart Disease, later).

When the aortic or pulmonic valve is stenotic, the increased resistance leads to increased afterload on the ventricles, which usually leads to a **concentric hypertrophy.** Aortic or pulmonic insufficiency, on the other hand, leads to increased volume load on the heart, as a fraction of the ejected blood leaks back. This leads to **dilation** of the affected ventricle. Mitral or tricuspid stenosis leads to blood "backing up" in the atria, resulting in atrial enlargement. Mitral or tricuspid regurgitation places an extra volume load on the ventricles. The ventricles pump their stroke volume both forward in the correct direction and backward to the atria through the incompetent valve. On the next stroke, this extra blood gets dumped from the atria back into the ventricles. The result of both volume and pressure overload leads to cardiomyopathy, increased oxygen demand, and impaired hemodynamics.

Table 12-3. Valvular lesions

Lesion	Symptoms	Signs
Mitral stenosis	Dyspnea, orthopnea, PND	Diastolic rumble Concomitant MR
Mitral regurgitation (MR)	Pulmonary edema, fatigue, right heart failure (secondary to left heart failure)	Holosystolic blowing murmur at the apex
Mitral prolapse	Chest pain, similar to MR	Midsystolic click, late systolic murmur
Aortic stenosis	Chest pain, syncope, presyncope, LV failure	Harsh systolic crescendo-decrescendo murmur at the right upper sternal borders
Aortic regurgitation	LV failure, arrhythmias	High pitched diastolic murmur at the right upper sternal border;
Austin-Flint murmur Quincke's	widened	pulse pressure; pulses; water-hammer pulse; Duroziez's sign
Tricuspid stenosis	RV failure, lower extremity edema, hepatic congestion	Tricuspid opening snap at the left lower sternal border
Tricuspid regurgitation	RV failure, lower extremity edema, hepatic congestion	Large v wave on JVP; blowing systolic murmur at the left lower sternal border

PND = paroxysmal nocturnal dyspnea; LV = left ventricle; RV = right ventricle; JVP = jugular venous pressure.

Signs & Symptoms

The symptoms can be deduced from the predicted hemodynamic effects of each lesion (Table 12-3). Murmurs caused by the different valves are best heard in specific areas of the chest (Fig. 12-36).

Diagnosis

Diagnosis is based on echocardiography, with Doppler visualization of the regurgitation or stenosis. In stenosis, valve area can be estimated from the measured velocity of blood flow through that valve.

Treatment

General management involves (1) treating underlying pathology (e.g., endocarditis, rheumatic fever); (2) management of general symptoms and hemodynamic compromise (e.g., CHF); (3) antibiotic prophylaxis against endocarditis for dental procedures, surgery, and so on; and (4) correction of the valvulopathy (valvuloplasty or valve replacement). Prosthetic valves are either mechanical or bioprosthetic (usually porcine). Bioprostheses have the advantage of not requiring chronic anticoagulation (strangely, the endocardium eventually grows over the valves, so there is little intravascular hemolysis). The disadvantage is that they don't last long (5–10 years). Mechanical valves come in various designs and have the advantage of durability (life span about 10–15 years), so they are a better option in the younger patient. The disadvantage is that they require chronic anticoagulation.

Rheumatic Fever

After a streptococcal infection (group A β-hemolytic), rheumatic fever can develop, leading to damage of heart valves (most commonly the mitral > aortic > tricuspid). The pathology involves an undetermined autoimmune process, likely involving cross-reactivity of a bacterial antigen with a native endocardial antigen.

Signs & Symptoms

An upper respiratory tract infection, the classic "strep throat" prodrome, is often noted, with typical symptoms of acute pharyngitis: sore throat, fever, chills, cough. Strep throat most often affects young school-aged children. Two to 3 weeks after the prodrome, if untreated, the patient develops one or more of the following: chorea, arthralgias, rash, fever, and malaise. **Aschoff bodies** are the classic lesion seen on the pathologic heart specimen.

Diagnosis

The diagnosis is based on clinical symptoms of recent *Streptococcus* infection. This can be done with culture, rapid strep antigen test, or antistreptolysin O titer.

Treatment

Antibiotics. A 10-day course of penicillin is the antibiotic of choice. Aspirin is used if myocarditis is present because it's an anticoagulant for the myocarditis as well as an anti-inflammatory agent for the heart, joints, and so forth. The most important factor in long-term outcome is the amount of sustained cardiac damage. Once recovered, patients need to take antibiotic prophylaxis every time they see a dentist to prevent the transient bacteremia from seeding their damaged endocardium.

Bacterial Endocarditis

Bacterial endocarditis is a bacterial infection of the endocardium and valves, usually by gram-positive cocci. Intravenous drug users are more likely to be infected with staphylococci. Previous valve damage (e.g., rheumatic fever), prosthetic valves, or other niduses for infection predispose to endocarditis.

- **Acute endocarditis** is usually due to *Staphylococcus* spp.

- **Subacute bacterial endocarditis** is usually due to *Streptococcus viridans*.

- **Nonbacterial (marantic) endocarditis** has fibrin deposits. **Libman-Sacks** lesions are nonbacterial endocardial vegetations seen in lupus patients.

Signs & Symptoms

The classic description of clinical findings in endocarditis likely result from microembolism of infectious vegetations to the distal end organs. Fever, a new unexplained murmur, cutaneous stigmata (Osler nodes, Janeway lesions, petechiae, splinter hemorrhages), Roth spots (eyes), and end-organ damage (e.g., nephritis, embolic stroke) are all possible.

Diagnosis

Valvular vegetations can be seen on echocardiography, the diagnostic tool of choice. Positive blood cultures are also required.

Treatment

Appropriate antibiotics.

Systemic Shock

Shock can be simply defined as the inadequate delivery of blood flow to the peripheral tissues, resulting in end-organ dysfunction, systemic hypoxia, and eventually death. Shock is classified as follows:

- **Cardiogenic shock**: Pump failure leads to inadequate tissue perfusion. It can result from MI, valve disease, cardiac tamponade, massive pulmonary embolism, and arrhythmias.

- **Hypovolemic shock**: Exsanguination, diarrhea, vomiting, diabetes with polyuria, burns, pancreatitis, or severe dehydration lead to intravascular volume depletion.

- **Distributive shock**: Lowered systemic vascular resistance leads to decreased perfusion, because the pressure is too low. Distributive shock can arise from (1) sepsis or systemic inflammatory response syndrome, (2) anaphylaxis, or (3) autonomic dysfunction.

The end point of shock is inadequate end-organ perfusion, leading to altered mental status, myocardial ischemia, acute renal failure, bowel ischemia, and ischemia of the extremities. The body has several built-in compensatory mechanisms that kick in with progressive shock:

- Increased sympathetic tone: increases CO (increased rate and contractility) and systemic vascular resistance (arteriolar vasoconstriction), but it can lead to increased myocardial demand in the face of decreased coronary perfusion

- Hyper-renin state: leads to retention of intravascular volume but contributes to renal insufficiency

- Increased peripheral O_2 extraction

Signs & Symptoms

Hypotension. BP is normal in early shock, so the first signs are orthostatic. Next, resting tachycardia is seen, and finally, resting hypotension is seen with severe shock. Flat neck veins, dry mucous membranes, altered mental status, oliguria or anuria, presyncope or syncope, and tachypnea are present. The specific etiology determines other symptoms. Crackles of pulmonary edema suggests cardiogenic shock. Cool, clammy skin is not consistent with distributive shock, which usually presents with warm skin initially. Signs of trauma suggest hypovolemia, history of medication or atypical food intake suggests anaphylaxis, and fever may suggest sepsis.

Diagnosis

The etiology of shock must be determined to ensure proper management. Invasive hemodynamic monitoring is indicated if there is any uncertainty about the etiology of shock or about the patient's volume status. This is especially true when initial resuscitation fails to produce significant improvement.

Treatment

General principles: ABCs (airway, breathing, circulation), then noninvasive and invasive monitoring:

- Initiate intensive care unit (ICU) or critical care unit monitoring.
- Ensure adequate oxygenation and ventilation (give supplemental O_2).
- Monitor hemodynamic status.
- Ensure vascular access with large-bore peripheral intravenous lines or central venous access, or both.

Treatment of cardiogenic shock includes diuresis, inotropic agents, vasodilators if indicated, and intra-aortic balloon pump. Septic shock requires finding the source of infection, covering with appropriate antibiotics, and maintaining fluid status. Hypovolemia requires fluids and blood products. Anaphylactic shock is treated with epinephrine, steroids, and antihistamines.

Specific inotropics, vasopressors, and vasodilators are often used; these are discussed in chapter 4 and under Pharmacology, later.

Aneurysms

Aneurysms are abnormal dilations of the vasculature. Aneurysms can be true aneurysms, when all three vessel wall layers are dilated, or pseudoaneurysms, where the intima dilates into the media and adventitia. In a dissection, a split in the intima lets blood and clot track into the vessel wall between the medial and adventitial layers, forming a false lumen.

Aortic aneurysm is an abnormal, localized dilation of the aorta. Most aortic aneurysms occur in the abdomen, with the remainder in the thorax. Abdominal aortic aneurysms (AAAs) are usually caused by atherosclerosis, which gradually weakens the vascular wall. Hypertension, smoking, a family history of abdominal aneurysms, trauma, and vasculitis may contribute. Two other causes of abdominal aortic aneurysm, Marfan's syndrome and syphilis, are primary causes of thoracic (ascending) aortic aneurysms.

Signs & Symptoms

Sharp or tearing back pain radiating to the shoulders is the classic presentation for a dissecting aneurysm. If there is rupture, the outlook is grim; most patients don't even make it to the hospital. If they do, most die in the operating room (OR). Dissection is a true emergency.

Diagnosis

The initial workup requires ruling out diseases with similar presentations: MI, GI causes, and renal and pulmonary disease. BP of all four limbs is crucial because an aneurysm that involves the innominate artery or left subclavian causes the involved limb BP to be lower than the BP of other limbs. The patient may present in frank hypotensive shock. Ultrasound is a good means of imaging abdominal aortic aneurysms because the liver provides good acoustic access to the abdominal aorta. Thoracic aneurysms can be diagnosed best with angiography or CT. MRI is also a good diagnostic tool.

Treatment

Surgical candidates need to be taken immediately to the OR. BP must be controlled because excessive hypertension can worsen a possible dissection. Mortality is very high.

Diseases Involving the Pericardium

Cardiac Tamponade

Cardiac tamponade is an abnormally increased collection of fluid in the pericardial space. The fluid collection prevents the ventricles from filling properly, leading to a restrictive filling pattern, which can cause hemodynamic collapse. The causes are trauma, ventricular wall rupture, malignant effusion, infectious effusion, and rheumatologic effusion. It's important to realize that the fluid accumulation must be rather rapid because the heart and body can adapt to slowly accumulating fluid.

Signs & Symptoms

Decreased intensity of heart sounds, decreased pulse pressure, neck vein distention, pulsus paradoxus.

Diagnosis

CXR may show increased cardiac silhouette size, and ECG may show decreased voltage or electrical alternans. Echocardiography is the diagnostic tool of choice. PA catheterization shows equalization of diastolic pressures because the tamponade compresses the heart chambers and equalizes filling pressures.

Treatment

Tamponade is a medical emergency requiring drainage of the fluid either percutaneously or surgically.

Pericarditis

Pericarditis is inflammation of the pericardium, which may be acute or chronic. Chronic pericarditis leads to pericardial thickening and fibrosis as well as constriction.

Acute Pericarditis

The causes of acute pericarditis include infection by viruses, bacteria, mycobacteria (TB), or fungi (histoplasmosis); chemicals; MI or cardiac surgery (Dressler's syndrome); uremia; radiation; autoimmune disease; and idiopathic causes.

Signs & Symptoms

Sharp chest pain that changes with body position, friction rub on auscultation, pericardial effusion, and possibly tamponade.

Diagnosis

ECG may be diagnostic if diffuse ST elevations are seen with the chest pain, with PR segment depression. Echocardiography is the diagnostic tool of choice, demonstrating thickened pericardium, with or without an effusion. Treatable etiologies must be ruled out.

Treatment

Treat underlying etiologies, and otherwise, provide supportive care. Resolution usually occurs within 6–8 weeks. Corticosteroids and nonsteroidal anti-inflammatory drugs may help the inflammation and pain. Pericardectomy may be necessary in severe cases.

Constrictive Pericarditis

Constrictive pericarditis occurs with chronic pericardial inflammation that leads to fibrosis, impeding normal relaxation and filling of the ventricles. It has the same etiologies as acute pericarditis.

Signs & Symptoms

Dyspnea, tachycardia, peripheral edema, ascites, and fatigue, usually with insidious onset. A prominent y descent with elevated JVP is often noted. Kussmaul's sign may be present (increased neck vein elevation with inspiration).

Diagnosis

Echocardiography is the diagnostic tool of choice. Given similar physiology and signs and symptoms, constrictive pericarditis can be difficult to distinguish from restrictive cardiomyopathy.

Treatment

Patients may initially be managed conservatively with diuretics and dietary sodium restriction, but more severe cases benefit from pericardiectomy, which has a high perioperative morbidity in this patient population.

Myocarditis

Myocarditis is acute myocardial inflammation. Causes include infection of the myocardium (mainly viral, particularly coxsackie), production of a myocardial toxin (e.g., diphtheria), or an autoimmune inflammatory process (e.g., rheumatic fever). Bacterial infection is rare, but may be due to *Mycoplasma pneumoniae*, *Staphylococcus*, *Streptococcus*, or *Rickettsiae*. Parasites (e.g., trypanosomiasis) may also be the cause. Other causes include hypersensitivity reactions and radiation toxicity. There is reported to be an AIDS-associated cardiomyopathy.

Signs & Symptoms

Fever, dyspnea, palpitations, and chest pain. Patients may present in florid CHF.

Diagnosis

ECG shows nonspecific ST or T wave changes or arrhythmias with conduction system involvement.

Treatment

Antiarrhythmics if arrhythmias are present, treat the CHF, and give steroids if the etiology is clearly not infectious.

Vascular Disease and Vasculitis

Peripheral Arterial Vascular Disease

Intermittent claudication is a result of stenosis (usually atherosclerosis) of the lower extremities, leading to calf pain on exercise and relieved by rest.

Signs & Symptoms

Patients experience leg pain on exertion that is relieved by rest. The amount of walking that precipitates pain is usually reproducible (e.g., five blocks). Patients may also display signs of poor circulation, including pallor, poor pulses, and cool extremities.

Diagnosis

Differential BPs in all four limbs: The ankle brachial index (ABI) is an excellent predictor of disease. ABI is the ratio of BP in the ankle to that of the arm. ABI less than 0.3 signifies significant disease. Angiography is the gold standard for diagnosis.

Treatment

Pentoxifylline (Trental) is a drug that theoretically makes RBC membranes more pliant and thereby improves peripheral blood flow. The definitive treatment is surgical revascularization: Either native vein or synthetic grafts are used to bypass discrete lesions.

Polyarteritis Nodosa

Polyarteritis nodosa is the inflammation of medium-sized muscular arteries, leading to ischemia in the tissues supplied by these arteries. It is idiopathic but may be related to hypersensitivity reactions to drugs and viruses. Males are afflicted three times more often than females. The kidneys are the organ system most likely involved. A rapidly progressing glomerulonephritis may result. Cardiac involvement can lead to ischemia and MI. The GI, CNS, and skin can also be involved.

Signs & Symptoms

Pain and local ischemia in the affected area.

Diagnosis

Laboratory tests show elevated acute-phase reactants, urinalysis shows proteinuria and RBC casts, and complement may be low (from being depleted). Tissue biopsy is the definitive diagnostic tool. Blood test may be positive for pANCA, but the test is neither sensitive nor specific (systemic lupus erythematosus, inflammatory bowel disease, and vasculitis limited to the kidney can also give positive results).

Treatment

Corticosteroids and immunosuppressants.

Wegener's Granulomatosis

Wegener's granulomatosis is systemic necrotizing vasculitis, with necrotizing granuloma formation in the upper and lower respiratory tract and involvement of other vascular beds. Incidence peaks in the fourth to fifth decades of life.

Signs & Symptoms

Upper respiratory infections (nasal congestion, sinusitis, mastoiditis, otitis media, etc.), ocular involvement, and skin nodules. Symptoms include cough, dyspnea, and hemoptysis.

Diagnosis

Laboratory tests show elevated acute-phase reactant levels and positive cytoplasmic antineutrophil cytoplasmic antigen (cANCA). CXR demonstrates lung involvement, and definitive diagnosis requires tissue biopsy.

Treatment

Corticosteroids and cytotoxic agents.

Takayasu's Arteritis

Takayasu's arteritis is a vasculitis that favors the branches of the aortic arch. It is common in Asian females and known as "pulseless disease" because it results in absent arm pulses. BP is low but rarely symptomatic. The patients may show evidence of transient ischemic attacks (TIAs) and cerebrovascular insufficiency. Diagnosis is made by tissue biopsy, and treatment is with corticosteroids, although many patients do not require treatment.

Giant Cell (Temporal) Arteritis

Small and medium vessels are affected, and patients are usually older than age 50. Onset is usually insidious. Patients may note jaw claudication, headache, fatigue, vision changes, scalp tenderness, fever, weight loss, and malaise. Acute-phase reactants are elevated, and biopsy is required for definitive diagnosis. Treatment is with corticosteroids.

Raynaud's Phenomenon and Disease

Raynaud's phenomenon and disease are characterized by intermittent cyanosis of the fingers and toes caused by exposure to cold or emotional upset. Raynaud's disease is the idiopathic form caused by vasospasm of the digital arteries in a bilateral symmetric manner. Raynaud's phenomenon can be unilateral and limited to only one or two fingers. It can occur in the setting of rheumatoid arthritis, systemic lupus erythematosus, CREST, and mixed connective tissue disease. Young women are disproportionately affected.

Signs & Symptoms

Blue and/or pale fingers (and, less commonly, toes) following exposure to cold or emotional upset. During an attack, the fingers are stiff and painful. The digits can become markedly red and throbbing during recovery, due to compensatory hyperemia. Gangrenous ulcers may form on the fingertips.

Diagnosis

Evidence of other disorders (e.g., SLE, rheumatoid arthritis) on history and physical examination distinguish Raynaud's phenomenon from Raynaud's disease. Raynaud's can be differentiated from thromboangiitis obliterans (see below) because the former affects women and the latter men, and in the latter, peripheral pulses tend to be diminished.

Treatment

Treatment is to keep extremities warm and use calcium channel blockers, although the latter is controversial.

Thromboangiitis Obliterans (Buerger's Disease)

Thromboangiitis obliterans is a disease of young male smokers, most commonly in Ashkenazi Jews of Eastern European descent. It is characterized by peripheral ischemia secondary to inflammation and thrombosis of the arteries and veins.

Signs & Symptoms

You should be highly suspicious of the diagnosis of thromboangiitis obliterans if the patient is a male under 40 who smokes and demonstrates signs and symptoms of arterial insufficiency in the limbs: intermittent claudication, loss of distal arterial pulses, ischemic neuropathy, ulcers, or a cold distal foot or toe (often asymmetric). There may be a history of small, red, tender cords that are evidence of migratory superficial segmental thrombophlebitis. The course of the disease is usually intermittent, with flare-ups and remissions.

Diagnosis

History and physical examination. Absent peripheral pulses help differentiate thromboangiitis obliterans from Raynaud's disease and antiphospholipid antibody syndrome. The patient population is younger and may not have an established history of atherosclerosis, thus differentiating thromboangiitis obliterans from cholesterol atheroembolic disease.

Treatment

Smoking cessation is mandatory to prevent disease progression, which can lead to amputation of gangrenous fingers and toes.

Deep Venous Thrombosis

Deep venous thrombosis (DVT) is the development of a blood clot in a vein. **Thrombophlebitis** refers to a secondary inflammation of the clot, resulting in pain, tenderness, and warmth. DVT and thrombophlebitis most often occur in the lower extremities. The risk factors that may predispose to the development of **venous thrombi** are referred to as **Virchow's triad**: injury to the endothelium of the vessel (e.g., trauma), hypercoagulable states (e.g., malignancy, estrogen use), and stasis (e.g., postoperative states).

Varicose Veins

Varicose veins are distended, tortuous veins with incompetent valves. They can be caused by a bout with thrombophlebitis or occur congenitally. Most commonly, they result from conditions associated with increased lower-extremity venous pressure: pregnancy, prolonged standing, and ascites.

Signs & Symptoms

Many patients complain of the cosmetic disfiguration of varicosities in the superficial veins. There can be significant discomfort, relieved by elevation of the legs or elastic stockings. Chronic varicosities lead to venous insufficiency, with edema, hyperpigmentation, and ulcers (known as stasis dermatitis). Lymphatic obstruction must be considered in the differential diagnosis.

Diagnosis

Physical examination, with particular attention to the lower extremities.

Treatment

Compression stockings, with venous stripping or sclerosis of the saphenous vein as a last resort.

Cardiac Transplantation

Transplantation is indicated in severe heart failure. Candidates must be younger than 55 years old, free of other serious disease (e.g., diabetes, cancer), and have a life expectancy of less than 1 year. Most have ischemic cardiomyopathy, but many have idiopathic cardiomyopathy, idiopathic hypertrophic subaortic stenosis, severe valvular disease, or in children, congenital disease. Combined heart-lung transplantation is indicated in severe pulmonary hypertension. Preoperative patients can be sustained for some time with LV assist devices, intra-aortic balloon pump, or in children, extracorporeal membrane oxygenation (ECMO) with cardiopulmonary bypass.

After transplantation, transplant rejection is the most common complication. Immunosuppression is achieved with combinations of cyclosporine, azathioprine, prednisone, and antithymocyte globulin. Part of the rejection process involves accelerated coronary atherosclerosis in the donor heart.

Congenital Heart Disease

Congenital heart disease usually manifests at birth or shortly thereafter, although it's usually present before birth. Congenital defects are classified as cyanotic or noncyanotic. Cyanotic lesions are ones that result in a right-to-left shunt, bypassing the lungs and causing deoxygenated blood to be pumped to the body.

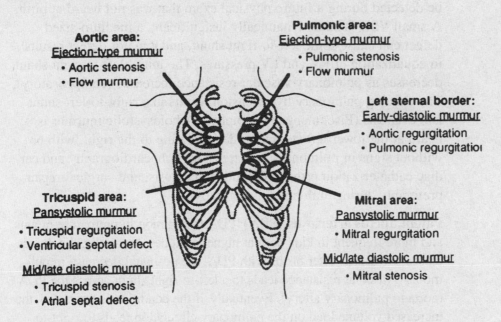

Aortic area:
Ejection-type murmur
• Aortic stenosis
• Flow murmur

Pulmonic area:
Ejection-type murmur
• Pulmonic stenosis
• Flow murmur

Left sternal border:
Early-diastolic murmur
• Aortic regurgitation
• Pulmonic regurgitation

Tricuspid area:
Pansystolic murmur
• Tricuspid regurgitation
• Ventricular septal defect

Mid/late diastolic murmur
• Tricuspid stenosis
• Atrial septal defect

Mitral area:
Pansystolic murmur
• Mitral regurgitation

Mid/late diastolic murmur
• Mitral stenosis

Fig 12-36 Locations where the murmors presented in this chapter demonstrate their maximum intensities.

Noncyanotic Congenital Heart Defects

- **Situs inversus:** Failure of organ rotation during development leads to reversal of organ location along the longitudinal axis of the body. The heart can be displaced to the right (dextroversion) or flipped around its axis so that the apex points to the right (dextrocardia), or both. In the case of situs inversus in Kartagener's syndrome (ciliary dysmotility syndrome), there is also bronchiectasis, chronic sinusitis, and infertility. Patients are usually asymptomatic except for Kartagener's syndrome. ECG is characteristic, and CXR is diagnostic. In general, patients have a normal life span.

- **Atrial septal defect** (ASD): Defects in the atrial septum occur in various locations. **Ostium secundum** defects are near the fossa ovalis. **Ostium primum** defects are located near the low atrial septum. **Sinus venosus** defects are near the RA and vena cava junction. Patients are often asymptomatic until adulthood, when prolonged left-to-right shunt leads to pulmonary hypertension and heart failure. Occasionally, a systolic murmur with fixed splitting of the S2 is heard. Echocardiography and cardiac catheterization provide definitive diagnosis, and surgical repair, preferably during childhood, is corrective.

- **Ventricular septal defect** (VSD): VSD is the most common congenital cardiac defect (>25% of all cases). It occurs most often in the membranous (superior) portions of the septum. The defect usually gets smaller as the patient grows. When this happens, a murmur may be detected during a future physical exam that was not heard at birth. A small VSD is hemodynamically insignificant, a medium-sized defect can cause some left-to-right shunt, and a major defect results in equalization of RV and LV pressures. The initial left-to-right shunt decreases as pulmonary vascular resistance increases (compensatory). The ensuing pulmonary hypertension results in a right-to-left shunt and cyanosis (Eisenmenger's complex). A holosystolic murmur is heard at the lower left sternal border, radiating to the right, with or without signs of pulmonary hypertension. Echocardiography and cardiac catheterization provide definitive diagnosis, and surgical repair, preferably during childhood, is corrective.

- **Patent ductus arteriosus (PDA):** PDA is common in premature infants and more frequent in kids born at higher altitudes. Normally, the ductus closes 4–8 weeks after birth. With PDA, the postnatal decrease in pulmonary vascular resistance leads to a left-to-right shunt across the PDA (aorta to pulmonary artery). Eventually, if the condition is untreated, the increased volume load on the pulmonary circulation leads to right-to-left shunt along with pulmonary hypertension and right heart failure (Eisenmenger's complex). At that stage, the patient has pink fingers (supplied by the innominate and subclavian arteries before merging with the PDA) but cyanotic toes, which are supplied by blood mixed with PDA unoxygenated blood. Treatment is surgical repair, and the operation carries a low risk. If the PDA is detected early (e.g., premature babies), it can be treated with indomethacin; it would be prudent to ensure that the PDA is not helping the baby survive other congenital heart defects like tricuspid atresia or transposition of the great vessels!

- **Pulmonic stenosis (PS)**: PS can be valvular, subvalvular, or supravalvular. A systolic murmur is heard at the left upper sternal border, and signs of right heart failure are present. Diagnosis is made by echocardiography. Surgical repair and valvuloplasty are treatment options.

- **Aortic stenosis**: A bicuspid aortic valve is the most common congenital cardiac anomaly seen in adults and is seen in 2% of the population. Congenital aortic stenosis is usually more symptomatic. A systolic murmur is heard at the right upper sternal border with radiation to the carotids. The murmur is louder with squatting and softer with Valsalva or handgrip. Diagnosis is made by echocardiography and catheterization. Valvuloplasty and surgical valve replacement are corrective.

- **Coarctation of the aorta**: This is a narrowing of the aorta that can be located anywhere from the aortic root to the descending aorta. It is usually located just distal to the left subclavian artery and ductus arteriosus. It's associated with a bicuspid aortic valve in 25% of cases. Other comorbid conditions include circle of Willis anomalies and Turner's syndrome. BP of arms and legs are markedly different, with upper-extremity hypertension and lower-extremity hypotension. Catheterization is useful to assess collateral circulation and any associated lesions. A CXR may show notching of the ribs because of diversion of blood through the internal mammary and intercostal arteries. Treatment is surgical repair.

Cyanotic Lesions

Cyanotic lesions are due to right-to-left shunting of blood. Deoxygenated blood bypassing the lungs is mixed with the oxygenated blood coming from the pulmonary capillary bed. Hypoxemia and cyanosis are the hallmark symptoms.

- **Transposition of the great vessels**: The aorta and coronary arteries exit the RV, and the pulmonary trunk exits the LV. As a result (and just for you physics buffs), the pulmonary and systemic circulations flow in parallel instead of in series. The only way the newborn can survive is if there is a fect connecting the two circuits: a PDA, ASD, or VSD. There is usually bidirectional shunting, and the more shunting there is, the more likely the patient is to survive. Diagnosis is made by echocardiography and catheterization. Treatment is corrective surgery. The PDA can be kept open prior to surgery with prostaglandin administration.

- **Total anomalous pulmonary venous return**: Oxygenated blood returning from the lungs enters the RA instead of the LA. An ASD is usually present, and so the RA blood (mixed with venous return blood) enters the LA through the ASD. The increased fraction of deoxygenated blood results in cyanosis. Increased pulmonary flow leads to pulmonary hypertension. Diagnosis and treatment are the same as above.

TIP: You can remember which congenital defects are cyanotic because they begin with T.

- **Truncus arteriosus**: One big vessel with a bicuspid valve leaves a single ventricle, replacing the normal aorta and pulmonary trunk. Because the lungs and body see the same blood oxygenation and blood pressure, severe cyanosis and pulmonary hypertension result. Diagnosis and treatment are the same as above.

- **Tetralogy of Fallot:** This is the most common cyanotic congenital anomaly seen in adults. It includes:

  VSD
  Pulmonic stenosis
  An aorta that overrides the VSD
  RV hypertrophy (a result of the other defects)

With the VSD, a left-to-right shunt is initially seen, leading to right heart volume overload. But because the VSD is large and the pulmonic stenosis limits flow to the pulmonary circulation, there is usually no pulmonary hypertension or right heart failure. The right ventricle hypertrophies, and the shunt then eventually becomes right-to-left, resulting in cyanosis. Patients have "spells" of cyanosis, hyperpnea, and syncope as a result of intermittent increases in right-to-left shunting. Without treatment, the pulmonic stenosis worsens gradually, leading to increased cyanosis. Diagnosis is with echocardiography and catheterization, and treatment is surgical. Because of the extensive right heart involvement, postsurgical heart block and other arrhythmias are fairly common.

- **Tricuspid artesia**: The tricuspid valve is absent, and so the RA and RV do not connect. The patients survive because there is usually an associated ASD and VSD. Treatment is surgical correction.

Neoplasms of the Cardiovascular System

There really aren't a whole lot of tumors that affect the heart (fortunately). The most common primary tumor is the **myxoma**, which is usually benign. It arises from the endocardial surface, mostly in the LA, but can be found anywhere. According to the 10/10 rule, 10% of myxomas are from the LA, and 10% of myxomas are malignant. Other malignant tumors include sarcomas (e.g., angiosarcoma and rhabdosarcoma). Metastatic tumors are much more common than primary neoplasms and include hematologic malignancies, melanoma, and lung and breast cancer. They tend to involve the pericardium and cause pericarditis and hemorrhagic effusions.

Signs & Symptoms

The patient may have signs of heart failure, a possible stroke from cancer or clot embolization, or other systemic symptoms (e.g., fever, night sweats, weight loss).

Diagnosis

On examination, a "plop" may sometimes be heard from the pedunculated myxoma falling onto the mitral valve. A murmur is common, and it may change with body position. Echocardiography is the diagnostic tool of choice.

Treatment

Surgical excision.

Pharmacology

Adrenergic agonists and antagonists are discussed in chapter 4. Specific applications are discussed in each disease entity.

Direct Vasodilators

Direct vasodilators are used primarily for control of hypertension in the acute situation (ICU, emergency room, OR) (Table 12-4).

Antihypertensives

The four major classes of antihypertensive drugs are as follows:

- β-Blockers
- Calcium channel blockers
- Diuretics

Table 12-4. Vasodilators

Drug	Mechanism	Toxicities
Nitroprusside	Similar to nitric oxide; direct smooth muscle relaxant	Hypotension; prolonged use leads to cyanide toxicity
Nitrates Nitroglycerin Isosorbide dinitrate	Similar to nitric oxide; direct smooth muscle relaxant (used for hypetension and angina)	Hypotension
Hydralazine, minoxidil	Direct smooth muscle relaxant	Hypotension
Terazosin	α-antagonist	Orthostatic hypotension, loss of sympathetic tone, syncope
Clonidine	CNS α_2 agonist	Hypotension

Table 12-5. Angiotensin-converting enzyme (ACE) inhibitors

Drug	Mechanism	Toxicities
Captopril, lisinopril, enalapril	Blocks ACE, disrupting the renin-angiotensin system	Hypotension, cough, leukopenia
Losartan	Angiotensin II receptor inhibitor	Vasodilation, decreased venous return; less cough than ACE inhibitors

Table 12-6. Classes of antiarrhythmics

Class	Mechanism	Effects
Class IA	Na^+ channel blocker	Prolongs the action potential duration
Class IB	Na^+ channel blocker	Reduces maximum velocity of AP upstroke
Class IC	Na^+ channel blocker	Prolongs refractory period
Class II	β-Blockers	Slows conduction through the AV junction
Class III	K^+ channel blocker	Prolongs action potential
Class IV	Ca^{+2} channel blocker	Blocks slow inward current

AP = action potential; AV = atrioventricular.

- ACE inhibitors

β-Blockers are discussed in chapter 4, and diuretics are discussed in chapter 14. Calcium channel blockers are discussed later. The major ACE inhibitors are listed in Table 12-5.

Antiarrhythmics

Antiarrhythmics are classified according to four classes (Table 12-6). Specific antiarrhythmics are listed in Tables 12-7 through 12-9.

Antiarrhythmics can be pretty daunting. The following are some high-yield facts:

- Lidocaine is the first-line agent for prophylaxis against and treatment of ventricular arrhythmias (ventricular tachycardia and the dreaded ventricular fibrillation). Beware its side effects: tremors, anxiety, seizures, and confusion. Also be aware that lidocaine accidentally given intravenously during administration of local anesthesia can *cause* arrhythmias.

- Amiodarone may be the best antiarrhythmic drug, in terms of efficaciousness and proven survival benefits. It is effective in most types of arrhythmias. Important side effects are pulmonary fibrosis and thyroid function abnormalities.

- Adenosine is a very short-acting drug that slows AV node conduction. It can be used to aid in diagnosis of a supraventricular tachycardia, and it can also break an AV nodal arrhythmia.

Digoxin

Digoxin is a drug with multiple effects. It blocks the cell membrane Na^+/K^+ pump, prevents Na^+ extrusion from the cell, which then inhibits the Na^+/Ca^{2+} exchanger, resulting in increased intracellular calcium. The increased intracellular calcium directly increases contractility. The secondary effect of digoxin is a slowing of conduction through the AV node.

Uses include the following:

- CHF, for increased contractility

- Supraventricular arrhythmias, including atrial fibrillation

Side effects include premature beats, tachycardia, and fibrillation. Severe digitalis toxicity can cause cardiac arrest. Treatment for digoxin toxicity includes the following:

- K^+: antagonizes effect on Na^+/K^+ pump

- Magnesium: antagonizes calcium

- Digoxin immune Fab (Digibind): antibodies directed against digoxin

Table 12-7. Class I, II, and III antiarrhythmics

Drug	Mechanism	Uses	Side effects
Quinidine	Class IA	Long-term treatment of atrial and ventricular arrhythmias (atrial fibrillation, atrial flutter, SVT)	Hypotension, GI distress, cinchonism, rash, "quinidine syncope"; raises blood levels of digoxin
Procainamide	Class IA	Same as quinidine	Drug-induced lupus, nausea and vomiting, psychosis
Disopyramide	Class IA	Same as quinidine	Urinary retention, CHF, constipation, blurred vision, glaucoma
Lidocaine	Class IB	Acute ventricular arrhythmias	Dizziness, paresthesias, confusion, coma
Phenytoin	Class IB	Treats arrhythmias due to digitalis toxicity	Stupor, ataxia, rash, gingival hypertrophy
Mexiletine	Class IB	Same as lidocaine	CNS and GI effects
Tocainide	Class IB	Ventricular tachyarrhythmias	Similar to lidocaine
Flecainide	Class IC	Ventricular arrhythmias (last resort drug)	CHF, increased ventricular tachyarrhythmias
Propafenone	Class IC	Ventricular and supraventricular arrhythmias	Dizziness, blurred vision
Sotalol	Class II	Chronic treatment of ventricular arrhythmias	—
Carvedilol	Class II	Atrial and ventricular arrhythmias in the context of acute MI; affects myocardial remodeling	CHF
Bretylium	Class III	Life-threatening ventricular arrhythmias unresponsive to other agents	Orthostatic hypotension, arrhythmias, nausea and vomiting
Amiodarone	Class III, IV activity	Same as bretylium	Paresthesia, thyroid dysfunction, pulmonary fibrosis crystalline deposits in the skin and corneas

SVT = supraventricular tachycardia; CHF = congestive heart failure; MI = myocardial infarction; GI = gastrointestinal.

Thrombolytics

In acute MI, coronary occlusion is thought to involve a combination of mechanical occlusion and local activation of the clotting cascade, leading to thrombus formation within the coronaries. Thrombolytics are often used in acute MI. Thrombolytics and anticoagulants (e.g., warfarin, heparin) are discussed in chapter 7.

Table 12-8. Calcium channel blockers

Drug	Mechanism	Uses	Toxicities
Nifedipine	Class IV	Coronary and peripheral vasodilation, hypertension, Prinzmetal's angina	Hypotension, nausea and vomiting, bradycardia, left ventricular failure
Diltiazem	Class IV	Supraventricular tachyarrhythmias	Same as nifedipine
Verapamil	Class IV	Supraventricular tachyarrhythmias	Same as nifedipine
Long-acting agents: Amlodipine Felodipine	Class IV	Long-term treatment of hypertension	Same as nifedipine

Table 12-9. Miscellaneous antiarrhythmics

Drug	Mechanism	Uses	Toxicities
Adenosine	Endogenous nucleoside, slows atrioventricular conduction, duration of action <10 seconds	Supraventricular tachyarrhythmias, especially in emergent situations	Minimal
Magnesium	Antagonizes effects of calcium	Digitalis toxicity, torsades de pointes, ventricular tachyarrhythmias	Tingling, neuropathy, flushing, dizziness
Potassium	Increased potassium	Treats hypokalemia, especially in the face of digitalis toxicity	Use with caution: arrhythmias, gastrointestinal distress
Atropine	Anticholinergic agent	Bradyarrhythmias, particularly asystole	Anticholinergic syndrome

Cholesterol- and Lipid-Lowering Agents

Clinical studies have very clearly demonstrated the improvement in survival and reduction of adverse events with the use of lipid-lowering agents in both primary and secondary prevention of CAD. Table 12-10 lists common cholesterol- and lipid-lowering agents.

Table 12-10. Cholesterol- and lipid-lowering agents

Drug	Mechanism	Uses	Toxicities
Cholestyramine	Intraluminal GI lipid-binding resin	Elevated LDL	Constipation, heartburn, bloating, malabsorption
Neomycin	Poorly absorbed antibiotic that acts as a lipid-binding resin	Elevated LDL, familial hyper-cholesterolemia	Nausea and vomiting, diarrhea, systemic toxicity if absorbed, renal failure
Lovastatin, pravastatin, simvastatin	HMG-CoA reductase inhibitor; inhibits mevalonate (cholesterol precursor) synthesis	Elevated LDL, elevated triglycerides	Myopathy, hepatotoxicity (monitor CK levels and LFTs every few months)
Gemfibrozil, clofibrate	Increases the activity of lipoprotein lipase	Elevated LDL, VLDL, or triglycerides	Myalgia, liver dysfunction, rash, nausea and vomiting
Niacin	Decreases cholesterol, VLDL synthesis	Elevated LDL, familial hyper-lipidemias	Flushing, rash, liver dysfunction
Probucol	Antioxidant; increases LDL and cholesterol destruction and excretion	Hypercholesterolemia, familial hyper-cholesterolemias	Arrhythmias

LDL = low-density lipoprotein; HMG-CoA = 3-hydroxy-3-methylglutaryl coenzyme A; VLDL = very low–density lipoprotein; CK = creatine kinase; LFT = liver function tests.

CHAPTER 13

The Gastrointestinal System

Anatomy

Gross anatomy of the gastrointestinal (GI) system is shown in Fig. 13-1. Following are the major organs of the GI system:

- Salivary glands: **Sialolithiasis** (salivary stones) is more likely in the submandibular and sublingual glands because their secretions are more mucinous, whereas the parotid's are more serous. Remember that the facial nerve runs through the parotid gland and is in danger of damage during surgery.

- Tongue: The **genioglossus** muscle is responsible for keeping the tongue from relaxing posteriorly and obstructing respiration.

- Tonsils: The palatine and pharyngeal tonsils form **Waldeyer's ring**, which is a structure of lymphoid tissue producing immunoglobulin A (IgA) to bind to ingested antigens. A botched tonsillectomy can result in damage to the carotid artery, which is an emergency!

- Esophagus: The top third of the esophagus is skeletal muscle; the remainder is smooth muscle. The esophagus has no peritoneal lining, so esophageal tumors spread locally very easily. The muscle undergoes a transition from striated proximally to smooth distally as conscious **deglutition** (swallowing) leads to automatic **peristalsis**. The lower esophagus has azygous venous drainage anastomosing with the stomach's portal drainage, and these are the veins that form varices in portal hypertension. The **gastroesophageal** (or cardiac) **sphincter** is not a true histologic sphincter, although it does tonically constrict to prevent reflux.

- Stomach: The antrum is the part of the stomach just proximal to the pylorus. It contains the G cells that make gastrin to increase acid production. Thus, an antrectomy treats hyperacidity.

- Duodenum: The duodenum is divided into four parts. The second part of the duodenum features the **ampulla of Vater** (with its **sphincter of**

G cells make gastrin.

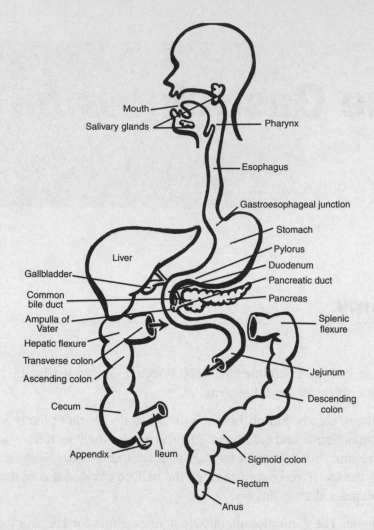

Mouth
Salivary glands
Pharynx
Esophagus
Gastroesophageal junction
Stomach
Pylorus
Liver
Duodenum
Gallbladder
Pancreatic duct
Common bile duct
Pancreas
Ampulla of Vater
Splenic flexure
Hepatic flexure
Transverse colon
Jejunum
Ascending colon
Descending colon
Cecum
Appendix
Ileum
Sigmoid colon
Rectum
Anus

Fig. 13-1. General overview of the gastrointestinal system.

Oddi), where the pancreatic and bile ducts drain, and dye can be introduced to visualize these ducts. The **ligament of Treitz** at the fourth part of the duodenum separates the upper GI tract from the lower. Roughly speaking, bleeding from the upper GI tends to show up as **melena** (dark, tarry stools), but bleeding from the lower GI appears as **hematochezia** (bright red blood) because upper GI bleeds have a chance to be digested.

- Gallbladder: During gallbladder removal, the anatomic landmark for surgeons is the **triangle of Calot**, made up of the liver edge, the common hepatic duct, and the cystic duct. The cystic artery runs right through the triangle and must be ligated during surgery.

- Jejunum and ileum: **Intussusception** occurs when the jejunum or ileum telescopes over itself. Venous drainage is via the **superior mesenteric vein**, which picks up contributions from colic veins and joins the splenic vein to form the **portal vein**, which supplies two-thirds of the liver's blood (Fig. 13-2). (The rest comes from the hepatic artery.)

- Appendix: The **appendiceal artery** is a branch of the ileocolic artery, which comes off the **superior mesenteric artery**. The ileocolic artery must be tied off during an appendectomy to avoid intraabdominal bleeding.

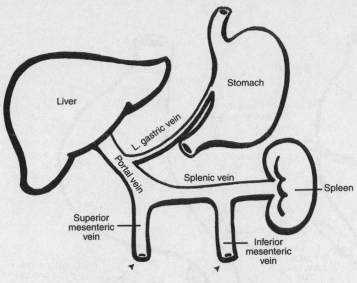

Fig. 13-2. The portal vein.

- Small intestine
- Cecum
- Ascending colon
- Transverse colon

- Descending colon
- Sigmoid colon
- Rectum

- **Colon, rectum, anus:** The portacaval anastomosis between the superior and the middle inferior rectal veins is the third site of varices with portal hypertension (along with the esophageal and umbilical veins) and can lead to the formation of hemorrhoids.

- **Liver:** Formed from four lobes all converging at the porta hepatis (the area on the inferior part of the liver housing the gallbladder and inferior vena cava [IVC]), the liver gets most of its blood flow from the gut, which explains why most metastatic GI cancers occur in the liver.

- **Pancreas:** Tumors in the pancreatic head may announce themselves early by causing symptoms such as biliary obstruction. Tumors in the tail are much more insidious. Fortunately, 80% of tumors are in the head.

- **Peritoneum:** Reflections of the peritoneum form mesenteries, which envelop intraperitoneal organs. These sharp angles taken by the peritoneum form channels and gutters, which you can use to predict where fluid and pus will flow.

Embryology

The gut tube is made out of **endoderm**, one of the three basic embryonic tissues. The developing tube is suspended anteriorly by the ventral mesentery, in which the liver and ventral pancreas grow, and posteriorly by the dorsal mesentery, in which the dorsal pancreas and spleen arise. When the stomach rotates and the liver takes its place on the right, the ventral pancreas swings around to form the head and uncinate process, fusing with the body and tail (Fig. 13-3). If this migration is abnormal, the pancreas may form a ring of tissue (**annular pancreas**) around the duodenum, resulting in bilious emesis.

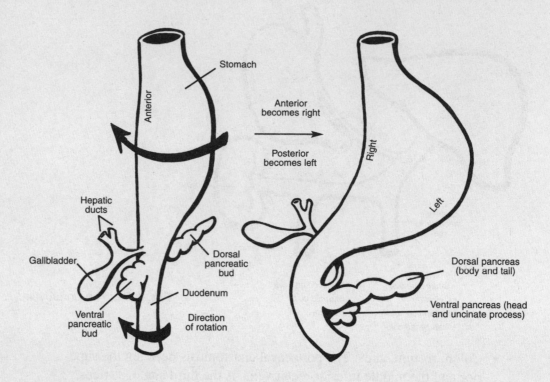

Fig. 13-3. The axial rotation of the primitive gut.

The embryonic gut is connected to the yolk sac by the **vitelline stalk** (yolk stalk), which acts as a pivot point for the intestines to twist around counterclockwise (Fig. 13-4). The cecum ends up making a 270-degree journey to its final destination in the right lower quadrant. However, this journey may be interrupted at any point (**malrotation**), resulting in an adult with an appendix in the right upper quadrant or even on the left!

The vitelline stalk has two other important anatomic associations. The first is that when all this rotation and growth is going on, the guts are seemingly "pulled" by the vitelline stalk out of the abdominal cavity. If they don't manage to sneak back in before the wall closes off, the herniation of bowel through peritoneum is called an **omphalocele**. **Gastroschisis** is a similar-appearing herniation caused by a wall muscle defect, but it is not related to the vitelline stalk herniation. The second consequence of the vitelline stalk is **Meckel's diverticulum**, a remnant of the vitelline duct behind the belly button. Present in 2–4% of the population, this gut outpouching may contain heterotopic pancreatic or gastric tissue, resulting in bleeding or inflammation.

Other congenital malformations, such as biliary atresia, are discussed under Genetic and Congenital Disorders, later.

Rule of 2s for Meckel's diverticulum:

• 2% of population
• Usually presents before age 2
• 2 inches long
• 2 feet proximal to the ileocecal valve
• May have 2 types of tissue

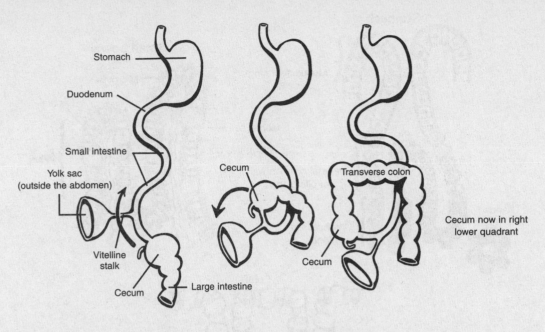

Fig. 13-4. The vitelline stalk and the rotation of the intestines.

Histology

- Esophagus: The muscularis externa undergoes a gradual transition from skeletal muscle to smooth muscle as it goes down. The mucosal epithelium is nonkeratinized stratified squamous epithelium rather than the simple columnar epithelium seen from the stomach to the rectum.

- Stomach: The stomach has several additional oblique muscle layers. Lining is thrown into folds call **rugae**. Mucus cells form the majority of the epithelium, but in the body and fundus, there are also **parietal cells** and **chief cells** (Fig. 13-5).

- Duodenum: The only segment with **Brunner's submucosal glands**, which secrete bicarbonate to neutralize stomach acid.

- Jejunum: The jejunum has pronounced **plicae circularis** (small transverse folds in the mucosa and submucosa).

- Ileum: The ileum has prominent **Peyer's patches** (lymphoid nodules) and many **goblet cells**, which secrete mucus.

- Colon: The colon has no villi, only crypts, and many goblet cells. Haustra with tinea coli are also characteristic (Fig. 13-6).

- Liver: The **portal triad** is made up of the portal vein, bile ductule, and hepatic artery (Fig. 13-7). Between the sinusoid epithelium and the hepatocytes is the space of Disse. Fenestrations allow macromolecules to reach this space. The liver is the site of phagocytic Kupffer cells.

Brunner's glands secrete bicarrbonate.

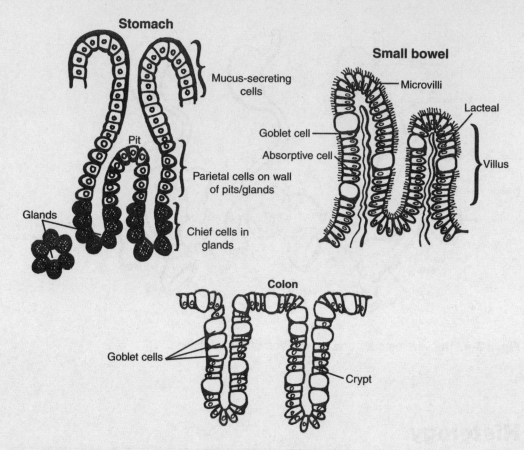

Fig. 13-5. Mucosa of the stomach, small bowel, and colon.

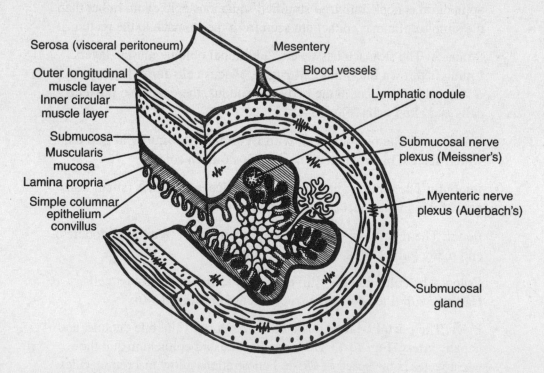

Fig. 13-6. Transverse section through the gut wall.

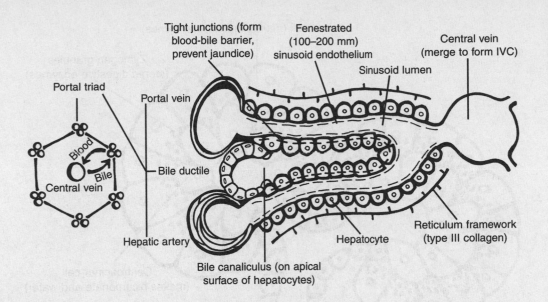

Fig. 13-7. Structure of the hepatic lobule. Embryologically, the liver is an evagination of gut endoderm. So the gut lumen is equivalent (and connected to) the bile canaliculi. (IVC = inferior vena cava.)

- Pancreas: **Acinar cells** make digestive enzymes that are stored as granules (Fig. 13-8). Centroacinar cells make bicarbonate and water.

Normal Physiology

Endocrine and Neural Regulatory Systems

Hormones

If you try to learn all the different GI hormones, it won't help you all that much. You should learn the basics about the "big three" (gastrin, cholecystokinin [CCK], and secretin), and you should know that **histamine** increases acid secretion, which is why we use H_2 blockers (Table 13-1).

Innervation

The gut has both extrinsic and intrinsic innervation. The **extrinsic system** has **afferent** fibers carrying sensory information back to the brain, letting you know when you have a tummy ache or gas. The brain poorly localizes sensory information from the viscera, which is why appendicitis begins as diffuse periumbilical pain before focusing in the right lower quadrant when it starts irritating the more precise peritoneal nerve endings. The **efferent** half of the extrinsic system consists of two parts. The parasympathetic fibers travel down the vagus and pelvic nerves to synapse in the gut wall and promote motility and secretion while resting and digesting. The sympathetic fibers synapse in prevertebral ganglia and cause the gut to shut down during the fight-or-flight response.

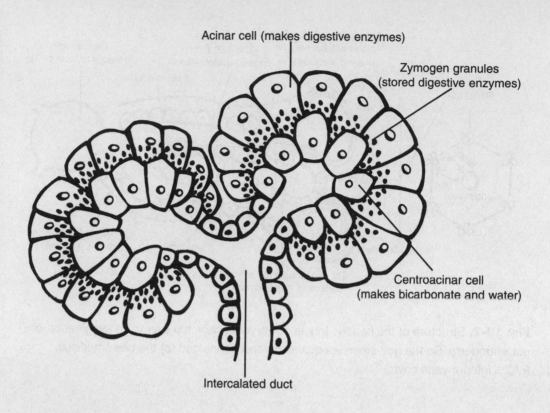

Fig. 13-8. Exocrine pancreas.

Table 13-1. Major gastrointestinal hormones

Hormone	Stimulus	Effect
Gastrin	Released from G cells of antrum in response to amino acids, stomach distention, and the vagus nerve Inhibited by low gastric pH (negative feedback)	Causes secretion of hydrochloric acid from the parietal cells **Zollinger-Ellison syndrome** is an ectopic gastrin-secreting tumor (**gastrinoma**) that causes ulcers.
Cholecystokinin	Released from I cells of duodenum in response to fatty acids and amino acids	Causes gallbladder contraction and pancreatic enzyme secretion, which is why gallstone pain is worse after fatty meals
Secretin	Released from S cells of duodenum in response to acid and fatty acids	Causes pancreas to release HCO_3^-, which neutralizes stomach acid and lets the pancreatic enzymes work

Gastrin, from the stomach, for the stomach.

Cholecystokinin means gall + bladder + get moving.

Secretin is nature's secret antacid.

Table 13-2. Gut innervation

Nerve plexus	Location	Function
Myenteric plexus (Auerbach's) (myo = muscle)	Gut muscle	Controls **m**otility (i.e., muscle)
Submucosal plexus (Meissner's)	Submucosa	Controls **s**ecretion

The **intrinsic system** consists of the **myenteric** and **submucosal** plexuses, which receive information from the extrinsic system and relay it within the gut (Table 13-2).

Gastrointestinal Motility

With the notable exceptions of the upper third of the esophagus (used when you want to swallow) and the external anal sphincter (used when you're in a car with no restroom in sight), the whole GI tract has smooth muscle. Sphincters are contracted tonically, but the rest of the tube has phasic contractions called *peristalsis*, which propel food boluses (Fig. 13-9).

Gastric emptying is faster when the contents are isotonic. Fat slows it down via CCK, and H⁺ in the duodenum slows it via a local reflex.

Vomiting

As anyone who has taken gross anatomy can attest, there are many different triggers that can stimulate **emesis** (vomiting). This is because you have both a **vomiting center** in the medulla (which responds to vestibular disturbances, throat tickling, and gastric distention) and a **chemoreceptor zone** in the fourth ventricle of the brain, which is stimulated by emetics and radiation. Vomiting is nothing more than reverse peristalsis emanating from the duodenum.

Electrolyte abnormalities associated with vomiting are alkalemia (you're losing acid), hypokalemia, and hyponatremia.

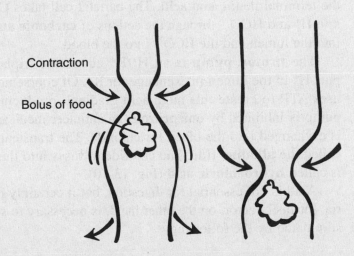

Contraction

Bolus of food

Fig. 13-9. Peristalsis.

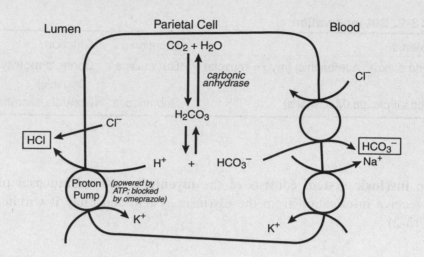

Fig. 13-10. The proton pump.

Secretory Products and Processes

Salivation

There are exactly three interesting things about saliva:

- Saliva has lots of mucins for lubrication and protection of the mucosa. It also has **amylase** for digesting starch and **lingual lipase** for breaking up fats. You may notice that the pancreas also puts out these enzymes, so serum tests for amylase and lipase, common in the workup of pancreatitis, may actually point to salivary pathology.

- The salivary ducts are similar to renal tubules in that under the influence of aldosterone, they resorb more Na^+ and secrete more K^+ than baseline.

- Both the sympathetic and the parasympathetic nervous system stimulate salivary secretion. Note that anticholinergics such as atropine (which block the parasympathetics) cause dry mouth.

Gastric Secretion

Parietal cells make two things: **intrinsic factor**, which aids vitamin B_{12} uptake in the terminal ileum, and **acid**. The parietal cell takes CO_2 and H_2O, converts them into H^+ and HCO_3^- through the actions of **carbonic anhydrase**, and pumps the H^+ into the lumen and the HCO_3^- into the blood.

The **proton pump** is an H^+/K^+ adenosine triphosphatase (ATPase), which puts H^+ in the lumen in exchange for K^+. Of course nothing is free, and the pump uses ATP to create this huge acid gradient, producing a pH as low as 0.8. This pump is inhibited by **omeprazole**, an antiulcer medication. Meanwhile, the HCO_3^- is exchanged into the blood for chloride. The transient excess base in the blood is called the **alkaline tide**. The chloride diffuses into the lumen; that's why the acid is called **hydrochloric acid** (Fig. 13-10).

Acid is not essential for digestion, but it certainly helps kill off ingested bacteria. Intrinsic factor, on the other hand, is necessary to sustain life. Acid secretion is stimulated by the following:

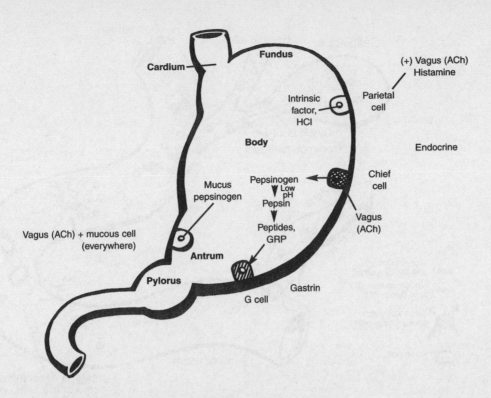

Fig. 13-11. Overview of gastric secretion. (ACh = acetylcholine.)

- Gastrin

- Parasympathetic nervous system (which is why they used to cut the vagus nerve for peptic ulcer disease [PUD])

- Histamine binding to H_2 receptors (the source of billion-dollar competition among cimetidine, ranitidine, and all the other H_2 blockers)

Acid secretion is inhibited by the following:

- Gastric pH less than 3.0 (via negative feedback on gastrin)

- Secretin released from the duodenum in response to acid

- Prostaglandins (aspirin blocks the production of prostaglandins and can lead to gastritis)

Chief cells secrete **pepsinogen**, which in the presence of acid, converts to the proteolytic enzyme **pepsin**. **G cells** secrete **gastrin**. **Mucous cells** make mucus, which coats, soothes, and relieves (i.e., protects the gastric mucosa from acid) (Fig. 13-11).

Pancreatic Secretion

The pancreas's **acinar cells** make the initial digestive juice, which is mainly water and NaCl. The **ductal cells** secrete HCO_3^- (for neutralizing the duodenal contents) and absorb the chloride. People with **cystic fibrosis** have a defect in the chloride channel, which controls these secretions, resulting in thickened secretions that eventually gum up the ducts and lead to autodigestion of the pancreas by trapped digestive enzymes.

Pancreatic secretion is stimulated by **secretin**, **CCK**, and the parasympathetic nervous system.

Pepsi is Coke's **chief** competitor. (Pepsin comes from chief cells.) The products of G cells and mucous cells are obvious from their names. Parietal cells make everything else.

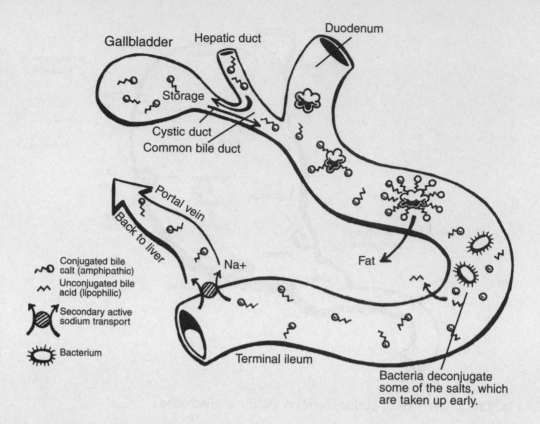

Fig. 13-12. The recycling of bile.

Bile Secretion

Bile is a greenish mixture of bile salts, cholesterol, phospholipids, and bile pigments (basically just bilirubin). **Bile salts**, like phospholipids, are **amphipathic**, meaning they are hydrophilic on one end and hydrophobic on the other. Thus, they can form **micelles** around fatty material in the duodenum. Once the fats are **emulsified** (made soluble in water) they can be broken down further and eventually shuttled across the intestinal wall.

    Bile acids are the precursors to bile salts and are made from cholesterol by hepatocytes. Once they're **conjugated** with a polar group (glycine or taurine), they're called *bile salts* and are stored in the gallbladder, where they wait for CCK to stimulate contraction. After they've done their job in the gut, bile salts are taken up in the terminal ileum by **secondary active transport** and surf the portal vein up to the liver for recycling (Fig. 13-12). Some bile salts may have their polar group clipped off by bacteria (**deconjugation**) and be reabsorbed across the lipophilic gut too early. **Steatorrhea** (fatty feces caused by fat malabsorption) may therefore result from either terminal ileectomy or from bacterial overgrowth, leading to early deconjugation and reuptake of bile salts.

Digestion and Absorption

The villi and microvilli that form the **brush border** of the small intestine greatly increase the surface area for absorption.

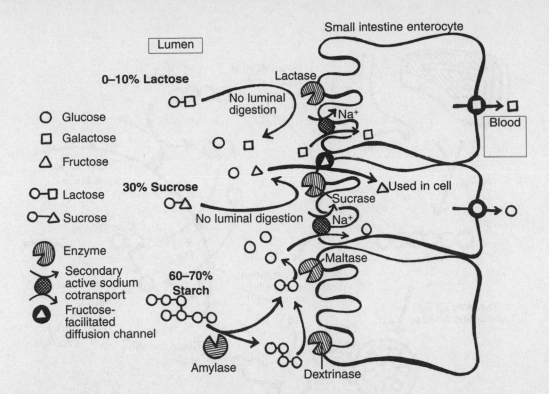

Fig. 13-13. Carbohydrate digestion and absorption.

Carbohydrates

Because it is a lipid bilayer, the gut wall absorbs only monosaccharides; anything larger is just too hydrophilic. Within the lumen, amylase from the pancreas and salivary glands works on breaking down starch (a polymer of glucose) into oligosaccharides ("few sugars"), such as maltose and α-dextrin. The brush border has three enzymes that cleave oligosaccharides and disaccharides into monosaccharides.

Maltase breaks maltose (a dimer of glucose) down into glucose, which is carried across the membrane by **secondary active sodium cotransport**. In other words, a cotransporter grabs a glucose and a sodium and shuttles them both across. It's powered by a sodium gradient maintained by the Na^+/K^+ ATPase on the basolateral membrane, which pumps Na^+ out of the cell. Once inside the cell, the glucose exits the basolateral membrane into the blood along its concentration gradient by **facilitated diffusion**.

α-**Dextrinase** breaks down some of the larger branched oligosaccharides into glucose.

Lactase breaks down lactose (glucose + galactose) into its monosaccharides. Galactose is shuttled by sodium cotransport, just like glucose (Fig. 13-13). **Lactase deficiency** (lactose intolerance) results in lactose being left in the lumen, where it "drags" water out of the intestinal wall by osmosis. Hence, it causes an **osmotic diarrhea**.

Sucrase breaks down sucrose (glucose + fructose). The fructose is unusual in that it does not undergo cotransport. Fructose enters the cell by facilitated diffusion (i.e., it has a carrier, but no ATP is expended), following its own gradient maintained by rapid use within the cell. Everyone loves fruit for this sweet sugar, and the intestinal cell is no exception.

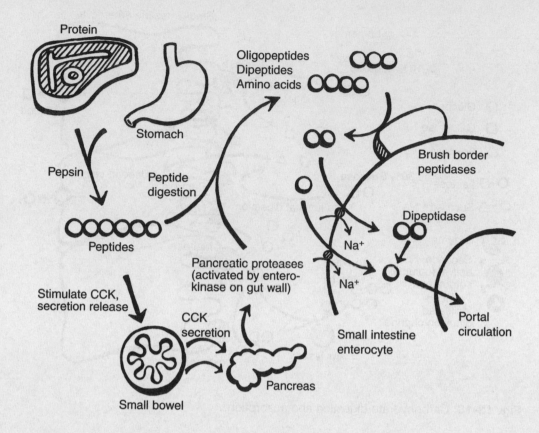

Fig. 13-14. Protein digestion and absorption. (CCK = cholecystokinin.)

Proteins

Unlike carbohydrates, proteins don't have to be broken all the way down into single amino acids. Some dipeptides and tripeptides are lipophilic enough to get across.
Several enzymes digest proteins:

- Pepsin from the stomach

- Endopeptidases, which cleave interior peptide bonds

- Exopeptidases, which cleave from the end

- Pancreatic proteases: There are many of these. They're secreted in an inactive form (**zymogens**) to be activated in the duodenum. Basically, **enterokinase** (on the brush border) converts trypsinogen into **trypsin**, which activates the rest. These two activators are themselves peptidases and can activate each other.

Amino acids and oligopeptides are absorbed by four different secondary active sodium cotransporters for acidic, basic, neutral, and imino peptides (Fig. 13-14).

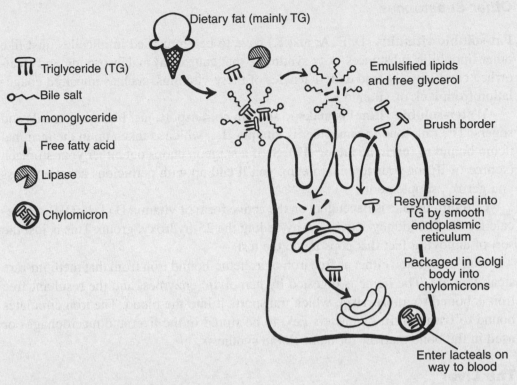

Triglyceride (TG)

Bile salt

monoglyceride

Free fatty acid

Lipase

Chylomicron

Dietary fat (mainly TG)

Emulsified lipids and free glycerol

Brush border

Resynthesized into TG by smooth endoplasmic reticulum

Packaged in Golgi body into chylomicrons

Enter lacteals on way to blood

Fig. 13-15. Lipid digestion and absorption.

Lipids

Pancreatic enzymes, such as **lipase** and **phospholipase**, hydrolyze the lipids (e.g., phospholipids, triglycerides) in the intestinal lumen. The resulting products are free fatty acids, monoglycerides, and cholesterol. The bile salt micelles solubilize the lipids and shuttle them across the **unstirred water layer** (water on the gut wall). The products then diffuse across the cell membrane (Fig. 13-15).

Inside the cell, the subunits are reconstituted into triglycerides and phospholipids. These are lumped along with the cholesterol into lipid droplets coated by **apoproteins**. The resulting particles, fatty on the inside and hydrophilic on the outside (just like a micelle), are called **chylomicrons**. The chylomicron traverses the membrane via **exocytosis** into a **lacteal**, which is basically an intestinal lymphatic channel.

Water and Electrolytes

Sodium follows the gradient established by Na^+/K^+ ATPase. Along the way, it generously helps sugars and amino acids get across. Water, as is its nature, follows sodium, as does chloride.

Just as the intestine can absorb ions, it can also secrete ions. **Cholera toxin** increases chloride secretion, dragging sodium and water into the lumen, resulting in copious watery diarrhea.

Potassium is passively absorbed in the small intestine. The large intestine acts much like the renal collecting tubule. Under the influence of **aldosterone**, it resorbs more sodium and secretes more potassium than normal. Another similarity is that, just as diuresis causes potassium wasting by presenting the collecting duct with a lot of dilute urine that sucks out potassium, diarrhea causes **hypokalemia** by the same mechanism.

Other Substances

Fat-soluble vitamins (D, E, A, and K) have to be emulsified in micelles, just like other lipophilic substances. Any syndrome that causes fat malabsorption and steatorrhea can naturally lead to deficiencies of these vitamins, such as impaired coagulation from lack of vitamin K.

Water-soluble vitamins undergo sodium cotransport, just like amino acids and sugars. The only one to remember is vitamin B_{12}, which is taken up in the terminal ileum bound to **intrinsic factor (IF)**. So if a surgeon chops out either your stomach (source of IF) or your terminal ileum, you'll end up with pernicious anemia unless you get B_{12} supplements.

Calcium uptake is dependent on the active form of vitamin D (1,25[OH]$_2$ cholecalciferol). The kidney activates it by adding the 25-hydroxyl group. This is just the sort of annoying fact that pops up on the test.

Iron is ingested either as free iron or as heme-bound iron from that medium-rare steak you ate. The heme is digested by hemolytic enzymes, and the resultant free iron is bound to **apoferritin**, which transports it into the blood. The iron circulates bound to **transferrin** ("transfers Fe") to be stored in the liver and macrophages or used in the bone marrow for hemoglobin synthesis.

The Liver

If you were a cell, what kind of cell would you want to be? A myocyte? You'd just be doing sit-ups all day. A neuron? Just passing on messages you heard. But the unheralded **hepatocyte** has a varied and interesting job description. Unlike the pancreas, with its beta cells and acinar cells and others, the liver has no specialization. Every hepatocyte does everything.

Here is a quick overview of the synthetic and metabolic functions of this gut-derived organ that serves as the metabolic jack-of-all-trades for the entire body:

- Filters blood from the intestine, cleansing the blood of bacteria (actually a function of the Kupffer cell, a hepatic macrophage).

- Metabolizes carbohydrate. Liver makes and stores glycogen and turns fructose and galactose into glucose. It also acts as a **glucose buffer**, storing sugar after a meal and releasing it several hours later (e.g., when answering the last few questions of the Boards before the lunch break). Gluconeogenesis and the creation of specialized sugars from intermediate steps in metabolic pathways also occur here.

- Metabolizes protein. Liver manufactures plasma proteins, such as albumin, makes urea for disposing of ammonia and other nitrogenous wastes and deaminates amino acids, making them available for use in the body's metabolic pathways. It also transforms and synthesizes the nonessential amino acids.

- Metabolizes lipid. Liver makes the lipoproteins for transportation of fats around the body, manufactures cholesterol and phospholipids for use in bile and cell membranes, and oxidizes fatty acids to provide energy. It is responsible for most of your body's conversion of sugars and protein into fats and for making your pants too tight.

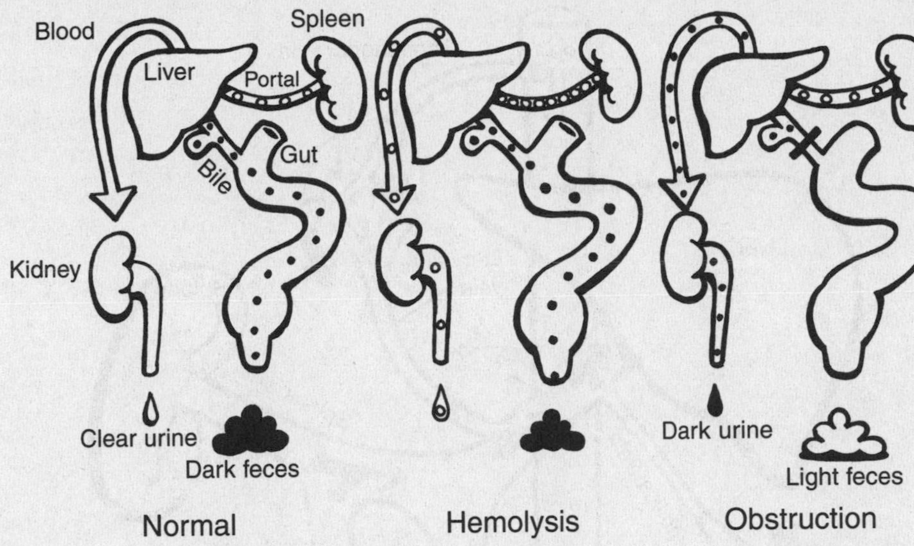

Fig. 13-16. The bilirubin pathway.

Factors II, VII, IX, and X are vitamin K dependent.

- Stores iron in the form of **ferritin** (iron + apoferritin = ferritin). Ferritin provides iron for hemoglobin synthesis when you need it.

- Makes **clotting factors**. One of the symptoms of end-stage liver disease is bleeding. Factors II, VII, IX, and X are vitamin K dependent.

- Stores vitamins.

- **Detoxifies**. The liver excretes many substances into the bile. Other toxins are chemically altered so that the kidney can dispose of them. Liver damage causes excess serum levels of many different drugs and hormones.

- Metabolizes bilirubin.

Heme is broken down in the **reticuloendothelial system** (RES) of the spleen and liver. The resultant **unconjugated** (indirect) bilirubin is insoluble; it must be carried in the blood by albumin. Hepatocytes take up the bilirubin and make it soluble and therefore excretable by **conjugating** it with a sugar (glucuronic acid). The conjugated (direct) bilirubin is placed in the bile and ends up in the intestinal lumen. Bacteria in the intestine metabolize it to urobilinogen (uro = urine) and then stercobilinogen (sterco = feces). Some of the urobilinogen gets reabsorbed and excreted in the urine, providing its yellow color.

With biliary obstruction, the conjugated bilirubin can't enter the gut and ends up in the blood (Fig. 13-16). The urine becomes brownish with all the excess bilirubin, whereas the stools are pale because they don't have enough bilirubin. With hemolysis and an increase in blood levels of unconjugated bilirubin, the urine looks normal because it's the conjugated bilirubin that adds the dark color.

The Gallbladder

The gallbladder stores bile, waiting for CCK to signal that a fatty meal has arrived and that some bile salts are needed to solubilize the fat. CCK causes the gallbladder smooth muscle to contract and the sphincter of Oddi to relax. While waiting for this

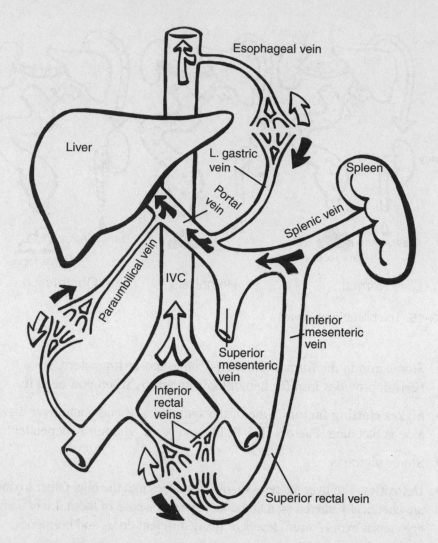

Fig. 13-17. The portacaval anastomoses and portal hypertension. Elevated portal blood pressure favors shunting along the white arrows to the caval system. (IVC = inferior vena cava.)

signal, the gallbladder concentrates the bile, reabsorbing Na^+, Cl^-, and bicarbonate. Water follows passively.

Enterohepatic Circulation

The liver processes about 1,500 ml of blood a minute, roughly 30% of the cardiac output. About 30% of this flow comes from the hepatic artery; the remainder is venous blood coming from the gut via the portal vein. Both systems drain into the liver sinusoids, from which the blood percolates past the hepatocytes into the central vein.

Normally, the blood pressure in the portal vein is around 9 mm Hg, whereas that of the hepatic vein and IVC is essentially zero. If liver parenchyma is replaced with fibrous tissue (a process known as **cirrhosis**), which contracts around the blood vessels, the portal pressure rises, and the blood from the gut has to find an alternate way back to the heart. The increased flow through veins, joining the portal and systemic drainage systems, causes the venous dilatation seen in esophageal varices, hemorrhoids, and caput medusa (Fig. 13-17). Portal hyper-

"Gut, butt, caput"

tension may also result from hepatic vein thrombosis, a condition known as **Budd-Chiari syndrome**.

Role of the Gut in Host Defense

Given how often we humans eat food that has been left out on the counter overnight, it's a good thing that our guts have developed specific measures to combat ingested pathogens:

- Acid and proteolytic enzymes in the lumen for digesting pathogens

- IgA in GI secretions for binding to pathogens and preventing them from attaching to the mucosa

- Gut-associated lymphoid tissue (such as tonsils in the pharynx and Peyer's patches in the ileum) for mounting a systemic immune response to ingested antigens

- Extravasation of leukocytes, such as neutrophils, to fight bacterial gut infections

- Macrophages (Kupffer cells) in the hepatic sinuses to phagocytose antigens

- Resident colonies of bacteria (normal flora), which are adapted to life in the gut and which out-compete pathogenic bacteria for resources

Repair and Regeneration

Because of continuous sloughing, the mucosal epithelium of the gut is one of the fastest-dividing tissues in the body. Therefore, GI distress is one of the earliest manifestations of generalized cytotoxic insults, such as chemotherapeutics and radiation. These **labile cells** tend to grow from the pits of the mucosa out toward the villi, just as your fingernails grow from the base outward.

Other tissues in the GI system do not regenerate nearly as fast. An example is the liver. Hepatocytes are **stable cells**; they retain the ability to proliferate if needed. Unless the reticulin network forming the "skeleton" of the liver is intact, however, the hepatocytes regenerate haphazardly and fail to line up into proper canaliculi.

Repair is the body's response to death of **permanent cells**. The end result of repair is fibrosis and scarring, as is seen in a cirrhotic liver.

Genetic and Congenital Disorders

Hypertrophic Pyloric Stenosis

Projectile nonbilious vomiting in an infant within the first 2 months of life is the hallmark of hypertrophic pyloric stenosis, a congenital hypertrophy of the gastric outflow tract muscle. Physical examination reveals a palpable **olive-like mass** in the epigastrium, representing the overly muscular pylorus. Food can't get through, so it

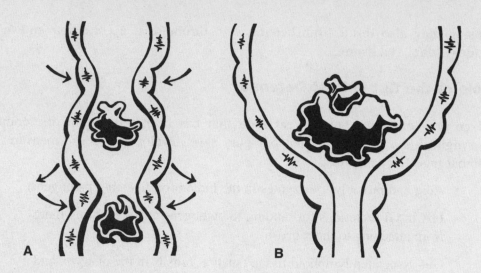

Fig. 13-18. Hirschsprung's disease contrasted with normal colonic peristalsis. **A.** In normal colonic peristalsis, waves of contraction and relaxation are mediated by nervous plexuses in the gut wall. **B.** In Hirschsprung's disease, the lower segment lacks nervous plexuses and is unable to contribute to peristalsis.

is sprayed across the room. Treatment is **pyloroplasty**—surgical alteration of the sphincter. Sometimes adults can acquire pyloric stenosis, either from inflammatory fibrosis due to an ulcer or from a tumor.

Biliary Atresia

Despite its name (*atresia* means congenital absence or narrowing), biliary atresia more often involves destruction of the extrahepatic bile ducts after birth, usually by viral infection or autoimmunity. Presenting in infancy as a severe obstructive jaundice with elevated direct bilirubin, the diagnosis is confirmed by showing a closed duct by cholangiography (injection of radiopaque dye into the duct and taking an X-ray). Surgery can sometimes establish a bypass for the bile, but usually the obstruction causes liver fibrosis, and the only hope for living beyond age 2 is a liver transplant.

Hirschsprung's Disease

Hirschsprung's disease—a disease of infants—that is more accurately known as **congenital aganglionic megacolon**, develops when neural crest tissue fails to migrate to a segment of the large intestine, so the embryo has no nerve plexuses in this part of the colon. Lacking neuronal control, the section of gut is functionally obstructed (Fig. 13-18). The child presents with absent bowel movements and abdominal distention. Stool builds up behind the affected segment, dilating the colon and eventually perforating. Diagnosis is made by biopsy, which shows lack of ganglion cells in the gut wall. Treatment is surgical removal of the affected segment.

Meconium Ileus

One of the first manifestations of cystic fibrosis in infants is abdominal distention and failure to have bowel movements. Just as thick mucus plugs up the pancreas and lungs, so do the first stools (meconium) of the CF baby become thickened and stuck. Treatment is a strong enema.

Wilson's Disease

Wilson's disease, a genetic disorder also known as **hepatolenticular degeneration** (for its involvement of the eye as well as the liver), essentially boils down to faulty **copper** excretion from the liver into the bile. The basic defect has been narrowed down to a copper-transporting protein found in normal livers. The excess copper ends up getting deposited throughout the body, most notably in the liver, brain, and eye. Because you would expect half the amount of this protein to handle the body's load of copper, you could surmise that Wilson's disease is an autosomal recessive disorder, which it is.

Signs & Symptoms

Because copper is deposited in so many organs, the disease can present in many different ways, but liver disease (jaundice, hepatomegaly) and neurologic disease (Parkinson-like tremor, rigidity, psychosis) are most common. It should always be on the differential diagnosis in liver disease in a child or young adult. The classic physical finding is the Kayser-Fleischer ring, a grayish green deposit on the rim of the cornea (Descemet's membrane).

Diagnosis

Diagnosis is based on showing elevated levels of urinary copper or decreased plasma ceruloplasmin (a copper carrier).

Treatment

Much of the destruction can be prevented by using copper chelators, such as penicillamine. Late-diagnosed cases may respond only to liver transplantation. Prevention is aimed at identifying affected relatives and starting chelator therapy.

Inflammatory, Infectious, and Immunologic Disorders

Esophagitis

Inflammation of the esophagus may have many different causes. The most common is **reflux esophagitis** (gastroesophageal reflux disease [GERD]) from ascent of gastric acid through the gastroesophageal sphincter. Among the many predisposing factors to GERD are an incompetent sphincter, impaired esophageal clearance of refluxed acid, and a hiatal hernia.

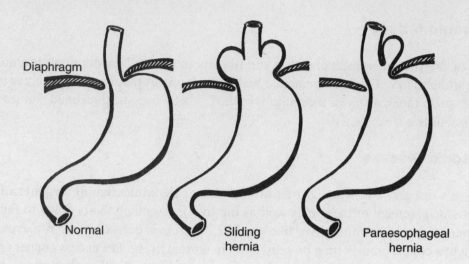

Diaphragm

Normal   Sliding   Paraesophageal
              hernia   hernia

Fig. 13-19. Hiatal hernias.

Barrett's esphagus may progress to esophageal adenocarcinoma.

The most important complication of long-standing GERD is **Barrett's esophagus**, which is metaplasia of the squamous epithelium into columnar epithelium (diagnosed by endoscopy and biopsy). Barrett's esophagus progresses to esophageal adenocarcinoma in up to 10% of cases.

Hiatal hernias are very common, occuring in up to 20% of adults. The crura of the diaphragm normally help to anchor the gastroesophageal junction. When the cardium of the stomach slips up in between the crura, it is a **sliding hiatal hernia**. When another part of the stomach pokes up beside the esophagus, it is a **paraesophageal hiatal hernia** (much rarer) (Fig. 13-19). Hiatal hernias are usually asymptomatic. Among people with severe erosive esophagitis hiatal hernia is almost always present, indicating that the loss of diaphragmatic anchoring allows easier passage of acid into the esophagus.

A second cause of esophagitis is infection, either from disseminated bacteremia or viremia in normal hosts or from cytomegalovirus or candidal infection in immunocompromised hosts. Odynophagia, or painful swallowing, is typical. A third common cause is ingestion of caustic agents, such as acids, bases, alcohol, hot substances, or drugs such as nonsteroidal anti-inflammatory drugs (NSAIDs) or antibiotics.

Signs & Symptoms

The hallmark symptom is heartburn, usually occurring 30–60 minutes after a meal or when the patient lies down (and loses the benefit of gravity).

Diagnosis

Diagnosis is usually made by proving that antacids relieve the pain, although more definitive tests such as endoscopy or esophageal pH monitoring may be necessary in atypical cases.

Treatment

Treatment may include H_2 antagonists, promotility agents (e.g., cisapride), proton-pump inhibitors (e.g., omeprazole), and repeated endoscopies for tumor surveillance.

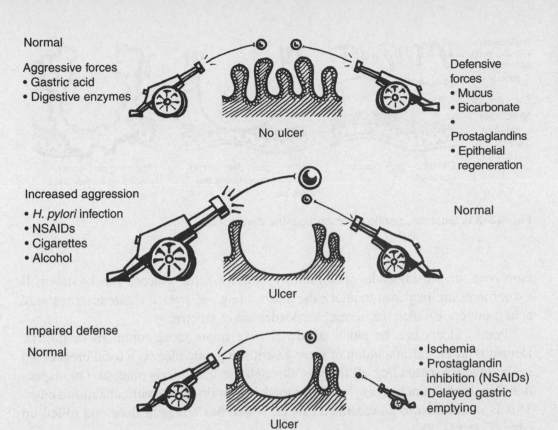

Normal

Aggressive forces
• Gastric acid
• Digestive enzymes

Defensive forces
• Mucus
• Bicarbonate
• Prostaglandins
• Epithelial regeneration

No ulcer

Increased aggression
• *H. pylori* infection
• NSAIDs
• Cigarettes
• Alcohol

Normal

Ulcer

Impaired defense

Normal

• Ischemia
• Prostaglandin inhibition (NSAIDs)
• Delayed gastric emptying

Ulcer

Fig. 13-20. The forces acting on the gastric and duodenal mucosa.

Gastritis

Gastritis can be acute (mainly neutrophils, superficial inflammation) or chronic (mainly lymphocytes, progressive mucosal atrophy, and scarring). The acute variety is also known as *erosive gastritis* for its tendency to cause upper GI bleeds. NSAIDs, alcohol, direct trauma, and shock (which shuts down splanchnic circulation) are among the many causes of acute gastritis. Patients are typically asymptomatic, although they may present with epigastric pain, nausea and vomiting, or hematemesis. Diagnosis is by endoscopy. Treatment involves avoiding the trigger (e.g., aspirin or alcohol) and medication with either H$_2$ blockers to reduce acid or sucralfate to protect the stomach lining.

Chronic gastritis is often due to infection with the gram-negative rod *Helicobacter pylori*. Because the irritation is usually asymptomatic and many people are colonized with the bacteria, treatment with antibiotics is usually delayed until the patient presents with a peptic ulcer. The other notable etiology of chronic gastritis is autoimmune, involving antibodies against the parietal cells and intrinsic factor. These patients present with anemia, not from bleeding but from vitamin B$_{12}$ deficiency. The other thing to remember about chronic gastritis is that it raises the risk of getting gastric cancer.

People with chronic gastritis are at increased risk of getting gastric cancer.

Peptic Ulcer

The mucosa of the stomach and duodenum is a battleground (Fig. 13-20). The normal forces waging war on the mucosa are gastric acids and digestive enzymes. The mucosa counters with its defensive measures: mucus, bicarbonate, prostaglandins, and the ability to regenerate cells. In peptic ulcer disease (PUD), there is an imbalance in these forces. If the defense is impaired (e.g., by ischemia, delayed gastric

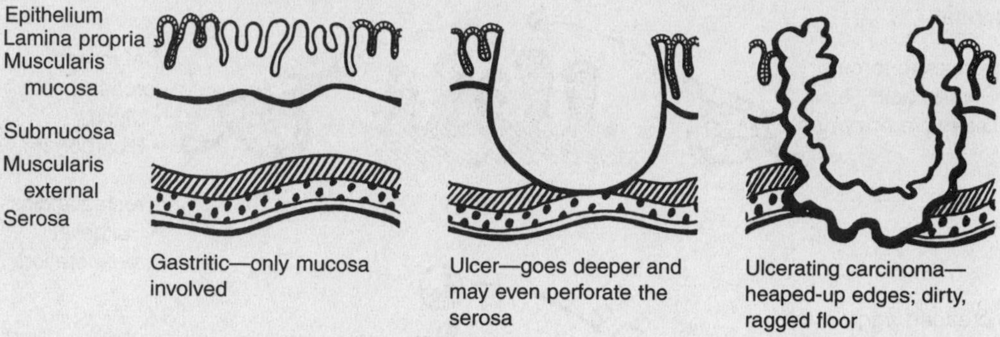

Epithelium
Lamina propria
Muscularis
  mucosa

Submucosa

Muscularis
  external
Serosa

Gastritic—only mucosa involved

Ulcer—goes deeper and may even perforate the serosa

Ulcerating carcinoma—heaped-up edges; dirty, ragged floor

Fig. 13-21. Gastritis, peptic ulcer, and gastric carcinoma.

emptying, or prostaglandin inhibition by NSAIDs), the mucosa breaks down. If extra forces are recruited to attack the mucosa (e.g., *H. pylori*, cigarettes, increased acid production), then the normal barricades are overcome.

Peptic ulcers can be either duodenal (five times more common) or gastric. Deeper than the inflammation of mere gastritis, a peptic ulcer is a focal breakdown in the mucosa, extending all the way through the muscularis mucosa. On inspection they look "punched out," with a smooth, clean floor and without a raised edge. This is in contrast to an ulcerated cancer, which has a ragged floor and rolled-up edge (Fig. 13-21).

Signs & Symptoms

Although 80–90% of ulcers present with epigastric pain (usually burning or "boring," worse at night and after meals), many are asymptomatic or are found when the patient comes in with bleeding, anemia, or perforation. Duodenal ulcers may cause gastric outlet obstruction, with vomiting of undigested food.

Diagnosis

Diagnosis is usually made by endoscopy, including biopsy (to rule out carcinoma; Fig. 13-21) and culturing for *H. pylori*.

Treatment

Treatment is aimed at tipping the balance of power back to the side of mucosal protection. H_2 blockers, such as cimetidine and ranitidine, inhibit histamine's contribution to acid production by blocking H_2-histamine receptors. Proton-pump inhibitors, such as omeprazole, directly block the acid-producing H^+/K^+ ATPase. Sucralfate binds to the ulcerated mucosa, providing a protective barrier. Misoprostol is a prostaglandin analogue that counters the antiprostaglandin effect of NSAIDs. Finally, eradication of *H. pylori* with antibiotics (metronidazole, amoxicillin, or clarithromycin) in conjunction with either proton-pump inhibitors or bismuth compounds (such as Pepto-Bismol) cures about 90% of *H. pylori*–associated ulcers and keeps them from coming back. Naturally, quitting smoking and cutting down on NSAIDs are keys to prevention as well. Remember that PUD is the primary cause of upper GI bleeding.

Food Poisoning

Family reunion—potato salad—all those aunts and uncles laid up with anorexia and vomiting. Food poisoning is actually a general description for a wide spectrum of acute illnesses ranging from a viral gastroenteritis to a life-threatening hemorrhagic fever. The causes can be classified as ingestion of either a preformed toxin or the organism itself.

One cause is ingestion of premade bacterial toxins (clostridia, staphylococci), resulting in an abrupt onset of intense vomiting or diarrhea. **Botulism** is a form of food poisoning arising from eating a paralytic toxin made by *Clostridium botulinum*.

Other food poisonings involve GI infection with various organisms. There may be a mild to moderate course of diarrhea (e.g., from *Salmonella*, *Campylobacter*, *Vibrio cholerae*, and many viruses), requiring little more than fluid and electrolyte replacement. The more severe bloody diarrhea (**dysentery**) comes from such organisms as *Shigella* or enteroinvasive *Escherichia coli*. The difference is due to the invasiveness of the bacteria. Some strains may cause dysentery in some people and no symptoms in others.

Because most of these illnesses are self-limited, antibiotics are reserved for severe cases or special situations, such as *Shigella*, in which only a tiny amount of bacteria causes infection. As gut pathogens, these organisms are transmitted by the fecal-oral route. Prevention is best summarized by the public safety warning: "Employees must wash hands before returning to work."

Traveler's Diarrhea

Traveler's diarrhea is merely a special form of food poisoning seen among tourists. When people travel, they encounter new foods, new methods of food preparation, and new gut pathogens. The typical story is a tourist having ten or more loose stools per day for several days. Most cases are due to bacterial infection from unsanitary food handling. Enterotoxigenic *E. coli*, *Campylobacter*, and *Shigella* are among the usual suspects. Treatment involves preventing dehydration until the infection clears, using antibiotics only if it's protracted or severe. Some travelers take bismuth subsalicylate or antibiotics prophylactically, but the best prevention is to avoid improperly handled food and drink.

Pancreatitis

Inflammation of the pancreas may take an acute or chronic form. **Acute pancreatitis** results from pancreatic enzymes leaking out to damage the pancreas and surrounding tissues. The vast majority of cases are due to either biliary tract disease (e.g., when a gallstone obstructs pancreatic outflow) or alcohol (through unclear mechanisms). Drugs, hyperlipidemias, and hypercalcemia are some of the other culprits.

Signs & Symptoms

Most patients present with acute epigastric pain, severe, steady, and often radiating to the back (because the pancreas is retroperitoneal). Other symptoms include nausea and vomiting. Physical examination shows tenderness, often with fever, hypotension, and jaundice. Patients may have periumbilical blueness (Cullen's sign) or blueness on the flank (Grey Turner's sign) if retroperitoneal hemorrhage is occurring.

You have to **turn** around to see Grey **Turner's** sign.

Diagnosis

Notable laboratory values include leukocytosis and elevated amylase and lipase (pancreatic enzymes). Computed tomography (CT) shows an enlarged, edematous pancreas and may turn up some of the many complications of pancreatitis, such as pseudocyst (a collection of pancreatic fluid), hemorrhage, or abscess.

Treatment

Prognosis of acute pancreatitis is determined by the **Ranson criteria**, a collection of findings that basically state the obvious fact that if you're old, infected, bleeding, or have dysfunction of other organs, you won't do as well (up to 100% mortality with seven positive criteria). Acute pancreatitis is treated by resting the bowel and pancreas (withholding food) and controlling pain until the inflammation subsides, usually after several days. Complications such as infection and **pseudocyst** each have their own treatment, often including surgical drainage.

    Chronic pancreatitis is usually recurrent acute pancreatitis, most often in alcoholics and persons suffering from malnutrition. Relapsing inflammation eventually leads to fibrosis and calcification. As with acute pancreatitis, the key to treatment is to cure the offending factor (e.g., managing the gallbladder disease, quitting alcohol consumption, correcting the hyperlipidemia). Pancreatic enzymes are replaced with oral supplementation.

Cholecystitis

Cholecystitis is inflammation of the gallbladder from the chemical irritation of stagnating bile, often followed by bacterial superinfection. In 90% of cases, it is caused by gallstones obstructing biliary outflow.

Signs & Symptoms

The patient is very ill, with right upper quadrant pain and tenderness, nausea and vomiting, fever and leukocytosis, and sometimes obstructive jaundice if the common bile duct is obstructed. Patients may also have referred pain to the right shoulder because of diaphragmatic and right phrenic nerve irritation.

Diagnosis

Most gallstones cannot be seen on X-ray, so ultrasound is more useful. Nuclear scans are also done.

Treatment

Most cases resolve on their own or with conservative management (bowel rest, pain control), although if the inflammation is severe enough or gangrenous, removal of the gallbladder (cholecystectomy) may be indicated. Some additional picky terminology that surgeons love: Cholelithiasis is stones in the gallbladder, and choledocholithiasis is stones in the common bile duct. Either of these can lead to cholecystitis.

    Chronic cholecystitis simply refers to long-standing, low-grade gallbladder inflammation with fibrosis. The symptoms are often more vague than in the acute form. Acalculous cholecystitis is gallbladder inflammation without stones, either from bacterial seeding, ischemia, or gallbladder disuse (as in anorexics or patients on parenteral nutrition).

Hepatitis

Although the liver can be involved in any blood-borne infection, when we talk about hepatitis we are usually referring to primary inflammation of the liver, most often caused by viruses, alcohol, or drugs.

Viral Hepatitis

Several viruses have a special predilection for the liver. Although they come from different families of viruses, they are all called "hepatitis virus" and are designated from A to E. They are discussed in more detail in chapter 5, but here's a quick summary:

Hepatitis A virus (HAV, a picornavirus) produces the most common acute hepatitis; it frequently appears in the news as epidemics of hepatitis traced to various foods. Transmitted by the fecal-oral route, HAV differs from the other hepatitides by causing **diarrhea** as well as the usual symptoms of acute hepatitis: malaise, fever, and nausea and vomiting, followed by jaundice. Other findings common to any viral hepatitis include icterus, hepatomegaly, elevated bilirubin, and high alkaline phosphatase and transaminase levels (indicative of liver damage). Acute hepatitis resulting from any of these viruses typically subsides after a couple of weeks. In addition to diarrhea, the other features specific to HAV are a short incubation time (about 3 weeks instead of 10) and low levels of viremia, so it doesn't cause chronic infections.

Hepatitis B virus (HBV, a hepadnavirus) has a longer incubation and prodrome than HAV. It also tends to be more severe, with 1% developing **fulminant hepatitis**, a massive necrosis of the liver marked by acute onset of jaundice, mental status changes (**hepatic encephalopathy**), liver failure, and usually death. Because HBV is blood-borne, 1 in 10 people with the virus become **chronic carriers**, able to continue passing on the virus through bodily fluids (e.g., blood transfusions, needle sharing, sexual intercourse). Most chronic carriers are asymptomatic, but those who fail to make antibody against the surface antigen (HBsAg) develop **chronic hepatitis**, which may continue to assault the liver until it becomes cirrhotic, and the patient dies. Another dreaded complication of HBV is its ability to cause **hepatocellular carcinoma** (also known as hepatoma).

HBV is transmitted by blood, breast-feeding, birth, and boinking.

Research into HBV antigens has made it possible to screen the donated blood supply for HBV, produce a vaccine against the surface antigen, and diagnose various stages of the illness, as illustrated in Fig. 13-22.

During the incubation and acute illness you may detect HBV surface antigen in the blood. While the patient is recovering (and if the patient has had the vaccine), you will find IgG against the surface antigen (anti-HBs). In between these two periods is a window where the only marker you may find is IgM against the core antigen (anti-HBc). The way to distinguish vaccinated cases from true cases is that only people exposed to the actual virus have antibodies against the core antigen. A final antigen to remember is HBeAg, which is a predictor of transmissibility: Low HBeAg = low transmission.

To distinguish vaccinated people from cases of hep B infection, recall that antibodies against the core antigen are only seen in infected people.

Hepatitis C virus (HCV) is similar to HBV in its mode of transmission and its ability to cause chronic hepatitis and carrier states. However, unlike HBV, which only becomes chronic 10% of the time, more than 70% of people with HCV develop chronic hepatitis. Since the advent of widespread testing for HBV, the majority of

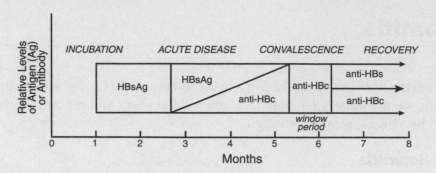

Fig. 13-22. Hepatitis B virus antigens and antibodies.

transfusion-associated hepatitis cases have been HCV, although it is on the decline now that tests for HCV have come out.

Hepatitis D virus (HDV, or delta virus) is a **defective virus**, meaning that it is only infective in the presence of HBV. HBV carriers who contract HDV have a higher risk of fulminant or chronic hepatitis.

Hepatitis E can be fatal in pregnant women.

Hepatitis E virus (HEV), like HAV, is transmitted by fecal-oral route; thus it's common in developing countries with poor sanitation. The remarkable thing about this otherwise unremarkable virus is how dangerous it is to pregnant women (10–20% mortality).

Prevention of viral hepatitis depends on hand-washing and good sanitation for the fecal-oral viruses, and needle care, safe sex, blood screening, and avoidance of frivolous transfusions for the blood-borne viruses. HBV vaccination is 90% effective and is now being given to babies born in the United States. If a person is suspected of recent exposure, administration of immunoglobulin (anti-HBs) may thwart illness. Treatment of active infection is generally limited to symptomatic care (bed rest, fluids). There is some evidence that α-interferon helps in HCV infection.

Alcoholic Hepatitis

One of the several manifestations of alcoholic liver disease (discussed later) is liver inflammation. Alcoholic hepatitis, like viral hepatitis, may take on an acute or chronic form. One finding that may help the physician distinguish between alcoholic and viral hepatitis (aside from a drinking history) is the ratio of serum transaminases. Although both alanine aminotransferase (ALT or SGPT) and aspartate aminotransferase (AST or SGOT) are elevated in both forms of hepatitis, the ratio of AST to ALT tends to be low in viral hepatitis and greater than 2:1 in alcoholics.

GO fAST (SGOT = AST).

Drug-Induced Hepatitis

As the body's main detox center, the liver is particularly susceptible to damage caused by medications. Some drugs are predictably hepatotoxic, with greater doses causing greater damage in a linear fashion. The most famous is probably acetaminophen, large doses of which cause hepatic necrosis in the absence of the antidote, *N*-acetylcysteine (known as Mucomyst). Tetracyclines and carbon tetrachloride are other predictable hepatotoxins. Other drugs cause idiosyncratic reactions, in which it can't be predicted which patients will have liver damage and which won't. Aspirin, chloramphenicol, and isoniazid fall into this group. Certain wild mushrooms are also hepatotoxic.

Reye's syndrome is fulminant acute hepatic failure that follows certain viral infections (e.g., varicella, influenza), usually in children. Nobody knows what causes it, but it is definitely associated with aspirin. With a 40% mortality rate, it's no surprise that nobody gives aspirin to kids, only acetaminophen.

Human Immunodeficiency Virus Infection and Acquired Immunodeficiency Syndrome

In addition to suffering a greater frequency of standard infections, acquired immunodeficiency syndrome (AIDS) patients are susceptible to a number of ailments that rarely affect immunocompetent hosts. Candidal esophagitis is among the most common AIDS infections. Diarrhea is a huge problem in AIDS, partly because even in the absence of superinfections, the human immunodeficiency virus (HIV) itself can cause diarrhea (**AIDS enteropathy**), presumably due to a direct viral effect on the gut epithelium. Furthermore, the parasite *Cryptosporidium*, which causes a benign, self-limited diarrhea in normal hosts, leads to a chronic watery diarrhea in AIDS patients. It is notoriously difficult to treat. **Pseudomembranous colitis**, caused by the anaerobe *Clostridium difficile*, usually arises in normal hosts only when their gut flora has been altered by antibiotics, but it is common in AIDS. Treatment is with metronidazole, a good drug for anaerobic bacteria and many parasites.

Appendicitis

Appendectomy is the most common acute surgery of the abdomen. Peaking in the teens and 20s (10% of population), appendicitis presents first as vague periumbilical pain, nausea and vomiting, anorexia, fever, and elevated white cell count. By the time the pain has localized to the right lower quadrant, with guarding and rebound tenderness, the peritoneum has become inflamed. Surgeons should accurately diagnose appendicitis about 85% of the time, preferring to open a few healthy bellies rather than risking a perforation by waiting out an equivocal case. Diagnosis is made by history and physical examination.

The instigating factor in appendicitis is obstruction of the lumen (usually by a fecalith) followed by distention, vascular compromise, necrosis, and eventual rupture.

Diverticulitis

The presence of mucosal outpouchings through the muscular layer of the colon (**diverticulosis**) is extremely common (60% of people at age 85), especially in Western countries, where the low-fiber diet predisposes to it. Diverticulosis typically involves the sigmoid and descending colon. It is usually asymptomatic but may be associated with occult or massive bleeding.

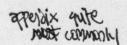
appendix quite most commonly

These patients will probably never come to your attention until one of the diverticula becomes obstructed and inflamed (**diverticulitis**). Similar to appendicitis in its etiology, diverticulitis also shares the symptoms of acute abdominal pain, fever, and leukocytosis. However, the pain is more suprapubic or left lower quadrant because more diverticula occur in the sigmoid colon. Diagnosis is usually by history and physical examination. Most patients respond to antibiotics (covering for anaerobes and gram-negative rods, the two most common groups of bowel bacteria) and, if severe, bowel rest. Some patients (e.g., perforations, abscesses, unresponsive to medical therapy) require surgical intervention.

Peritonitis

Inflammation of the abdominal lining is a common result of nearly any inflammatory or infectious process in the abdomen. Using appendicitis as an example, we note the onset of peritonitis when irritation of the finely discriminating peritoneal pain fibers localizes the patient's pain to the right lower quadrant. The abdomen becomes exquisitely tender, with "rebound tenderness" (increased pain when pressure on the belly is suddenly released, due to sudden movement of the peritoneum). The abdominal muscles reflexively tense up to prevent you from palpating deeply (a phenomenon known as "guarding"). The patient is febrile and very ill-appearing, with an elevated white cell count. Surgery is required imminently.

Another type of peritonitis is found in patients with chronic liver disease and ascites (fluid in the abdomen). Called **spontaneous bacterial peritonitis** due to its lack of an obvious infectious source, this illness presents in much the same way as typical secondary peritonitis: abdominal pain and fever. Thus, you must rule out other causes of infection. The bacteria don't really arise spontaneously but rather travel across the bowel and find this wonderful culture medium in the abdominal fluid. Diagnosis is made simply by tapping the ascites (paracentesis) and finding neutrophils or bacteria. Early treatment with appropriate antibiotics can reduce mortality from 50% to 10%.

When peritonitis is incompletely treated, the immune system attempts to isolate the bacteria by building a fibrous capsule around them. Known as an **abscess**, this bag of bacteria and leukocytes presents clinically with pain, fever, and chills, which may be intermittent due to periodic escape of bacteria into the blood. Diagnosis is made by CT scan followed by drainage procedures and antibiotics. Often abscesses can be found in the tissue of various organs, particularly the liver.

Inflammatory Bowel Disease

Inflammatory bowel disease (IBD) is a chronic, relapsing, life-long illness of autoimmunity. Actually a spectrum of illnesses, IBD is traditionally divided into **Crohn's disease** and **ulcerative colitis**, each of which has its own specific features but shares the common etiology of unchecked inflammation (Table 13-3). The gut is on the front line of the battle between bacteria and body. In the normal host, inflammation is constantly deployed to fend off infection. But the body has mechanisms to keep the inflammation under control, putting out the fire before it rages. In IBD, these mechanisms (which are essentially unknown) are faulty.

Like many autoimmune diseases, IBD features a genetic predisposition. Many sufferers also have other autoimmune diseases, such as ankylosing spondylitis or erythema nodosum. Onset peaks in the 20s. Treatment for both types of IBD focuses on damping the immune response. Salicylates, such as sulfasalazine, corticosteroids, and mercaptopurine, suppress immune function. Patients with IBD are at increased risk of developing colon adenocarcinoma and require regular surveillance with colonoscopy.

Table 13-3. Ulcerative colitis compared to Crohn's disease

Ulcerative colitis	Crohn's disease
Continuous inflammation starting at the rectum and heading north; usually involves only colon (may have backwash ileitis.	**Skip** lesions (i.e., not continuous) involving both colon and small intestine
Inflammation involves **mucosa** and **submucosa** only	**Transmural** inflammation
Ulceration without thickening; friable, hyperemic mucosa; pseudopolypos; **no granulomas**.	Wall thickens and forms fissures ("**cobblestone pattern**"); has **granulomas**
Presentation: abdominal pain, weight loss, chronic diarrhea with blood and mucus	Chronic diarrhea, pain, fever, weight loss; sometimes a palpable mass, perianal disease (fistulae, fissures)
Complications: toxic megacolon, colonic carcinoma at an early age	Malabsorption, obstruction, fistulae between bowel loops
Surgery: often done to prevent carcinoma; mandatory for toxic megacolon	Often aggravated by surgery, so surgery generally reserved for obstructions and fistulae
Increased risk of colon cancer	

Mechanical, Metabolic, Physiologic, and Regulatory Disorders

Achalasia

Achalasia is sort of like the Hirschsprung's disease of the esophagus. The difference is the age of presentation, with achalasia patients presenting between ages 25 and 60 with progressive **dysphagia** (impaired swallowing) and regurgitation of undigested food. As with Hirschsprung's, there is loss of the ganglion cells in the myenteric plexus, leading to impaired motility and progressive dilatation of the segment above the defect. Some cases are due to **Chagas' disease**. Diagnosis is supported by barium esophagram showing "bird's beak" tapering of the distal esophagus. Esophageal manometry (pressure measurements) shows absence of peristalsis, incomplete relaxation of the lower sphincter, and overall high pressures in the esophagus.

Traditional treatment relies on surgery or balloon inflation to open up the distal esophagus. Recently, locally injected botulinum toxin has been successfully used to relax the sphincter. As long as treatment occurs before severe dilatation, patients can swallow normally. The most feared complication of achalasia is a 16-fold increase in squamous carcinoma of the esophagus. squamous© – 16x↑!

Achalasia is associated with an increased risk of squamous cell cancer of the esophagus.

Intestinal Obstruction

There are many reasons the lumen of the intestine can get blocked off (Fig. 13-23).

- Crohn's disease (the gut wall becomes thickened and adherent)
- Hernias (the gut slips through a wall of muscle and gets trapped)

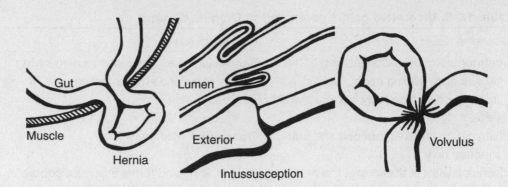

Fig. 13-23. Hernia, intussusception, and volvulus.

- Intussusception (the gut telescopes in on itself)

- Surgical adhesions (the gut gets scarred up and sticks together after being manipulated)—the most common cause of small bowel obstruction

- Tumors or hematomas (the gut lumen gets impinged or directly plugged)

- Volvulus (the gut twists around on itself, like the twists on a balloon animal)

With any obstruction, the patient presents with cramping abdominal pain, vomiting, and obstipation (complete constipation and no gas from below—a trait your friends may actually appreciate). As the bowel behind the obstruction dilates, the pain becomes constant. X-rays are used to aid diagnosis, and a barium swallow can definitively demonstrate the obstruction. The main complication of obstruction is stoppage of blood supply (**strangulation**), which requires prompt surgical correction.

Paralytic Ileus

Ileus is the loss of peristalsis for reasons other than obstruction. Because both ileus and obstruction cause similar symptoms (pain, vomiting, obstipation, distention), it is difficult to distinguish them clinically. Ileus tends to be less painful than obstruction, and the pattern of bowel sounds is different. Bowel sounds are rare or absent in ileus (no contractile action), whereas in obstruction you might hear high pitched "tinkles" as air squeaks through tight lumens with forceful peristalsis trying to move things along.

To generate a list of causes of ileus, think about things that might startle the bowel into shutting down: abdominal surgery, major illness, peritonitis. Many medicines, particularly opioids and anticholinergics, inhibit the bowel and cause ileus. To treat the ileus, treat the underlying cause.

Irritable Bowel Syndrome

Irritable bowel syndrome (IBS) is a catch-all phrase for a bunch of abdominal complaints with no clear etiology. With millions of adults having symptoms that fit IBS, this is a common, but frustrating, diagnosis for physicians. Among the typical complaints are intermittent crampy pain, fluctuating bowel habits, and distention or bloating, all lasting at least 3–6 months. The physician should try to rule out treatable illnesses, such as IBD, malabsorption, and neoplasms. Physical examination and laboratory tests are remarkable only for the lack of findings.

The ultimate causes of IBS are varied. Among the possibilities are abnormal motility, increased pain response, and psychosocial issues. The mainstay of therapy is to nonjudgmentally reassure the patient that although his or her symptoms are real, they aren't life-threatening.

Malabsorption

When nutrients fail to get soaked up from the intestinal lumen into the bloodstream, the patient is said to have **malabsorption**. If you consider all the different hurdles a food particle must overcome to cross the gut wall, you can see that many different physical and biochemical abnormalities can cause malabsorption. Although the signs and symptoms are subtly different for each etiology, most malabsorption syndromes are marked by some combination of malnutrition, diarrhea, and weight loss.

First, let's consider malabsorption due to **defective intraluminal hydrolysis**. In adults, a scarcity of digestive enzymes from the pancreas may be an end result of chronic pancreatitis. In children, the leading cause of pancreatic enzyme deficiency is cystic fibrosis. Either way, the patient has a lot of difficulty digesting fats, and the lipids end up in the stool (steatorrhea). Protein deficiency isn't much of a problem, probably because the stomach's acid and pepsin are sufficient. Lipid malabsorption is also seen in **bile salt deficiency**, which is usually caused by bacterial overgrowth secondary to impaired motility. The bacteria deconjugate the bile salts, leading to early reuptake before the bile can emulsify the fats. Unlike pancreatic insufficiency, bile salt deficiency also causes impaired uptake of vitamins D, E, A, and K, with the resultant clinical syndromes.

The second site of malabsorption is the gut wall itself. These **primary intestinal disorders** can be divided into biochemical and morphologic defects. Recall from Physiology that the enzymes for breaking disaccharides into monosaccharides reside on the brush border. Absence of any of these enzymes results in that sugar being left in the lumen. If the sugar is present in sufficient quantities, it causes an **osmotic diarrhea** by "pulling" water into the lumen. The most famous of these disaccharidase deficiencies is **lactose intolerance** (lactase deficiency). After birth, levels of lactase decline steadily, especially among people of non-European descent. With a small amount of dairy products, you get crampy pains, bloating, and flatulence. If you raid the entire dairy section, you'll have osmotic diarrhea. Stool pH is used in diagnosis. Treatment is to avoid lactose or take lactase caplets.

The best-known morphologic defect causing malabsorption is **celiac sprue**, also known as gluten enteropathy. These patients have widespread damage to the mucosa of their proximal small intestine, with loss of villi. The extent of malabsorption depends on the length of intestine involved. The apparent instigator in this disorganization of the epithelium is **gluten**, the protein in many grains. Removal of gluten from the diet (rice and corn are okay) is essential. **Crohn's disease** also causes malabsorption if it involves enough of the small bowel. People who have had segments of their small intestines removed may have **short bowel syndrome** (also known as "dumping syndrome"), which is malabsorption due to insufficient absorptive area.

The third site of malabsorption is found after nutrients travel across the gut wall. **Lymphatic obstruction** impairs the ability of chylomicrons and lipoproteins to enter the lacteals.

Malabsorption has several **infectious causes**. **Whipple's disease** refers to infection with the bacillus *Tropheryma whippelii*. Many organs are affected, including the small intestine, where it causes malabsorption. **Giardiasis** is an infectious diarrhea caused by the parasite *Giardia lamblia*. In some patients (particularly AIDS patients) the diarrhea may progress to chronic malabsorption. **Tropical sprue** manifests as malabsorption in travelers to tropical areas. Caused by overgrowth of enterotoxin-producing bacteria, tropical sprue has pathologic changes similar to those of celiac sprue, but it may be seen throughout the small intestine.

A useful test for diagnosing various forms of malabsorption is the **fecal fat test**. Normal people lose only about 6 g of fat in their stool a day. Anything more than 10 g is definitely steatorrhea. In cases of severe fat malabsorption, fat loss may total 100 g or more (if the person ate a burger and fries that day). The **D-xylose test** helps to determine whether the malabsorption is a primary intestinal disorder. Because the sugar xylose does not require pancreatic or biliary secretions, any xylose that you give a patient ends up in the stool if there's a problem with the gut wall itself. Naturally, the most specific test for differentiating among the various diseases is intestinal wall biopsy and culture.

Introduction to Liver Disease

The liver is a resilient organ, but even the remarkable regenerative capacities of the liver are no match for chronic, repeated insults. Damage to the liver is manifested in many ways. One of the tools used to differentiate the various causes of liver disease is the battery of **liver function tests** (LFTs). Actually, some of these assays for serum levels of different markers test for liver function and others test for liver destruction. Don't worry about learning normal values for the boards; they'll be provided.

- Bilirubin: **Direct** (already conjugated by the liver) bilirubin is elevated in intra- or extrahepatic obstruction. **Indirect** (**un**conjugated, **in**soluble) bilirubin is elevated when hemolysis releases it from red blood cells (RBCs) or in rare genetic deficiencies in conjugating enzymes.

- Albumin: Albumin is a multipurpose serum protein synthesized in the liver. It is decreased when disease is prolonged enough to deplete the blood level.

- Prothrombin time (PT): This measures the function of liver-produced clotting factors. Prolongation of the PT is one of the most sensitive prognosticators of severe liver disease.

- Transaminases: These enzymes spill into the blood from necrosing liver. The ratio of AST to ALT can be helpful, with AST:ALT greater than 2:1 suggesting alcoholic liver disease and less than 1:1 suggesting viral hepatitis.

- Alkaline phosphatase: This enzyme is released during liver damage, particularly necrosis and cholestasis.

Abnormal LFTs may be the first clue that something bad is happening to the liver. Conversely, the first sign of liver disease may be jaundice and scleral icterus, seen when the bilirubin exceeds 3 mg/dl or so. Jaundice is frequently accompanied by pruritus (itching). The most common type of jaundice is **neonatal jaundice**, seen in newborns who do not have a sufficient quantity of **glucuronyl transferase**, the enzyme used for conjugation. Because bilirubin is very toxic to the neonatal brain (**kernicterus**), UV light is used to isomerize the bilirubin, which prevents it from crossing the blood-brain barrier.

Other clinical presentations of liver disease include hepatitis (fever, pain, malaise, jaundice), cirrhosis or portal hypertension (ascites, varices, splenomegaly), and hepatic failure (metabolic abnormalities, coagulopathy, encephalopathy). Naturally, these presentations overlap. **Hepatic encephalopathy** describes the mental status changes that accompany the metabolic derangements of liver failure. Although the accumulation of many toxins is responsible for encephalopathy, the most commonly followed serum toxin is **ammonia**. **Lactulose**, an indigestible carbohydrate, is given in cases of encephalopathy to reduce ammonia levels. Lactulose is digested by colonic bacteria, lowering the gut pH. The excess acid converts ammonia to ammonium ion, which cannot cross back into the bloodstream. The result, along with an osmotic diarrhea, is a depletion of blood ammonia.

Hyperbilirubinemia

Diseases that elevate blood levels of bilirubin fall into one of these four categories of disorder:

- Increased bilirubin production

- Decreased bilirubin uptake by the liver

- Impaired conjugation in the liver

- Decreased excretion of bilirubin into the bile (**cholestasis**)

The first three types are unconjugated hyperbilirubinemias (indirect bilirubin, normal stool and urine color), but the last one shows increased conjugated bilirubin (direct bilirubin, dark urine, light stools).

Increased unconjugated bilirubin is usually due to hemolysis. The liver works fine but is overwhelmed by the bilirubin load. The patient may be anemic and have a reticulocytosis, indicative of high RBC turnover. **Ineffective erythropoiesis**, with destruction of abnormal blood cells in the bone marrow, is another cause of bilirubin overproduction.

Decreased bilirubin uptake due to interference with membrane transport proteins is a rare drug side effect.

Impaired conjugation is a result of decreased activity of **glucuronyl transferase** (UGT), the conjugating liver enzyme. This enzyme is immature at birth (**neonatal jaundice**) but usually kicks in within a few weeks. There are a few hereditary forms of UGT deficiency. **Gilbert's syndrome** is a common disease, causing small, benign elevations in bilirubin during times of stress (e.g., illness) due to decreased UGT activity. There may also be a component of impaired uptake. **Crigler-Najjar syndrome** comes in two forms. In type II UGT activity is decreased, causing very yellow skin but no other problems. Type I is the absence of UGT activity. This rare disorder inevitably causes death in infancy from kernicterus.

Dubin-Johnson and Rotor's cause increased DiRect bilirubin, but Gilbert's and Crigler-Najjar are the opposite.

[handwritten margin notes]

Primary biliary cirrhosis
↑ AMA
↑ ALP

Primary sclerosing cholangitis
beads on a string
(cholangiography)

Decreased excretion (cholestasis) of conjugated bilirubin encompasses many diseases, both inside and outside the liver. There are two hereditary forms. **Dubin-Johnson syndrome** is a harmless impairment in bile excretion into the canaliculi. For some reason these patients end up with a black pigmented liver. **Rotor's syndrome** is also a benign disease. Also caused by a defect in some unknown excretory protein, Rotor's syndrome differs in that the liver is not black.

The other causes of cholestasis are best divided up anatomically. **Canalicular** defects include not only Dubin-Johnson and Rotor, but also **recurrent jaundice of pregnancy**, which affects canalicular transport for some unknown reason. **Hepatocanalicular** and **hepatocellular** cholestasis refer to hepatic injury, with elevated transaminases and alkaline phosphatase. Inflammation of the liver tissue obstructs bile flow. Typical causes include drugs (e.g., chloramphenicol, anabolic steroids), hepatitis, and alcohol.

Ductal cholestasis results from destruction of interlobular bile ducts, with increasing alkaline phosphatase and transaminases. One form of ductal disease is **primary biliary cirrhosis**, a <u>fatal</u> autoimmune disease (usually of women) that attacks the bile ducts and forms granulomas. The patients have a high antimitochondrial antibody titer and very high alkaline phosphatase. The liver eventually becomes shrunken and fibrotic (**cirrhosis**), causing <u>death by hepatic failure</u>. A second form of ductal disease is **primary sclerosing cholangitis**, in which stricturing of the biliary tree causes a beads-on-a-string appearance on cholangiography. Seen more in men, and frequently in association with ulcerative colitis, primary sclerosing cholangitis has a high alkaline phosphatase, but the antimitochondrial antibody level is normal. The cause is unknown. Once again, it is a progressive, fatal disease.

The final location for cholestasis is outside the liver. Most commonly, gallstones blocking the bile duct are responsible for backup of bile flow.

Alcoholic Liver Disease and Cirrhosis

Excessive alcohol consumption is the most common cause of reversible liver disease; many of the changes seen in the liver can improve with cessation of drinking. Alcohol is also the most common cause of **irreversible** liver disease, with alcoholic cirrhosis being one of America's leading causes of death. The following paragraphs delineate the stages of alcoholic liver disease.

Fatty liver (**hepatic steatosis**) forms after short-term ingestion of 80 g of ethanol a day (about eight beers). Metabolism of ethanol yields the reduced form of nicotinamide-adenine dinucleotide (NADH), which is used in lipid synthesis. The fat accumulates in the hepatocytes, enlarging the liver. The patient is usually completely asymptomatic. Fatty liver is completely reversible.

Alcoholic hepatitis often acutely follows binges of heavy drinking. Women are more at risk of getting it than men, possibly due to lower levels of alcohol dehydrogenase in the stomach. The patient usually complains of malaise, upper abdominal pain, anorexia, and weight loss. Some patients are critically ill (10% die with each bout of hepatitis). Laboratory tests show high bilirubin and alkaline phosphatase. The AST:ALT ratio is generally above 2:1. Liver biopsy shows hepatocyte necrosis, Mallory bodies (deranged cytoskeleton), and neutrophil infiltrate. If the patient can stop drinking and improve nutrition, these liver changes may reverse. Otherwise, repeated episodes of alcoholic hepatitis will lead to cirrhosis.

Cirrhosis is the liver's response to repeated injury. First fibrous septae segregate the hepatocytes into **micronodules**. The liver continues to become more nodular and fibrotic. Eventually the fibrosis overtakes the nodules, and the liver becomes shrunken and hard. Blood flow through the liver is deranged, elevating the portal blood pressure and sending the blood through the portacaval anastomoses (esophageal, hemorrhoidal, umbilical). The shunting of blood decreases liver perfusion, causing more necrosis. The spleen enlarges from impaired venous drainage. Starling's forces (increased hydrostatic pressure, decreased oncotic pressure from hypoalbuminemia) squeeze fluid out into the peritoneal cavity (ascites).

Patients with cirrhosis may present with weakness and anorexia. Or they may roll in by ambulance after vomiting blood (**hematemesis**) from esophageal varices. They may even present with hormonal dysfunction (amenorrhea, gynecomastia, decreased libido, palmar erythema) due to the liver's role in metabolizing sex steroids. Later manifestations include edema (ascites, pleural effusions, ankle swelling), encephalopathy, and **hepatorenal syndrome** (renal failure caused by liver failure for unclear reasons).

Except for liver transplantation, treatment is generally aimed at ameliorating the consequences of cirrhosis. For ascites, diuretics and paracentesis are helpful. For portal hypertension, surgical shunts known as TIPS (for transjugular intrahepatic portosystemic shunt) and β-blockers are used. Esophageal varices may be managed with sclerotherapy (injecting a hardening agent) or rubber-banding via endoscope. Encephalopathy may respond to lactulose. Spontaneous bacterial peritonitis requires antibiotics. Anemia and coagulopathy necessitate vitamin therapy and transfusions.

Ethanol is not the only cause of cirrhosis; it is merely the most common. Because cirrhosis is a response to injury, any chronic injury may lead to it. Viral hepatitis and biliary disease are second and third on the list. **Hemochromatosis** is excessive iron deposition in the liver and throughout the body. Hemochromatosis has a primary genetic form in which the gut absorbs too much iron as well as a secondary acquired form, where excess iron may come from RBC breakdown or some other source. Treatment is iron chelators and bloodletting (really!). Rarer causes of cirrhosis include Wilson's disease (discussed earlier) and **α_1-antitrypsin deficiency**, where the patients lack an enzyme that inhibits a protease that can break down tissue. Patients get cirrhosis as well as emphysema, from a similar process in the lungs.

Cholelithiasis

Cholelithiasis refers to the presence of stones in the gallbladder. Stones form when one of the components of bile is present in too high a concentration, causing it to precipitate out of solution. In the United States, with its fast-food chains, the precipitant is usually cholesterol. More common in obese people and women, gallstones usually aren't a problem as long as they remain in the gallbladder. When they migrate down into the ducts (**choledocholithiasis**), however, they cause **biliary** colic, a sharp right-upper-quadrant pain, sometimes with referred pain to the right shoulder (due to the proximity to the diaphragm and phrenic nerve, which shares nerve roots that innervate the shoulder). The pain is most common after fatty meals, when the duct squeezes down around the stone.

Risk factors for gallstones: **F**emale, **F**at, **F**orty, **F**air (skinned), and **F**ertile

The stones are visible on ultrasound. If symptomatic, gallstones can be treated by cholecystectomy, endoscopic stone extraction through the sphincter of Oddi, oral

black *white*

Table 13-4. Esophageal neoplasms

	Squamous cell carcinoma	Adenocarcinoma
Pathology	Can arise anywhere in the esophagus	Glandular tumor usually arising in distal esophagus in region of glandular metaplasia (Barrett's esophagus)
Signs and symptoms	Progressive dysphagia (difficulty swallowing), weight loss; usually presents late in the disease	Same
Diagnosis	Barium esophagram shows lesion; endoscopy with biopsy confirms diagnosis	Same
Treatment	Poor prognosis; surgery is done to improve ability to eat, but is rarely curative; radiation may help	Same
Contributing factors (targets for prevention)	Poor diet combined with chronic ingestion of toxins (cigarette smoke, alcohol); also more common in people who have had achalasia	Long-standing GERD causes Barrett's esophagus, which predisposes to adenocarcinoma

GERD = gastroesophageal reflux disease.

administration of bile salts (which dissolve the stones by restoring the proper ratio of bile components), or breaking up the stones with sound waves (**lithotripsy**).

One of the most important complications of choledocholithiasis is secondary bacterial infection of the biliary ducts (**cholangitis**). The bacteria generally crawl up through the sphincter of Oddi. The expected gut flora are seen, namely, gram-negative rods such as *E. coli* and anaerobes such as *Bacteroides*. The classic findings are called **Charcot's triad**: right upper quadrant pain, fever and chills, and jaundice. Other findings include elevated conjugated bilirubin and alkaline phosphatase (which suggest obstruction of hepatic outflow and liver damage). Diagnosis can be confirmed by **cholangiography** (introduction of radiopaque dye into the ducts, followed by X-ray imaging). The dye can be placed either by needle through the skin and liver or by an endoscope through the sphincter of Oddi, which has the added benefit of allowing you to try to extract any stones.

Neoplastic Disorders

Neoplastic disorders of the GI tract are described in Tables 13-4 through 13-9.

Besides colorectal carcinoma, there are a lot of other things you might see growing in people's colons when you stick a colonoscope up there (Fig. 13-24).

- Inflammatory polyps: The "pseudopolyps" seen in ulcerative colitis; these are islands of inflamed mucosa surrounded by ulceration.

- Hyperplastic polyps: The vast majority of polyps. Little domes of mucosal cells on top of a fold in the colon wall. No malignant potential.

Table 13-5. Stomach neoplasms

	Gastric adenocarcinoma	*Leiomyoma*
Pathology	Most common form is ulcerated but may also be polypoid or diffusely infiltrative	After the uterus, stomach is the most common site for this benign smooth muscle tumor
Signs and symptoms	Epigastric pain, weight loss, anemia due to occult bleeding Usually presents late in the disease	Asymptomatic or obstructive symptoms
Diagnosis	Endoscopy with biopsy	Same
Treatment	Surgical resection Treatment may be palliative to limit obstruction or bleeding	Surgical resection, with good prognosis
Contributing factors (targets for prevention)	Much more common outside the United States (e.g., Japan), which may be related to a high-nitrosamine diet *Helicobacter pylori* is a strong risk factor	None
Other	In Japan, where the cancer is much more common, screening programs are used to detect early carcinoma Early resection improves 5-year survival from 5% to >90%	None

Table 13-6. Small intestine neoplasms

	Metastatic cancer and lymphoma	*Carcinoid tumor*
Pathology	Cancers arising elsewhere are among the most common malignant neoplasms in any part of the gastrointestinal system, but especially in the small bowel, where primary tumors are exceedingly rare	Malignant tumor of neuroendocrine cells Can produce endocrinopathies (e.g., Cushing's, Zollinger-Ellison), based on its secretory products (usually if metastatic to liver)
Signs and symptoms	Pain, nausea, obstruction, bleeding, anemia	Same symptoms as metastatic, plus diarrhea with cutaneous flushing and other signs of endocrine abnormalities
Diagnosis	Barium radiography; confirmed by enteroscopy and biopsy	Abnormal hormone levels
Treatment	Surgery	Same
Contributing factors (targets for prevention)	Unknown	Unknown

Table 13-7. Colorectal adenocarcinoma

Pathology	Forms include a polypoid mass, an ulceration, and a constricting annular mass ("napkin ring")
	Most are found in the descending colon and rectum
Signs and symptoms	Right colon: anemia due to occult blood loss
	Sigmoid colon: obstructive symptoms, pencil-thin stools,
	Rectum: pain, gross blood, tenesmus
Diagnosis	Barium enema followed by colonoscopy with biopsy
Treatment	Surgical resection with chemotherapy
Contributing factors (targets for prevention)	Low-fiber diet; familial polyposis syndromes and ulcerative colitis also raise risk
Other	Third leading killer among cancers (after lung and breast)
	Routine sigmoidoscopy is recommended for people older than age 40

Table 13-8. Liver neoplasms

	Hepatocellular carcinoma	Hepatocellular adenoma
Pathology	Malignant hepatocytes that invade large vessels	Hypervascular sheets of hepatocytes without portal triads
Signs and symptoms	Cachexia (wasting), weakness, and weight loss	Right upper quadrant mass, may rupture and hemorrhage
Diagnosis	Elevated alpha-fetoprotein; CT scan followed by liver biopsy	Same
Treatment	Surgery or chemotherapy (poor prognosis)	Surgical resection (good prognosis)
Contributing factors (targets for prevention)	Most arise in cirrhotic livers or in conjunction with hepatitis B or C viruses	Almost exclusively seen in women; associated with oral contraceptive use

- Hamartomatous polyps: Non-neoplastic mixture of normal gut constituents. The juvenile type has lots of mucin-filled cysts. The **Peutz-Jeghers type** is associated with increased pigmentation of the lips and buccal mucosa. No malignant potential.

- Neoplastic polyps: **Tubular adenomas** are pedunculated (on a stalk) growths of closely packed glands. These may undergo malignant change, especially if they are large, and should be removed (polypectomy). **Villous adenomas** are sessile (no stalk) with fingerlike projections. They frequently become malignant, so a polypectomy is indicated. **Familial adenomatous polyposis** is a genetic predisposition to getting hundreds of neoplastic polyps. Patients usually have cancer before age 40. Complete colectomy is indicated.

Table 13-9. Pancreatic and biliary neoplasms

	Pancreatic carcinoma	Bile duct carcinoma (cholangiocarcinoma)
Pathology	Nearly all arise in the ductal epithelium, grow slowly, and are usually incurable by the time they're noticed	Pale, nonpigmented tissue arising from ductal epithelium
Signs and symptoms	Obstructive jaundice, epigastric pain to the back, weight loss	Asymptomatic or obstructive jaundice
Diagnosis	CT, MRI, or endoscopic retrograde cholangiopancreatography (ERCP)	Same
Treatment	Combined radiation and chemotherapy may be palliative	Same
Contributing factors (targets for prevention)	Incidence is on the rise, but causes are uncertain Smoking, fatty diet, and chemical carcinogens play a role	Parasitic infection with *Clonorchis* is associated
Other	Cancers in the head may cause early cholestatic symptoms and therefore may be curable	Poor prognosis

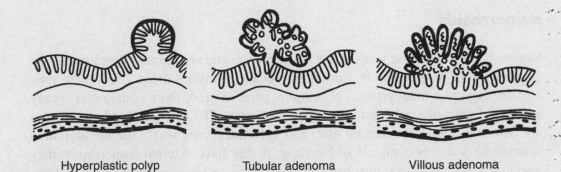

Hyperplastic polyp   Tubular adenoma   Villous adenoma

Fig. 13-24. Colonic polyps.

Vascular Disorders of the Gastrointestinal System

Ischemia

Ischemia of the intestine may be chronic (due to atherosclerosis) or acute (due to embolus, thrombosis, intussusception, volvulus, vasculitis, or systemic hypotension). Both present with pain, although the time course is different. If the bowel actually infarcts, the patient has lactic acidosis, hypotension, and abdominal distention. Antibiotics should be started (because they could rupture anytime) and surgical attempts may be made to restore blood flow. Otherwise, the ischemic bowel must be surgically resected.

Occlusion of a vein leading from the intestine, as is seen in **mesenteric vein thrombosis**, causes similar symptoms to arterial embolism, because they both cause tissue ischemia or infarction. They are also treated the same way.

Ischemic colitis results from poor circulation to the large bowel. Because the colon has good collateral flow, infarction is rare. The most likely place to see it is at the **splenic flexure**, which is a watershed area between the superior and inferior mesenteric arteries. The presentation is difficult to distinguish from IBD: crampy lower abdominal pain and diarrhea, which may be bloody. Ischemic colitis may occur after abdominal aortic aneurysm repair, resulting in compromise of the colonic blood supply. This may occasionally be cured by simply tanking up the vascular volume with lots of fluids but can require surgical resection of necrotic tissue.

Angiodysplasia

Also known as **vascular ectasias** or **arteriovenous malformations**, these tufts of dilated blood vessels are most commonly seen in the right colon, usually in elderly people. They typically present with bleeding, either as anemia, hematochezia, or occult blood. They may be treated with endoscopic cautery or even surgical removal of the involved segment.

Hemorrhoids

Hemorrhoids are dilated veins in the lower rectum and anal canal. They are present in about 5% of the population. Caused by elevated pressures in the veins, these varicosities may be a manifestation of portal hypertension, or more commonly, simply a result of chronic straining to pass hardened stool. The two types of hemorrhoids are **internal** (above the dentate line) and **external** (down where the epithelium is squamous). Patients complain of bleeding. If they have external hemorrhoids they also note pain and discomfort, because this area is well innervated with pain fibers. Internal hemorrhoids may prolapse out of the anus but are usually painless. If one of the dilated veins thromboses, the pain increases markedly.

Hemorrhoids are easy to diagnose by visualization with an anoscope. It is important to take a look because many things can masquerade as a hemorrhoid. Rectal or anal cancer, anal fissures (a crack in the anal mucosa), and anal fistulas (an abnormal passageway from the skin to the anal canal) may all present with pain and bleeding. Most hemorrhoids improve with increasing dietary fiber (to soften stools) and anesthetic ointments or suppositories. If that doesn't work, you can take some of the same measures used to treat esophageal varices, namely rubber-banding or sclerotherapy.

Pharmacology

See Tables 13-10 through 13-13 for information about the pharmacology associated with the disorders of the GI system.

Table 13-10. Normal flora of the colon

Nonpathogenic bacteria

Bifidobacterium
Eubacterium
Lactobacterium

Pathogenic bacteria	Extraintestinal disease
Coliforms (Escherichia coli)	UTI's
Bacteroides (B. fragilis)	Perforation-associated peritonitis
Streptococcus feacalis	Endocarditus, UTIs
Pseudomonas aeruginosa	Various nosocomial infections
Clostridium (C. perfingens)	Gas gangrene

Table 13-11. Absorption

DIFFUSION		ACTIVE TRANSPORT	
Simple	Facilitated	Primary	Secondary
H_2O	Na^+	$Na^+/K^+ATPase$	glucose/Na^+
CO_2	K^+	$K^+/H^+ATPase$	galactose/Na^+
	HCO_3^-		$Na^+/K^+/2Cl^-$
	fructose		dipeptides/H^+
	glucose		tripeptides/H^+

Table 13-12. Antacids and antisecretory drugs

Drug	Mechanism	Uses	Side effects, other
Antacids Aluminum hydroxide Magnesium hydroxide Calcium carbonate	Neutralize gastric acid	Symptomatic relief for GERD, PUD	Constipation Diarrhea Hypercalcemia Can be in toxic renal failure patients
H_2 antagonists	Inhibit histamine's stimulation of acid secretion	PUD, GERD, Zollinger-Ellison	All associated with impotence
Cimetidine			Slows metabolism of several drugs (warfarin, diazepam, phenytoin) by inhibiting cytochrome P-450 system
Ranitidine			
Famotidine			Most potent H_2 blocker
Proton pump inhibitors Omeprazole Lansoprazole	Irreversibly block the H^+/K^+ ATPase	PUD, GERD, Zollinger-Ellison	Total inhibition of acid leads to bacterial overgrowth
Sucralfate	Selectively binds to ulcer tissue, acts as a barrier by coating mucous layer	PUD	Requires low pH to be activated, so an acid blocker should not be given simultaneously

PUD = peptic ulcer disease; GERD = gastroesophageal reflux disease.

Table 13-13. Motility and antimotility drugs

Drug	Mechanism	Uses	Side effects, other
Motility drugs Cisapride Metoclopramide	Accelerate transit of gut contents by increasing ACh release from gut nerves	GERD, gastroparesis (impaired motility)	CNS effects (metoclopramide) due to actions on ACh and dopamine pathways

Antiemetics
Dopamine antagonists
    Promethazine
    Prochlorperazine
    Metoclopramide
	Block dopamine receptors in chemoreceptor trigger zone		Sedation, extrapyramidal symptoms, dystonias

Serotonin antagonist Ondansetron	Serotonin blockade in the CNS	Nausea and vomiting from chemotherapy and postoperatively	Marijuana derivatives (THC) are also used for this application
Pancreatic enzymes Pancreatin Pancrelipase (lipase enriched)	Purified extracts of hog pancreas to replace missing digestive enzymes	Cystic fibrosis, chronic pancreatitis	As proteins they have a high uric acid content, so renal stones may occur
Antidiarrheals Diphenoxylate Loperamide	Inhibit ACh release in the enteric nervous system	Diarrhea (used if the diarrhea is prolonged)	Similar action to opioids, which are also effective antidiarrheals

CNS = central nervous system; GERD = gastroesophageal reflux disease; ACh = acetylcholine; THC = tetrahydrocannabinol.

Table 13-14. Laxatives

Drugs	Mechanism	Uses	Side effects, other

Irritant laxatives
    Castor oil
    Senna
    Bisacodyl
	Locally irritate mucosa, increasing motility	Constipation	Chronic use creates dependence by damaging myenteric plexus

Bulk laxatives
    Psyllium, fiber
    Lactulose
    Saline enemas
	Distend the colon, causing reflex contraction	Constipation	Indigestible carbohydrates (psyllium, bran fiber) are good for long-term use (and reduce colon cancer)

Emollient laxatives
    Mineral oil
    Docusate
	Soften the stool	Constipation	Any laxative may be a drug of abuse, particularly in people with eating disorders
			Abuse may cause electrolyte imbalances

Cathartics
    Sorbitol
    Magnesium salts
	Remove toxins by stimulating emesis	Toxic ingestion (e.g., pills)	Avoid magnesium in renal patients

Table 13-15. Immunosuppressives and antineoplastic agents

Drug	Mechanism	Uses	Side effects, other
Salicylates 5-Aminosalicylic acid Sulfasalazine	Inhibit cyclooxy-genase	IBD; also used topically for distal colitis	Salicylates are complexed to other molecules to minimize gastric irritation, bleeding Overdose causes tinnitus, acidosis
Corticosteroids Prednisone Hydrocortisone ACTH	Inhibit cyclooxy-genase and phospholipase A_2	IBD, colitis	Overuse causes Cushing's syndrome
Cytotoxic drugs Azathioprine Mercaptopurine	Inhibit purine bio-synthesis, killing dividing cells (immune cells, cancer)	IBD, cancers	Bone marrow suppression (anemia, leukopenia)
Antineoplastic 5-Fluorouracil (5-FU)	Complexes with folic acid and inhibits thymidylate synthesis	Carcinoma of the esophagus, stomach, pancreas, and colon	Many chemotherapeutic agents are used in GI cancers, but 5-FU is the most common Myelosuppression is the major toxicity

IBD = inflammatory bowel disease; ACTH = adrenocorticotropic hormone; GI = gastrointestinal.

CHAPTER 14

Renal and Urinary Systems

Anatomy

The urinary system consists of a pair of kidneys, a pair of ureters, one bladder, and a urethra (Fig. 14-1).

- The **kidneys** are located in the retroperitoneum and lie in the L1–L4 region. Remember that the right kidney is usually lower than the left because the liver gets in the way.

- The **ureters** are also retroperitoneal and travel along the psoas muscle. The ureters can be obstructed by renal calculi (stones) at three sites of constriction: (1) the ureteropelvic junction (where it meets the renal pelvis), (2) the crossing of the pelvic brim, and (3) the ureterovesicular junction (where it meets the bladder). The ureter has a muscular wall that propels urine to the bladder by a peristaltic wave.

- The **detrusor** muscle of the bladder squeezes urine into the urethra when stimulated by parasympathetic signals.

- The **renal arteries** branch lies just inferior to the superior mesenteric artery (Fig. 14-2). Because the aorta lies slightly to the left of center, the right renal artery must travel further to reach the kidney than the left. The inferior vena cava (IVC) lies just to the right of center, so the left renal vein travels further than the right. The renal veins pass in front of the arteries. The testicular and ovarian arteries arise from the aorta and cross the ureters anteriorly.

- The **sphincter urethrae** muscle lies within the urogenital diaphragm and helps keep urine from leaking out (Fig. 14-3). Besides having autonomic innervation, we can even control this sphincter voluntarily, which is especially helpful on long road trips.

- In men, the **prostate** sits between the bladder and the sphincter urethrae muscle. As men get older, many develop benign prostatic

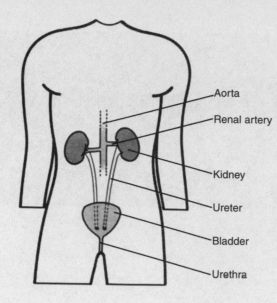

Fig. 14-1. The urinary system. (Reprinted with permission from PR Wheater, HG Burkitt, VG Daniels. *Functional Histology: A Text and Colour Atlas* [rev ed]. Edinburgh: Churchill Livingstone, 1987;236.)

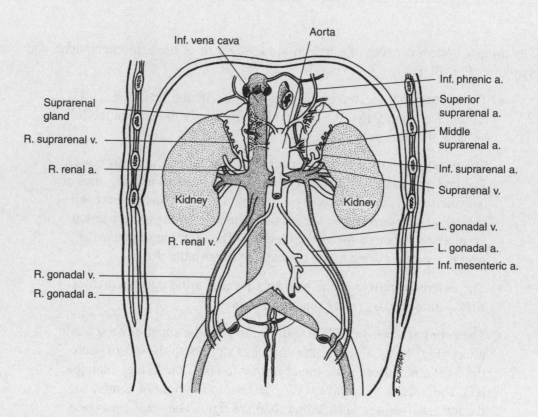

Fig. 14-2. Location of kidneys, ureters, and associated vasculature.

hyperplasia (BPH), in which the prostate gets larger around the urethra, compressing it and making it difficult to urinate.

- Women have a shorter urethra than men and are more prone to horribly uncomfortable **urinary tract infections** (UTIs). Women may develop **stress incontinence** (losing urine with a laugh or cough) after childbirth

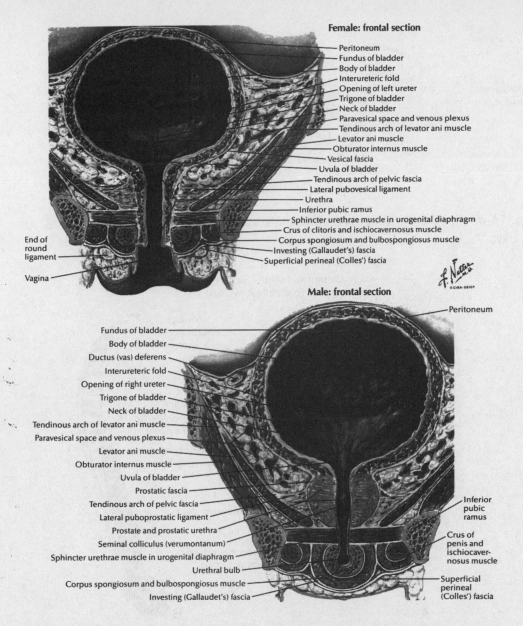

Female: frontal section

- Peritoneum
- Fundus of bladder
- Body of bladder
- Interureteric fold
- Opening of left ureter
- Trigone of bladder
- Neck of bladder
- Paravesical space and venous plexus
- Tendinous arch of levator ani muscle
- Levator ani muscle
- Obturator internus muscle
- Vesical fascia
- Uvula of bladder
- Tendinous arch of pelvic fascia
- Lateral pubovesical ligament
- Urethra
- Inferior pubic ramus
- Sphincter urethrae muscle in urogenital diaphragm
- Crus of clitoris and ischiocavernosus muscle
- Corpus spongiosum and bulbospongiosus muscle
- Investing (Gallaudet's) fascia
- Superficial perineal (Colles') fascia

End of round ligament

Vagina

Male: frontal section

- Peritoneum

- Fundus of bladder
- Body of bladder
- Ductus (vas) deferens
- Interureteric fold
- Opening of right ureter
- Trigone of bladder
- Neck of bladder
- Tendinous arch of levator ani muscle
- Paravesical space and venous plexus
- Levator ani muscle
- Obturator internus muscle
- Uvula of bladder
- Prostatic fascia
- Tendinous arch of pelvic fascia
- Lateral puboprostatic ligament
- Prostate and prostatic urethra
- Seminal colliculus (verumontanum)
- Sphincter urethrae muscle in urogenital diaphragm
- Urethral bulb
- Corpus spongiosum and bulbospongiosus muscle
- Investing (Gallaudet's) fascia

- Inferior pubic ramus
- Crus of penis and ischiocavernosus muscle
- Superficial perineal (Colles') fascia

Fig. 14-3. Anatomy of the urinary bladder. (Reprinted with permission from FH Netter. *Atlas of Human Anatomy.* Summit, NJ: CIBA–GEIGY, 1989.)

because the levator ani and muscles of the urogenital diaphragm are stretched and weakened as the baby passes through the vaginal canal.

Embryology

- During the fourth week, nephrotomes develop from intermediate mesoderm (Fig. 14-4) and later give rise to the **pronephric**, **mesonephric**, and **metanephric** systems.

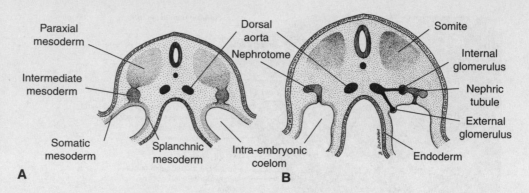

Fig. 14-4. Origin of the kidney and collecting system. **A.** Nephric tubule at 21 days. **B.** At 25 days.

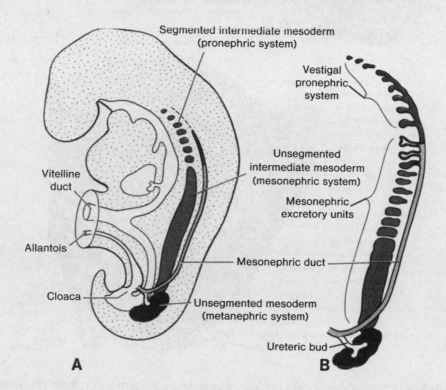

Fig. 14-5. A. Relationship of pronephric, mesonephric, and metanephric systems. **B.** Development of the mesonephros.

- The **pronephros** appears first in the cervical region (Fig. 14-5A). It degenerates for the most part, except for the pronephric ducts, which interact with the mesonephric system and form the mesonephric tubules.

- The **mesonephros** goes through some elaborate development but ultimately regresses (Fig. 14-5B). It is important because it stimulates the formation of the müllerian (paramesonephric) ducts, which is critical to the development of female sex organs; in men, the mesonephric duct transforms into the ejaculatory system (epididymis to ejaculatory duct).

- The **metanephros** is called the *permanent kidney* and develops into the real deal. The **ureteric bud** grows from the bottom of the mesonephric duct and is encompassed by the metanephric blastema

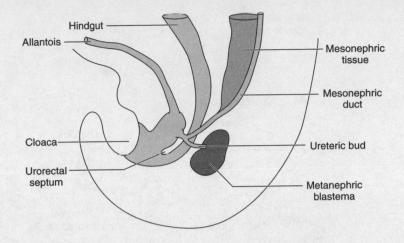

Fig. 14-6. Origin of the permanent kidney, from interactions between the ureteric bud and metanephric blastema.

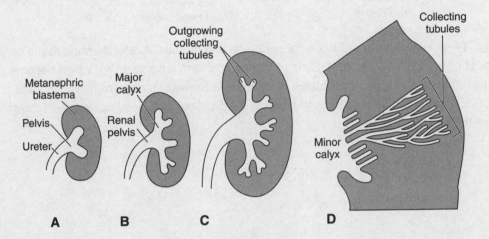

Fig. 14-7. Development of the excretory system. **A.** 6 weeks. **B.** End of sixth week. **C.** 7 weeks. **D.** Newborn.

(Fig. 14-6). The ureteric bud goes through multiple divisions and extensions to form the ureter, pelvis, major and minor calyces, and the collecting tubules (Fig. 14-7).

- The new collecting tubules stimulate the metanephric tissue to form tubules for the rest of the nephron. The proximal part of the metanephric tubule forms **Bowman's capsule**, and as it invaginates, it engulfs the glomerulus. The metanephric tubules extend to form the proximal convoluted tubule, the loop of Henle, and the distal convoluted tubule. The distal part of the metanephric tubules fuses with the collecting tubules to form a patent conduit for urine flow (Fig. 14-8).

- The cloaca is divided by the urorectal septum to form the primitive urogenital sinus and anorectal canal. The **urinary bladder** then develops from the urogenital sinus and remains attached to the umbilicus by the urachus (the final remnant of the allantois) (Fig. 14-9). The urethra comes from the definitive urogenital sinus.

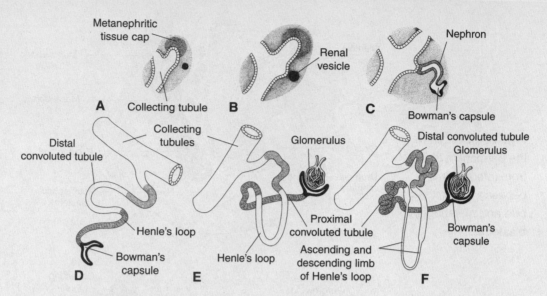

Fig. 14-8. Development of the renal corpuscle and tubules. **A.** Metanephric tissue caps cover collecting tubules. **B, C.** Cells of tissue caps form renal vesicles, which become small tubules. **C, D.** Proximal tubule develops into Bowman's capsule, which indents. **E, F.** Excretory tubule lengthens to become the proximal and distal convoluted tubules and the loop of Henle.

- During fetal development, the kidney rises out of the pelvis while the gonads descend (Fig. 14-10). The kidneys start to excrete urine into the amniotic cavity by the middle of the pregnancy. Although the kidneys make urine, they are not responsible for removing waste products from the fetus because that job is done by the placenta. Fetal urine is dilute.

Histology

The Kidney

All highways to and from the kidney are located at the **hilum**. These roads include the renal artery, renal vein, and ureter. The kidney is divided into an outer **cortex** and an inner **medulla** (Fig. 14-11).

The medulla consists of multiple medullary pyramids. The base of the pyramid is surrounded by cortex; the apex is called the **renal papilla**. Urine passes from renal papilla, minor calyx, major calyx, and renal pelvis to ureter. Portions of the cortex (the renal columns) extend between the pyramids. The kidney is covered by a fibrous capsule as well as a thick layer of fat, which help to protect against some traumatic injuries.

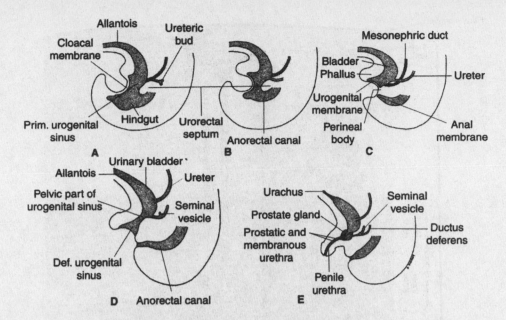

Fig. 14-9. Origin of the urinary bladder. Development of urogenital sinus and anorectal canal at the end of the fifth week (**A**), 7 weeks (**B**), and 8 weeks (**C**). Development of urinary bladder (**D**) and penile urethra (**E**) from urogenital sinus.

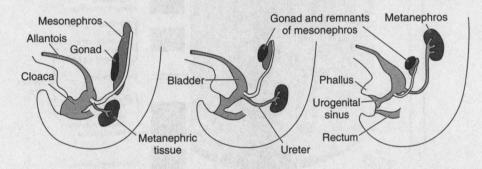

Fig. 14-10. Development of the urinary bladder. Relative development of kidneys and gonads during development.

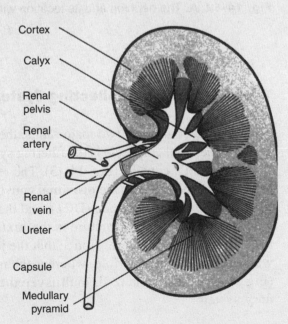

Fig. 14-11. Anatomy of the kidney. (Reprinted with permission from PR Wheater, HG Burkitt, VG Daniels. *Functional Histology: A Text and Colour Atlas* [rev ed]. Edinburgh: Churchill Livingstone, 1987;237.)

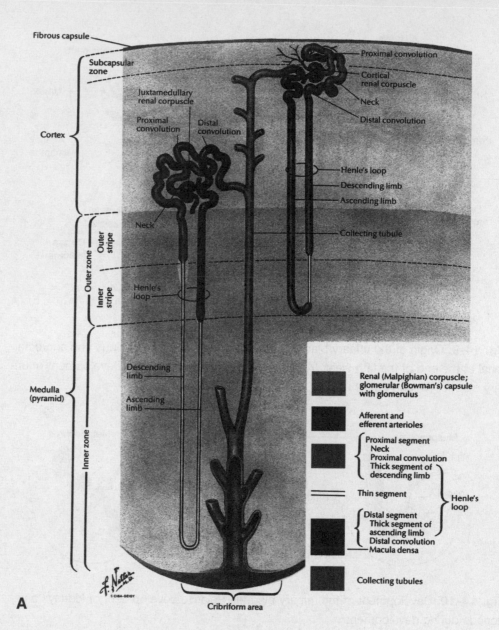

Fig. 14-12. A. The nephron and its location within the cortex and medulla.

The Nephron and Collecting System

The nephron consists of two major units, the renal **corpuscle** and renal **tubule** (Fig. 14-12). The renal corpuscle is the filtering system, which consists of the **glomerulus** plus **Bowman's capsule** (Fig. 14-13). The renal tubule carries the filtrate to the collecting duct and includes the **proximal convoluted tubule** (PCT), the **loop of Henle**, the **distal convoluted tubule** (DCT), and the **collecting tubule**.

Another important structure is the **juxtaglomerular apparatus**, which helps to regulate blood pressure. Notice that the juxtaglomerular cells are located in the wall of the afferent arteriole, whereas the macula densa is in the wall of the DCT (Fig. 14-14). A specialized, multilayered **transitional epithelium** lines the urinary system.

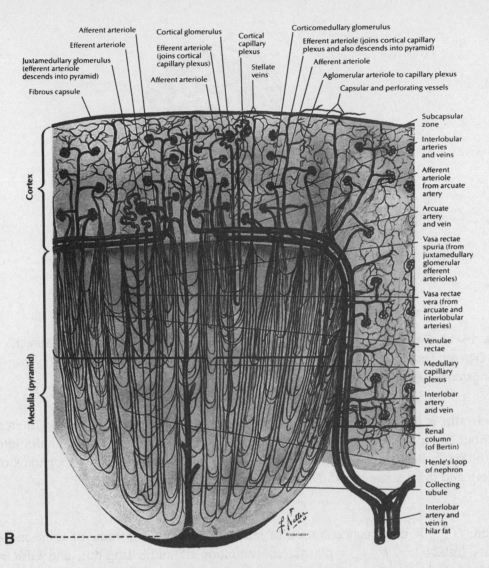

Afferent arteriole
Efferent arteriole
Juxtamedullary glomerulus
(efferent arteriole
descends into pyramid)
Fibrous capsule
Cortical glomerulus
Efferent arteriole
Efferent arteriole
(joins cortical
capillary plexus)
Afferent arteriole
Cortical
capillary
plexus
Stellate
veins
Corticomedullary glomerulus
Efferent arteriole (joins cortical capillary
plexus and also descends into pyramid)
Afferent arteriole
Aglomerular arteriole to capillary plexus
Capsular and perforating vessels

Cortex

Medulla (pyramid)

Subcapsular
zone
Interlobular
arteries
and veins
Afferent
arteriole
from arcuate
artery
Arcuate
artery
and vein
Vasa rectae
spuria (from
juxtamedullary
glomerular
efferent
arterioles)
Vasa rectae
vera (from
arcuate and
interlobular
arteries)
Venulae
rectae
Medullary
capillary
plexus
Interlobar
artery
and vein
Renal
column
(of Bertin)
Henle's loop
of nephron
Collecting
tubule
Interlobar
artery and
vein in
hilar fat

B

Fig. 14-12. B. Renal vasculature. (Reprinted with permission from FH Netter. *Atlas of Human Anatomy*. Summit, NJ: CIBA–GEIGY, 1989.)

Physiology

Glomerular Filtration and Hemodynamics

Renal Clearance

Clearance measures how fast a certain substance is removed from the blood (in milliliters per minute) and excreted in the urine. It can be calculated using the following formula:

$$C = (U \times V)/P$$

where C = clearance (ml/min), U = concentration in urine (mg/ml), V = volume of urine made per minute (ml/min), and P = concentration in plasma (mg/ml).

Clearance is affected by how easily a substance is filtered at the glomerulus, secreted by the tubules, or reabsorbed by the tubules. The clearance formula is important because it can be used to determine the **glomerular filtration rate** (GFR).

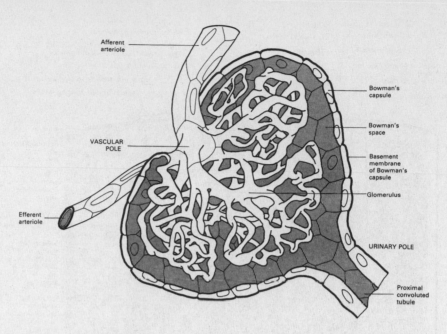

Fig. 14-13. Renal corpuscle. (Reprinted with permission from PR Wheater, HG Burkitt, VG Daniels. *Functional Histology: A Text and Colour Atlas* [rev ed]. Edinburgh: Churchill Livingstone, 1987;241.)

Inulin is a substance that can be used to determine GFR because it is filtered without being secreted or reabsorbed. All you need to do is inject some inulin into the blood, collect urine for the next 24 hours (or any time period, just keep track of units), and draw some blood. Now using the formula, you have:

$$C = \text{GFR} = (U_{\text{inulin}} \times V)/P_{\text{inulin}}$$

where U_{inulin} = urine concentration of inulin (mg/ml), V = volume of urine in 24 hours (ml/24 hr), P_{inulin} = plasma concentration of inulin (mg/ml), and GFR = (ml/24 hr), then convert to ml/min.

Besides inulin, **mannitol** and **sorbitol** are commonly used to determine GFR. Now that you have the inulin clearance as a standard, you can compare the clearance of any other substance to see if it's freely filtered, secreted, or reabsorbed.

In the hospital, **blood urea nitrogen (BUN)** and **creatinine** are used to estimate GFR. BUN is a measure of nitrogen from proteins that were eaten, whereas creatinine measures nitrogen from muscle breakdown. If GFR decreases, the BUN and creatinine both increase (there's more left in the blood). As we get older, GFR normally decreases, but the creatinine level doesn't change because our bodies usually have less muscle mass. The main problem to be aware of is that the rate of drug excretion decreases in older patients with decreased GFR.

Another way to determine GFR is by using the **Starling equation**:

$$\text{GFR} = K_f \, [(P_{\text{glom}} - P_{\text{BS}}) - (\neq_{\text{glom}} - \neq_{\text{BS}})]$$

where K_f = filtration coefficient, P_{glom} = hydrostatic pressure in the glomerular capillary, P_{BS} = hydrostatic pressure in Bowman's space, $\neq_{\text{glom}}$ = oncotic pressure in the glomerular capillary, and $\neq_{\text{BS}}$ = oncotic pressure in Bowman's space.

GFR increases with constriction of the efferent arteriole or dilation of the afferent arteriole (P_{glom} increases).

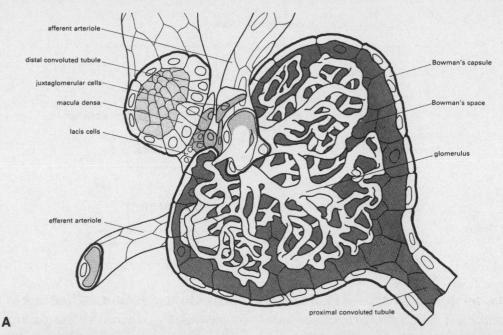

A

B

Fig. 14-14. Diagram (**A**) and light microscopy (**B**) of the juxtaglomerular apparatus. (MD = macula densa; A = afferent arteriole; J = juxtaglomerular cells; L = lacis cells.) (Reprinted with permission from PR Wheater, HG Burkitt, VG Daniels. *Functional Histology: A Text and Colour Atlas* [rev ed]. Edinburgh: Churchill Livingstone, 1987;254.)

Renal Blood Flow

Blood flow to the kidneys follows the same general principles discussed in chapter 12. The same formula can be used to determine renal blood flow (RBF):

$$Q = \Delta P/R$$

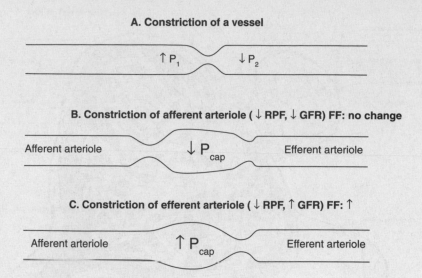

Fig. 14-15. Alterations in renal plasma flow (RPF), glomerular filtration rate (GFR), and filtration fraction (FF) with constriction of afferent and efferent arterioles. (P_{cap} = pressure within glomerular capillary; P_1 = pressure proximal to constriction; P_2 = pressure distal to constriction.)

where Q = RBF, $\Delta P = P_{renal\ artery} - P_{renal\ vein}$ = renal perfusion pressure, and R = resistance. RBF decreases if R increases or ΔP decreases; RBF increases if R decreases or ΔP increases.

Although the systemic blood pressure may vary, the kidney keeps its blood flow relatively constant by a process called **autoregulation**. This is done by adjusting renal vascular resistance to keep RBF constant, as systemic arterial pressures fluctuate between 100 and 200 mm Hg (Fig. 14-15).

Exercise increases sympathetic tone, which causes constriction of the afferent arteriole, decreasing RBF, and shunting blood to active muscles.

RBF is determined indirectly by calculating the renal plasma flow (RPF). Instead of using inulin, **para-aminohippuric acid** (PAH) is used to determine clearance with the formula above, and this value is a close estimate of RPF. Because the hematocrit (Hct) measures the percentage of blood volume taken up by RBCs, and plasma is the blood "fluid" without RBCs:

$$RBF\ (1 - Hct) = RPF$$

$$RBF = RPF/(1 - Hct)$$

Filtration fraction (FF) refers to how much RPF is filtered through the glomerular capillary membrane. It can be calculated by the following equation:

$$FF = GFR/RPF$$

In general, FF is 20%, which means that 80% of the RPF passes into the efferent arterioles. Table 14-1 shows how constriction and dilation of the afferent and efferent arterioles affect GFR, RPF, and FF. Increased resistance = constriction; decreased resistance = dilation. Think through each scenario to make sure it makes sense.

Table 14-1. Effects of changes in renal vascular resistance with a constant renal perfusion

Renal arteriolar vascular resistance		Renal plasma flow (ml/min)	Glomerular filtration rate (ml/min)	Filtration fraction
Afferent	Efferent			
↑		Decreased	Decreased	No change
↓		Increased	Increased	No change
	↑	Decreased	Increased	Increased
	↓	Increased	Decreased	Decreased

Note that the glomerular filtration rate and renal plasma flow exhibit parallel shifts with changes in afferent arteriolar resistance but exhibit divergent shifts with changes in efferent arteriolar resistance. Increases in vascular resistance always lead to a decline in renal plasma flow, and decreases in arteriolar resistance always lead to an increase in renal plasma flow. In the first two columns, upward arrows denote the effect of vasoconstriction, and downward arrows denote the effect of vasodilation.

Tubular Mechanisms for Reabsorption and Secretion

Reabsorption and Secretion Rates

You already know the basics for doing this calculation. All you do is take the equation used to determine clearance and break it down:

$$\text{GFR (ml/min)} \times P \text{ (mg/dl)} = \text{Filtered load}$$

$$U \text{ (mg/dl)} \times V \text{ (ml/min)} = \text{Excretion rate}$$

The filtered load describes how much stuff was filtered per minute; the excretion rate describes how much stuff was excreted in the urine per minute. If the excretion rate is *greater* than the filtered load, then tubular secretion has occurred (by subtracting the two values, you get the actual rate of secretion). If the excretion rate is *less* than the filtered load, then reabsorption has occurred, with the rate expressed as the difference.

Titration Curves

The reabsorption and secretion of substances can be represented graphically (Fig. 14-16). First, let's use glucose as an example of a substance that is reabsorbed.

The amount of glucose filtered is directly proportional to the plasma concentration of glucose. Remember, $\text{GFR} \times P_{glu}$ = filtered load.

Glucose is reabsorbed from the PCT by a **sodium-glucose cotransporter**. These cotransporters can reabsorb all the glucose that is delivered as long as the glucose concentration is less than 300 mg/dL. If the concentration goes any higher, the cotransporters become saturated and are incapable of working overtime. The **transport maximum** (T_m) is the point at which the cotransporters are giving all they've got. The extra glucose that is delivered to the PCT gets excreted at a rate that is directly proportional to the plasma concentration of glucose above the T_m.

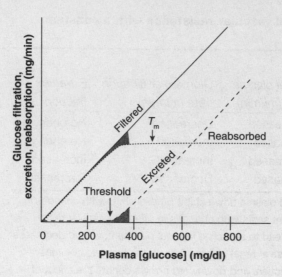

Fig. 14-16. Titration curve for a substance that is reabsorbed. (T_m = transport maximum.)

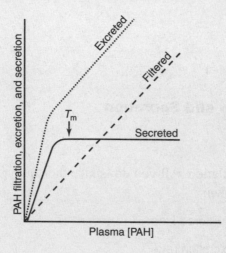

Fig. 14-17. Titration curve for a substance that is secreted. (PAH = para-aminohippuric acid; T_m = transport maximum.)

Now let's compare this to a secreted substance, PAH (Fig. 14-17). The filtration curve is exactly the same as the one for glucose, except that the T_m curve is shifted to the left. PAH is secreted by carriers in the PCT: As the concentration of PAH increases, the secretion increases accordingly. Because PAH is filtered as well as secreted, the excretion is the sum of the two (shown as the excretion curve). Once the concentration of PAH reaches a certain level, the carriers are working at full capacity, and the secretion rate cannot increase any further. This is referred to as the T_m for PAH. After the T_m is reached, the excretion rate follows the slope of the filtration curve and is directly proportional to the plasma concentration of PAH.

Sodium Management

Two-thirds of all filtered Na$^+$ is reabsorbed at the PCT (Fig. 14-18). The early PCT uses **cotransporters** to reabsorb Na$^+$ along with glucose, phosphate, amino acids, or lactate. The cotransporter uses the energy derived from Na$^+$ moving down its concentration gradient to drive the active reabsorption of the other molecules against their concentration gradients. Another cotransporter exchanges Na$^+$ from the tubular lumen with H$^+$ from the cell, which also depends on the amount of filtered HCO$_3^-$. The favorable Na$^+$ gradient is maintained by a **Na$^+$/K$^+$ adenosine triphos-**

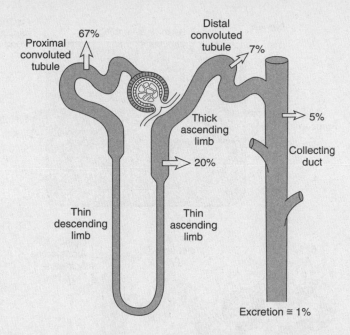

Fig. 14-18. Reabsorption of NaCl.

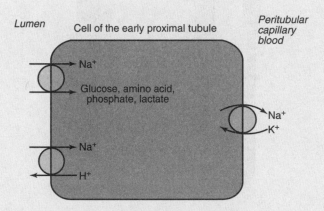

Fig. 14-19. Na$^+$ transporters in the cells of the proximal convoluted tubule.

phatase (**ATPase**), which uses ATP to pump Na$^+$ out of the cell as it pumps K$^+$ in. Cl$^-$ is reabsorbed with Na$^+$ in the middle and late PCT (Fig. 14-19). **Carbonic anhydrase inhibitors** work on the PCT.

Glomerulotubular balance refers to the PCT's ability to maintain the reabsorption rate of Na$^+$ no matter how much fluid is delivered. This is explained by the Starling forces. If extracellular (ECF) volume decreases (dehydration), the peritubular capillary fluid will have a lower hydrostatic pressure, P_{cap}, and a higher protein concentration, which increases π_{cap}. Both forces increase the movement of fluid from tubules to blood and enhance reabsorption. If ECF volume increases (overzealous water ingestion), P_{cap} increases and π_{cap} decreases, which both decrease reabsorption.

Some 20% of filtered Na$^+$ is reabsorbed by the **thick ascending limb of the loop of Henle (a-loop)** (Fig. 14-20). The cells use a **Na$^+$/K$^+$-2Cl$^-$ cotransporter**, in which Na$^+$ is passively absorbed while providing the energy for active K$^+$ absorption. Although Na$^+$ and Cl$^-$ are both absorbed, the cells of the a-loop are impermeable to water. **Loop diuretics** (e.g., furosemide) act here.

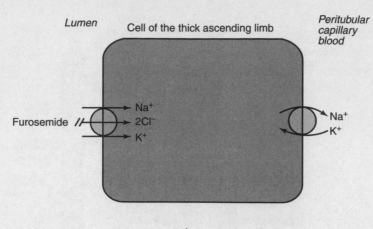

Fig. 14-20. The Na⁺/K⁺-2Cl⁻ cotransporter in the cells of the a-loop.

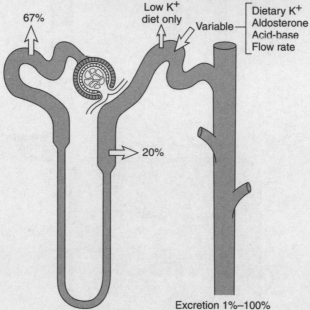

Excretion 1%–100%

Fig. 14-21. K⁺ management.

Some 12% of filtered Na^+ is reabsorbed in the DCT and collecting ducts. The early distal tubule has a Na^+/Cl^- cotransporter and is impermeable to water (very similar to the a-loop). **Thiazide diuretics** have their main action here.

The late DCT and collecting duct have **principal cells** and **intercalated cells**. The principal cells reabsorb Na^+ and secrete K^+, which is mediated by **aldosterone**. This section of the DCT is also affected by antidiuretic hormone (ADH), which increases water reabsorption. This is the site of action for the **K⁺-sparing diuretics**, such as spironolactone. The intercalated cells are also stimulated by aldosterone, which increases K^+ reabsorption and H^+ secretion.

Potassium Management

K^+ is freely filtered at the glomerulus. K^+ reabsorption is similar to that of Na^+ in that two-thirds is reabsorbed at the PCT (along with Na^+ and water) and 20% is reabsorbed at the a-loop (by the Na^+/K^+-$2Cl^-$ cotransporter) (Fig. 14-21). K^+ is reabsorbed or secreted at the DCT and collecting tubules depending on the following factors:

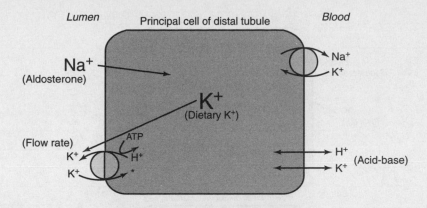

Fig. 14-22. K⁺ secretion by cells of the distal convoluted tubule.

- Amount of K⁺ in diet

- Level of aldosterone

- Acid-base status

- Diuretics

- Anions in tubules

K⁺ is reabsorbed in the intercalated cells of the DCT by a **H⁺/K⁺-ATPase**. This is also one of the major ways that acid-base status is regulated.

K⁺ secretion is kind of sneaky (Fig. 14-22). First, the Na⁺/K⁺-ATPase makes sure that there's a higher concentration of K⁺ inside the cell. Then, K⁺ is passively secreted into the tubular lumen depending on the factors mentioned above.

When more K⁺ is consumed in the diet, the concentration of K⁺ in the principal cell increases, so that the K⁺ gradient is even stronger (K⁺ inside the cell is greater than K⁺ concentration in the lumen), and more K⁺ is passively secreted (Fig. 14-23). A diet low in K⁺ is just the opposite: The K⁺ gradient is smaller, so less K⁺ is secreted and more is saved.

Aldosterone increases the amount of Na⁺ that enters the cell and stimulates the Na⁺/K⁺-ATPase to increase the amount of K⁺ pumped into the cell. Again, because there's even more K⁺ inside the cell than out, K⁺ secretion increases. If the aldosterone level is too high (**hyperaldosteronism**), this can lead to hypokalemia (too little K⁺ in the blood). If the aldosterone level is too low (**hypoaldosteronism**), the K⁺ gradient is smaller than normal, less K⁺ is secreted, and this can lead to hyperkalemia (too much K⁺ in the blood).

If a patient is acidotic (too much H⁺ in the blood), the excess H⁺ gets pulled into the cell in exchange for K⁺ out of the cell. Less K⁺ in the cell means a smaller gradient, less K⁺ secretion, and hyperkalemia. In alkalosis, there's too little H⁺ in the blood. Now, H⁺ is kicked out of the cell in exchange for K⁺ moving into the cell. This generates a higher K⁺ gradient, more K⁺ is secreted, and the patient becomes hypokalemic.

Loop diuretics and thiazides increase the flow of fluid to the distal tubule. This effectively decreases the K⁺ concentration in the lumen and increases the K⁺ gradient (remember, the other way to increase the gradient is by putting more K⁺ into the cell, as in hyperaldosteronism) (Fig. 14-24). As a result, K⁺ secretion increases, and the patient can become hypokalemic.

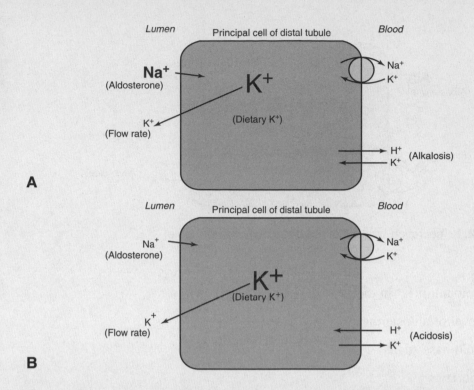

A

B

Fig. 14-23. A. K$^+$ secretion in the setting of high dietary K$^+$, hyperaldosteronism, or alkalotic states. **B.** K$^+$ secretion in the setting of low dietary K$^+$, hypoaldosteronism, or acidotic states.

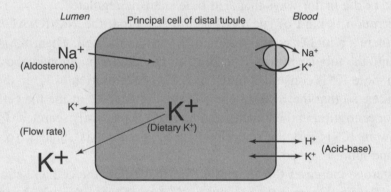

Fig. 14-24. Effects of loop diuretics on K$^+$ secretion.

Hypokalemia can be prevented in the setting of diuretic use by adding a K$^+$-sparing diuretic, such as spironolactone or amiloride. These prevent K$^+$ secretion either indirectly (spironolactone is an aldosterone antagonist) or directly (amiloride works on the DCT).

K$^+$ secretion may also increase if there are excess anions in the tubular lumen (opposites attract!).

Calcium

Only 60% of Ca^{+2} in the plasma is filtered across the glomerular membrane. However, 90% of this filtered Ca^{+2} is reabsorbed in the PCT and the a-loop. Ca^{+2} is absorbed passively along with Na$^+$ reabsorption. Because loop diuretics block Na$^+$

reabsorption, Ca^{+2} reabsorption is also inhibited. Loop diuretics are therefore helpful in treating **hypercalcemia** (too much Ca^{+2} in the blood).

About 9% of Ca^{+2} is actively reabsorbed by the DCT and collecting duct. **Parathyroid hormone** (PTH) stimulates the DCT to increase Ca^{+2} reabsorption. (PTH is released when blood Ca^{+2} levels are low.) Thiazides also increase Ca^{+2} reabsorption by the DCT. Patients who have renal stones precipitated by hypercalciuria (too much Ca^{+2} in the urine) may therefore benefit from treatment with thiazides.

Magnesium

Mg^{+2} is reabsorbed by the PCT, DCT, and the a-loop. Mg^{+2} and Ca^{+2} compete for the same transporters in the ascending limb, so if excess Ca^{+2} is in the blood, more Ca^{+2} is filtered. This excess Ca^{+2} will overpower the Mg^{+2} and be transported at the expense of Mg^{+2}, which will be excreted. The tables are turned, however, if there is excess Mg^{+2} in the blood. Now Mg^{+2} will win and be transported, while the loser, Ca^{+2}, is excreted.

Phosphate

About 85% of phosphate is reabsorbed by the PCT by cotransport with Na^+. Because the rest of the nephron cannot reabsorb phosphate, 15% of the phosphate is excreted! Phosphate reabsorption is inhibited by PTH, which stimulates adenylate cyclase and increases cyclic adenosine monophosphate (c-AMP).

Urea

The PCT reabsorbs 50% of the filtered urea. Urea is also reabsorbed by the inner medullary collecting ducts only when they are stimulated by ADH. Urea is then used to help concentrate urine when volume status is low (e.g., dehydration or hemorrhage).

Urinary Concentration and Dilution

Concentration of Urine

Urine is concentrated by a countercurrent multiplier system (Fig. 14-25). It's countercurrent because the three limbs have fluid flow in alternating directions.

As you travel deeper into the medulla, the osmotic gradient becomes progressively higher. This corticopapillary gradient is what allows for efficient water retention. The gradient is mostly NaCl and urea.

Just like Na^+, two-thirds of the water is reabsorbed in the PCT.

In the **descending limb of the loop of Henle (d-loop)**, water moves from the tubule to the interstitium, which has a much higher osmolarity. Because this concentrates the tubular fluid, it's called the **concentrating segment**. The d-loop is fairly impermeable to NaCl and urea, so most of it stays within the tubule.

In the a-loop, urea moves down its concentration gradient and into the lumen. NaCl gets pumped out of the lumen and into the interstitium: This is one source of the high corticopapillary osmotic gradient. Because the a-loop is impermeable to water, and more NaCl leaves than urea enters, the tubular fluid left behind is more dilute. This is why the a-loop is called the **diluting segment**.

The early DCT is also impermeable to water, so the tubular fluid is diluted even further. However, water (and urea) can be reabsorbed in the late DCT, especially when ADH is around.

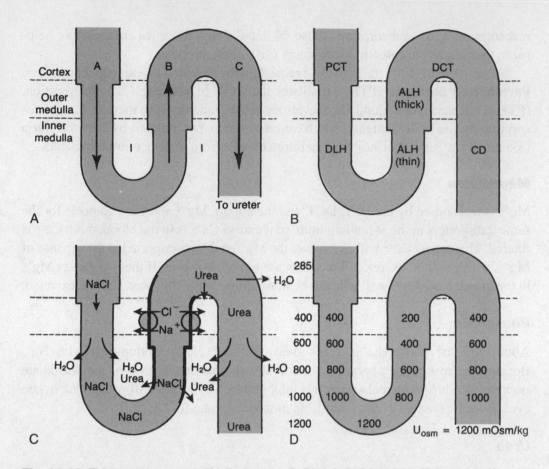

Fig. 14-25. The countercurrent multiplier system. **A.** Direction of fluid flow. **B.** Location of tubule segments. **C.** Movement of NaCl, H₂O, and urea. **D.** Osmolarity inside and outside tubules. (PCT = proximal convoluted tubule; DLH = descending loop of Henle; ALH = ascending loop of Henle; DCT = distal convoluted tubule; CD = collecting duct; U$_{osm}$ = urine osmolarity.)

In the collecting ducts, urea passively moves down its concentration gradient into the interstitium. This movement is even better in the presence of ADH, which increases urea permeability in the collecting ducts. As the collecting ducts extend into the inner medulla, water and urea are both reabsorbed (also improved by the presence of ADH). Some of the urea enters the a-loop as mentioned previously, but most gets stuck in the interstitium and adds to the strong corticopapillary osmotic gradient.

The **vasa recta** are the countercurrent exchangers (Fig. 14-26). They follow the tubules into the medulla and are permeable to water and solutes. As blood passes into the descending limb of the vasa recta, the osmotic gradient causes NaCl and urea to move into the capillaries while water moves into the interstitium. After the vasa recta make a U-turn, the plasma is super concentrated, so NaCl and urea return to the interstitium, and water moves back into the capillaries. The net effects are that solutes are trapped in the interstitium, hence maintaining the osmotic gradient (important for water reabsorption), and water is returned to the circulation. Figure 14-27 describes how the body retains water in a water deprivation state.

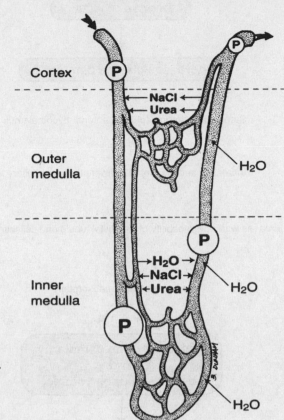

Cortex

Outer
medulla

Inner
medulla

← NaCl ←
← Urea ←

→ H_2O →
← NaCl →
← Urea →

H_2O

H_2O

H_2O

Fig. 14-26. The importance of vasa
recta in preserving the osmotic gradient.
(P = plasma concentration; the larger
the P, the higher the concentration.)

Dilution of Urine

Now let's imagine that you've been lounging around, drinking water all day long.
Again, two-thirds of the water is reabsorbed at the PCT. The tubular fluid is also
diluted in the a-loop (NaCl is actively removed) and early DCT. The difference is
that without the presence of ADH, the late DCT and collecting ducts remain impermeable to water. No matter what the osmotic gradient is, water is stuck within the
tubules and is excreted as dilute urine (Fig. 14-28).

Free Water Clearance

Free water clearance (FWC) tells you how much water is excreted or reabsorbed.
When ADH is present, water is reabsorbed, and FWC is negative. When ADH is
absent, water is excreted, and FWC is positive. To calculate the FWC, you need to
know the urine flow rate (V), and the osmolar clearance (C_{osm}).

$$FWC = V - C_{osm}$$

Remember, $C_{osm} = (U_{osm} \times V)/P_{osm}$.

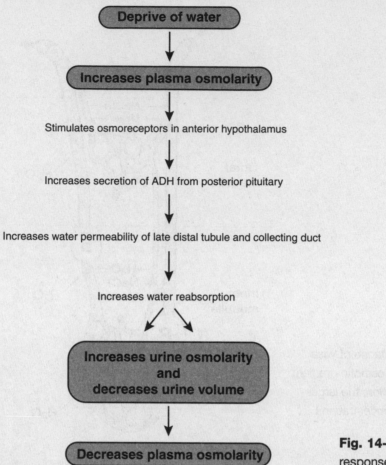

Fig. 14-27. Physiologic response to water deprivation.

The C_{osm} tells you how many osmoles are cleared from the urine each minute. If C_{osm} is low (i.e., there's a low concentration of osmoles in the urine), whatever is left over must be water. A high osmolar clearance can only occur when the urine is well concentrated; water is reabsorbed, which is reflected as a negative FWC. The clinical examples listed in Table 14-2 should reinforce this concept.

Body Fluid Compartments

Distribution of Body Water

Total body water (TBW) is about 60% of the body weight in men. It's a little bit lower in women, which is attributed to more relative adipose tissue.

Intracellular fluid (ICF) is about two-thirds of TBW. K^+ and Mg^{+2} are the major cations, whereas protein and organic phosphates (e.g., ATP) are the major anions.

Exracellular fluid (ECF) is then about one-third of TBW. Na^+ is the major cation; Cl^- and HCO_3^- are the major anions. About three-fourths of the ECF is located in the interstitium, and the other one-fourth is found in plasma (Fig. 14-29). Albumin and immunoglobulins comprise the major plasma proteins. Because interstitial fluid is almost identical to plasma, except that it lacks proteins, it is called an **ultrafiltrate**.

Specific markers can be used to measure the amount of fluid in each compartment, which is called the *volume of distribution* (V_D). The markers used are listed in

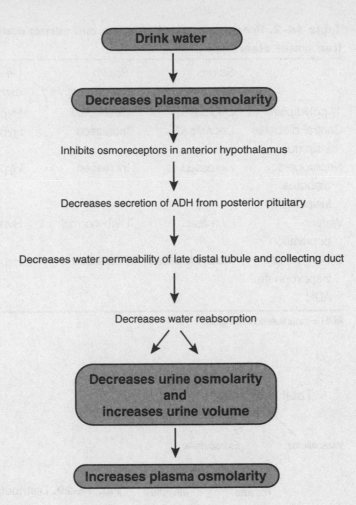

Fig. 14-28. Physiologic response to water overload.

Table 14-3. The basic principle is as follows: A certain amount of marker is injected into the blood, it is allowed to equilibrate, and then the resulting concentration is measured. Now plug and chug:

$$V_D \text{ (liters)} = \text{Marker (mg)/concentration (mg/liter)}$$

Because mannitol is a large molecule, it cannot cross into cells, so it's a perfect marker for measuring the ECF.

Water Shifts

In general, water moves between the ECF and ICF to maintain an equal osmolarity in both compartments. The scenarios described in Fig. 14-30 and Table 14-4 describe different effects on ICF and ECF.

Volume expansion states (overhydration) can be achieved with hyperosmotic (fluid osmolality > plasma osmolality), **isosmotic** (fluid osmolality = plasma osmolality), or **hyposmotic** (fluid osmolality < plasma osmolality) fluids:

- Excessive NaCl ingestion, or infusion with hypertonic saline can lead to **hyperosmotic overhydration**. ECF osmolarity increases directly, and this draws water out of the ICF. The result is that ECF volume increases, and as ICF volume decreases, ICF osmolarity increases to equilibrate with the ECF.

**Table 14-2. Processes affecting urine and serum osmolarity and
free water clearance**

	Serum ADH	Serum osmolarity/[NA+]	Urine osmolarity	Free water clearance
1° polydipsia	Decreased	Decreased	Hyposmotic	Positive
Central diabetes insipidus	Decreased	Increased	Hyposmotic	Positive
Nephrogenic diabetes insipidus	Increased	Increased	Hyposmotic	Positive
Water deprivation	Increased	High–normal	Hyperosmotic	Negative
Syndrome of inappropriate ADH	Much increased	Decreased	Hyperosmotic	Negative

ADH = antidiuretic hormone.

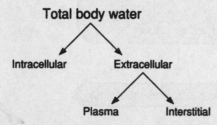

Fig. 14-29. Distribution of total body water.

Table 14-3. Markers used for evaluation of fluid compartments

Compartment	Marker
Total body water (TBW)	Tritiated H_2O or D_2O
Extracellular fluid (ECF)	Inulin
	Mannitol
	Sulfate
Intracellular fluid	ECF minus plasma volume
Plasma volume	Radiolabeled albumin
	Evans blue
Interstitial	TBW minus ECF

- **Isosmotic overhydration** occurs with isotonic NaCl infusion.
  Although ECF volume increases, there's no change in osmolarity, so
  no water shifts out of the ICF. Extra fluid in the ECF dilutes plasma
  proteins and RBCs, which lowers the hematocrit.

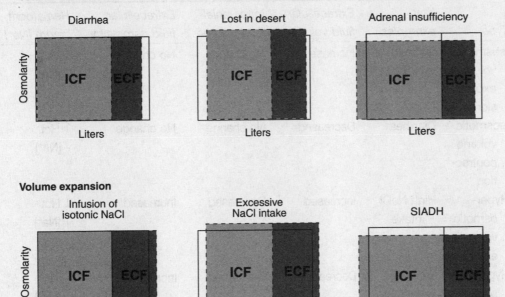

Fig. 14-30. Alterations in extracellular fluid (ECF) and intracellular fluid (ICF) under different physiologic stressors. (SIADH = syndrome of inappropriate antidiuretic hormone.)

- Syndrome of inappropriate ADH (SIADH) is an example of **hyposmotic overhydration**. Excess water is retained, which increases ECF volume but lowers osmolarity. Water then shifts from ECF to ICF, thereby expanding ICF volume but lowering ICF osmolarity until it equilibrates with the ECF. You would think that the hematocrit would decrease because of dilution effects (as in isosmotic overhydration), but the hematocrit stays the same because the water also shifts into RBCs.

Volume contraction states (dehydration) can also be the result of hyperosmotic, isosmotic, or hyposmotic fluid loss:

- **Hyperosmotic dehydration** can be caused by profuse sweating. ECF volume decreases, and because sweat is hyposmotic, ECF osmolarity increases. Water then shifts from ICF to ECF, which lowers ICF volume and increases ICF osmolarity until it equilibrates with the ECF. The hematocrit remains unchanged because water shifts out of the RBCs to maintain RBC concentration.

- **Diarrhea** is one way to lose isotonic fluid and lower ECF volume while maintaining ECF osmolarity. As a result, no water shifts between the ECF and ICF, so ICF volume remains the same. Hematocrit increases because the RBCs are concentrated (from volume loss) and because there is no water shift out of or into the RBCs (osmolarity is unchanged).

Table 14-4. Changes in volume and osmolarity of body fluids

Type	Key examples	Extracellular fluid volume	Intracranial fluid volume	Extracellular fluid osmolarity	Hematocrit, serum [Na$^+$]
Isosmotic volume expansion	Isotonic NaCl infusion	Increased	No change	No change	↓ Hct – [Na$^+$]
Isosmotic volume contraction	Diarrhea	Decreased	No change	No change	↑ Hct – [Na$^+$]
Hyperosmotic volume expansion	High NaCl intake	Increased	Decreased	Increased	↓ Hct ↑ [Na$^+$]
Hyperosmotic volume contraction	Sweating Fever Diabetes insipidus	Decreased	Decreased	Increased	– Hct ↑ [Na$^+$]
Hyposmotic volume expansion	Syndrome of inappropriate diuretic hormone	Increased	Increased	Decreased	– Hct ↓ [Na$^+$]
Hyposmotic volume contraction	Adrenal insufficiency	Decreased	Increased	Decreased	↑ Hct ↓ [Na$^+$]

- **Hyposmotic dehydration** can occur with adrenal insufficiency. If there isn't enough aldosterone around, the DCT cannot reabsorb NaCl at a normal rate, so more NaCl is lost relative to water. As a result, ECF volume decreases along with ECF osmolarity. Water then shifts from the ECF to ICF, increasing ICF volume but decreasing ICF osmolarity until equilibration occurs. The RBCs are more concentrated (from decreased ECF volume) and larger (lower ECF osmolarity causes water to shift into the RBCs), so the hematocrit increases.

Acid-Base Balance

Buffer Systems

Buffers help to prevent pH changes when the concentration of H$^+$ changes. HCO$_3^-$ is the major extracellular buffer, whereas proteins and organic phosphates are the

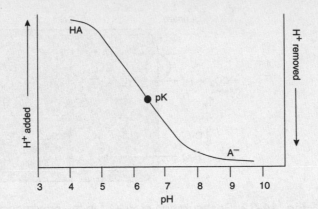

Fig. 14-31. Titration curve for a weak acid (HA) and its base (A⁻).

major intracellular buffers. In general, a buffer pair system works the best when the pH range is within 1.0 pH unit of the pK (dissociation constant). You can calculate pH using the Henderson-Hasselbalch equation:

$$pH = pK + \log [A^-]/[HA]$$

where $pH = -\log_{10}[H^+]$, $pK = -\log_{10}K$, $[A^-]$ = concentration of base, and $[HA]$ = concentration of acid.

You can also graph a titration curve to show how the concentrations of acid and base change as H^+ increases. The concentration of acid equals the concentration of base when pH equals pK (Fig. 14-31).

HCO_3^- Regulation

HCO_3^- is produced from the following reaction:

$$CO_2 + H_2O \leftrightarrow H_2CO_3 \leftrightarrow H^+ + HCO_3^-$$

The formation of H_2CO_3 from CO_2 and H_2O is catalyzed by carbonic anhydrase (CA). Most of the HCO_3^- is reabsorbed in the PCT. Intracellular CA produces H^+, which is secreted into the tubular lumen by the Na^+/H^+ exchanger. The H^+ combines with filtered HCO_3^-, and this gets converted to CO_2 and H_2O by a CA within the brush border of the PCT cell. The CO_2 and H_2O diffuse into the cell and are then used by the intracellular CA to make H^+ and HCO_3^-. The H^+ is sent back into the lumen as before, and the HCO_3^- is reabsorbed into the blood. The net result with one of these cycles is that a molecule of HCO_3^- is reabsorbed (H^+ is not secreted) (Fig. 14-32).

If the amount of filtered HCO_3^- increases, reabsorption will also increase; however, eventually the mechanism will be saturated, and any excess HCO_3^- is excreted. This is part of the compensation for metabolic alkalosis.

If P_{CO_2} increases, more CO_2 is delivered to the PCT, leading to more intracellular CO_2, more H^+ production, and more HCO_3^- reabsorption. This is how the kidney compensates for respiratory acidosis. The exact opposite occurs in the setting of respiratory alkalosis.

Titratable Acid ($H_2PO_4^-$)

Another fate for H^+ is that it's pumped into the lumen by H^+-ATPase, where it encounters a filtered HPO_4^{-2} and forms $H_2PO_4^-$. This is excreted as titratable acid. The net result is that H^+ is secreted, lowering urine pH, and HCO_3^- is reabsorbed (Fig. 14-33).

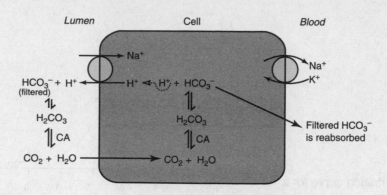

Fig. 14-32. Reabsorption of HCO_3^- in the proximal collecting tubule.

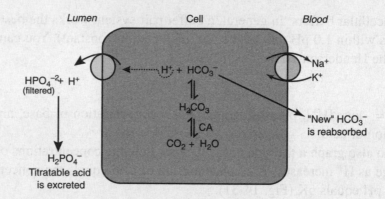

Fig. 14-33. Formation and excretion of titratable acid.

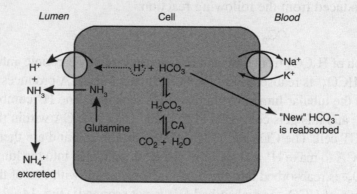

Fig. 14-34. Formation and excretion of NH_4^+. (CA = carbonic anhydrase.)

NH_4^+

H^+ may also combine with NH_3 in the tubular lumen to produce NH_4^+. Again, H^+ is pumped into the lumen by H^+-ATPase. NH_3 is derived from glutamine as a result of protein degradation, and it follows its concentration gradient into the lumen (Fig. 14-34). Once NH_4^+ is produced, the H^+ is excreted in a process called **diffusion trapping**. HCO_3^- is also reabsorbed. This process is essential for responding to acidosis because NH_3 diffusion into the lumen can reach 10 times normal!

Table 14-5. Summary of hormones that act on the kidney

Hormone	Stimulus for secretion	Actions on kidneys	Location
Parathyroid hormone	↓ Plasma [Ca^{2+}]	↓ Phosphate reabsorption ↑ Ca^{2+} reabsorption Stimulates 1α-hydroxylase	Proximal and distal tubules
Antidiuretic hormone	↑ Plasma osmolarity ↓ Blood volume	↑ H_2O permeability	Distal tubule and collecting duct
Aldosterone	↓ Blood volume (via renin-angiotensin II) ↑ Plasma [K^+]	↑ Na^+ reabsorption ↑ K^+ secretion ↑ H^+ secretion	Distal tubule
Atrial natriuretic factor	↑ Atrial pressure	↑ GFR ↓ Na^+ reabsorption	—
Angiotensin II	↓ Blood volume (via renin)	↑ Na^+ –H^+ exchange and HCO_3^- reabsorption	Proximal tubule

Renal Oxygen Consumption

Next to the heart, the kidney is ranked second for oxygen consumption. The arteriovenous oxygen concentration difference is extremely small, so that the blood is effectively being shunted through the renal capillaries. This is the reason that blood returning to the IVC has a higher oxygen content than blood from the superior vena cava.

Oxygen consumption is fairly proportional to RBF but really depends on how much Na^+ is actively reabsorbed. If RBF decreases, GFR decreases, less Na^+ is filtered, and less oxygen is required by the kidney.

Hormones

- **Renin** is produced by the juxtaglomerular cells of the juxtaglomerular apparatus. It is a crucial hormone in the management of blood pressure.

- **Erythropoietin** (EPO) is believed to be secreted by the extraglomerular mesangial cells. EPO acts on bone marrow precursors to stimulate RBC production.

- 1,25-Dihydroxycholecalciferol is the active form of **vitamin D**, and it facilitates the absorption of Ca^{+2} from the gastrointestinal (GI) tract.

These hormones are discussed in more detail in chapters 7 and 16. See Table 14-5 for information about other hormones and their effect on the kidney.

Normal Micturition

Micturition, or urination, is a process that we all take for granted. However, a number of physiologic processes must be tightly coordinated. The detrusor muscle is innervated by

parasympathetic fibers via the pelvic nerves from S2 and S3. The **urogenital diaphragm**, which contains the external bladder sphincter, has **somatic innervation** via the pudendal nerve. The ureters have both sympathetic and parasympathetic innervation. Urine accumulating in the pelvis triggers a peristaltic wave, propelling urine into the bladder. The ureters join the bladder obliquely at the trigone. This unusual angle is important for preventing urine reflux into the ureters during detrusor contraction.

As the bladder fills with urine, the bladder wall stretches, which is sensed by the sensory arm of the parasympathetic fibers. This stimulates a reflex contraction of the detrusor muscle such that pressure within the bladder increases and is maintained long enough to expel the urine. The reflex eventually fatigues, and the detrusor relaxes.

Of course, the brain ultimately has the final word on when micturition occurs. The brain keeps the external bladder sphincter clamped down even when micturition reflexes occur. Once you're in an appropriate setting, the brain can not only relax the external sphincter but also facilitate a micturition reflex. These responses are also enhanced by "bearing down."

Genetic and Congenital Disorders

Polycystic Kidney Disease

There are two forms of polycystic kidney disease. The juvenile form is autosomal recessive, whereas the adult form is autosomal dominant. The theory is that the collecting tubules and metanephric tubules fail to join. The urine that's produced then accumulates in the tubules, causing dilation and formation of cysts. Both kidneys are large, riddled with multiple cysts, and function poorly. Some of these patients are unlucky enough to also have intracranial aneurysms.

Signs & Symptoms

Patients with this disease may develop gross hematuria or frequent UTIs. Eventually, kidney function decreases, leading to hypertension and elevated levels of BUN and creatinine. Some may develop subarachnoid hemorrhages from the intracranial aneurysms.

Diagnosis

The large kidneys and cysts can be visualized with an ultrasound or intravenous urogram.

Treatment

Treatment of UTIs and hypertension may prolong kidney function. Dialysis is required in the setting of renal failure. Transplantation is unlikely because half of family members are affected. The patient and family may benefit from genetic counseling.

Renal Agenesis

The theory of renal agenesis is that the ureteric bud degenerates and fails to stimulate the development of the metanephric tissue. This is most commonly unilateral (1 in 1,500), although bilateral agenesis occurs rarely.

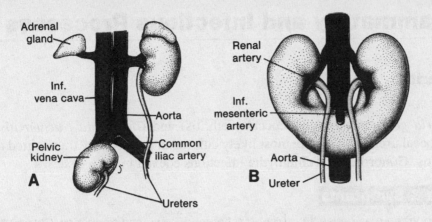

Fig. 14-35. Pelvic (**A**) and horseshoe (**B**) kidneys. (Adapted from TW Sadler. *Langman's Medical Embryology* [5th ed]. Baltimore: Williams and Wilkins, 1985.)

In the case of bilateral agenesis, oligohydramnios develops (too little amniotic fluid) because the fetus cannot excrete the amniotic fluid that it swallows. The fetus can still develop because the placenta is in charge of clearing waste products, but the neonate may only live a few days after birth.

Pelvic Kidney

If the kidney fails to ascend into the abdomen properly, it will remain in the pelvis near the common iliac artery (Fig. 14-35A). The adrenal gland on the affected side is in its normal position.

Horseshoe Kidney

Occasionally, as the kidneys ascend, they travel so close together that the lower poles fuse (Fig. 14-35B). The kidneys can only travel to the lower lumbar region because the bottom of the horseshoe gets caught on the inferior mesenteric artery. This abnormality occurs in 1 in 600 people.

Urachal Fistula and Cyst

Normally, the allantois is obliterated, and a fibrous cord called the **urachus** takes its place. If the lumen of the allantois persists, urine can drain directly from the bladder out the umbilicus. This is called a *urachal fistula*. If only a small portion of the allantois lumen persists, it can continue its secretory activity and cause a dilation, called a *urachal cyst*.

Cystinuria

The basic amino acids—cysteine, ornithine, arginine, and lysine—are moved into the cell against their concentration gradient by a specific transport system, the γ-glutamyl cycle. The amino acids form a dipeptide with glutathione, which is then transported into the cytoplasm. A defect in this system leads to the excretion of all four amino acids in the urine.

Inflammatory and Infectious Processes

Urethritis

Neisseria gonorrhoeae (gonococcal urethritis) and *Chlamydia trachomatis* (non-gonococcal urethritis) are the most likely culprits in the sexually transmitted disease urethritis. Gonorrhea and chlamydia infections coexist in 50% of cases.

Signs & Symptoms

Gonorrhea may cause a purulent discharge, dysuria, and frequency. Chlamydia may also cause a mucopurulent discharge, but many patients are asymptomatic.

Diagnosis

The diagnosis is made by finding gram-negative diplococci within white blood cells (WBCs) or if there is a positive Thayer-Martin culture. If the Gram's stain is negative, chlamydia is assumed to be the etiology, but an immunofluorescence stain may be sent off to confirm. New detection systems have also been developed to check the urine for these infections.

Treatment

Ceftriaxone for gonorrhea and doxycycline for chlamydia (erythromycin may be used as a substitute in pregnant women). Both are normally given because the rate of coinfection is so high.

Cystitis

Commonly known as a UTI, cystitis is an infection of the bladder that is more common in women due to shorter urethras. *Escherichia coli* is the most common etiology in all patients; however, *Staphylococcus saprophyticus* is seen in sexually active women. Diabetics are susceptible to *Staphylococcus aureus* infections.

Signs & Symptoms

Dysuria, urinary frequency, urgency, nocturia, and suprapubic pain.

Diagnosis

A "clean catch" midstream urine specimen reveals that WBCs are present or a bacteria count greater than 10^5. A culture may be used to check for antibiotic sensitivities.

Treatment

Trimethoprim-sulfamethoxazole is adequate, but you can always use your sensitivity results to tailor the antibiotic appropriately.

Prostatitis

The prostate can be infected by the same gram-negative GI bacteria (e.g., *E. coli*) that cause cystitis. Prostatitis may be caused by reflux of contaminated urine into the prostatic ducts.

Signs & Symptoms

Symptoms are the same as those for UTIs plus perineal or low back pain. In the acute setting, the patient may have a fever; chronic cases present with recurrent UTIs. On examination, the prostate is tender and "boggy."

Diagnosis

A sample of the seminal fluid usually shows high bacterial counts and lots of WBCs.

Treatment

Trimethoprim-sulfamethoxazole.

Pyelonephritis

Pyelonephritis is an infection of the renal parenchyma. It is usually caused by *E. coli* that refluxes from a lower UTI.

Signs & Symptoms

In addition to the symptoms for cystitis, the patient may note flank pain, fever, chills, nausea, and vomiting. The patient has costovertebral angle tenderness on the side with the affected kidney.

Diagnosis

The urinalysis may demonstrate WBC casts, which can distinguish it from cystitis.

Treatment

Hospitalization with intravenous antibiotics for the first couple days. A third-generation cephalosporin or a fluoroquinolone is appropriate, and treatment continues for at least 2 weeks.

Immunologic Disorders

Nephritic Syndrome

Nephritic syndrome is characterized by **oliguria** (usually <400 ml of urine excreted per day), **azotemia** (elevated BUN and creatinine), **hypertension**, and **hematuria** (with red cell casts, which are diagnostic of glomerulonephritis). It has a number of causes but is classically associated with **poststreptococcal (acute) glomerulonephritis**.

After an infection with certain group A β-hemolytic streptococci (either a throat or skin infection), immune complexes form between antibodies and streptococcal antigens. These complexes get lodged in the glomeruli, causing an acute inflammatory response. They can be seen using immunofluorescent stains as "lumpy-bumpy" glomeruli with subepithelial humps on electron microscopy. **Antistreptolysin O** titers may be high, and **serum C3** levels may be low (both signifying a recent strep infection). Antibiotics are useful only if the patient has a persistent infection.

Goodpasture's disease usually affects young men and involves direct damage of the glomerular and pulmonary alveolar membranes by rogue antibodies. Patients usually develop hemoptysis as well. Treatment may include high-dose corticosteroids or plasmapheresis.

Rapidly progressive (crescentic) glomerulonephritis is a nephritic syndrome which quickly progresses to renal failure (with uremia in 3–9 months). Half of these cases are the result of poststreptococcal disease; about 10% turn out to be Goodpasture's. Histologic findings include crescents (half-moons) from Bowman's capsule wrapped around the glomerular capillaries.

Alport's syndrome is an X-linked disorder that affects the glomerular basement membrane because of defective type IV collagen. The syndrome includes an associated sensorineural deafness. Treatment is with dialysis and transplantation (in renal failure patients). Genetic counseling may also be helpful.

Acute Interstitial Nephritis

Acute interstitial nephritis is considered a hypersensitivity reaction that is often the result of drug-induced damage to the interstitial cells of the kidney. It can be caused by a number of different drugs, including antibiotics (penicillin derivatives, aminoglycosides, amphotericin B), nonsteroidal anti-inflammatory drugs and acetaminophen, and diuretics. The patient usually develops acute renal failure, rash, fever, and eosinophilia. Treatment requires removal of the offending drug and supportive care for the acute renal failure.

Transplant Rejection

Hyperacute rejection is immediate and presumably due to an ABO mismatch (extremely uncommon these days).

Acute rejection often occurs within the first 2 months after transplantation. The patient may develop fever, hypertension, graft tenderness, oliguria (with decreased creatinine clearance), and azotemia. The interstitium shows an impressive infiltration by lymphocytes. Immunosuppressive agents are used to prevent further damage to the graft, but when they are unsuccessful, the graft must be removed.

Chronic rejection usually occurs after 2 months after transplantation. The symptoms are often the same as for acute rejection but much more insidious. Pathology slides show lots of plasma cells in the interstitium and intimal fibrosis (of the cortical arteries), which leads to renal ischemia, interstitial fibrosis, and tubular atrophy. At 5 years after transplantation, only 5% of grafts are lost to chronic rejection, but most grafts eventually succumb with time. Unfortunately, there is no way to prevent it.

Traumatic and Mechanical Disorders

Urolithiasis (Kidney Stones)

Calcium is most commonly found in urinary stones; therefore, hypercalciuria is a risk factor. Idiopathic hypercalciuria accounts for more than half of all kidney stones. Other causes of hypercalciuria should be pursued, including hyperparathyroidism. **Struvite stones**, composed of magnesium ammonium phosphate, are the result of urea-splitting bacteria (e.g., *Pseudomonas* or *Proteus*) and account for 10–15% of cases.

Signs & Symptoms

Renal colic is excruciating pain that results when urine excretion is blocked by the stone. The pain usually starts in the flank, radiates around the side and into the groin and can last 30 minutes to an hour. Symptoms for pyelonephritis may also be present. Hematuria is possible if the stone doesn't cause complete obstruction.

Diagnosis

An abdominal X-ray can spot calcium stones (it's less sensitive for struvite stones). Stones can also be seen as filling defects on an intravenous pyelogram (IVP).

Treatment

Treat the pain first; narcotics are often necessary. Small stones may be shattered by ultrasound waves (lithotripsy). If lithotripsy doesn't work, stones may be removed surgically. Calcium stones can be prevented by drinking lots of water. Patients with idiopathic hypercalcinuria may benefit from thiazide diuretics. Struvite stones can be avoided by treating UTIs aggressively.

Ureteral Reflux

The most common reason urine flows from bladder to ureter is a misconnection between bladder and ureter during fetal development. Hydronephrosis may develop from increased pressure in the ureter, and these patients are at risk for pyelonephritis. Children who present with persistent UTIs should be evaluated with a voiding cystourethrogram.

Treatment possibilities range from doing nothing (mild cases) to surgery (severe cases). UTIs must be treated aggressively.

Neurogenic Bladder

A neurogenic bladder is the result of abnormalities in cerebral control, sensation, or motor function. Diabetics have an associated neuropathy that prevents them from sensing when the bladder is full. It can also occur in the setting of patients with acute spinal cord injury; once they've recovered, the bladder can work autonomously, with reflex filling and emptying. The poliovirus can damage motor neurons, which inhibits proper detrusor muscle function.

Diagnosis

Urodynamic studies can evaluate the sensory loop, bladder capacity, and sphincter control. Urinary obstruction and reflux are picked up on a voiding cystourethrogram.

Treatment

Treatment may involve medications that enhance sphincter control, relax a spastic detrusor, or stimulate the autonomic nerves. The patient may opt for frequent catheterization or for a urinary diversion (surgery).

Trauma to the Urinary System

The kidneys are fairly well protected, but any blow to the flank near ribs 10–12 (often accompanied by flank discoloration) may indicate kidney damage. The bladder and urethra are at great risk during automobile accidents, because pelvic fractures often cause the bladder to shear off the urethra (ouch!). These injuries can cause peritonitis and other nasty problems and should be suspected if blood is noted at the urethral meatus or a lower abdominal mass is present.

Renal Failure

Acute Renal Failure

The most common cause of acute renal failure is acute tubular necrosis secondary to ischemic damage (shock, rhabdomyolysis, or surgery) or toxins. Glomerulonephritis, renovascular disease, and interstitial nephritis can also lead to acute renal failure.

Diagnosis

Patients have azotemia (elevated BUN and creatinine) because of a decreased GFR, oliguria, and possibly uremic symptoms. ·

Treatment

Treatment requires close monitoring of fluids to prevent overload, electrolyte monitoring, decreased protein intake, and dialysis if things look bad. Full recovery may take weeks (if ever).

Chronic Renal Failure

Because the kidney has an incredible functional reserve, you normally don't see symptoms of chronic renal failure until 90% of the nephrons are lost. The two major causes are diabetes and hypertension. Other causes include glomerulonephritis, adult polycystic kidney disease, obstructive uropathy, and tubulointerstitial disease.

Diagnosis

Azotemia is usually the first sign of trouble. Because the kidneys can't save Na^+, serum Na^+ is low, but K^+ and H^+ are high (hyperkalemic metabolic acidosis). Decreased production of EPO leads to anemia. Decreased activation of vitamin D leads to decreased Ca^{2+} absorption and phosphate retention, leading to renal osteodystrophy (bone breakdown in an attempt to raise serum Ca^{2+}).

Treatment

Treatment includes restriction of dietary protein and correction of metabolic abnormalities. Dialysis and transplantation are reserved for refractory cases.

Uremic Syndrome

With renal failure, the patient may have neurologic problems, including encephalopathy, drowsiness, seizures, peripheral neuropathy (in chronic renal failure), and **asterixis** (a hand flap that occurs when the patient pretends to hold up a wall). Cardiac abnormalities include hypertension and congestive heart failure from volume overload. Relative to the GI system, nausea, vomiting, and anorexia are common, plus a bad taste in the mouth. **Uremic frost** (urea crystals from sweat) may be seen (and smelled) on the skin, which is usually yellow-brown. Laboratory findings are the same as for chronic renal insufficiency (CRI), and osmolality of urine and plasma are comparable because the kidney has lost its concentrating abilities. Treatment is the same as for CRI.

Cortical and Papillary Necrosis

Diffuse Cortical Necrosis

Diffuse cortical necrosis is a result of infarction of the renal cortices without damage to the medulla. It's classically associated with **obstetric emergencies** (e.g., eclampsia, abruptio placentae) and may occur in the setting of septic or cardiogenic shock. If it occurs diffusely and bilaterally, the patient develops anuria and dies a uremic death, but if it has a patchy distribution, there may be hope. The pathology suggests that end-organ vasospasm and disseminated intravascular coagulation ultimately cause the damage.

Renal Papillary Necrosis (Necrotizing Papillitis)

Renal papillary necrosis occurs most often as a result of diabetes mellitus, in which the tips of the renal papillae develop ischemic necrosis. It may also be a rare result of acute pyelonephritis or long-term use of phenacetin combined with aspirin (which also leads to cortical tubulointerstitial nephritis).

Signs & Symptoms

Symptoms associated with phenacetin-induced papillitis include GI disturbances, headache, hypertension, and anemia.

Diagnosis

Urine samples show pyuria (in 100% of cases) and occasionally gross hematuria. The diagnosis can sometimes be made by IVP.

Treatment

Underlying infections should be treated and offending drugs removed.

Nephrotic Syndrome

Nephrotic syndrome is a combination of findings due to increased basement membrane permeability and loss of plasma proteins. There must be **more than 3 g of protein** in the urine per day, **hypoalbuminemia** (because of all the albumin lost in the urine), generalized **edema** (from decreased plasma oncotic pressure), and **hypercholesterolemia** (think of it as an overeager liver that tries to compensate by making more proteins but also ends up producing more cholesterol). Other symptoms may include ascites, pulmonary edema, and hypotension because of low serum proteins.

Nephrotic syndrome is caused by several diseases:

- **Minimal change disease (MCD)** is the most common cause in kids. Although the glomeruli look normal on light microscopy, an electron microgram shows fusing of the epithelial podocytes. Corticosteroids are used for treatment, and prognosis is good, although MCD may recur.

- **Focal segmental glomerulosclerosis** occurs in older patients but has clinical similarities to MCD. It's focal because only some of the glomeruli are affected and segmental because only part of the glomerulus is affected.

- **Membranous glomerulonephritis** (MGN) is a major cause of nephrotic syndrome in teens and young adults. The pathology has characteristic findings, such as thickened capillary walls, intramembranous and subepithelial immune complex deposition, and a **"spike and dome"** appearance on electron microscopy (domes of immune complexes separated by thin spikes of basement membrane). Immunofluorescence picks up IgG and C3 in a granular distribution. It can be associated with the following:

  Infections, such as hepatitis B and syphilis
  Drugs, such as gold salts, penicillamine
  Malignancy
  Systemic lupus erythematosus (SLE; 10% of patients)

  MGN shows a poor response to steroid treatment.

  Diabetes, amyloidosis, and SLE may also cause nephrotic syndrome and are discussed separately.

Tubular Disorders

Acute Tubular Necrosis

Acute tubular necrosis is the most frequent etiology of acute renal failure. It is often the result of renal ischemia secondary to shock (e.g., septic or hemorrhagic), but it may also be associated with rhabdomyolysis (and myoglobinuria) or direct toxic effects of numerous drugs and chemical substances. Although it can lead to death, appropriate medical management leads to complete recovery within 2–3 weeks. The underlying cause must be treated and offending drugs removed.

Renal Tubular Acidosis

Renal tubular acidosis (RTA) is a result of tubules that are unable to either excrete H^+ or generate HCO_3^-. Urinary pH and serum K^+ can be used to differentiate the forms, as shown in Table 14-6. All forms develop a hyperchloremic metabolic acidosis, and most produce acidified urine, but serum K^+ varies.

Type I RTA is a result of defective H^+ secretion in the DCT. As a result, more K^+ is excreted, so the patient is hypokalemic. This is the one case in which the urine can't be acidified appropriately, resulting in a urine pH exceeding 5.5.

Table 14-6. Renal tubular acidosis

Renal tubular acidosis (types)	Renal defect	Glomerular filtration rate	Serum [K+]	Distal H+ secretion (minimal urine pH)
I. Classic distal	Distal H+ secretion	Normal	Decreased	>5.5
II. Proximal	Proximal HCO_3^- reabsorption	Normal	Decreased	<5.5
III. Glomerular insufficiency	NH_3 production	Decreased	Normal	<5.5
IV. Hyporeninemic hypoaldosteronism	Distal Na+ reabsorption, K+ secretion, and H+ secretion	Decreased	Increased	<5.5

Type II RTA is caused by a defective PCT, which can't reabsorb filtered HCO_3^-. This can occur iatrogenically with CA inhibitors. Hypokalemia results from increased HCO_3^- delivery to the DCT (K+ is electrically drawn into the tubules). Thiazides may be used to induce volume contraction and stimulate HCO_3^- retention.

Type III RTA results from decreased GFR and a secondary inability to produce enough NH_3. Serum K+ is normal. It is not really a *tubular* process.

Type IV RTA is the only form that causes hyperkalemia. It is a result of aldosterone deficiency, which can occur in the setting of hyporeninemia (induced by diabetic, hypertensive, interstitial, or human immunodeficiency virus–related kidney damage). You don't want to give anything to these patients that would increase serum K+ (e.g., angiotensin-converting enzyme [ACE] inhibitors or spironolactone).

Nephrogenic Diabetes Insipidus

The end result of nephrogenic diabetes insipidus is the same as with central diabetes insipidus. In this case, however, even though there's enough ADH around, the renal tubules fail to respond appropriately. It may be familial in origin or develop secondary to amyloidosis, sickle cell anemia, or drug use (e.g., lithium).

Signs & Symptoms

Patients develop polydipsia, polyuria (with a low osmolality), and hypernatremia. The difference is that these patients do not respond when exogenous ADH is given.

Treatment

Thiazide diuretics may actually be helpful in these patients because, as they lower the circulating volume, they induce more Na+ and water reabsorption at the PCT (instead of reabsorption occurring at the collecting tubules). This decreases urine volume and bypasses the ADH system.

Benign Prostatic Hyperplasia

As men get older, few can escape the development of BPH. Because it's most often periurethral, urinary obstruction occurs.

Signs & Symptoms

Symptoms include hesitancy, decreased force of urine stream, and dribbling. Urinary retention may lead to urge incontinence and nocturia. UTI may occur with its associated symptoms.

Diagnosis

On rectal examination, the prostate may be large and fleshy, but it may be normal (because growth is often periurethral). Therefore, transrectal ultrasound may be a more sensitive test.

Treatment

Treatment with α-blockers (terazosin, prazosin) inhibits urinary bladder sphincter contractions, making it easier to urinate. Surgical treatment with a transurethral prostatectomy may be necessary to relieve the obstruction.

Neoplastic Disorders

Bladder Carcinoma

The most common bladder cancer is **transitional cell carcinoma**, which makes sense because these are the cells that line the bladder. **Smoking, aniline dyes,** and **schistosomiasis** infection are all risk factors. Men get it three times as often as women.

Signs & Symptoms

The most common finding is hematuria, although as the tumor gets larger, it may cause obstruction and cystitis. If it gets big enough, you may even be able to palpate a suprapubic mass.

Diagnosis

Malignant cells may be found in urine cytology, and an IVP may show a filling defect consistent with a tumor mass. A definitive diagnosis can be made by actual visualization (cystoscopy) and biopsy.

Treatment

Treatment includes surgical resection, radiation, and chemotherapy, depending on the tumor stage. Patients require close monitoring because these tumors often recur.

Renal Cell Carcinoma

Renal cell carcinoma (RCC) is an **adenocarcinoma**, which is the most common kidney tumor to affect adults. **Hematuria, flank pain**, and an **abdominal mass** are the classic symptoms, although weight loss, fever, and hypertension can occur. Hematuria is present in more than 70% of cases and may be the only sign. EPO production may be increased, leading to **polycythemia**. Ultrasound, IVP, and CT and MRI scan can demonstrate tumor size and extent. The only treatment option is surgery.

Wilms' Tumor

Wilms' tumor is the most common kidney tumor to affect children, with most cases occurring before age 4. Only 10% of patients have this disease bilaterally. The symptoms and diagnostic tests are the same as for RCC. Treatment includes surgical resection and chemotherapy (occasionally radiotherapy) and results in a good prognosis.

Prostate Carcinoma

Adenocarcinoma of the prostate usually develops in the peripheral regions of the prostate (compared to the periurethral location of BPH). It accounts for 18% of new cancers in men, ranking it second, just behind lung cancer.

Signs & Symptoms

Patients may be asymptomatic but may have BPH symptoms (from urinary obstruction) as well as hematuria. Some patients may only present with bony pain from metastatic lesions.

Diagnosis

Serum prostate-specific antigen (PSA) and acid phosphatase levels are usually elevated. The prostate may be nodular, firm, or irregular to palpation. Diagnosis can be made by ultrasound and biopsy. Metastatic lesions can be picked up with a bone scan.

Treatment

Treatment may include radical prostatectomy or radiation, or "watchful waiting" (i.e., doing nothing, because tumor progression is fairly slow). If caught early, prognosis is good. PSA levels can be used as a screening test, although PSA levels may also be high in patients with BPH.

Vascular Disorders

Renal Artery Stenosis

Although vascular disorders are uncommon causes of hypertension, they're important because they're often the most correctable. Renal artery stenosis leads to decreased blood flow to the kidney. The affected kidney reacts as if the blood pressure for the entire body were too low, stimulating the renin-angiotensin-aldosterone system in a mistaken attempt to "normalize" blood flow.

In younger patients, the main cause is **fibromuscular dysplasia**. The most common cause in adults is renal artery atherosclerosis, which affects men twice as much as women and is often seen in 50 year olds. Other unusual causes include aneurysm,

Takayasu's arteritis, hypercoagulable states, external trauma, instrumentation, and compression from external sources, such as a tumor.

Signs & Symptoms

In addition to hypertension, patients may have an abdominal bruit, hypokalemia, and metabolic alkalosis.

Diagnosis

Diagnosis can be made by doing an IVP, which demonstrates a small kidney and a delayed appearance of contrast on the abnormal side (because of decreased delivery of blood to the affected kidney). Renal angiography then shows exactly where the lesion is. Another method is to measure the amount of renin in the renal veins— the affected side has higher levels.

Treatment

Treatment choices include the use of antihypertensive drugs, surgical correction, balloon angiography, and stent placement.

Renal Arterial Embolism

Embolism causes a functional stenosis with all the sequelae of renal artery stenosis. The source can be a clot (e.g., atrial fibrillation, myocardial infarction), an infectious emboli (e.g., infective endocarditis, artificial heart valves), or an atheromatous plaque.

Signs & Symptoms

Acute renal artery occlusion may cause acute renal failure along with flank pain and hematuria.

Diagnosis

Lactate dehydrogenase may be elevated because of tissue necrosis (from ischemic kidney damage). Diagnosis can be made by angiography.

Treatment

Treatment may require anticoagulation with heparin or stent placement.

Renal Vein Thrombosis

Etiologies of renal vein thrombosis include a number of different processes, such as clots extending from the IVC, tumor invasion of the renal vein, renal amyloidosis, and diseases causing nephrotic syndrome (especially membranous glomerulonephritis).

Signs & Symptoms

If the clot evolves slowly, the patient may be asymptomatic; however, an acute renal vein thrombosis can present with pain, costovertebral angle tenderness, and hematuria.

Diagnosis

Diagnosis can be made on an IVP, demonstrating an enlarged affected kidney (the blood has trouble leaving the kidney, so it causes the kidney to swell). Doppler ultrasonography, which may show an absence of blood flow in the affected renal vein, can also be used.

Treatment

Just like deep vein thrombosis, it's thought that a renal vein thrombosis may cause a pulmonary embolism. Treatment, then, consists of long-term anticoagulation (3–6 months) with warfarin.

Effects of Systemic Disease on the Kidney

Diabetic Nephropathy

Five to 15% of all patients with diabetes develop end-stage renal disease (ESRD). Over a third of patients with insulin-dependent diabetes develop ESRD in 20 years. Although the exact cause of renal disease isn't known, disease progression is fairly predictable. **Microalbuminuria** occurs first (tiny amounts of protein in the urine), followed by **gross proteinuria** (after 15 years of diabetes), nephrotic syndrome and azotemia (3–5 years later), and ESRD (1–5 years after that).

Pathology slides demonstrate thickening of the glomerular basement membrane and mesangium (**diffuse glomerulosclerosis**) as well as nodular thickening within the glomeruli (nodular glomerulosclerosis), called **Kimmelstiel-Wilson nodules**.

Disease progression may be achieved with tight control of serum glucose (at the microalbuminuria stage; this is controversial), a low-protein diet (believed to preserve nephron function), ACE inhibitors, and treating hypertension. ESRD is treated by dialysis or transplantation.

Lupus Nephritis

Lupus nephritis refers to a number of different lesions, which are all possible sequelae of SLE. There are four major lesions, which usually occur during the first year of clinical SLE. The majority of the major lesions clinically present with a combination of proteinuria, hematuria, azotemia, nephrotic syndrome, and renal insufficiency (kind of a blend between nephritic and nephrotic syndromes). Special serologic studies, in general, show a positive fluorescent antinuclear antibody, anti-DNA antibodies, and decreased levels of C3 and C4. Remission occurs in one-third to one-half of patients, but relapses are common. Finally, one form may make a transition to another form and acquire its associated prognosis. Treatment involves the use of glucocorticoids with or without cytotoxic drugs. The following descriptions highlight the differences.

- **Focal proliferative**: The lesions are focal in that they involve only some of the glomeruli (usually less than half) and proliferative because there is segmental proliferation of endothelial and mesangial cells (i.e., only certain regions of the glomeruli are affected). Nephrotic syndrome is rare.

- **Diffuse proliferative**: This is the most severe form. Proliferation of mesangial and endothelial cells occurs in almost all glomeruli. It has the characteristic **wire-loop abnormality**, which results from immune complex deposits causing thickening of the glomerular basement membrane. On electron microscopy, this is seen as subendothelial deposits. More than half of these patients present with nephrotic syndrome, and it is unavoidable for almost all patients. Hypertension occasionally occurs. Only 50% of patients are alive at 5 years.

- **Membranous**: This has the same characteristics as membranous glomerulonephritis (mentioned previously). The mortality rate at 5 years is 10%.

- **Mesangial**: The biopsy shows an increase in mesangial cells and matrix. Many patients with this form are asymptomatic. There isn't any disease progression unless it makes a transition to diffuse proliferative or membranous.

Henoch-Schönlein Purpura

Henoch-Schönlein purpura is a systemic disease seen mainly in children. Clinical findings are preceded by vaccination, an infection, or drugs. The classic **rash** usually affects legs and buttocks, nephritis occurs in 30% of cases, and there is often arthritis, abdominal pain, and GI bleeding. Immunofluorescent staining of the biopsy is positive for IgA in the mesangium. Prognosis in general is good, which is lucky because no treatments have proven to be beneficial.

Renal Amyloidosis

Renal amyloidosis can also cause nephrotic syndrome. The amyloid fibrils can be seen throughout the glomerulus, interstitium, and in blood vessel walls. Amyloid may be revealed with a Congo red stain examined by birefringence under polarized light. The glomeruli eventually get obliterated, which leads to renal failure and uremia.

Kidney-Related Electrolyte Abnormalities

Hypernatremia

Serum Na^+ that is too high (>155 mEq/liter) may be a result of dehydration from fluid losses (e.g., diarrhea, vomiting, sweating, burns, diabetes insipidus) or decreased fluid intake.

Signs & Symptoms

If untreated, symptoms include central nervous system (CNS) disturbances, such as coma or seizures, and even death.

Treatment

Treatment is to give back free water. ADH should be given to patients with central diabetes insipidus. The free water must be replaced slowly to prevent cerebral edema.

Hyponatremia

Serum Na^+ that is too low (<135 mEq/liter) often occurs when ADH levels are too high. SIADH is a primary cause of elevated ADH. Secondary causes include nephrotic syndrome, congestive heart failure, cirrhosis, and with the use of some diuretics. **Pseudohyponatremia** means that the serum Na^+ appears low even though there's probably enough Na^+ around. This can occur with hyperlipidemia, which makes it appear that plasma volume is increased so that Na^+ concentration is decreased.

Signs & Symptoms

Symptoms are the same as for hypernatremia.

Treatment

Serum Na^+ needs to be elevated with hypertonic saline or fluid restriction. If done too quickly, you may precipitate **central pontine myelinolysis**. These patients develop severe CNS disease, in which they're left with only their eye movements intact.

Hyperkalemia

Serum K^+ that is too high (>5.5 mEq/liter) may be a result of decreased K^+ excretion from any cause of acute and chronic renal failure, defective renal secretory function (e.g., interstitial nephritis or obstructive uropathy), K^+-sparing diuretics (e.g., spironolactone), or hypoaldosteronism. Excessive K^+ release into the serum may result from massive cell damage from burn injuries or hemolysis.

Signs & Symptoms

Clinically, the patients may develop weakness or arrhythmias, which can be deadly.

Treatment

Treatment involves removing serum K^+ by diuretics (e.g., furosemide, thiazides) or K^+-binding compounds excreted in the stool. K^+ may also be shifted into cells using glucose or insulin, and calcium may prevent arrhythmias.

Hypokalemia

Serum K^+ that is too low (<3.5 mEq/liter) is a common problem in hospitalized patients. This may occur with diuretics (e.g., furosemide, thiazide), some renal tubular diseases, and hyperaldosteronism. Anise-containing licorice can precipitate hypokalemia because of its ability to reproduce aldosterone's effects. Patients receiving too much insulin may also drop their serum K^+ as insulin drives potassium along with glucose into the cells.

Signs & Symptoms

Symptoms are the same as for hyperkalemia.

Treatment

Treatment is K^+ replacement in oral or intravenous form.

Pharmacology

Table 14-7 lists the actions, indications, and toxicities of common diuretics.

Table 14-7. Diuretics

Agents	Mechanism of action	Uses	Toxicities
Carbonic anhydrase (CA) inhibitors (acetazolamide)	Causes $NaHCO_3$ wasting at the PCT and blocks CA^{2+} in the eye	Glaucoma, metabolic alkalosis, urinary alkalinization, rarely used as a diuretic	Metabolic acidosis, paresthesias, hypokalemia
Loop diuretics (furosemide)	Inhibits Na^+ reabsorption in the thick ascending limb, causes K^+ and Ca^{2+} wasting, may saturate the uric acid transporter	Volume overload (CHF, acute pulmonary edema, nephrotic syndrome, cirrhosis), hypertension, hyperkalemia, hypercalcemia	Hypokalemia (± metabolic alkalosis) hyponatremia, dehydration, hypotension, ototoxicity, hyperuricemia (± gout), interstitial nephritis/allergic reactions
Ethacrynic acid	Same	Same; tolerated by patients allergic to furosemide (a sulfa-containing drug)	Same, except no hyperuricemia or allergic reactions
Thiazide diuretics (hydrochlorothiazide)	Blocks NaCl absorption in the DCT, causes K^+ wasting but stimulates Ca^{2+} reabsorption	Less effective than furosemide, but longer action; essentially the same indications as furosemide; also treats hypercalciuria and nephrolithiasis	Hypokalemia (± metabolic alkalosis) hyponatremia, dehydration, hypotension, hyperlipidemia hyperglycemia, hyperuricemia, and allergic reactions
K^+-sparing diuretics (amiloride/triamterene)	Directly acts on the DCT to increase Na^+ excretion, and decrease K^+ wasting	Weak diuretic used with other diuretics to prevent hypokalemia	Hyperkalemia, hyponatremia, dehydration
Aldosterone antagonists (e.g., spironolactone)	Competitively blocks the actions of aldosterone on the DCT and collecting ducts	Hyperaldosterone states (e.g., cirrhosis, CHF)	Same as K^+ sparing plus endocrine disturbances (antiandrogen effects, gynecomastia, menstrual irregularities
Antidiuretic hormone (ADH) antagonists (lithium)	Blocks ADH action on collecting ducts	SIADH, secondary causes of increased ADH (CHF, cirrhosis, nephrotic syndrome)	CNS disturbances, interstitial nephritis, nephrogenic diabetes insipidus
Osmotic agents (mannitol)	Causes water and Na^+ diuresis by osmotic forces	Acute cerebral edema (from stroke or trauma), acute renal failure, acute glaucoma	Acute intravascular expansion may cause hypertension or pulmonary edema; dehydration later, nausea, vomiting, headache

PCT = proximal convoluted tubule; DCT = distal convoluted tubule; CHF = congestive heart failure; CNS = central nervous system; SIADH = syndrome of inappropriate ADH.

CHAPTER 15

Reproduction

Fetal Development

Overview of Embryogenesis

Fertilization defines the contact between a spermatozoa and an ovum, a process that can last an entire day! Generally, fertilization occurs while the ovum is still traversing the fallopian tube, which is why any scarring in the fallopian tube can predispose to an ectopic pregnancy. Initially, the sperm passes through the ovum's corona radiata by releasing **hyaluronidase**. Next the zona pellucida is penetrated, and the remaining enzymes are released from the spermatozoa's **acrosome** (Fig. 15-1). Finally, the membranes of the sperm and ovum fuse, placing the sperm's contents in the ovum. This fusion produces metabolic signals that prevent any additional sperm from fertilizing the same ovum and that tell the ovum to complete its meiotic divisions.

Soon after fertilization is completed, mitosis begins. Initially, the overall mass remains the same, and each cell is **totipotent**, meaning that no differentiation has occurred and each individual cell can still develop into a mature organism. At approximately 16 cells, this quality is lost (i.e., differentiation begins), and the total cytoplasmic mass begins to increase. At this point the cell cluster is called a **morula** (Fig. 15-2).

Eventually a cavity develops in the cell mass, creating a central area (embryoblast) that develops into the embryo, and a surrounding layer, the **trophoblast**, that will comprise the fetal contribution to the placenta. The embryo is called a **blastula**, and it is at this stage that implantation into the uterine wall occurs (5–7 days postfertilization).

After implantation, both layers divide further. The trophoblast separates into the **syncytiotrophoblast** and the **cytotrophoblast**. The syncytiotrophoblast makes the lytic enzymes that allow for further burrowing into the endometrium. The cytotrophoblast layer is surrounded by blood from the maternal sinusoids, creating an early circulation.

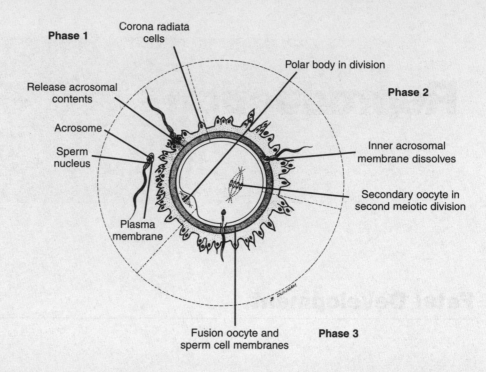

Fig. 15-1. The phases of fertilization.

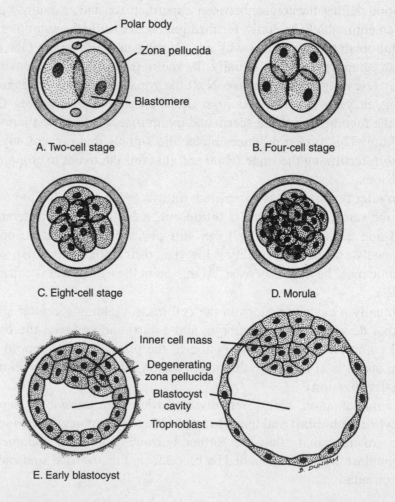

Fig. 15-2. Embryonic development.

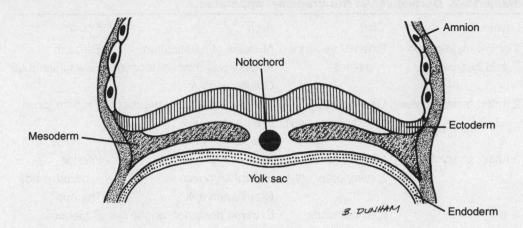

Fig. 15-3. Trilaminar embryo.

Table 15-1. Adult derivatives of the trilaminar embryo

Ectoderm	Mesoderm	Endoderm
Epidermis (e.g., hair and nails)	Dermis	Gut epithelium
Nervous system	Cardiovascular	Glands
Brain	structures	Germ cells
Spinal cord	Lymphatics	Branchial pouches
Neural crest cells (e.g., autonomic ner-	Connective tissue	
vous system, pia, melanocytes, chro-	Muscle	
maffin cells of adrenal medulla)	Bone	
Otic placode	Genitourinary parenchyma	
Otic cup	Serous linings	
Lens placode	Dura	
Branchial clefts	Spleen	
	Branchial arches	

Meanwhile, the embryo divides into an **ectoderm** and an **endoderm**. The endoderm surrounds the primitive yolk sac, whereas the endoderm forms part of the amnion cavity. The cells destined to become ectoderm also contribute to the **mesoderm**, which separates the original two layers. One cylindrical portion of mesoderm is known as the **notochord** (Fig. 15-3). It induces formation of the neural tube from the ectoderm and later goes on to form the nucleus pulposus of the vertebral disks. Some other derivatives of these germ layers that are useful to know are listed in Table 15-1.

The Branchial Apparatus

One potential source for embryology questions involves adult derivatives of the branchial clefts, arches, and pouches (Table 15-2), but don't get too carried away. You can already derive many of the relationships from your knowledge of anatomy because structures (e.g., muscles and nerves) that are functionally related tend to originate from the same level.

Table 15-2. Derivatives of the branchial apparatus

Level	Cleft	Arch	Pouch
1 (think mastication and hearing)	External auditory meatus	Muscles of mastication Anterior two-thirds of tongue Cranial nerve V	Eardrum Eustachian tube
2 (think facial expression)	Cervical sinus (temporary only)	Muscles of facial expression, plus stapedius Cranial nerve VII	Palatine tonsil
3 (think pharynx)	Cervical sinus (temporary only)	Posterior tongue Stylopharyngeus Cranial nerve IX	Inferior parathyroids Thymus
4–6	Cervical sinus (temporary only) Persistence = branchial cyst	Extreme posterior tongue Throat cartilage Laryngeal muscles Fourth arch = cranial nerve X Sixth arch = recurrent laryngeal	Superior parathyroids Parafollicular cells of the thyroid

Reproductive Tract Development

Although the sex of a child is determined at conception, the development of the male and female reproductive systems do not begin until about 7 weeks' gestation. The period before this is termed the "indifferent" stage of sexual development, when the **mesonephros** (precursor of the urogenital tract) develops sex cords, which can develop into either male or female organs.

Female Reproductive Development

If there is no Y chromosome present (e.g., the fetus is XX), the cortical sex cords begin developing into ovaries at about week 10. At 16 weeks, these break up to form primordial follicles, each of which carries a primordial oocyte, or oogonia. During this time, active division occurs to increase the number of **oogonia**—once the child is born, no further oogonia production occurs. Unlike males, who produce new germ cells throughout life after puberty, females are born with their full complement of germ cells. This fact explains the concern about female exposure to radiation and mutagens even in a pediatric setting.

Two sets of ducts—the **wolffian** (mesonephric) **duct** and the **müllerian** (paramesonephric) **duct**—are present in both sexes during development. If the embryo has ovaries or no testes, the mesonephric duct regresses and the paramesonephric duct develops into most of the female reproductive tract, including the uterus and the fallopian tubes. The vagina and labia develop from the urogenital sinus. The gubernaculum, a layer of tissue that follows during the descent of the ovaries, becomes the ovarian ligament and the round ligament of the uterus.

Male Reproductive Development

The presence of a Y chromosome causes the development of the sex cords into the testes and seminiferous tubules. The seminiferous tubules give rise to precursor **Leydig cells**, which secrete testosterone and determine development of the male external genitalia. **Müllerian inhibiting factor** is synthesized by precursor **Sertoli cells**. These two substances cause the mesonephric ducts to develop and the para-mesonephric ducts to regress. The mesonephric ducts eventually develop into the vas deferens and seminal vesicles. Urogenital folds, under the influence of andro-gens, elongate and form the penis.

Anatomy

You are unlikely to be asked to recall complex anatomic detail of the reproductive tract, but the following clinically significant functional relationships are useful to understand.

Arterial Supply and Lymphatic Drainage of the Ovaries and Testes

When the ovaries and testes descend during fetal life they carry their own blood sup-ply and lymphatic drainage with them. So, although the other reproductive struc-tures are supplied by the iliacs and drain to the inguinal lymph nodes, the ovaries and testes are supplied by branches of the descending aorta and drain to nodes in the posterior abdominal wall. This is clinically significant in searching for metastatic ovarian and testicular cancers.

Hernias

The first type of hernia to remember is the **indirect inguinal hernia**, which retraces the testicular descent down the inguinal canal, passing through the deep and superficial inguinal rings. This is in contrast to the **direct inguinal hernia**, which simply pouches through the superficial ring only. Because the inferior epi-gastric artery separates these two rings (it lies medial to the deep ring and lateral to the superficial ring), it provides a useful landmark for distinguishing between these two hernias (Fig. 15-4).

Relationship of the Ovaries and Fallopian Tubes

Although the fallopian tube and ovary both lie together in the **broad ligament**, the ovary does not connect directly to the fallopian tube (Fig. 15-5). Instead, the fim-briae at the end of the fallopian tube "catch" the ovum released by the ovary. (A miss could result in a peritoneal **ectopic pregnancy**.)

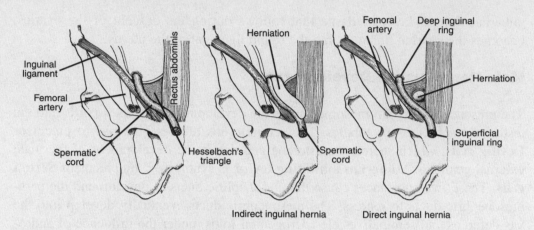

Fig. 15-4. Direct and indirect inguinal hernias.

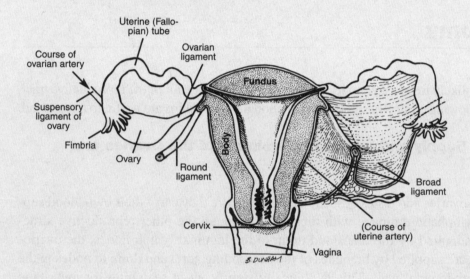

Fig. 15-5. Female reproductive anatomy.

Histology

Spermatogenesis and the Blood-Testis Barrier

Spermatogenesis occurs in the seminiferous tubules of the testes. The key players are the **Leydig cells** and the **Sertoli cells**. The Leydig cells are in the underlying interstitial tissue and influence spermatogenesis by secreting testosterone. The Sertoli cells extend from the basement membrane to the lumen of the tubule, forming tight junctions with one another that comprise the **blood-testis barrier**. (An injury to the tubules that exposes mature sperm to the blood can create an autoimmune reaction and lead to male infertility).

The immature spermatogonia begin their journey from the basement membrane and make their way past the Sertoli cells (which provide structural and metabolic support) to the lumen of the tubule (Fig. 15-6). Along the way they undergo meio-

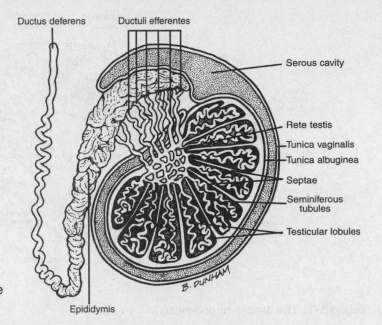

Fig. 15-6. Histology of the testis.

Labels: Ductus deferens, Ductuli efferentes, Serous cavity, Rete testis, Tunica vaginalis, Tunica albuginea, Septae, Seminiferous tubules, Testicular lobules, Epididymis

B. DUNHAM

sis I and II before arriving at the tubule. From there they are transported from the rete testis to the efferent ductules, and finally to the epididymis, where they complete their maturation. The mature sperm are carried by the vas deferens and converge at the urethra at the site of the prostate, where the prostatic glandular tissue secretes up to 75% of the final ejaculate. The prostatic secretion is rich in citric acid and, more important, fibrinolysin, which liquefies the semen. Overall, the process of spermatogenesis and transport takes about 3 months.

Oogenesis

As noted earlier, the ovary develops all its oocytes during embryogenesis, and they lie dormant until puberty, arrested in prophase of meiosis I. Each oocyte is encapsulated by follicular cells and is known as a **primordial follicle**. Starting at puberty, approximately 10 follicles begin to grow under the influence of follicle-stimulating hormone (FSH) during each menstrual cycle. Usually only one of these follicles develops to maturity, although we know there are exceptions (e.g., nonidentical twins). The follicle that becomes dominant suppresses the other follicles in a process known as *follicular atresia*. Meiosis I is completed (with the expulsion of polar bodies containing the unused DNA) and meiosis II begins. The surrounding follicular cells also mature and become the **thecal layer** and **granulosa layer** (Fig. 15-7). The granulosa cells produce progesterone and act in concert with the thecal cells to produce estrogen.

Before puberty, oocytes are arrested in prophase of meiosis I.

The Cervical Transition Zone

The cervix is divided anatomically into the exocervix, which projects into the vagina, and the endocervix. Histologically there is also a division that correlates roughly with the anatomic division but changes throughout life. The exocervix is lined by nonkeratinized, stratified squamous epithelium, whereas the endocervix is lined by mucin-

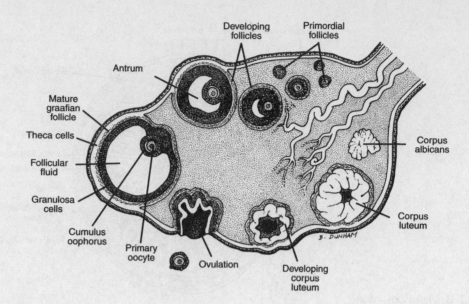

Fig. 15-7. The stages of oogenesis.

secreting columnar epithelium. The **transition zone** refers to the border of these two epithelia, which makes a gradual transition rather than an abrupt one. The transition zone is the site of most cervical cancers, which are usually squamous cell carcinomas.

Changes Associated with Senescence

Vaginal Atrophy

Although vaginal atrophy is an early consequence of the low-estrogen state of menopause, it might be considered its own entity, and it can be reversed with local application of estrogen cream. The vaginal mucosa thins, leading to decreased vaginal lubrication. The normal deep rugae of the vagina are lost, and pelvic examination reveals a pale, smooth surface.

Benign Prostatic Hyperplasia

The hyperplasia that the prostate frequently undergoes in elderly men also is thought to be due to an alteration of the hormonal milieu. Some consequences of the obstructive hyperplasia can seem less than benign; these are covered in chapter 14.

Reproductive Endocrinology

Hypothalamic and Pituitary Hormones

The hypothalamus is responsible for producing gonadotropin-releasing hormone (**GnRH**), which is carried by the portal circulation to the anterior pituitary where it

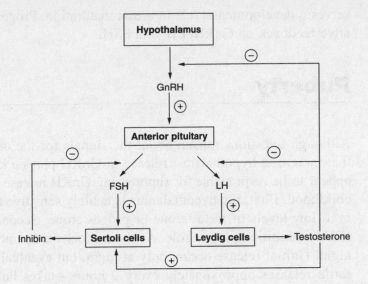

Fig. 15-8. Male reproductive hormones. (GnRH = gonadotropin-releasing hormone; FSH = follicle-stimulating hormone; LH = luteinizing hormone.)

causes the release of **luteinizing hormone** (LH) and **follicle-stimulating hormone** (FSH). GnRH only causes hormone release by the pituitary if secreted in pulsatile bursts. A steady infusion of GnRH actually causes pituitary suppression. GnRH gets feedback inhibition from progesterone and testosterone.

In the male, FSH acts on the Sertoli cells to stimulate support of spermatogenesis. The Sertoli cells produce the hormone **inhibin**, which downregulates FSH in a feedback loop. LH acts on the Leydig cells to promote testosterone release. In feedback inhibition, testosterone not only suppresses GnRH, but it also directly lowers LH release from the pituitary (Fig. 15-8).

In females, LH acts on the ovarian thecal cells to promote progesterone production. Diffusion carries the progesterone to the neighboring granulosa cells, where it is converted first to testosterone and then to estrogen. The effects of FSH and LH in females are discussed in more detail later.

Effects of Testosterone, Estrogen, and Progesterone

Testosterone is converted to dihydroxytestosterone, its more active form, locally at the tissue level by **5α-reductase**. As discussed earlier, testosterone plays a role in prenatal wolffian duct maturation and later in spermatogenesis. It is also important in the development of secondary male sexual characteristics and overall growth during puberty. In addition to increasing libido, testosterone increases secretory activity throughout the male reproductive tract.

Estrogen and testosterone are in many ways analogous, but estrogen has even more varied effects. Estrogen is responsible for the development of both primary and secondary female sex characteristics. In addition, estrogen upregulates not only its own receptor, but also those for LH and progesterone. Estrogen generally exerts a negative feedback on LH and FSH, but midway through the menstrual cycle, a positive feedback effect predominates, which causes a surge of LH and FSH that triggers ovulation. Estrogen (along with progesterone) is essential in maintaining pregnancy. Progesterone plays a key role in maintaining the glandular activity of the endometrium during the latter half of the menstrual cycle. It also serves a developmental role in breast maturation. Progesterone always exerts negative feedback on GnRH, LH, and FSH.

Puberty

Although questions remain about the signals for the onset of puberty, it is clear that increased hypothalamic release of GnRH plays a key role. Two mechanisms appear to be responsible for suppressing GnRH release (and thus puberty) during childhood. First, the hypothalamus is acutely sensitive to negative feedback from even low levels of testosterone or progesterone. Second, central nervous system (CNS) inhibition plays a role. As these blocks are removed, GnRH is released at night. (Initial release occurs only at night, but eventually the adult pattern—pulsatile releases approximately every 2 hours—takes hold.) Androgen production from the adrenals also plays a role in initiating development of secondary sexual characteristics.

Menarche defines the start of menstrual periods. The age at menarche varies by culture, geographic area, and nutritional status and weight. In the Western world, the average age at menarche is 12.8 years.

Menstrual Cycle

Understanding the normal menstrual cycle hinges on interactions at four different levels: hypothalamus, pituitary, ovaries, and endometrium. An idealized cycle length is 28 days (although the range of normal includes somewhat shorter and longer cycles). Day 1 is defined as the first day of menstruation, with the first four days of the cycle comprising the **menstrual phase**. Days 5–14 are the **proliferative phase** (the follicular phase) and are separated from days 15–28, known as the **secretory** (or luteal) **phase**, by ovulation (Fig. 15-9 and Table 15-3).

Intercourse and Orgasm

- Sexual excitation leading to orgasm in males and females involves both psychological and physical stimuli.

- Penile and clitoral erection are mediated by the parasympathetic nervous system, which causes arterial dilatation and engorgement of potential spaces, as well as stimulating lubricating secretions.

- Emission and ejaculation by the male and orgasm in the female are mediated by the sympathetic nervous system. Ejaculation involves rhythmic muscular contractions that propel the sperm deep into the vagina and even past the cervix!

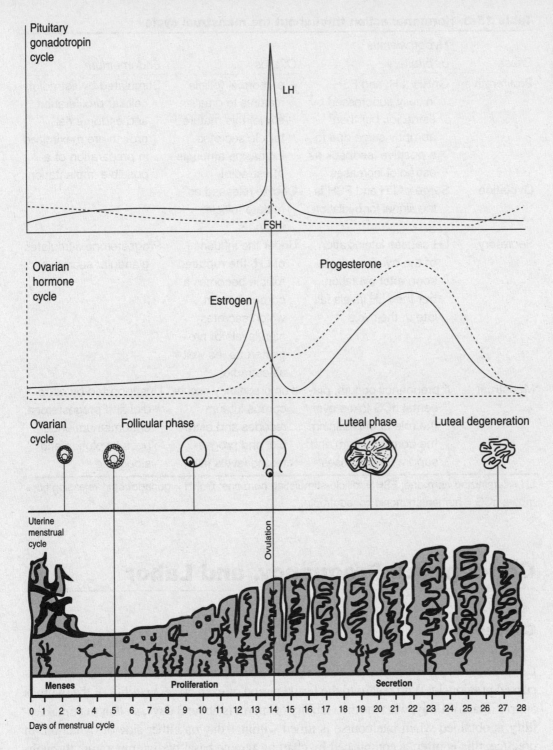

Fig. 15-9. The menstrual cycle. (LH = luteinizing hormone; FSH = follicle-stimulating hormone.)

Table 15-3. Hormonal action throughout the menstrual cycle

Phase	Hypothalamus or pituitary	Ovaries	Endometrium
Proliferative	GnRH, LH, and FSH initially suppressed by estradiol, but then abruptly surge due to a positive feedback as estradiol increases	A primordial follicle matures to graafian stage; this mature follicle secretes increasing amounts of estradiol	Stimulated by estradiol, cellular proliferation and endometrial growth are maximized in preparation of a possible implantation
Ovulation	Surge of LH and FSH is the signal for ovulation	Oocyte released as mature follicle ruptures	—
Secretory	LH causes luteinization of the ovarian follicle soon after ovulation, but then LH levels fall late in the cycle	Under the influence of LH, the ruptured follicle becomes a corpus luteum, which secretes high levels of progesterone, as well as estradiol	Progesterone stimulates glandular secretions
Menstrual	If pregnancy occurs, placental hCG takes over the role of maintaining the corpus luteum and suppressing menses	If no pregnancy occurs, corpus luteum recedes and estradiol and progesterone levels fall	Unsupported by estradiol and progesterone, endometrium undergoes involution and sloughing

LH = luteinizing hormone; FSH = follicle-stimulating hormone; GnRH = gonadotropin-releasing hormone; hCG = human chorionic gonadotropin.

Conception, Pregnancy, and Labor

Conception

Conception and *fertilization* are used synonymously, and the mechanism has been discussed previously. With regard to the fertile period of each cycle, viability of the ovum is approximately 1 day, whereas the viability of sperm is about 3 days, so that maximal fertility is obtained when intercourse is timed within 1 day on either side of ovulation. In practice, this is often accomplished by charting female basal body temperature throughout the cycle because progesterone mildly raises core temperature after ovulation.

Pregnancy

Most of the changes that occur during pregnancy are related to hormonal signals, although the size and metabolic demands of the fetus also necessitate other physiologic changes. After fertilization and implantation, the placenta must take over the role of the pituitary, producing LH to maintain the corpus luteum. This is a key function because the estrogen and progesterone produced by the corpus luteum are essential in maintaining the secretory response of the decidual cells of the endometrium (initially the chief source of nutrition for the developing embryo). The placenta produces a hormone that is analogous to LH called **human chorionic gonadotropin** (hCG). Detection of this hormone in the blood and urine is the basis for pregnancy testing.

Eventually, the placenta (more specifically, the syncytial trophoblasts) overtakes the corpus luteum as a source of estrogen and progesterone. The placenta uses precursors produced by the maternal and fetal adrenal glands to produce these hormones. Estrogen is a signal for enlargement of the uterus and external genitalia. It also relaxes the pelvic ligaments for easier passage of the fetus through the birth canal. In addition, estrogen stimulates prolactin production. Together with progesterone, these hormones cause enlargement of the breast ductal system, although estrogen blocks the prolactin receptor so that lactation does not begin. Progesterone also decreases the contractility of the uterus to prevent spontaneous abortion. The incompletely understood hormone **human chorionic somatomammotropin** is also produced by the placenta in large amounts. One known action of this hormone is to decrease maternal insulin sensitivity so that more nutrients are available to the fetus.

The suggested weight gain associated with a pregnancy is approximately 25–35 lb. Some of this weight gain represents the need for stores of vitamins, calcium, and especially iron, which the fetus extracts from the mother. Maternal blood volume increases 30% by the end of the pregnancy. Cardiac output increases to supply the placenta adequately, and the extra blood compensates for normal blood losses during birth.

A normal pregnancy is considered to be 40 weeks, ±2 weeks on each side. Remember that by convention these weeks are counted from the last normal menstrual period and not from the date of conception.

Labor

The exact mechanisms that signal for the onset of labor (also called *parturition*) are not known, but the following factors are thought to contribute. Late in pregnancy, estrogen, which tends to increase uterine contractions, rises relative to progesterone, which suppresses contractility. The posterior pituitary hormone **oxytocin** increases uterine responsiveness, and its rate of production considerably increases during labor. Mechanical factors also play a role as reflexive responses to the pain of contractions provide an urge to push.

After delivery of the baby and the placenta, estrogen and progesterone levels decline rapidly. This releases the prolactin receptor blockade, and lactation can proceed. Oxytocin plays a role in milk "let-down," with both oxytocin and prolactin being stimulated by suckling.

Fetal and Neonatal Physiology: Placental Exchange

As fetal demands become greater toward the end of pregnancy, the placental barrier becomes thinner. After the fourth month, it consists only of a syncytial membrane and the endothelium of the fetal capillary. Oxygen and carbon dioxide diffuse readily across this barrier. In the same manner, most metabolic substrates also cross by simple diffusion. The fetal demand for glucose is so great that a carrier is used for facilitated diffusion. A few nutrients (such as certain amino acids) are needed in greater concentration in the fetal blood than in the maternal blood and are transported actively. Excretion of fetal waste products is the mirror image, with diffusion occurring down gradients from fetal to maternal blood.

Menopause and Male Climacteric

Menopause

Technically, menopause denotes the actual cessation of menstruation. In practical usage, it also refers to the 1- to 3-year phase of declining flow and decreasing frequency of menstruation, plus the cluster of responses that accompany a changing hormone balance. Physiologically, menopause can be understood to be due to the limited number of ovarian follicles that are able to respond to stimulation by FSH and LH. Follicles are lost either to ovulation or degeneration with each cycle so that, by the late 40s or early 50s, most women have a minimal number of follicles, and estrogen and progesterone production by the ovaries decreases. With the removal of feedback inhibition from estrogen and progesterone, levels of FSH, LH, and GnRH are elevated. This likely contributes to the hot flashes, night sweats, and insomnia often associated with menopause. Elevated FSH and LH are used to diagnose premature menopause (**ovarian failure**), and low estrogen is implicated in osteoporosis and atherosclerosis.

Because **hormone-replacement therapy** (HRT) counteracts these changes, as well as lowering low-density lipoprotein and increasing high-density lipoprotein cholesterol, it has received wide advocacy. Recently, it has been noted that administration of unopposed estrogen increases the risk of endometrial cancer, but the addition of progestin to the regimen alleviates this concern. There is also worry over a small increase in the incidence of breast cancer associated with HRT. This has led to the recommendation that physicians should help the patient assess her relative individual risks regarding HRT. Side effects include breakthrough menstrual bleeding, weight gain, and fluid retention. Estrogen is metabolized in the liver, and HRT is contraindicated in patients with hepatic disease or gallbladder disease.

Male Climacteric

Although there is no true equivalent of menopause in males, beginning in the late 40s or early 50s most males begin to note a gradual decrease in sexual function. This is known as *male climacteric* and is attributed to a decrease in testosterone production, which actually begins earlier. As with menopause, this process is reversible with administration of hormones, including testosterone, synthetic androgens, or even estrogen.

Congenital Reproductive Defects

Klinefelter's Syndrome

Klinefelter's syndrome was the first sex chromosome abnormality to be recognized. It occurs in phenotypic males who are born with an extra X chromosome (47,XXY). It remains inapparent until puberty. The incidence is 1 in 1,000 live births, but half of all 47,XXY conceptions result in spontaneous abortion. The female equivalent of this disorder, **trisomy X**, usually results in phenotypically normal females.

Signs & Symptoms

Klinefelter's syndrome is generally noted when secondary sexual characteristics fail to develop. Particularly notable are hypogonadism and gynecomastia. Klinefelter's syndrome almost always causes infertility due to azoospermia. Psychosocial disturbance is also commonly reported.

Pathology

As might be expected, Klinefelter's syndrome results from chromosomal nondisjunction. This can occur in maternal or paternal meiosis I or meiosis II, or from a later mitotic error. The penetrance can vary due to mosaicism, usually through loss of one X chromosome.

Diagnosis

Physical examination and elevated levels of LH, FSH, and prolactin all increase suspicion of Klinefelter's, but karyotyping is the gold standard. A new polymerase chain reaction (PCR) technique is also available.

Treatment

As is the case with most congenital abnormalities, treatment is limited.

XYY Syndrome

Use of the word *syndrome* may overstate the significance of having an extra Y chromosome. Unlike other aneuploidies, no specific phenotypic cluster is associated with a 47,XYY phenotype, probably because there's so little genetic information on the Y chromosome. Nevertheless, it has been implicated as a cause of behavioral problems.

Signs & Symptoms

This genotype was first noted in higher proportion in prison and mental institution populations than in the general public. Prospective studies from newborn screening have confirmed the increased incidence of behavioral problems and show a tendency for males with this phenotype to be taller than average.

Pathology

This karyotype results from a nondisjunction during paternal meiosis II, leading to a YY sperm.

Diagnosis

This karyotype is only noted during karyotypic screening evaluations.

Treatment

Behavioral problems are addressed individually.

Turner's Syndrome

Turner's syndrome is caused when the second sex chromosome is lost, and only an X chromosome remains, so that the karyotype is 45,X. It is less common than some of the other sex chromosome aneuploidies, but its classic features are often noticeable before the onset of puberty.

Signs & Symptoms

Typical findings are short stature, gonadal dysgenesis (usually streak ovaries), and typical facial and truncal abnormalities, including a low posterior hairline, webbing of the neck, and a broadened chest with widely spaced nipples. Renal and cardiovascular abnormalities, particularly coarctation of the aorta, are occasionally present.

Pathology

Turner's syndrome usually results from a nondisjunctional error that leaves either the ovum or sperm without a sex chromosome. In about 25% of cases, a mosaic pattern is noted, indicating that the chromosome was lost after fertilization.

Diagnosis

Recognition of physical findings, with subsequent karyotyping. Occasionally this diagnosis is made prenatally by ultrasound or immediately after birth because many of the dysmorphologies are present. Some cases are not recognized until a workup for infertility takes place.

Treatment

Supplemental estrogen can restore the maturation of secondary sexual characteristics and initiate normal menses, but it does not confirm fertility. Growth hormone may help to increase stature if administered in youth.

Female Pseudohermaphrodism

Unlike the extremely rare cases of true hermaphrodism, where an individual is born with both testes and ovaries, pseudohermaphrodism occurs when apparent sexual phenotype does not correlate with genotype. In females, this is generally due to virilization resulting from abnormally elevated androgen levels, caused by an enzymatic deficiency in biosynthetic pathways.

Signs & Symptoms

Female pseudohermaphrodism is generally discovered due to ambiguous genitalia, which are noted in the initial infant screening examination, but it may not become apparent until later in childhood. It also may be picked up from a salt-losing crisis, because often there is also a block in the production of mineralocorticoids.

Pathology

The most common cause of female pseudohermaphrodism is **congenital adrenal hyperplasia**, which is usually due to an autosomal recessive defect in **21-hydroxylase**. Because this enzyme is in the pathway that converts cholesterol to corticosteroids, loss of this enzyme shunts precursors toward androgen production. The low levels of glucocorticoids exacerbate the problem by signaling for increased precursor synthesis.

Diagnosis

A diagnosis is made using anatomic investigation, including radiographic studies, with contributing evidence from measurements of various steroids, glucocorticoids, and precursors. In males with 21-hydroxylase deficiency the more obvious anatomic evidence is absent, so that the first sign is a salt-losing crisis. This has led to increased use of heel-stick screening of both female and male infants for this deficiency.

Treatment

Except for rare cases that are diagnosed late, gender assignment matches chromosomal sex, and surgery is performed to restore the normal female external genitalia. Emphasis is placed on early treatment because glucocorticoid administration can arrest the virilization, maintain fertility, and prevent a salt-losing crisis.

Male Pseudohermaphrodism

Male pseudohermaphrodism results from undervirilization of a male embryo. During normal embryogenesis, the primary pathway produces female sexual characteristics; exposure to androgens alters differentiation toward a male phenotype. A breakdown in either androgen production or target tissue response can lead to male pseudohermaphrodism. Target tissue response is most often the cause and is called **androgen insensitivity syndrome** (formerly known as *testicular feminization*).

Signs & Symptoms

This disorder produces apparently normal female genitalia externally but with a blind-ended vagina and no uterus, ovaries, or fallopian tubes. Functional testes, which produce elevated levels of testosterone remain undescended in the abdomen or inguinal canal. There is minimal axillary or pubic hair.

Pathology

Androgen insensitivity syndrome is an X-linked recessive disorder that results in failure to produce functional androgen-binding receptors. A similar phenotype occurs in the autosomal recessive inherited defect of 5α-reductase (described earlier), the enzyme that converts testosterone to its active form at the tissues.

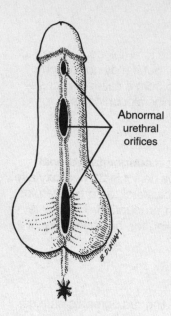

Abnormal
urethral
orifices

Fig. 15-10. Hypospadias.

Diagnosis

Prepubertal diagnosis is usually made when the testes are associated with hernias or mistaken for hernias. Otherwise, diagnosis is usually delayed until a postpubertal workup is done for primary amenorrhea.

Treatment

Removal of the testes is important because of the increased risk of cancer in undescended testes. This procedure generally is postponed until after puberty because the hormone production from the testes still leads to essentially normal female secondary sexual characteristics. Pain from the testes is an indication for prepubertal removal and hormone supplementation.

Hypospadias

If fusion of the urethral folds during male embryogenesis is incomplete, abnormal openings in the urethra can occur along the ventral (inferior) aspect of the penis (Fig. 15-10).

Signs & Symptoms

Hypospadias is usually overtly visible at birth. Examination can involve looking for urine loss through the abnormal orifices.

Pathology

This developmental defect is thought to be related to an incomplete response to androgens during development. It is also seen in cases of maternal progesterone intake during early pregnancy.

Diagnosis

Hypospadias is found during normal screening examination of male infants. It often occurs in association with other developmental errors.

Treatment

Surgery.

Epispadias

In contrast to hypospadias, epispadias involves abnormal urethral meatus displacement to the dorsal aspect of the penis.

Signs & Symptoms

The displaced urethral orifice is usually evident. Both hypospadias and epispadias, if not corrected, can be associated with urinary tract infections and infertility.

Pathology

Precursor tissues for the urethra and glans become inverted early in development.

Diagnosis

Made on physical examination.

Treatment

Surgery.

Cryptorchidism

Cryptorchidism refers to undescended or partially descended testes, either unilaterally or bilaterally.

Signs & Symptoms

By definition, the chief finding is the lack of one or both testes in the scrotum. Cryptorchidism is frequently associated with inguinal hernias.

Pathology

Cryptorchidism can involve arrest of descent of one or both testes at any point in their developmental journey from the abdomen, through the inguinal canal, and down into the scrotum. If a testis remains undescended for longer than about 2 years, germ cell development becomes compromised. The malpositioned testis is also more vulnerable to injury. There is an approximately 10-fold increase in the risk of testicular cancer, and this risk is not removed by surgical repositioning. Cryptorchidism in female pseudohermaphrodites has been previously discussed.

Diagnosis

Physical examination. Descent can be completed after birth during the first year of life, particularly in premature infants. Cryptorchidism must be distinguished from normal testis retraction reflexes on examination.

Treatment

Surgical repositioning should be undertaken before spermatogenesis is compromised. Removal of a nonfunctional testis reduces risk for malignancy.

Male Genital Inflammation

Inflammation of the male reproductive tract is nearly always related to extension of local or systemic infection through the blood or lymph supply, or by retrograde passage along the vas deferens.

Epididymitis

Chlamydia, gonorrhea, and tuberculosis are important infections that have a predilection for the epididymis. In addition, any urinary tract infection can extend to the epididymis and eventually may also cause orchitis.

Signs & Symptoms

Classically, patients present with unilateral testicular pain, swelling, tenderness, and fever. A concomitant urethritis may also be present.

Pathology

Inflammation is due to a nonspecific neutrophil and lymphocyte response, in the case of sexually transmitted pathogens, and a typical granulomatous response in epididymal tuberculosis.

Diagnosis

Urethral swabs and urine culture may reveal the organism causing the epididymitis. A purified protein derivative (PPD) should be placed to rule out tuberculosis. Especially in young men presenting with unilateral pain, torsion (twisting of the spermatic cord) must be ruled out because ischemic damage can rapidly result. Doppler ultrasound examination or nuclear scan with labeled erythrocytes can be used to demonstrate blood flow.

Treatment

Treatment focuses on antibiotic coverage appropriate to the probable causative organisms. Lack of improvement raises suspicion for testicular cancer.

Orchitis

Viral orchitis is the leading cause of acquired testicular failure in adult men, and mumps should always be considered as a cause of testicular inflammation. The other classically important infection with a predilection for the testes is syphilis.

Signs & Symptoms

Unilateral or bilateral pain and swelling of the testes usually occurs about 1 week after the parotitis of mumps and is accompanied by systemic viral symptoms.

Pathology

Viral orchitis is a rare finding in prepubertal males who develop mumps but occurs in about one-fourth of postpubertal cases. The inflammation usually remains interstitial and usually does not permanently disturb testicular function. However, direct viral involvement of the seminiferous tubules, or ischemia from excess pressure related to swelling, can lead to lasting damage. The syphilitic response is typical of that seen in other areas, with gummas, inflammation, and obliterative endarteritis.

Diagnosis

A diagnosis of mumps is generally made clinically, although saliva cultures and antibody titers can be confirmatory. Syphilis is diagnosed by the presence of an antibody reaction.

Treatment

There is no antiviral medicine that is active against mumps, so treatment of orchitis focuses on pain control and the use of ice and corticosteroids to limit inflammation. Syphilis normally responds well to penicillin.

Gynecologic Disorders

Vulvovaginitis

Mild inflammation and infection of the vulva and vagina is typically caused by one of three organisms: *Candida*, *Trichomonas vaginalis*, and *Gardnerella*. More severe infections are caused by *Chlamydia* and other sexually transmitted diseases. Atrophic vaginitis has been previously discussed.

Signs & Symptoms

Patients may experience itching and burning with malodorous discharge, depending on the cause. Candidal infections are accompanied by a thick, white discharge, and trichomonal infections are accompanied by an odorous, greenish gray, frothy discharge. *Gardnerella* infections (also known as bacterial vaginosis) cause a grayish, malodorous discharge that is not as profuse as in trichomonal infections.

Pathology

Vaginal smears are treated with KOH and normal saline. Candidal infections show budding yeast with pseudohyphae. Trichomonal infections show motile flagellated organisms. *Gardnerella* infections show "clue cells," which are vaginal epithelial cells coated with coccobacilli.

Diagnosis

History and vaginal smears.

Treatment

Candida is treated with topical antifungals, such as clotrimazole. Both *Trichomonas* and *Gardnerella* are treated with metronidazole. Sexual partners should be treated as well to prevent reinfection.

Pelvic Inflammatory Disease

Pelvic inflammatory disease (PID), also known as *acute salpingitis*, is caused by ascending infection of the upper reproductive tract. Typically, microorganisms advance from the vagina and cervix to the uterus, fallopian tubes, and ovaries.

Signs & Symptoms

Severe cervical motion tenderness, lower abdominal pain, and vaginal discharge.

Pathology

The most common causative organisms are sexually transmitted, and include *Neisseria gonorrhoeae* and *Chlamydia trachomatis*. Risk factors for the development of PID include multiple sexual partners, sexually transmitted diseases, and intrauterine device (IUD) use. Complications include chronic salpingitis, abscess formation, ectopic pregnancy, and infertility.

Diagnosis

Made by history and cultures but should always include a pregnancy test to rule out ectopic pregnancy. Laparoscopy is sometimes needed to differentiate PID from appendicitis, a ruptured ovarian cyst, or an ovarian torsion.

Treatment

Early and aggressive antibiotic administration is the mainstay of therapy. Depending on the degree of illness, it may necessitate hospitalization for intravenous antibiotics.

Mastitis and Breast Abscesses

Mastitis and breast abscesses occur in nursing mothers, usually after the second or third week postpartum. Cracks or fissures develop in the nipple during nursing and may act as the source of entry for organisms, usually from the skin flora. Patients experience localized pain and redness and are best treated with antibiotics and local heat application. During the infection, patients can continue feeding with breast milk; however, the milk should be pumped manually rather than breast-feeding directly.

Uterine Prolapse

Uterine prolapse refers to a weakening of support of the uterus, which leads to its descent into the vagina. Most commonly, this occurs as a delayed result of stretching during childbirth.

Signs & Symptoms

Patients typically note a vaginal mass. In severe cases, the prolapse can lead to pain or discomfort, usually most prominent when the patient is walking or sitting.

Pathology

Weakness in the transverse cervical and uterosacral ligaments is the chief cause of uterine prolapse. The levator musculature and perineal body can help to compensate, so any damage to or weakness in these structures can contribute to prolapse.

Diagnosis

History and pelvic examination.

Treatment

A surgical solution must be tailored to the reproductive desires of the woman and can range from hysterectomy with partial obliteration of the vagina to plication of the suspensory ligaments. An inflatable vaginal counter-pressure device is available for women who do not desire surgery, or in whom surgery is contraindicated.

Urinary Incontinence

Urinary incontinence is the involuntary loss of urine. Traditionally, intermittent incontinence has been divided into three main categories: urge incontinence, overflow incontinence, and stress incontinence. **Urge incontinence** is caused by a hyperreflexive bladder with or without diminished sphincter tone. **Overflow incontinence** results from prolonged urinary retention. **Stress incontinence** is caused by laxity of the muscles making up the pelvic floor. Because it is seen mainly in multiparous women, stress incontinence is the focus of discussion.

Signs & Symptoms

Stress incontinence can usually be recognized by a history of urine loss with activities that increase intra-abdominal pressure, such as coughing, laughing, or lifting. These symptoms are more severe in upright than in supine positions.

Pathology

Pregnancy and childbirth can cause damage to the normally strong suspensory ligaments that hold the urethra in close proximity to the pubis, increasing urethral resistance. Nevertheless, these changes are often not experienced until aging causes a weakening of the pelvic floor, and the urethra drops with relation to the pubis.

Diagnosis

Urinalysis should always be performed because subclinical urinary tract infection can be an easily treatable source of incontinence, especially in the elderly. The physician can perform a stress test, where the patient is observed while coughing with a full bladder, but the diagnosis can often be made on history.

Treatment

Medical treatment focuses on improving sphincter tone with the use of α-adrenergic agonists. Estrogen replacement has also been shown to counteract atrophic changes. Anatomic resistance can be improved through the use of physical therapy, where the patient learns exercises to strengthen the pelvic diaphragm (Kegel exercises). Surgery also focuses on increasing anatomic resistance by stabilizing the urethra.

Menstrual Disorders

Definition of Terms

- **Hypermenorrhea** or **menorrhagia**: These terms are synonymous and refer to regular cyclic menses characterized by abnormally heavy bleeding, either due to increased flow or duration. This can be a sign of many abnormalities, including inadequate progesterone levels, clotting disorders, inflammation, and neoplasms.

- **Hypomenorrhea**: Diminished menstrual flow during regular menses. Can include vaginal spotting.

- **Metrorrhagia**: Also known commonly as *breakthrough bleeding*, it is bleeding or spotting that occurs at midcycle (between normal menses). Usually due to inadequate midcycle estrogen. This is a common problem with low-dose oral contraceptives.

- **Menometrorrhagia**: Unusually heavy bleeding that occurs irregularly between menses.

- **Oligomenorrhea**: Infrequent menstruation that tends to involve sparse flow.

- **Polymenorrhea**: Menstrual bleeding more often than every 21 days.

Dysmenorrhea

Dysmenorrhea is pain associated with menses. In younger women the pain may or may not be associated with other pathologic findings, but in older women a secondary cause usually exists. Secondary causes of dysmenorrhea include PID, endometriosis, submucosal myoma, IUD use, and cervical stenosis.

Signs & Symptoms

The pain is usually in the lower midline of the abdomen and often occurs in conjunction with cramping, headache, nausea, diarrhea, and flushing. It may last for 1 or more days in the time leading up to or during menses.

Pathology

The pain of primary dysmenorrhea is produced by constriction and anoxia in the uterus due to cramping initiated by prostaglandins.

Diagnosis

Contrast imaging studies or laparoscopy are sometimes necessary to rule out other causes and make this diagnosis. However, primary dysmenorrhea is a relatively common disorder, and in a younger woman with no other findings, a trial of nonsteroidal anti-inflammatory drugs (NSAIDs) can help to make the diagnosis.

Treatment

NSAIDs are useful both for their analgesic and anti-inflammatory activity. The treatments for PID and endometriosis are discussed separately.

Table 15-4. Differential diagnosis of amenorrhea

Hormonal state	Differential diagnosis
Low estrogen	Reversible insults, such as illness, anorexia, stress, and strenuous exercise
Low FSH (problem is central)	Hypothalamic or pituitary tumors
	Congenital GnRH deficiency (primary only)
Low estrogen	Turner's syndrome (primary)
High FSH (ovarian failure)	Female pseudohermaphrodism (primary)
	Premature menopause (secondary)
High androgen (adrenals vs. ovaries)	Adrenal tumor or hyperplasia
	Ovarian tumor
	Polycystic ovary syndrome
	Anabolic steroids
High prolactin	Prolactinoma
	Breast-feeding
	Drugs (dopamine inhibiting or depleting)
	Hypothyroidism

FSH = follicle-stimulating hormone; GnRH = gonadotropin-releasing hormone.

Amenorrhea

Amenorrhea is divided into two main categories: **primary amenorrhea**—a lack of menses onset by age 16, and **secondary amenorrhea**—the absence of menses for 3 consecutive months after menarche. There is a great deal of etiologic overlap between the two categories, and most of the causes can be understood in terms of the disturbances they cause in the endocrine system (Table 15-4).

Pregnancy must always be considered as a cause of both primary and secondary amenorrhea. Administration of progestin is often used as a diagnostic test to see if the uterus is capable of responding normally on progestin withdrawal.

Infertility

Infertility is defined as failure to conceive after 1 year of unprotected intercourse. About 1 in 5 couples experience infertility. Approximately 40% of cases are due to "male factors," such as abnormal sperm function or the presence of a varicocele. Fifty percent of cases are due to "female factors," with about 30% due to tubal dysfunction, 15% due to ovarian dysfunction, and the remaining 5% due to cervical factors. About 10% of cases are unexplained.

The first level of evaluation of infertile couples includes semen analysis, ovulation studies, and assessment of tubal function. Semen analysis involves testing for sperm count, motility, and morphology. Normal sperm count is greater than 20 million per ml. Ovulation studies include looking for signs of normal ovulation (e.g., regular menses and basal body temperature changes) as well as measurement of an elevated progesterone during the luteal cycle. Tubal function is assessed by a contrast imaging study (hysterosalpingogram) and laparoscopy to assess patency of the tubes and look for pelvic adhesions.

The second phase of evaluation searches for cervical factors, luteal phase problems, and special sperm tests. Cervical factors are tested by the postcoital test, in which the woman's midcycle cervical mucus is tested 12 hours after intercourse for quality and quantity of surviving sperm.

Luteal phase insufficiency is treated with clomiphene citrate to trigger ovulation. Sperm are tested by the hamster egg penetration assay, in which the sperm are mixed with hamster eggs in which the zona pellucida has been removed, and the ability to fertilize is evaluated.

Treatment includes in vitro fertilization, surgical correction, and surrogacy, if the above factors cannot be easily corrected.

Polycystic Ovary Syndrome

Polycystic ovary syndrome is characterized by anovulation in the presence of steadily high levels of estrogen, LH, and androgen. This hormonal milieu can support the development of follicles, which become cysts because they are not ovulated. This syndrome affects 2–5% of women of reproductive age.

Signs & Symptoms

Infertility and hirsutism are present, and amenorrhea or abnormal menses are common. Forty percent of patients with this syndrome are obese.

Pathology

Although the primary lesion leading to this syndrome is unknown, there are clues as to contributing factors. Elevated levels of androgen from adrenal hyperplasia or tumors are known to cause this syndrome. Presumably, obesity exacerbates this syndrome because androgens are converted to estrone in the fat. Estrone is believed to suppress FSH, with a relative increase in LH leading to constant ovarian stimulation. Persistently elevated estrogen levels place these patients at higher risk for cancer.

Diagnosis

Made chiefly on the basis of history and hormone levels, but transvaginal ultrasound is also diagnostic.

Treatment

If fertility is desired, ovulation can be induced with clomiphene. Otherwise, oral contraceptives can be used to restore normal cycling.

Endometriosis

Endometriosis is the presence of endometrial tissue in places outside the uterus. The most common sites for implantation of endometrial tissue are the cul-de-sacs, ovaries, and fallopian tubes. However, sites as distant as the lung and kidney have been documented.

Signs & Symptoms

Notable mostly for an aching pain that begins up to a week before the onset of menses and becomes worse until menstrual flow occurs. It can also be a cause of infertility. There may be signs specific to the site involved (e.g., bloody stools from gastrointestinal involvement).

Pathology

Although the mechanism is unclear, possibilities include retrograde menstruation, spontaneous metaplasia, and vascular or lymphatic dissemination.

Diagnosis

Definitive diagnosis requires the documentation of endometrial glands and stroma in the tissue at the site under suspicion. Although the differential diagnosis for lower abdominal pain is broad, usually only PID and endometriosis consistently produce pain associated with menses.

Treatment

A variety of 6- to 9-month hormonal regimens, often including GnRH analogues and oral contraceptives, are used with the goal of inhibiting ovulation and lowering overall hormone levels. During this time it is hoped that the endometrial implants will recede. If unsuccessful, surgical removal can be performed. In women who still desire fertility, this involves systematic removal of the ectopic tissue, now often with laser surgery. Otherwise, hysterectomy with removal of the ovaries and fallopian tubes is usually performed.

Sexual Dysfunction

This topic encompasses diverse etiologies, including physical and psychological causes. A loss of sexual function usually signals physical (versus mental) illness or a side effect of treatment. Although organic causes of female sexual dysfunction have not been as extensively researched, most of the causes apply to both males and females. Systemic illness and musculoskeletal pain (e.g., arthritis) often play an overlooked role.

- **Neurologic**: Any pathology that leads to decreased sensory input can contribute to sexual dysfunction. The most common neurologic cause of sexual dysfunction is diabetic neuropathy.

- **Vascular**: The inability to engorge erectile tissues with blood stems from arterial insufficiency, with atherosclerosis being a common cause. Inability to maintain engorgement is usually caused by venous insufficiency, though it may also be caused by arterial steal to supply other tissues.

- **Pharmacologic**: The long list of drugs that cause male impotence includes such broad categories as hypertensive medications (especially β-blockers and diuretics), antihistamines, psychiatric medications (especially selective serotonin-reuptake inhibitors), and drugs of abuse (especially alcohol and nicotine).

- **Endocrine**: In both males and females testosterone levels are critical to the maintenance of libido. Thyroid and pituitary dysfunction may also be related.

- **Genital factors**: Local infections, atrophic vaginitis, endometriosis, and penile scarring (Peyronie's disease) can be causes.

- **Trauma**: Damage to the local nervous system or vascular supply, especially as a result of surgery, is a frequent cause. In males, retrograde ejaculation (ejaculation into the bladder) can be caused by damage to the bladder neck, particularly during prostate surgery.

- **Psychiatric**: Low self-esteem, depression, and anxiety are all common causes of sexual dysfunction. Interpersonal difficulties with sexual partners can also play a role. A history of abuse may be common in such circumstances. Of particular note in females is **vaginismus**, a condition in which the pubococcygeal muscles spasm on contact, making penetration painful. This disorder can be treated by stepwise desensitization. In males, a psychogenic etiology is suspected if the patient experiences normal early-morning erections during sleep.

Treatment

Treatment is specific to the etiology. Lack of libido responds to testosterone replacement. Changing medications often restores sexual function. In males, if the vascular supply is intact (as in the case of neuropathy), injection of prostaglandins into the penis can lead to erection. If the vascular supply is disrupted, many males can achieve a satisfactory erection using a vacuum constriction device or an implanted prosthesis. Vascular reconstructive surgery is also an option.

Neoplastic Diseases

Leiomyoma

Also known as **fibroids**, leiomyomata are benign uterine neoplasms composed of smooth muscle. They are the most common tumors seen in women. Leiomyomas may be estrogen-sensitive because they are most commonly seen during the reproductive years and tend to shrink during menopause. However, contraceptive pills appear to have no effect on fibroid size.

Signs & Symptoms

Patients may be asymptomatic or experience pain, bleeding, or urinary disorders caused by pressure.

Pathology

Grossly, leiomyomas are firm, white, circumscribed nodules. They are found in three locations: subserosal, intramural, and submucosal. Submucosal fibroids compose only about 10% of leiomyomata but are the most symptomatic.

Diagnosis

Ultrasound.

Treatment

Medical treatments include GnRH analogues and mifepristone (RU-486), both of which have been found to shrink fibroids. If bleeding or pain is severe, surgical removal of the tumor (myomectomy) or hysterectomy may be indicated.

Cervical Cancer

Cervical cancer is associated with **human papillomavirus** (HPV) subtypes 16 and 18, which are sexually transmitted. Risk factors for the development of cervical cancer include multiple partners, early age at first intercourse, and smoking. More than 75% are squamous cell carcinomas. The remaining cases are adenocarcinoma and are associated with mothers who used **diethylstilbestrol** during pregnancy.

Signs & Symptoms

Patients may be asymptomatic or may experience breakthrough or postcoital bleeding.

Pathology

Grossly, the cervical lesion may be fungating or ulcerative. Microscopically, cells are evaluated both for precancerous dysplasia and evidence of invasive disease. The classification system of precancerous dysplasia is known as the **cervical intraepithelial neoplasia** (CIN) system. Atypia in the superficial cell layers is known as **koilocytosis** and constitutes stage CIN I. Stage CIN II consists of atypia in both superficial and basal cell layers, and stage CIN III is atypia throughout with minimal maturation. CIN III is carcinoma in situ and is the same as stage 0 invasive carcinoma (Fig. 15-11).

Diagnosis

Asymptomatic patients are usually diagnosed by abnormal Papanicolaou (Pap) smear. Abnormal Pap smears or symptomatic patients receive colposcopy and biopsy, and excision if necessary.

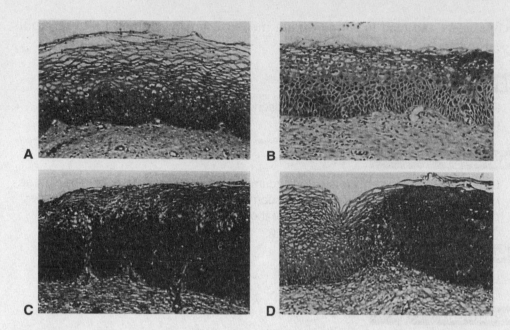

Fig. 15-11. Cervical intraepithelial neoplasia (CIN). **A.** Normal ectocervix. **B.** Moderate dysplasia—CIN II. **C.** Severe dysplasia—CIN III. **D.** Carcinoma in situ—CIN III. (Reprinted with permission from P Wheater, G Burkitt, A Stevens, J Lowe. *Basic Histopathology. A Colour Atlas and Text* [2nd ed]. Edinburgh: Churchill Livingstone, 1991;177.)

Treatment

Early detection through screening has led to excellent survival times. Stage 0 (carcinoma in situ) has a 100% cure rate, with stage I (confined to cervix) rates at 85–90%. Stage IV (disseminated disease) has a 10–15% survival rate.

Endometrial Carcinoma

Adenocarcinoma of the endometrium is the second most common cancer of the female genital tract. It is most often seen in postmenopausal women. Risk factors include nulliparity, diabetes, obesity, polycystic ovary syndrome, and prolonged use of unopposed estrogen.

Signs & Symptoms

Abnormal bleeding is usually the presenting symptom. Such bleeding in a postmenopausal female is a particularly ominous sign. In some cases, blockage of the cervix limits bleeding but predisposes to infection of the uterus and fallopian tubes.

Pathology

The majority of carcinomas are adenocarcinomas. Both stage and grade are important for prognosis.

Diagnosis

Endometrial carcinomas are occasionally diagnosed by Pap smear, but the Pap smear is not designed to be specific for this cancer. Endometrial biopsy is the gold standard of diagnosis.

Treatment

Treatment involves hysterectomy, with radiotherapy unless the adenocarcinoma is low grade and confined to the uterine corpus. Prognosis for metastasis outside of the true pelvis is poor, with 5-year survival rates of about 5%.

Vulvar Carcinoma

Carcinoma of the vulva is squamous in origin. It shares many similarities with cervical cancer, including an association with HPV infections and a classification system for vulvar intraepithelial neoplasia (VIN). Carcinoma is associated with prolonged irritation and genital warts caused by HPV types 16, 18, and 31.

Signs & Symptoms

Genital warts, pruritus, and bloody discharge are all early signs. Later lesions may appear as a mass or ulceration.

Pathology

VIN I represents hyperplasia, VIN II represents dysplasia, and VIN III is carcinoma in situ. If the basement membrane has been compromised, it is important to distinguish microinvasive carcinoma (stage Ia) from later stages because it can be treated less radically.

Diagnosis

Biopsy is essential for diagnosis. An abscess of the Bartholin's gland is a frequent cause of a tender vulvar mass not associated with cancer.

Treatment

For carcinoma in situ and microinvasive carcinoma, local removal is usually sufficient. Later stages require radical vulvectomy with lymph node dissection.

Ovarian Cancers

Because of the variety of tissues in the ovary, several types of neoplasms can arise. Although the majority of ovarian tumors prove to be benign, ovarian cancer is the fourth leading cause of cancer death among women. This is primarily attributable to the tendency of ovarian cancers to remain asymptomatic until significant growth has occurred. Table 15-5 shows a simple classification scheme for some ovarian tumors.

Signs & Symptoms

Abdominal pain, bloating, ascites, and palpable mass are symptoms of advanced disease.

Pathology

Specific cell type is determined by tissue examination and classified as benign, having low malignant potential, or malignant. Ovarian cancer has a familial association, with a 5% lifetime risk in women with an affected first-degree relative. A familial breast cancer–ovarian syndrome exists, and specific genetic mutations are being discovered in such families.

Table 15-5. Classification of ovarian cancers

Type	Specific neoplasms	Remarks
Surface epithelial	Serous Mucinous Endometrioid	Accounts for 75% of ovarian neoplasms but 95% of those leading to malignancy
Germ cell neoplasms	Cystic teratomas are the only common neoplasms	15–20% of ovarian neoplasms but only 2–4% of malignancies; occurs mostly in young women
Sex cord gonadal stromal	Granulosa cell Thecal cell Sertoli or Leydig cell Lipid cell	5–10% of ovarian neoplasms but 1–3% of malignancies

Diagnosis

Ideally, diagnosis is made early by palpation of an ovarian mass on routine pelvic examination. An elevated level of CA-125 is a tumor marker present in up to 80% of patients with epithelial ovarian cancer.

Treatment

Benign neoplasms involve removal of the tumor only or the entire affected ovary. Malignant neoplasms are usually treated with hysterectomy, bilateral oophorectomy, and chemotherapy.

Testicular Cancer

Although testicular cancer is uncommon, it is the most common neoplasm in men between 15 and 35 years of age. Testicular tumors are divided into seminomas and nonseminomatous germ cell tumors (NSGCTs).

Signs & Symptoms

Patients may note a testicular mass or have a sense of heaviness. About 10% of patients have pain at the time of presentation as a result of intratesticular hemorrhage.

Pathology

Histologic classification of the tumor is important for treatment. The division between seminomas and NSGCT is aided by serum tumor markers. LDH is elevated in both types of cancer, but α-fetoprotein and hCG are more elevated in NSGCT.

Diagnosis

Ultrasound may aid in diagnosis, but unilateral orchiectomy is ultimately done to make the tissue diagnosis.

Treatment

Treatment has traditionally involved orchiectomy and chemotherapy. However, more conservative approaches in low-grade tumors now involve using orchiectomy alone and following serial tumor marker levels to diagnose recurrence.

Table 15-6. Differential diagnosis of a breast mass

Diseases	Histology	Remarks
Benign diseases with little increased risk of breast cancer	Fibrocystic change (believed to be caused by fluctuating estrogen levels)	Microscopic findings include cysts, papillomatosis, adenosis, and ductal epithelial hyperplasia
Benign diseases with increased risk for breast cancer	Fibroadenoma	Occurs as a firm discrete nodule in younger women; generally treated by excision
Carcinoma in situ	Ductal carcinoma in situ (confers increased risk for ipsilateral carcinoma)	Epithelial transformation that has not violated histologic boundaries; treatment is excision and observation
	Lobular carcinoma in situ (confers increased risk for bilateral carcinoma)	
Invasive carcinoma	Ductal carcinoma (76%) Lobular carcinoma (14%) Mucinous carcinoma (2%) Medullary carcinoma (2%) Tubular or cribriform (3%)	The most important predictors of prognosis are size, grade, and axillary node involvement Estrogen and progesterone receptor status also significant
Unrelated lesions	Breast abscess Fat necrosis	Abscess usually caused by *Staphylococcus aureus* during lactation Fat necrosis result of trauma

Breast Carcinoma

Breast carcinoma is the most common malignant neoplasm in females, with the estimated lifetime risk now as high as 11%. Risk factors for developing breast cancer include early menarche, late menopause, late childbearing, family history, and exposure to radiation. Oral contraceptives and HRT are controversial as risk factors. Environmental factors are suspected because rates of breast cancer vary significantly across cultures.

Signs & Symptoms

Masses may or may not be painful (Table 15-6). **Paget's disease** of the breast is an uncommon type of lobular carcinoma that can cause nipple contraction and an eczematoid skin reaction known as "peau d'orange" (orange-peel texture). Breast cancer can produce warmth and redness in the overlying skin. (This is particularly true of cancers that arise during pregnancy.)

Pathology

Breast cancer spreads initially by local infiltration. Lymphatic spread is mainly to axillary lymph nodes but can involve the internal mammary chain. Hematogenous spread is mainly to the lungs and liver but can also involve bone, pleura, adrenals, ovaries, and brain.

Diagnosis

Mammographic screening is designed to diagnose clinically inapparent malignancies early. Ultrasound can be used to distinguish cysts from solid masses. Other diagnostic tools involve fine-needle aspiration, which has the advantage of allowing a diagnosis to be made before surgery. However, the test has a high false-negative rate. Open breast biopsy is the most sensitive diagnostic tool.

Treatment

Initially breast cancer was treated with radical mastectomy, which consisted of removal of the entire breast, the pectoralis major and minor, and the axillary contents. It was later found that similar cure rates were achieved leaving the muscle intact, and this procedure, known as the *modified radical mastectomy*, became the standard. Studies are now demonstrating that local excision of small primary tumors ("lumpectomy"), followed by radiation therapy, can achieve similar results. Because it is now clear that breast cancer is often a systemic disease at the time of presentation, adjuvant chemotherapy is now widely used. In tumors that test positive for estrogen receptors, therapy with tamoxifen (an antiestrogen) is proving to be beneficial. This is especially true in the elderly, who often cannot tolerate aggressive systemic chemotherapy.

Obstetric Problems

Multiple Gestation

Multiple gestation, defined as the presence of two or more fetuses, is viewed correctly as a complication of pregnancy because it confers increased maternal and fetal risk of morbidity and mortality. The frequency of twinning is approximately 1 in 90 in North America, but there is considerable variability throughout the world based on race, hereditary factors, maternal age, maternal parity, and the use of fertility drugs. The zygosity of multiple gestations reveals the mechanism responsible for the twinning, as well as defining some different risks. **Monozygotic** (identical) twins result from the division of a fertilized egg at various stages of embryogenesis. Depending on the stage, the two fetuses may share an amniotic and chorionic sac, an amniotic sac only, or neither. Conjoined twins are formed when the division takes place 2 or more weeks after fertilization. **Dizygotic** (fraternal) twins result when more than one fertilized egg develops. This always leads to two amnions, and two chorions, and can also lead to different sexes.

Abortion

Abortion is often thought of in two categories. **Spontaneous abortion** is known in lay terms as "miscarriage" and is an unexpected loss of a pregnancy before the fetus can survive outside of the mother. To avoid confusion, therapeutic or **elective abortions** (as they are known in lay terms) are often referred to as a termination of pregnancy by the medical community. Such terminations may be performed by pharmacologic, surgical, or other mechanical means, often involving cervical dilatation and premature induction of labor.

The incidence of spontaneous abortions is unknown and difficult to study, but is estimated to be 10–15%. There are multiple etiologies, the most common being fetal chromosome anomalies. Most of these arise from sporadic events and are not inherited. Maternal infection, environmental exposure, and systemic disease can all contribute to spontaneous abortion. Abnormal uterine and cervical anatomy may also be important. Because the fetus represents foreign tissue in the mother, the maternal immune system must be suppressed against nonself to maintain pregnancy. Although incompletely understood, it is now felt that lack of such suppression can lead to spontaneous abortion.

Another possible cause of spontaneous abortion is erythrocyte antigen incompatibility between mother and fetus. The prototype for this situation is an Rh-negative mother who is sensitized and makes antibody against the Rh antigen on the erythrocytes of an Rh-positive fetus. To identify this possible problem, Rh-negative mothers are screened to see if they have been sensitized and are producing Rh antibody. At-risk pregnancies are closely monitored by serial testing of the amniotic fluid for evidence of fetal hemolysis (**erythroblastosis fetalis**). In an attempt to prevent sensitizations, Rh-negative mothers are given IgG antibody against Rh factor (RhoGAM) after labor and delivery. The RhoGAM clears any fetal erythrocytes that spill into the maternal circulation so that sensitization does not take place.

Ectopic Pregnancy

Ectopic pregnancy refers to implantation of a gestation anywhere but the endometrial cavity of the uterus. About 98% of the time, such pregnancies are in the fallopian tubes and presumably occur when transport of the ovum is impaired. The chief risk factors for such an implantation are a history of PID (which accounts for at least half of all ectopic pregnancies), previous surgery of the fallopian tubes, and prolonged IUD use.

Because the fallopian tube is prone to rupture, which can lead to severe intra-abdominal blood loss, it is important that this diagnosis be considered in any patient of reproductive age presenting with abdominal pain. Other supporting symptoms include amenorrhea, although this is unreliable because bleeding can occur as a result of the ectopic pregnancy or as a result of inadequate hCG production from the improperly implanted gestation. In fact, measurement of serial hCG, which shows sluggish increases, is an important diagnostic tool for recognizing an ectopic pregnancy. For the same reason, a low level of progesterone in the setting of a positive hCG is also suspicious. Ultrasound and laparoscopy are often used to confirm the diagnosis. Treatment can involve removal of the involved portion of the fallopian tube by open surgery or laparoscopy. Alternatively, methotrexate (a folic acid inhibitor) can be used to halt the growth of the trophoblast by inhibiting DNA synthesis. The ectopic pregnancy is then resorbed.

Third-Trimester Bleeding

There are three major sources of bleeding that occur late in pregnancy. **Placenta previa** is partial or complete blockage of the internal cervical os by the placenta. Unless blood loss is severe, management involves bed rest until the fetus is deemed mature enough for delivery. **Abruptio placentae** describes a premature separation of the placenta from the uterine wall. This is a more serious complication, which demands aggressive monitoring of fetus and mother, and often leads to prompt delivery. The most grave source of bleeding is **uterine rupture**, which can occur before or during labor, usually in the setting of a previously weakened uterus. Rapid intervention with surgical closure or hysterectomy is required.

Preeclampsia and Eclampsia

Preeclampsia describes a condition of pregnancy defined by the following triad of symptoms: **increased blood pressure**, **proteinuria**, and **edema**. A diagnosis of eclampsia includes these findings plus seizures. Preeclampsia is a relatively common condition (up to 7% of pregnancies) that can occur from about the twentieth week through the end of pregnancy. The cause is not known, though the symptoms reverse rapidly after delivery. Treatments to date have been ineffective. If the symptoms are mild or moderate, bed rest is used until the fetus is believed to have matured to a fully viable state. Severe preeclamptic symptoms or the onset of eclampsia require immediate delivery once the mother has stabilized from seizure.

Gestational Diabetes

The role of placentally derived human chorionic somatomammotropin in reducing maternal insulin sensitivity has already been discussed. Increased levels of estrogen and progesterone have similar functions. Glucose intolerance that first manifests itself during this state is called *gestational diabetes*. This condition is screened for with a **glucose tolerance test** during pregnancy because hyperglycemia is known to create maternal and fetal problems. Elevated blood sugars in the first trimester can lead to congenital anomalies. In addition, persistently elevated glucose levels can lead to large-for–gestational age babies, which can lead to prematurity or present a problem for vaginal delivery. Finally, the high levels of circulating insulin in the mother (and therefore the baby) may lead to a hypoglycemic crisis in the baby after delivery.

Cord Compression

Cord compression is either a partial or complete constriction of the umbilical cord. Typically this happens during labor or delivery, and it may occur regularly with uterine contractions. The central blood pressure of the fetus raises acutely, causing a reflex bradycardia. Therefore the onset and severity of the compression is judged by a deceleration of the fetal heart rate.

Postpartum Hemorrhage

Postpartum hemorrhage is a major cause of maternal morbidity. The leading cause of bleeding in the time immediately after parturition is **uterine atony**. This is a failure of the uterus to contract after separation of the placenta, leading to continued blood loss through the arterioles that supplied the placenta. In such cases, an infusion of oxytocin can stimulate contraction to physiologically clamp off bleeding vessels. Birth trauma is the next most common cause of postpartum hemorrhage, followed by incomplete delivery of the placenta.

Postpartum Disseminated Intravascular Coagulation and Sepsis

Infection is another leading postpartum complication. In pregnant and nonpregnant women, the vagina contains many organisms as part of the normal flora, including potential pathogens. The overgrowth of these bacteria is held in check by the relatively acidic local environment of the vagina. In contrast, the uterus has no normal bacterial flora. After parturition, the amniotic fluid alkalinizes the vagina, thus promoting bacterial growth. Furthermore, the trauma of birth can allow introduction of these bacteria into the uterus, where the rich endometrium provides an excellent growth medium (endometritis). The open communication of the blood supply to the uterus provides a portal of entry for the bacteria, leading to bacteremia and sepsis.

Overwhelming sepsis can be a potent stimulus to the coagulation pathway. Also, the release of tissue factors into the circulation during delivery may stimulate coagulation. In such cases, factors that are supposed to act locally (e.g., thrombin) begin to be systemically activated, leading to disseminated intravascular coagulation (DIC). The clotting factors and platelets are used faster than they can be produced, which leads to increased bleeding time. Although transfusions can be used to replace these blood products, treatment requires resolution of the underlying condition.

Postpartum Depression

Most women describe a mild dysphoria within the first 6 months of the birth of a child. This phenomenon is often called the "postpartum blues" and is thought to be due to hormonal factors, with varying contribution from emotional issues. With support and reassurance, these feelings may resolve without worsening. If more severe symptoms of depression develop, the patient should be treated for clinical depression (discussed in chapter 18).

Fetal Prematurity

Labor beginning before the thirty-seventh week of pregnancy is deemed to be premature. This is a clinically significant definition because fetal prematurity is implicated in 85% of fetal illness and death. Common risk factors for the onset of premature labor include premature rupture of the extraembryonic membranes, urinary tract infections, pharmacologic effects (including drugs of abuse), multiple gestation, prior surgery or trauma to the abdomen or uterus, and a past history of premature delivery.

In some cases, early recognition of contractions followed by bed rest can reverse the onset of labor. If medical treatment becomes necessary, magnesium sulfate administered intravenously is often effective in halting contractions. β-Adrenergic agonists are also effective because the smooth muscle of the uterus is under sympathetic control.

In some cases of premature labor (as well as maternal or fetal illness) an assessment of the fetal maturity is indicated because timely delivery is desirable. The ability of the neonate to survive outside the mother hinges on lung development. More specifically, the development of **surfactant**, which lowers the surface resistance to lung inflation, is a critical step toward independent oxygenation. Traditionally, the amniotic fluid has been sampled to test levels of **lecithin** and **sphingomyelin**, two components of surfactant. An increasing ratio of lecithin to sphingomyelin indicates maturing lungs. Now additional components of surfactant that are believed to be markers of maturity have been identified. Use of corticosteroids administered before or after delivery is under investigation as a means to promote faster development of the lungs. Externally administered surfactant is also being investigated.

Lactation Problems

Mothers are encouraged to breast-feed largely because the breast milk contains maternal antibodies that transfer passive immunity to the baby. Even if prolonged breast-feeding is not planned, there is benefit to some initial breast-feeding because colostrum, the secretion of the breasts for 3–6 days after delivery, is particularly rich in nutrients. A lack of milk production can be caused by several factors, including inadequate prolactin or oxytocin or an overabundance of estrogen or progesterone. Other hormones, such as cortisol, also play a role, perhaps explaining why stress can limit milk production. In addition, breast-feeding can be limited by a mother's need to take medications that are secreted in breast milk and can adversely affect the baby.

The nutritional requirements of the mother while breast-feeding are extensive. In particular, iron, vitamin B_{12}, and calcium depletion is of concern, and it is suggested that new mothers continue their prenatal vitamin regimen.

Postcoital Contraception and Abortifacients

See Table 15-7 for a comparison of contraceptive methods.

Up to 99% of pregnancies can be prevented with postcoital administration of estrogen or estrogen-progesterone in higher doses than are given in oral contraceptive regimens. Drawbacks of this protocol are frequent nausea and teratogenicity if pregnancy is not prevented.

RU-486, a competitive inhibitor at the progesterone receptor, is also effective as a single dose within 72 hours of coitus. When it is followed by an oral or vaginal prostaglandin, it results in termination of up to 95% of pregnancies less than 7 weeks. Adverse effects include vomiting, diarrhea, and pain, with up to 5% of patients having vaginal bleeding that requires intervention. RU-486 is not currently approved for use in the United States.

Intramuscular methotrexate followed a week later by vaginal misoprostol gives similar results. In cases where these regimens fail, teratogenicity is an issue.

Fertility Drugs

The use of **clomiphene citrate** has been mentioned earlier as a treatment for infertility. It is a partial estrogen agonist and appears to act at the level of the hypothalamus and pituitary to increase FSH and LH. It often induces the ovulation of more than one ovum, and the incidence of multiple pregnancy is about 10%. Other adverse effects include mild hot flashes and occasional visual disturbances. The use of pulsed-dose GnRH to increase FSH and LH has also been discussed. The main drawback to this therapy is that it necessitates implantation of a pump. If ovulation is suppressed by high levels of prolactin (as occurs physiologically during breast-feeding), bromocriptine can be used to suppress prolactin levels. It is an ergot derivative that binds dopamine receptors in the pituitary. Bromocriptine should only be used after a prolactinoma is excluded. It can also be effective in infertility associated with polycystic ovary syndrome.

Teratogens

Teratogenesis is abnormal development of the fetus caused by exposure to a drug or a drug metabolite. Although most drugs cross the placenta and may act on the fetus, for a drug to be classified as a teratogen, it must result in a characteristic malformation or cluster of malformations of the same fetal target tissues. This relationship is dose-dependent and reflects that the drug has its teratogenic effect at a specific stage of development. Because most organogenesis takes place in the first trimester, this is the most vulnerable time period for the fetus with respect to teratogenesis, although the development of some organs, such as the CNS, continues until after birth (consider the fetal alcohol syndrome). The mechanism of most teratogens is not understood, although some relationships can be predicted (e.g., depletion of folic acid is a known cause of neural tube defects).

Anabolic Steroids

The androgenic effects of testosterone have been previously discussed. In addition, testosterone and its derivatives are known to have a trophic effect on the development of muscle mass. Anabolic steroids are compounds that have been synthesized in an attempt to exploit the trophic effects while minimizing androgenic effects. This division has not been achieved fully, and high doses of anabolic steroids lead to virilizing effects in females and cause testicular atrophy in males. Besides HRT, postulated uses for anabolic steroids include stimulation of erythropoiesis in refractory anemia and stimulation of a pubertal growth spurt. However, the androgenic side effects and concern about increased cancer risk have limited these therapeutic uses of anabolic steroids.

Table 15-7. A comparison of contraceptive methods

Type	Mechanism	Failure (per year)	Side effects	Advantages
Oral contraceptives Combination estrogen and progesterone Progesterone only (minipill)	Inhibits ovulation by pituitary suppression Decreases the likelihood of implantation by altering the endometrium and fallopian tube secretions	3%	Hypercoagulability Weight gain Depression Nausea or headache Acne Hypertension Breakthrough bleeding Contraindicated if hepatoma or gallbladder disease	Decreased risk of endometrial cancer Decreased incidence of benign breast disease Decreased menstrual flow Decreased pain with cycling
Norplant (levonorgestrel)	Subdermally implanted hormone is released slowly to thin the uterine lining and prevent implantation	0.2%	Irregular bleeding Worsens liver disease, breast cancer Requires surgical implantation and removal	Lasts up to 5 years No effort to comply Lipid reduction
Depo-Provera (medroxyprogesterone)	Progestin is only injection that blocks the LH surge, thickens the cervical mucus, and alters the endometrium to prevent implantation	0.3%	Weight gain Slight reversible bone loss Breakthrough bleeding Delayed return of fertility	Lasts 3–5 months Easier compliance
Intrauterine device	Creates an inflammatory reaction that inhibits implantation Inhibits sperm and ovum motility	<2%	Cramping Bleeding Increased PID Increased ectopic pregnancy Uterine rupture	Inexpensive Long-acting

Method	Mechanism	Failure rate	Side effects	STD protection
Male or female condom	Physically collects sperm	12%	Latex allergy	Provides the best protection from STDs
Diaphragm	Physical barrier to fertilization	18%	Increased risk of toxic shock Increased UTIs Cervical irritation Requires fitting	Reduces rates of STDs
Spermicides (nonoxynol-9)	Kills or inactivates sperm Some barrier function Lubricating	21%	Allergy	Reduces rates of STDs

LH = luteinizing hormone; PID = pelvic inflammatory disease; UTIs = urinary tract infections; STDs = sexually transmitted diseases.

CHAPTER 16

Endocrinology

Hypothalamus and Pituitary Gland

Embryology

The hypothalamus and pituitary, which sit at the base of the brain, are key players in many of the endocrine functions of the body. The hypothalamus is real brain tissue, arising from the diencephalon (which gives rise to all structures with "thalamus" in their names: epithalamus, thalamus, subthalamus, and hypothalamus).

The pituitary, on the other hand, is made up of two different origins. The posterior pituitary, or neurohypophysis, also arises from neuroectoderm — the infundibulum, to be precise. The anterior pituitary, or adenohypophysis, rises up from the oral ectoderm — known as Rathke's pouch — between weeks 4 and 6 of development. The connection between the pouch and oral cavity degenerates, but if remnants persist, they may later give rise to craniopharyngiomas.

Anatomy

The hypothalamus is connected to the pituitary gland in two ways. First, nerve fibers travel directly from the hypothalamus to the **posterior pituitary** (Fig. 16-2). The hormones **vasopressin** (antidiuretic hormone, ADH) and **oxytocin** are synthesized in these nuclei and travel down into the bloodstream of the posterior pituitary.

The anterior pituitary is connected to the hypothalamus through a portal blood supply, which allows blood to travel between two separate capillary beds before returning to the heart, like the liver portal system. The **superior hypophyseal arteries** descend on each side and divide to become a capillary network within the anterior pituitary. This blood supply carries many releasing hormones from the hypothalamus, which stimulate secretion in the anterior pituitary. These hormones include **gonadotropin-releasing hormone** (GnRH), **somatostatin**, **growth hormone–releasing hormone** (GHRH), **thyrotropin-releasing hormone** (TRH), **dopamine**, and **corticotropin-releasing hormone** (CRH). The pituitary hormones are listed in table 16-1.

One way to remember the hormones released by the anterior pituitary is to use a mnemonic based on the histological staining of the cells. "GPa" reminds you of **GH** and prolactin, which are produced in acidophilic cells. "b-FLAT" refers to FSH, LH, ACTH, and TSH, which are produced in basophilic cells. Interestingly, FSH, LH, and TSH have identical a subunits and differentiate themselves through their b subunits.

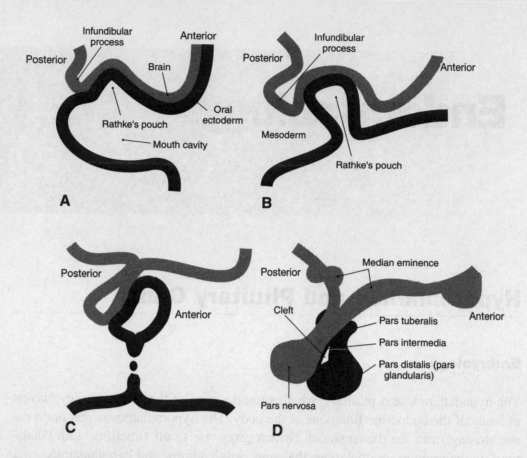

Fig. 16-1. Pituitary development. **A.** Beginning formation of Rathke's pouch and infundibular process. **B.** Neck of Rathke's pouch constricted by growth of mesoderm. **C.** Rathke's pouch pinched off. **D.** Mature form.

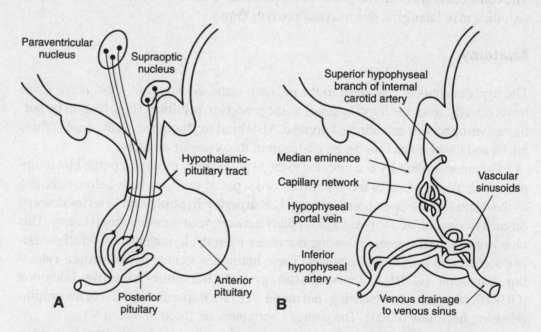

Fig. 16-2. Hypothalamic-pituitary connections. **A.** Hypothalamohypophyseal tract. **B.** Hypophyseal portal system.

Table 16-1. Pituitary hormones

Anterior pituitary	Posterior pituitary
Follicle-stimulating hormone (FSH)	Oxytocin
Luteinizing hormone (LH)	Vasopressin (antidiuretic hormone)
Growth hormone (GH)	
Thyroid-stimulating hormone (TSH)	
Prolactin	
Adrenocorticotropic hormone (ACTH)	
Melanocyte-stimulating hormone (MSH)	

Another useful fact to remember about the anterior pituitary hormones is that ACTH is derived from proopiomelanocortin, or **POMC**, a precursor which also gives rise to MSH, b-lipotropin, and b-endorphin. A disorder which causes elevated ACTH levels will also cause stimulation of melanocytes, a phenomenon which explains the darkening of crural folds seen in **Addison's disease**.

Because the pituitary sits above the optic chiasm, a pituitary tumor may cause visual disturbances.

Panhypopituitarism

If there is a deficiency of all pituitary hormones (panhypopituitarism), whether congenital or acquired (e.g., trauma), FSH and LH are usually the first to decrease, resulting in **menstrual irregularities** and **genital atrophy**. Adrenocorticotropic hormone (ACTH) and thyroid-stimulating hormone (TSH) are the next to fall, leading to **hypoadrenalism, hypotension, hyperkalemia**, and **hypothyroidism**.

Clinical scenarios in which you should suspect panhypopituitarism include patients with the above findings who have a history consistent with pituitary adenomas or brain tumors, trauma, stroke, surgery to the brain, or postpartum pituitary necrosis (**Sheehan's syndrome**). The pituitary tumor may be a component of **multiple endocrine neoplasia (type I)**, discussed later in this chapter. Treatment is with replacement hormones.

Vasopressin

Vasopressin causes the collecting tubules of the kidneysreabsorb water back from the urine (hence, its other name, antidiuretic hormone). It also acts directly on peripheral arterioles, causing vasoconstriction. Both of these actions serve to increase blood pressure.

Vasopressin release is regulated by osmoreceptors in the **paraventricular** and **supraoptic nuclei** of the hypothalamus. When the hypothalamus detects a rise in plasma osmolality (for example, when a patient is dehydrated), it stimulates the release of vasopressin from the posterior pituitary.

The Supraoptic nucleus helps you "sop" up water from the kidneys.

Diabetes Insipidus

Lack of ADH causes excretion of large amounts of dilute urine. "Central" diabetes insipidus, or ADH insufficiently stemming from pituitary or hypothalamic dysfunction, is caused by head trauma, neurosurgery, or an intracranial neoplasm. **Nephrogenic DI** occurs when the kidneys are abnormal and do not respond to ADH properly. Treatment is with vasopressin or its analogues.

A classic case of central DI would be a patient who begins to produce large amounts of low-osmolality urine after head trauma. The differential diagnosis for large volumes of low-osmolality urine would be central DI, nephrogenic DI, or psychogenic polydipsia (in other words, the patient is drinking extremely excessive amounts of water). The osmolality of the plasma would differentiate polydipsia from DI: if the plasma osmolality is high, then DI is the culprit. If the plasma osmolality is low, the patient is drinking too much water. Another test to differentiate the two entities would be to deprive the patient of water: In patients with DI, the urine osmolality remains unchanged, but in patients with polydipsia, the urine osmolality rises.

The next step would be to differentiate central from nephrogenic DI. In central DI, the plasma ADH level is low, and urine osmolality rises following intravenous administration of ADH. If the DI is nephrogenic, on the other hand, the plasma ADH levels may be normal or high, and intravenous ADH would not affect the urine osmolality since the kidneys simply cannot respond to the hormone.

Syndrome of Inappropriate Antidiuretic Hormone Secretion

Too much ADH causes excess free water absorption in the kidneys relative to the body's needs. The results are hyponatremia in the setting of overly concentrated urine. There are many etiologies, including pulmonary disease, cranial lesions, and ectopic ADH production – (oat cell carcinoma of the lung is a classic example). Treatment is water restriction and treatment of the underlying disorder. Demeclocycline blocks the action of ADH on the collecting ducts.

Making the diagnosis of SIADH is not trivial. The patient must have hyponatremia in the presence of plasma hypo-osmolality, since artifactual hyponatremia can arise from disorders like hyperglycemia and hyperlipidemia. The urine must also be inappropriately concentrated, which differentiates SIADH from excessive water intake. Euvolemia must be present; in other words, rule out congestive heart failure, cirrhosis, and nephrotic syndrome. Finally, the patient must not have any renal, adrenal, or thyroid insufficiency, which could cause salt wasting.

Growth Hormone

Growth hormone (GH), or **somatotropin**, acts on the skeletal system to increase lineara growth. GH acts on the liver to promote the synthesis of insulin-like growth factor, (IGF-1, also known as somatomedin C), which then act on chondrocytes in the bone to increase cell division. Related actions of GH include increased protein synthesis and increased lipolysis. GH is also a counter-regulatory hormone—that is, it counters the actions of insulin on carbohydrate metabolism by increasing glucose release by the liver and decreasing glucose uptake in tissue.

Regulation of GH is varied (Fig. 16-3). Increased secretion of GH is triggered by multiple factors, including secretion of GHRH by the hypothalamus, sleep, stress, hypoglycemia, increased serum amino acids, and dopamine. Decreased secretion occurs during hypothalamic secretion of somatostatin (also known as *growth hormone–inhibiting hormone*), obesity, hyperglycemia, cortisol, and, of course, high levels of GH.

Acromegaly occurs when excess growth hormone is produced by a pituitary tumor in adults (after the epiphyseal plates have fused in bones). Bony overgrowth (jaw) as well as soft tissue overgrowth (heart) are common.

Diabetes mellitus due to glucose intolerance can occur, albeit rarely, from excess growth hormone activity. Treatment is via transsphenoidal surgery or local radiation.

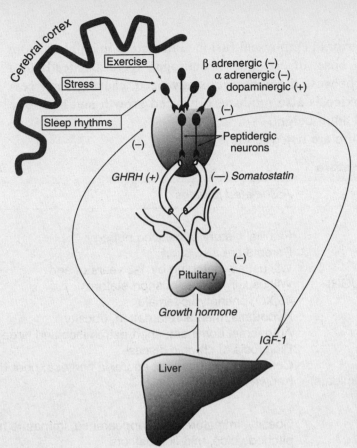

Fig. 16-3. Growth hormone feedback loop. (GHRH = growth hormone–releasing hormone.)

Short Stature

The number of non-endocrine and endocrine causes of short stature is rather extensive (Table 16–2). Common causes of short stature include constitutional short stature, genetic short stature, and malnutrition. A child with constitutional short stature has physiologically but not mentally delayed development and will reach normal or low-normal height after a delayed puberty. In genetic short stature, other family members are also short, and the child does not have a delayed bone age or delay in reaching puberty.

The benefits of GH therapy for short children depends greatly on the cause of short stature. Children with classic growth hormone deficiency (a diagnosis that is difficult to make, as various factors can influence the results of a GH challenge test) have proven benefit. Children with Turner's syndrome and renal failure have some benefit, as do extremely short children with delayed bone age and very slow growth velocities, as defined by a research protocol. For other children with short stature, it is unclear whether GH treatment results in an increase in adult height.

Tall Stature

Non-endocrine causes of tall stature include constitutional tall stature and genetic tall stature. In constitutional tall stature, the child may be taller than his or her peers throughout childhood but grows at a normal velocity with a moderately advanced bone age. The final height is usually within normal range for the child's family. Genetic tall stature refers to a tall child who comes from a tall family. The child's growth velocity is normal, as is his or her bone age.

Endocrine disorders that can cause tall stature include pituitary gigantism, commonly from a GH-secreting adenoma. The somatic features of acromegaly are present, and the individual also undergoes excessive linear growth because the GH excess is present prior to epiphyseal fusion. Tall stature in children from sexual precocity, or early onset of estrogen or androgen secretion, leads to a paradoxically short adult because the bone age is advanced, causing early cessation of growth. Thyrotoxicosis also produces advanced growth and bone age that can lead to decreased adult height.

The causes of tall stature are listed in table 16-3.

Table 16–2. Causes of short stature

Cause	Associated findings
Non-endocrine	
Constitutional short stature	Familial history of delayed puberty
Genetic short stature	Parents are also short
Prematurity	Will usually catch up by 1-2 years of age
Intrauterine growth retardation(IUGR)	Will usually remain of short stature
Turner's syndrome	45,XO; phenotypic female
Prader-Willi syndrome	Hypotonia, mental retardation, obesity
Achondroplasia	Autosomal dominant, short extremities and large head
Chronic disease	Diagnosis of chronic disease
Malnutrition	Consider food faddism, anorexia nervosa, poor diet
Drugs (e.g., high-dose methylphenidate)	Known drug use
Endocrine	
Congenital GH deficiency	Obesity, immature facial appearance, immature high-pitched voice, mid-line defects
Acquired GH deficiency	History of tumor
Psychosocial dwarfism	History of abuse (ignored or severely disciplined child)
Hypothyroidism	Low free T4, apathy, bradycardia
Cushing's syndrome	Buffalo hump, moon facies, central obesity
Rickets (Vitamin D deficiency)	Bow-legged, chest deformity

Table 16–3. Causes of tall stature

Cause	Associated findings
Non-endocrine	
Constitutional tall stature	Advanced bone age, no other disorders, possible obesity
Genetic tall stature	Tall parents, normal bone age
Syndromes	
Marfan's syndrome	Long thin fingers, hyperextension of joints, heart murmur, lens subluxation
XYY syndrome	Abnormal karyotype
Klinefelter's syndrome	XXY karyotype, gynecomastia, hypogonadism
Beckwith-Wiedemann syndrome	Overweight, macroglossia, omphalocele, hypoglycemia
Cerebral gigantism	Prominent forehead, high-arched palate, sharp chin, hypertelorism, mental retardation
Homocystinuria	Phenotype similar to Marfan's syndrome, mental retardation, seizures, osteoporosis, thromboembolism
Endocrine	
Pituitary gigantism	Acromegaly, pituitary adenoma
Sexual precocity	Early puberty, short adult height
Thyrotoxicosis	Advanced bone age, short adult height

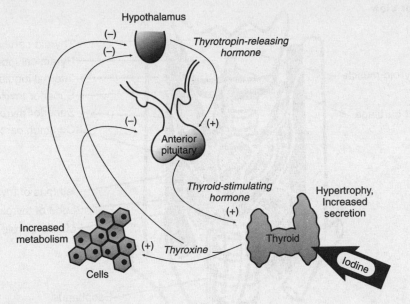

Fig. 16-4. Thyroid hormone feedback loop.

Thyroid Gland

Physiology

The thyroid gland secretes hormones that act on the nucleus and mitochondria of cells all over the body. Their main role is activating metabolic activity. Some effects of thyroid hormone include increased synthesis of protein, increased degradation of glycogen and fat, and increased heart rate and contractility.

The release of thyroid hormone is regulated by the hypothalamus and anterior pituitary gland (Fig. 16-4). **TRH** triggers the release of **TSH** from the pituitary. This in turn stimulates the synthesis and release of thyroid hormone from the thyroid gland. Thyroid hormone in the bloodstream then exerts a negative feedback effect on both the pituitary and hypothalamus. In addition, the thyroid gland has some capacity for self-regulation. When iodine is deficient, iodine transport is increased; as iodine becomes overabundant, iodine transport is inhibited. Complete inhibition of iodine transport due to excess iodine is known as a **Wolff-Chaikoff affect**.

Development

The thyroid gland is the first endocrine gland to develop in humans, starting around weeks 3–4. A downgrowth of ectoderm from the floor of the pharynx descends in the neck while maintaining its connection to the tongue by a tube known as the **thyroglossal duct**. Although the thyroglossal duct usually atrophies, remnants may form thyroglossal cysts and sinuses, which present later in life. The site of origin of the thyroglossal duct is known as the **foramen cecum**. In some cases, the thyroid may fail to descend, or may descend incompletely, resulting in a lingual thyroid or an accessory thyroid gland in the tongue or neck.

Anterior view

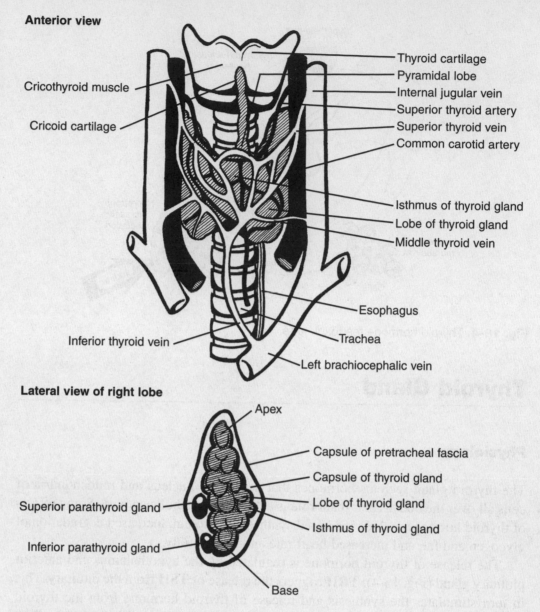

- Cricothyroid muscle
- Cricoid cartilage
- Thyroid cartilage
- Pyramidal lobe
- Internal jugular vein
- Superior thyroid artery
- Superior thyroid vein
- Common carotid artery
- Isthmus of thyroid gland
- Lobe of thyroid gland
- Middle thyroid vein
- Esophagus
- Inferior thyroid vein
- Trachea
- Left brachiocephalic vein

Lateral view of right lobe

- Apex
- Capsule of pretracheal fascia
- Capsule of thyroid gland
- Lobe of thyroid gland
- Isthmus of thyroid gland
- Superior parathyroid gland
- Inferior parathyroid gland
- Base

Fig. 16-5. Anatomy of the thyroid gland.

Anatomy and Histology

The thyroid glands consist of two lobes, connected across the midline by an isthmus across the second to fourth tracheal rings. Blood supply arises primarily from the superior thyroid artery (off the common carotid artery) and inferior thyroid artery(off the subclavian artery); venous drainage is from the superior, middle, and inferior thyroid veins (Fig. 16-5).

Histologically, the thyroid gland consists of multiple follicles filled with **colloid**, a gelatinous substance (Fig. 16-6). These follicles are lined by simple cuboidal epithelium, which synthesizes the thyroid hormones thyroxine (T_4) and triiodothyronine (T_3). **Parafollicular cells** are also present in the follicles and secrete **calcitonin**.

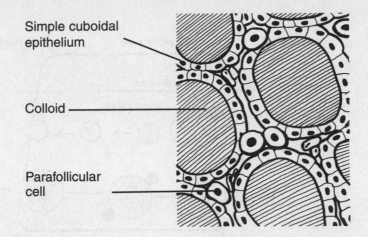

Simple cuboidal
epithelium

Colloid

Parafollicular
cell

Fig. 16-6. Histology of the
thyroid gland.

Thyroid Hormone Synthesis

During thyroid hormone synthesis, the thyroid gland takes up iodide, a nutrient rapidly absorbed in the gastrointestinal (GI) tract. Uptake occurs via active transport aided in the thyroid by an Na^+/K^+-adenosine triphosphatase (ATPase). The iodide is then oxidized and attached to thyroglobulin, a glycoprotein synthesized by the thyroid gland. This results in **monoiodotyrosine** (MIT), which subsequently acquires another iodide and becomes **diiodotyrosine** (DIT). Two molecules of DIT are then joined together to form T_4, or one molecule of DIT and one MIT can be joined to form T_3 (Fig. 16-7). T_4 and T_3 are released into the bloodstream as required.

Once T_3 and T_4 are in the serum, they can remain free or else can be bound to thyroid hormone transport proteins. Only the free forms are biologically active; therefore, variations in the quantity of thyroid-binding proteins can alter total serum T_3 and T_4 without changing the amount of free forms available. Most T_4 is bound to T_4-binding globulin (TBG), and the remainder is bound to T_4-binding prealbumin (TBPA) and albumen. T_3 is also bound primarily to TBG, although a small amount is found bound to albumin as well.

Although free T_4 is found in higher concentrations in the blood than free T_3, T_3 is about four times more potent than T_4. In general, T_4 is converted locally to T_3 so that tissues have the benefit of the stronger hormone. T_4 may also be converted to reverse T_3, an inactive form. Most T_3 in the blood comes from the metabolism of T_4.

Thyroid Function Tests

The first step in assessing thyroid dysfunction (after a history and physical examination) involves checking the status of the pituitary. Levels of TSH are low when the thyroid is hyperactive and high when the thyroid is hypoactive as a result of feedback suppression, assuming that the pituitary is functioning correctly. Assessing the levels of thyroid hormone is done by checking T_4 levels because it is much more difficult to check T_3 levels. T_4 levels vary depending on the amount of free T_4 and the binding capacity of proteins in the serum. In conditions such as pregnancy, hepatitis, and cirrhosis, there is an increased thyroid-binding capacity, whereas in situations of protein loss or steroid use, there is a decrease of binding capacity. Therefore, hypo- or hyperthyroidism can be missed by placing too much stock in "normal" total T_4 levels.

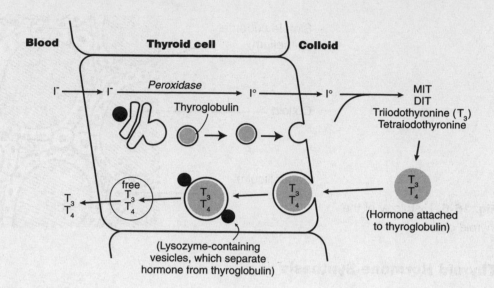

Fig. 16-7. Thyroid hormone synthesis. (MIT = monoiodotyrosine; DIT = diiodotyrosine; T_4 = thyroxine.)

To determine binding capacity, a resin T_3 uptake measurement can be performed. This measure, along with the total T_4 level, can provide the **free T_4 index**, which is proportional to the amount of free T_4 in the serum.

To evaluate thyroid nodules, a **thyroid scan** is performed. A thyroid scan uses small doses of radioactive iodine or technetium, which is taken up by the metabolic activity of the thyroid gland. This makes it possible to visualize the gland and is useful in determining whether a nodule is "hot" (overactive) or "cold" (underactive) relative to the rest of the thyroid. Fine-needle aspiration (FNA), core biopsy, and excision are also used to establish a diagnosis.

Hypothyroidism

Congenital Hypothyroidism (Cretinism)

Congenital deficiency of thyroid hormone is due to iodine deficiency or inborn errors of thyroid hormone synthesis. Infants display poor feeding, coarse skin, excessive somnolence, and a hoarse cry. Their appearance is stocky with enlarged tongue and wide-set eyes. These children must be treated with thyroid replacement as soon as possible to avoid the development of mental retardation.

Sick Euthyroid Syndrome

Sick euthyroid syndrome is a laboratory phenomenon found in acutely ill patients. Serum T_4 and T_3 levels are low, but the TSH level is normal. No treatment is necessary.

Hashimoto's Thyroiditis

Hashimoto's thyroiditis is an autoimmune disorder, most common in middle-aged women. The thyroid becomes enlarged, nodular, and nontender and eventually becomes small and fibrotic. Thyroid function tests may be normal unless the patient is hypothyroid (20% of cases). **Serum antithyroglobulin antibodies** are present.

Treatment consists of thyroid replacement therapy, even in patients with normal thyroid function tests, because it helps to reduce the size of the thyroid.

Iatrogenic Hypothyroidism

There are many causes of iatrogenic hypothyroidism, including thyroid surgery, neck irradiation, and chronic lithium therapy. Therapeutic use of iodine-131 for thyrotoxicosis may lead to hypothyroidism.

Signs & Symptoms

Lethargy, cold intolerance, constipation, weight gain despite reduced appetite, and irregular menses. Coarse hair and dry skin with nonpitting edema (myxedema) and slowed relaxation phase of deep tendon reflexes are noted. Women may experience menorrhagia.

Diagnosis

Serum T_4 is decreased. TSH is high in primary hypothyroidism.

Treatment

Treatment consists of thyroid replacement therapy and regular TSH monitoring.

Hyperthyroidism

Graves' Disease

Graves' disease is an autoimmune disorder that is the most common cause of hyperthyroidism. Patients develop antibodies that bind to the thyroids TSH receptors and stimulate thyroid hormone synthesis.

Signs & Symptoms

Tremors, anxiety, weight loss despite increased appetite, diarrhea, palpitations, heat hypersensitivity, insomnia, and occasionally exophthalmos (big, bulging eyeballs like Marty Feldman). Signs include tachycardia, widened pulse pressure, tremor, warm skin, and occasional atrial fibrillation.

Diagnosis

Elevated T_3, T_4, and the presence of anti-TSH receptor antibodies. Antimicrosomal antibodies are also seen.

Treatment

Surgery, radioactive iodine, or antithyroid medications, such as propylthiouracil (PTU) and methimazole. A thyroidectomy would leave the patient hypothyroid and requiring lifelong thyroid replacement therapy. Also, remember that the recurrent laryngeal nerve runs through the thyroid gland and may be damaged during surgery, resulting in vocal cord paralysis on the affected side.

Symptomatic relief can be given with propranolol.

Subacute Thyroiditis

Subacute thyroiditis (also known as de Quervin's thyroiditis) is most likely viral in etiology, with symptoms of mild hyperthyroidism and fever.

Signs & Symptoms

Patients are often asymptomatic or have a tender, enlarged thyroid gland with neck pain.

Diagnosis

Laboratory tests show decreased radioactive iodine uptake and elevated sedimentation rate.

Treatment

Anti-inflammatory agents, including glucocorticoids are used, and β-blockers are used for cardiovascular symptom control. Patients may need temporary thyroid replacement therapy for periods of hypothyroidism which follow the hyperthyroidism.

Toxic Adenoma and Toxic Multinodular Goiter

Toxic adenoma and toxic multinodular goiter are hyperthyroid conditions that occur when thyroid nodules begin to function autonomously. These patients exhibit the classic signs of hyperthyroidism.

Struma ovarii

Ovarian teratomas may contain thyroid tissue. The tissue may hyperfunction independently due to a toxic nodule, or it may secrete excess hormone in parallel with the thyroid in Grave's disease or toxic multinodular goiter.

Diagnosis

Excess T_3 and T_4 are noted, along with depressed pituitary TSH production. Thyroid scan shows one or more "hot spots" with a hypoactive background.

Treatment

Treatment is with surgery or radioiodine.

Thyrotoxicosis Factitia

Thyrotoxicosis factitia is caused by ingestion of excessive quantities of thyroid hormone, sometimes done for weight loss. The treatment is obvious (to stop taking the hormone!), and the patient may need to be referred for psychiatric evaluation.

Thyroid Storm

Thyroid storm is a medical emergency in which patients present with extreme manifestations of thyrotoxicosis, such as arrhythmias and tremors. This condition can be triggered by surgery, illness, or other stress in patients with baseline thyroid abnormalities.

β-Blockers, PTU, or methimazole are given to control symptoms, and glucocorticoids may inhibit the conversion of T_4 to T_3. Intravenous sodium iodide also blocks hormone release via the Wolff-Chaikoff effect. Definitive treatment by surgery or radioactive iodine postponed until the patient is euthyroid.

Thyroid Nodules and Goiters

Any enlargement of the thyroid gland that is *not* the result of a neoplasm is termed a **goiter**. It can be associated with hyperthyroidism (Graves' disease, toxic nodular goiter), euthyroidism (iodine deficiency), or hypothyroidism (Hashimoto's thyroiditis). Thyroid enlargement may result from overstimulation with TSH or a TSH-like substance or may be due to inflammation. **Endemic goiter** is present when a large proportion of a population has a goiter, and it is usually due to iodine deficiency.

Approximately 5% of people in the United States have thyroid nodules. The majority of thyroid nodules are benign, although malignancy must always be considered in the workup. If benign, a nodule may produce appropriate or excessive amounts of thyroid hormone. Malignant tumors typically do not produce hormone and are therefore "cold" on thyroid scan. Risk of malignancy is increased in the following:

- Young, male patients

- Previous history of head or neck irradiation

- "Cold" nodule on radionuclide scan

- Solid nodule rather than cystic

Evaluation usually includes a thyroid scan, ultrasound, and FNA. Benign nodules require treatment (surgery or iodine-131) if symptoms of hyperthyroidism are present. Treatment for malignant nodules is discussed later.

Thyroid Carcinoma

Thyroid cancer is the most common endocrine cancer, with four types of malignancy.

Papillary Carcinoma

Papillary carcinoma is the most common thyroid malignancy, with the best prognosis. This slow-growing tumor often metastasizes to local cervical nodes. It is strongly associated with previous irradiation and is often found in women under age 40.

On microscopic examination, the tumor consists of papillary structures covered with glandular epithelium. Small, calcified bodies known as **psammoma bodies** are often present.

Follicular Carcinoma

Follicular carcinoma is more common in older patients, with a poorer prognosis than papillary. Spread occurs via blood to bone, lung, brain, and liver. The follicular pattern may be difficult to distinguish from benign adenomas. Because spread occurs through the bloodstream, vessel invasion is common.

Anaplastic Carcinoma

Anaplastic carcinoma, which occurs in the elderly, is the least common type of thyroid cancer and has the poorest prognosis. Local invasion of the neck and trachea often causes **hoarseness** and **dysphagia**. On microscopic examination, sheets of poorly differentiated cells are seen.

Medullary Carcinoma

Medullary carcinoma is a malignancy of the **parafollicular C cells**, which produce calcitonin, thus an elevated serum calcitonin is characteristic. Prognosis is poor. This tumor often occurs as a component of familial multiple endocrine neoplasia, type II (MEN II).

Signs & Symptoms

The most common presentation of thyroid malignancy is an asymptomatic nodule noted by the patient or physician.

Diagnosis

Diagnosis is by thyroid scan, ultrasound, and biopsy.

Treatment

Surgery, with subsequent ablation of remaining thyroid tissue using radioactive iodine, is the usual treatment. Thyroid hormone–replacement therapy is necessary after surgery.

Parathyroid Glands & Calcium Regulation

Physiology

The parathyroid glands secrete the parathyroid hormone (PTH). PTH is responsible for elevating serum calcium. It mobilizes calcium stores by:

- Stimulating osteoclasts in bone

- Increasing reabsorption of calcium in the kidney

- Increasing the production of 1,25-dihydroxycholecalciferol (the active form of vitamin D), which increases calcium absorption from the GI tract

PTH also decreases phosphate reabsorption in the renal tubules, lowering serum phosphate. PTH levels are regulated directly by serum calcium levels. Increased serum calcium results in decreased PTH secretion, whereas decreased serum calcium triggers increased PTH secretion.

Calcitonin, a hormone synthesized by the parafollicular cells of the thyroid gland, also plays a role in calcium regulation. Calcitonin decreases serum calcium by inhibiting bone resorption and by increasing urinary excretion of calcium and phosphate.

PTH works in concert with calcitonin and vitamin D to regulate the body's calcium balance (Table 16-4). Calcitonin is a hormone synthesized by the parafollicular cells of the thyroid gland. It decreases serum calcium by inhibiting bone resorption and by increasing urinary excretion of calcium and phosphate. Vitamin D, on the other hand, is a sterol hormone that assists in increasing serum calcium concentrations by increasing uptake of calcium from the jejunum and ileum through direct action on enterocytes. It also enhances calcium and phosphate reabsorption from the kidney. Its action on the bone includes stimulation of both osteoblast and osteoclast activity.

The influence of PTH on the production of 1,25-dihydroxycholecalciferol [1,25-(OH)2D], the most active form of vitamin D, links vitamin D activity to the regulation of calcium homeostasis. Endogenous vitamin D3, or cholecalciferol, is synthesized in the skin by the action of ultraviolet rays on 7-dehydrocholesterol. (Vitamin D2, or ergo-calciferol, is taken in through fortified milk. It is equipotent to cholecalciferol and undergoes an identical metabolic pathway.) The next step is hydroxylation in the liver to produce 25-hydroxycholecalciferol [25-(OH)D]. 25-(OH)D can be stored in fat as a reservoir of vitamin D. The final activation step is conversion of 25-(OH)D to 1,25-(OH)2D in the proximal tubule of the kidney by the enzyme 1a-hydroxylase. Factors that boost 1a-hydroxylase activity include decreased serum calcium, increased PTH levels (which also arise from decreased serum calcium), and decreased serum phosphate levels (which can be secondary to increased PTH activity). Large amounts of dietary phosphate can depress 1a-hydroxylase activity.

Table 16–4. Calcium regulation

Effects	Serum Calcium	Serum Phospha-te	Bone	Kidney	Intestine	Stimulus for Activity
PTH	Increase	Decrease	Incresed reaorption	Increased calcium reuptake, decreased phosphate reuptake	Increased calcium uptake (indirect through vitamin D)	Decreased serum calcium
Vitamin D	Increase	Increase	Stimulates osteoclasts and osteoblasts; increased resorption in vitamin D intoxication	Increased calcium reuptake, increased phosphate reuptake	Increased calcium uptake	Decreased serum calcium, increased PTH, decreased serum phosphate
Cacitonin	Decrease		Decreased resorption			Increased serum calcium

Development

The parathyroid glands derive from the third and fourth pharyngeal pouches (Fig. 16-9). Paradoxically, the glands from the third pouch travel further downward than those of the fourth pouch, which remain superior.

Anatomy and Histology

The parathyroid glands are located within the fascia of the thyroid gland, usually along the posterior border. Typically, there are four parathyroid glands, which share the thyroid's blood supply. Histologically, the parathyroid is composed of **chief cells**, which secrete PTH, and **oxyphil cells**, whose function is unknown.

Symptoms of hyperparathyroidism: "Bones, stones, abdominal groans, and psychic moans."

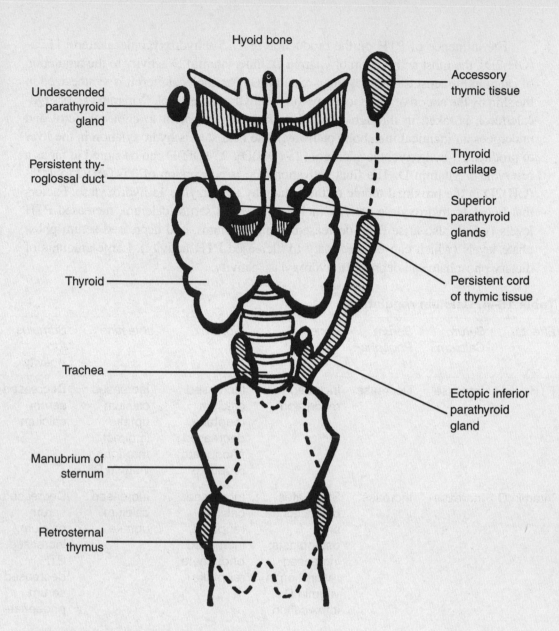

Hyoid bone

Undescended parathyroid gland

Persistent thyroglossal duct

Thyroid

Trachea

Manubrium of sternum

Retrosternal thymus

Accessory thymic tissue

Thyroid cartilage

Superior parathyroid glands

Persistent cord of thymic tissue

Ectopic inferior parathyroid gland

Fig. 16-9. Parathyroid gland development.

Primary Hyperparathyroidism

Primary hyperparathyroidism occurs when excess PTH is secreted by the parathyroid gland. A single, benign adenoma is responsible in 80% of cases. Hyperplasia of all four glands accounts for most of the other cases. Parathyroid cancer is rare, comprising less than 2% of primary hyperparathyroidism. Patients with primary hyperparathyroidism are usually older women.

Signs & Symptoms

The disorder is often asymptomatic, but evidence of hypercalcemia (GI disturbances, muscle weakness, emotional lability), osteoporosis, or renal stones may be present.

Diagnosis

Laboratory tests reveal high PTH, with the resulting high calcium and low phosphorus.

Treatment

Treatment is surgical. Beware of postoperative hypocalcemia, as "hungry bones," freed from the power of PTH, take up the available calcium.

Secondary Hyperparathyroidism

Secondary hyperparathyroidism is parathyroid hypertrophy that develops in response to low serum calcium. Common causes of low serum calcium are vitamin D deficiency or malabsorption, renal tubular problems causing calcium loss (renal tubular acidosis, Fanconi syndrome), and certain antiseizure medications that interfere with vitamin D metabolism (phenytoin, phenobarbital). Serum phosphorus is low, unless there is renal insufficiency, which results in phosphorus retention. The underlying disorder is treated.

Aldosterone phones a "collect" call to the connecting ducts.

Hypoparathyroidism

Hypoparathyroidism occurs when parathyroid glands fail to develop (**DiGeorge syndrome**), when they are removed by surgery, or when target tissues are not responsive (**pseudohypoparathyroidism**).

Signs & Symptoms

The ensuing hypocalcemia causes tingling of the lips and fingers and can lead to tetany. A positive **Chvostek's sign** occurs when a tap on the cheek causes facial muscle spasms. **Trousseau's sign** is present when a blood pressure cuff inflated on the arm induces carpal spasm.

Diagnosis

Low levels of PTH, causing low calcium and high phosphorus.

Treatment

Calcium and vitamin D supplementation.

Hypercalcemia

Hyperparathyroidism and malignancy are the most common causes of hypercalcemia. **Bony metastases** and osteolytic tumors (multiple myeloma, lymphoma, leukemia) may raise calcium levels by increasing bone resorption. Certain cancers (e.g., **bronchogenic tumors**) can also secrete a parathyroid hormone-related protein that results in hypercalcemia, low serum phosphate, and bone resorption in the presence of low serum PTH (**a paraneoplastic syndrome**). Prolonged bed rest may aggravate hypercalcemia in cancer patients. Other causes include:

- Increased intestinal absorption (sarcoidosis, hypervitaminosis A or D)

- Increased renal reabsorption (thiazide diuretics, Addison's disease)

- Ingestion of large amounts of calcium carbonate and milk (**milk-alkali syndrome**)

Signs & Symptoms

"Stones, bones, abdominal groans, and psychic moans." Renal stones may result in acute urinary tract obstruction. Polyuria occurs because the excess calcium blocks ADH receptor sites in the distal convoluted tubules. Also, potentiation of digoxin may occur, resulting in arrhythmias.

Diagnosis

A large proportion of calcium is bound to albumin in the serum. Patients with low albumin levels have low total calcium levels, although their free calcium level may be normal. To adjust for the effect of low albumin, the lower limit of normal for calcium should be shifted down by 0.8 mg/dl for every 1 g/dl of albumin below normal. For example, if the normal albumin level is 4.0, and the patient's albumin level is 3.0, a total calcium level of 7.6 mg/dl (0.8 mg/dl below normal) would still be considered normal.

Treatment

Aggressive, continuous hydration, followed by furosemide to promote calciuria after patient is well hydrated. Pamidronate and calcitonin help reduce bone resorption.

Hypocalcemia

Etiologies include hypoparathyroidism, vitamin D abnormalities (deficiency, malabsorption, or impaired metabolism), renal tubular defects, and acute pancreatitis (the released fats chelate calcium).

Magnesium deficiency (common in alcoholics) causes hypocalcemia by decreasing PTH secretion and decreasing PTH's effect on target organs. In this case, magnesium supplementation must be added to calcium and vitamin D.

Signs & Symptoms

Tetany in severe cases. Chvostek's sign and Trousseau's sign may be present.

Diagnosis

Serum phosphate is high in hypoparathyroidism and renal failure, but not in vitamin D deficiency.

Treatment

Calcium and magnesium supplementation.

From out to in—salt, sugar, sex: aldosterone, glucocorticoids, androgens.

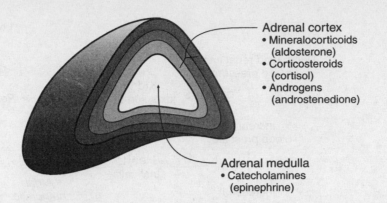

Adrenal cortex
• Mineralocorticoids
  (aldosterone)
• Corticosteroids
  (cortisol)
• Androgens
  (androstenedione)

Adrenal medulla
• Catecholamines
  (epinephrine)

Fig. 16-10. Adrenal gland: cortex and medulla.

Adrenal Glands

Physiology

The adrenal gland consists of two types of endocrine tissue. The adrenal **cortex** secretes steroid hormones, specifically **aldosterone**, **cortisol**, and **androgens**, whereas the adrenal **medulla** secretes **catecholamines**, such as epinephrine (Fig. 16-10). The adrenal cortex is further subdivided into three zones, the **glomerulosa**, the **fasciculata**, and the **reticularis**, each of which is responsible for the synthesis of a particular class of steroids (Fig. 16-11).

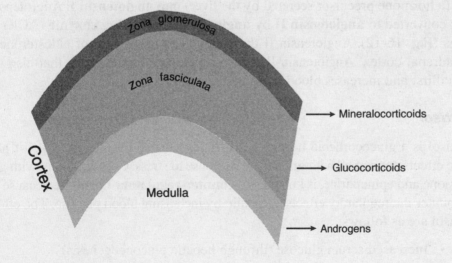

Zona glomerulosa
Zona fasciculata
Medulla
Cortex

→ Mineralocorticoids
→ Glucocorticoids
→ Androgens

Aldosterone phones a "collect" call to the collecting ducts.

Fig. 16-11. Zones of the adrenal cortex.

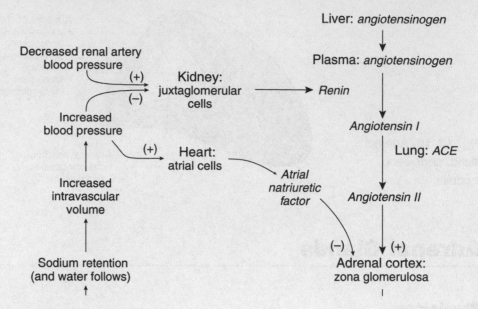

Fig. 16-12. Aldosterone actions.

Aldosterone

Aldosterone acts on the distal tubules and collecting ducts of the kidney to increase the absorption of sodium, exchanging it for potassium and hydrogen ions. As sodium is resorbed, more water molecules are retained as well. This leads to increased volume and increased blood pressure.

Aldosterone is regulated by the renin-angiotensin system. In the juxtaglomerular apparatus of the kidney, the hormone renin is secreted when fluid volumes drop, as in dehydration or hemorrhage. In the bloodstream, renin converts **angiotensinogen** (a hormone precursor secreted by the liver) into **angiotensin I**. Angiotensin I is then converted to **angiotensin II** by **angiotensin-converting enzyme** (ACE) in the lungs (Fig. 16-12). Angiotensin II then stimulates the release of aldosterone from the adrenal cortex. Angiotensin II is also a potent vasoconstrictor that also stimulates thirst and increases blood pressure centrally.

Cortisol

Cortisol is a glucocorticoid hormone that is responsible for a wide range of physiologic effects concerned with immediate response to stress. Cortisol, along with growth hormone and epinephrine, is known as a **counter-regulatory hormone** because it acts to counter the regulatory effects of insulin by increasing blood glucose. The effects of cortisol are as follows:

- Increased serum glucose (through hepatic gluconeogenesis)

- Increased serum amino acids (through protein catabolism)

- Increased plasma lipids and ketone bodies (through lipolysis)

- Increased concentration of neutrophils

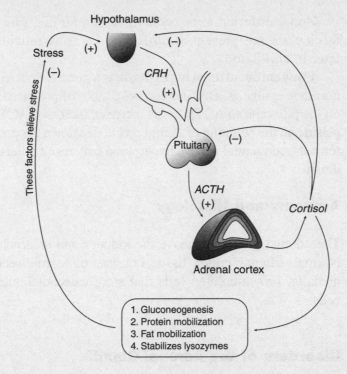

Fig. 16-13. Cortisol feedback loop. (CRH = corticotropin-releasing hormone; ACTH = adrenocorticotropic hormone.)

- Decreased concentration and migration of other white blood cells (through inhibition of IL-2 production)

- Decreased synthesis of inflammatory mediators, such as prostaglandins and histamine

Cortisol is regulated by the secretion of corticotropin-releasing hormone (CRH) from the hypothalamus and ACTH from the anterior pituitary (Fig. 16-13). Levels of cortisol rise and fall through the day in a circadian rhythm, with the highest levels just before waking and the lowest levels in the late evening. Cortisol is bound to corticosteroid-binding globulin (CBG) and albumin in the blood; just like T_4, only free cortisol is biologically active. Free cortisol levels provide negative feedback to the hypothalamus and pituitary, acting to decrease the secretion of CRH and ACTH.

Adrenal Androgens

Adrenal androgens are generally present in tiny amounts when compared to the amounts secreted by the gonads. The two most significant androgens, **dehydroepiandrosterone** (DHEA) and **androstenedione**, are weak androgens and are converted to more potent androgens peripherally.

Development

The adrenal cortex and the adrenal medulla develop from different sources. The adrenal cortex arises from **mesoderm**. The adrenal medulla arises from **neural crest cells** from adjacent sympathetic ganglia.

Zonal differentiation occurs late in fetal life. The zona glomerulosa and zona fasciculata are present at birth, but the zona reticularis does not develop until later in childhood.

Congenital adrenal hyperplasia is a genetic deficiency of the enzymes of adrenal hormone synthesis. Because cortisol cannot be produced, there's no negative feedback on the pituitary, so ACTH levels increase. Increased ACTH then causes adrenal hyperplasia and the shunting of steroid precursors down the paths that produce androgens. In females, congenital adrenal hyperplasia may result in hirsutism and pseudohermaphroditism.

Anatomy and Histology

The adrenal glands lie above the kidneys and are enclosed within the renal fascia. Normal adrenal cortex tissue consists of steroid-secreting cells. In the adrenal medulla, brown-colored cells that store catecholamines are known as **chromaffin cells**.

Disorders of the Adrenal Gland

Primary Corticoadrenal Insufficiency (Addison's Disease)

Destruction of both adrenal glands results in a deficiency of mineralocorticoids (most significantly aldosterone) and glucocorticoids (most significantly cortisol). Etiology is usually autoimmune, infectious (tuberculosis, fungal), or hemorrhagic (eg, armpits, oneral folds, back of the neck).

Signs & Symptoms

Symptoms are nonspecific: including fatigue, weakness, weight loss, nausea, and vomiting. A notable feature is hyperpigmentation of the skin (**acanthosis nigricans**), which develops because ACTH and melanocyte-stimulating hormone are made from the same precursor. When ACTH increases in an attempt to stimulate cortisol production, melanocyte-stimulating hormone increases as well, causing darkening, especially of the folds of the skin (e.g., armpits, crural folds, back of the neck).

Diagnosis

Loss of aldosterone causes hyponatremia, with associated dehydration and orthostatic hypotension, and hyperkalemia. Eosinophilia is also characteristic, although the etiology of this is unknown.

An ACTH stimulation test assesses serum cortisol before and after ACTH is given. No increase in cortisol, along with a high serum ACTH, is diagnostic, because the adrenals are already nonfunctioning and more ACTH doesn't help to increase cortisol production.

Treatment

Glucocorticoid and mineralocorticoid replacement. Glucocorticoid doses should be increased in times of stress and illness. If they aren't, patients may develop an "addisonian crisis," which can cause profound weakness, shock, fever, and even coma.

Secondary Corticoadrenal Insufficiency

This adrenal hypofunction is due to a lack of ACTH. It most commonly occurs in patients who have received corticosteroids for more than 4 weeks. Exogenous steroids suppress ACTH, thus allowing the adrenal glands to atrophy. If steroid use is abruptly discontinued, the adrenals are not able to produce a sufficient supply of endogenous steroid. Because of this phenomenon, patients should be tapered off steroid medications. Symptoms are the same as in primary disease, and a **corticosteroid taper** is sufficient treatment.

Cushing's Syndrome

Many things can lead to excess glucocorticoids:

- **Cushing's disease** refers specifically to Cushing's syndrome caused by a pituitary adenoma. The adenoma produces ACTH, which causes adrenal hyperplasia. ACTH levels may be normal or elevated. (Either is inappropriate because the high levels of cortisol in blood should suppress ACTH secretion.) High doses of glucocorticoids do suppress cortisol levels somewhat because the pituitary still has some feedback regulation intact. Treatment is transsphenoidal removal of the pituitary tumor.

- **Ectopic ATCH production** is usually associated with a lung tumor. If the tumor is not resectable for cure, treatment is symptomatic. This ACTH production is not suppressible, even with high-dose glucocorticoids.

- An **adrenal cortical tumor** may produce high levels of cortisol. ACTH levels are suppressed, and cortisol production is not suppressible with glucocorticoids. Treatment is with surgical resection of the tumor. Glucocorticoids must be given postsurgically, while the remaining atrophied adrenal gland tissue recovers.

- **Chronic glucocorticoid therapy** is required for a number of diseases, from asthma to lupus. The problem is that prolonged steroid use can have many negative consequences. Besides the signs and symptoms discussed below, these patients may develop cataracts, glaucoma, hypertension, and osteoporosis, to name a few.

Signs & Symptoms

Central obesity with a "buffalo hump," moon facies, and peripheral muscle wasting. Other symptoms include vertebral fractures from osteoporosis, atrophic skin with purple striae, easy bruising, hypertension, and psychiatric changes (depression, agitation, or euphoria). In women, high adrenal androgens may cause hirsutism, acne, and menstrual irregularities. In men, cortisol may inhibit gonadotropin secretion by the pituitary, causing impotence and loss of libido.

Diagnosis

The dexamethasone suppression test is performed. Dexamethasone is a potent glucocorticoid analogue. In normal people, 1–2 mg dexamethasone, given at night, feeds back to inhibit ACTH release from the pituitary and results in lower serum cortisol levels the next morning. This serum cortisol suppression does not occur in people with Cushing's syndrome.

Adrenogenital Syndrome

Adrenogenital syndrome includes any condition in which high levels of adrenal androgens cause virilization. Effects are more obvious in women and can include hirsutism, baldness, acne, voice changes, amenorrhea, and clitoral hypertrophy. The condition can be congenital, in which an enzyme defect causes precursors of cortisol and aldosterone synthesis to be shunted to androgen synthesis. Later in life, adrenal hyperplasia, adenoma, or adenocarcinoma can increase androgen production and cause symptoms.

Hyperaldosteronism

Primary hyperaldosteronism (**Conn's syndrome**) is caused by adrenal hyperplasia or adrenal adenoma. Patients have hypertension and hypokalemia. Treatment is with the aldosterone antagonist, spironolactone. Adenomas are surgically resected.

Secondary aldosteronism is caused by increased activity of the renin-angiotensin system. The most common cause is a decrease in the blood pressure perceived by the juxtaglomerular cells, as in congestive heart failure, cirrhosis, and nephrotic syndrome. The underlying disorder is treated.

Pheochromocytoma

This rare tumor of the adrenal medulla or sympathetic ganglion secretes bursts of catecholamines, usually epinephrine. The increased sympathetic activity causes episodic hypertension, headaches, palpitations, and anxiety. Diagnosis is confirmed when 24-hour urine collection shows elevated levels of catecholamines and their metabolites. Treatment is surgical, though symptoms may be temporarily controlled with α- and β-blockers.

Endocrine Pancreas

Physiology

Insulin's job is to store energy for our bodies from the foods we eat in the form of glucose, amino acids, and lipids. Insulin is synthesized in the pancreas and acts on almost all tissues, except the brain and red blood cells. When blood sugar or amino acids levels rise, insulin secretion is triggered. Fat intake does not trigger insulin secretion. The functions of insulin include these:

- Increased synthesis of glycogen, lipids, and proteins in the liver

- Increased synthesis of fatty acids from glucose and decreased lipolysis in peripheral adipose tissues

- Increased glucose and amino acid uptake in skeletal muscle

Glucagon is a catabolic hormone that works to oppose the actions of insulin and provides energy to your body when there isn't a meal in sight. It acts mainly on the liver to degrade and release glucose, lipids, and ketones into the bloodstream. It also stimulates gluconeogenesis.

Somatostatin is secreted by the pancreas and appears to play a local regulatory role in the secretion of insulin and glucagon, as well as some role in GI function.

Development

During development of the pancreas (described in more detail in chapter 13), **endocrine cells** form groupings amidst the **exocrine pancreas** glandular tissue. These groups of cells, known as the islets of Langerhans, contain three hormone-secreting types of cells, The first, known as **alpha cells**, secretes glucagon. **Beta cells**, the most numerous endocrine cell in the islets, secrete insulin. **Delta cells** secrete somatostatin.

Diabetes Mellitus (Type I)

Type I diabetes is also called *juvenile-onset diabetes* or *insulin-dependent diabetes*. Patients lose their ability to produce endogenous insulin. The mechanism is unknown, but it is thought to be autoimmune, as patients generally have anti–islet cell antibodies. Type I diabetes is associated with the MHC class II molecules HLA-DR3, HLA-DR4, and HLA-DQw3.2, and it may run in families. The average age of onset is 11–13 years.

Signs & Symptoms

The classic triad of symptoms is **polyuria** (caused by osmotic diuresis from glucose dumping in the urine), **polydipsia** (to replenish water loss), and **polyphagia** (in a futile effort to increase available energy). Weight loss occurs because energy from glucose cannot get into the tissues. Accelerated fat breakdown, in an effort to provide energy to the body's cells, leads to ketoacidosis, and patients may present with nausea and vomiting, air hunger (known as **Kussmaul's respirations**), or coma. In general, the onset of symptoms is rapid.

Diagnosis

One of the following is present:

- Elevation of random plasma glucose and classic symptoms of diabetes

- Fasting plasma glucose >126 mg/100 ml on 2 separate days

- Positive oral glucose tolerance test on more than one occasion (plasma glucose >200 mg/100 ml 2 hours after an oral glucose load)

Treatment

Insulin injections are required. Insulin doses and combinations must be titrated to maintain optimal blood glucose levels. Patients must be taught how to monitor their glucose level at home (fingerstick monitoring) and how to adjust diet and insulin accordingly.

Type I diabetics often have a "honeymoon" period shortly after their diabetes is diagnosed, during which endogenous insulin levels rise. Therapy may not be needed for several months, but symptoms and insulin requirements inevitably return.

Diabetes Mellitus (Type II)

Type II diabetes is also called *adult-onset diabetes* or *non–insulin dependent diabetes*. This type of diabetes arises when the body's response to insulin decreases, and the tissues become increasingly resistant to insulin. Initially, the pancreas responds by increasing insulin production, but the beta cells' capacity to produce insulin may wane later in the disease. Thus, depending on the stage of disease at the time of diagnosis, insulin levels may be low, normal, or even high. Although patients may need insulin therapy (insulin-requiring non–insulin dependent diabetes), endogenous insulin production is usually sufficient to protect against diabetic ketoacidosis (discussed later). Obesity and a positive family history for type II diabetes are common, but there is no association with any HLA type. Typical onset occurs after age 40, and it is diagnosed the same way that type I diabetes is.

Signs & Symptoms

Although the classic symptoms are the same as in type I, onset is more insidious, and ketoacidosis does not occur. Patients may complain of blurry vision due to osmotic changes in the lens.

Treatment

- Diet should be low in concentrated sugar to minimize serum glucose fluctuations. The patient should be taught to monitor serum glucose with fingersticks.

- Weight loss and exercise may increase insulin sensitivity in the tissues.

- Oral hypoglycemic agents, called sulfonylureas, stimulate insulin secretion. Insulin injections are required in type II patients who do not respond to more conservative measures.

- A newer class of medications, called biguanides, may increase peripheral glucose uptake by increasing the effects of insulin on muscle cells.

Ketoacidosis

Insulin normally inhibits peripheral lipolysis. When insulin is extremely low, triglycerides are degraded into free fatty acids, which are then converted to ketoacids by the liver. The three types of ketones seen are acetone, acetoacetate, and β-hydroxybutyrate. Diabetic ketoacidosis (DKA) occurs most commonly in type I diabetics who do not take their insulin. It also occurs when infection or myocardial infarction has increased the body's insulin requirements. Type II diabetics usually produce enough insulin of their own to protect against DKA.

Signs & Symptoms

The prodrome involves 12–24 hours of weakness, polyuria, and polydipsia. The patient may hyperventilate and take deep, rapid breaths (Kussmaul's respirations) in an attempt to compensate for the metabolic acidosis caused by ketone bodies. A fruity, acetone odor may be smelled on the breath. Abdominal pain and vomiting are also common, but care must be taken to determine if GI complaints are due to ketoacidosis or to a precipitating infection. As dehydration worsens, mental status changes can occur.

Diagnosis

Serum glucose is 300–800 mg/dl.

Treatment

Hydration and insulin. Potassium must also be given and monitored carefully. The diuresis leads to depletion of the body's K$^+$ stores. Then, with treatment, insulin causes potassium to enter cells, and if it is not replaced, hypokalemia can cause fatal cardiac arrhythmias.

Hyperosmolar Coma

This complication of type II diabetes usually occurs after many days of infection or other illness.

Signs & Symptoms

The symptoms of polyuria, polydipsia, and dehydration are similar to those of ketoacidosis; however, because some insulin is present, lipolysis and ketoacidosis do not occur. Therefore, there is no hyperventilation or acetone smell to the breath, but dehydration is profound and causes significant mental status changes. Dehydration may not be immediately apparent, because urine output remains normal due to osmotic diuresis. Hemoconcentration may lead to stroke.

Diagnosis

Serum glucose is 600–2,000 mg/dl, much higher than in DKA.

Treatment

Treatment is similar to that of DKA.

Hypoglycemia/Hyperinsulinism

Several clinical entities can cause hypoglycemia. **Reactive hypoglycemia,** also known as postprandial hypoglycemia, is lowered blood glucose that occurs 2–4 hours after eating. A pancreatic islet cell tumor, or insulinoma, can produce excess insulin, causing hypoglycemia. Iatrogenic hypoglycemia can result from administration of too much insulin (remember Klaus von Bulow?) or, less frequently, from excessive oral hypoglycemics.

Signs & Symptoms

The symptoms of hypoglycemia fall into two categories. Faintness, weakness, tremulousness, palpitations, sweating, and hunger are the symptoms of a hypercatecholamine state, as epinephrine induces glycogen mobilization. The other type of symptoms are CNS-related: headache, confusion, and personality changes.

Diagnosis

Reactive hypoglycemia is diagnosed if hypoglycemia coincides with the occurrence of typical symptoms and are relieved by carbohydrate ingestion. Elevated insulin in the presence of hypoglycemia indicates insulinoma or an exogenous insulin source. A favorite board question is hypoglycemia in the presence of high levels of insulin, particularly in a patient with access to exogenous insulin (for example, the family member of a diabetic). If the plasma C peptide (the non-functional portion of insulin that is clipped off when the body produces endogenous insulin) is low, then the insulin must have been administered exogenously.

Treatment

Eating frequent small meals improves reactive hypoglycemia. Surgery is required to treat insulinoma. For iatrogenic hypoglycemia, increased care should be used in monitoring glucose and administering insulin.

Chronic Complications of Diabetes

Most chronic complications are due to **microvascular disease**. Development of complications is more severe in patients with poorly controlled diabetes and seems to be associated with chronic exposure to high levels of glucose, although the mechanism is unknown.

- **Retinopathy**: In background retinopathy, effects include micro-aneurysms, blot hemorrhages, infarcts, hard exudates, and macular edema. Changes are seen early and do not usually cause visual loss until macular edema develops. In proliferative retinopathy, new vessels grow on the retinal surface (**neovascularization**). These vessels are fragile and prone to hemorrhage. Fibrosis occurs during healing and may put traction on the retina, leading to retinal detachment and visual loss. Laser therapy can slow the progression of proliferative retinopathy.

- **Renal disease**: The first sign is proteinuria, with a subsequent decrease in creatinine clearance after 1–3 years. End-stage renal disease, requiring dialysis or transplant, typically occurs 3 years after that. Preventative measures include keeping strict control of plasma glucose, eating a low-protein diet, controlling hypertension (especially with ACE inhibitors), avoiding contrast dye, and aggressively treating urinary tract infections.

- **Atherosclerosis**: Coronary artery disease, stroke, and peripheral vascular disease are more common in diabetics. Peripheral vascular disease presents as intermittent claudication (leg pain with exercise due to ischemia) or nonhealing foot ulcers. Diabetics are also prone to having "silent" heart attacks (only detected by electrocardiography later) and may not have anginal symptoms because they often have a concomitant neuropathy.

- **Neuropathy**: Bilateral symmetric sensory impairment usually begins in the feet and progresses proximally. Patients may complain of pain or numbness. Foot ulcers may develop and become infected without patients' noticing, so diabetic patients should be trained to examine their feet regularly for ulcerations. Autonomic dysfunction can include impotence, orthostatic hypotension, constipation or diarrhea, and silent myocardial infarction. Finally, mononeuropathies may be caused by infarction of a single nerve, frequently a cranial nerve. Pain is followed by a palsy, which usually resolves in several months.

Multiple Endocrine Dysfunction

Multiple Endocrine Neoplasia (MEN) Syndromes

This group of autosomal dominant syndromes involves hyperplasia or neoplasms in more than one endocrine gland. All patients who have hyperplasia or neoplasms in one endocrine gland should be evaluated for these syndromes, and the family history should be thoroughly reviewed. The features of MEN syndromes are listed in Table 16-5.

Pharmacology

See Tables 16-6 through 16-9 for a description of the drugs used to treat the disorders that were discussed in this chapter.

Table 16-5. Multiple endocrine neoplasias (MEN)

Syndrome	Characteristics
MEN I (Wermer's syndrome)	Parathyroid adenomas
	Pancreatic adenomas
	Pituitary adenomas
MEN II (Sipple's syndrome)	Medullary thyroid carcinoma
	Pheochromocytomas
	Parathyroid adenomas
MEN III (or MEN IIa)	Like MEN II but with neuromas

Table 16-6. Thyroid-related drugs

Agent	Mechanism	Uses	Toxicities
Levothy-roxine (T_4)	Acts directly at thyroid receptor (converted to T_3)	Thyroid replacement therapy	Periodic TSH checks; T_4 levels not accurate in assessing thyroid function if taking levothyroxine; large doses cause thyrotoxicosis
Propyl-thiouracil	Prevents iodine metabolism and T_4 to T_3 conversion	Hyperthyroidism	Teratogenic to fetal thyroid
Iodine	Inhibits T_4 release	Thyrotoxicosis	—
Methimazole	Prevents iodine metabolism	Hyperthyroidism	Teratogenic to fetal thyroid

T_3 = triiodothyronine; TSH = thyroid-stimulating hormone.

Table 16-7. Calcium-related drugs

Agent	Mechanism	Uses	Toxicities
Calcium carbonate	Increases serum calcium	Osteoporosis Renal failure Hypocalcemia	Renal stones Hypercalcemia
Vitamin D (calcitriol)	Increases calcium absorption	Renal failure Hypocalcemia Hypoparathyroidism	Renal stones Hypercalcemia
Calcitonin	Inhibition of bone resorption	Paget's disease Osteoporosis Hypercalcemia	—
Mithramycin	Cytotoxic antibiotic that inhibits osteoclasts	Paget's disease Hypercalcemia	Hepatic and renal toxicity Thrombocytopenia
Bisphosphonates (e.g., etidronate)	Reduces bone turnover by reducing osteoclasts	Hypercalcemia Osteoporosis Paget's disease	Electrocardiographic changes Renal failure

Table 16-8. Corticosteroids

Agent	Mechanism	Uses	Toxicities
Prednisone	Acts at cortisol receptor; weakly active at mineralocorticoid receptors	Asthma Autoimmune disorders	4 times more potent than cortisol
Hydrocortisone	Acts at cortisol receptor; weakly active at mineralocorticoid receptors	Addison's disease Inflammatory bowel disease (enemas)	As potent as cortisol
Dexamethasone	Acts at cortisol receptor	Adrenal evaluation High intracranial pressure	Rapid action
Triamcinolone	Acts at cortisol receptor; no mineralocorticoid effects	Adrenal hormone replacement Dermatitis (topical)	30 times more potent than cortisol
Beclomethasone	Acts at cortisol receptor	Allergic rhinitis (spray)	Few systemic effects
Spironolactone	Antagonist at mineralocorticoid receptor; acts as diuretic	Hyperaldosteronism Hirsutism	Hyperkalemia
Aminoglutethimide	Blocks steroid synthesis by blocking conversion of cholesterol to pregnenolone	Cushing's disease ACTH tumors Hormone-sensitive tumors	—
Fludrocortisone	Acts at mineralocorticoid receptor	Addison's disease	Hypertension Hypokalemia

ACTH = adrenocorticotropic hormone.

Table 16-9. Diabetic agents

Agent	Mechanism	Uses	Comments
Rapidly acting insulin (e.g., regular insulin)	Acts at insulin receptor	Diabetes mellitus (I and II)	Onset: 30 mins to 2 hours Duration: 5–12 hours
Intermediate-acting insulin (e.g., NPH insulin)	Acts at insulin receptor	Diabetes mellitus (I and II)	Onset: 2–4 hours Duration: 16–24 hours
Long-acting insulin (e.g., Ultralente insulin)	Acts at insulin receptor	Diabetes mellitus (I and II)	Onset: 4–8 hours Duration: 36–48 hours
Glipizide	Stimulates insulin secretion from beta cells of pancreas	Type II diabetes mellitus	May cause hypoglycemia Onset: 1–3 hours Duration: 10–24 hours
Glyburide	Stimulates insulin secretion from beta cells of pancreas	Type II diabetes mellitus	May cause hypoglycemia Onset: 1–3 hours Duration: 24–72 hours
Chlorpropamide	Stimulates insulin secretion from beta cells of pancreas	Type II diabetes mellitus	May cause hypoglycemia Longest half-life (3–5 days)
Tolbutamide	Stimulates insulin secretion from beta cells of pancreas	Type II diabetes mellitus	May cause hypoglycemia Shortest half-life (6–12 hours)
Biguanides (e.g., metformin)	Increases tissue sensitivity to insulin	Type II diabetes mellitus Insulin resistance	**Lactic acidosis** rare but fatal; does not cause hypoglycemia
Thiazdidinediones (e.g., pioglitazone, rosiglitazone)	Increases tissue sensitivity to insulin	Type II Diabetes mellitus	Check LFT's for hepatotoxicity; does not cause hypoglycemia

CHAPTER 17

Biostatistics and Epidemiology

Epidemiology

Central Tendency

The central tendency measures (mean, median, mode) describe the central values of a given data set. For example, say you're given the ages of a group of medical students (22, 21, 22, 23, 22, 24):

The **mean**, also known as the average, is calculated by adding all the values together and then dividing by the number of values in the series. With the numbers above, the mean age is 22.3 (sum of 134 divided by 6).

$$\text{Mean} = \frac{\text{Sum}}{\text{Number of values}}$$

The **median** value divides the group of data in half. To calculate the median, the data is rearranged in ascending number order (the medical students' ages are then reordered like this: 21, 22, 22, 22, 23, 24). If there is an odd number of data points, the central value is the median value. If there is an even number of data points, the median value is the average of the two central values. There are six values (an even number), so the median is the average of the two central values (44/2), which equals 22.

Median =
Number in the middle

The **mode** is the most commonly occurring value in the data set. Because the number 22 appears the most in this data set (three times), it is also the mode. It's important to remember that the mean, median, and mode are not necessarily equal to each other. In general, the median is considered the best measure of central tendency.

Mode =
Most popular number

Variability

The variability describes how scattered the data points are from the middle values. Suppose you are given a group of patients with the following serum cholesterol levels: 142, 221, 330, 286, 199, 212, 256.

The **range** of the data is calculated by subtracting the highest value from the lowest value. In this case, the range is $330 - 142 = 188$.

The **variance** (s^2) is a little more complicated to calculate and is mainly used to subsequently calculate the standard deviation. First, you need to calculate the mean as above. In this case, it's about 235 (1,646 divided by 7). Then, just plug it into the equation below to calculate the difference, or deviation, of each data point from the

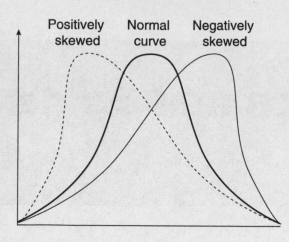

Fig. 17-1. Positive and negative skew.

mean. The differences are squared, added up, and divided by the total number of data points minus 1. The formula is as follows:

$$\text{Variance} = s^2 = \frac{\sum(\text{Average value} - \text{individual value})^2}{\text{Total number of data points} - 1}$$

The sum of the squares of the deviation is 22,737 (8,649 + 196 + 9,025 + 2,601 + 1,296 + 529 + 441). The total number of data points minus 1 is 6. Therefore, the variance is 22,737 divided by 6, or about 3,790.

The **standard deviation** is the square root of the variance:

$$\text{Standard deviation} = s = \sqrt{\text{variance}}$$
$$\sqrt{3,790} = {\sim}62$$

Probability

Probability is the likelihood of a particular event taking place within a given number of possible outcomes. Probability is expressed as a value between 0 (no likelihood of the event occurring) and 1 (100% likelihood that the event will occur).

Probability distributions are different ways to display data graphically so that you can determine the likelihood of a particular event occurring. The standard "normal" distribution, or gaussian "bell-shaped" curve, is an example of a probability distribution (Fig. 17-1). Other distributions include bimodal, rectangular, and skewed curves. If the *tail* of a curve skews to the right, it's **positively skewed**. If it skews to the left, it's **negatively skewed**.

In a perfect bell-shaped curve, the mean equals the median and the mode. Also, if you know the standard deviation and the mean, you can use percentiles to describe the values in your data set. In a bell-shaped distribution, 68% of values are within one standard deviation of the mean, 95% are within two standard deviations, and more than 99% are within three standard deviations (Fig. 17-2). The median value is always at the fiftieth percentile, regardless of whether the distribution is normal or skewed.

1 SD = 68%
2 SD = 95%
3 SD = 99%

Assume that the Step 1 test scores are distributed in a bell-shaped curve, with a mean score of 200 and a standard deviation of 20. This means that about 68% of test-takers will score between 180 and 220 and about 95% will score between 160 and 240. Many of the defined normal ranges on laboratory tests assume a standard

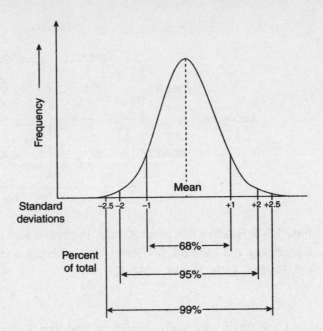

Fig. 17-2. Standard deviation
distribution of bell-shaped curves.
(Reprinted with permission from
RS Breaden, C Denenberg,
KC Feibusch, SN Gomperts.
*Prescription for the Boards:
USMLE Step 2* [1st ed]. Boston:
Little, Brown, 1996;419.)

distribution, and the top and bottom levels of the range correspond to a standard
deviation of 2, encompassing 95% of all values.

Prevalence and Incidence

The **incidence** of a disease is the number of *new* cases of the disease that occur over
a period of time. The formula is as follows:

$$\text{Incidence} = \frac{\text{Number of new cases of a disease over a given period}}{\text{Total population}}$$

Incidence does not tell you anything about the number of cases that already
exist. To measure that, we look at the **prevalence**:

$$\text{Prevalence} = \frac{\text{Number of existing cases of a disease}}{\text{Total population}}$$

Incidence is expressed over a given period (e.g., per month, per year), whereas
prevalence describes a specific point in time. Prevalence also depends on the length
of survival after contracting the disease—a long survival increases the number of
"existing cases." The incidence of a disease may exceed the prevalence (a newly discovered disease that kills rapidly, e.g., Ebola virus), but in most cases the prevalence
exceeds the incidence, which reflect the chronic course of diseases such as diabetes
and chronic obstructive pulmonary disease.

Case Fatality Rates

Case fatality rates refer to the number of people with a particular condition who
die over a given period of time.

$$\text{Case fatality} = \frac{\text{Number of people with the disease who die}}{\text{Number of people with the disease}}$$

Disease

	Present	Absent	
Present	a	b	a + b
Absent	c	d	c + d
	a + c	b + d	a + b + c + d = N

Exposure (row label)

Fig. 17-3. Relative risk or odds ratio. (Reprinted with permission from RS Breaden, C Denenberg, KC Feibush, SN Gomperts. *Prescription for the Boards: USMLE Step 2* [1st ed]. Boston: Little, Brown, 1996;421.)

Case fatality rates *do not* indicate the risk of dying from a particular disease in the general population—only the risk for people who *already* have the disease! For a given illness, the case fatality rate may be 100%, but to decide whether this is an important problem at the population level, you need to know the prevalence and the incidence as well.

Assessing Risk

Risk factors: variables associated with a disease.

Risk factors are variables that may be associated with the development of a particular disease. For example, smoking is believed to be a strong risk factor for the development of coronary artery disease. Risk factors are identified when a variable is found to be associated to a particular outcome. However, association alone does not mean that the risk factor actually causes the disease. For example, there is an association between low-birth-weight babies and inner-city neighborhoods, but it is not correct to assume that being born in an inner-city neighborhood causes low birth weight.

Risk difference is calculated by subtraction of the risks.

The **risk difference**, also known as the *excess risk*, is the risk of developing a disease in an exposed group minus that risk in an unexposed group. For example, if the risk of developing lung cancer in smokers is 14 per 100 smoking years, and the risk of developing lung cancer in nonsmokers is 1 per 100 nonsmoking years, the risk difference is $14 - 1 = 13$ per 100 years.

Relative risk is a ratio of the risk in an exposed population to the risk in an unexposed population.

The **relative risk** is the risk that an exposed population has of contracting a particular condition compared to an unexposed population. A relative risk of 5.0 means that the exposed population is 5 times more likely to get the disease than the unexposed population.

Relative risks can only be calculated with data from cohort studies (Fig. 17-3). In case-control studies, an approximation of the relative risk, known as the **odds ratio**, can be calculated. Cohort and case-control studies are discussed later in the chapter.

Odds ratio ≈ relative risk if $a \ll b$ and $c \ll d$ because $a + b \approx b$ and $c + d \approx d$

$$\text{Relative risk} = \frac{\text{Incidence rate among the exposed population}}{\text{Incidence rate among the unexposed population}} = \frac{a/(a + b)}{c/(c + d)}$$

$$\text{Odds ratio} = \frac{a/b}{c/d} = \frac{ad}{bc}$$

		True Diagnosis: Diseased	True Diagnosis: Not diseased	
Screening Test	⊕	a (True-positive)	b (False-positive)	a + b
	⊖	c (False-negative)	d (True-negative)	c + d
		a + c	b + d	N

Fig. 17-4. Sensitivity and specificity.

Sensitivity, Specificity, and Predictive Values

Sensitivity is the percentage of diseased individuals who test positive with a diagnostic test (Fig. 17-4).

Mnemonic for sensitivity is PID, or "positive in disease.

$$\text{Sensitivity} = \frac{\text{Number of true-positives}}{\text{Number of true-positives + false-negatives}} = \frac{a}{a + c}$$

Specificity is the percentage of healthy individuals who test negative with the diagnostic test.

Mnemonic for specificity is NIH, or "negative in health."

$$\text{Specificity} = \frac{\text{Number of true-negatives}}{\text{Number of true-negatives + false-positives}} = \frac{d}{b + d}$$

SNout = sensitivity rules out
SPin= specificity rules in

Sensitivity and specificity reflect how good a test is at picking up or ruling out a disease.The higher the sensitivity, the better a test is at ruling out a disease if the patient tests negative. The higher the specificity, the better a test is at ruling in a disease if the patient tests positive.

PPV = a/(a + b)

The **positive predictive value** (PPV) is the probability of having a disease given a positive test result.

$$\text{PPV} = \frac{\text{Number of true-positives}}{\text{Number of true-positives + false-positives}} = \frac{a}{a + b}$$

NPV = d/(c + d)

The **negative predictive value** (NPV) is the probability of not having the disease, given a negative test.

$$\text{NPV} = \frac{\text{Number of true-negatives}}{\text{Number of true-negatives + false-negatives}} = \frac{d}{c + d}$$

Know these formulas cold—it's common for the Step 1 test to give you a bunch of numbers and ask you to calculate the sensitivity, specificity, PPV, and NPV.

The sensitivity and specificity are qualities of the test used and do not vary with the populations being tested. The positive predictive value and negative predictive value, on the other hand, do vary depending on the prevalence of the disease in a population. If the disease has a high prevalence in the population being tested, then the positive predictive value of a test improves and the negative predictive value worsens. If a disease has a low prevalence, then the positive predictive value goes down and the negative predictive value improves.

		Actual case	
		H_0 is true	H_0 is false (H_1 is true)
Decision based on study	Accept H_0	Correct decision	Type II error (β)
	Reject H_0 (assume H_1 is true)	Type I error (α)	Correct decision

Fig. 17-5. Errors in hypothesis testing. (H_0 = null hypothesis; H_1 = alternate hypothesis.) (Reprinted with permission from RS Breaden, C Denenberg, KC Feibush, SN Gomperts. *Prescription for the Boards: USMLE Step 2* [1st ed]. Boston: Little, Brown, 1996;424.)

When screening for a disease such as HIV, serial tests are used to confirm the diagnosis. The first test used should have a very high sensitivity to avoid missing disease-positive cases. The positive cases can then undergo a second test, which should have a high specificity to ascertain that positive results are truly disease-positive. In HIV, the screening ELISA has a >99.9% sensitivity, and the confirmatory Western blot has a >99.9% specificity when combined with the ELISA.

Statistical Significance and Power

The **null hypothesis**, H_0, is the assumption that there is no difference between two populations. The **alternate hypothesis**, H_1, states that there is a difference between the two populations. It is assumed that the null hypothesis is correct unless it is "rejected," that is, we can show that the differences in a population did not occur randomly.

To show a significant difference between two populations, there are multiple statistical tests, such as the chi-square test and the *t*-test, which allow us to calculate a **p value**, or probability that the test results could have occurred by chance alone. A *p* value less than 0.05 indicates that there is less than a 5% chance that the two populations were different due to random error alone. **Confidence intervals** are another way to show that a difference is significant: If the intervals you are given span a range that contains the value 1, it indicates that the difference is not statistically significant.

p <0.05 is statistically significant.

A **type I error** (α error) is the possibility that H_0 is rejected when it's actually true (Fig. 17-5). In other words, a real difference did not exist, but the test led you to believe that one did. The likelihood of a type I error equals the *p* value; it's usually less than 5% (0.05).

A **type II error** (β error) occurs when H_0 is accepted but is actually false. In this case, there really was a difference, but it was missed. A type II error is associated with the power of a study (power $= 1 - \beta$). *Power* is the ability of a study to actually detect the difference you were looking for and depends on the size of the populations studied. A typical value for β is 0.10 or 0.20.

Observational Studies

Cohort studies are prospective; they follow one population over a period of time. They are expensive and time-consuming, but they can provide complete data on a number of exposures and allow you to calculate relative risks between different populations.

Case-control studies look at populations with and without a certain disease and attempt to determine exposure patterns. Case-control studies are quicker, easier, and less expensive than cohort studies and better at studying rare diseases. Recall bias is more likely (see below), however, and only an odds ratio may be calculated, not relative risk. If the disease is rare in the population, an odds ratio is a good approximation of relative risk.

Cross-sectional studies look at a population at one point in time. These are generally inexpensive, but they are not good for studying rare exposures or studying the effects of exposure over time.

Case series are reports on a set of clinical subjects with a particular exposure or outcome (e.g., a group of people undergoing an experimental surgery). There is usually no information about a control group (people who did not undergo the procedure), and the results cannot be extrapolated to the general population.

Community surveys look at multiple factors in a particular group of people (e.g., African-American or senior community). These studies are similar to cross-sectional studies but are generally broader in the amount of information obtained.

Experimental Studies

Clinical trials are performed to compare the effects of two different clinical interventions. A common example is studying the efficacy of a new drug. The subjects are randomly divided into two groups and given the new drug or the older, gold standard medication (or a placebo, if there is no gold standard drug). Neither the subject nor the researchers should know which group is getting the drug ("double-blind"). Clinical trials allow a number of factors to be controlled but are expensive and lengthy.

Community intervention trials are performed when the "subject" is the whole community; for example, one town undergoes fluoridation of its water and is compared to a town that does not. Community intervention trials can provide a lot of data because there may be many subjects, but are subject to the possibility that there are differences in the two populations other than the intervention itself.

Validity

Validity describes the ability of a test to measure what it was designed to measure. **Internal validity** refers to the question of whether a given exposure caused an observed change. Threats to internal validity include

- Extraneous events
- Maturation (changes during the intervention)
- Instrumentation (differences in observers or calibration)
- Selection bias

External validity is the generalizability of the results to the rest of the population. Threats to external variability include pretesting (sensitizes them to treatment) and reactive effects of testing (people who know they are being tested act differently).

Bias

Bias is the possible effect that systematic error may have on the results of a study. Many different types of bias exist:

- **Confounding bias**: When a third factor is associated with both the risk factor and the disease, the study results can be attributed to the third factor (e.g., smoking is associated with fatal motorcycle accidents, but only because both smoking and not wearing a helmet are seen in "risk takers").

- **Selection bias**: The people who are selected for an intervention are different than those who aren't (e.g., if selected from hospitalized patients, subjects might be sicker than average).

- **Lead-time bias**: Because screening may diagnose a disease earlier, "survival time" appears longer, but it isn't.

- **Length bias**: Screening detects slowly progressive cases (those with aggressive disease are missed because they're dead or cured).

- **Volunteer bias**: The type of people who volunteer for studies may be fundamentally different than those who don't (e.g., more compliant, different socioeconomic status).

- **Withdrawal bias**: The type of people who are withdrawn from a study are fundamentally different from those who aren't (e.g., people who died might be classified as "lost to follow-up" instead).

- **Compliance bias**: The type of people who are compliant with a regimen may be different from the noncompliant (e.g., people who cannot adhere to strict dietary regimens may be at higher risk for disease than people who are accustomed to adhering to a strict diet).

- **Recall bias**: The data collected may depend on a patient's recollection (notoriously unreliable), and the cases may be asked more details about exposure than controls.

- **Attention bias**: Subjects may change their behavior once they know they are being observed.

Organization and Costs of Health Care

As everyone knows, health care in the United States is changing rapidly. In the past, patients usually paid separately for each visit to the doctor (**fee-for-service**) or had health insurance that reimbursed the health care providers. As health insurance became more prevalent (as a benefit with employment), people did not care what fees were charged for medical care, and physician's prices went up. In the 1970s, the idea of **health maintenance organizations** (HMOs)—health plans that would be reimbursed a set amount per patient no matter how much money is spent on each patient (known as **capitation**)—took hold. The advantage was that by only paying a certain amount, health plans had an incentive to keep people healthy. However, as HMOs have become more prevalent, there is concern that the HMO providers may also have an incentive to withhold necessary care as well. In the 1960s, Congress authorized **Medicare** (medical insurance for people aged 65 and older) and **Medicaid** (medical insurance for the indigent). Many other industrialized nations have nationalized, state-sponsored health care systems that provide health care for the full population.

Medical Ethics

Nonmaleficence and Beneficence

Nonmaleficence is the translation of the basic medical tenet *"Primum non nocere,"* or "First, do no harm." This means no deliberate harmful acts (of course!) but also that we should consider the risks and benefits involved in any toxic therapies. **Beneficence** is the responsibility to go a step further and actually do something beneficial for the patient. Our duty for beneficence is not just to individual patients but to the community at large (e.g., public health interventions).

Informed Consent

Informed consent is the power of the patient to choose and refuse interventions after understanding the options. The requirements include the following:

- Discussion of pertinent information, including the nature of the proposed interventions as well as risks, benefits, and alternative treatments
- Voluntary patient agreement with treatment plan with no coercion from any party

Informed consent is *not* required in the following situations:

- Emergency situations, in which there is a **doctrine of implied consent**
- When the patient lacks mental capability to understand the situation and make decisions—in this case, an appropriate surrogate (e.g., parent, spouse) must make the decisions.

Confidentiality

Confidentiality, or the idea that all communication between a patient and physician is private, can be waived in the following circumstances:

- The patient waives the right (e.g., allows you to tell family members).
- There is a possibility of serious potential harm to patient or others (e.g., suicidal or homicidal plans).

- The patient has a **"reportable" illness** (it must be reported to the public health department). This includes some infectious diseases, such as gonorrhea and tuberculosis (human immunodeficiency virus [HIV] reporting varies from state to state due to fears of discrimination), child or elder abuse, and possible impairment of driving (e.g., epileptics with frequent loss of consciousness).

Death and Dying

Elizabeth Kübler-Ross named the following five stages as common human ways of coping with death, dying, and loss.

- **Denial**: The patient may be in a state of shock and deny the diagnosis or the presence of physical impairment.

- **Anger**: The patient may feel frustrated and angry at what may seem to be "bad luck."

- **Bargaining**: The patient may make promises of good behavior to God, family, or doctor in exchange for being saved or cured.

- **Depression**: The patient may have symptoms similar to clinical depression, including insomnia, hopelessness, and possible suicidal ideation. This should not be accepted as normal: It requires psychiatric evaluation.

- **Acceptance**: The patient acknowledges the prognosis and can make and accept long-term decisions.

Birth-Related Issues

The U.S. Supreme Court has upheld that **abortion** cannot be denied to women in the first 3 months of pregnancy. After this, state laws vary until the stage of viability, at about 24 weeks gestation. "Late-term" abortions may be performed in cases in which the mother's life is at risk, although this is controversial.

Research Participation

Patients must be able to provide informed consent in order to participate in research. **Conflicts of interest** include situations in which what is best for the study is not necessarily what is best for the patient. These situations must always be resolved in favor of the patient. If placebos are used, the patient must be informed, and the existence of any known effective treatment makes the use of a placebo unethical.

Referral to Other Physicians

It is unlawful in most states to refer a patient to a physician group or health-related facility (e.g., laboratory or X-ray facility) in which the referring physician may have a financial interest, unless it is disclosed to the patient before the referral.

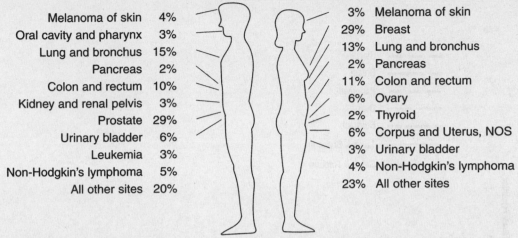

Melanoma of skin	4%	3%	Melanoma of skin
Oral cavity and pharynx	3%	29%	Breast
Lung and bronchus	15%	13%	Lung and bronchus
Pancreas	2%	2%	Pancreas
Colon and rectum	10%	11%	Colon and rectum
Kidney and renal pelvis	3%	6%	Ovary
Prostate	29%	2%	Thyroid
Urinary bladder	6%	6%	Corpus and Uterus, NOS
Leukemia	3%	3%	Urinary bladder
Non-Hodgkin's lymphoma	5%	4%	Non-Hodgkin's lymphoma
All other sites	20%	23%	All other sites

Fig. 17-6. Cancer incidence, 1999 (excludes basal and squamous cell cancer and carcinoma in situ except bladder). (Reprinted from SH Landis, T Murray, S Bolden, PA Wingo. Cancer statistics, 1999. CA Cancer J Clin 1999; 49:16.)

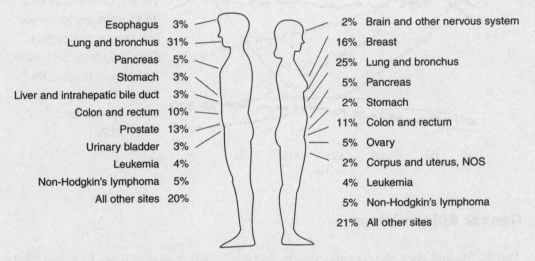

Esophagus	3%	2%	Brain and other nervous system
Lung and bronchus	31%	16%	Breast
Pancreas	5%	25%	Lung and bronchus
Stomach	3%	5%	Pancreas
Liver and intrahepatic bile duct	3%	2%	Stomach
Colon and rectum	10%	11%	Colon and rectum
Prostate	13%	5%	Ovary
Urinary bladder	3%	2%	Corpus and uterus, NOS
Leukemia	4%	4%	Leukemia
Non-Hodgkin's lymphoma	5%	5%	Non-Hodgkin's lymphoma
All other sites	20%	21%	All other sites

Figure 17-7. Cancer deaths, 1999 (excludes basal and squamous cell cancer and carcinoma in situ except bladder). †These two cancers tied for a ranking of 10. (Reprinted from SH Landis, T Murray, S Bolden, PA Wingo. Cancer statistics, 1999. CA Cancer J Clin 1999; 49:16.)

Epidemiology

Prevention

- **Primary prevention** is the prevention of disease. Education aimed at avoiding alcohol and using seatbelts are examples of primary prevention.

- **Secondary prevention** is early detection of disease. Pap smears and fecal occult blood tests are some examples.

- **Tertiary prevention** attempts to keep a disease from getting worse. Treatment and rehabilitation after a heart attack or stroke are examples of tertiary prevention.

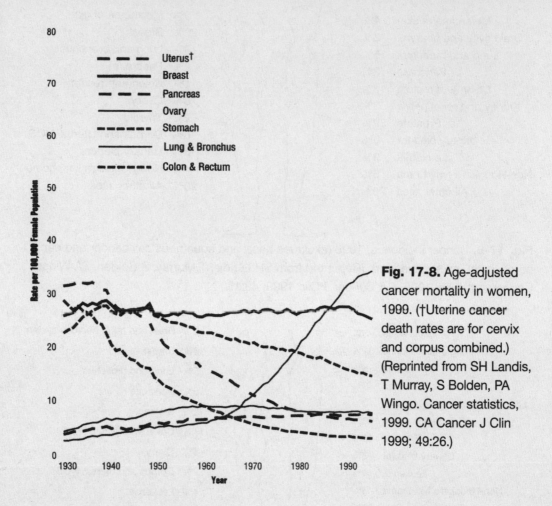

Fig. 17-8. Age-adjusted cancer mortality in women, 1999. (†Uterine cancer death rates are for cervix and corpus combined.) (Reprinted from SH Landis, T Murray, S Bolden, PA Wingo. Cancer statistics, 1999. CA Cancer J Clin 1999; 49:26.)

Cancer Epidemiology

The 10 leading sites of new cancer cases and deaths are shown in Figs. 17-6 and 17-7. Memorize these—they are common easy questions on the Boards.

The age-adjusted cancer death rate trends are shown in Figs. 17-8 and 17-9. Notice that the number of lung cancer deaths has been going up, but the number of stomach cancer deaths has been coming down.

Mortality Rates

Tables 17-1 lists the top 10 causes of death for the U.S. population. In addition to those statistics, there are some other notable trends when the data is analyzed by race and age:

- **Homicide** is the leading cause of death in African-American and Hispanic males aged 15–24 years.

- **Cancer** is the top killer in women until age 75, at which time **heart disease** takes over as the top cause of mortality. Remember that! You need to put your postmenopausal patients on hormone-replacement therapy to prevent heart disease.

- **Accidents** are the leading cause of death in males and females aged 1–39.

- **HIV/AIDS** had been the leading killer in all males aged 25-44, but more recent reports no longer support that finding, probably due to the intervention of antiviral therapy.

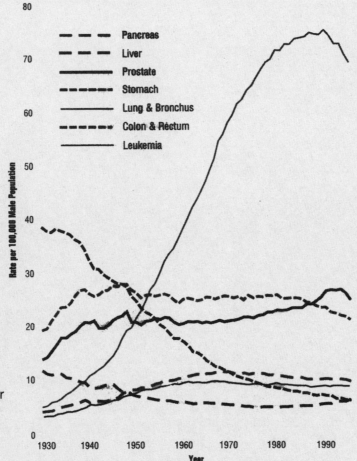

Fig. 17-9. Age-adjusted cancer mortality in men, 1999. (Reprinted from SH Landis, T Murray, S Bolden, PA Wingo. Cancer statistics, 1999. CA Cancer J Clin 1999; 49:27.)

Tables 17-1. Mortality rates for 1995 in the United States, all ages

Cause	Rate (per 100,000 people)
1. Heart disease	205
2. Cancer	169
3. Cerebrovascular disease	42
4. Chronic obstructive pulmonary disease	30
5. Accidents (including automobile)	32
6. Pneumonia and influenza	21
7. Diabetes mellitus	18
8. Human immunodeficiency virus/acquired immunodeficiency syndrome	13
9. Suicide	11
10. Disease of Arteries	8

Psychiatry

Diagnosis of Mental Disorders

The standard basis for classification in the United States and abroad is the *Diagnostic and Statistical Manual of Mental Disorders, Fourth Edition, Revised* (*DSM-IVR*). Given the scope of the USMLE, the entire *DSM-IVR* isn't included here, just the highlights that you should know. Some points about the *DSM-IVR*:

- Each mental disorder is seen as a behavioral or psychological pattern that is not associated with socially or culturally expected responses to a given situation (e.g., bereavement over a loss is not considered a disorder).

- Each disorder has a descriptive categorization according to symptoms, and many disease entities overlap. Also, patients may have multiple DSM diagnoses.

To be complete about evaluating and managing patients, psychiatrists classify problems according to five **axes**:

- **Axis I** is the clinical mental diagnosis (e.g., schizophrenia).

- **Axis II** lists any personality disorders or mental retardation.

- **Axis III** includes any general medical conditions.

- **Axis IV** lists any psychosocial or environmental problems (e.g., unemployment).

- **Axis V** is the global assessment of functioning (GAF) on a scale from 1 to 100. Typically, 70–100 is the range for mild or minimal symptoms. Below 50 indicates serious impairment (e.g., suicidal ideation).

Neurotransmitters

Recent research in psychiatry has focused on neurotransmitters and their actions in the central nervous system. Table 18-1 lists the major neurotransmitters and their proposed abnormalities in different psychiatric disorders.

Table 18-1. Neurotransmitters

Neurotransmitter	CNS pathway	Abnormality	Medication
Dopamine (5 types of receptors, D1–D5)	Nigrostriatal (coordination of movement) Mesolimbic and mesocortical (control of emotions and behavior) Periventricular (control of food intake) Hypothalamic (prolactin regulation and release)	Schizophrenia ("dopamine hypothesis" involving D2 receptors) Mood disorders (depression, mania) Parkinson's disease	Neuroleptics Dopa analogues (e.g., L-dopa)
Serotonin (5-HT) (15 receptor subtypes)	Median and dorsal raphe nuclei Locus ceruleus Pineal body	Low levels may allow low catecholamines to cause depression High levels may cause mania	Antidepressants, especially selective serotonin-reuptake inhibitors
Norepinephrine (NE), Epinephrine	Locus ceruleus Lateral tegmental neurons	"Monoamine hypothesis"—underactivity of NE and 5-HT may cause depression, and increased activity leads to mania Panic disorder associated with α_2-receptors	Tricyclic antidepressants MAO inhibitors
Acetylcholine	Corpus striatum Nucleus accumbens Motor cortex Thalamus	Alzheimer's dementia	Complicated interactions with anticholinesterases
GABA (2 receptor subtypes)	Inhibitory neurons throughout CNS	?Schizophrenia	Benzodiazepines

GABA = γ-aminobutyric acid; MAO = monoamine oxidase.

Table 18-2. Apgar score

Feature	0 points	1 point	2 points
Heart rate	0	100	>100
Respiratory effort	0	Irregular	Regular
Muscle tone	Limp	Some activity	Moving limbs, crying
Reflex irritability	None	Grimace	Grimace and cough
Color	Blue-gray	Pink trunk	Pink all over

Normal Infant Development

A typical USMLE question will list a number of tasks a child can do and test your ability to gauge whether the child is age-appropriate. Be sure you know those development milestones.

Apgar Score

The Apgar score is a commonly used but seldom useful scoring system for newborns, evaluated at 1 and 5 minutes after birth. The 5-minute score correlates best with long-term outcome. A 10 is a perfect score. As you can see in Table 18-2, these are very crude assessments.

Cognitive Development

Piaget's stages of development are as follows:

- **Birth to 2 years—sensorimotor phase**: Children gain knowledge about their environment through assimilation. Children gain the skills of **object permanence** (knowing something still exists even though she cannot see it) around age 2. **Stranger anxiety** begins around 8 months.

- **2–7 years—preoperational phase**: Language acquisition and symbolic thinking begins. The child can have magical or illogical thinking, and this is the time of egocentrism: The child is only aware of his own point of view (the terrible twos).

- **7–11 years—operational phase**: Logical thinking begins, as well as awareness of other points of view. The child begins to understand concepts of conservation of mass and volume.

- **11 years to adolescence—abstract phase**: Hypothetical and deductive reasoning begins, and there is increased flexibility and awareness of one's own thoughts.

Motor and Language Development

- **Newborn to 2 months**: Can regard face, respond to sounds, and move all extremities. May be able to lift head, smile, and vocalize.

- **2–6 months**: Grasps objects and can follow through 180 degrees. Smiles and laughs spontaneously. Starts to make rudimentary one-syllable noises. Can roll over.

- **6-9 months**: Can sit independently and pull to stand. Uses pincer grasp. Feeds self and waves "bye-bye." Babbles and can say "mama" and "dada" nonspecifically.

- **12–18 months**: Walks well and drinks from a cup. Has a small vocabulary and can indicate desires. Scribbles. Points to four body parts.

- **2-2 1/2 years**: Solves single-piece puzzles. Pulls up pants. Jumps, kicks ball, and rides tricycle using pedals. Imitates horizontal and vertical line drawings. Combines 2-3 words.

- **3-3 1/2 years**: Copies circle and cross. Throws ball overhand. Toilet trained. Puts on shirt. Walks up stairs with alternating feet. Balances on one foot for a few seconds. Gives full name, age, and sex. Names 2 colors.

- **4-4 1/2 years**: Hops on one foot and broad-jumps 24 inches. Dresses self. Can boss, criticize, and show off. Identifies some letters and numbers. Understands prepositions and opposites. Asks "how" and "why." Can copy square.

- **5 years**: Prints first name. Counts 10 objects. Skips with alternating feet. Ties shoes. Asks meaning of words.

Psychosocial Development

Erik Erikson's stages of psychosocial development are as follows:

- **0–18 months: Trust vs. mistrust**: Important that daily needs are taken care of to develop trust.

- **18 months to 3 years: Autonomy vs. shame**: Trying to assert independence but feeling doubt and shame. Gauges other people's reactions.

- **4–6 years: Initiative vs. guilt**: Starts to make plans and carry them through. Guilt regarding "right" and "wrong."

- **6–13 years: Industry vs. inferiority**: School attendance and ranking amongst peer group are important. Able to establish identity away from home setting.

- **11–20 years: Identity vs. role confusion**: Establishment of identity as separate from parents, includes the "trying on" of many roles.

- **20–35 years: Intimacy vs. isolation**: Identity established, now tries to establish relationships with others.

- **35–65 years: Generativity vs. stagnation**: Sense of continuity with bringing in next generation. Sense of making a contribution as well as personal fulfillment.

- **65 and up: Integrity vs. despair**: Maintenance of dignity and establishment that life has been productive and worthwhile.

Table 18-3. Mental retardation ranking

Level of mental retardation	IQ
Mild	50–55 to 70
Moderate	35–40 to 50–55
Severe	20–25 to 35–40
Profound	<20–25

Early-Onset Disorders

Mental Retardation

Mental retardation is defined as an IQ below 70. Mentally retarded persons experience significant delays in developmental and social milestones. Mental retardation is associated with early fetal insults, such as congenital infections and alcohol exposure. Certain genetic syndromes, such as Down syndrome, are also associated with mental retardation. The classification for mental retardation is shown in Table 18-3.

Motor Skill and Learning Disorders

The following are classified as **learning disorders**:

- Reading disorder

- Mathematics disorder

- Disorders of written expression

These are present if the skills are "substantially below chronologic age" (as measured by standardized tests) and significantly affect academic achievement.

Developmental coordination disorder is classified as a **motor skill disorder**. It consists of marked delays in motor milestones and "clumsiness" that is not attributable to a general medical condition (e.g., cerebral palsy or muscular dystrophy).

Communication Disorders

The following are classified as **communication disorders**:

- Expressive language disorder

- Mixed receptive-expressive language disorder

- Phonologic disorders: disorders in which a child fails to develop speech sounds appropriately for age

- Stuttering: in addition to "classic" stuttering (sound and syllable repetitions), includes pauses and circumlocutions (word substitutions to avoid potentially problematic words)

Developmental Disorders

This classification includes the following:

- **Autistic disorder** is characterized by increased nonverbal behaviors, lack of social and emotional responsiveness, delays in language development, stereotyped body movements (e.g., finger twisting), and inflexible adherence to routine.

- **Asperger's disorder** is just like autism in terms of movements and emotional development, except the children seem to have normal language and cognitive development.

- **Rett's disorder** is characterized by a completely normal pregnancy, birth, and development; then, at age 5–30 months, growth and development begin to be lost. Stereotyped movements accompany a loss of previously acquired motor skill.

- **Childhood disintegrative disorder** is just like Rett's disorder in that the children develop normally for the first 2 years but then start losing language, motor, and other skills before age 10.

Impulse-Control Disorders

Impulse-control disorders include

- **Attention-deficit/hyperactivity disorder** (ADHD): This is a popular one—kids suffer from inattention to school lessons or other tasks and are easily distractible. The classic case is a little boy who is constantly fidgeting in school and has difficulty with self-control (e.g., blurts out answers). Medication with amphetamines (e.g., dextroamphetamine or methylphenidate) usually does the trick, oddly enough!

- **Conduct disorder**: These are the kids who set fires and torture animals at a young age, in addition to committing other crimes. Onset can occur in childhood or adolescence and is classified from mild to severe. There is an increased risk of developing antisocial personality disorder in adulthood.

- **Oppositional defiant disorder**: Kids develop a pattern of negative, hostile behavior in which they argue with adults and seem very irritable.

Other Childhood Disorders

Other disorders are listed in Table 18-4. Note that for these definitions to apply, none of these things can be caused by a medical condition.

Table 18-4. Other childhood disorders

Disorder	Definition
Pica	Craving and eating non-nutritive substances, such as dirt
Rumination	Regurgitating and rechewing food
Feeding disorder	Not eating enough to gain weight
Tourette's disorder	Uncontrolled tics (sudden, rapid, and recurrent vocalization or motor movement); the classic tic (uncontrolled swearing) less common
Transient tic disorder	Tic disorder that doesn't last more than 12 months
Encopresis	Having a bowel movement in an inappropriate setting
Enuresis	Urinating in an inappropriate setting
Separation anxiety	Excessive worry and physical symptoms when separated from caregiver
Selective mutism	Doesn't talk in particular situations
Reactive attachment disorder	Inappropriate social interactions—either cannot establish them or exhibits excessive attachment
Stereotypic movement	Repetitive, nonfunctional motor habits, often self-injurious

Table 18-5. Dissociative disorders

Disorder	Definition
Dissociative amnesia	Unable to recall personal information, usually due to a traumatic event
Dissociative fugue	Sudden and unexpected travel that cannot be recalled, along with confusion about identity and loss of memory
Dissociative identity disorder (formerly called *multiple personality disorder*)	At least two distinct states in which one cannot recall what the other has done
Depersonalization	Persistent feeling of detachment, as if subject is in a dream or fog

Dissociative Disorders

The various dissociative disorders are listed in Table 18-5.

Delirium and Dementia

Delirium

Delirium is a *disturbance of consciousness* with the inability to focus attention and preserve cognition. The problem develops over a short time, with a fluctuating course.

Signs & Symptoms

Altered cognition, impaired attention, fluctuating course. Tremor and hallucinations are common.

Diagnosis

Rule out medical causes, such as electrolyte disturbances, hypoxia, drug overdose, trauma, or infection.

Treatment

Supportive care, with treatment of the underlying disease.

Dementia

Dementia is memory impairment and cognitive disturbance, with a gradual, insidious onset. Alzheimer's disease is the number one cause of dementia. Other causes include multiple infarcts, drug toxicity, and vitamin deficiency. Dementia is discussed in more detail in chapter 8.

Signs & Symptoms

The above may be accompanied by aphasia, apraxia, or agnosia.

Diagnosis

Electroencephalography may show diffuse slowing.

Treatment

Treatment of underlying disorder.

Substance Use Disorders

The following definitions are useful in understanding substance disorders:

- **Intoxication**: Intoxication is a reversible symptom caused by substance use, resulting in "maladaptive behavior."

- **Abuse**: This is a pattern of recurrent substance use that results in failure at work, home, school, and other areas.

- **Dependence**: A pattern of recurrent substance use results in tolerance (needing more for the same effect) or withdrawal (see below). These people have tried to stop using the substance and spend a lot of time trying to get more.

- **Withdrawal**: A substance-specific syndrome of symptoms (say that three times fast!) develops after cessation of use.

Table 18-6. Symptoms associated with substance use

Drug	Intoxication	Withdrawal
Alcohol	Slurred speech, ataxia, nystagmus, and impaired memory and attention	Tremors, hyperactivity, insomnia, increased pulse and blood pressure, hallucinations, seizures
Amphetamines and cocaine	Tachycardia, dilated pupils, sweating, psychomotor agitation, cardiac arrhythmias	Dysphoric mood, fatigue, bad dreams, increased appetite
Nicotine	Decreased nervousness, decreased appetite	Dysphoria, insomnia, irritability, anxiety, difficulty concentrating
Caffeine	Nervousness, flushing, diuresis, tachycardia	Severe headache
Marijuana	Impaired coordination, euphoria or anxiety, slowing of time sense, increased appetite, tachycardia, social withdrawal	None
Opioids	Drowsiness, slurred speech, impaired attention, no pain	Nausea and vomiting, muscle aches, sweating, diarrhea, yawning, pupillary dilation

Common symptoms of intoxication and withdrawal of various substances are listed in Table 18-6.

Psychotic Disorders

Schizophrenia

Schizophrenia is characterized by disturbed language, thought, and perceptions. Onset usually occurs in the second or third decade of life, and may be gradual or sudden. Schizophrenia has a genetic basis, although environment and family play important roles in its development.

Patients with schizophrenia may experience **hallucinations**, or false perceptions without an external stimulus, or delusions, or false beliefs held with conviction despite evidence to the contrary (note the difference between hallucinations and **illusions**, which are incorrect interpretations of real stimuli).

Signs & Symptoms

Patients initially present with social withdrawal, psychosis, or depression. **"Positive" symptoms** include hallucinations, delusions, and disorganized speech. **"Negative" symptoms** include social withdrawal, emotional blunting, cognitive deficits, and poverty of speech and motor activity.

Diagnosis

DSM-IVR diagnostic criteria are as follows:

- At least two of the following: delusions, hallucinations, disorganized speech, disorganized or catatonic behavior, or any negative symptoms (listed above).

- Social or occupational dysfunction.

- Duration of at least 6 months and exclusion of other related disorders, such as schizoaffective disorder, mood disorders, developmental disorders, or substance abuse. If the symptoms last less than 6 months, it is called schizophreniform disorder.

Treatment

Combined pharmacologic and psychosocial treatment. Neuroleptics and good support systems are helpful, along with a good therapeutic alliance with the physician. Patients with schizophreniform disorder require acute treatment with neuroleptics and may be at increased risk for suicide.

Neuroleptic Malignant Syndrome

Neuroleptic malignant syndrome is a rare but acute illness caused by the use of neuroleptics. Patients experience fever, muscle rigidity, autonomic dysfunction, and delirium. The neuroleptic should be withdrawn, and the patient should receive bromocriptine (a dopamine agonist) and supportive care. Mortality is greater than 20% if untreated.

Schizoaffective Disorder

Schizoaffective disorder is a mixture of schizophrenic symptoms and mood disorder symptoms, such as depression. It is usually seen in young adults. It is classified as either bipolar type (with manic symptoms) or depressive type (with depressive symptoms).

Signs & Symptoms

See diagnostic criteria, below.

Diagnosis

DSM-IVR diagnostic criteria are as follows:

- Major depressive or manic episode is concurrent with schizophrenic symptoms.

- At least 2 weeks of delusions or hallucinations occur.

- Other medical causes are excluded.

Treatment

Patients require neuroleptics with either lithium or carbamazepine for the bipolar type, or antidepressants for the depressive type.

Brief Psychosis

A brief psychosis may occur as a reaction to overwhelming stress, such as a death in the family. The patient experiences symptoms of schizophrenia for a period of 1 day to 1 month. It is treated with neuroleptics, anxiolytics, and therapy.

Mood Disorders

Depression

Depression has a lifetime prevalence of 10–20%, and the incidence is higher in women than men. The **monoamine transmitter** hypothesis suggests that norepinephrine and serotonin are involved. Patients with depression often have a family history of depression as well as increased rates of alcohol and drug abuse. A depressive episode can be characterized as catatonic, melancholic, atypical, or associated with the postpartum period. **Seasonal affective disorder** is the presence of depressive episodes at a particular time of year, usually fall or winter.

Signs & Symptoms

Patients experience feelings of hopelessness, anhedonia, and low self-worth. Symptoms include low energy and changes in sleep, weight, and eating patterns.

Diagnosis

DSM-IVR diagnostic criteria of a major depressive episode are five or more of the following over 2 weeks, accompanied by depressed mood:

- Anhedonia (loss of interest in pleasurable activities)

- Weight loss or gain

- Insomnia or hypersomnia

- Psychomotor agitation or retardation

- Fatigue

- Feelings of worthlessness or guilt

- Inability to concentrate

- Thoughts of death or plans to commit suicide

Mnemonic:
SIG E CAPS
Suicidal ideation
Interest (decreased)
Guilt
Energy (decreased)
Concentration (decreased)
Appetite (change)
Psychomotor (change)
Sleep disturbances

Treatment

Pharmacologic treatment includes tricyclic antidepressants, selective serotonin-reuptake inhibitors (SSRIs), and monoamine oxidase (MAO) inhibitors, which are accompanied by psychotherapy.

Grief versus Depression

A common test question describes a grieving family member and asks you to make the distinction between normal grief, pathological grief, and depression. Since depressive symptoms are a normal part of the grief process, this distinction can be hard to make.

- In **normal grief**, severe depressive symptoms should abate after several months, whereas they tend to persist longer in depression. Suicidal ideation, particularly with a plan, is not a part of the grieving process, although the individual may express a desire to join the deceased. The intense feeling of sadness and loneliness usually occurs in "pangs" interspersed with periods of normal feeling, and self-blame and guilt feelings are usually focused on the deceased. In depression, on the other hand, the sadness and loneliness is more continuous, and the feelings of guilt and worthlessness usually are centered around the self, not just in regard to the deceased. The grieving welcome emotional support and feel better after venting their feelings, whereas those suffering major depression tend to withdraw from support.

- **Pathological grief** can manifest as **absent or delayed grief**, in which the feelings of grief are repressed and denied, only to come back later as a more prolonged and distorted grief. Individuals who experience delayed grief are at greater risk for developing major depression. Distorted grief occurs when a facet of the grieving process becomes disproportionately prolonged or overshadows the others. Disabling "survival guilt" is one example of distorted grief. Another example is the individual who over-identifies with the deceased to the point where he may forsake his own interests to pursue those of the deceased. Other examples of distorted grief include conversion disorder, in which the individual develops symptoms identical to those of the deceased, and denial of loss, in which the individual attempts to leave the room and belongings of the deceased completely unchanged.

Manic Disorder

Manic disorder is characterized by elevated, expansive, or irritated moods. Patients often have feelings of increased productivity and creativity. They experience euphoria, delusions, and hallucinations and have a decreased need for sleep. A fascination with social interaction, music, outlandish clothing, and even public disrobing can be seen. Manic speech is rapid and difficult to interpret. Episodes can last days to weeks. **Hypomania** is a shorter, less severe manic episode that lasts less than 4 days.

Bipolar Disorder

Bipolar patients experience depression with episodes of manic symptoms. There are several subtypes of bipolar disorder, which are beyond the scope of the USMLE. Other disorders, especially schizophrenia and schizoaffective disorder, must be ruled out for this diagnosis. Treatment is with lithium or neuroleptics.

Cyclothymia is a "blunted" version of bipolar disorder in which the patient experiences short cycles of depression and hypomania. These patients may be "stimulus seekers"—that is, drawn to risky hobbies and having volatile work histories and social relationships. This condition is treated with lithium and anti-depressants.

Dysthymia

Dysthymia is a chronic, "neurotic" type of depression, in which patients experience poor self-esteem and depressed feelings throughout life. Symptoms of depression may be present. Treatment is with psychotherapy.

Anxiety Disorders

Anxiety disorders are characterized by persistent or irrational fears (**phobias**) or generalized uncomfortable emotional states (**anxiety**). They are believed to be multifactorial, including genetic predisposition, learned responses, and environmental patterns. Abnormalities in the γ-aminobutyric acid (GABA) receptor have been implicated because most anxiolytics work at this site.

Phobias

A multitude of phobias can be experienced. The important ones are as follows:

- **Agoraphobia**: A fear of being caught in a situation from which one cannot escape, leading to embarrassment and panic (e.g., supermarket, elevator). This is often associated with feelings of being closed in and crowded by other people.

- **Social phobia**: A fear of embarrassment and humiliation in social situations (e.g., public speaking, parties).

- **Specific phobia**: A fear of a specific thing, such as animals, blood, or heights.

Treatment of phobias includes psychotherapy, behavior modification, and drugs for somatic symptoms.

Panic Disorder

Patients with this condition experience episodes of fear and anxiety accompanied by feelings of impending doom. The constellation of physical symptoms includes palpitations, tachycardia, trembling, dizziness, and chest pain. The episodes may last for several minutes. Panic disorder may be accompanied by agoraphobia. Treatment is with anxiolytics.

Generalized Anxiety Disorder

Patients with this disorder experience excessive anxiety or worry, which often persists for several months. The anxiety leads to difficulty concentrating, restlessness, fatigue, muscle tension, and insomnia. Treatment with SSRIs, anxiolytics, and relaxation therapy are helpful.

Post-Traumatic Stress Disorder

A small percentage of people who experience a psychologically traumatic experience that is "outside the range of usual human experience" develop post-traumatic stress disorder (PTSD). The traumatic incident can include war experiences, major personal trauma, natural disasters, and sexual abuse. Patients with PTSD often try to self-medicate with drug or alcohol abuse.

Signs & Symptoms

The patient experiences recurrent, intrusive recollections of the event with persistent nightmares and a sense of reliving the experience. The patient feels emotional distress and tries to avoid situations that remind him or her of the event.

Diagnosis

Presence of the above symptoms with a history of traumatic experience.

Treatment

Acute PTSD (e.g., shell-shock during World War II) is treated by having the patient resume all normal function as soon as possible. Chronic PTSD is treated with anti-depressants and therapy.

Obsessive-Compulsive Disorder

Obsessions are repetitive, intrusive images or impulses. These often focus on harming others or acquiring or spreading contamination. **Compulsions** are repetitive thoughts or rituals that are done to relieve anxiety. Common compulsions include cleaning, checking things, or avoiding certain objects.

Obsessive-compulsive disorder (OCD) appears to have a genetic link and has been associated with serotonin dysfunction. Onset is usually in the teens through 30s and can often occur in conjunction with a pre-existing depression. Treatment includes SSRIs and behavioral modification. Neuroleptics may also be used, and surgical ablation in the limbic system may work in refractory cases.

Somatoform Disorders

One of the differences between somatoform disorders is the type of gain involved.

- **Primary gain** occurs when internal conflicts are outside the patient's awareness, so the symptoms are symbolic.

- **Secondary gain** refers to tangible benefits, such as getting out of work or school when you're sick.

Malingering

Malingering is the conscious faking of symptoms for secondary gain—for example, someone pretending to have a back injury so as to receive disability payments.

Factitious Disorders

In factitious disorders, patients fake symptoms for unconscious psychiatric reasons, for example, preferring the "sick" role. There is no evidence of any organic pathology. These patients are at increased risk for unnecessary operations and procedures. They require psychiatric evaluation because they are unable to control their behavior.

Somatization Disorders

Patients with somatization disorder complain of many vague symptoms, usually involving several organ systems, especially gastrointestinal (GI), genitourinary, and cardiopulmonary problems. Before a patient receives this label, you must rule out other possible multiorgan diseases, such as multiple sclerosis or systemic lupus erythematosus.

Conversion Disorders

Conversion disorder patients experience loss of neurologic function with no identified organic pathology. Common conversion disorder symptoms include paralysis, blindness, deafness, and seizures. Symptoms may occur abruptly, after an acute stress. Patients sometimes appear indifferent to the accompanying loss of function, known as "la belle indifference."

Hypochondriasis

Patients with hypochondriasis exhibit an abnormal preoccupation with minor symptoms and disease possibilities (think: medical student). Physical symptoms may be accompanied by signs of anxiety or depression.

Personality Disorders

Personality disorders are inflexible and maladaptive personality traits that cause significant impairment in social or occupational functioning. They usually manifest in adolescence and continue throughout adulthood. They are divided into different clusters based on similar traits. Therapy is the treatment of choice, although it is rarely successful.

Cluster A

- **Paranoid personality disorder**: A pattern of pervasive distrust or suspicion of others. More common in men than women and may have a genetic basis.

- **Schizoid personality disorder**: A pattern of detachment from social relationships and limited range of emotional expression. Patients are usually detached, self-absorbed loners.

- **Schizotypal personality disorder**: Social and interpersonal deficits, along with eccentricities of behavior and perception. Speech may be idiosyncratic or peculiar. There is a genetic link to schizophrenia.

Cluster B

- **Antisocial personality disorder**: Disregard for the rights of others, beginning in childhood. It is more common in males and people of lower socioeconomic status. Approximately 75% of prison inmates are estimated to have this disorder.

- **Borderline personality disorder**: Instability in interpersonal relationships and self-image, along with impulsivity. These patients are preoccupied with the possibility of real or imagined abandonment, yet they fear loss of identity in intimate relationships.

- **Histrionic personality disorder**: Excessive emotionality and attention-seeking behavior, accompanied by dysphoria with loss or rejection. May be related to separation difficulties in childhood.

- **Narcissistic personality disorder**: Grandiosity, need for admiration, and lack of empathy. These patients are often considered pretentious and self-important. This condition may be induced by repeated insults to self-esteem in childhood.

Cluster C

- **Avoidant personality disorder**: Social discomfort, hypersensitivity to criticism and rejection, and marked timidity. There is often associated depression, anger, and anxiety, with failure to develop personal relationships.

- **Dependent personality disorder**: Excessive need to be taken care of that leads to submissiveness, clinging behavior, and fear of separation. The patient may be depressed and experience intense anxiety when left alone.

- **Obsessive-compulsive personality disorder**: A preoccupation with orderliness, perfectionism, and interpersonal control. This is different from OCD in that OCD-related obsessions and compulsions are not necessarily related to neatness and disorder.

Ego Defenses

Ego defenses are ways that everyone, including normal people, deal with reality. They are classified based on the stage of development in which they are used. Ego defenses are common Step 1 questions. The case history describes a patient behavior and asks you to identify the ego defense from a list of choices. You may not need to know each one in detail, but it is important to be able to recognize differences between them.

Narcissistic defenses are used by children or psychotic persons. Table 18-7 lists the most common narcissistic defense mechanisms.

Immature defenses are used by teens and patients with depression or anxiety disorders, such as OCD (Table 18-8).

Neurotic defenses are seen in OCD and persons with mild personality disorders (Table 18-9). They are used by normal adults under some stressful circumstances.

Mature defenses are considered normal adaptive functioning (Table 18-10).

Table 18-7. Narcissistic ego defenses

Defense	Definition	Other information
Denial	Refusal to acknowledge a negative event	In psychotic patients, may be replaced by fantasy; in normal persons, usually used after a fatal diagnosis (as a higher-level ego defense)
Distortion	Extreme reshaping or reinterpretation of events	May accompany wish-fulfilling delusions
Primitive idealization and splitting	Classifies things as either all good or all bad	Objects may be rapidly shifted from one category to another
Projection	Unacceptable traits or feelings are transferred to an outside source	May take the form of paranoid delusions; also a higher-level ego defense if mild

Abuse

Child Abuse

Child abuse is a common problem that is grossly underreported. Up to 4,000 children die each year as a result of abuse. These children are often brought to the physician for multiple injuries with vague explanations. Many children deny abuse out of fear of repercussions.

Signs & Symptoms

Multiple visits to different emergency rooms (ERs) along with other unexplained injuries are common. The children may or may not be unkempt or malnourished. Burn injuries may have unusual distributions, and injuries to the back are common.

Diagnosis

X-rays may show multiple healing fractures.

Treatment

Suspected child abuse MUST be reported to local authorities.

Table 18-8. Immature ego defenses

Defense	Definition	Other information
Acting out	Expressing an unconscious or unacceptable wish by immediate action	Extreme immediate misbehavior
Blocking	Inhibition of a feeling	Similar to repression, but they feel more tension about it
Hypochondriasis	Transference of feelings of reproach and shame of others into personal complaints of somatic pain	May coexist with depression or anxiety disorders
Identification and introjection	Feelings of similar identity with another person, out of guilt or love	For example, Jewish persons were made guards in Nazi camps and participated in torture of fellow prisoners
Passive-aggressive behavior	Passivity and indirect behavior instead of open confrontation of reality	For example, doing something badly instead of just telling your significant other that you refuse to do it
Regression	Reverting back to earlier developmental stages	Classic example is bedwetting in older children during periods of stress
Schizoid fantasy	Use of an isolated fantasy to avoid conflict resolution	—
Somatization	Conversion of unresolved conflicts into somatic symptoms	Not the same as somatization disorder
Turning against self	Unacceptable urge toward others is redirected to self	For example, causing injury to self instead of hurting others

Spousal Abuse

A woman is beaten every 12 seconds in the United States. Almost half of the injured women seen in the ER are victims of abuse. Abuse may be part of a chronic, maladaptive relationship within a couple. The abusing spouse may have an accompanying alcohol or drug problem, and victims often blame themselves for "rocking the boat," which leads to underreporting.

Signs & Symptoms

Unexplained injuries that may be repetitive or may be concentrated in areas of the body that are usually hidden by clothing.

Diagnosis

As for child abuse. Try to document with photos if possible.

Table 18-9. Neurotic defenses

Defense	Definition	Other information
Controlling	Excessive management to avoid anxiety	Tight scheduling and overplanning of treatment, for example
Displacement	Unconscious shifting of feelings to another object	May displace feelings of love onto other more, attainable object
Dissociation	Emotional separation of identity to avoid emotional distress	Coldly participating in abuse or a crime without feelings
Doing and undoing	Symbolic action of something unacceptable, followed by its opposite	—
Inhibition	Limitation of actions to avoid anxiety or conflict	—
Intellectualization	Emotional control by overanalysis	May think about and mentally "defend" actions to avoid feelings
Isolation	Separation of feelings from ideas	May involve repression or displacement as well
Rationalization	Justification with reasons for actions performed that would otherwise be unacceptable	Arguing that special treatment for a friend would have been performed anyway
Reaction formation	Opposite of an unacceptable impulse becomes character trait	A person with homosexual impulses may lead antigay group
Repression	Unconscious withholding of an idea or feeling	Forgetting the anniversary of a loved one's death; compare to suppression
Sexualization	Attributing sexual significance to someone to avoid personal impulses	Calling someone "a slut" to avoid dealing with attraction to him or her

Table 18-10. Mature defenses

Defense	Definition	Example
Altruism	Constructive service to others	Personal satisfaction obtained by identification and introjection
Anticipation	Overconcern about the future to allay anxiety	May try to think about all positive and negative outcomes
Asceticism	Elimination of the pleasurable portions of an activity	Pleasure derived from renouncing "base actions"
Humor	Overt feelings of mirth to avoid feelings of pain	A form of distraction used commonly in medicine (e.g., jokes about seriously ill patients)
Sublimation	Gratification of an inappropriate impulse through a more acceptable channel	Feelings of competitiveness directed toward sports instead of classmates
Suppression	Conscious withholding of an idea or feeling	Trying not to think about an upcoming test while partying; compare to repression

Treatment

Offer support services and shelter information. If the victim refuses to leave the situation, do not be judgmental; offer support whenever he or she is ready. Most states require reporting to the police.

Elder Abuse

Elder abuse is extremely underreported and often manifests as signs of neglect rather than abuse. Signs of dehydration and malnourishment should alert you to the possibility, and it MUST be reported to the authorities if suspected.

Psychoanalysis

Freudian Theory

Freud's theory is a structural theory in which three parts of the psychic apparatus explain human development, emotions, and illness. The three parts are as follows:

- **Id**: The collection of raw impulses and drives, such as sex, fear, and aggression
- **Superego**: The conscience of the mind, full of things you "should" do
- **Ego**: The rational mediator between the expectations of the superego and the desires of the id

According to Freudian theory, the psychosexual stages of development (listed below) must each be completed or else patients develop a **fixation** at a particular point:

- **Oral stage (0–18 months)**: Associated with the mouth and breast-feeding
- **Anal stage (18–36 months)**: Associated with bowel control, autonomy, and self-control issues
- **Genital stage (3–5 years)**: Active male and passive female conceptions develop, along with genitals as pleasure-providing organs

Jungian Theory

Jungian theory involves the **collective unconscious**, an inherited commonality to all humankind in thought and ideas. **Archetypes** are universal images found across cultures in religion and myth.

Adlerian Theory

Adlerian theory focuses on socially mediated phenomena. Feelings of inferiority drive an infant's sense of helplessness, and willpower is a personal drive that influences social interactions. In this theory, birth order is very important and strongly influences individual behavior patterns.

Pharmacology

Neuroleptics

The actions of neuroleptics are not fully understood. Most neuroleptics are associated with blockade of the dopamine and serotonin receptors in the central nervous system (Table 18-11). Because the actions appear to be nonselective, however, a number of undesirable side effects can occur, including the following:

- **Parkinsonism and other extrapyramidal symptoms**, such as muscle rigidity and tremor, may occur. These can be reversed with concurrent administration of anticholinergics, such as benztropine.

- **Tardive dyskinesia** may develop after long-term therapy with neuroleptics. Patients may develop irreversible choreoathetoid movements of the mouth and extremities. No treatment exists, and anticholinergics, which are usually given to decrease the risk of extrapyramidal signs, may worsen these symptoms.

- **Neuroleptic malignant syndrome** (discussed earlier in the chapter).

Other, less serious side effects include anticholinergic effects, such as dry mouth, urinary retention, and constipation.

Antidepressants

Until recently, **tricyclic antidepressants** were the mainstay of treatment for depression for more than 30 years (Table 18-12). With the introduction of **SSRIs**, however, tricyclics are used much less frequently. Tricyclic medications have numerous side effects, including sedation, weight gain, orthostatic hypotension, and a withdrawal syndrome. Also, if taken as an overdose, tricyclic antidepressants are cardiotoxic and often lethal. By comparison, SSRIs have low rates of toxicity, although GI symptoms and headache are seen. SSRIs are also less of a concern in patients with suicidal ideation because overdose is not lethal. **MAO inhibitors**, previously second-line agents in the treatment of depression, are also rarely used these days due to multiple side effects.

Table 18-11. Neuroleptics

Agents	Toxicities and other information
Chlorpromazine	Most toxic of the neuroleptics; acute dystonia, tardive dyskinesia, neuroleptic malignant syndrome, and endocrine effects; orthostatic hypotension and antiadrenergic effects
Thioridazine	Possible cardiotoxicity; fewer extrapyramidal signs
Haloperidol	Used for acute psychosis; has severe extrapyramidal side effects
Prochlorperazine	Also used for treatment of nausea and vomiting
Thiothixene	Less tardive dyskinesia
Clozapine	Has significant D4-blocking action; used as a second-line agent; fewer extrapyramidal effects; agranulocytosis may occur in 2–3%

Table 18-12. Antidepressants

Agent	Mechanism	Uses	Toxicities
Tricyclic antidepressants (e.g., nortriptyline, amitriptyline)	Blocks reuptake of monoamines at the receptor (e.g., norepinephrine, serotonin, dopamine)	Depression Chronic pain syndromes Panic attacks	Sedation, dry mouth, weight gain; cardiotoxicity in large amounts; abrupt withdrawal causes flulike syndrome, so must be tapered
Selective serotonin-reuptake inhibitors (e.g., fluoxetine, sertraline, paroxetine)	Blocks serotonin reuptake at the receptor	Depression Obsessive-compulsive disorder	Nausea, vomiting, diarrhea, dizziness, insomnia, and headache; impotence in males
Monoamine oxidase inhibitors (e.g., selegiline, isocarboxazid)	Blocks metabolism of monoamines (e.g., norepinephrine, serotonin, dopamine) by enzyme inhibition	Depression Narcolepsy	Cannot eat tyramine-containing foods (e.g., wine, cheese); hypotension, hepatotoxicity
Miscellaneous agents (e.g., bupropion)	Unknown	Depression	Induces P-450 enzymes; seizures; minimal anticholinergic effects

Lithium is not an antidepressant but is used in the treatment of bipolar disorder. The mechanism of action is unknown. Adverse effects are common and include tremor, sedation, leukocytosis, and endocrine problems, such as thyroid dysfunction and diabetes insipidus. Lithium levels should be monitored regularly.

Anxiolytics

Anxiolytics, primarily benzodiazepines, are discussed in chapter 4.

Index

Note: Page numbers followed by *f* indicate figures; page numbers followed by *t* indicate tables.

Notes

www.review.com

Expert Advice

Talk About It

Pop Surveys

www.review.com

Paying for it

www.review.com

The Princeton Review

Getting in

Word du Jour

www.review.com

Find-O-Rama School & Career Search

www.review.com

Best Schools

Finding it

FIND US...

International

Hong Kong
4/F Sun Hung Kai Centre
30 Harbour Road, Wan Chai,
Hong Kong
Tel: (011)85-2-517-3016

Japan
Fuji Building 40, 15-14
Sakuragaokacho, Shibuya Ku,
Tokyo 150, Japan
Tel: (011)81-3-3463-1343

Korea
Tae Young Bldg, 944-24,
Daechi- Dong, Kangnam-Ku
The Princeton Review- ANC
Seoul, Korea 135-280,
South Korea
Tel: (011)82-2-554-7763

Mexico City
PR Mex S De RL De Cv
Guanajuato 228 Col. Roma
06700 Mexico D.F., Mexico
Tel: 525-564-9468

Montreal
666 Sherbrooke St.
West, Suite 202
Montreal, QC H3A 1E7 Canada
Tel: (514) 499-0870

Pakistan
1 Bawa Park - 90 Upper Mall
Lahore, Pakistan
Tel: (011)92-42-571-2315

Spain
Pza. Castilla, 3 - 5° A, 28046
Madrid, Spain
Tel: (011)341-323-4212

Taiwan
155 Chung Hsiao East Road
Section 4 - 4th Floor,
Taipei R.O.C., Taiwan
Tel: (011)886-2-751-1243

Thailand
Building One, 99 Wireless Road
Bangkok, Thailand 10330
Tel: (662) 256-7080

Toronto
1240 Bay Street, Suite 300
Toronto M5R 2A7 Canada
Tel: (800) 495-7737
Tel: (716) 839-4391

Vancouver
4212 University Way NE,
Suite 204
Seattle, WA 98105
Tel: (206) 548-1100

locations

National (U.S.)
We have over 60 offices around the U.S. and run courses in over 400 sites. For courses and locations within the U.S. call 1 (800) 2/Review and you will be routed to the nearest office.

More expert advice from **The Princeton Review**

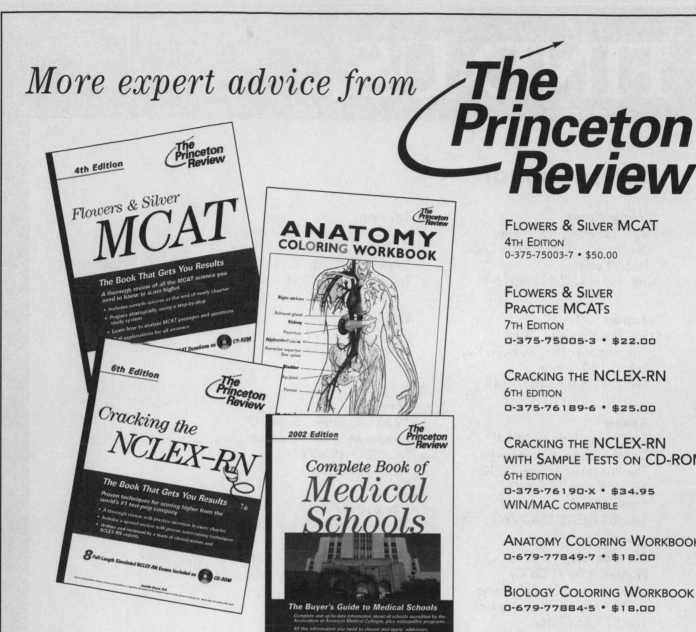

FLOWERS & SILVER MCAT
4TH EDITION
0-375-75003-7 • $50.00

FLOWERS & SILVER
PRACTICE MCATs
7TH EDITION
0-375-75005-3 • $22.00

CRACKING THE NCLEX-RN
6TH EDITION
0-375-76189-6 • $25.00

CRACKING THE NCLEX-RN
WITH SAMPLE TESTS ON CD-ROM
6TH EDITION
0-375-76190-X • $34.95
WIN/MAC COMPATIBLE

ANATOMY COLORING WORKBOOK
0-679-77849-7 • $18.00

BIOLOGY COLORING WORKBOOK
0-679-77884-5 • $18.00

HUMAN BRAIN
COLORING WORKBOOK
0-679-77885-3 • $17.00

PHYSIOLOGY
COLORING WORKBOOK
0-679-77850-0 • $18.00

THE COMPLETE BOOK OF
MEDICAL SCHOOLS
2002 EDITION
0-375-76212-4 • $22.00

GUIDE TO CAREERS IN THE
HEALTH PROFESSIONS
0-375-76158-6 • $24.95

If you want to give yourself the best chance for getting into the medical school of your choice, we can help you get the highest test scores, make the most informed choices, and make the most of your experience once you get there. Whether you want to be an M.D., a nurse, or any other kind of health care professional, we can even help you ace the tests and make a career move that will let you use your skills and education to their best advantage.

AVAILABLE AT YOUR LOCAL BOOKSTORE
www.randomhouse.com/princetonreview